# Leadership

**Research Findings, Practice, and Skills**

# Leadership

## Research Findings, Practice, and Skills

Sixth Edition

ANDREW J. DuBRIN

*Rochester Institute of Technology*

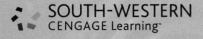

SOUTH-WESTERN
CENGAGE Learning™

Australia • Brazil • Japan • Korea • Mexico • Singapore • Spain • United Kingdom • United States

## SOUTH-WESTERN
### CENGAGE Learning™

*To Rosie, Clare, Camila, Sofia, Eliana, and Carson*
***Leadership: Research Findings, Practice and Skills**, Sixth Edition*
Andrew DuBrin

Publisher: Jack Calhoun

Editor-in-Chief: Melissa Acuna

Development Editor: Suzanna Bainbridge

Executive Acquisitions Editor: Joe Sabatino

Senior Content Project Manager:
  Shelley Dickerson

Editorial Assistant: Ruth Belanger

Art/Design Manager: Jill Haber

Senior Photo Editor: Jennifer Meyer Dare

Composition Buyer: Chuck Dutton

Print Buyer: Miranda Klapper

Marketing Manager: Clint Kernen

Cover image: © DLTLLC/Corbis

Compositor: Pre-Press PMG

> For product information and technology assistance, contact us at
> **Cengage Learning Customer & Sales Support, 1-800-354-9706**
>
> For permission to use material from this text or product,
> submit all requests online at **www.cengage.com/permissions**
> Further permissions questions can be emailed to
> **permissionrequest@cengage.com**

Library of Congress Control Number: 2008943262

Student Edition:

ISBN-13: 978-0-547-14396-5

ISBN-10: 0-547-14396-6

**South-Western**
5191 Natorp Blvd.
Mason, OH 45040
USA

Cengage Learning products are represented in Canada by Nelson Education, Ltd.

For your course and learning solutions, visit **www.cengage.com**

Purchase any of our products at your local college store or at our preferred online store **www.ichapters.com**

PRINTED IN UNITED STATES OF AMERICA
3 4 5 6 7 8 9 12 11 10

# Brief Contents

# Contents

CHAPTER 3   ## Charismatic and Transformational Leadership   66

# Preface

Welcome to the Sixth Edition of *Leadership: Research Findings, Practice, and Skills*. The new edition of this text is a thorough update of the Fifth Edition, which has been used widely in both graduate and undergraduate courses in leadership.

Leadership is now a course by itself after long having been a key topic in several disciplines. Many scholars and managers alike are convinced that effective leadership is required to meet most organizational challenges. Today organizations recognize that leadership transcends senior executives. As a result, organizations require people with appropriate leadership skills to inspire and influence others in small teams, task forces, and units at all organizational levels.

Without effective leadership at all levels in organizations, it is difficult to sustain profitability, productivity, and good customer service. In dozens of different ways, researchers and teachers have demonstrated that leadership does make a difference. Many curricula in business schools and other fields, therefore, now emphasize the development of leadership skills. With the recent exposures of the dark side of business leadership, such as CEOs finding ways to create fortunes for themselves at the expense of employees and stockholders, more attention than ever is being paid to the values and personal characteristics of leaders. Toward that end, this text continues its emphasis on the qualities of effective leaders, including an entire chapter on leadership ethics and social responsibilities.

## PURPOSE OF THE TEXT

The purpose of this text is implied by its title—*Leadership: Research Findings, Practice, and Skills*, Sixth Edition. It is designed for undergraduate and graduate courses in leadership that give attention to research findings about leadership, leadership practice, and skill development. The text best fits courses in leadership that emphasize application and skill building. *Leadership* is also designed to fit courses in management development that emphasize the leadership aspect of management. In addition, it can serve as a supplement to organizational behavior or introductory management courses that emphasize leadership.

The student who masters this text will acquire an overview of the voluminous leadership literature that is based both on research and experience. Information in this text is not restricted to research studies and syntheses of research and theories;

it also includes the opinions of practitioners, consultants, and authors who base their conclusions on observations rather than empirical research.

What the text is *not* also helps define its nature and scope. This book does not attempt to duplicate the scope and purpose of a leadership handbook by integrating theory and research from several thousand studies. At the other extreme, it is not an evangelical approach to leadership espousing one leadership technique. I have attempted to find a midpoint between a massive synthesis of the literature and a trade book promoting a current leadership fad. *Leadership: Research Findings, Practice, and Skills,* Sixth Edition, is designed to be a mixture of scholarly integrity, examples of effective leadership in action, and skill development.

*Leadership* is not intended to duplicate or substitute for an organizational behavior text. Because almost all organizational behavior texts are survey texts, they will mention many of the topics covered here. My approach, however, is to emphasize skill development and prescription rather than to duplicate basic descriptions of concepts and theories. I have tried to minimize overlap by emphasizing the leadership aspects of any concept presented here that might also be found in an organizational behavior or management text. Often when overlap of a topic exists, the presentation here focuses more on skill development than on a review of theory and research. For example, the section on motivation emphasizes how to apply basic explanations of motivation such as expectancy theory and equity theory, but I do not present an overview of motivation theories as is found in an organizational behavior text.

One area of intentional overlap with organizational behavior and management texts does exist: a review of all basic leadership theories. In such instances, however, I emphasize skill development and ideas for leadership practice stemming from these older theories.

## FEATURES OF THE BOOK

To accomplish its purpose, this text incorporates many features into each chapter in addition to summarizing and synthesizing relevant information about leadership:

- **Chapter Outlines** giving the reader a quick overview of the topics covered
- **Learning Objectives** to help focus the reader's attention on major outcomes
- Boldfaced **key terms,** listed at the end of the chapter and defined in a **Glossary** at the back of the text
- Real-life and hypothetical **examples** throughout the text
- **Leader in Action** inserts describing the leadership practices, behaviors, and personal attributes of real-life leaders
- **Leadership Self-Assessment Quizzes** relating to both skills and personal characteristics
- **Leadership Skill-Building Exercises,** including role plays, to emphasize the activities and skills of effective leaders
- End-of-chapter **Summaries** that integrate all key topics and concepts
- End-of-chapter **Guidelines for Action and Skill Development**, giving additional suggestions for improving leadership skill and practice

- **Discussion Questions and Activities** suited for individual or group analysis
- Two **Leadership Case Problems** per chapter, which illustrate the major theme of the chapter and contain questions for individual or group analysis
- A **Leadership Portfolio** skill-building exercise in each chapter that instructs the student to record progress in developing leadership skills and behaviors
- **Internet Skill-Building Exercises** that reinforce the Internet as another source of useful information about leadership. Where possible, the student is directed toward an interactive exercise.
- A **Knowledge Bank** section in each chapter that directs the student toward the textbook website to access supplementary information, such as additional research or knowledge from organizational behavior that fits the subject at hand. We also selectively place in the Knowledge Bank some material that was found in the last two editions, but dropped from the current edition of the text.

### Framework of the Text

The text is a blend of description, skill development, insight development, and prescription. Chapter 1 describes the meaning, importance, and nature of leadership, including leadership roles and the importance of followership. Chapter 2 identifies personal attributes associated with effective leaders, a subject that has experienced renewed importance in recent years. Charismatic and transformational leadership, an extension of understanding the personal attributes of leadership, is the subject of Chapter 3.

Chapter 4 surveys behaviors and practices associated with effective leadership in a variety of situations, and describes leadership styles. Chapter 5 extends the study of styles by describing the contingency and situational aspects of leadership. Chapter 6 focuses on leadership ethics and social responsibility. Chapter 7 describes how leaders use power and politics. Chapter 8 extends this topic by analyzing the tactics leaders use to influence people. Chapter 9 describes how leaders foster teamwork and empower team members.

The next five chapters deal with specific leadership skills: motivating and coaching skills (Chapter 10), which constitute the basis of many leadership positions; creativity and innovation (Chapter 11); communication (including nonverbal and cross-cultural communication) and conflict resolution skills (Chapter 12); vision and strategy creation and knowledge management (Chapter 13); and effective leadership in international and culturally diverse settings (Chapter 14).

Chapter 15 concludes the book with an overview of approaches to leadership development and learning. In addition, there is a discussion of leadership succession, and the challenges facing a new leader.

## CHANGES IN THE SIXTH EDITION

The Sixth Edition of *Leadership: Research Findings, Practice, and Skills* is a thorough update of the Fifth Edition. Some of the changes in this edition reflect the recent leadership information I felt should be included in the new edition. Many changes, though, reflect suggestions made by adopters and reviewers. For example, one reviewer suggested that I include more about global leadership skills, and another that I include how a leader can apply equity theory to motivate subordinates. To make way for the new material, I have selectively pruned older examples and research findings, and shifted some information to the online Knowledge Bank. A comprehensive list of changes appears in the "Transition Guide" at the beginning of the *Instructor's Resource Manual*. The following list highlights the changes in the Sixth Edition:

## Changes Throughout the Text

- Several new Internet exercises at the end of each chapter
- Fourteen new chapter introductions
- Fifteen new Leader in Action boxes
- Twenty-six new cases and two updated cases from the Fifth Edition
- More emphasis on leaders of less well-known firms, middle managers in larger firms, small-business owners, and sports leaders
- New examples throughout
- Several new Guidelines for Action and Skill Development
- Nine new Skill-Building Exercises
- One new Leadership Self-Assessment Quiz

## Content Changes Within Chapters

Chapter 1 now contains an analysis of followership classified by level of engagement. Chapter 2 presents information about executive intelligence as a cognitive skill. Chapter 3 presents a few new company visions, developing a personal brand, management by storytelling, and the impact of transformational and charismatic leadership on team performance. Chapter 4 describes management openness as a leadership behavior, and the 2006 version of the Leadership Grid.® Chapter 5 provides more clarification on Fiedler's Contingency Model and the application of the normative decision model, and describes evidence-based leadership. Chapter 6 has discussions of extraordinary executive compensation and building a sustainable environment. Chapter 7 describes the dependence theory of power and the blunder of writing embarrassing or incriminating email messages.

Chapter 8 includes a description of leadership influence for organizational change. Chapter 9 contains an expanded discussion of practicing e-leadership in virtual teams. Chapter 10 includes a description of how to use equity and social comparison for worker motivation. Chapter 11 includes two new business examples of thinking outside the box, as well as recognizing the hidden opportunities when products and ideas flop. Chapter 12 contains a discussion of the appropriate use of business jargon, nonverbal communication challenges with videoconferencing, and making the rounds as a leadership communication technique. Chapter 13 describes contrarian thinking as part of strategy. Chapter 14 presents a modern set of cultural value dimensions, success factors in international positions, and cross-cultural motivation. Chapter 15 includes a discussion of developing self-awareness through understanding lopsided leadership, growing inside-outside leaders for CEO positions, and the challenges of being a new leader.

## Supplements

Several supplements that facilitate teaching accompany this edition.

***Instructor's companion website at www.cengage.com/management/dubrin.*** This password-protected website provides valuable resources for designing and teaching your course. Content includes downloadable files from the instructor's manual, PowerPoint® slides for downloading, links to the text-specific video segments from the DVD, and the video guide.

***Instructor's Manual.*** This manual features chapter outlines and lecture notes, possible answers to discussion questions and case questions, and comments on exercises in the text.

***Computerized Test Bank.*** This computerized version of the test bank allows instructors to select, edit, and add questions, or generate randomly selected questions to produce a test master for easy duplication. Online Testing and Gradebook functions allow instructors to administer tests via their local area network or the World Wide Web, set up classes, record grades from tests or assignments, analyze grades, and compile class and individual statistics. This program can be used on both PCs and Macintosh computers.

***PowerPoint® slide presentation.*** These slides have been specially developed for this book to enhance the teaching and learning experience. The Premium PowerPoint slides embed multimedia content including graphics, tables, weblinks, and more.

***DVD.*** The video package focuses on important leadership and teamwork skills and concepts found throughout the text. A Video Guide with segment overviews and discussion questions is also available.

***Instructor's CD-ROM.*** Key instructor ancillaries, including the *Instructor's Resource Manual*, Test Bank, ExamView, and PowerPoint slides, are provided on CD-ROM, giving instructors the ultimate tools for customizing lectures and presentations.

***Web Tutor.*** Jumpstart your course with customizable, text-specific content within this Course Management System! Access a wealth of resources, including web quizzes, games, leadership assessments, KnowledgeBank activities, student-facing PowerPoint® slides, and more. Supplement the classroom experience and further prepare students for professional success. This resource is ideal as an integrated solution for your distance learning or web-enhanced course.

Students will also have access to support materials that have been developed to help them obtain a strong understanding of the Leadership course.

***Premium Student Website.*** In addition to the companion site (www.cengage.com/managment/dubrin), you can also choose to package your text with the Premium Student Website. This pincode-protected website is an optional package, and provides students with value-added content including student-facing PowerPoint® slides, interactive quizzes and games, flashcards, leadership assessments, and more. Ask your sales representative about this optional package, or visit www.cengage.com/login to add Leadership to your bookshelf and access the Premium Student Website.

## Acknowledgments

Any project as complex as this one requires a team of dedicated and talented people to see that it achieves its goals. First, I thank the many effective leaders whom I have observed in action for improving my understanding of leadership. Second, I thank the following professors who offered suggestions for improving this and previous editions:

Steven Barry, *University of Colorado–Boulder*
John Bigelow, *Boise State University*
Meika Bowden McFarland, *Albany Technical College*
Bruce T. Caine, *Vanderbilt University*
Felipe Chia, *Harrisburg Area Community College*
Jeewon Cho, *Montclair State University*
Conna Condon, *Upper Iowa University*
Emily J. Creighton, *University of New Hampshire*
Rawlin Fairbough, *Sacred Heart University*
Janice Feldbauer, *Austin Community College*
Justin Frimmer, *Jacksonville University*
Barry Gold, *Pace University*
George B. Graen, *University of Cincinnati*
Stephen G. Green, *Purdue University*
James R. Harris, *North Carolina Agricultural and Technical State University*
Paul Harris, *Lee College*
Nell Hartley, *Robert Morris College*
Linda Hefferin, *Elgin Community College*
Winston Hill, *California State University, Chico*
Avis L. Johnson, *University of Akron*
Marvin Karlins, *University of South Florida*
Nelly Kazman, *University of La Verne*
David Lee, *University of Dayton*
Brian McNatt, *University of Georgia*
Ralph Mullin, *Central Missouri State University*
Linda L. Neider, *University of Miami*
Rhonda S. Palladi, *Georgia State University*
Joseph Petrick, *Wright State University*

Mark Phillips, *University of Texas at San Antonio*
Judy Quinn, *Kutztown University*
Clint Relyea, *Arkansas State University*
Gary Renz, *Webster University*
Howard F. Rudd, *College of Charleston*
Tom J. Sanders, *University of Montevallo*
Robert Scherer, *Wright State University*
Marianne Sebok, *Community College of Southern Nevada*
Charles Seifert, *Siena College*
Kimberley L. Simons, *Madisonville Community College*
Randall G. Sleeth, *Virginia Commonwealth University*
Ahmad Tootoonchi, *Frostburg State University*
David Van Fleet, *Arizona State University West*
John Warner, *University of New Mexico*
Velvet Weems-Landingham, *Kent State University—Geauga*

The editorial and production team at Cengage Learning also receives my gratitude. By name they are Lise Johnson, Joe Sabatino, Suzanna Bainbridge, Ruth Belanger, Shelley Dickerson, Clint Kernen, Danny Bolan, Katie Huha, and Michael Farmer. Sara Planck of Matrix Productions and Rebecca Roby also receive my gratitude for their contributions to this book. Writing without loved ones would be a lonely task. My thanks, therefore, also go to my family members—Drew, Douglas and Gizella, Melanie and Will, Rosie, Clare, Camila, Sofia, Eliana, and Carson.

A.J.D.

## ABOUT THE AUTHOR

Andrew J. DuBrin is a Professor of Management emeritus in the College of Business at the Rochester Institute of Technology, where he teaches courses and conducts research in leadership, organizational behavior, and career management. He also served as department chairman and team leader in previous years. He received his Ph.D. in Industrial Psychology from Michigan State University.

DuBrin has business experience in human resource management, and consults with organizations and individuals. His specialties include leadership, influence tactics, and career development. DuBrin is an established author of both textbooks and trade books, and contributes to professional journals, magazines, newspapers, and online shows. He has written textbooks on organizational behavior, management, and human relations. His trade books cover many topics including charisma, team play, coaching and mentoring, office politics, and self-discipline.

## CHAPTER 1

# The **Nature** and **Importance** of **Leadership**

## LEARNING OBJECTIVES

After studying this chapter and doing the exercises, you should be able to

- Explain the meaning of leadership and how it differs from management.
- Describe how leadership influences organizational performance.
- Pinpoint several important leadership roles.
- Identify the major satisfactions and frustrations associated with the leadership role.
- Describe a framework for understanding leadership.
- Recognize how leadership skills are developed.
- Pinpoint several traits, behaviors, and attitudes of a successful follower.

## CHAPTER OUTLINE

Five months into her job as WellPoint Inc.'s chief executive, Angela Braly was on a three-week tour rallying the troops at the health insurance behemoth's operation across fourteen states.

On the agenda that morning: giving a pep talk to managers at the company's Empire Blue Cross Blue Shield in New York. Along with other insurers, Empire had recently come under fire from the state's attorney general over whether its planned doctor-rating programs simply tried to steer members to less-expensive physicians. Ms. Braly told the assembled managers that, despite the flak the company had been getting, measuring physicians would help guide consumers, just as other WellPoint initiatives had, like selling less-expensive plans to the uninsured and providing counseling for people who need complex and costly drugs. Several weeks later, as if to underline Ms. Braly's point, her company reached an agreement with the New York attorney general on criteria that Empire will use in measuring and disclosing physicians' performance.

> "Part of the reason we're a lightning rod is that we have to be the disciplinarians around health care costs," Ms. Braly said. "But we have to remind our employees how they're making a difference in people's lives. We're in a very personal business."

The 46-year-old Ms. Braly sees rousing WellPoint's 42,000 employees with her can-do pluck as no small part of her job. As the health insurance giant's new CEO, she became arguably the most powerful woman in corporate America in 2007. With $60 billion in annual sales and nearly 35 million members in its Blue Cross Blue Shield plans across the country, WellPoint is the company's largest insurer. A mother of three, Ms. Braly has a personable nature that belies her steeliness and skill as a tough-minded negotiator, colleagues and acquaintances say.[1]

The characterization of Angela Braly touches on many leadership topics to be covered in this book, including the ideas that energizing employees is part of a leader's job, that an important leadership role is to be a spokesperson for the organization, that a leader should be personable, and that a leader should have good negotiating skills.

Our introductory chapter begins with an explanation of what leadership is and is not. We then examine how leaders make a difference, the various roles they play, and the major satisfactions and frustrations they experience. The chapter also includes an explanation of how reading this book and doing the various quizzes and exercises will enhance your own leadership skills. It concludes with a discussion of "followership"—giving leaders good material to work with.

## THE MEANING OF LEADERSHIP

You will read about many effective organizational leaders throughout this text. The common characteristic of these leaders is their ability to inspire and stimulate others to achieve worthwhile goals. Thus we can define **leadership** as the ability to inspire confidence and support among the people who are needed to achieve organizational goals.[2]

A Google search of articles and books about leadership in organizations indicates 188 million entries. In all those entries, leadership has probably been defined in many ways. Here are several other representative definitions of leadership:

- Interpersonal influence, directed through communication toward goal attainment
- The influential increment over and above mechanical compliance with directions and orders
- An act that causes others to act or respond in a shared direction
- The art of influencing people by persuasion or example to follow a line of action
- The principal dynamic force that motivates and coordinates the organization in the accomplishment of its objectives[3]
- A willingness to take the blame (as defined by legendary football quarterback Joe Montana)[4]
- First figuring out what's right, and then explaining it to people, as opposed to first having people explain to you what's right, and then just saying what they want to hear (as defined by former New York mayor and presidential candidate Rudy Giuliani).[5]

A major point about leadership is that it is not found only among people in high-level positions. Leadership is needed at all levels in an organization and can be practiced to some extent even by a person not assigned to a formal leadership position. For example, working as a junior accountant, a person might take the initiative to suggest to management that they need to be more careful about what they classify as a true sale. A recent analysis suggests that for improved business results to come about, it will be because managers below the "C suite" (such as CEO, COO, and CFO) take the initiative and risks to drive the company in a different direction. Change needs to come about from leaders at lower levels, rather than relying exclusively on leadership from the top.[6]

An extreme example of the importance of workers exercising leadership is Roadway Express, Inc. After implementing a program of employee involvement in productivity improvement, Roadway management concluded that if Roadway is to compete in an industry in which net profit margins are less than 5 percent in a good year, every one of its 28,000 employees must be a leader. The shared leadership approach appears to have worked because Roadway grew to $1.643 billion in annual sales six years later, and was profitable.[7]

The ability to lead others effectively is a rare quality. It becomes even more rare at the highest levels in an organization because the complexity of such positions requires a vast range of leadership skills. This is one reason that firms in search of new leadership seek out a select group of brand-name executives with proven track records. It is also why companies now emphasize leadership training and development to create a new supply of leaders throughout the firm.

## Leadership as a Partnership

The current understanding of leadership is that it is a long-term relationship, or partnership, between leaders and group members. According to Peter Block, in a **partnership** the leader and the group members are connected in such a way that the power between them is approximately balanced. Block also describes partnership as the opposite of parenting (in which one person—the parent—takes responsibility for the welfare of the other—the child). Partnership occurs when control shifts from the leader to the group member, in a move away from authoritarianism and toward shared decision making.[8] Four things are necessary for a valid partnership to exist:

1. *Exchange of purpose.*  In a partnership, every worker at every level is responsible for defining vision and values. Through dialogue with people at many levels, the leader helps articulate a widely accepted vision.
2. *A right to say no.*  The belief that people who express a contrary opinion will be punished runs contrary to a partnership. Rather, a person can lose an argument but never a voice.
3. *Joint accountability.*  In a partnership, each person is responsible for outcomes and the current situation. In practice, this means that each person takes personal accountability for the success and failure of the organizational unit. (See Joe Montana's definition of leadership stated earlier.)
4. *Absolute honesty.*  In a partnership, not telling the truth to one another is an act of betrayal. When power is distributed, people are more likely to tell the truth because they feel less vulnerable.[9]

Block's conception of leadership as a partnership is an ideal to strive toward. Empowerment and team building—two major topics in this book—support the idea of a partnership. Looking at leadership as a partnership is also important because it is linked to an optimistic view of group members who want to perform well for the good of the organization.

## Leadership as a Relationship

A modern study of leadership emphasizes that leadership is a relationship between the leader and the people being led. In the words of popular leadership theorist Ken Blanchard, "Leadership isn't something you do to people. It's something you do with them."[10] Research indicates that having good relationships with group members is a major success factor for the three top positions in large organizations. James Kouzes and Barry Posner conducted an online survey asking respondents to indicate, among other questions, which would be more essential to business success in five years: social skills or Internet skills. Seventy-two percent indicated social skills, and 28 percent, Internet skills. The authors concluded that the web of people matters more than the web of technology.[11] (Yet a person who lacks Internet skills may not have the opportunity to be in a position to manage relationships.) Building relationships with people is such an important part of leadership that the theme will be introduced at various points in this text.

## Leadership Versus Management

To understand leadership, it is important to grasp the difference between leadership and management. We get a clue from the standard conceptualization of the functions of management: planning, organizing, directing (or leading), and controlling. Leading is a major part of a manager's job, yet a manager must also plan, organize, and control.

Broadly speaking, leadership deals with the interpersonal aspects of a manager's job, whereas planning, organizing, and controlling deal with the administrative aspects. Leadership deals with change, inspiration, motivation, and influence. Table 1-1 presents a stereotype of the differences between leadership and management. As is the case with most stereotypes, the differences tend to be exaggerated.

**TABLE 1-1** Leaders Versus Managers

| LEADER | MANAGER |
| --- | --- |
| Visionary | Rational |
| Passionate | Business-like |
| Creative | Persistent |
| Inspiring | Tough-minded |
| Innovative | Analytical |
| Courageous | Structured |
| Imaginative | Deliberative |
| Experimental | Authoritative |
| Independent | Stabilizing |
| Shares knowledge | Centralizes knowledge |
| Trusting | Guarded |
| Warm and radiant | Cool and reserved |
| Expresses humility | Rarely admits to being wrong |
| Initiator | Implementer |
| Acts as coach, consultant, teacher | Acts as a boss |
| Does the right things | Does things right |
| Inspires through great ideas | Commands through position |
| Knows results are achieved through people | Focuses on results |

*Source*: Genevieve Capowski, "Anatomy of a Leader: Where Are the Leaders of Tomorrow?" *Management Review*, March 1994, p. 12; David Fagiano, "Managers Versus Leaders: A Corporate Fable," *Management Review*, November 1997, p. 5, Keki R. Bhote, *The Ultimate Six Sigma* (New York: AMACOM, 2002); "Leaders: Salespeople in Disguise?" *Manager's Edge*, Special Issue, 2007, p. 3.

According to John P. Kotter, a prominent leadership theorist, managers must know how to lead as well as manage. Without being led as well as managed, organizations face the threat of extinction. Following are several key distinctions between management and leadership:

- Management produces order, consistency, and predictability.
- Leadership produces change and adaptability to new products, new markets, new competitors, new customers, and new work processes.
- Leadership, in contrast to management, involves having a vision of what the organization can become and mobilizing people to accomplish it.
- Leadership requires eliciting cooperation and teamwork from a large network of people and keeping the key people in that network motivated by using every manner of persuasion.
- Leadership produces change, often to a dramatic degree, such as by spearheading the launch of a new product or opening a new market for an old product. Management is more likely to produce a degree of predictability and order.
- Top-level leaders are likely to transform their organizations, whereas top-level managers just manage (or maintain) organizations.
- A leader creates a vision (lofty goal) to direct the organization. In contrast, the key function of the manager is to implement the vision. The manager and his or her team thus choose the means to achieve the end that the leader formulates.[12]

If these views are taken to their extreme, the leader is an inspirational figure and the manager is a stodgy bureaucrat mired in the status quo. But we must be careful not to downplay the importance of management. Effective leaders have to be good managers themselves, or be supported by effective managers. A germane example is the inspirational entrepreneur who is so preoccupied with motivating employees and captivating customers that he or she neglects internal administration. As a result, costs skyrocket beyond income, and such matters as funding the employee pension plan and paying bills and taxes on time are overlooked. In short, the difference between leadership and management is one of emphasis. Effective leaders also manage, and effective managers also lead.

## THE IMPACT OF LEADERSHIP ON ORGANIZATIONAL PERFORMANCE

An assumption underlying the study of leadership is that leaders affect organizational performance. Boards of directors—the highest-level executives of an organization—make the same assumption. A frequent antidote to major organizational problems is to replace the leader in the hope that the newly appointed leader will reverse performance problems. Here we will review some of the evidence and opinion, pro and con, about the ability of leaders to affect organizational

## ◉ Leader in Action

### A Full-Time Manager for a Law Firm?

Do big law firms need full-time managers at the helm? The question arises following the breakdown of merger talks between Dewey Ballantine LLP and Orrick, Herrington & Sutcliffe LLP. The proposed merger failed for many reasons, but their contrasting leadership styles were one factor.

Dewey, a 526-lawyer firm based in New York, follows the law-firm tradition with a chairman who is an active and successful practicing lawyer. In one year, Morton Pierce spent 3,300 hours on billable work for clients—or about 12.6 hours, on average, every weekday. That left relatively little time for management and administration issues. "Management is not my passion," he said in an interview.

By contrast, Orrick Chairman Ralph Baxter Jr. hasn't practiced law since 1992. He spends his days traveling to the firm's eighteen offices worldwide, scouting lawyers and other law firms, meeting with clients, and communicating with colleagues. He holds quarterly town-hall meetings via videoconference for Orrick's roughly 1,000 lawyers and sends out informational webcasts more frequently.

As law firms have grown larger and more global in recent decades, more have followed Orrick's path. Their leaders increasingly resemble public-company CEOs, focusing on managing others at the firms. "Ralph Baxter is the epitome of the twenty-first-century law-firm leader," says David Wilkins, the director of Harvard Law School's Program on the Legal Profession. "Firms that have radically moved themselves up the prestige ladder and the profitability ladder and expanded their geographic scope have had full-time leaders," he says.

Some law firms still take the traditional view. At New York's Cravath, Swaine & Moore LLP, a manager's credibility depends on "your credibility as a practitioner," says firm head Evan Chesler, who spends three-fourths of his time on legal work.

Chesler says Cravath lawyers believe that the law is a profession—not merely a business. He notes that Cravath is relatively easier to run than other large firms, in part because the 500-lawyer firm has only two offices, New York and London.

Wilkins of Harvard Law School agrees that firms of Cravath's size "can get away with part-time managers." He says lawyer-managers "do have more authority because their partners see them as true participants." But Wilkins thinks that most firms need a full-time manager.

### Questions

1. Why does having a full-time leader/manager of a law firm sometimes make a contribution to the success of the firm?
2. If the manager of a law firm still practices law, what leadership role is he or she carrying out while practicing law?
3. How effective could a leader/manager be who spends 3,300 hours a year working with clients or customers?

*Source:* Nathan Koppel, "Law Firms Try New Idea: Manager-Focused CEO," *The Wall Street Journal*, January 22, 2007, p. B3.

performance. The Leader in Action profile provides a positive example of the importance of effective leadership in a professional organization, yet also looks at the other side of the argument.

### Research and Opinion: Leadership Does Make a Difference

The idea that leaders actually influence organizational performance and morale is so plausible that there is not an abundance of research and opinion that deals with this issue. (Nor do we have loads of studies demonstrating that sleeping reduces fatigue.) Here we look at a sample of the existing research and opinion.

A team of researchers investigated the impact of transactional (routine) and charismatic (inspirational) leadership on financial performance.[13] The researchers analyzed 210 surveys completed by senior managers from 131 *Fortune 500* firms. Transactional and charismatic leadership styles were measured with a leadership questionnaire. Each participant was asked to think about the CEO of his or her company and rate that individual on the leadership scale. Because an uncertain environment often makes having a strong leader more important, participants also completed a questionnaire that measured perceived environmental uncertainty. Organizational performance was measured as net profit margin (NPM), computed as net income divided by net sales. The performance data were gathered from public information about the companies.

The results of the study disclosed that (1) transactional leadership was not significantly related to performance, (2) charismatic leadership showed a slight positive relationship with performance, and (3) when the environment is uncertain, charismatic leadership is more strongly related to performance.

In another study, a group of researchers analyzed 200 management techniques as employed by 150 companies over ten years. The aspect of the study evaluating the effects of leadership found that CEOs influence 15 percent of the total variance (influencing factors) in a company's profitability or total return to shareholders. The same study also found that the industry in which a company operates also accounts for 15 percent of the variance in profitability. So the choice of a CEO leader is as important as the choice of whether to remain in the same industry or enter a different one.[14]

An analysis of the franchise industry points to the importance of leadership. The report noted that it can be difficult to pinpoint a specific formula for franchise success, yet conversations with successful franchise operators emphasized the importance of enthusiasm, leadership, and an ability to work with people. (Enthusiasm and the ability to work with people are important components of leadership.) One of the franchisers included in the report was Steven J. Greenbaum, the founder of PostNet International Franchise Corp., which offers copying, printing, packing, and shipping services. Greenbaum says that "Leadership is critical. You are required to have a vision of what the business can be, and communicate the vision to the company officers and franchisees."[15]

An overview of research on managerial succession over a recent 20-year period provides more support for the idea that leadership has an impact on organizational performance. A consistent relationship was found between who is in charge and how well an organization performed as measured by a variety of indicators. Using different methodologies, these studies arrived at the same conclusion that changes in leadership are followed by changes in company performance. Statistical analyses suggest that the leader might be responsible for somewhere between 15 percent and 45 percent of a firm's performance.[16] How leaders impact organizational (or unit) performance is essentially the subject of this book. For example, good results are attained by developing teamwork and formulating the right strategy.

In addition to tangible evidence that leadership makes a difference, the perception of these differences is also meaningful. An understanding of these perceptions derives from **attribution theory**, the theory of how we explain the causes of events. Gary Yukl explains that organizations are complex social systems of patterned interactions among people. In their efforts to understand (and simplify) organizational events, people interpret these events in simple human terms. One especially strong and prevalent approach is to attribute causality to leaders. They are viewed as heroes and heroines who determine the fates of their organizations.[17] The extraordinary success of Southwest Airlines Co. during the 1990s is thus attributed to Herb Kelleher, its flamboyant chief executive. Kelleher initiated no-frills, low-cost air service and built Southwest into a highly profitable airline. (Ultimately, new competitors modeled after Southwest, such as JetBlue Airlines, took away some of Southwest's profitability.) Most organizational successes are attributed to heroic leaders—according to attribution theory.

## Research and Opinion: Formal Leadership Does Not Make a Difference

In contrast to the previous argument, the antileadership argument holds that leadership has a smaller impact on organizational outcomes than do forces in the situation. To personalize this perspective, imagine yourself appointed as the manager of a group of highly skilled investment bankers. How well your group performs could be attributed as much to their talent and to economic conditions as to your leadership. The three major arguments against the importance of leadership are substitutes for leadership, leadership irrelevance, and complexity theory.

**Substitutes for Leadership**    At times competent leadership is not necessary, and incompetent leadership can be counterbalanced by certain factors in the work situation. Under these circumstances, leadership itself is of little consequence to the performance and satisfaction of team members. According to this viewpoint, many organizations have **substitutes for leadership**. Such substitutes are factors in the work environment that provide guidance and incentives to perform, making the leader's role almost superfluous,[18] as shown in Figure 1-1.

*Closely knit teams of highly trained individuals.*    When members of a cohesive, highly trained group are focused on a goal, they may require almost no leadership to accomplish their task. Several researchers have studied air traffic controllers who direct traffic into San Francisco and pilots who land jet fighters on a nuclear aircraft carrier. With such groups, directive (decisive and task-oriented) leadership

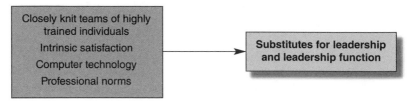

**FIGURE 1-1** Substitutes for Leadership.

is seemingly unimportant. When danger is the highest, these groups rely more on each other than on a leader.

***Intrinsic satisfaction.*** Employees who are engaged in work they find strongly self-motivating, or intrinsically satisfying, require a minimum of leadership. Part of the reason is that the task itself grabs the worker's attention and energy. The worker may require little leadership as long as the task is proceeding smoothly. Many information technology firms provide a minimum of leadership and management to information technology professionals, who may be totally absorbed in such tasks as combating the latest computer virus.

***Computer technology.*** Some companies today use computer-aided monitoring and computer networking to take over many of the supervisor's leadership functions. The computer provides productivity and quality data, and directions for certain tasks are entered into the information system. Even error detection and goal setting are incorporated into some interaction systems. Instead of asking a supervisor for assistance, some employees use the computer network to ask for assistance from other workers. (We could argue here that the computer is being used to control rather than to lead workers.)

***Professional norms.*** Workers who incorporate strong professional norms often require a minimum of supervision and leadership. A group of certified professional accountants may not need visionary leadership to inspire them to do an honest job of auditing the books of a client or advising against tax fraud.

Although the leadership substitute concept has some merit, it reflects naiveté about the role of organizational leadership. The late Bernard M. Bass, professor of management, notes that self-management by groups and individuals requires delegation by a higher authority. In addition, higher-ranking managers provide guidance, encouragement, and support.[19]

More recent research study suggests that the theory of substitutes for leadership may be flawed and that leadership does indeed have an impact on group effectiveness. A team of researchers conducted a study of forty-nine organizations with at least fifty employees and two levels of management. The sample consisted of 940 employees and 156 leaders. Measures of substitutes for leadership were similar to the information presented here, such as "I am a member of a professional group whose standards and values guide me in my work." In short, the study suggested that "leadership matters." The likeability of the leader and whether the leader provides rewards for good performance were found to be the major correlates of performance.[20]

**Leadership Irrelevance** According to the theorizing of Jeffrey Pfeffer, leadership is irrelevant to most organizational outcomes. Rather, it is the situation that must be carefully analyzed. Pfeffer argues that factors outside the leader's control have a larger impact on business outcomes than do leadership actions.[21] During the late 1990s and continuing into the 2000s, cell phone ownership surged throughout the world, with 80 percent of adults in the United States owning cell phones. The sales boom in this electronic equipment could be better attributed to an outside force than to inspirational leadership within telecommunications companies.

Another aspect of the leader irrelevance argument is that high-level leaders have unilateral control over only a few resources. Furthermore, the leader's control of these resources is limited by obligations to stakeholders like consumers and stockholders. Finally, firms tend to choose new organizational leaders whose values are compatible with those of the firm. The leaders therefore act in ways similar to previous leaders.

Jim Collins, who has extensively researched how companies endure and how they shift from average to superior performance, also doubts the relevance of leadership. According to his earlier research, corporate leaders are slaves of much larger organizational forces. Collins makes the analogy of children holding a pair of ribbons inside a coach and imagining they are driving the horse. It is not the leader's personality that makes a difference; more important is the organization's personality. For example, Collins notes that Jack Welch was the product rather than the producer of GE's success during his long reign.[22]

Another argument for leadership irrelevance is that in the modern organization effective leadership means widespread collaboration in obtaining ideas, rather than the heroic leader doing all the innovating. According to this point of view, instead of centralizing leadership in the hands of a few, authority and power are shared, and people lead themselves.[23] (The concept of shared leadership will surface at several places in the text.)

The leader irrelevance argument would have greater practical value if it were recast as a *leader constraint theory*, which would hold that leaders are constrained in what they can do but still have plenty of room to influence others.

**Complexity Theory** Similar to the pessimistic outlook of leader irrelevance is the perspective of *complexity theory*, which holds that organizations are complex systems that cannot be explained by the usual rules of nature. Leaders and managers can do little to alter the course of the complex organizational system. The same view holds that forces outside the leader or manager's control determine a company's fate. Managers cannot predict which business strategies or product mixes will survive. The best they can hope for is to scramble or innovate in order to adapt to outside forces. Ultimately all companies will die but at different times, because it is the system, not leadership and management, that dominates.[24]

A useful perspective on whether leadership makes a difference is to ask the right question as framed by J. Richard Hackman and Ruth Wageman. Instead of asking if leaders make a difference, we should be asking *under what conditions leaders make a difference.*[25] A crisis mode is an example of a situation in which a strong leader usually makes a difference, such as getting field units back on track after a hurricane or product recall.

## LEADERSHIP ROLES

Another way to gain an understanding of leadership is to examine the various roles carried out by leaders. A *role* in this context is an expected set of activities or behaviors stemming from one's job. Leadership roles are a subset of the managerial roles studied by Henry Mintzberg and others.[26] Before reading ahead to the summary of leadership roles, you are invited to complete Leadership Self-Assessment Quiz 1-1.

 ### Leadership Self-Assessment Quiz 1-1

**Readiness for the Leadership Role**

**Instructions:** Indicate the extent to which you agree with each of the following statements, using the following scale: 1, disagree strongly; 2, disagree; 3, neutral; 4, agree; 5, agree strongly.

1. It is enjoyable to have people count on me for ideas and suggestions.

    1       2       3       4       5

2. It would be accurate to say that I have inspired other people.

    1       2       3       4       5

3. It's a good practice to ask people provocative questions about their work.

    1       2       3       4       5

4. It's easy for me to compliment others.

    1       2       3       4       5

5. I like to cheer people up even when my own spirits are down.

    1       2       3       4       5

6. What my team accomplishes is more important than my personal glory.

    1       2       3       4       5

7. Many people imitate my ideas.

    1       2       3       4       5

8. Building team spirit is important to me.

    1       2       3       4       5

9. I would enjoy coaching other members of the team.

    1       2       3       4       5

## Quiz 1-1 (continued)

**10.** It is important to me to recognize others for their accomplishments.

    **1**     **2**     **3**     **4**     **5**

**11.** I would enjoy entertaining visitors to my firm even if it interfered with my completing a report.

    **1**     **2**     **3**     **4**     **5**

**12.** It would be fun for me to represent my team at gatherings outside our unit.

    **1**     **2**     **3**     **4**     **5**

**13.** The problems of my teammates are my problems too.

    **1**     **2**     **3**     **4**     **5**

**14.** Resolving conflict is an activity I enjoy.

    **1**     **2**     **3**     **4**     **5**

**15.** I would cooperate with another unit in the organization even if I disagreed with the position taken by its members.

    **1**     **2**     **3**     **4**     **5**

**16.** I am an idea generator on the job.

    **1**     **2**     **3**     **4**     **5**

**17.** It is fun for me to bargain whenever I have the opportunity.

    **1**     **2**     **3**     **4**     **5**

**18.** Team members listen to me when I speak.

    **1**     **2**     **3**     **4**     **5**

**19.** People have asked me to assume the leadership of an activity several times in my life.

    **1**     **2**     **3**     **4**     **5**

**20.** I have always been a convincing person.

    **1**     **2**     **3**     **4**     **5**

**Total score:** _____

***Scoring and Interpretation:*** Calculate your total score by adding the numbers circled. A tentative interpretation of the scoring is as follows:

- **90–100:** High readiness for the leadership role
- **60–89:** Moderate readiness for the leadership role
- **40–59:** Some uneasiness with the leadership role
- **39 or less:** Low readiness for the leadership role

If you are already a successful leader and you scored low on this questionnaire, ignore your score. If you scored surprisingly low and you are not yet a leader, or are currently performing poorly as a leader, study the statements carefully. Consider changing your attitude or your behavior so that you can legitimately answer more of the statements with a 4 or a 5. Studying the rest of this text will give you additional insights that may be helpful in your development as a leader.

Leading is a complex activity, so it is not surprising that Mintzberg and other researchers identified nine roles that can be classified as part of the leadership function of management.

1. *Figurehead.* Leaders, particularly high-ranking managers, spend some part of their time engaging in ceremonial activities, or acting as a figurehead. Four specific behaviors fit the figurehead role of a leader:
   a. entertaining clients or customers as an official representative of the organization
   b. making oneself available to outsiders as a representative of the organization
   c. serving as an official representative of the organization at gatherings outside the organization
   d. escorting official visitors

2. *Spokesperson.* When a manager acts as a spokesperson, the emphasis is on answering letters or inquiries and formally reporting to individuals and groups outside the manager's direct organizational unit. As a spokesperson, the managerial leader keeps five groups of people informed about the unit's activities, plans, capabilities, and possibilities (vision):
   a. upper-level management
   b. clients or customers
   c. other important outsiders such as labor unions
   d. professional colleagues
   e. the general public

Dealing with outside groups and the general public is usually the responsibility of top-level managers.

3. *Negotiator.* Part of almost any manager's job description is trying to make deals with others for needed resources. Researchers have identified three specific negotiating activities:
   a. bargaining with superiors for funds, facilities, equipment, or other forms of support
   b. bargaining with other units in the organization for the use of staff, facilities, equipment, or other forms of support
   c. bargaining with suppliers and vendors for services, schedules, and delivery times

4. *Coach and motivator.* An effective leader takes the time to coach and motivate team members, and sometimes to inspire large groups of people inside the organization. This role includes five specific behaviors:
   a. informally recognizing team members' achievements
   b. providing team members with feedback concerning ineffective performance
   c. ensuring that team members are informed of steps that can improve their performance
   d. implementing rewards and punishments to encourage and sustain good performance
   e. inspiring people through such means as being charismatic, creating visions, telling interesting stories, and being highly ethical

5. *Team builder.* A key aspect of a leader's role is to build an effective team. Activities contributing to this role include:
   a. ensuring that team members are recognized for their accomplishments, such as through letters of appreciation
   b. initiating activities that contribute to group morale, such as giving parties and sponsoring sports teams
   c. holding periodic staff meetings to encourage team members to talk about their accomplishments, problems, and concerns

6. *Team player.* Related to the team-builder role is that of the team player. Three behaviors of team players are:
   a. displaying appropriate personal conduct
   b. cooperating with other units in the organization
   c. displaying loyalty to superiors by supporting their plans and decisions fully

7. *Technical problem solver.* It is particularly important for supervisors and middle managers to help team members solve technical problems. Two activities contributing to this role are:
   a. serving as a technical expert or adviser
   b. performing individual contributor tasks on a regular basis, such as making sales calls or repairing machinery

8. *Entrepreneur.* Although not self-employed, managers who work in large organizations have some responsibility for suggesting innovative ideas or furthering the business aspects of the firm. Three entrepreneurial leadership role activities are:
   a. reading trade publications and professional journals to keep up with what is happening in the industry and profession
   b. talking with customers or others in the organization to keep aware of changing needs and requirements
   c. getting involved in situations outside the unit that could suggest ways of improving the unit's performance, such as visiting other firms, attending professional meetings or trade shows, and participating in educational programs

9. *Strategic planner.* Top-level managers engage in strategic planning, usually assisted by input from others throughout the organization. Carrying out the strategic-planner role enables the manager to practice strategic leadership. Specific activities involved in this role include:
   a. setting a vision and direction for the organization and providing innovative ideas to pursue
   b. helping the firm deal with the external environment
   c. helping develop organizational policies

A common thread in the leadership roles of a manager is that the managerial leader in some way inspires or influences others. An analysis in the *Harvard Business Review* concluded that the most basic role for corporate leaders is to release the human spirit that makes initiative, creativity, and entrepreneurship possible.[27] An important practical implication is that managers at every level can exercise leadership. For example, a team leader can make an important contribution to the firm's thrust for quality by explaining to team members how to minimize duplications in a mailing list. Leadership Skill-Building Exercise 1-1 provides an opportunity to apply role analysis to yourself.

Up to this point, we have described the meaning of leadership, how leadership affects organizational performance, and the many activities carried out by leaders. You have had an opportunity to explore your attitudes toward occupying the leadership role, and personally apply leadership role analysis. We now further personalize information about leadership.

# THE SATISFACTIONS AND FRUSTRATIONS OF BEING A LEADER

The term *leader* has a positive connotation for most people. To be called a leader is generally better than to be called a follower or a subordinate. (The term *follower* has virtually disappeared in organizations, and the term *subordinate* has fallen out of favor. The preferred term for a person who reports to a leader or manager is *team member, group member,* or *associate.* Researchers, however, continue to use the terms *subordinate* and *follower* for technical purposes.) Yet being a leader, such as a team leader, vice president, or COO (chief operating officer), does not always bring personal satisfaction. Some leadership jobs are more fun than others, such as being the leader of a successful group with cheerful team members.

Because most of you are contemplating becoming a leader or moving further into a leadership role, it is worthwhile to examine some of the potential satisfactions and frustrations many people find in being an organizational leader.

## Satisfactions of Leaders

The types of satisfactions that you might obtain from being a formal leader depend on your particular leadership position. Factors such as the amount of money you are paid and the type of people in your group influence your satisfaction. Nevertheless, as Gloria Molina, who was chair of the Los Angeles County Board of Supervisors several years ago, said, "It was never easy, but there is great satisfaction in leadership."[28] Leaders often experience seven sources of satisfaction.

**1. *A feeling of power and prestige.*** Being a leader automatically grants you some power. Prestige is forthcoming because many people think highly of people who are leaders. In some organizations, top-level leaders are addressed as Mr., Mrs., or Ms., whereas lower-ranking people are referred to by their surnames. Yet many leaders encourage others to call them by their first name.

**2. *A chance to help others grow and develop.*** A leader works directly with people, often teaching them job skills, serving as a mentor, and listening to personal problems. Part of a leader's job is to help other people become managers and leaders. A leader often feels as much of a "people helper" as does a human resource manager or a counselor.

## ◎ Leadership Skill-Building Exercise 1-1

### My Leadership Role Analysis

Here is an opportunity for you to think through your current level of skill or potential ability to carry out successfully the nine leadership roles already described. Each role will be listed along with a reminder of one of its key aspects. Check next to each role whether it is an activity you could carry out now, or something for which you will need more experience and preparation. For those activities you check as "capable of doing it now," jot down an example of your success in this area. For example, a person

who checked "capable of doing it now" for Role 7, technical problem solver, might have written: "I helped the restaurant where I was an assistant manager bring in more revenue during off-peak hours. I promoted an early-bird supper for senior citizens."

Few readers of this book will have had experience in carrying out most of these roles. So relate the specific roles to any leadership experience you may have had, including full-time work, part-time work, volunteer work, clubs, committees, and sports.

| LEADERSHIP ROLE | CAPABLE OF DOING IT NOW | NEED PREPARATION AND EXPERIENCE |
|---|:---:|:---:|
| 1. Figurehead (Engage in ceremonial activities; represent the group to outsiders.) | ☐ | ☐ |
| 2. Spokesperson (Answer inquiries; report information about the group to outsiders.) | ☐ | ☐ |
| 3. Negotiator (Make deals with others for needed resources.) | ☐ | ☐ |
| 4. Coach and motivator (Recognize achievements; encourage; give feedback and advice; inspire people.) | ☐ | ☐ |
| 5. Team builder (Contribute to group morale; hold meetings to encourage members to talk about accomplishments and concerns.) | ☐ | ☐ |
| 6. Team player (Correct conduct; cooperate with others; be loyal.) | ☐ | ☐ |
| 7. Technical problem solver (Help group members solve technical problems; perform individual contributor tasks.) | ☐ | ☐ |
| 8. Entrepreneur (Suggest innovative ideas and further business activity of the group; search for new undertakings for the group.) | ☐ | ☐ |
| 9. Strategic planner (Set direction for others based on external environment.) | ☐ | ☐ |

*Interpretation:* The more of the nine roles you are ready to perform, the more ready you are to function as a manager or to perform managerial work. Your study of leadership will facilitate carrying out more of these roles effectively. For purposes of skill development, choose one of the roles in which you need preparation and experience. Read some information

in this text or elsewhere about the role, and then practice that role when the opportunity arises. Or, create an opportunity to practice that role. For example, assume you have a valuable skill such as web site design. During the next couple of weeks, coach a beginner in web site design.

**3. *High income.*** Leaders, in general, receive higher pay than team members, and executive leaders in major business corporations typically earn several million dollars per year. A handful of business executives receive compensation of over $100 million per year and several have received over $150 million as compensation for being fired. If money is an important motivator or satisfier, being a leader has a built-in satisfaction. In some situations a team leader earns virtually the same amount of money as other team members. Occupying a leadership position, however, is a starting point on the path to high-paying leadership positions.

**4. *Respect and status.*** A leader frequently receives respect from group members. He or she also enjoys a higher status than people who are not occupying a leadership role. Status accompanies being appointed to a leadership position on or off the job. When an individual's personal qualifications match the position, his or her status is even higher.

**5. *Good opportunities for advancement.*** Once you become a leader, your advancement opportunities increase. Obtaining a leadership position is a vital first step for career advancement in many organizations. Staff or individual contributor positions help broaden a person's professional experience, but most executives rise through a managerial path.

**6. *A feeling of "being in on" things.*** A side benefit of being a leader is that you receive more inside information. For instance, as a manager you are invited to attend management meetings. In those meetings you are given information not passed along to individual contributors. One such tidbit might be plans for expansion or downsizing.

**7. *An opportunity to control money and other resources.*** A leader is often in the position of helping to prepare a department budget and authorize expenses. Even though you cannot spend this money personally, knowing that your judgment on financial matters is trusted does provide some satisfaction. Many leaders in both private and public organizations control annual budgets of several million dollars.

## Dissatisfactions and Frustrations of Leaders

About one out of ten people in the work force is classified as a supervisor, administrator, or manager. Not every one of these people is a true leader. Yet the problems these people experience often stem from the leadership portions of their job. Many individual contributors refuse to accept a leadership role because of the frustrations they have seen leaders endure. These frustrations include the following:

**1. *Too much uncompensated overtime.*** People in leadership jobs are usually expected to work longer hours than other employees. Such unpaid hours are called casual overtime. People in organizational leadership positions typically spend about fifty-five hours per week working. During peak periods of peak demands, this figure can surge to eighty hours per week.

**2. *Too many "headaches."*** It would take several pages to list all the potential problems leaders face. Being a leader is a good way to discover the validity of Murphy's law: "If anything can go wrong, it will." A leader is subject to a batch of problems involving people and things. Many people find that a leadership position is a source of stress, and many managers experience burnout.

**3. *Facing a perform-or-perish mentality.*** Many leaders face an enormous amount of pressure to either perform or be fired. These pressures often can be found in companies owned by private equity (or buyout) firms. The head of each company owned by an equity firm is expected to make the company profitable through such means as slashing costs, boosting sales in international markets, and paying down debt. There is also considerable pressure on the CEO to improve operations by making them more efficient.[29]

**4. *Not enough authority to carry out responsibility.*** People in managerial positions complain repeatedly that they are held responsible for things over which they have little control. As a leader, you might be expected to work with an ill-performing team member, yet you lack the power to fire him or her. Or you might be expected to produce high-quality service with too small a staff and no authority to become fully staffed.

**5. *Loneliness.*** As former Secretary of State and five-star general Colin Powell says, "Command is lonely." The higher you rise as a leader, the lonelier you will be in a certain sense. Leadership limits the number of people in whom you can confide. It is awkward to confide negative feelings about your employer to a team member. It is equally awkward to complain about one group member to another. Some people in leadership positions feel lonely because they miss being "one of the gang."

**6. *Too many problems involving people.*** A major frustration facing a leader is the number of human resource problems requiring action. The lower your leadership position, the more such problems you face. For example, the office supervisor spends more time dealing with problem employees than does the chief information officer.

**7. *Too much organizational politics.*** People at all levels of an organization, from the office assistant to the chairperson of the board, must be aware of political factors. Yet you can avoid politics more easily as an individual contributor than you can as a leader. As a leader you have to engage in political byplay from three directions: below, sideways, and upward. Political tactics such as forming alliances and coalitions are a necessary part of a leader's role. Another troublesome aspect of organizational politics is that there are people lurking to take you out of the game, particularly if you are changing the status quo. These enemies within might attack you directly in an attempt to shift the issue to your character and style and avoid discussing the changes you are attempting to implement. Or, your superiors might divert you from your goals by keeping you overwhelmed with the details of your change effort.[30] In addition, backstabbers may agree with you in person but badmouth you to others.

**8. *The pursuit of conflicting goals.*** A major challenge leaders face is to navigate among conflicting goals. The central theme of these dilemmas is attempting to grant others the authority to act independently, yet still getting them aligned or pulling together for a common purpose.[31] Many of the topics relating to these conflicting goals are discussed at later points in the text.

**9. *Being perceived as unethical, especially if you are a corporate executive.*** The many corporate financial scandals made public in recent years have led to extreme perceptions that CEOs, in particular, are dishonest, unethical, and almost criminal in their behavior. Even if 95 percent of corporate leaders are honest and devoted to their constituents, the leader still has to deal with the possibility of being perceived as dishonest.

# A FRAMEWORK FOR UNDERSTANDING LEADERSHIP

**(KB) Knowledge Bank**
A table of these dilemmas as identified by a group of bank executives can be found online in the Knowledge Bank section of the web site for this text.

**www.cengage.com/ management/dubrin**

Many different theories and explanations of leadership have been developed because of the interest in leadership as a practice and as a research topic. Several attempts have been made to integrate the large number of leadership theories into one comprehensive framework.[32] The framework presented here focuses on the major sets of variables that influence leadership effectiveness. The basic assumption underlying the framework can be expressed in terms of a simple formula with a profound meaning:

$$L = f(l, gm, s)$$

The formula means that the leadership process is a function of the leader, group members (or followers), and other situational variables. Bruce J. Avolio emphasizes that leadership is a function of both the leader and the led and the complexity of the context (setting and environment).[33] In other words, leadership does not exist in the abstract but takes into account factors related to the leader, the person or persons being led, and a variety of forces in the environment. A charismatic and visionary leader might be just what a troubled organization needs to help it achieve world-class success. Yet a group of part-time telemarketers might need a more direct and focused type of leader to help them when their telephone calls mostly meet with abrupt rejection from the people solicited.

The model presented in Figure 1-2 extends this situational perspective. According to this model, leadership can best be understood by examining its key variables: leader characteristics and traits, leader behavior and style, group member characteristics, and the internal and external environment. At the right side of the framework, **leadership effectiveness** refers to attaining desirable outcomes such as productivity, quality, and satisfaction in a given situation. Whether or not the leader is effective depends on the four sets of variables in the box.

Beginning at the top of the circle, *leader characteristics and traits* refers to the inner qualities, such as self-confidence and problem-solving ability, that help a leader function effectively in many situations. *Leader behavior and style* refers to the activities engaged in by the leader, including his or her characteristic approach, that relate to his or her effectiveness. A leader who frequently coaches group members and practices participative leadership, for example, might be effective in many circumstances.

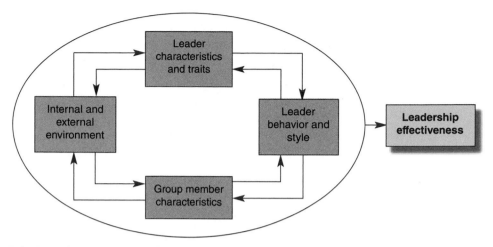

**FIGURE 1-2** A Framework for Understanding Leadership.

*Source: Managing Today!* by Stephen P. Robbins, © 1997. Reprinted by permission of Prentice-Hall, Inc. Upper Saddle River, N.J.

*Group member characteristics* refers to attributes of the group members that could have a bearing on how effective the leadership attempt will be. Intelligent and well-motivated group members, for example, help the leader do an outstanding job. The *internal and external environment* also influences leadership effectiveness. A leader in a culturally diverse environment, for example, will need to have multicultural skills to be effective. All of the topics in this text fit somewhere into this model, and the fit will be more obvious at some places than at others. Table 1-2 outlines how the elements of the leadership model line up with chapters in the text.

The arrows connecting the four sets of variables in Figure 1-2 suggest a reciprocal influence among them. Some of these linkages are stronger than others. The most pronounced linkage is that a leader's characteristics and traits will typically influence the leader's style. If a given individual is extraverted, warm, and caring, it will be natural for him or her to adopt a people-oriented leadership style. Another linkage is that the group members' characteristics might influence the leader's style. If the members are capable and self-sufficient, the leader is likely to choose a leadership style that grants freedom to the group. It will be easier for the leader to empower these people. A final linkage is that the internal and external environment can influence or mediate the leader's traits to some extent. In an environment in which creativity and risk taking are fostered, leaders are more likely to give expression to their tendencies toward creative problem solving and risk taking.

## SKILL DEVELOPMENT IN LEADERSHIP

Leadership skills are in high demand. Executives seeking candidates for high-level management jobs list leadership skills as the top attributes they want. After these come industry-specific experience and functional/technical expertise.[34] Leadership

**TABLE 1-2** Relationship Between Chapter Topics and the Framework for Understanding Leadership

| COMPONENT OF THE MODEL | RELEVANT CHAPTER OR CHAPTERS |
| --- | --- |
| Leader characteristics and traits | Chapter 2, "Traits, Motives, and Characteristics of Leaders" |
| | Chapter 3, "Charismatic and Transformational Leadership" |
| | Chapter 6, "Leadership Ethics and Social Responsibility" |
| | Chapter 11, "Creativity, Innovation, and Leadership" |
| | Chapter 12, "Communication and Conflict Resolution Skills" |
| Leader behavior and style | Chapter 4, "Leadership Behaviors, Attitudes, and Styles" |
| | Chapter 6, "Leadership Ethics and Social Responsibility" |
| | Chapter 8, "Influence Tactics of Leaders" |
| | Chapter 9, "Developing Teamwork" |
| Group member characteristics | Chapter 5, "Contingency and Situational Leadership" |
| | Chapter 10, "Motivation and Coaching Skills" |
| Internal and external environment | Chapter 13, "Strategic Leadership and Knowledge Management" |
| | Chapter 14, "International and Culturally Diverse Aspects of Leadership" |
| | Chapter 7, "Power, Politics, and Leadership" |
| | Chapter 15, "Leadership Development and Succession" |

skills are also sought in candidates for entry-level professional positions. Although students of leadership will find this information encouraging, developing leadership skills is more complex than developing a structured skill such as inserting an additional memory card into a computer. Nevertheless, you can develop leadership skills by studying this text, which follows a general learning model:

**1. *Conceptual information and behavioral guidelines.*** Each chapter in this text presents useful information about leadership, including a section titled "Guidelines for Action and Skill Development."

**2. *Conceptual information demonstrated by examples and brief descriptions of leaders in action.*** Much can be learned by reading about how effective (or ineffective) leaders operate.

**3. *Experiential exercises.*** The text provides an opportunity for practice and personalization through cases, role plays, and self-assessment quizzes. Self-quizzes are emphasized here because they are an effective method of helping you personalize

Leadership Skill-Building Exercise 1-2

### My Leadership Portfolio

Here, we ask you to begin developing a leadership portfolio that will be a personal document of your leadership capabilities and experiences. In each chapter, we will recommend new entries for your portfolio. At the same time, you are encouraged to use your imagination in determining what constitutes a suitable addition to your leadership portfolio.

We suggest you begin your portfolio with a personal mission statement that explains the type of leadership you plan to practice. An example might be, "I intend to become a well-respected corporate professional, a key member of a happy and healthy family, and a contributor to my community. I aspire to lead many people toward constructive activities." Include your job résumé in your portfolio, and devote a special section to leadership experiences. These experiences can be from the job, community and religious activities, and sports. (See Leadership Self-Assessment Quiz 1-2.)

the information, thereby linking conceptual information to yourself. For example, you will read about the importance of assertiveness in leadership and also complete an assertiveness quiz.

**4. *Feedback on skill utilization, or performance, from others.*** Feedback exercises appear at several places in the text. Implementing some of the skills outside of the classroom will provide additional opportunities for feedback.

**5. *Practice in natural settings.*** As just implied, skill development requires active practice. A given skill has to be practiced many times in natural settings before it becomes integrated comfortably into a leader's mode of operation. A basic principle of learning is that practice is necessary to develop and improve skills. Suppose, for example, that you read about giving advice in the form of questions, as described in Chapter 10. If you practice this skill at least six times in live settings, you will probably have acquired an important new skill for coaching others.

Leadership Skill-Building Exercise 1-2 gives you the opportunity to begin developing your leadership skills systematically.

 Leadership Self-Assessment Quiz 1-2

#### The Leadership Experience Audit

***Instructions:*** Readers of this book vary considerably in their leadership, managerial, and supervisory experience. Yet even readers who have not yet occupied a formal leadership position may have had at least a taste of being a leader. Use the following checklist to record any possible leadership experiences you might have had in the past or have now.

☐ Held a formal leadership position, such as vice president, department head, manager, assistant manager, team leader, group leader, or crew chief

☐ Seized the opportunity on the job to take care of a problem, although I was not assigned such responsibility

☐ Headed a committee or task force

☐ Was captain or co-captain of an athletic team

☐ Held office in a club at high school, career school, or college

☐ Was editor of a campus newspaper or section of the newspaper such as sports

☐ Organized a study group for a course

☐ Organized an ongoing activity to sell merchandise at people's homes, such as for Avon, Mary Kay, or Tupperware

☐ Worked in multilevel sales and recruited and guided new members

☐ Organized a charity drive for a school or religious organization

☐ Organized a vacation trip for friends or family

☐ Took charge during a crisis, such as by helping people out of a burning building or a flooded house

☐ Was head of a choir or a band

☐ Headed a citizens' group making demands on a company or the government

☐ Organized a group of friends to help out people in need, such as physically disabled senior citizens

☐ Other

*Interpretation:* The more experiences you checked, the more leadership experience you already have under your belt. Leadership experience of any type can be valuable in learning to work well with people and coordinate their efforts. Many CEOs in a variety of fields got their start as assistant fast-food restaurant managers.

# FOLLOWERSHIP: BEING AN EFFECTIVE GROUP MEMBER

**KB Knowledge Bank**
Contains a Leadership Skill-Building Exercise that will give you more insight into the multidimensional nature of effective group membership.

**www.cengage.com/ management/dubrin**

To be an effective leader, one needs good followers. Leaders cannot exist without followers. As we mentioned at the outset of this book, the word *followers* suffers from political incorrectness, yet it is a neutral term as used by leadership researchers. A point of view that represents a modern view of leadership, as explained by J. Richard Hackman and Ruth Wageman, is that leaders are also followers and followers also exhibit leadership. Each boss is also a subordinate, such as a team leader reporting to a middle manager.[35] And each subordinate will often carry out a leadership role, such as heading up a short-term project—or even organizing this year's holiday party.

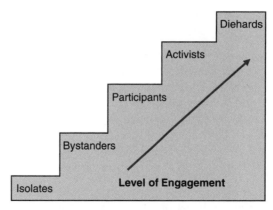

**FIGURE 1-3** Followers Classified by Level of Engagement.

Most of the topics in our study of leadership are aimed at inspiring, motivating, and influencing group members to want to achieve organizational goals. It is also valuable, however, to focus on three key aspects of being an effective group member: types of followers, the personal characteristics of productive followers, and the importance of collaboration between leaders and followers.

## Types of Followers

A major challenge in being a leader is to recognize that followers differ substantially in talent and motivation. Similarly, a challenge in becoming an effective follower is to understand your basic approach to being a group member. Barbara Kellerman offers a typology that helps explain how followers differ from one another. She focuses on the defining factor of the level of engagement with the leader or group to arrive at five types of follower, as illustrated in Figure 1-3. At one end of the continuum is "feeling and doing nothing." At the other end is "being passionately committed and deeply involved."[36]

**1. *Isolates*** are completely detached, and passively support the status quo by not taking action to bring about changes. They do not care much about their leaders, and just do their job without taking an interest in the overall organization. Isolates need coaching, yet sometimes firing them is the only solution.

**2. *Bystanders*** are free riders who are typically detached when it fits their self-interests. At a meeting, a bystander is more likely to focus on the refreshments, and taking peeks at his or her personal text messages. Bystanders have low internal motivation, so the leader has to work hard to find the right motivators to spark the bystander into action.

**3. *Participants*** show enough engagement to invest some of their own time and money to make a difference, such as taking it on their own to learn new technology that would help the group. Participants are sometimes for, and sometimes against, the leader and the company. The leader has to review their work and attitudes carefully to see if the participant is being constructive.

**4. *Activists*** are considerably engaged, heavily invested in people and processes, and eager to demonstrate their support or opposition. They feel strongly, either positively or negatively, about their leader and the organization and act accordingly. An activist might be enthusiastic about reaching company goals, or so convinced that the company is doing the wrong thing that he or she blows the whistle (reports the company to an outside agency). The leader has to stay aware of whether the activist is for or against the company.

**5. *Diehards*** are super-engaged to the point that they are willing to go down for their own cause, or willing to oust the leader if they feel he or she is headed in the wrong direction. Diehards can be an asset or a liability to the leader. Diehards have an even stronger tendency to be whistleblowers than do activists. A diehard, for example, might take it on her own to test the lead quantity of paint in children's furniture sold by the company. Leaders have to stay in touch with diehards to see if their energy is being pointed in the service of the organization.

The categorization of followers just presented adds a touch of realism to understanding the challenging role of a leader. Not everybody in the group is super-charged and eager to collaborate toward attaining organizational goals.

## Essential Qualities of Effective Followers

As observed by Robert E. Kelley, effective followers share four essential qualities:[37]

1. ***Self-management.*** The key to being a good follower is to think for oneself and to work well without close supervision. Effective group members see themselves as being as capable as their leaders.
2. ***Commitment.*** Effective followers are committed to something beyond themselves, be it a cause, product, department, organization, idea, or value. To a committed group member, the leader facilitates progress toward achieving a goal.
3. ***Competence and focus.*** Effective followers build their competence and focus their efforts for maximum impact. Competence centers on mastering skills that will be useful to the organization. Less effective group members rarely take the initiative to engage in training and development.
4. ***Courage.*** Effective followers establish themselves as independent, critical thinkers and fight for what they believe is right. A good follower, for example, might challenge the company's policy of taking ninety days to make good on accounts payable, or of recruiting key people almost exclusively from people with demographic characteristics similar to those of top management.

This list is illustrative, since almost any positive human quality would contribute directly or indirectly to being an effective group member or follower. Another way of framing the qualities of effective followers is to say that such followers display the personal characteristics and qualities of leaders. Although leaders cannot be expected to change the personalities of group members, they can take steps to encourage these qualities. Interventions such as coaching, empowerment, supportive communication, and frequent feedback would support effective followership.

### Collaboration Between Leaders and Followers

A key role for followers is to collaborate with leaders in achieving organizational goals. As described by leadership guru Warren Bennis, the postbureaucratic organization (a type of organization that came after the bureaucratic era, such as team-based organizations) requires a new kind of alliance between leaders and the led. When high-level leaders do not make all of the decisions but solicit input from knowledgeable group members, leaders and followers work together more closely. In the words of Bennis:[38]

> Today's organizations are evolving into federations of networks, clusters, cross-functional teams, temporary systems, ad hoc task forces, lattices, modules, matrices—almost anything but pyramids with their obsolete TOPdown leadership. The new leader will encourage healthy dissent and value those followers courageous enough to say no.

A related point here is that the new leader and the led are close allies. Great leaders are made by great groups; every organizational member needs to contribute energy and talent to help leaders carry out their roles successfully.

## SUMMARY

Leadership is the ability to inspire confidence in and support among the people who are needed to achieve organizational goals. Leading is a major part of a manager's job, but a manager also plans, organizes, and controls. Leadership is said to deal with change, inspiration, motivation, and influence. In contrast, management deals more with maintaining equilibrium and the status quo. A current development is to regard leadership as a long-term relationship, or partnership, between leaders and group members.

Many people attribute organizational performance to leadership actions. Some research evidence supports this widely accepted view. For example, one study showed that when the environment is uncertain, charismatic leadership is strongly related to performance. Others argue that certain factors in the work environment, called substitutes for leadership, make the leader's role almost superfluous. Among these factors are closely knit teams of highly trained workers, intrinsic satisfaction with work, computer

technology, and professional norms. Another antileadership argument is that the leader is irrelevant in most organizational outcomes because the situation is more important and the leader has unilateral control over only a few resources. Moreover, since new leaders are chosen whose values are compatible with those of the firm, those values actually are more important.

Complexity theory argues that leaders and managers can do little to alter the course of the complex organizational system. The system, rather than the leader, dictates that all companies ultimately die.

Examining the roles carried out by leaders contributes to an understanding of the leadership function. Nine such leadership roles are the figurehead, spokesperson, negotiator, coach and motivator, team builder, team player, technical problem solver, entrepreneur, and strategic planner. An important implication of these roles is that managers at every level can exert leadership.

Leadership positions often are satisfying because they offer such things as power, prestige, the opportunity to help others, high income, and the opportunity to control resources. At other times being a leader carries with it a number of frustrations, such as facing a perform-or-perish mentality, insufficient authority, having to deal with human problems, and too much organizational politics. The leader also has the difficult task of balancing workers' need to be independent with their need to commit to a common purpose.

The framework for understanding leadership presented here is based on the idea that the leadership process is a function of the leader, group members, and other situational variables. According to the model, leadership can best be understood by examining its key variables: leader characteristics and traits, leader behavior and style, group member characteristics, and the internal and external environment.

Leadership effectiveness is dependent on all four sets of variables.

Leadership skills can be developed by following a general learning model that involves acquiring conceptual knowledge, reading examples, doing experiential exercises, obtaining feedback, and practicing in natural settings.

A major challenge facing leaders is that followers differ substantially in characteristics, including level of engagement from feeling and doing nothing to total passion, commitment, and involvement. To be an effective leader, one needs good followers with characteristics such as self-management, commitment, competence and focus, and courage. A key role for followers is to collaborate with leaders in achieving organizational goals. The postbureaucratic organization requires a new kind of alliance between leaders and the led.

## KEY TERMS

**Leadership**
**Partnership**
**Attribution theory**

**Substitutes for**
**leadership**

**Leadership**
**effectiveness**

##  GUIDELINES FOR ACTION AND SKILL DEVELOPMENT

Vast amounts of information have been gathered about leaders and leadership, and many different leadership theories have been developed. Many leadership research findings and theories are confusing and contradictory. Nevertheless, from this thicket of information emerge many useful leadership concepts and techniques to guide you toward becoming a more effective leader.

As you work toward leadership effectiveness, first be familiar with the approaches to leadership described in this text. Then choose the formulation that seems best to fit the leadership situation you face. For example, if you are leading a team, review the information about team leadership. Typically an effective leader needs to combine several leadership approaches to meet the demands of a given situation. For instance, a leader might need to

combine creative problem solving and emotional support to members to help the team rebound from a crisis.

The eclectic (choosing from among many) approach we recommend is likely to be more effective than accepting an idea such as "there are six secrets to leadership success."

### Discussion Questions and Activities

1. What forces in the environment or in society have led to the surge in interest in the subject of leadership in recent years?
2. Companies spend considerable amounts of money and time helping first-level supervisors become good leaders. What sense does this investment of time and money make?

3. Give an example of how you have exerted leadership on or off the job in a situation in which you did not have a formal leadership position. Explain why you describe your activity as leadership.
4. What would a boss of yours have to do to demonstrate that he or she is an effective leader and an effective manager?
5. Identify a business or sports leader who you think is highly effective, and explain why you think he or she is highly effective.
6. Based on an informal survey, many people who were voted "the most likely to succeed" in their high school yearbooks became leaders later on in their career. How can you explain this finding?

7. Top-level leaders of major business corporations receive some of the highest compensation packages in the work force. Why are business leaders paid so much?
8. Suppose that a big company like Home Depot or Ford Motor Company loses money in a given year. Explain whether you think company leadership should be asked to take a pay cut (or be fined).
9. Which of the nine leadership roles do you think you are the most suited for at this stage in your career? Explain your reasoning.
10. In what way might being an effective follower help prepare a person for becoming an effective leader?

## Leadership Case Problem A

### Highland Homes Goes for the Green

Bob Shallenberger and John Cavanagh enjoy having company over. Both live in homes built by their company, Highland Homes, based in St. Louis, Missouri. Both use them as models to show potential customers what they can do. The two fraternity brothers from St. Louis University used "creative financing" and credit cards to launch their vision in 2003. "We did everything except rob banks," says Shallenberger.

Highland Homes isn't your typical builder. Each new home comes with a plasma TV and the option of special packages like "Elvis live," which includes a stereo, karaoke machine, CD player, and iPod Nano. Those are fun extras, but the real difference comes down to Highland's environmentally friendly building methods: sustainably grown wood, rooftop decks, underground parking, lots of park-like green space, and high-efficiency heating and cooling systems.

Says Cavanagh about green building, "It's difficult and it's expensive to learn. It's challenging, and there's some risk in it. We see it as a big growth segment of the market." Their next move? "Being recognized as the top green residential builder in the country is the goal for us," Cavanagh says.

There's a definite spark to Shallenberger and Cavanagh when they discuss Highland Homes and the future of the business. "When we design a building, we live and breathe it," says Shallenberger. They have no shortage of projects lined up and no shortage of future homeowners looking to buy into their affordable and hip green urban developments. "We've got a bunch of cool people working for us," Shallenberger continues. "The people that we sell to are all really cool, too."

The two business owners believe that if you surround yourself with entrepreneurial-minded employees, you'll gain a creative, dedicated work force and a constant infusion of creative ideas.

### Questions

1. In what way are Bob Shallenberger and John Cavanagh exercising leadership?
2. What leadership roles are Shallenberger and Cavanagh carrying out as they attract cool people to work with them?
3. Why would cool people be attracted to working for Highland Homes?
4. What roles might Shallenberger and Cavanagh need to carry out to attain their goal of being recognized as the top green residential builder in the United States?

*Source*: Amanda C. Kooser, "Young Millionaires," *Entrepreneur*, October 2007, p. 88.

## Leadership Case Problem B

### The Subprime Department Blues

Mary Chen had been the manager of the subprime mortgage department of a large bank for several years. Although her department was small, she and top-level management thought that their mission was important. As Chen explains it, "We make it possible for people with less than prime credit ratings to become homeowners. We create mortgages for honest, hardworking people who for many reasons do not have excellent credit records. So our group is doing some good in this world, despite a few foreclosures here and there."

As interest rates climbed on adjustable rate mortgages (ARMs), the number of late payers tripled, and the number of foreclosures doubled. Every day the media pounded the subprime lenders, blaming them for a potential recession and a sharp decline in the stock market.

Supervising the people in her department became increasingly more difficult. As Chen said, "As the subprime mess progressed, I saw fewer smiles in my department. Workers were calling in sick more frequently. One-half the people in the department requested a transfer to the mortgage department that provided mortgages to customers with first-rate credit records. Even my best workers looked stressed out."

Malcolm Flynn, a mortgage specialist with four years' experience, described the working conditions in the subprime department in these words: "This is bad. We feel we are looked upon like we are drug dealers. People think we are rotten because we lent money to people who didn't have the means to pay back the loan.

"Most of us won't admit the kind of work we are in when talking to people outside the bank. We come to work every day hoping the work will be more fun, but it never is."

When Chen discussed the morale problems she was facing within her group, her manager advised Chen "to be a better leader." Her manager also said that a true leader can guide a group through rough times.

Chen thought to herself, "This advice looks good on paper, but I don't know what to do next."

### Questions

1. What advice might you offer Mary Chen to pick up morale in her department?
2. Which leadership roles should Chen emphasize to lead the group out of its funk?
3. To what extent do you believe the statement of Chen's manager that "a true leader can guide a group through rough times"?

## Internet Skill-Building Exercise

### Key Leadership Topics

Visit the Center for Creative Leadership (CCL), www.ccl.org, to develop additional insight into major topics in leadership. Glance at the titles of articles about leadership to become sensitive to some of the major issues. Note the topics of three articles or books, and check the index to this textbook to see if the same topics are considered important here; make the same check at the Center for Creative Leadership site. While visiting CCL, think through whether the leadership courses offered by the center would interest you.

Apply the chapter concepts! Visit the Web and complete this Internet skill-building exercise to learn more about current leadership topics and trends.

# Traits, Motives, and Characteristics of Leaders

CHAPTER 2

## LEARNING OBJECTIVES

After studying this chapter and doing the exercises, you should be able to

- Identify general and task-related traits that contribute to leadership effectiveness.
- Describe how emotional intelligence contributes to leadership effectiveness.
- Identify key motives that contribute to leadership effectiveness.
- Describe cognitive factors associated with leadership effectiveness.
- Discuss the heredity versus environment issue in relation to leadership effectiveness.
- Summarize the strengths and weaknesses of the trait approach to leadership.

## CHAPTER OUTLINE

**Personality Traits of Effective Leaders**
General Personality Traits
Task-Related Personality Traits

**Leadership Motives**
The Power Motive
The Drive and Achievement Motive
Tenacity and Resilience

**Cognitive Factors and Leadership**
Cognitive (or Analytical) Intelligence
Knowledge of the Business or Group Task
Creativity
Insight into People and Situations
Farsightedness and Conceptual Thinking
The WICS Model of Leadership in Organizations

**The Influence of Heredity and Environment on Leadership**

**The Strengths and Limitations of the Trait Approach**

**Summary**

31

Don Thompson is the star of the show. At McDonald's annual Peak Experience in Las Vegas—a conference for company management—attendees line up to shake his hand, take a picture with him, or just shoot the breeze as he walks through the event's massive expo hall. The affable yet focused executive is an attraction in his own right, unable to make it through the crowd to peruse the countless supplier displays. Among those in the queue to press the flesh is Tilmon F. Brown, CEO of New Horizons Baking Co. Brown, who supplies buns to some 1,300 McDonald's restaurants, is all smiles. Business is good, he says, and he offers words of greetings and continued success to Thompson.

As president of McDonald's USA, the largest division of the mammoth restaurant chain, Thompson is responsible for ensuring the financial success of McDonald's 13,700 locations in the United States. And judging by his reception, he is good at it. Some 24 hours earlier, the 44-year-old executive gave a rousing speech to the 16,000 attendees in which he discussed the state of the business, the company, future growth pans, and the importance of each conference attendee, calling them ambassadors of the brand. Describing the mood as festive would be an understatement. Pyrotechnic displays shot flames dramatically into the air while musical performances entertained the crowd, many of whom were on their feet dancing and slamming noisemakers together.

"The place was rocking," recalls the Chicago native with a smile. "The noise level, the energy, the cheering, you would have thought you were in the middle of some major conference."

Much of McDonald's growth in the mid-2000s was the result of initiatives derived from Thompson's leadership: a more appealing breakfast menu, specialty coffees, and healthier menu options such as Asian Salad and Snack Wrap.

Thompson, who has a degree in electrical engineering from Purdue University, began his career at McDonald's in 1990 as a restaurant systems engineer. Since then, he has excelled in a slew of positions that have one common thread: They performed better from a business and financial standpoint after his arrival. He did it by focusing on quality, not quantity; expanding menu offerings; and improving customer satisfaction and efficiency. In recognition, he has earned numerous promotions throughout the $21.6 billion corporation. He also earned the title Black Enterprise 2007 Corporate Executive of the Year.

To obtain restaurant experience, in 1995 Thompson traded in his suit and tie for a crew uniform and went to work with a franchise in South Chicago. For six months, he flipped burgers, cleaned toilets, worked as a cashier, and co-managed the restaurant. He loved it. When the six months were up, Thompson said to the senior vice president, "If you can leave me in the restaurant and continue to pay me a director's salary, I'll be just fine."[1]

The vignette just presented describes a highly placed manager who has several of the leadership traits discussed in this chapter, particularly cognitive skills, extraversion, and a sense of humor. His charisma is evident also. When people evaluate managers in terms of their leadership effectiveness, they often scrutinize the managers' traits and personal characteristics. Instead of focusing only on the results the managers achieve, those making the evaluation assign considerable weight to the manager's attributes, such as adherence to high standards. Many people believe intuitively that personal characteristics strongly determine leadership effectiveness.

The trait-based perspective on leadership has reemerged in recent years after having fallen out of favor for decades. Stephen J. Zacarro notes that traits tend to help understand leadership behavior and effectiveness when integrated in meaningful ways.[2] For example, the leader described earlier emphasizes traits related to interpersonal skills with cognitive traits to attain company goals. The trait-based perspective also acknowledges that the situation often influences which trait to emphasize, such as a supervisor of highly technical workers needing to emphasize problem-solving ability. In contrast, a supervisor of workers performing nontechnical, repetitive work might need to emphasize enthusiasm as a motivator.

This chapter and the following chapter concentrate on personal characteristics; Chapter 4 describes the behaviors and skills that contribute to leadership effectiveness. Recognize, however, the close association between personal characteristics and leadership skills and behaviors. For example, creative thinking ability (a characteristic) helps a leader formulate an exciting vision (leadership behavior).

Characteristics associated with leadership can be classified into three broad categories: personality traits, motives, and cognitive factors. These categories of behavior serve as helpful guides. However, they are not definitive: a convincing argument can often be made that an aspect of leadership placed in one category could be placed in another. Nevertheless, no matter how personal characteristics are classified, they point toward the conclusion that effective leaders are made of the *right stuff*. Published research about the trait perspective first appeared in the mid-nineteenth century, and it continues today. Since a full listing of every personal characteristic ever found to be associated with leadership would take several hundred pages, this chapter discusses only the major and most consistently found characteristics related to leadership effectiveness.

## PERSONALITY TRAITS OF EFFECTIVE LEADERS

Observations by managers and human resource specialists, as well as dozens of research studies, indicate that leaders have certain personality traits.[3] These characteristics contribute to leadership effectiveness in many situations as long as the leader's style fits the situation reasonably well. For example, an executive might perform admirably as a leader in several different high technology companies with different organizational cultures. However, his intellectual style might make him a poor fit with production workers. Leaders' personality traits can be divided into two groups: general personality traits such as self-confidence and trustworthiness, and task-related traits, such as an internal locus of control.

### General Personality Traits

We define a general personality trait as a trait that is observable both within and outside the context of work. That is, the same general traits are related to success

**FIGURE 2-1** General Personality Traits of Effective Leaders.

and satisfaction in both work and personal life. Figure 2-1 lists the general personality traits that contribute to successful leadership.

***Self-Confidence***   Self-confidence improves one's performance in a variety of tasks, including leadership.[4] A leader who is self-assured without being bombastic or overbearing instills self-confidence in team members. A self-confident team leader of a group facing a seemingly impossible deadline might tell the group, "We are understaffed and overworked, but I know we can get this project done on time. I've been through tough demands like this before. If we work like a true team, we can pull it off."

Self-confidence was among the first leadership traits researchers identified, and it has recently received considerable attention as a major contributor to leadership effectiveness.[5] In addition to being self-confident, the leader must project that self-confidence to the group. He or she may do so by using unequivocal wording, maintaining good posture, and making appropriate gestures such as pointing an index finger outward.

Self-confidence is not only a personality trait. It also refers to a behavior and an interpersonal skill that a person exhibits in a number of situations. It is akin to being cool under pressure. We can conclude that a person is a self-confident leader when he or she maintains composure when dealing with a crisis, such as while managing a large product recall. The interpersonal skill comes in being able to keep others calm during turmoil.

***Humility***   Although self-confidence is a key leadership trait, so is humility, or being humble at the right times. Part of humility is admitting that you do not know everything and cannot do everything, as well as admitting your mistakes to team

**KB Knowledge Bank**
Includes suggestions for developing self-confidence as required for leadership effectiveness.

**www.cengage.com/ management/dubrin**

members and outsiders. A leader, upon receiving a compliment for an accomplishment, may explain that the group deserves the credit. The case for humility as a leadership trait is made strongly by Stephen G. Harrison, the president of a consulting firm, in his comment about how the definition of great leadership has changed: "Great leadership is manifested or articulated by people who know how to understate it. There is leadership value in humility, the leadership that comes from putting people in the limelight, not yourself. Great leadership comes from entirely unexpected places. It's understatement, it's dignity, it's service, it's selflessness."[6]

Research by Jim Collins on what makes companies endure and dramatically improve their performance supports the importance of humility. He uses the term *Level 5 Leader* to describe the most accomplished leaders. Level 5 Leaders are modest yet determined to accomplish their objectives.[7]

**Trustworthiness**   Evidence and opinion continue to mount that being trustworthy and/or honest contributes to leadership effectiveness.[8] An effective leader or manager is supposed to *walk the talk*, thereby showing a consistency between deeds (walking) and words (talk). In this context, **trust** is defined as a person's confidence in another individual's intentions and motives and in the sincerity of that individual's word.[9] Leaders must be trustworthy, and they must also trust group members. Given that so many people distrust top-level business leaders, as well as political leaders, gaining and maintaining trust is a substantial challenge. A Watson Wyatt *Work/USA* study found that 72 percent of employees believe their immediate managers act with honesty and integrity in their work, but only 56 percent believe that about company leadership.[10] The following trust builders are worthy of a prospective leader's attention and implementation:[11]

- Make your behavior consistent with your intentions. Practice what you preach and set the example. Let others know of your intentions and invite feedback on how well you are achieving them.
- When your organization or organizational unit encounters a problem, move into a problem-solving mode instead of looking to blame others for what went wrong.
- Honor confidences. One incident of passing along confidential information results in a permanent loss of trust by the person whose confidence was violated.
- Maintain a high level of integrity. Build a reputation for doing what you think is morally right in spite of the political consequences.
- Tell the truth in ways people can verify. It is much easier to be consistent when you do not have to keep patching up your story to conform to an earlier lie. An example of verification would be for a group member to see if the manager really did attempt to buy new conference room furniture as he or she said.
- Admit mistakes. Covering up a mistake, particularly when everybody knows that you did it, destroys trust quickly.
- Make trust pay in terms of receiving rewards. Trust needs to be seen as a way of gaining advantage.

It takes a leader a long time to build trust, yet one brief incident of untrustworthy behavior can permanently destroy it. Leaders are usually allowed a fair share of honest mistakes. In contrast, dishonest mistakes quickly erode leadership effectiveness.

When a leader is perceived as trustworthy, the organization benefits. Kurt T. Dirks and Donald L. Ferrin examined the findings and implications of research during the last four decades about trust in leadership. The review involved 106 studies and 27,103 individuals. The meta-analysis (quantitative synthesis of studies) emphasized supervisory leadership based on the importance of trust in day-to-day interactions with group members. Trusting a leader was more highly associated with a variety of work attitudes of group members. The highest specific relationships with trust were as follows:[12]

- Job satisfaction ($r = .51$)
- Organizational commitment ($r = .49$)
- Turnover intentions ($r = .40$) (If you trust your leader, you are less likely to intend to leave.)
- Belief in information provided by the leader ($r = .35$)
- Commitment to decisions ($r = .24$)
- Satisfaction with the leader ($r = .73$)
- LMX ($r = .69$) (LMX refers to favorable exchanges with the leader.)

The relationship of trust to job performance was statistically significant but quite low ($r = .16$). One reason may be that many people perform well for a leader they distrust out of fear of being fired or bad-listed.

Being trustworthy and earning trust is considered so essential to effective leadership that some companies use these factors to evaluate leaders and managers. For example, IBM evaluates its leaders on ten key factors, one of which is *earning trust*. A leader who earns trusts "does what is right for the long-term good of relationships inside and outside of IBM." As with the other traits (some of which are really behaviors), the relevance of earning trust was uncovered from interviews with thirty-three IBM executives who had been regarded as outstanding leaders within the company.[13]

Leadership Self-Assessment Quiz 2-1 gives you the opportunity to examine your own tendencies toward trustworthiness.

 ## Leadership Self-Assessment Quiz 2-1

### Behaviors and Attitudes of a Trustworthy Leader

*Instructions:* Listed here are behaviors and attitudes of leaders who are generally trusted by their group members and other constituents. After you read each characteristic, check to the right whether this is a behavior or attitude that you appear to have developed already, or whether it does not fit you at present.

## Quiz 2-1 (continued)

| | Fits Me | Does Not Fit Me |
|---|---|---|
| 1. Tells people he or she is going to do something, and then always follows through and gets it done | ☐ | ☐ |
| 2. Is described by others as being reliable | ☐ | ☐ |
| 3. Is good at keeping secrets and confidences | ☐ | ☐ |
| 4. Tells the truth consistently | ☐ | ☐ |
| 5. Minimizes telling people what they want to hear | ☐ | ☐ |
| 6. Is described by others as "walking the talk" | ☐ | ☐ |
| 7. Delivers consistent messages to others in terms of matching words and deeds | ☐ | ☐ |
| 8. Does what he or she expects others to do | ☐ | ☐ |
| 9. Minimizes hypocrisy by not engaging in activities he or she tells others are wrong | ☐ | ☐ |
| 10. Readily accepts feedback on behavior from others | ☐ | ☐ |
| 11. Maintains eye contact with people when talking to them | ☐ | ☐ |
| 12. Appears relaxed and confident when explaining his or her side of a story | ☐ | ☐ |
| 13. Individualizes compliments to others rather than saying something like "You look great" to many people | ☐ | ☐ |
| 14. Does not expect lavish perks for himself or herself while expecting others to go on an austerity diet | ☐ | ☐ |
| 15. Does not tell others a crisis is pending (when it is not) just to gain their cooperation | ☐ | ☐ |
| 16. Collaborates with others to make creative decisions | ☐ | ☐ |
| 17. Communicates information to people at all organizational levels | ☐ | ☐ |
| 18. Readily shares financial information with others | ☐ | ☐ |
| 19. Listens to people and then acts on many of their suggestions | ☐ | ☐ |
| 20. Generally engages in predictable behavior | ☐ | ☐ |

***Scoring and Interpretation:*** These statements are mostly for self-reflection, so no specific scoring key exists. However, the more of these statements that fit you, the more trustworthy you are—assuming you are answering truthfully. The usefulness of this self-quiz increases if somebody who knows you well also answers it about you. Your ability and willingness to carry out some of the behaviors specified in this quiz could have an enormous impact on your career because so many business leaders in recent years have not been perceived as trustworthy. Being trustworthy is therefore a career asset.

*Authenticity*    Embedded in the trait of being trustworthy is **authenticity**—being genuine and honest about your personality, values, and beliefs as well as having integrity. Bill George, a Harvard Business School professor and former chairman and CEO of Medtronic, developed the concept of authentic leadership. In his words, "Authentic leaders demonstrate a passion for their purpose, practice their values consistently, and lead with their hearts as well as their heads. They establish long-term meaningful relationships and have the self-discipline to get results. They know who they are."[14] To become an authentic leader, and to demonstrate authenticity, be yourself rather than attempt to be a replica of someone else. Others respond to your leadership, partly because you are genuine rather than phony. The authentic leader can emphasize different values and characteristics to different people without being phony. For example, a corporate-level manager at Goodyear service centers might engage in more banter when he visits a service center than when meeting with financial analysts.

You are most likely to find an authentic leader among the ranks of middle managers, small-business owners, and athletic coaches in non-name athletic programs. (Observe that the models provided are not usually strongly power-oriented glory seekers.) However, George offers the example of Daniel Vasella, the chairman and CEO of the pharmaceutical firm Novartis. He helped build a global health care company that could help people through developing lifesaving new drugs. The cornerstones of the Novartis culture are compassion, competence, and competition.

George and several colleagues conducted an intensive leadership development study of 125 diverse business leaders to understand how they became and remain authentic. The authentic leaders typically learned from their experiences by reflecting on them. They also took a hard look at themselves to understand what they really believe, such as whether they really care if their workers are satisfied. The authors of the study concluded that the leader being authentic is the only way to create long-term, positive business results.[15]

*Extraversion*    Extraversion (the scientific spelling for *extroversion*) has been recognized for its contribution to leadership effectiveness because it is helpful for leaders to be gregarious and outgoing in most situations. Also, extraverts are more likely to want to assume a leadership role and participate in group activities. A meta-analysis of seventy-three studies involving 11,705 subjects found that extraversion was the most consistent personality factor related to leadership effectiveness and leadership emergence.[16] (*Emergence* refers to someone being perceived as having leadership qualities.) Extraversion may be an almost innate personality characteristic yet most people can move toward becoming more extraverted by consciously attempting to be more friendly toward people including smiling and asking questions. An example is, "How are things going for you today?"

Even though it is logical to think that extraversion is related to leadership, many effective leaders are laid-back and even introverted. Michael Dell, the famous founder of Dell Inc., is a reserved individual who is sometimes described as having a vanilla personality. Yet Dell has been working to become more extraverted.

*Assertiveness*   Letting others know where you stand contributes to leadership effectiveness, and also contributes to being or appearing extraverted. **Assertiveness** refers to being forthright in expressing demands, opinions, feelings, and attitudes. Being assertive helps leaders perform many tasks and achieve goals. Among them are confronting group members about their mistakes, demanding higher performance, setting high expectations, and making legitimate demands on higher management. A director of her company's cell phone service unit was assertive when she said to her staff, "Our cell service is the worst in the industry. We have to improve." An assertive person is reasonably tactful rather than being aggressive and obnoxious.

Leadership Self-Assessment Quiz 2-2 gives you the opportunity to determine how assertive you are.

 ## Leadership Self-Assessment Quiz 2-2

### The Assertiveness Scale

*Instructions:* Indicate whether each of the following statements is mostly true or mostly false as it applies to you. If in doubt about your reaction to a particular statement, think of how you would *generally* respond.

|  | Mostly True | Mostly False |
|---|:---:|:---:|
| 1. It is extremely difficult for me to turn down a sales representative when he or she is a nice person. | ☐ | ☐ |
| 2. I express criticism freely. | ☐ | ☐ |
| 3. If another person is being very unfair, I bring it to that person's attention. | ☐ | ☐ |
| 4. Work is no place to let your feelings show. | ☐ | ☐ |
| 5. It is no use asking for favors; people get what they deserve. | ☐ | ☐ |
| 6. Business is not the place for tact; say what you think. | ☐ | ☐ |
| 7. If a person looks as if he or she is in a hurry, I let that person in front of me in a supermarket line. | ☐ | ☐ |
| 8. A weakness of mine is that I am too nice a person. | ☐ | ☐ |
| 9. If my restaurant bill is even 50 cents more than it should be, I demand that the mistake be corrected. | ☐ | ☐ |
| 10. If the mood strikes me, I will laugh out loud in public. | ☐ | ☐ |
| 11. People would describe me as too outspoken. | ☐ | ☐ |
| 12. I am quite willing to have the store take back a piece of furniture that was scratched upon delivery. | ☐ | ☐ |

## Quiz 2-2 (continued)

| | Mostly True | Mostly False |
|---|:---:|:---:|
| 13. I dread having to express anger toward a coworker. | ☐ | ☐ |
| 14. People often say that I am too reserved and emotionally controlled. | ☐ | ☐ |
| 15. I have told friends and work associates exactly what it is about their behavior that irritates or displeases me. | ☐ | ☐ |
| 16. I fight for my rights down to the last detail. | ☐ | ☐ |
| 17. I have no misgivings about returning an overcoat to the store if it does not fit me right. | ☐ | ☐ |
| 18. After I have an argument with a person, I try to avoid him or her. | ☐ | ☐ |
| 19. I insist that my spouse (or roommate or partner) do his or her fair share of undesirable chores. | ☐ | ☐ |
| 20. It is difficult for me to look directly at another person when the two of us are in disagreement. | ☐ | ☐ |
| 21. I have cried among friends more than once. | ☐ | ☐ |
| 22. If someone near me at a movie keeps up a conversation with another person, I ask him or her to stop. | ☐ | ☐ |
| 23. I am able to turn down social engagements with people I do not particularly care for. | ☐ | ☐ |
| 24. It is in poor taste to express what you really feel about another individual. | ☐ | ☐ |
| 25. I sometimes show my anger by swearing at or belittling another person. | ☐ | ☐ |
| 26. I am reluctant to speak up at a meeting. | ☐ | ☐ |
| 27. I find it relatively easy to ask friends for small favors such as giving me a ride to work while my car is being repaired. | ☐ | ☐ |
| 28. If another person is talking very loudly in a restaurant and it bothers me, I inform that person. | ☐ | ☐ |
| 29. I often finish other people's sentences for them. | ☐ | ☐ |
| 30. It is relatively easy for me to express love and affection toward another person. | ☐ | ☐ |

### *Scoring Key*

| | | | |
|---|---|---|---|
| **1.** Mostly false | **6.** Mostly true | **11.** Mostly true | **16.** Mostly true |
| **2.** Mostly true | **7.** Mostly false | **12.** Mostly true | **17.** Mostly true |
| **3.** Mostly true | **8.** Mostly false | **13.** Mostly false | **18.** Mostly false |
| **4.** Mostly false | **9.** Mostly true | **14.** Mostly false | **19.** Mostly true |
| **5.** Mostly false | **10.** Mostly true | **15.** Mostly true | **20.** Mostly false |

## Quiz 2-2 (continued)

| | | | |
|---|---|---|---|
| **21.** Mostly true | **24.** Mostly true | **27.** Mostly true | **29.** Mostly true |
| **22.** Mostly true | **25.** Mostly true | **28.** Mostly true | **30.** Mostly true |
| **23.** Mostly true | **26.** Mostly false | | |

***Scoring and Interpretation:*** Score 1 for each of your answers that agrees with the scoring key.

- **0–15:** Nonassertive
- **16–24:** Assertive
- **25+:** Aggressive

Do this exercise again about thirty days from now to see how stable your answers are. You might also discuss your answers with a close friend to determine if that person has a similar perception of your assertiveness.

A score in the nonassertive range could suggest that you need to develop your assertiveness and self-confidence and become less shy to enhance those aspects of your leadership that involve face-to-face interaction with people. To help verify the accuracy of this score, ask a current or former boss whether he or she agrees that you are nonassertive.

***Enthusiasm, Optimism, and Warmth***   In almost all leadership situations, it is desirable for the leader to be enthusiastic. Group members tend to respond positively to enthusiasm, partly because enthusiasm may be perceived as a reward for constructive behavior. Enthusiasm is also a desirable leadership trait because it helps build good relationships with team members. A leader can express enthusiasm both verbally ("Great job"; "I love it") and nonverbally (making a "high five" gesture). An executive newsletter made an enthusiastic comment about enthusiasm as a leadership trait:

> People look to you for [enthusiasm] to inspire them. It is the greatest tool for motivating others and for getting things done. As a leader, you have to get out in front of your people. Even the most enthusiastic employee is loath to show more of it than his or her boss. If you don't project a gung-ho attitude, everybody else will hold back.[17]

Enthusiasm often takes the form of optimism, which helps keep the group in an upbeat mood and hopeful about attaining difficult goals. The optimistic leader is therefore likely to help bring about exceptional levels of achievement. Yet, there is a potential downside to an optimistic leader. He or she might not develop contingency plans to deal with projects that do not go as well as expected.[18] An overly optimistic IT manager, for example, might not take into account that an earthquake could hit the geographic area where company data are stored.

Being a warm person and projecting that warmth is part of enthusiasm and contributes to leadership effectiveness in several ways. First, warmth helps establish rapport with group members. Second, the projection of warmth is a key component of charisma. Third, warmth is a trait that helps provide emotional support to group members. Giving such support is an important leadership behavior. Fourth, in the words of Kogan Page, "Warmth comes with the territory. Cold fish don't make good leaders because they turn people off."[19]

**Sense of Humor**   Whether humor is a trait or a behavior, the effective use of humor is an important part of the leader's role. Humor adds to the approachability and people orientation of a leader. Laughter and humor serve such functions in the workplace as relieving tension and boredom and defusing hostility. Because humor helps the leader dissolve tension and defuse conflict, it helps him or her exert power over the group. Self-effacing humor is the choice of comedians and organizational leaders alike. By being self-effacing, the leader makes a point without insulting or slighting anybody. Instead of criticizing a staff member for being too technical, the leader might say, "Wait, I need your help. Please explain how this new product works in terms that even I can understand."

Humor as used by leaders has been the subject of considerable serious inquiry, and here are a few recommendations based on this research:[20]

- People who occupy high-status roles joke at a higher rate than those of lesser status and tend to be more successful at eliciting laughter from others. (Did you know that Al Gore, the environmentalist/investment banker/presidential candidate, has been on *Saturday Night Live*?)
- Self-enhancing humor (building up your self) facilitates the leader's acquisition of power from superiors by increasing the leader's appeal.
- Self-defeating (self-effacing to the extreme) humor is negatively related to power, and may lead to the perception that the leader is too playful and not serious.
- Aggressive humor can be used to victimize, belittle, and cause others some type of disparagement—and will lead to negative outcomes such as stress and counter-hostility among group members. (No surprise to readers here.)

Leadership Skill-Building Exercise 2-1 provides an opportunity to use humor effectively.

## Task-Related Personality Traits

Certain personality traits of effective leaders are closely associated with task accomplishment. The task-related traits described here are outlined in Figure 2-2.

**Passion for the Work and the People**   A dominant characteristic of effective leaders is their passion for their work and to some extent for the people who help them accomplish the work. The passion goes beyond enthusiasm and often expresses itself as an obsession for achieving company goals. Many leaders begin their workday at 6:00 A.M. and return to their homes at 7:00 P.M. After dinner they retreat to their home offices to conduct business for about two more hours. Information technology devices, such as personal digital assistants and cell phones, feed the passion for work, making it possible to be in touch with

## ⊙ Leadership Skill-Building Exercise 2-1

### A Sense of Humor on the Job

This is an exercise for six persons in both scenarios. *Scenario 1: Windmill Plant Manager.* One person plays the role of the head of the manufacturing plant that makes windmills to help other companies and communities reduce energy sources that send too many pollutants into the air. The manager has called a meeting to discuss some somber news: the plant has been cited by the Environmental Protection Agency for spewing too many toxic wastes into the air. Improvements must be made in a hurry. He or she should make a few humorous introductory comments that will relieve some of the tension and worry. The five other people, who play the roles of department heads in the windmill factory, should also make effective use of humor in responding to the CEO's comments.

*Scenario 2: Staff Resignations.* One person plays the role of the company CEO, who has scheduled a staff meeting. The CEO's task is to inform employees that the seventh top manager in the last year has just resigned. He or she should make a few humorous introductory comments that will relieve some of the tension and worry. The five other people, who play the roles of the remaining staff members, should also make effective use of humor in responding to the CEO's comments.

the office even during golf or a family picnic. The downside to extreme passion for work is that it can lead to work addiction, thereby interfering with other joys in life.

Passion for their work is especially evident in entrepreneurial leaders, no matter what size and type of business. A given business, such as refurbishing engines, might appear mundane to outsiders. The leader of such a business, however, is willing to talk for hours about tearing down old engines and about the wonderful people who help do the job.

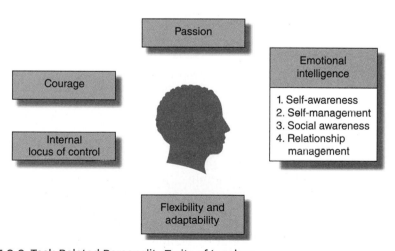

**FIGURE 2-2** Task-Related Personality Traits of Leaders.

Being passionate about the nature of the business can be a major success factor in its survival. Randy Komisar, a strategy consultant to many dot-com business firms, argues that the purpose of business cannot be simply to make lots of money. He says that too many business startups lack a deep foundation in values and are managed by a drive for success, not by passion. "Drive pushes you toward an objective, and you can deny part of yourself by sheer will to achieve a goal," Komisar explains. "Passion irresistibly pulls you toward the need to express yourself and has to come from within and be nurtured." A problem with drive alone is that the end justifies the means.[21]

One of the ways for an entrepreneur to inject passion into a business is to tell a *creation story* (your company, not the Bible). The story should inspire people to understand how your product or cause will make the world a better place. Howard Schultz, the founder and chairman of Starbucks, provides an example.[22]

> Schultz's story begins in 1961, when his father broke his ankle at work and was left without income, insurance or any way to support his family. The family's fear inspired change. Schultz grew up driven to create a company in which employees have a safety net woven of respect and dignity.

***Emotional Intelligence***    Many different aspects of emotions, motives, and personality that help determine interpersonal effectiveness and leadership skill have been placed under the comprehensive label of *emotional intelligence*. **Emotional intelligence** refers to the ability to do such things as understand one's feelings, have empathy for others, and regulate one's emotions to enhance one's quality of life. This type of intelligence generally has to do with the ability to connect with people and understand their emotions. Many of the topics in this chapter (such as warmth) and throughout the text (such as political skill) can be considered related to emotional intelligence.

Based on research in dozens of companies, Daniel Goleman discovered that the most effective leaders are alike in one essential way: they all have a high degree of emotional intelligence. Cognitive intelligence (or general mental ability) and technical skills are considered threshold capabilities for success in executive positions. Yet, according to Goleman, without a high degree of emotional intelligence, a person can have excellent training, superior analytical skills, and loads of innovative suggestions, but he or she still will not make a great leader. His analysis also revealed that emotional intelligence played an increasingly important role in high-level management positions, where differences in technical skills are of negligible importance. Furthermore, when star performers were compared with average ones in senior leadership positions, differences in emotional intelligence were more pronounced than differences in cognitive abilities.[23]

Four key factors in emotional intelligence are described next, along with a brief explanation of how each factor links to leadership effectiveness. The components of emotional intelligence have gone through several versions, and the version presented here is tied closely to leadership and interpersonal skills. The leader who scores high in emotional intelligence is described as *resonant*.[24]

**1. *Self-awareness.*** The ability to understand your own emotions is the most essential of the four emotional intelligence competencies. Having high self-awareness allows people to know their strengths and limitations and have high self-esteem. Resonant leaders use self-awareness to accurately measure their own moods, and they intuitively understand how their moods affect others. (Effective leaders seek feedback to see how well their actions are received by others. A leader with good self-awareness would recognize such factors as whether he or she was liked or was exerting the right amount of pressure on people.)

**2. *Self-management.*** This is the ability to control one's emotions and act with honesty and integrity in a consistent and adaptable manner. The right degree of self-management helps prevent a person from throwing temper tantrums when activities do not go as planned. Resonant leaders do not let their occasional bad moods ruin their day. If they cannot overcome the bad mood, they let work associates know of the problem and how long it might last. (A leader with high self-management would not suddenly decide to fire a group member because of one difference of opinion.)

**3. *Social awareness.*** This includes having empathy for others and intuition about organizational problems. Socially aware leaders go beyond sensing the emotions of others by showing they care. In addition, they accurately size up political forces in the office. (A team leader with social awareness, or empathy, would be able to assess whether a team member had enough enthusiasm for a project to assign it to him. A CEO who had empathy for a labor union's demands might be able to negotiate successfully with the head of the labor union to avoid a costly strike.)

**4. *Relationship management.*** This includes the interpersonal skills of being able to communicate clearly and convincingly, disarm conflicts, and build strong personal bonds. Resonant leaders use relationship management skills to spread their enthusiasm and solve disagreements, often with kindness and humor. (A leader with good relationship management skills would not burn bridges and would continue to enlarge his or her network of people to win support when support is needed. A leader or manager with good relationship management skills is more likely to be invited by headhunters to explore new career opportunities.)

If leaders do not have emotional intelligence, they may not achieve their full potential despite their high cognitive intelligence. Steve Heyer, a former executive at Coca-Cola, is a case in point. He was hired into Coca-Cola as a person with the potential to become the next CEO. But Heyer's personality ran against the company's ingrained culture, and he did not pick up on the subtle cues about how he should behave (part of emotional intelligence). He was harsh with people and flaunted his position. Because Coke depends on its bottlers, company executives have a saying: "If your bottler drives a Cadillac, *you* drive a Buick. If your bottler drives a Buick, *you* drive a Ford. If your bottler drives a Ford, *you* walk." Heyer drove a Mercedes. Heyer was denied promotion to CEO, and he left the company in June 2004.[25] He also clashed with key people in his next executive position, as an executive in an investment banking firm.

After the banking firm, Heyer became the CEO at Starwood Hotels & Resorts Worldwide, but his low emotional intelligence caught up with him again. He quickly developed the reputation of being brusque and often had difficult relations with employees. Heyer was finally dismissed when an anonymous letter accused him of sending inappropriate and suggestive emails and text messages to a young, female employee. According to another claim, Heyer had an inappropriate physical encounter with a female employee outside a restaurant restroom. Heyer denied all the preceding accusations.[26]

Most of the leaders described in this book have good emotional intelligence. Here are two examples of making good use of emotional intelligence on the job:[27]

■ Your company is approached about merging. The due diligence process suggests everything is favorable, yet your gut instinct says something is amiss. Rather than ignore your intuition, use it to motivate yourself to gather more information on the principals in the company.

■ Your stomach knots as you prepare for a presentation. Your anxiety may stem from your sense that you are not well prepared. The emotionally intelligent response is to dig into the details and rehearse your presentation until the knots are replaced by a sense of welcome anticipation and confidence.

Research on emotional intelligence and leadership has also focused on the importance of the leader's mood in influencing performance. Daniel Goleman, Richard Boyatzis, and Annie McKee believe that the leader's mood and his or her associated behaviors greatly influence bottom-line performance. One reason is that moods are contagious. A cranky and ruthless leader creates a toxic organization of underachievers (who perform at less than their potential). In contrast, an upbeat and inspirational leader breeds followers who can surmount most challenges. Thus mood finally affects profit and loss. The implication for leaders is that they have to develop emotional intelligence regarding their moods. It is also helpful to develop a sense of humor, because lightheartedness is the most contagious of moods.[28]

***Flexibility and Adaptability***   A leader is someone who facilitates change. It therefore follows that a leader must be flexible enough to cope with such changes as technological advances, downsizings, global outsourcing, a shifting customer base, and a changing work force. **Flexibility**, or the ability to adjust to different situations, has long been recognized as an important leadership characteristic. Leaders who are flexible are able to adjust to the demands of changing conditions, much as antilock brakes enable an automobile to adjust to changes in road conditions. Without the underlying trait of flexibility, a person could be an effective leader in only one or two situations. The manufacturing industry exemplifies a field in which situation adaptability is particularly important because top executives are required to provide leadership for both traditional production employees as well as highly skilled professionals.

***Internal Locus of Control***   People with an **internal locus of control** believe that they are the prime mover behind events. Thus, an internal locus of control helps a leader in the role of a take-charge person because the leader believes fundamentally in his or her innate capacity to take charge. An internal locus of control is closely related to self-confidence. A strong internal locus facilitates self-confidence because the person perceives that he or she can control circumstances enough to perform well.

A leader with an internal locus of control is likely to be favored by group members. One reason is that an "internal" person is perceived as more powerful than an "external" person because he or she takes responsibility for events. The leader with an internal locus of control would emphasize that he or she can change unfavorable conditions, as did many courageous managers whose offices were destroyed during the World Trade Center attacks on September 11, 2001.

Leadership Skill-Building Exercise 2-2 provides you with an opportunity to begin strengthening your internal locus of control. Considerable further work would be required to shift from an external to an internal locus of control.

*Courage*    Leaders need courage to face the challenges of taking prudent risks and taking initiative in general. Courage comes from the heart, as suggested by the French word for heart, *coeur*. Leaders must face up to responsibility and be willing to put their reputations on the line. It takes courage for a leader to suggest a new undertaking, because if the undertaking fails, the leader is often seen as having failed. Many people criticized Steve Jobs and his management team when they initiated Apple stores because they saw no useful niche served by these retail outlets. The Apple stores were an immediate and long-lasting success, vindicating the judgment of Jobs and his team. The more faith people place in the power of leaders to cause events, the more strongly they blame leaders when outcomes are unfavorable.

According to Kathleen K. Reardon, courage in business is a special kind of calculated risk taking that comes about with experience. One of the requirements of taking an intelligent gamble is having contingency plans.[29] For example, if the Apple stores failed, the properties could have been sold to other posh retailers, thereby reducing possible losses.

# LEADERSHIP MOTIVES

Effective leaders, as opposed to nonleaders and less effective leaders, have frequently been distinguished by their motives and needs. In general, leaders have an intense desire to occupy a position of responsibility for others and to control them. Figure 2-3 outlines three specific leadership motives or needs. All three motives can be considered task related.

## The Power Motive

Effective leaders have a strong need to control resources. Leaders with high power motives have three dominant characteristics: (1) they act with vigor and determination to exert their power; (2) they invest much time in thinking about ways to alter the behavior and thinking of others; and (3) they care about their personal standing with those around them.[30] The power motive is important because it

## Leadership Skill-Building Exercise 2-2

### Developing an Internal Locus of Control

A person's locus of control is usually a deeply ingrained thinking pattern that develops over a period of many years. Nevertheless, you can begin developing a stronger internal locus of control by analyzing past successes and failures to determine how much influence you had on the outcome of these events. By repeatedly analyzing the relative contribution of internal versus external factors in shaping events, you may learn to feel more in charge of key events in your life. The following events are a good starting point.

1. *A contest or athletic event that you either won or made a good showing in*

   What were the factors within your control that led to your winning or making a good showing?

   _____

   _____

   _____

   What were the factors beyond your control that led to your winning or making a good showing?

   _____

   _____

   _____

2. *A course in which you received a poor grade*

   What were the factors within your control that led to this poor grade?

   _____

   _____

   _____

What were the factors beyond your control that led to this poor grade?

_____

_____

_____

3. *A group project to which you were assigned that worked out poorly*

   What were the factors within your control that led to this poor result?

   _____

   _____

   _____

   What were the factors beyond your control that led to this poor result?

   _____

   _____

   _____

After you have prepared your individual analysis, you may find it helpful to discuss your observations in small groups. Focus on how people could have profited from a stronger internal locus of control in the situations analyzed.

means that the leader is interested in influencing others. Without power, it is much more difficult to influence others. Power is not necessarily good or evil; it can be used for the sake of the power holder (personalized power motive) or for helping others (socialized power motive).[31]

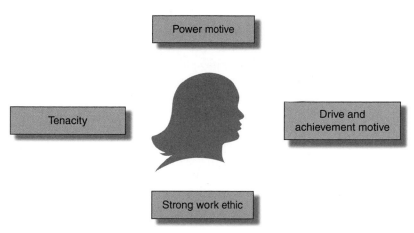

**FIGURE 2-3** Leadership Motives.

***Personalized Power Motive*** Leaders with a personalized power motive seek power mostly to further their own interests. They crave the trappings of power, such as status symbols, luxury, and money. In recent years, some leaders have taken up power boating, or racing powerful, high-speed boats. When asked how he liked his power-boating experience, an entrepreneurial leader replied, "It's fun, but the startup costs are about $350,000."

Because of his love for the trappings of power, Donald Trump® is seen as a leader with a strong personalized power motive. Even the name *Donald Trump* is registered; that is, it is supposed to be written with the "registered" symbol upon first mention. Trump has a penchant for naming yachts, hotels, and office buildings after himself. His drive for power is intertwined with his immodesty and lack of humility. Trump's television show, *The Apprentice,* helped make him a national symbol of power, and his firm even tried to make the term *"You're fired"* a registered trademark.

Despite Trump's elevated personalized power motive, he does not fit all three characteristics stated earlier. Trump gives his financial managers considerable latitude in managing his enterprises. In contrast to Trump, some leaders with strong personalized power motives typically enjoy dominating others. Their need for dominance can lead to submissive subordinates who are frequently sycophants and yes-persons.

Another characteristic of leaders with a personalized power motive is that they do not worry about everybody liking them. They recognize that as you acquire power, you also acquire enemies. In the words of successful college football coach Steve Spurrier, "If people like you too much, it's probably because they are beating you."[32]

***Socialized Power Motive*** Leaders with a socialized power motive use power primarily to achieve organizational goals or a vision. In this context, the term *socialized* means that the leader uses power primarily to help others. As a result, he or she is likely to provide more effective leadership. Leaders with socialized power motives tend to be more emotionally mature than leaders with personalized power motives. They exercise power more for the benefit of the entire organization and are less likely to manipulate others through the use of power. Leaders with socialized power motives are also less defensive and more willing to accept expert advice. Finally, they have longer-range perspectives.[33]

It is important not to draw a rigid line between leaders with personalized power motives and those with socialized power motives. The distinction between doing good for others and doing good for oneself is often made on the basis of very subjective criteria. A case in point is H. Ross Perot, the highly successful business founder, social activist, and two-time candidate for U.S. president. Perot supporters attest to his genuine desire to create a good life for others and to serve the public. His detractors, however, regard Perot as a leader obsessed with power and self-importance.

## The Drive and Achievement Motive

Leaders are known for working hard to achieve their goals. **Drive** refers to a propensity to put forth high energy into achieving goals and to a persistence in applying that energy. Drive also includes **achievement motivation**—finding joy in accomplishment for its own sake. Entrepreneurs and high-level corporate managers usually have strong achievement motivation. Such people have a consistent desire to:

1. Achieve through their efforts and take responsibility for success or failure
2. Take moderate risks that can be handled through their own efforts
3. Receive feedback on their level of performance
4. Introduce novel, innovative, or creative solutions
5. Plan and set goals[34]

## Tenacity and Resilience

A final observation about the motivational characteristics of organizational leaders is that they are *tenacious*. Tenacity multiplies in importance for organizational leaders because it takes a long time to implement a new program or to consummate a business deal, such as acquiring another company. Resilience is part of tenacity because the tenacious person will bounce back from a setback through continuous effort. Prescription drug wholesaler Stewart Rahr is the owner of Kinray, a privately held company. He attributes much of his success to his ability to overcome rejection and keep trying. In reflecting on his early days, he says, "I remember Charlie Cohen of Cohen's Pharmacy telling me, 'Nothing for you today,' and hanging up on me over and over again." Rahr's persistence eventually brought orders, if only for a few bottles of aspirin. Today his company provides drugs, bandages, and orthopedic shoes to 3,000 corner pharmacies in seven states.[35] Rahr will probably need to be persistent and resilient again as the online and mail-order sales of drugs gain a bigger share of the market.

A study of 150 leaders conducted by Warren Bennis reinforces the link between leadership effectiveness and tenacity. All interviewees embodied a strongly developed sense of purpose and a willful determination to achieve what they wanted. "Without that," said Bennis, "organizations and individuals are not powerful. The central ingredient of power is purpose."[36]

Leadership Self-Assessment Quiz 2-3 gives you the opportunity to obtain a tentative measure of your resilience.

 **Leadership Self-Assessment Quiz 2-3**

### Personal Resiliency Quiz

**Instructions:** Answer each of the following statements *mostly agree* or *mostly disagree* as it applies to yourself. In taking a questionnaire such as this, it can always be argued that the true answer to any one particular statement is "It depends on the situation." Despite the validity of this observation, do your best to indicate whether you would mostly agree or disagree with the statement.

| | Mostly Agree | Mostly Disagree | Score (see key) |
|---|---|---|---|
| 1. Winning is everything. | ☐ | ☐ | _____ |
| 2. If I have had a bad day at work or school, it tends to ruin my evening. | ☐ | ☐ | _____ |
| 3. If I just keep trying, I will get my share of good breaks. | ☐ | ☐ | _____ |
| 4. It takes me much longer than most people to shake the flu or a cold. | ☐ | ☐ | _____ |
| 5. If it were not for a few bad breaks I have received, I would be much further ahead in my career. | ☐ | ☐ | _____ |
| 6. There is no disgrace in losing. | ☐ | ☐ | _____ |
| 7. I am a generally self-confident person. | ☐ | ☐ | _____ |
| 8. Finishing last beats not competing at all. | ☐ | ☐ | _____ |
| 9. I like to take a chance, even if the probability of winning is small. | ☐ | ☐ | _____ |
| 10. If I have two reversals in a row, I do not worry about it being part of a losing streak. | ☐ | ☐ | _____ |
| 11. I am a sore loser. | ☐ | ☐ | _____ |
| 12. It takes a lot to get me discouraged. | ☐ | ☐ | _____ |
| 13. Every "no" I encounter is one step closer to a "yes." | ☐ | ☐ | _____ |
| 14. I doubt I could stand the shame of being fired or being downsized. | ☐ | ☐ | _____ |
| 15. I enjoy being the underdog once in a while. | ☐ | ☐ | _____ |

**Scoring Key:** Give yourself 1 point for each statement you responded to that is in agreement with the following answer key. If your response does not agree with the key, give yourself a zero. Add your points for the 15 statements to obtain your total score.

| | | |
|---|---|---|
| **1.** Mostly disagree | **3.** Mostly agree | **5.** Mostly disagree |
| **2.** Mostly disagree | **4.** Mostly disagree | **6.** Mostly agree |

## Quiz 2-3 (continued)

**7.** Mostly agree

**8.** Mostly agree

**9.** Mostly agree

**10.** Mostly agree

**11.** Mostly disagree

**12.** Mostly agree

**13.** Mostly agree

**14.** Mostly disagree

**15.** Mostly agree

***Scoring and Interpretation:*** Your score on the Personal Resiliency Quiz gives you a rough index of your overall tendencies toward being able to back bounce from adversity. The higher your score, the more resilient you are in handling disappointment, setbacks, and frustration. The following breakdown of scores will help you determine your degree of resiliency.

- **13+ *Very Resilient:*** You are remarkably effective in bouncing back from setback, or being resilient. Your resiliency should help you lead others when setbacks arise.

- **4–12 *Moderately Resilient:*** Like most people, you probably cope well with some type of adversity but not others.

- **0–3 *Not Resilient:*** You are the type of individual who has difficulty coping with adversity. Focusing on learning how to cope with setbacks and maintain a courageous outlook could help you in your development as a leader.

# COGNITIVE FACTORS AND LEADERSHIP

Mental ability as well as personality is important for leadership success. To inspire people, bring about constructive change, and solve problems creatively, leaders need to be mentally sharp. Another mental requirement is the ability to sort out essential information from less essential information and then store the most important information in memory. Problem-solving and intellectual skills are referred to collectively as **cognitive factors**. The term *cognition* refers to the mental process or faculty by which knowledge is gathered. We discuss six cognitive factors that are closely related to cognitive intelligence, as shown in Figure 2-4. The descriptor *cognitive* is somewhat necessary to differentiate traditional mental ability from emotional intelligence. The accompanying Leader in Action profile illustrates how a leader uses cognitive skills to perform well in his position, and to obtain a position.

### Cognitive (or Analytical) Intelligence

Being very good at solving problems is a fundamental characteristic of effective leaders in all fields. Business leaders, for example, need to understand how to analyze company finances, use advanced software, manage inventory, and deal with international trade regulations. Research spanning 100 years has demonstrated that leaders receive higher scores than most people on mental ability tests, including IQ (a term for a test score that for many people is synonymous with intelligence). A

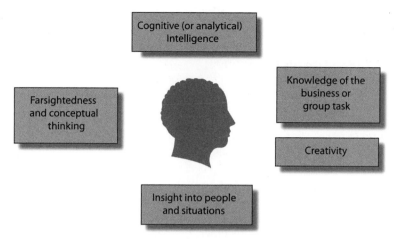

**FIGURE 2-4** Cognitive Factors and Leadership.

meta-analysis of 151 studies found a positive relationship between intelligence and job performance of leaders in many different settings. The relationship is likely to be higher when the leader plays an active role in decision making and is not overly stressed. The researchers also found support for the old idea that intelligence contributes the most to leadership effectiveness when the leader is not vastly smarter than most group members.[37]

One of thousands of potential examples of a leader with good cognitive intelligence is Ratan N. Tata, the chairman of the Tata Group—India's biggest conglomerate. Although he is over 70 years old, his associates are amazed at his command of numbers and technical details of the wide-ranging Tata companies.[38]

## Knowledge of the Business or Group Task

Intellectual ability is closely related to having knowledge of the business or the key task the group is performing. An effective leader has to be technically competent in some discipline, particularly when leading a group of specialists. It is difficult for the leader to establish rapport with group members when he or she does not know what they are doing and when the group does not respect the leader's technical skills.

A representative example of the contribution of knowledge of the business to leadership effectiveness is the situation of Jim Press, the former executive vice president and chief operating officer of Toyota Motor Sales, U.S.A., Inc. At age 60 he joined Chrysler in 2007 as vice chairman and chief product strategist. Press is considered to be one of the most influential executives in the American auto industry, and enjoys a reputation as perhaps the savviest sales and marketing executive in the business. He regularly conducted pep rallies with Toyota employees. Press has a rare blend of attributes. As a thirty-nine-year veteran who has mastered Toyota's highly regarded engineering and manufacturing systems, his interpersonal skills combined with his intimate knowledge of auto manufacturing gave him enormous clout within Toyota, and then within Chrysler as well as the U.S. automotive industry in general.[39]

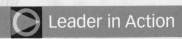 Leader in Action

### Former Nike and Coors Leader Frits van Paasschen Tries the Hotel Business

Five months after the abrupt departure of its chief executive officer, Starwood Hotels & Resorts Worldwide Inc. tapped the beer industry for a new CEO, hoping his experience in managing brands, especially overseas, could propel the hotel giant.

Starwood named Coors Brewing Co. chief executive Frits van Paasschen, 46 years old, as its new chief—the second time Starwood has turned to the beverage industry for leadership. Its previous chief, Steven Heyer, who left Starwood after a stormy 2½-year tenure, came from Coca-Cola. (Heyer was mentioned in the section about emotional intelligence earlier in this chapter.)

Van Paasschen has no hotel industry experience. In addition to Molson Coors Brewing Co.'s Coors unit, Paasschen's résumé includes stints at Nike Inc. and Walt Disney Co. At Starwood, the corporation behind well-known brands including Westin, Sheraton, and le Meridien, he will oversee a lodging empire that leases or manages about 871 hotels with approximately 266,000 rooms in 100 countries.

Starwood is betting that van Paasschen's experience with brands and overseas operations will be relevant to its sprawling hotel operations. At Coors, he was credited with helping increase sales of Coors Light and Keystone Light, using straightforward marketing messages—"cold" and "refreshing" for Coors Light, and "smooth" for Keystone Light—a discount brand. Marketing an array of distinct brands is important at Starwood, where in addition to its already formidable lineup of hotel names, the company is in the process of introducing two new brands, Aloft and Element.

At Nike, van Paasschen oversaw Nike's business in Europe, the Middle East, and Africa over a four-year period, increasing profit along the way. Starwood says that its new chief's global experience is especially relevant to Starwood—half of its planned 105,000 hotel rooms in the pipeline are outside North America.

Starwood's directors wanted their next leader to be someone "with strong moral values and upright character," the person close to the matter said. As part of the screening process, the front-runners had to craft their initial 100-day plan describing how they would lead the business and had to be interviewed by every Starwood board member. Van Paasschen's 100-day plan assessed the company's current strategy and suggested ways to tweak it. "That's when Frits pulled ahead," the source said. His thoughtful proposal "struck just the right tone on how he would lead. His command would be very inclusive, very hands-on—but very involving," this person added.

#### Questions

1. What evidence is presented in this story that Frits van Paasschen has good cognitive skills?
2. Why should Starwood directors care about a CEO's moral character so long as he can increase profits at the company?
3. What hints about Paasschen's approach to leadership do you find?

*Source:* Tamara Audi, Joann S. Lublin, and David Kesmodel, "Starwood Taps Beer Industry Executive for a New Chief Executive," *The Wall Street Journal (Central Edition)*, September 1–2, 2007, p. A3. Copyright 2007 by Dow Jones & Company, Inc. In the format Textbook via Copyright Clearance Center.

The importance of knowledge of the business is strongly recognized as an attribute of executive leadership. Leaders at every level are expected to bring forth useful ideas for carrying out the mission of the organization or organizational unit. Newspaper executive Gary Pruitt explains that today is the age of architect CEOs, who have to decide whether to gut, scale down, expand, or build new divisions for their companies. "This is an era when CEOs have to be hands-on, deeply engaged and knowledgeable about operations."[40] Furthermore, it is widely believed that in Silicon Valley, the most successful info tech companies are best run by leaders steeped in technology knowledge, preferably the founders. Several years ago Jerry Yang, the cofounder and former Chief Yahoo! of Yahoo!, was appointed as the new CEO.[41]

Knowledge of the business or the group task is particularly important when developing strategy, formulating mission statements, and sizing up the external environment. Chapter 13 deals with strategy formulation at length.

## Creativity

Many effective leaders are creative in the sense that they arrive at imaginative and original solutions to complex problems. Creative ability lies on a continuum, with some leaders being more creative than others. At one end of the creative continuum are business leaders who think of innovative products and services. One example is Steve Jobs of Apple Inc. and Pixar Animation Studios. Jobs has contributed creative product ideas to both firms, including endorsing the development of the iPod and then the iPhone. At the middle of the creativity continuum are leaders who explore imaginative—but not breakthrough—solutions to business problems. At the low end of the creativity continuum are leaders who inspire group members to push forward with standard solutions to organizational problems. Creativity is such an important aspect of the leader's role in the modern organization that the development of creative problem-solving skills receives separate attention in Chapter 11.

## Insight into People and Situations

Another important cognitive trait of leaders is **insight**, a depth of understanding that requires considerable intuition and common sense. Intuition is often the mental process used to provide the understanding of a problem. Insight helps speed decision making. Lawrence Weinbach, the former chairman, president, and CEO of Unisys, puts it this way: "If we want to be leaders, we're going to have to make decisions with maybe 75 percent of the facts. If you wait for 95 percent, you are going to be a follower."[42] Jeff Bezos of Amazon.com believes that the bigger the decision, such as whether or not to enter a particular business, the greater the role of insight and intuition.

Insight into people and situations involving people is an essential characteristic of managerial leaders because it helps them make the best use of both their own and others' talents. For example, it helps them make wise choices in selecting people for key assignments. Insight also enables managers to do a better job of training and developing team members because they can wisely assess the members' strengths and weaknesses. Another major advantage of being insightful is that the leader can size up a situation and adapt his or her leadership approach accordingly. For instance, in a crisis situation, group members welcome directive and decisive leadership. Being able to read people helps the manager provide this leadership.

You can gauge your insight by charting the accuracy of your hunches and predictions about people and business situations. For example, size up a new coworker or manager as best you can. Record your observations and test them against how that person performs or behaves many months later. The feedback from this type of exercise will help sharpen your insights.

Psychologist Justin Menkes has formulated a concept of the intelligence and thinking of leaders that combines analytical intelligence and insight. Labeled ***executive intelligence***, the concept refers to superior reasoning and problem-solving skills that enable the executive to cut through conflicting data to create a solution that uniquely fits the situation at hand. Andrea Jung, CEO and chairwoman of Avon, is presented as a person with executive intelligence.

One example of Jung's critical thinking was her decision while in charge of product marketing. She consulted with and cultivated Avon's direct sales force rather than simply forcing change through a top–down directive. The mostly female sales force was objecting to a shift to higher-priced lines of perfume, which they feared would be a tough sell with their current customers. At meetings throughout the country, Jung polled reps as to how many actually used Avon products themselves. Most conceded that they didn't and quickly came around to Jung's belief that the company's merchandise had become too downmarket.[43]

## Farsightedness and Conceptual Thinking

To develop visions and corporate strategy, a leader needs **farsightedness**, the ability to understand the long-range implications of actions and policies. A farsighted leader recognizes that hiring talented workers today will give the firm a long-range competitive advantage. A more shortsighted view would be to hire less-talented workers to satisfy immediate employment needs. The farsighted leader/manager is not oblivious to short-range needs but will devise an intermediate solution, such as hiring temporary workers until people with the right talents are found.

Conceptual thinking refers to the ability to see the overall perspective, and it makes farsightedness possible. A conceptual thinker is also a *systems thinker* because he or she understands how the external environment influences the organization and how different parts of the organization influence each other. A good conceptual thinker recognizes how his or her organizational unit contributes to the firm or how the firm meshes with the outside world.

Being farsighted benefits the leadership of basic businesses as well as that of high-technology firms. An example is that many successful real estate developers restore distressed properties in cities, and then rent the properties or sell them at hefty profits. Much of the renovation of downtown Detroit has been the product of farsighted thinking by private developers.

## The WICS Model of Leadership in Organizations

Robert J. Sternberg has developed an approach to understanding leadership based on cognitive factors. **WICS** is a systems model of leadership that provides an understanding of leadership as a set of decision processes that embodies wisdom, intelligence, and

**FIGURE 2-5** The WICS Model of Leadership.

*Source:* Robert J. Sternberg, "WICS: A Model of Leadership in Organizations," *Academy of Management Learning and Education*, December 2003, p. 387. Updated with Sternberg, "A Systems Model of Leadership: WICS," *American Psychologist*, January 2007, pp. 34–42. *Academy of Management Learning and Education* by Robert J. Sternberg. Copyright 2003 by *Academy of Management Learning and Education*. Reproduced with permission of *Academy of Management Learning and Education* in the format Textbook via Copyright Clearance Center.

creativity, as well as other higher cognitive processes. To be a highly effective leader, one needs these three components, working together or synthesized, as diagrammed in Figure 2-5.

Creativity generates the ideas a leader needs; analytical or academic intelligence evaluates whether the ideas are good or bad. Creativity is also essential for helping to create the stories that leaders tell to inspire and motivate followers. For example, a product manager for baby food might tell true stories about how underweight babies grew healthy and strong when their parents switched to the company's brand of baby food. Practical intelligence is applied to implement the ideas and persuade others of their worth. Wisdom is applied to balance the interests of all stakeholders and to ensure that the actions of the leader seek a common good. Practical intelligence refers to the ability to solve everyday problems—sometimes referred to as *street smarts*—by using experience-based knowledge to adapt to and shape the environment. Wisdom is the most important quality a leader can have, but it is relatively rare.[44] The insight and intuition referred to earlier in the chapter are much like wisdom.

Jim Press of Chrysler, described earlier, might classify as a leader with intelligence, creativity, and wisdom because he has contributed to the design and manufacture of high-quality vehicles and to the creation of thousands of jobs. The WICS model emphasizes that cognitive factors are indeed useful for leadership. Personality factors, however, are still a key part of being an effective leader.

To help personalize the information about key leadership traits presented so far, do Leadership Skill-Building Exercise 2-3.

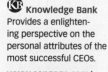

**Knowledge Bank**
Provides a enlightening perspective on the personal attributes of the most successful CEOs.

**www.cengage.com/ management/dubrin**

# THE INFLUENCE OF HEREDITY AND ENVIRONMENT ON LEADERSHIP

Does heredity or environment contribute more to leadership effectiveness? Are leaders born or made? Do you have to have the right stuff to be a leader? Many people ponder these issues now that the study of leadership is more in vogue. The

**Leadership Skill-Building Exercise 2-3**

### Group Feedback on Leadership Traits

The class organizes into groups of about seven people. A volunteer sits in the middle of each group. Each group member looks directly at the person in the "hot seat" and tells him or her what leadership trait, characteristic, or motive he or she seems to possess. It will help if the feedback providers offer a few words of explanation for their observations. For example, a participant who is told that he or she has self-confidence might also be told, "I notice how confidently you have told the class about your success on the job." The group next moves on to the second person, and so forth. (We assume that you have had some opportunity to observe your classmates prior to this exercise.)

Each member thus receives positive feedback about leadership traits and characteristics from all the other members in the group. After all members have had their turn at receiving feedback, discuss as a group the value of the exercise.

most sensible answer is that the traits, motives, and characteristics required for leadership effectiveness are caused by a combination of heredity and environment. Personality traits and mental ability traits are based on certain inherited predispositions and aptitudes that require the right opportunity to develop. Cognitive intelligence is a good example. We inherit a basic capacity that sets an outer limit to how much mental horsepower we will have. Yet people need the right opportunity to develop their cognitive intelligence so that they can behave brightly enough to be chosen for a leadership position.

Evelyn Williams, who directs the leadership development program at Stanford University, makes the following metaphor: "I think leadership is a combination of nature and nurture. Just as some musicians have a special talent for playing instruments, some people seem to be born with leadership abilities. But whatever their natural talent, people can certainly learn to be better musicians—and better leaders."[45]

The physical factor of energy also sheds light on the nature-versus-nurture issue. Some people are born with a biological propensity for being more energetic than others. Yet unless that energy is properly channeled, it will not help a person become an effective leader.

The nature-versus-nurture issue also surfaces in relation to the leadership characteristic of creativity and innovation. Important genetic contributors to imaginative thinking include brainpower and emotional expressiveness. Yet these traits require the right environment to flourish. Such an environment would include encouragement from others and ample opportunity to experiment with ideas.

Research about emotional intelligence reinforces the statements made so far about leadership being a combination of inherited and learned factors. The outermost areas of the brain, known as the neocortex, govern analytical thinking and technical skill, which are associated with cognitive or traditional intelligence. The innermost areas of the brain govern emotions, such as the rage one feels when being criticized by a customer. Emotional intelligence originates in the neurotransmitters of the limbic system of the brain, which governs feelings, impulses, and drives.

A person therefore has genes that influence the emotional intelligence necessary for leadership. However, experience is important for emotional intelligence because it increases with age,[46] and a person usually becomes better at managing relationships the more practice he or she has. As one turnaround manager said, "I've restructured five different companies, and I've learned to do it without completely destroying morale."

A final note is that some leadership traits are more difficult to awaken or develop than others, with passion for work and people being an example. Jonathan Byrnes, a consultant and senior lecturer at MIT, says that you have to have the right people to develop into leaders. "You can't teach passion for the work to someone who can't wait to go home."[47]

# THE STRENGTHS AND LIMITATIONS OF THE TRAIT APPROACH

A compelling argument for the trait approach is that the evidence is convincing that leaders possess personal characteristics that differ from those of nonleaders. Based on their review of the type of research reported in this chapter, Kirkpatrick and Locke concluded: "Leaders do not have to be great men or women by being intellectual geniuses or omniscient prophets to succeed. But they do need to have the 'right stuff' and this stuff is not equally present in all people."[48] The current emphasis on emotional intelligence, charisma, and ethical conduct, which are really traits, attitudes, and behaviors, reinforces the importance of the trait approach.

Understanding the traits of effective leaders serves as an important guide to leadership selection. If we are confident that honesty and integrity, as well as creativity and imagination, are essential leadership traits, then we can concentrate on selecting leaders with those characteristics. Another important strength of the trait approach is that it can help people prepare for leadership responsibility and all of the issues that accompany it. A person might seek experiences that enable him or her to develop vital characteristics such as self-confidence, good problem-solving ability, and assertiveness.

A limitation to the trait approach is that it does not tell us which traits are absolutely needed in which leadership situations. We also do not know how much of a trait, characteristic, or motive is the right amount. For example, some leaders get into ethical and legal trouble because they allow their ambition to cross the borderline into greed and gluttony. In addition, too much focus on the trait approach can breed an elitist conception of leadership. People who are not outstanding on key leadership traits and characteristics might be discouraged from seeking leadership positions.

The late Peter Drucker, a key figure in the modern management movement, was skeptical about studying the qualities of leaders. He believed that a leader cannot be categorized by a particular personality type, style, or set of traits. Instead, a leader should be understood in terms of his or her constituents, results, behaviors, and responsibilities. A leader must look in the mirror and ask whether the image there is the kind of person he or she wants to be. (However, Drucker in this instance may have been alluding to the leader's traits and values!)[49]

A subtle limitation to the trait approach is that it prompts some people to believe that to be effective, you have to have a high standing on almost every leadership characteristic. In reality, the majority of effective leaders are outstanding in many characteristics but are low on others. Jim Press, the automotive executive, is an inspiring leader and a great conceptual thinker. Yet at times he may get a little bogged down in details such as telling engineers how they should change the dimensions of cup holders on the minivan.

A balanced perspective on the trait approach is that certain traits, motives, and characteristics increase the probability that a leader will be effective, but they do not guarantee effectiveness. The leadership situation often influences which traits will be the most important.[50] At the same time different situations call for different combinations of traits. Visualize yourself as managing a restaurant staffed by teenagers who had never worked previously. You would need to emphasize warmth, enthusiasm, flexibility, and adaptability. Less emphasis would be required on cognitive skills and the power motive.

## Reader's Roadmap

In this chapter we focused on the traits, motives, and characteristics of the leader—his or her inner qualities. In the next chapter we dig further into leadership qualities by studying charismatic and transformational leadership.

## SUMMARY

The trait-based perspective of leadership contends that certain personal characteristics and skills contribute to leadership effectiveness in many situations. General personality traits associated with effective leadership include (1) self-confidence, (2) humility, (3) trustworthiness, (4) authenticity, (5) extraversion, (6) assertiveness, (7) enthusiasm, optimism, and warmth, and (8) sense of humor.

Some personality traits of effective leaders are closely associated with task accomplishment. Among them are (1) passion for the work and the people, (2) emotional intelligence, (3) flexibility and adaptability, (4) internal locus of control, and (5) courage. Emotional intelligence is composed of four traits: self-awareness, self-management, social awareness, and relationship management.

Certain motives and needs associated with leadership effectiveness are closely related to task accomplishment. Among them are (1) the power motive, (2) the drive and achievement motive, and (3) tenacity and resilience.

Cognitive factors are also important for leadership success. They include cognitive (or analytical) intelligence and knowledge of the business or group task: that is, technical competence. Creativity is another important cognitive skill for leaders, but effective leaders vary widely in their creative contributions. Insight into people and situations, including the ability to make effective judgments about business opportunities, also contributes to leadership effectiveness. Farsightedness and conceptual thinking help leaders to understand the long-range implications of actions and policies and to take an overall perspective. Being open to experience is yet another cognitive characteristic associated with effective leaders. The WICS model of leadership in organizations emphasizes that leaders must synthesize wisdom and intelligence—both analytical and practical, and creativity (all cognitive factors).

The issue of whether leaders are born or bred frequently surfaces. A sensible answer is that the traits, motives, and characteristics required for leadership effectiveness are a combination of heredity and environment.

The trait approach to leadership is supported by many studies showing that leaders are different from nonleaders and that effective leaders are different from less effective leaders. Nevertheless, the trait approach does not tell us which traits are most important in which situations or how much of a trait is required. Also, different situations call for different combinations of traits.

## KEY TERMS

Trust
Authenticity
Assertiveness
Emotional intelligence
Flexibility

Internal locus of control
Drive
Achievement motivation
Cognitive factors
Insight

Executive intelligence
Farsightedness
WICS

## ✔ GUIDELINES FOR ACTION AND SKILL DEVELOPMENT

Because emotional intelligence is so important for leadership success, many organizations sponsor emotional intelligence training for managers. One way to get started on improving emotional intelligence would be to attend such a training program. However, like all forms of training, emotional intelligence training must be followed up with consistent and determined practice. A realistic starting point in improving your emotional intelligence is to work with one of its four components at a time, such as the empathy aspect of social awareness.

Begin by obtaining as much feedback as you can from people who know you. Ask them if they think you understand their emotional reactions and how well they think you understand them. It is also helpful to ask someone from another culture or someone who has a severe disability how well you communicate with him or her. (A higher level of empathy is required to communicate well with somebody much different from you.) If you have external or internal customers, ask them how well you appear to understand their position.

If you find any area of deficiency, work on that deficiency steadily. For example, perhaps you are not perceived as taking the time to understand a point of view quite different from your own. Attempt to understand other points of view. Suppose you believe strongly that money is the most important motivator for practically everybody. Speak to a person with a different opinion and listen carefully until you understand that person's perspective.

A few months later, obtain more feedback about your ability to empathize. If you are making progress, continue to practice. Then, repeat these steps for another facet of emotional intelligence. As a result of this practice, you will have developed another valuable interpersonal skill.

A constructive approach to applying trait theory to attain your goals in a given situation is to think through which combination of traits is the most likely to lead to positive outcomes in the situation at hand. Finding the right cluster of traits to emphasize is usually much more useful than emphasizing one trait. You might be leading a group, for example, that is worried because it needs a creative idea to become more productive. Here you might emphasize your cognitive skills, be assertive about expressing your ideas, and also express enthusiasm about the group's chances for success.

### Discussion Questions and Activities

1. How much faith do voters place in the trait theory of leadership when they elect public officials?
2. Suppose a college student graduates with a major for which he or she lacks enthusiasm. What might this person do about becoming a passionate leader?
3. Describe a leadership setting or situation in which being extraverted and assertive might not be an asset.
4. What would a manager to whom you report have to do to convince you that he or she has emotional intelligence?
5. Describe any leader or manager whom you know personally or have watched on television who is unenthusiastic. What effect did the lack of enthusiasm have on group members?
6. What would lead you to conclude that a leader was non-authentic (phony)?
7. What are your best-developed leadership traits, motives, and characteristics? How do you know?
8. A disproportionate number of people who received an M.B.A. at elite business schools are top executives in *Fortune 500* business firms. How does this fact fit into the evidence about the roles of heredity and environment in creating leaders?
9. Visualize the least effective leader you know. Identify the traits, motives, and personal characteristics in which that person might be deficient.
10. Many people who disagree with the trait approach to leadership nevertheless still conduct interviews when hiring a person for a leadership position. Why is conducting such interviews inconsistent with their attitude toward the trait approach?

## Leadership Case Problem A

### The Methodical John Thain Takes Over at Merrill

A few years back, Merrill Lynch & Co. chose John Thain, the chief of NYSE Euronext, as its new chief executive. The move was interpreted as signaling that after years of inner turmoil and risky expansion, the board of the beleaguered financial giant wanted a pair of steady hands at the helm.

Wall Street executives said that the companies that appeared to emerge relatively unscathed from the credit risks that gripped some of the nation's biggest banks were led by men who knew the innards of their businesses. Also, they couldn't be fooled too easily by bond traders and were hands-on to a fault.

Thain, who studied electrical engineering at Massachusetts Institute of Technology and has a Harvard M.B.A., revels in the nitty-gritty of the businesses he has run. The 52-year-old spent twenty-four years at Goldman, holding various jobs from mortgage-bond trader to chief financial officer before rising to president in 1999. He took the NYSE job to have a chance to take a CEO role and work to turn around an important financial institution facing governance and technological challenges.

Thain said he accepted the offer from Merrill because it has a "great franchise" with strong positions in wealth management, investment banking, and sales and trading, among other areas. "It's got one problem area," he said, "and I know a lot about that area" from running Goldman's mortgage desk from 1985 to 1990. The problem was reflected in an $8 billion after-tax loss for 2007, along with $22 billion in writedowns.

Known for a somewhat robotic personality, Thain deflected concerns during an interview that he doesn't have the charisma to lead a firm known for its "thundering herd" of 16,000 brokers. "I think I have better interpersonal skills than people give me credit for," he said. He added that he has taken a lot of time to get to know the Big Board's floor traders, a task somewhat akin to one challenge at Merrill: winning the support of its army of stockbrokers.

Another selling point for the Merrill board is that Thain was known to be a consensus builder, and has the ability to attract and retain talent. His predecessor, Stan O'Neal, was known for driving away potential challengers and firing executives who were a threat to his power.

Some Merrill alumni expressed surprise that their alma mater would turn to an outsider and a former rival. "It's shocking they picked someone from a Goldman Sachs background," said former Merrill CEO Dan Tully. He added that Thain didn't seem to be a folksy "people person" consistent with the culture of Merrill, which has a huge brokerage force. "I understand he's very cerebral," Tully said. As a youth, Thain put together a ham radio for his mother.

At a meeting with a consultant at the NYSE on its lower trading floor, Thain jumped in with questions about what color the prices and data on the screen should be to make the job easier for traders. Two years earlier, a visit to the Chicago Board Options Exchange ran long when Thain asked a series of questions about how the floor traders on that exchange used technology. "There's an awful lot of substance there," says William Brodsky, the CEO of the Chicago Board Options exchange. "Merrill is lucky to have him."

Thain at times grew frustrated with parts of the job at the NYSE, especially the ceremonial ones.

Early on, he preferred to stay away from twice-a-day bell-ringings on the balcony above the trading floor. Later he showed up at bell-ringings more often, using them as an opportunity to show CEOs and other business leaders in person what actually happened on the trading floor. "He's a detail person and understands the inner workings, but he also appreciates the big picture and is well connected," says Amy Butte, a former NYSE finance executive.

One of Thain's biggest accomplishments was in getting the Euronext deal done, in the face of a bid by Frankfurt's Deutsche Borse that many European politicians preferred. So despite his reputation as an operations person, he showed he could get a tough deal done through delicate negotiations. "That really impressed the board" of Merrill said one person close to the board.

Adding to the board's confidence was Thain's extensive experience in some of the very areas bedeviling Merrill Lynch: mortgage trading. Thain is also known to be willing to take bold action when necessary. Faced with major losses in 2008, he facilitated the sale of Merrill Lynch to Bank of America Corp. Thain was thought to be a contender to become the CEO of the combined company.

## Questions

1. Which traits and characteristics of Thain are revealed by this story?
2. What emphasis did the Merrill board place on cognitive characteristics in their selection of Thain?
3. Based on the information presented, what advice can you offer John Thain about emphasizing the right traits to be successful as the head of Merrill?
4. How strong does Thain's power motive appear to be?

*Source*: Randall Smith and Aaron Lucchetti, "Merrill Taps NYSE's Thain as CEO," *The Wall Street Journal*, November 15, 2007, pp. A1, A21; Dwight Cass and Richard Beales, "Merrill's Gold-Star Move," www.breakingnews.com, November 15, 2007.

## Leadership Case Problem B

### Amy Touchstone Wants to Shape Up the Club

Amy Touchstone, 27, is feeling great these days, having just been promoted to director of operations at the East End Athletic Club. For two years previously she worked as an administrator and receptionist at the club, which offers a wide range of fitness equipment, ten indoor tennis courts, six squash courts, one basketball court, and a variety of fitness programs including massages.

Reporting to Touchstone is a staff of ten people, three of whom are full-time workers, and seven of whom are part-timers. Her main responsibilities are to ensure that the club is running smoothly, outside of athletic programs and marketing. The billing office and custodial staff report to Touchstone.

When Touchstone asked her boss, the club manager, what she was supposed to accomplish as the director of operations, she was told, "East End isn't nearly as efficient, clean, and sharp as it should be for the rates we charge. So go fix it." Touchstone liked these general directives, but she thought that she would need to arrive at a few specific ideas for improvement.

Based on a technique she learned in a marketing course, Touchstone decided to dig into the responses in the club member suggestion box that is located at the front desk. Amy dug back into three months of suggestions. The key themes for improving the club as revealed by these suggestions were as follows:

- Stop charging us for everything, such as using the tennis courts, if we are already paying hefty monthly dues.
- The men's locker room is horrible because of the way the guests throw their towels on the floor. These guys have no respect for the club.

- Some of the staff don't seem interested in the members. Sometimes they are talking to each other when they should be paying attention to us. We are put on hold far too often when we call the club.
- Some of the people who work here act like they are doing us a favor to let us use the facilities.

Amy reviewed the negative themes she found among the suggestions, and then discussed them with Joe Pellagrino, a fitness coach whom she had known for several years. Pellagrino said, "Don't worry about a handful of complainers. Only the people with a gripe bother to put something in the suggestion box."

Amy thought to herself, "Joe could have a point. Yet those suggestions seem pretty important. I should start taking action on improvements tomorrow. I have to think of a good way to approach the staff."

### Questions

1. What personal characteristics of a leader should Touchstone emphasize in bringing about improvements in the operation of the East End Athletic Club?
2. What leadership roles (review Chapter 1) should Touchstone emphasize in bringing about improvements in the operation of the club?
3. What do you recommend that Touchstone do next to carry out her leadership responsibility of improving operations?

## ◎ Leadership Skill-Building Exercise 2-4

### My Leadership Portfolio

For this addition to your leadership portfolio, first select five of the traits, motives, and characteristics described in this chapter that you think you have already exhibited. For each of these attributes, explain why you think you have it. An example would be as follows:

*Insight into people and situations:* As a restaurant manager, my job was to help hire an assistant manager who would share some of the responsibilities of running the restaurant. I invited a friend of mine, Laura, to apply for the position even though she had never worked in a restaurant. I noticed that she was businesslike and also had a good touch with people. Laura was hired, and she proved to be a fantastic assistant manager. I obviously sized her up correctly.

Second, select several leadership traits, motives, or characteristics that you think you need to develop to enhance your leadership skills. Explain why you think you need this development and how you think you might obtain it. An example would be as follows:

*Passion for the work and people:* So far I am not particularly passionate about any aspect of work or any cause, so it is hard for me to get very excited about being a leader. I plan to read more about my field and then interview a couple of successful people in this field to find some aspect of it that would be a joy for me to get involved in.

## Internet Skill-Building Exercise

### Measuring Your Emotional Intelligence

Go to www.queendom.com and take the Emotional IQ Test, which is the equivalent of emotional intelligence. The Emotional IQ Test will evaluate several aspects of your emotional intelligence and will make suggestions for enhancing it. After completing the test, you will receive a Snapshot Report with an option to purchase the full results. See if the report touches on other characteristics mentioned in this chapter.

Apply the chapter concepts! Visit the Web and complete this Internet skill-building exercise to learn more about current leadership topics and trends.

## CHAPTER 3

# Charismatic and Transformational Leadership

## LEARNING OBJECTIVES

After studying this chapter and doing the exercises, you should be able to

- Describe many of the traits and behaviors of charismatic leaders.
- Explain the visionary component of charismatic leadership.
- Explain the communication style of charismatic leaders.
- Have an action plan for developing your charisma.
- Explain the nature of transformational leadership.
- Identify several of the impacts of charismatic and transformational leadership on performance and behavior.
- Describe the concerns about charismatic leadership from the scientific and moral standpoint.

## CHAPTER OUTLINE

In its formative years, Xerox Corporation was widely acclaimed for its innovation and cutting-edge technology. As competitors in the document-processing field swooped in, the company reputation for innovation lost some strength. Xerox has turned around in recent years, to a large extent because the company has again become a powerful innovator. Xerox has created new technologies that can read, understand, route, and protect documents, among other useful functions.

A lead person in the new technology thrust is Sophie Vandebroek, 45, the company's chief technology officer for several years. Her primary role is to keep Xerox at the leading edge of advances in information technology that translate into improved company profits and an enhanced stock price. Vandebroek was born and raised in Belgium, and she earned a doctorate in electrical engineering from Cornell University. Here are a couple of excerpts from an interview that a *Fortune* reporter conducted with her.

*Innovation may be the hottest topic in business. How can it be a competitive advantage for Xerox?*

The major focus is ensuring that our customers constantly want to buy our products and services. The ultimate meaning of innovation is delighting the customer, and bringing about excellent economic returns for Xerox. Innovation only exists when it provides a benefit to the customer.

*So what is your vision?*

It's assisting our customers deal more effectively with their business processes involving documents. That means making sure they have the information they need when and where they need it, with the history and context of the information they need. It also means seamlessly bridging the digital and physical, and making it easy and fast to get to information. I want the document to be smart enough so I don't need to worry about it.[1]

The words of chief technology officer Sophie Vandebroek illustrate an important topic in this chapter: A major contributor to a company transformation is the visionary thinking of leaders. Charismatic and transformational leaders think big. The study of charismatic and transformational leadership, an extension of the trait theory, has become an important way of understanding leadership. One of the many reasons that charisma is important is that it facilitates leaders in carrying out their roles. In the opinion of Jack and Suzy Welch, charisma makes the leader's job much easier. In today's fiercely competitive global economy, leaders need to energize their constituents more than ever. Helping people attain stretch goals and understand why change is necessary is done more quickly with charisma than relying solely on reasoning and logic.[2]

In this chapter we examine the meaning and effects of charismatic leadership, the characteristics of charismatic leaders, how such leaders form visions, and how one develops charisma. We also describe the closely related and overlapping subject of transformational leadership. Finally, we look at the dark side of charismatic leadership.

# THE MEANINGS OF CHARISMA

Charisma, like leadership itself, has been defined in various ways. Nevertheless, there is enough consistency among these definitions to make charisma a useful concept in understanding and practicing leadership. *Charisma* is a Greek word meaning "divinely inspired gift." In the study of leadership, **charisma** is a special quality of leaders whose purposes, powers, and extraordinary determination differentiate them from others.[3] In general use, the term *charismatic* means to have a charming and colorful personality, such as that shown by basketball star Yao Ming or soccer star Mia Hamm.

The various definitions of charisma have a unifying theme. Charisma is a positive and compelling quality of a person that makes many others want to be led by that person. The phrase *many others* is chosen carefully. Few leaders are perceived as charismatic by *all* of their constituents. A case in point is Steve Jobs of Apple Inc. and Pixar, whose name surfaces frequently in discussions of charisma. Several years ago he was nominated *Time* magazine person of the year by an entertainment executive, and given this accolade: "He is a true visionary who continues to lead the technological revolution. Year after year, Apple creates must-have products that shape how we live our lives. Jobs and Apple continue to lead us into a wonderful new technological future."[4] In contrast, a news reporter and novelist describes Jobs as "a brilliant but short-tempered figure known for his outsize ego and penchant for control."[5] This last statement is hardly characteristic of an inspiring leader.

Given that charisma is based on perceptions, an important element of charismatic leadership involves the *attributions* made by group members about the characteristics of leaders and the results they achieve. According to attribution theory, if people perceive a leader to have a certain characteristic, such as being visionary, the leader will more likely be perceived as charismatic. Attributions of charisma are important because they lead to other behavioral outcomes, such as commitment to leaders, self-sacrifice, and high performance.

A study of attributions and charisma found that the network a person belongs to influences the attributions he or she makes. The subjects in the study were police workers who rated the director of a police organization and students in an introductory business course who rated the charisma of their professors. The study found that network members influenced to some extent whether the study participants perceived their leader or professor to be charismatic and that perceptions of charisma were the closest among friends within networks.[6] What about you? Are your perceptions of the charisma of your professors influenced by the opinions of your network members?

## Charisma: A Relationship Between the Leader, Group Members, and Other Stakeholders

A key dimension of charismatic leadership is that, like all leadership, it involves a relationship or interaction between the leader and the people being led. Furthermore, the people accepting the leadership must attribute charismatic qualities to the leader. John Gardner believes that charisma applies to leader–constituent relationships in

**Knowledge Bank**
Contains a sampling of additional definitions of charisma.

**www.cengage.com/ management/dubrin**

which the leader has an exceptional gift for inspiration and nonrational communication. At the same time the constituents' response is characterized by awe, reverence, devotion, or emotional dependence.[7] The late Sam Walton, founder of Wal-Mart Stores, had this type of relationship with many of his employees. Walton's most avid supporters believed he was an inspired executive to whom they could trust their careers.

Charismatic leaders use impression management to deliberately cultivate a certain relationship with group members. In other words, they take steps to create a favorable, successful impression, recognizing that the perceptions of constituents determine whether they function as charismatic leaders.[8] Impression management seems to imply that these leaders are skillful actors in presenting a charismatic face to the world. But the behaviors and attitudes of truly charismatic leaders go well beyond superficial aspects of impression management, such as wearing fashionable clothing or speaking well. For example, a truly charismatic leader will work hard to create positive visions for group members.

A notable aspect of charismatic and transformational leaders is that their influence extends beyond the immediate work group and beyond reporting relationships. An example is that some consumers are influenced to purchase products from a company, and some suppliers want to do business with it, based partly on the charisma of a company leader.[9] Andrea Jung, the stylish chairperson of Avon, is a case in point. After seeing a story about Jung in a business magazine, or seeing her interviewed on television, many consumers are willing to give Avon products a try.

Another way in which the highly charismatic leader influences external stakeholders is that he or she becomes the symbol of the organization. If the leader meets the stakeholders' (or followers') needs, such as wanting to identify with a powerful figure, the stakeholders will have favorable interactions with the organization. Visualize a teenage girl wanting to identify with a successful mother figure, who regards Jung as cool. She might then become a loyal Avon customer. A middle-age male who perceived Jung to be the type of woman he wanted to have a relationship with might purchase company stock on that basis.

Charismatic leadership is possible under certain conditions. The constituents must share the leader's beliefs and must have unquestioning acceptance of and affection for the leader. The group members must willingly obey the leader, and they must be emotionally involved both in the mission of the charismatic leader and in their own goals. Finally, the constituents must have a strong desire to identify with the leader.[10]

## The Effects of Charisma

Jane A. Halpert performed a statistical analysis of the effects charismatic leaders have on followers, and found that three dimensions are the most important, as shown in Figure 3-1. One key dimension is **referent power**, the ability to influence others because of one's desirable traits and characteristics. If we like a leader, he or she might be able to exercise referent power. Another dimension is **expert power**, the ability to influence others because of one's specialized knowledge, skills, or abilities. An important part of Steve Jobs' charisma stems from his expert powers reflected in imagining and designing electronic devices such as the iMac and iPod.

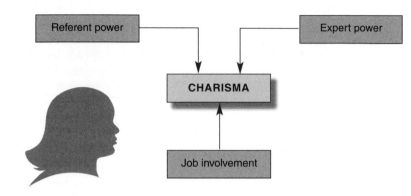

**FIGURE 3-1** Halpert's Dimensions of Charisma.

A third dimension of charismatic leadership is the ability to get group members excited about their work, or to experience **job involvement.**[11]

Job involvement is a key component of job satisfaction, and one empirical study has provided evidence of the relationship between charismatic leadership and job satisfaction. Using a sample of state government employees, the researchers found that managers who rated their own managers as high on charisma tended to have high job satisfaction with supervision. The study also found that working for a charismatic leader enhanced commitment to the organization.[12]

Another way of understanding the effects of charisma is to understand that top-level leaders sometimes lose their power and position because they are perceived as not being charismatic enough to get constituents to accomplish important goals. An example is Zoe Cruz, the former co-president and heir apparent at Morgan Stanley. Cruz had oversight over the part of the investment bank that suffered losses in the mortgage credit crisis of several years ago. It appeared she had escaped the bloodletting following the losses. But she also suffered from criticisms of her leadership style by many of her colleagues, who said that she lacked charisma and ease with people. Cruz may have been the victim of political infighting at Morgan Stanley.[13] Yet if you are well liked, you are less likely to be a political victim.

The information just presented is useful for the aspiring charismatic leader. To be charismatic, one must exercise referent power and expert power and must get people involved in their jobs. Also, not being charismatic enough can sometimes make it difficult to hold on to a high-level leadership position.

## TYPES OF CHARISMATIC LEADERS

The everyday use of the term *charisma* suggests that it is a straightforward and readily understood trait. As already explained, however, charisma has different meanings and dimensions. As a result, charismatic leaders can be categorized into five types: socialized charismatics, personalized charismatics, office-holder charismatics, personal charismatics, and divine charismatics.[14]

Following the distinction made for the power motive, some charismatic leaders use their power for the good of others. A **socialized charismatic** is a leader who restrains the use of power in order to benefit others. This type of leader also attempts to bring group members' values in line with his or her values. The socialized charismatic formulates and pursues goals that fulfill the needs of group members and provide intellectual stimulation to them. Followers of socialized charismatics are autonomous, empowered, and responsible. A study conducted in a health care organization indicated that direct reports of leaders perceived to be socialized charismatics are less likely to engage in workplace deviance (such as lying, stealing, and cheating). Part of the reason is that the socialized charismatic imparts positive values to group members.[15]

The effect of the socialized charismatic on followers provides more insight into this type of charismatic. In the socialized relationship, the followers have a clear sense of who they are and a clear set of values. The charismatic relationship gives them an opportunity to express their important values within the framework of being a group member, such as wanting to work together to preserve the planet. In a socialized relationship, the followers derive a sense of direction and self-expression not from identifying with the leader but from the leader's message.[16] The message of the socialized charismatic in this situation might be, "We want to make money but we want to contribute to a sustainable environment at the same time."

A second type of charismatic leader is the **personalized charismatic**. Such individuals serve primarily their own interests and so exercise few restraints on their use of power. Personalized charismatics impose self-serving goals on constituents, and they offer consideration and support to group members only when it facilitates their own goals. Followers of personalized charismatics are typically obedient, submissive, and dependent. They also identify more with the leader than the leader's message, and therefore might follow the leader down an unethical path such as granting homeowner loans that will most likely result in a high foreclosure rate.[17]

Another type of charismatic leader is the *office-holder charismatic*. For this type of leader, charismatic leadership is more a property of the office occupied than of his or her personal characteristics. The chief executive officer of the Procter & Gamble Company, for example, might have considerable luster but would lose much of it immediately after leaving office. Office-holder charismatics attain high status by occupying a valuable role.

In contrast to office-holder charismatics, *personal* (not *personalized*) *charismatics* gain very high esteem through the faith others have in them. A personal charismatic exerts influence whether he or she occupies a low- or high-status position because he or she has the right traits, characteristics, and behaviors. Former Secretary of State Colin H. Powell would qualify in the eyes of many as a personal charismatic. After retiring from his position as the top-ranking U.S. Army general, Powell was deluged with offers to serve on corporate boards and to make speaking appearances. He was eventually appointed as secretary of state in the George W. Bush administration and served during Bush's first term; he later remained an influential figure on the world stage.

A historically important type of charismatic leader is the *divine charismatic*. Originally, charismatic leadership was a theological concept: a divine charismatic was someone endowed with a gift of divine grace. In 1924 Max Weber defined a charismatic leader as a mystical, narcissistic, and personally magnetic savior who would arise to lead people through a crisis. For millions of people, Joe Montana of Notre Dame and the San Francisco 49ers was the ultimate quarterback, and he also possessed a warm, magnetic personality. His expert power in football and his referent power as a person combined to help his post-football business, Joe Montana's Recipes, succeed. (Are you familiar with Comeback Kid Coleslaw or Overtime Oatmeal Cookies, among other tasty treats?)

## CHARACTERISTICS OF CHARISMATIC LEADERS

The outstanding characteristic of charismatic leaders is that they are charismatic, and therefore they can attract, motivate, or lead others! They also have other distinguishing characteristics. Because charisma is a key component of transformational leadership, many of these characteristics also apply to transformational leaders. A **transformational leader** is one who brings about positive, major changes in an organization. Many charismatic leaders, however, are not transformational. Although they inspire people, they may not bring about major organizational changes. As we look at the characteristics of charismatic leaders,[18] you will note that many of these characteristics apply to leaders in general.

First, charismatic leaders are *visionary* because they offer an exciting image of where the organization is headed and how to get there. A vision is more than a forecast; it describes an ideal version of the future of an entire organization or an organizational unit. The next section provides additional information about vision in leadership, including guidelines on how to develop a vision. Chapter 13, in discussing the leadership aspects of business strategy, also contains information about formulating visions.

Charismatic leaders also have *masterful communication skills*. To inspire people, the charismatic leader uses colorful language and exciting metaphors and analogies. (More about the communication skills of charismatic leaders is presented later in this chapter.) Another key characteristic is the *ability to inspire trust*. Constituents believe so strongly in the integrity of charismatic leaders that they will risk their careers to pursue the chief's vision. Charismatic leaders are also *able to make group members feel capable*. Sometimes they do this by enabling group members to achieve success on relatively easy projects. They then praise the group members and give them more demanding assignments.

Charismatic people are typically tactful in social situations based partly on their ability to read other people's emotions (part of emotional intelligence). Related to reading emotions is the ability to connect with people, as in the now overdone phrase, "I feel your pain." Don Thompson, the McDonald's executive described in Chapter 2, represents a sterling example of somebody who connects with people, as evidenced by the people who wait in line to shake his hand.

In addition, charismatic leaders have an *energy and action orientation*. Like entrepreneurs, most charismatic leaders are energetic and serve as role models for getting things done on time. *Emotional expressiveness and warmth* are also notable. A key characteristic of charismatic leaders is the ability to express feelings openly. A bank vice president claims that much of the charisma people attribute to her can be explained very simply: "I'm up front about expressing positive feelings. I praise people, I hug them, and I cheer if necessary. I also express my negative feelings, but to a lesser extent." Nonverbal emotional expressiveness, such as warm gestures and frequent (nonsexual) touching of group members, is also characteristic of charismatic leaders.

Because emotional expressiveness is such an important part of being and becoming charismatic, you are invited to take Leadership Self-Assessment Quiz 3-1. It will help you think about a practical way of developing charismatic appeal.

Another trait of charismatic leaders is that they *romanticize risk*. They enjoy risk so much that they feel empty in its absence. Jim Barksdale, now a venture capitalist for online startup companies and former CEO of Netscape, says that the fear of failure is what increases your heart rate. As great opportunists, charismatic people yearn to accomplish activities others have never done before. Risk taking adds to a person's charisma because others admire such courage. In addition to treasuring risk, charismatic leaders use *unconventional strategies* to achieve success. The charismatic leader inspires others by formulating unusual strategies to achieve important goals. Anita Roddick, the late founder of the worldwide chain of cosmetic stores called The Body Shop, accomplished her goals unconventionally: she traveled around the world into native villages, searching out natural beauty products that in the manufacturing process would not harm the environment or animals.

Charismatic leaders often have a *self-promoting personality*. They frequently toot their own horn and allow others to know how important they are. Richard Branson, the colorful chairman of the Virgin Group, has relied on self-promotion to build his empire, a collection of about 200 companies with the Virgin trademark. Among his antics have been flying around the world in a balloon and sliding down the side of a silver ball attached to a New York City building. He also conducts much of his business electronically from his private island in the Virgin Islands. More will be said about Sir Richard later in the chapter.

Another characteristic observed in many charismatic leaders is that they challenge, prod, and poke. They test your courage and your self-confidence by asking questions like "Do your employees really need you?" Donald Trump regularly asks his builders why they cannot construct a part of a building to look better, yet at lower cost.

A final strategy for becoming more charismatic is really an amalgam of the ideas already introduced: being *dramatic and unique* in significant, positive ways is a major contributor to charisma. This quality stems from a combination of factors, such as being energetic, promoting yourself, romanticizing risk, and being emotionally expressive. Oprah Winfrey is dramatic and unique in the sense that she expresses love for so many of her constituents.

**Leadership Self-Assessment Quiz 3-1**

### The Emotional Expressiveness Scale

***Instructions:*** Indicate how well each of the following statements describes you by circling the best answer: very inaccurately (VI), inaccurately (I), neutral (N), accurately (A), very accurately (VA).

|  | VI | I | N | A | VA |
|---|---|---|---|---|---|
| 1. While watching a movie, I sometimes shout in laughter or approval. | 1 | 2 | 3 | 4 | **(5)** |
| 2. During a group meeting, I have occasionally shouted my approval with a statement such as "Yes" or "Fantastic." | 1 | 2 | 3 | **(4)** | 5 |
| 3. During a group meeting, I have occasionally expressed disapproval by shouting an expression such as "Absolutely not" or "Horrible." | 1 | 2 | 3 | **(4)** | 5 |
| 4. Several times, while attending a meeting, someone has said to me, "You look bored." | 5 | **(4)** | 3 | 2 | 1 |
| 5. Several times while attending a social gathering, someone has said to me, "You look bored." | 5 | **(4)** | 3 | 2 | 1 |
| 6. Many times at social gatherings or business meetings, people have asked me, "Are you falling asleep?" | 5 | **(4)** | 3 | 2 | 1 |
| 7. I thank people profusely when they do me a favor. | 1 | 2 | 3 | **(4)** | 5 |
| 8. It is not unusual for me to cry at an event such as a wedding, graduation ceremony, or engagement party. | 1 | 2 | 3 | **(4)** | 5 |
| 9. Reading about or watching news events, such as an airplane crash, brings tears to my eyes. | 1 | 2 | 3 | **(4)** | 5 |
| 10. When I was younger, I got into more than my share of physical fights or shouting matches. | 1 | 2 | 3 | 4 | **(5)** |
| 11. I dread having to express anger toward a coworker. | 5 | 4 | **(3)** | 2 | 1 |
| 12. I have cried among friends more than once. | 1 | 2 | 3 | 4 | **(5)** |
| 13. Other people have told me that I am affectionate. | 1 | 2 | 3 | 4 | **(5)** |
| 14. Other people have told me that I am cold and distant. | **(5)** | 4 | 3 | 2 | 1 |
| 15. I get so excited watching a sporting event that my voice is hoarse the next day. | 1 | 2 | 3 | 4 | **(5)** |
| 16. It is difficult for me to express love toward another person. | **(5)** | 4 | 3 | 2 | 1 |
| 17. Even when alone, I will sometimes shout in joy or anguish. | 1 | 2 | 3 | **(4)** | 5 |
| 18. Many people have complimented me on my smile. | 1 | 2 | 3 | 4 | **(5)** |
| 19. People who know me well can easily tell what I am feeling by the expression on my face. | 1 | 2 | 3 | 4 | **(5)** |
| 20. More than once, people have said to me, "I don't know how to read you." | **(5)** | 4 | 3 | 2 | 1 |

## Quiz 3-1 (continued)

***Scoring and Interpretation:*** Add the numbers you circled, and use the following as a guide to your level of emotionality with respect to being charismatic and dynamic.

- **90–100:** Your level of emotionality could be interfering with your charisma. Many others interpret your behavior as being out of control.
- **70–89:** Your level of emotionality is about right for a charismatic individual. You are emotionally expressive, yet your level of emotional expression is not so intense as to be bothersome.
- **20–69:** Your level of emotionality is probably too low to enhance your charisma. To become more charismatic and dynamic, you must work hard at expressing your feelings.

If you believe that emotional expressiveness is a trait and behavior out of your reach or inclination, direct your efforts toward developing other traits and behaviors associated with charisma. For example, you could work on developing vision and taking risks.

## THE VISION COMPONENT OF CHARISMATIC LEADERSHIP

A major buzzword in leadership and management is **vision**, the ability to imagine different and better future conditions and ways to achieve them. A vision is a lofty, long-term goal. An effective leader is supposed to have a vision, whereas an ineffective leader either lacks a vision or has an unclear one. Being a visionary is far from an ordinary task, and recent research in neuroscience suggests that visionary leaders use their brain differently than others.

Studies conducted at Arizona State University by Pierre Balthazard required participants to think about the future. Brain activity was measured through EEG technology. A key finding was that levels of brain activity differed significantly between those participants considered visionaries and non-visionaries. Classifying a business, academic, or political leader as "visionary" was based on interview observations. Visionaries showed much higher levels of brain activity in the areas of the brain associated with visual processing and the organization of information. For example, visionaries showed higher activity in the occipital lobe, which is associated with visual processing and procedural memory.[19]

Many people use the terms *vision* and *mission* interchangeably, yet management theorists see them differently. According to organizational change specialist Peter M. Senge, a mission is a purpose, and reason for being, whereas a vision is a picture or image of the future we seek to create.[20] A mission of a company that rents private warehouse space to consumers and small business might be, "To extend the living and working space of responsible people." The same company's vision might be, "To create a more comfortable, less cramped world for the decades ahead."

Creating a vision is one of the major tasks of top management, yet quite often vision statements fail to inspire constituents. According to Jim Collins, a vision statement is likely to be more inspirational when it combines three elements:

1. A reason for being beyond making money
2. Timeless, unchanging core values
3. Ambitious but achievable goals

Mechanisms should then be established that set the values into action. A well-known example is that 3M encourages scientists to spend 15 percent of their time on whatever they want; this policy supports the company vision of being a world-class innovator.[21] A vision is also considered an important part of strategy implementation. Implementing the vision (or ensuring that the vision is executed) is part of the leader's role. This is true despite the opinion that the leader creates the vision and the manager implements it. Visions have become so popular that some companies have them reproduced on wallet-size plastic cards, key rings, and coffee mugs. It has been said than an effective vision fits on a T-shirt. Here are several sample vision statements:

*Google:* To make nearly all information accessible to everyone all the time.
*Microsoft Corporation:* To enable people throughout the word to realize their potential.
*Sun Microsystems Inc.:* The Network is the Computer™
*Blackstone Group LP:* To become the pre-eminent global lodging company in the world.
*Estée Lauder Companies:* Bringing the best to everyone we touch.
*Progressive Insurance:* To reduce the human trauma and economic costs associated with automobile accidents. (A critical thinker might say this is a mission rather than a vision statement, despite being offered as a vision.)

Although many vision statements appear as if they could be formulated in fifteen minutes, managers invest considerable time in their preparation and often use many sources of data. To create a vision, obtain as much information from as many of the following sources as necessary:[22]

■ Your own intuition about developments in your field, the market you serve, demographic trends in your region, and the preferences of your constituents. Think through what are the top industry standards.
■ The work of futurists (specialists in making predictions about the future) as it relates to your type of work.
■ A group discussion of what it takes to delight the people your group serves. Analyze carefully what your customers and organization need the most.
■ Annual reports, management books, and business magazines to uncover the type of vision statements formulated by others.
■ Group members and friends; speak to them individually and collectively to learn of their hopes and dreams for the future.
■ For a vision for an organizational unit, the organization's vision. You might get some ideas for matching your unit's vision with that of the organization.

Leadership Skill-Building Exercise 3-1 gives you an opportunity to practice vision formulation. Keep in mind that a critic of vision statements once said that it is often difficult to tell the difference between a vision and a hallucination.

## Leadership Skill-Building Exercise 3-1

### Formulating a Vision

Along with your teammates, assume the role of the top management group of an organization or organizational unit that is in need of revitalization. Your revitalization task is to create a vision for the organization. Express the vision in not more than twenty-five words, using the guidelines for developing a vision described in the text. Come to an agreement quickly on the organization or large organizational unit that needs a vision. Or choose one of the following:

- The manufacturer of an electric-powered automobile
- A distributor of paid-for online music
- A waste disposal company
- A chain of home-improvement and hardware stores
- A manufacturer of watches retailing for a minimum of $25,000

# THE COMMUNICATION STYLE OF CHARISMATIC LEADERS

Charismatic and transformational leaders typically communicate their visions, goals, and directives in a colorful, imaginative, and expressive manner. In addition, they communicate openly with group members and create a comfortable communication climate. To set agendas that represent the interests of their constituents, charismatic leaders regularly solicit constituents' viewpoints on critical issues. They encourage two-way communication with team members while still promoting a sense of confidence.[23] Here we describe two related aspects of the communication style of charismatic leaders: management by inspiration and management by storytelling.

## Management by Inspiration

According to Jay A. Conger, the era of managing by dictate is being replaced by an era of managing by inspiration. An important way to inspire others is to articulate a highly emotional message. Roger Enrico, the long-time dynamic CEO of PepsiCo, Inc., directed a leadership development program for selected company managers. At the outset of the program, he knocked participants off balance by telling them "nobody in this room can look at the company's problems and blame the turkeys at the top. You're now one of them."[24] Conger has observed two major rhetorical techniques of inspirational leaders: the use of metaphors and analogies, and the ability to gear language to different audiences.[25]

***Using Metaphors and Analogies***   A well-chosen analogy or metaphor appeals to the intellect, to the imagination, and to values. The charismatic Mary Kay Ash (now deceased), founder of the cosmetics company Mary Kay Inc., made frequent use of metaphors during her career. To inspire her associates to higher performance, she often said: "You see, a bee shouldn't be able to fly; its body is too heavy for its wings. But the bumblebee doesn't know that and it flies very well." Mary Kay explained the message of the bumblebee metaphor in these terms: "Women come to us not knowing they can fly. Finally, with help and encouragement, they find their wings—and then they fly very well indeed."[26]

***Gearing Language to Different Audiences***   Metaphors and analogies are inspiring, but effective leaders must also choose the level of language that will suit their audience. This is important because constituents vary widely in verbal sophistication. One day, for example, a CEO might be attempting to inspire a group of Wall Street financial analysts, and the next day she or he might be attempting to inspire first-level employees to keep working hard despite limited salary increases.

An executive's ability to speak on a colloquial level helps create appeal. A person with the high status of an executive is expected to use an elevated language style. When the person unexpectedly uses the everyday language of an operative employee, it may create a special positive response. One of the many reasons Donald Trump is so popular with construction workers and tradespeople is that he often speaks to them in a tough-guy language familiar to them.

## Management by Storytelling

Another significant aspect of the communication style of charismatic and transformational leaders is that they make extensive use of memorable stories to get messages across. **Management by storytelling** is the technique of inspiring and instructing team members by telling fascinating stories. The technique is a major contributor to building a strong company culture. Jim Sinegal, cofounder and CEO of Costco, frequently tells a story that incorporates the values he has successfully built into the company:

> Back in 1996, Costco was doing a brisk business in Calvin Klein Jeans priced at $29.99. When a smart buyer got a better deal on a new batch of the jeans, company guidelines calling for a strict limit on price markups dictated a lower price of $22.99. Costco could have stuck to the original price and dropped seven dollars a pair straight into its own pocket. But I insisted on passing the savings on to customers because I saw the company's focus on customer value as the key to its success.

The story continues to circulate among Costco managers today. The short anecdote vividly communicates a message about the company's values, partly because Sinegal's cost-conscious behavior reinforces the message. He answers his own telephone, and draws the relatively small salary for a CEO of $350,000.[27]

Storytelling as a leadership tool has been elevated to such a level that some companies hire corporate storytelling consultants to help their executives develop the art.[28] Storytelling is regarded as a useful tool for getting people to embrace change, because a well-crafted story captures people's attention.

To get started developing the skill of management by storytelling, do Leadership Skill-Building Exercise 3-2.

**Leadership Skill-Building Exercise 3-2**

### Charismatic Leadership by Storytelling

***Instructions:*** Gather in a small problem-solving group to develop an inspiring anecdote about something that actually happened, or might have happened, at a current or former employer. Here are some guidelines:

1. Make up a list of core values the firm holds dear, such as quality, service, or innovation.

2. Think of an incident in which an employee strikingly lived up to (or violated) one of these values. Write it up as a story with a moral.

3. Share your stories with other members of the class, and discuss whether this exercise could make a contribution to leadership development.

*Source:* From "Management by Anecdote," *SUCCESS,* December 1992, p. 35. Copyright © 1992 SUCCESS Publishing Inc. Reprinted by permission.

## THE DEVELOPMENT OF CHARISMA

A person can increase his or her charisma by developing some of the traits, characteristics, and behaviors of charismatic people. Several of the charismatic characteristics described earlier in the chapter are capable of development. For example, most people can enhance their communication skills, become more emotionally expressive, take more risks, and become more self-promoting. In this section we examine several behaviors of charismatic people that can be developed through practice and self-discipline. Leadership Self-Assessment Quiz 3-2 gives you an opportunity to think through how much development you might need in terms of *personal magnetism*, a type of sparkle that attracts other people to you and that adds to your charisma.

 **Leadership Self-Assessment Quiz 3-2**

### The Personal Magnetism Deficit Inventory

***Instructions:*** Insufficient personal magnetism could be blocking your career growth, assuming you are already technically competent and hard working. To test how much magnetism you have, respond to the following statements in terms of Yes, No, or Not Applicable (NA).

|  | Yes | No | NA |
|---|---|---|---|
| 1. It has been a long time since you received new assignments and/or promotions in your job. | ☐ | ☒ | ☐ |
| 2. You have been a downsizing victim at two or more firms. | ☐ | ☒ | ☐ |

## Quiz 3-2 (continued)

|  | Yes | No | NA |
|---|---|---|---|
| **3.** People rarely ask for your opinion during a meeting. | ☐ | ☒ | ☐ |
| **4.** You were absent from a meeting and nobody commented later that you were missed. | ☐ | ☒ | ☐ |
| **5.** Almost nobody wants you to become a member of his or her network. | ☐ | ☒ | ☐ |
| **6.** When you join a new team, you are rarely nominated to be the leader. | ☐ | ☒ | ☐ |
| **7.** Your jokes and witty comments rarely receive much of a reaction from others. | ☐ | ☒ | ☐ |
| **8.** Coworkers or fellow students seldom mention your name during meetings or other gatherings. | ☐ | ☐ | ☐ |
| **9.** Other people rarely quote statements that you make. | ☐ | ☐ | ☐ |
| **10.** You frequently make a statement or volunteer your opinion during a meeting, and you barely receive a reaction. | ☐ | ☐ | ☐ |
| **11.** A person you know received a compliment for wearing a certain outfit, yet nobody complimented you when you wore almost the identical outfit. | ☐ | ☐ | ☐ |
| **12.** People you attempt to lead rarely act inspired. | ☐ | ☐ | ☐ |
| **13.** You rarely receive email messages or instant messages from contacts unless they are in response to your message. | ☐ | ☐ | ☐ |
| **14.** In school, you were never (or are never) nominated to be the captain of a team or the head of a club. | ☐ | ☐ | ☐ |
| **15.** Strangers rarely smile at you. | ☐ | ☐ | ☐ |
| **16.** When in a public building or airport, a stranger rarely opens the door for you. | ☐ | ☐ | ☐ |
| **17.** When at a social gathering, you usually have to initiate conversations because few people start talking to you spontaneously. | ☐ | ☐ | ☐ |
| **18.** You receive few compliments on the job, in school, or in personal life. | ☐ | ☐ | ☐ |
| **19.** People tend to yawn frequently in face-to-face interactions with you. | ☐ | ☐ | ☐ |
| **20.** You cannot recall anyone ever saying that you are dynamic or that you have a sparkling personality. | ☐ | ☐ | ☐ |

*Interpretation:* Very few people would be able to say that they have had none or only one of the twenty experiences just listed. But you may need to develop your personal magnetism and your charisma if you have had five or more of these experiences. The information in this section of the chapter and in the corresponding references could help you become more magnetic and charismatic.

## Techniques for Developing Charisma

*Create Visions for Others*   Being able to create visions for others will be a major factor in your being perceived as charismatic. A vision uplifts and attracts others. To form a vision, use the guidelines presented previously in the chapter. The visionary person looks beyond the immediate future to create an image of what the organization or unit is capable of becoming. A vision is designed to close the discrepancy between current and ideal conditions. The vision thus sees beyond current realities.

Another characteristic of an effective vision formulated by the leader is that it connects with the goals and dreams of constituents.[29] For example, the leader of a group that is manufacturing fuel cells for electric cars might listen to team members talk about their desires to help reduce pollution in the atmosphere and then base the vision statement on a "desire to save the planet" or "reduce global warming."

*Be Enthusiastic, Optimistic, and Energetic*   A major behavior pattern of charismatic people is their combination of enthusiasm, optimism, and high energy. Without a great amount of all three characteristics, a person is unlikely to be perceived as charismatic by many people. A remarkable quality of charismatic people is that they maintain high enthusiasm, optimism, and energy throughout their entire workday and beyond. Elevating your energy level takes considerable work, but here are a few feasible suggestions:

1. Get ample rest at night, and sneak in a fifteen-minute nap during the day when possible. If you have a dinner meeting where you want to shine, take a shower and nap before the meeting.
2. Exercise every day for at least ten minutes, including walking. No excuses are allowed, such as being too busy or too tired, or the weather being a handicap.
3. Switch to a healthy, energy-enhancing diet.
4. Keep chopping away at your To Do list so you do not have unfinished tasks on your mind, because they will drain your energy.

An action orientation helps you be enthusiastic, optimistic, and energetic. "Let's do it" is the battle cry of the charismatic person. An action orientation also means that the charismatic person prefers not to agonize over dozens of facts and nuances before making a decision.

*Be Sensibly Persistent*   Closely related to the high energy level of charismatics is their almost-never-accept-no attitude. I emphasize the word *almost* because outstanding leaders and individual contributors also know when to cut their losses. If an idea or a product will not work, the sensible charismatic absorbs the loss and moves in another, more profitable direction. An executive at a telecom company said, "A test of executive material in our company is whether the middle manager has the guts to kill a failed project. Some managers become so ego-involved in a product they sponsored, they fight to keep it alive long after it should have died. They twist and distort financial information to prove that there is still life left in their pet product. A person with executive potential knows when to fold his or her tent."

***Remember Names of People***   Charismatic leaders, as well as other successful people, can usually remember the names of people they have seen only a few times. (Sorry, no charisma credits for remembering the names of everyday work associates.) This ability is partly due to the strong personal interest charismatic leaders take in other people.

The surest way to remember names, therefore, is to really care about people. Failing that, the best way to remember a name is to listen carefully to the name, repeat it immediately, and study the person's face. You can also use the many systems and gimmicks available for remembering names, such as associating a person's name with a visual image. For example, if you meet a woman named Betsy Applewhite, you can visualize her with an apple (or a white personal computer) on her head. The best system of name retention remains to listen carefully to the name, repeat it immediately, and study the person's face.

***Develop Synchrony with Others***   A subtle, yet defining, aspect of a truly charismatic person is one who connects well with others. Psychology professor Frank Bernieri studies physical signals that people send to each other, and concludes that being in synch physically with other people is part of charisma. If someone is in synchrony with you, you tend to think he or she is charismatic. A practical method of being in synch with another person is to adjust your posture to conform to his or her posture. The other person stands up straight, and so do you; when he or she slouches, you do also. Charismatic people make these postural adjustments almost subconsciously, or at least without giving the process much thought. Highly skilled charismatic people through the timing of their breaths, gestures, and cadence can entrap listeners into synchrony to the point that they "breathe and sway in tune with the speaker."[30]

***Develop a Personal Brand, Including Making an Impressive Appearance***   A new trend in career advancement is to build a personal brand. Understanding your basket of strengths forms the basis for developing your **personal brand** (or, the *brand called you*). Your identity as shown on the Internet, including social networking sites such as Facebook, is also part of your personal brand. Your personal brand makes you unique, thereby distinguishing you from the competition.[31] Perhaps your brand will not reach the recognition of Nike or Rolex, but it will help develop your reputation. Your personal brand also helps you attract people to accept your leadership.

Another component of your personal brand is your appearance. By creating a polished appearance, a person can make slight gains in projecting a charismatic image. A few people can make great gains by looking good. Ralph Lauren, the most successful fashion designer in American history,[32] is a leader who has enhanced his charisma through his impeccable physical appearance. Given that he is in the fashion business, a "Ralph Lauren–like" appearance is important for his personal image as well as to help build a brand image.

However, in most cases the effect of appearance depends on the context. If exquisite clothing and good looks alone made a person a charismatic leader, those impressive-looking store associates in upscale department stores would all be charismatic leaders. Therefore, in attempting to enhance your charisma through appearance, it is necessary to analyze your work environment to assess what type of appearance is impressive. Ralph Lauren, with his exquisite suits, cuff links, and pocket handkerchief, would create a negative image at a Silicon Valley firm: his carefully cultivated appearance would detract from his charisma. (Of course, Lauren could enhance his charisma by wearing clothing from his sporty Polo line.)

Despite these caveats, there is much you can do to enhance your appearance. In recent years there has been a surge of image consultants who help businesspeople develop an appearance that is useful in influencing people and getting hired. These consultants perform such services as helping you shop for a new wardrobe, suggesting a new hairstyle, or helping you revamp your slouching posture.[33]

*Be Candid*   Charismatic people, especially effective leaders, are remarkably candid with people. Although not insensitive, the charismatic person is typically explicit in giving his or her assessment of a situation, whether the assessment is positive or negative. Charismatic people speak directly rather than indirectly, so that people know where they stand. Instead of asking a worker, "Are you terribly busy this afternoon?" the charismatic leader will ask, "I need your help this afternoon. Are you available?"

**Knowledge Bank**
Presents details of a study in charisma training.
**www.cengage.com/management/dubrin**

*Display an In-Your-Face Attitude*   The preferred route to being perceived as charismatic is to be a positive, warm, and humanistic person. Yet some people, including business and sports figures, earn their reputation for charisma by being tough and nasty. An in-your-face attitude may bring you some devoted supporters, although it will also bring you many detractors. The tough attitude is attractive to people who themselves would like to be mean and aggressive.

## TRANSFORMATIONAL LEADERSHIP

Transformational leadership focuses on what the leader accomplishes yet still pays attention to the leader's personal characteristics and his or her relationship with group members. As mentioned previously, the transformational leader helps bring about major, positive changes by moving group members beyond their self-interests and toward the good of the group, organization, or society. The essence of transformational leadership is developing and transforming people.[34] In contrast, the *transactional* leader focuses on more routine transactions, rewarding group members for meeting standards (contingent reinforcement). Extensive research by Bernard M. Bass indicates that the transformational-versus-transactional distinction has been observed in a wide variety of organizations and cultures.[35]

So who is a transformational leader? One example is Greg Brenneman, who is president and CEO of Quiznos (those toasted sub-sandwiches) and also operates Turn Works Inc., a private equity firm. The term "Turn" implies that the company does turnarounds, or revitalizing other companies. Quiznos is one the fastest-growing quick-service restaurants in decades.[36] In his previous position as chairman and CEO of Burger King Corporation, Brenneman helped revitalize the company's declining market share. Before Burger King, he was credited with helping turn around Continental Airlines, Inc., and the consulting arm of Pricewaterhouse Coopers International Limited. In his savior role at Burger King, he added new domestic units and focused on menu development to enhance same-store revenues. Shortly after Brenneman arrived, to boost morale he gave corporate staff members bonuses worth three times more than what they received the previous year. Because of his ability to revive a troubled company, Brenneman has been sought by several other companies, including Waste Management, Inc., to be their CEO.[37]

## How Transformations Take Place

Leaders often encounter the need to transform organizations from low performance to acceptable performance or from acceptable performance to high performance. At other times, a leader is expected to move a firm from a crisis mode to high ground. To accomplish these lofty purposes, the transformational leader attempts to overhaul the organizational culture or subculture. His or her task can be as immense as the process of organizational change. To focus our discussion specifically on the leader's role, we look at several ways in which transformations take place.[38] (See also Figure 3-2.)

**1.** *Raising people's awareness.* The transformational leader makes group members aware of the importance and values of certain rewards and how to achieve them. He or she might point to the pride workers would experience should the firm become number 1 in its field. At the same time, the leader should point to the financial rewards accompanying such success.

**2.** *Helping people look beyond self-interest.* The transformational leader helps group members look to "the big picture" for the sake of the team and the

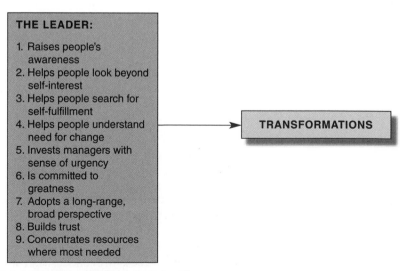

**THE LEADER:**

1. Raises people's awareness
2. Helps people look beyond self-interest
3. Helps people search for self-fulfillment
4. Helps people understand need for change
5. Invests managers with sense of urgency
6. Is committed to greatness
7. Adopts a long-range, broad perspective
8. Builds trust
9. Concentrates resources where most needed

→ **TRANSFORMATIONS**

**FIGURE 3-2** How Transformations Take Place.

organization. The executive vice president of a bank told her staff members, "I know most of you dislike doing your own support work. Yet if we hire enough staff to make life more convenient for you, we'll be losing money. Then the government might force us to be taken over by a larger bank. Who knows how many management jobs would then have to be cut."

**3. *Helping people search for self-fulfillment.*** The transformational leader helps people go beyond a focus on minor satisfactions to a quest for self-fulfillment. The leader might explain, "I know that making sure you take every vacation day owed you is important. Yet if we get this proposal out on time, we might land a contract that will make us the envy of the industry." (Being the envy of the industry satisfies the need for self-fulfillment.)

**4. *Helping people understand the need for change.*** The transformational leader must help group members understand the need for change both emotionally and intellectually. The problem is that change involves dislocation and discomfort. An effective transformational leader recognizes this emotional component to resisting change and deals with it openly. Organizational change is much like a life transition. Endings must be successfully worked through before new beginnings are possible. People must become unhooked from their pasts.

Dealing with the emotional conflicts of large numbers of staffers is obviously an immense task. One approach taken by successful leaders is to conduct discussion groups in which managers and workers are free to discuss their feelings about the changes. This approach has been used quite effectively when firms are downsized. Many of the "survivors" feel guilty that they are still employed while many competent coworkers have lost their jobs. Clearly, conducting these sessions requires considerable listening skill on the manager's part.

**5. *Investing managers with a sense of urgency.*** To create the transformation, the leader assembles a critical mass of managers and imbues in them the urgency of change. The managers must also share the top leader's vision of what is both necessary and achievable. To sell this vision of an improved organization, the transformational leader must capitalize on available opportunities.

**6. *Committing to greatness.*** Peter Koestenbaum argues that business can be an opportunity for individual and organizational greatness. By adopting this greatness attitude, leaders can ennoble human nature and strengthen societies. Greatness encompasses striving for business effectiveness such as profits and high stock value, as well as impeccable ethics. An emphasis on ethical leadership instills a desire for customer service and quality and fosters feelings of proprietorship and involvement.[39] (A commitment to greatness is, of course, important for all leaders, not just those who are charismatic.)

**7. *Adopting a long-range perspective and at the same time observing organizational issues from a broad rather than a narrow perspective.*** Such thinking on the part of the transformational leader encourages many group members to do likewise. Unless many people think with a future orientation, and broadly, an organization cannot be transformed.[40]

**8. *Building trust*.** Another useful process for transforming a firm is to build trust between leaders and group members, particularly because distrust and suspicion are rampant during a company revival. Executive Carlos Ghosn found that building trust was an essential ingredient of his turnaround efforts at Nissan Motors in Japan. One component of building trust was to impose transparency on the entire organization. In this way everyone knew what everyone else was doing.[41]

**9. *Concentrating resources on areas that need the most change*.** The turnaround artist or transformational leader cannot take care of all problems at once in a troubled organization. A practical strategy is to get around limitations on funds, staff, or equipment by concentrating resources on problem areas that are most in need of change and have the biggest potential payoff. For example, when police chief Bill Bratton turned around the much-maligned New York Police Department in the mid-1990s, he concentrated resources on the narcotics squad because so much crime is related to narcotics.[42] And Bill Brenneman added an Enormous Omelette Sandwich to the Burger King menu shortly after beginning his turnaround.

## Attributes of Transformational Leaders

Transformational leaders possess the personal characteristics of other effective leaders, especially charismatic leaders. In addition, a compilation of studies suggests that nine qualities are particularly helpful in enabling leaders to bring about transformations.[43]

Above all, transformational leaders are *charismatic*. Two key personality factors enhancing their charisma are agreeableness and extraversion, which combine to enhance their interpersonal relationships. Of these, extraversion had the biggest impact.[44] Unless they are the brutal slash-and-burn type of turnaround manager, transformational leaders have the respect, confidence, and loyalty of group members. One reason is that managers who use the transformational leadership style tend to score higher on *emotional intelligence*. A specific attribute here is that transformational leaders read emotions well.[45]

Charismatic, transformational leaders create a *vision*. By communicating a vision, they convey a set of values that guide and motivate employees. Moreover, although transformational leaders are often greatly concerned with organizational survival, they also take the time to *encourage the personal development of their staff*. As group members develop, their performance is likely to increase. Transformational leaders also give *supportive leadership,* such as by giving positive feedback to group members and recognizing individual achievements. Supportive leadership also contributes to the development of group members.

Transformational leaders, like most effective leaders and managers, practice *empowerment* by involving team members in decision making. John Chambers of Cisco, who is somewhat of a transformational leader, regards empowerment as the distinguishing feature of his leadership. *Innovative thinking,* another important characteristic, helps transformational leaders achieve their goals; for example, they might develop innovative ways to raise cash and cut costs quickly. Transformational leaders encourage their staff to think innovatively as well and give them challenging assignments. As with other effective leaders and managers, they also *lead by example*. During a period of cost-cutting, for example, a transformational leader might fly business coach and eat in the company cafeteria instead of having gourmet food catered to his or her office.

A study conducted with 132 managers and 407 subordinates indicated that managers who are perceived to be transformational score higher on a test of *moral reasoning* than do transactional leaders.[46] In contrast to the type of transformational leaders in the study just mentioned, those who specialize in rescuing failed corporations do not appear to score high in moral reasoning. Such actions include shutting down many company facilities, laying off much of the work force, and canceling contracts with various vendors.

Not every leader classified as transformational will have the nine characteristics just described. For example, some transformational leaders are brusque with people rather than agreeable. Furthermore, it is not always easy to determine whether a given leader can be accurately described as transformational. Sometimes situational forces contribute more heavily to the turnaround than do the leader's personal qualities. The director of an indoor-tennis club was complimented about how he transformed the club from one that was close to bankruptcy and short on membership. He replied, "It wasn't me. Two of our competitors closed down and we picked up a lot of their membership."

The accompanying Leader in Action profile tells a story about a transformational leader. As you read the sketch, look for the leader's transformational behaviors and attributes.

### The Impact of Transformational and Charismatic Leadership on Performance and Behavior

Although the current discussion deals primarily with transformational leadership, it would be artificial to separate its impact on performance from that of charismatic leadership. An important reason is that charismatic leadership, as already discussed, is a component of transformational leadership. The general picture of the impact of transformational leadership is that at its best it can arouse followers to a higher level of thinking. Transformational leaders appeal to the ideals and values of their constituents, thereby enhancing commitment to a carefully crafted vision. Followers are inspired to develop new ways of thinking about problems. Group members become more responsible because they are inspired, and they engage in more constructive behavior such as organizational citizenship behavior—or helping out even without the promise of a reward.[47] Workers who report to transformational leaders are even more likely to have a positive mood throughout the workday.[48]

Here we look at several empirical studies about the effects of charismatic and transformational leadership in work settings. We review an overall analysis of the impact of transformational leadership and two specific studies. The studies summarized here are also useful in understanding how transformational leadership affects behavior.

**Leader in Action**

## Swashbuckling Richard Branson of the Virgin Group

Where most see turmoil, some see opportunity. And few are more opportunistic than Sir Richard Branson, the swashbuckling founder of everything from airlines to health clubs and—soon—an outfit offering space travel, all under the Virgin Group brand. (Several polls have indicated that Branson is one of the three best-known people in Great Britain, along with the Prime Minister and the Queen.) So when a liquidity crisis sent British mortgage lender Northern Rock's share price plummeting, Branson was ready to come to the rescue—and add the bank to his growing roster of Virgin companies.

There's no deal yet, but Branson aims to fold Northern Rock's 76 branches and $200 billion in assets into an existing operation called Virgin Money. He has assembled a team of financial heavyweights such as insurer American International Group and investor Wilbur Ross, who together would inject up to $2 billion into the bank in exchange for a controlling interest. "The Northern Rock brand is broken . . . and it needs funding and liquidity, which Virgin and its partners can provide," says Jayne-Anne Gadhia, CEO of Virgin Money UK.

Can Branson's magic revive Northern Rock? So far, Virgin is far from a major player in finance, with just $6 billion in assets and an online-only operation. And Branson has overreached in the past, with relatively unsuccessful forays into soft drinks, cosmetics, clothing, and more. But Virgin Money is growing. Its British arm serves 2 million customers, offering savings accounts, loans, credit cards, and insurance, and it's getting high marks for its service. In recent years it has moved into Australia and South Africa.

In May 2007, Virgin paid $50 million for a controlling interest in CircleLending, and changed its name to Virgin Money USA. The outfit administers $200 million in loans between family and friends, charging fees of $100 to $2,000 to collect and insure

repayment. Soon, Virgin hopes to offer mortgages, mutual funds, and services requiring a partner with a banking license.

If Virgin snares Northern Rock, it will need to keep funding its $200 billion loan portfolio and pay off the $26 billion bailout Northern got from the Bank of England. Virgin says it can do so by wooing more online accounts to bolster Northern's deposit base and tapping its partners' deep pockets.

Once Virgin gets the Northern Rock operation back on its feet, it intends to ramp up offerings quickly. Gadhia plans to shift Northern's focus away from less profitable lending and to use Northern's branch network to promote Virgin credit cards, insurance, and mutual funds. And by continuing to expand internationally—Canada may be next—Virgin Money will be able to take smart ideas from one market and introduce them elsewhere. "What we do well," says Gordon McCallum, CEO of Virgin Management, which oversees the group's companies, "is design simple products and deliver them with great service."

### Questions

1. What hint does this story give that Richard Branson is charismatic?
2. In what way does it appear that Branson and the members of his management team are transformational leaders?
3. Branson is an extraordinarily wealthy person who has many intense interests outside of business, including sports and philanthropy. Why doesn't he just quit Virgin and stop worrying about things such as purchasing a giant financial institution?

*Source:* Excerpted from Kerry Capell and William Stanley Reed, "The International Bank of Branson," *Business Week*, October 29, 2007, p. 042.

*Overall Validity of Transformational Leadership*   Timothy A. Judge and Ronald F. Piccolo reviewed eighty-seven studies to examine the impact of transformational leadership on various measures of performance. The researchers also evaluated the impact of transactional leadership and laissez-faire leadership on performance. Laissez-faire leadership is a style that gives group members the freedom to do basically what they want with a minimum of direction. The three approaches to leadership were measured by questionnaires based on subordinates' perceptions.

Transformational leadership showed the highest overall relationships on six criteria: (a) follower job satisfaction, (b) follower leader satisfaction, (c) follower motivation, (d) leader job performance, (e) group or organization performance, and (f) rated leader effectiveness. Interestingly, transactional leadership was also shown to produce good results, and laissez-faire leadership was associated with negative results. Unlike previous studies, transactional leadership showed a strong positive relationship to transformational leadership. (Ordinarily, transformational leadership and transactional leadership are negatively related because transformational leaders are said not to engage in routine transactions with group members.) Transformational leadership was negatively related to laissez-faire leadership.[49] The explanation is most likely that transformational leaders are actively involved with group members.

*Business Unit Performance*   As part of a larger study, Jane M. Howell and Bruce J. Avolio investigated the relationship of transformational leadership to business unit performance. The sample included seventy-eight managers from the highest four levels of management in a large Canadian financial institution. At the time of the study, the firm was facing a turbulent external environment because of increased competition. A scale was developed to measure three aspects of transformational leadership: charisma, intellectual stimulation, and individual consideration. The measure of business unit performance represented the degree to which the manager reached goals for the year, calculated in terms of the percentage of goals met. Each goal was measured against criteria for expected, superior, and outstanding performance.

Data analysis revealed that leaders who displayed more individualized consideration, intellectual stimulation, and charisma positively contributed to business unit performance. Leaders who used the techniques of management by exception and contingent rewards (positive reinforcement) were less likely to increase unit performance. The authors concluded that the more positive contribution to business unit performance came from behaviors associated with transformational leadership.[50]

*Team Level Performance*   Transformational and charismatic leadership also have positive effects on work teams. A study investigated the relationship between transformational leadership behavior and group performance in 218 financial service teams in U.S. and Hong Kong branches of a large bank. A branch supervisor being perceived as transformational indirectly improved team performance as measured by supervisory ratings of team effectiveness. Three examples of statements measuring transformational leadership were as follows: "Talks about the future in an enthusiastic, exciting way," "Will not settle for second best," and "Shows concern for me as a person."

The study demonstrated that transformational leadership, as perceived by team members, helped the team feel more *potent*. Team potency is the generalized beliefs of members about the capabilities of the team to perform well with a variety of tasks in different situations. Team potency, in turn, improved team performance.[51]

# CONCERNS ABOUT CHARISMATIC LEADERSHIP

Up to this point, an optimistic picture has been painted of both the concept of charisma and charismatic leaders. For the sake of fairness and scientific integrity, contrary points of view must also be presented. The topic of charismatic leadership has been challenged from two major standpoints: the validity of the concept, and the misdeeds of charismatic leaders.

### Challenges to the Validity of Charismatic Leadership

Some leadership researchers doubt that charisma can be accurately defined and measured. Conducting research about charisma is akin to conducting research about high quality: you know it when you see it, but it is difficult to define in operational terms. Furthermore, even when one leader is deemed to be charismatic, he or she has many detractors. According to the concept of **leadership polarity**, leaders are often either revered or vastly unpopular. Martha Stewart is a prime example of a leader who experiences leadership polarity. Many of her fans are mesmerized by her personality and accomplishments. Many of her detractors detest her (perhaps based on envy) and were gleeful when Stewart was accused of insider trading and sent to prison.

Another problem with the concept of charisma is that it may not be necessary for leadership effectiveness. Warren Bennis and Burt Nanus have observed that very few leaders can accurately be described as charismatic. The organizational leaders the two researchers studied were "short and tall, articulate and inarticulate, dressed for success and dressed for failure, and there was virtually nothing in terms of physical appearance, personality, or style that set them apart from followers."

Based on these observations, Bennis and Nanus hypothesized that instead of charisma resulting in effective leadership, the reverse may be true: people who are outstanding leaders are granted charisma (perceived as charismatic) by their constituents as a result of their success.[52] A study conducted with eighteen CEOs of major U. S. corporations and 770 top management team members supports the same idea. A major finding was that good organizational performance was associated with subsequent perceptions of the CEO being charismatic. In contrast, perception that the CEO was charismatic was not associated with future performance of the firm.[53] The take-away lesson here is that if you are successful in attaining goals, it will enhance your charisma.

## The Dark Side of Charismatic Leadership

Some people believe that charismatic leadership can be exercised for evil purposes. This argument was introduced previously in relation to personalized charismatic leaders. Over forty years ago, Robert Tucker warned about the dark side of charisma, particularly with respect to political leaders:

> The magical message which mesmerizes the unthinking (and which can often be supplied by skilled phrase makers) promises that things will become not just better but perfect. Charismatic leaders are experts at promising Utopia. Since perfection is the end, often the most heinous actions can be tolerated as seemingly necessary means to that end.[54]

Some charismatic leaders are unethical and lead their organizations toward illegal and immoral ends. People are willing to follow the charismatic leader down a quasi-legal path because of his or her personal magnetism. Garry Winnick, the former chairman of Global Crossing Ltd., is a modern-day symbol of how gluttonous and destructive a charismatic leader can be. Winnick, a former junk bond broker, charmed thousands with his affable personality. He purchased several Rolls Royce automobiles as gifts for social friends and work associates. On the way to leading Global Crossing toward bankruptcy, he sold about $730 million of his own company stock. His work space was a replica of the White House Oval Office. While thousands of workers were being laid off, Winnick was building the most expensive private residence in the world for himself and his family. With renovations, the property in Bel Air, California, was valued at about $90 million.

Personality specialist Robert Hogan says that a potential problem with charismatic leaders is that some of them are narcissists (self-adoring to a fault). These leaders have the charisma attributes of being assertive, attractive, and powerful, but they often fail as leaders because they never admit mistakes. Charisma needs to be mixed with humility for full effectiveness.[55]

Boards of directors currently seek CEOs who do not overemphasize charisma and celebrity status at the expense of concentrating on running the business. In this way the dark side of charisma can be minimized. Recognize that a true charismatic and transformational leader is highly concerned about human welfare and attaining outstanding organizational performance.

## Reader's Roadmap

In Chapter 2 we focus on the traits, motives, and characteristics of the leader—or the inner qualities of him or her. Here we dug further into leadership qualities by studying charismatic and transformational leadership. In the next chapter we focus more sharply on the actions of leaders in terms of their behaviors, attitudes, and styles.

## SUMMARY

Charisma is a special quality of leaders whose purposes, powers, and extraordinary determination differentiate them from others. It is also a positive and compelling quality of a person that makes many others want to be led by that person. An important element of charismatic leadership involves the attributions made by group members about the characteristics of leaders and the results they achieve. Social network members often influence a person's attributions of charisma. The relationship between group members and the leader is important because of these attributions. Charismatic leaders frequently manage their impressions to cultivate relationships with group members.

One study showed that the effects of charismatic leadership can be organized into three dimensions: referent power, expert power, and job involvement. Charismatic leadership enhances job satisfaction. In a top-level executive position, being perceived as not having enough charisma can lead to your downfall.

Charismatic leaders can be subdivided into five types: socialized, personalized (self-interested), office-holder, personal (outstanding characteristics), and divine. Charismatic leaders have characteristics that set them apart from noncharismatic leaders: they have a vision, masterful communication skills, the ability to inspire trust, and the ability to make group members feel capable. They also are tactful, have an energy and action orientation, are emotionally expressive and warm, romanticize risk, use unconventional strategies, have a self-promoting personality, and emphasize being dramatic and unique.

The idea of vision is closely linked to charisma because charismatic leaders inspire others with an uplifting and attractive vision. Visionaries may have different levels of brain activities than non-visionaries in certain areas of the brain. A vision is more future-oriented than a mission. In formulating a vision, it is helpful to gather information from a variety of sources, including one's own intuition, futurists, and group members.

Charismatic and transformational leaders communicate their visions, goals, and directives in a colorful, imaginative, and expressive manner. Communication effectiveness allows for management by inspiration. One technique for inspiring others is to use metaphors, analogies, and organizational stories. Another is gearing language to different audiences. Charismatic and transformational leaders also extensively use memorable stories or anecdotes to get messages across.

A person can increase his or her charisma by developing some of the traits, characteristics, and behaviors of charismatic people. The suggestions presented here include creating visions for others; being enthusiastic, optimistic, and energetic; being sensibly persistent; remembering names of people; developing a personal brand and making an impressive appearance; being candid; and displaying an in-your-face attitude.

To bring about change, the transformational leader attempts to overhaul the organizational culture or subculture. Specific change techniques include raising people's awareness of the importance of certain rewards and getting people to look beyond their self-interests for the sake of the team and the organization. Transformational leaders help people search for self-fulfillment and understand the need for change, and they invest managers with a sense of urgency. The transformational leader also commits to greatness, adopts a long-range perspective, builds trust, and concentrates resources where change is needed the most.

Transformational leaders have characteristics similar to those of other effective leaders. In addition, they are charismatic, extraverted, create a vision, encourage personal development of the staff, and give supportive leadership. Emphasis is also placed on empowerment, innovative thinking, and leading by example. Transformational leaders are likely to be strong on moral reasoning.

Transformational leadership can arouse followers to a higher level of thinking, and to engage in more constructive behavior. Transformational leadership is positively related to the criteria of follower job satisfaction, leader satisfaction, follower motivation, leader job performance, group or organization performance, and rated leader effectiveness. Transactional leadership attains the same results to a lesser degree, whereas laissez-faire leadership is negatively related to such criteria. Empirical research indicates that leaders who display more individualized consideration, intellectual stimulation, and charisma (transformational leaders) have high business unit

performance. Transformational and charismatic leadership also have positive effects on work teams.

One concern about charismatic and transformational leadership is that the concept is murky. Many noncharismatic leaders are effective. Another concern is that some charismatic leaders are unethical and devious, suggesting that being charismatic does not necessarily help the organization. A true charismatic and transformational leader is highly concerned about human welfare and attaining organizational goals.

## KEY TERMS

| | | |
|---|---|---|
| **Charisma** | **Socialized charismatic** | **Management by storytelling** |
| **Referent power** | **Personalized charismatic** | **Personal brand** |
| **Expert power** | **Transformational leader** | **Leadership polarity** |
| **Job involvement** | **Vision** | |

##  GUIDELINES FOR ACTION AND SKILL DEVELOPMENT

Following are suggestions to help a person act in a charismatic manner. All of them relate to well-accepted interpersonal skill techniques.

1. **Be sure to treat everyone you meet as the most important person you will meet that day.** For example, when at a company meeting, shake the hand of every person you meet.
2. **Multiply the effectiveness of your handshake.** Shake firmly without creating pain, and make enough eye contact to notice the color of the other person's eyes. When you take that much trouble, you project care and concern. Think a positive thought about the person whose hand you shake.
3. **Give sincere compliments.** Most people thrive on flattery, particularly when it is plausible. Attempt to compliment only those behaviors, thoughts, and attitudes you genuinely believe merit praise. At times you may have to dig to find something praiseworthy, but it will be a good investment of your time.

4. **Thank people frequently, especially your own group members.** Thanking others is still so infrequently practiced that it gives you a charismatic edge.
5. **Smile frequently, even if you are not in a happy mood.** A warm smile seems to indicate a confident, caring person, which contributes to a perception of charisma. A smile generally says, "I like you. I trust you. I'm glad we're together."
6. **Maintain a childlike fascination for your world.** Express enthusiasm for and interest in the thoughts, actions, plans, dreams, and material objects of other people. Your enthusiasm directed toward others will engender enthusiasm in you.
7. **Be more animated than others.** People who are perceived to be more charismatic are simply more animated than others. They smile more frequently, speak faster, articulate better, and move their heads and bodies more often.[56]

## Discussion Questions and Activities

1. Identify a business, government, education, or sports leader whom you perceive to be charismatic. Explain the basis for your judgment.

2. Athletes and other celebrities who smile frequently and wave to the audience are often described as being "charismatic." What is wrong or incomplete about this use of the term *charisma*?

3. Describe how a person might write email messages to give an impression of being charismatic.

4. Explain why the presence of a charismatic leader tends to enhance the job satisfaction of group members.

5. A concern has been expressed that leaders who are charismatic are often incompetent. They simply get placed into key positions because they create such a good impression. What do you think of this argument?

6. Design a research study or survey to determine if being perceived as charismatic really helps a person advance in a managerial career.

7. If a transformational leader is supposed to be so smart and so visionary, why would he or she emphasize empowerment in his or her leadership approach?

8. Provide an example of an athletic coach who proved to be a transformational leader, and justify your opinion.

9. When Robert Nardelli was appointed CEO and chairman at Chrysler in 2007, some of his first steps were to shutter a number of factories and lay off about 20,000 workers in order to reduce costs. How might these actions impact his status as a transformational leader?

10. What opportunities might a first-level supervisor or team leader have to be a transformational leader?

## Leadership Case Problem A

### The Image Doctor Is In

"You are being googled, maybe even right now," William Arruda says to 150 people who have tuned into a CareerCoach Institute teleconference. He pauses for effect, then continues: "If you don't show up in Google, you don't exist."

Arruda, a former IBM marketing executive and the 45-year-old founder of Reach Communication Consulting in New York, pulled in $1 million last year milking the latest consulting gimmick, "personal branding." That means showing how, among other things, to pretty up the picture of yourself that shows up on search sites, YouTube, and blogs. Arruda says you need a presence as distinctive as a Nike swoosh—"What makes you unique makes you successful." Think of this work as something like repositioning a tired toothpaste brand.

Fee: up to $15,000. To find out what is promotional or problematic about the executives who hire him, Arruda interviews them, polls friends and colleagues—typical question: if this person were a car, what kind would he or she be?—and then tells them how to stand out by writing blogs, giving speeches, and changing the way they talk or dress.

Pierre Van Beneden, 53, says Arruda in 2001 helped him develop and promote an expertise in how technology affects education. Since then, at Arruda's urging, he has delivered speeches on the topic and created a slick web site. He credits Arruda with helping him get noticed and recruited in 2003. Now he is vice president of Adobe's business in Europe, Africa, and the Middle East.

Big companies tap Arruda to lead charisma-boosting workshops. Starwood Hotels & Resorts recently hired him to speak to 300 execs. He has gotten business from American Express, JPMorgan Chase, and Microsoft.

Some executives are uneasy self-promoters. Jane Swift, a program director at British Telecom in London, followed Arruda's advice to network with higher-ups—she hosted a lunch for women executives in the company—but she isn't convinced she needs her own web site. "I don't want a 'Who does she think she is?' response," she frets.

That's not the kind of thing that troubles Arruda. When he isn't doling out doses of oomph, he is busy recruiting coaches to help him build his own brand. Currently there are 150 Arrudaites around the world, preaching his gospel of personal branding. They pay him $3,200 for 60 hours of training plus a 5 percent cut of their consulting gigs.

## Questions

1. In which aspects of charisma is William Arruda providing coaching and training?
2. To what extent is Arruda professionally qualified to correct the personalities of his clients?
3. What is your reaction to Arruda's statement, "If you don't show up on Google, you don't exist"?
4. Explain whether you would invest your own money in having the CareerCoach Institute help you develop a personal brand.
5. Out of curiosity, if you were a car, what make and model would you be? What about the instructor of this course?

*Source:* Excerpted from Suzanne Hoppough, "You Inc.: Image Doctor," *Forbes*, February 26, 2007, p. 60. Reprinted by permission of Forbes Magazine © 2008 LLC.

## Leadership Case Problem B

### Time to Rebound at Willow Pond

Heather Osaka had worked ten years in the hospital administration field, at two hospitals, one HMO, and one nursing home. However, she had yet to hold a chief administrator position. One afternoon she received a text message from Jake Wofford, a former classmate who was now in the executive recruiting business. "Maybe a great opportunity for you. Get back," said the message.

Osaka did get back to Wofford quickly. The opportunity to which he referred was a position as the director of Willow Pond, a medium-size assisted living home in the same city where Osaka now lived. "Assisted living" refers to helping older residents who are not quite able to care for themselves, yet do not require the level of care provided by a nursing home. Jake was frank in informing Heather that Willow Pond was troubled, and that the previous director had been fired. Yet, the home still complied enough with state regulations to remain in operation.

The most recent problem at the home receiving publicity involved a man with a criminal record who walked into Willow Pond, sneaked into a resident's studio apartment, and sexually molested her. To gain entrance to the living area, the intruder donned a "Friends of Willow Pond" smock designated for volunteers. Wearing the smock facilitated his roaming the living area.

Before finally accepting the position, Heather spoke with the owners, who also operated several other homes for the elderly. She also consulted with a few of the supervisors and, with permission, interviewed four Willow Pond residents. The owners and Heather agreed that the following issues were among the most pressing:

- The residents and their families complain that the food is poor.
- Many of the residents are treated callously by the staff, and often told to "shut up" when they make

a special demand such as having a button sewn, or ask for an off-menu item.

■ The staff turnover is far higher than the industry average, with many young staffers just taking resident-care jobs as a last resort. Many of the people with experience in resident care who take a position at Willow Brook quickly leave for higher pay or for a more congenial atmosphere.

■ Sanitation at the facility barely meets state requirements, and the building has a grungy, neglected appearance.

■ Much of the equipment and furniture is old and shabby. Many of the TV sets produce blurry images.

■ Willow Brook does not have high-speed Internet access for the residents, leaving those with computers in their rooms and apartments struggling to use the Internet.

■ The physician and registered nurse service is not as reliable as at most assisted-care facilities.

■ Willow Pond has shown a slight operating loss for three consecutive years.

The first day on the job, Heather thought to herself, "This looks like a job for Superwoman, or at least a great turnaround artist. So where do I begin making a difference?"

### Questions

1. Why is this case included in a chapter about charismatic and transformational leadership?
2. What aspects of transformational leadership should Heather emphasize in her approach to rehabilitating Willow Pond?
3. How might emphasizing the charismatic aspects of her personality help Heather bring about the necessary changes?
4. Why might the job at Willow Brook prove to be a wonderful career opportunity for Heather Osaka?

## ◎ Leadership Skill-Building Exercise 3-3

### My Leadership Portfolio

How much charisma, or how many charismatic behaviors, have you exhibited this week? Think back to all your interactions with people in this last week or two. What have you done that might have been interpreted as charismatic? Review the characteristics of a charismatic leader described in the text and in the Guidelines for Action and Skill Development. For

example, did you smile warmly at someone, did you wave to a person you see infrequently and address him or her by name? Did you help your team, club, or group think seriously about its future? As part of this same exercise, record your charismatic behaviors for the upcoming week. Be alert to opportunities for displaying charisma.

## Internet Skill-Building Exercise

### Charisma Tips from the Internet

A section in this chapter offered suggestions for becoming more charismatic. Search the Internet for additional suggestions and compare them to the suggestions in the text. A good starting point is www.workstar.net/library/charisma.htm. Be alert to contradictions, and offer a possible explanation for each contradiction. You might want to classify the suggestions into two categories: those dealing with the inner person, and those dealing with more superficial aspects of behavior. A suggestion of more depth would be to become a visionary, and a suggestion of less depth would be to wear eye-catching clothing.

**Apply the chapter concepts!** Visit the Web and complete this Internet skill-building exercise to learn more about current leadership topics and trends.

# Leadership Behaviors, Attitudes, and Styles

## CHAPTER 4

## LEARNING OBJECTIVES

After studying this chapter and doing the exercises, you should be able to

- Explain the key leadership dimensions of initiating structure and consideration.

- Describe at least five task-oriented leadership behaviors and attitudes.

- Describe at least five relationship-oriented attitudes and behaviors.

- Explain how leaders use 360-degree feedback to improve their performance.

- Describe the autocratic and participative leadership styles.

- Present the case for the entrepreneurial style of leadership and for gender differences in leadership style.

- Determine how to choose the most appropriate leadership style.

## CHAPTER OUTLINE

Gary Hayes, cofounder of New York consultant firm Hayes Brunswick, worked with a law firm where a senior partner flung heavy law books across the room at an associate. "The associate told me it was all right since the partner intentionally threw to miss—not hit him," says Hayes. "But the associate moved to another firm."

The vice president of marketing at a Silicon Valley company attributes rapid turnover at many West Coast technology companies to what he calls "screaming bully bosses." One such boss, a bodybuilder who liked to show off his strength to managers by doing twenty-five pushups at the start of meetings, called him at all hours to scream about things that had gone wrong. A second bully boss,

the CEO of a semiconductor-network startup, ridiculed him and his colleagues publicly. "He'd pick up something I'd written and say, 'Who wrote this? A second grader? It's the stupidest thing I've ever read,'" the marketing vice president says.

On a trip to Japan, the CEO exploded after the marketing vice president spent two long hours on a Sunday looking for a gift for his wife. Back at headquarters, he was told he'd report to a lower-level executive. "It was my boss's way of punishing me," says the marketing vice president, who quit. Also quitting, in quick succession, were the vice president of engineering and the vice president of human resources, who were also tired of their boss's harangues.[1]

The misdeeds of the managers just presented carry a message: Despite the abundant information about appropriate behaviors and attitudes, some managers do not understand what it takes to effectively lead others. This chapter describes a number of key behaviors and attitudes that help a manager function as a leader. We also describe the closely related topic of leadership styles.

Frequent reference is made in this chapter, and at other places in the text, to leadership effectiveness. A working definition of an **effective leader** is one who helps group members attain productivity, including high quality and customer satisfaction, as well as job satisfaction. Leadership effectiveness is typically measured by two key measures or criteria.

The first criterion relates to objective data, such as those dealing with sales, production, safety, quality, number of patents produced by the group, cost-cutting, or staying within budget. Measures of job satisfaction and turnover are also used to measure leadership effectiveness. The second criterion focuses on judgments by others about the leader's effectiveness, such as a plant manager rating a supervisor or the board rating a CEO. Most of the research reported throughout this text includes measures of leadership effectiveness in the design of the study.

## THE CLASSIC DIMENSIONS OF CONSIDERATION AND INITIATING STRUCTURE

Studies conducted at Ohio State University in the 1950s identified 1,800 specific examples of leadership behavior that were reduced to 150 questionnaire items on leadership functions.[2] The functions are also referred to as *dimensions of leadership behavior*. This research became the foundation for most future research about leadership behavior, attitudes, and styles. The researchers asked team members to describe their supervisors by responding to the questionnaires. Leaders were also asked to rate themselves on leadership dimensions. Two leadership dimensions accounted for 85 percent of the descriptions of leadership behavior: "consideration" and "initiating structure."

**Consideration** is the degree to which the leader creates an environment of emotional support, warmth, friendliness, and trust. The leader creates this environment by being friendly and approachable, looking out for the personal welfare of the group, keeping the group abreast of new developments, and doing small favors for the group.

Leaders who score high on the consideration factor typically are friendly and trustful, earn respect, and have a warm relationship with team members. Leaders with low scores on the consideration factor typically are authoritarian and impersonal in their relationships with group members. Three questionnaire items measuring the consideration factor are as follows:

1. Do personal favors for people in the work group.
2. Treat all people in the work group as your equal.
3. Do little things to make it pleasant to be a member of the staff.

The relationship-oriented behaviors described later in this chapter are specific aspects of consideration. Another key example of consideration is *making connections* with people. Julia Stewart, president and CEO of IHOP, believes that making connections is one of her most essential leadership functions. Back in her days at Applebee's (now a division of IHOP), she spent about five minutes every day checking in with each of the nine managers who directly reported to her. They talked about such social topics as where they ate over the weekend (even if it was not Applebee's). Stewart says that leaders cannot afford *not* to take time to chitchat. "I worry about the bosses who are in the crisis mode 80 or 90 percent of the time. By spending the first couple of minutes each day with the employees, I have more of an understanding of what makes them tick."[3]

Low standing on the consideration factor can be a predictor of CEO failure. According to the case histories of management professor Terry Leap, individuals who exhibit rude behavior will most probably alienate the wrong person at the wrong time.[4]

**Initiating structure** means organizing and defining relationships in the group by engaging in such activities as assigning specific tasks, specifying procedures to be followed, scheduling work, and clarifying expectations for team members. A team leader who helped group members establish realistic goals would be engaged in initiating structure. Other concepts that refer to the same idea include *production emphasis*, *task orientation*, and *task motivation*. The task-related leadership behaviors and attitudes described later in this chapter are specific aspects of initiating structure.

Leaders who score high on this dimension define the relationship between themselves and their staff members, as well as the role that they expect each staff member to assume. Such leaders also endeavor to establish well-defined channels of communication and ways of getting the job done. Three self-assessment items measuring initiating structure are as follows:

1. Try out your own new ideas in the work group.
2. Emphasize meeting deadlines.
3. See to it that people in the work group are working up to capacity.

A positive example of a leader who emphasizes initiating structure is James Albaugh, the president and CEO of Boeing Integrated Defense Systems. While managing at a rocket engine division, Albaugh reorganized the assembly line and trained workers to improve their efficiency. Colleagues remember him as somewhat of an obsessive manager. For example, Albaugh once left a manager a Post-it® note with a cigarette butt stuck to it—a reminder that efficiency includes sweeping the floor.[5]

Leaders have been categorized with respect to how much emphasis they place on the two dimensions of consideration and initiating structure. As implied by Figure 4-1, the two dimensions are not mutually exclusive. A leader can achieve high or low status on both dimensions. For example, an effective leader might contribute to high productivity and still place considerable emphasis on warm human relationships. The four-cell grid of Figure 4-1 is a key component of several approaches to describing leadership style. We return to this topic later in this chapter and in Chapter 5.

A new study of the validity of consideration and initiating structure indicates that these classic dimensions do indeed contribute to an understanding of leadership because they are related to leadership outcomes. A meta-analysis showed that consideration is strongly related to the job satisfaction of group members, satisfaction with the leader, worker motivation, and leader effectiveness. Initiating structure was slightly more strongly related to job performance, group performance, and organization performance. However, initiating structure was also associated with satisfaction and performance.[6] These results are encouraging because they reinforce the importance of this pioneering research.

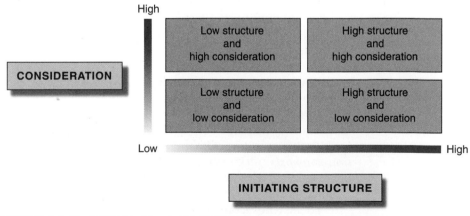

**FIGURE 4-1** Four Combinations of Initiating Structure and Consideration.

# TASK-RELATED ATTITUDES AND BEHAVIORS

The task-related versus relationship-related classification remains a useful framework for understanding leadership attitudes, behaviors, and practices. This section identifies and describes task-related attitudes and behaviors that are characteristic of effective leaders, as outlined in Table 4-1. Task-related in this context means that the behavior, attitude, or skill focuses more on the task to be performed than on the interpersonal aspect of leadership.

**1. *Adaptability to the situation.*** Effective leaders adapt to the situation. Adaptability reflects the contingency viewpoint: a tactic is chosen based on the unique circumstances at hand. A leader who is responsible for psychologically immature group members will find it necessary to supervise them closely. If the group members are mature and self-reliant, the leader will use less supervision. The adaptive leader also selects an organization structure that is best suited to the demands of the situation, such as choosing between a brainstorming group and a committee.

**2. *Direction setting.*** Given that a major responsibility of leadership is to produce change, the leader must set the direction of that change. Direction setting is part of creating a vision and a component of strategy. The strategy describes a feasible way of achieving the vision. Former GE executive turned business author Larry Bossidy believes that it is part of a business leader's job to communicate clearly where the business is going, why, and how the company will benefit if goals are achieved.[7]

Shortly after John Thompson took over as CEO of Symantec, he pointed the company in the direction of concentrating on Internet security software (including Norton AntiVirus software). He explained that security software would soon grow dramatically in importance.

**3. *High performance standards.*** Effective leaders consistently hold group members to high standards of performance. Jeff Immelt, CEO and chairman of GE says, "The ability to demand high performance without being heartless has been part of GE for a long time."[8] When performance is measured against these high standards, productivity is likely to increase, since people tend to live up to the expectations of their superiors. This is called the **Pygmalion effect**, and it works in a subtle, almost unconscious way. When a managerial leader believes that a group member will succeed, the manager communicates this belief without realizing it. Conversely,

**TABLE 4-1** Task-Related Leadership Attitudes and Behaviors

1. Adaptability to the situation
2. Direction setting
3. High performance standards
4. Concentrating on strengths of group members
5. Risk taking and execution of plans
6. Hands-on guidance and feedback
7. Ability to ask tough questions

when a leader expects a group member to fail, that person will not disappoint the manager. The manager's expectation of success or failure becomes a self-fulfilling prophecy because the perceptions contribute to success or failure.

**4.** *Concentrating on the strengths of group members.* An axiom of effective leadership and management is to make good use of the strengths of group members rather than concentrating effort on patching up areas for improvement. The effective leader helps people improve, yet still capitalizes on strengths. A team member might have excellent interpersonal skills, yet poor technical skills. It would be best to assign that person a role that emphasizes interpersonal skills, while at the same time helping him or her improve technical skills. Marcus Buckingham emphasizes that capitalizing on each person's unique pattern of skills saves time because group members are not laboring at tasks outside their capability and interest. The manager might even develop a job description that best fits each employee's uniqueness.[9] Suppose you are the manager of a call center, and one staffer is great at calming down angry customers. Other call center members are then asked to refer customers who have gone ballistic to your team member who can handle the rage well.

**5.** *Risk taking and execution of plans.* To bring about constructive change, the leader must take risks and be willing to implement those risky decisions. Larry Bossidy says about the importance of execution: "I'm an impatient person, and I get more satisfaction from seeing things get done than I do about philosophizing or building sand castles. Many people regard execution as detail work that's beneath the dignity of a business leader. That's wrong. It's a leader's most important job."[10]

**6.** *Hands-on guidance and feedback.* You will recall that technical competence and knowledge of the business are important leadership characteristics. They enable the leader to provide group members with hands-on guidance about how to accomplish important work. The leader who provides such guidance helps the group accomplish important tasks; at the same time, group members learn important skills. Too much guidance of this nature, however, can be a symptom of poor delegation and micromanagement (managing too closely). Too little guidance, and macromanagement is the result in which the manager gives too little or no direction to group members. Henry Mintzberg observes that the leader's strategy might suffer because he or she does not understand the operations of the business.[11]

To improve their hands-on management skills, about 150 officials of Loews Hotels are required to spend a day every year in an entry-level job at one of its eighteen U.S. and Canadian hotels. They share impressions with employees in their temporary departments and solicit ideas for making these jobs easier. One result was the installation of handlebars on room-service carts so they are easier for waiters to push.[12]

Closely related to guidance is giving frequent feedback on performance. The leader can rarely influence the actions of group members without appropriate performance feedback. This feedback tells group members how well they are doing so that they can take corrective action if needed. It also serves as a reinforcer that prompts group members to continue favorable activities. Leadership Skill-Building Exercise 4-1 provides practice in developing feedback skills.

The accompanying Leader in Action profile illustrates the importance top management at a health care firm attaches to hands-on experience for leaders.

## ▶ Leader in Action

### Top Brass Try Life in the Trenches

By 11:30 A.M. one recent day, Carolyn Kibler had been on her feet for nearly six hours, shuttling among sixteen dialysis patients at a DaVita Inc. clinic in Atlanta, Georgia. Her lower back ached from the unaccustomed strain. The outgoing and talkative former nurse had known little about dialysis before she joined DaVita in 2006. (Dialysis takes the place of nonfunctioning or poorly functioning kidneys in flushing wastes from the body.)

Kibler is a vice president of the nation's number 2 dialysis-treatment operator, earning a six-figure salary while overseeing forty-eight other clinics. For three days this spring, however, she helped treat seriously ill patients alongside technicians working up to thirteen-hour days for $14.30 an hour. "The job is definitely more physically demanding than I had imagined," the 48-year-old executive admits.

Kibler quickly feels the stress of the job. She must don a close-fitting surgical gown and plastic face visor. "It's real hot," she says. While wearing the protective gear, she helps a technician monitor patients' blood pressure, checks other vital signs, watches the machines' water purity, and completes paperwork.

After her hectic three-day stint, Kibler describes her technicians as "some of the most empathetic caregivers I have ever seen." DaVita's prosperity depends on front-line troops aiding patients. "Band-Aid by Band-Aid, piece of tape by piece of tape, and alarm by alarm," she continues.

Back in her office in another part of Atlanta, Kibler tries to integrate the lessons from her clinic experience into her leadership of a roughly 750-employee division. "I am more conscious of the power of my words and my actions and the impact they have down in the organization," she says.

So Kibler is more lenient when clinics fall behind on paperwork due to staffing shortages. She praises a nurse who skipped a conference call to discuss a clinic's quality report so she could fill in for an absent employee caring for patients. "When something like that comes up, I have a picture of the treatment floor, everyone scurrying around and patients waiting in their chairs," Kibler says. "Patient care comes first." At an evening staff meeting in another clinic on June 13, she thanked workers for "the gift of life they had given to each patient they touched that day."

DaVita requires managers to attend two days of classroom training before working in a clinic, and surveys participants after their visits. DaVita chief executive Kent J. Thiry created the immersion program for his senior managers in 2002. "The experience changes their view of the world," he says. "They are better leaders as a result."

### Questions

1. How would the kind of hands-on experience DaVita managers receive help them formulate visions?
2. Explain whether you think "life in the trenches" is valuable for a leader.
3. Leadership authority Edward Lawler favors the type of program presented here. Yet he cautions that executives' rare appearances in the trenches may suggest that these people are really out of touch. How do you react to this caution?

*Source:* Excerpted from Joann S. Lublin, "Top Brass Try Life in the Trenches," *The Wall Street Journal*, June 25, 2007, p. B1.

## ◎ Leadership Skill-Building Exercise 4-1

### Feedback Skills

After small groups have completed an assignment such as answering the case questions or discussion questions, hold a performance feedback session. Also use observations you have made in previous problem-solving activities as the basis for your feedback. Each group member provides some feedback to each other member about how well he or she thinks the other person performed. Use only volunteers, because this type of feedback may be uncomfortable and disturbing to some individuals. Students not receiving the feedback can serve as observers and later present their feedback on what took place during the exercise. To increase the probability of benefiting from this experience, feedback recipients must listen actively. Refer to the section in Chapter 10 on coaching skills and techniques for more information on feedback and active listening.

A convenient way to do this exercise is for everyone to sit in a circle. Choose one feedback recipient to begin. Going clockwise around the circle, each group member gives that person feedback. After all people have spoken, the feedback recipient gives his or her reactions. The person to the left of the first recipient is the next one to get feedback.

After everyone has had a turn receiving performance feedback, hold a general discussion. Be sure to discuss three key issues:

1. How helpful was the feedback?
2. What was the relative effectiveness of positive versus negative feedback?
3. Were some group members better than others in giving feedback?

7. *Ability to ask tough questions.* There are many times when leaders can be effective by asking tough questions rather than providing answers. A **tough question** is one that makes a person or group stop and think about why they are doing or not doing something. (A tough question might also be considered the *right* question.) In this way, group members are forced to think about the effectiveness of their activities. They might ask themselves, "Why didn't I think of that? It seems so obvious." Asking questions is important because quite often group members may have the solutions to difficult problems facing the organization.

When Alan R. Mulally was the newly appointed CEO at Ford Motor Co., he was told that the company loses close to $3,000 every time a customer buys a Focus compact. He asked, "Why haven't you figured out a way to make a profit?" Given a few excuses, Mulally hammered away again: "I want to know why no one figured a way to build this car at a profit, whether it has to be built in Michigan or China or India, if that's what it takes."[13]

Now that you have studied various components of task-oriented attitudes and behaviors, do Leadership Self-Assessment Quiz 4-1. It will further sensitize you to the task activities of leaders and managers.

## Leadership Self-Assessment Quiz 4-1

### Task-Oriented Attitudes and Behaviors

**Instructions:** Indicate whether you mostly agree or mostly disagree with the following statements. Relate the statements to any work situation, including sports, community activities, and school activities, in which you have been responsible for the work of others. If a work situation does not come to mind, imagine how you would act or think.

| | Mostly Agree | Mostly Disagree |
|---|---|---|
| 1. I keep close tabs on productivity figures and interpret them to the group. | ☐ | ☐ |
| 2. I send frequent email and text messages to group members, giving them information about work procedures. | ☐ | ☐ |
| 3. I clearly specify the quality goals our group needs to achieve. | | |
| 4. I maintain clear-cut standards of performance. | ☐ | ☐ |
| 5. When I conduct a meeting, the participants can count on a clear-cut agenda. | ☐ | ☐ |
| 6. I feel good about my workweek only if our team has met or exceeded its productivity goals. | ☐ | ☐ |
| 7. People should not be spending time with computers in the office unless the computers are actually increasing productivity. | ☐ | ☐ |
| 8. I freely criticize work that does not meet standards. | ☐ | ☐ |
| 9. I spend at least 20 percent of my workweek either planning myself or helping team members with their planning. | ☐ | ☐ |
| 10. I spend a good deal of time solving technical or business problems myself, or helping group members do the same. | ☐ | ☐ |

**Interpretation:** If you responded "mostly agree" to eight, nine, or ten of these statements, you have a strong task orientation. If you responded "mostly disagree" to four or more of the statements, you have below-average task-oriented behaviors and attitudes.

**Skill Development:** A task orientation is important because it can lead directly to goal attainment and productivity. Nevertheless, a task orientation must be balanced with a strong people orientation and interpersonal skills for maximum effectiveness.

# RELATIONSHIP-ORIENTED ATTITUDES AND BEHAVIORS

Leadership involves influencing people, so it follows that many effective leadership attitudes, behaviors, and practices deal with interpersonal relationships. Randy Komisar, who helps launch startup technology firms, was asked how he sweeps into companies and manages employees effectively. He replied: "I rely on relationship power, not traditional position power that comes from my title. I find that building relationships with people and inspiring them are the keys to my leadership. That's how I think any manager becomes a leader."[14]

Table 4-2 lists the seven relationship-oriented attitudes and behaviors that we will discuss next. (Most other parts of this book describe the interpersonal skill aspects of leadership.)

**1. *Aligning people.*** Getting people pulling in the same direction and collaborating smoothly is a major interpersonal challenge. To get people pulling together, it is necessary to speak to many people. The target population can involve many different stakeholders. Among them are managers and team leaders, higher-ups, peers, and workers in other parts of the organization, as well as suppliers, government officials, and customers. Anyone who can implement the vision and strategies or who can block implementation must be aligned.[15] After being aligned, organizational members can pull together toward a higher purpose. Alignment of people also incorporates getting the group working together smoothly.

Alignment is easier when the group has an agreed-upon mission or purpose. Paul Tagliabue, the former CEO of the National Football League (NFL), was noted for his ability to create harmony among players and owners. Gene Upshaw, the late head of the Players Association, made this comment about the mission Tagliabue helped develop: "I don't see this as us versus the owners, but instead it's us versus all the other entertainment choices out there: the movies, music, and theater."[16]

**2. *Openness to worker opinions.*** A major part of relationship-oriented leadership is to engage in **management openness**, or a set of leader behaviors particularly relevant to subordinates' motivation to voice their opinion.[17] When the leader is open in this way, subordinates perceive that their boss listens to them, is interested in their ideas, and gives fair consideration to suggestions. Being open

**TABLE 4-2** Relationship-Oriented Attitudes and Behaviors

**1.** Aligning people
**2.** Openness to worker opinions
**3.** Creating inspiration and visibility
**4.** Satisfying higher-level needs
**5.** Giving emotional support and encouragement
**6.** Promoting principles and values
**7.** Being a servant leader

to worker opinions is part of the consideration dimension, and also central to participative leadership.

**3. *Creating inspiration and visibility.*** As described in the discussion of charismatic and transformational leadership, inspiring others is an essential leadership practice. Inspiring people usually involves appealing to their emotions and values, such as when the head of a snowmobile business unit encourages workers to believe that they are making winters more enjoyable for people who live in regions that accumulate snow.

Because human contact and connections reinforce inspiration, another part of being inspirational is being visible and available. One of the many ways in which Sam Palmisano, the CEO of IBM, inspires people is through his visibility. He frequently interacts face-to-face with workers at all levels in the company. His ability to chat with almost anybody he meets makes him approachable to employees and customers.[18]

**4. *Satisfying higher-level needs.*** To inspire people, effective leaders motivate people by satisfying higher-level needs, such as needs for achievement, personal growth, a sense of belonging, recognition, self-esteem, and a feeling of control over one's life. Many leaders in organizations express an awareness of the importance of need satisfaction for building good relationships with workers. A robust method of satisfying higher-level needs is to help them grow professionally. Star executive W. James McNerney, now the Boeing Company CEO, says that he has been a successful executive at three major companies primarily through helping people perform better. McNerney contends that people who grow are open to change, have the courage to change, work hard, and are good team players. In his words, "What I do is figure out how to unlock that in people, because most people have that inside of them. But they often get trapped in a bureaucratic environment where they've been beaten about the head and shoulders."[19]

**5. *Giving emotional support and encouragement.*** Supportive behavior toward team members usually increases leadership effectiveness. A supportive leader gives frequent encouragement and praise, and also displays caring and kindness even about non-work-related matters such as the health of a worker's ill family member.[20] Keep in mind that encouragement means to fill with courage.[21] One of the many work-related ways of encouraging people is to allow them to participate in decision making. Emotional support generally improves morale and sometimes improves productivity. In the long term, emotional support and encouragement may bolster a person's self-esteem. Being emotionally supportive comes naturally to the leader who has empathy for people and who is a warm person.

**6. *Promoting principles and values.*** A major part of a top leader's role is to help promote values and principles that contribute to the welfare of individuals and organizations. This promotion can be classified as relationship-oriented because it deals directly with the emotions and attitudes of people, and indirectly with the task. Stephen Covey, who is widely quoted for his uplifting messages, advises that an organization's mission statement must be for all good causes.[22] Leaders who believe in these good causes will then espouse principles and values that lead people toward good deeds in the workplace. To encourage managers and all other employees to conduct their work affairs at a high moral level, many companies put their values in written form. The values might be placed in employee handbooks, on company intranets, or on company web sites.

What constitutes the right values depends on the leader's core beliefs. Bill George, the former chairman and CEO of Medtronic, Inc., and now Harvard Business School professor, has inspired many managers with his thoughts about authentic leadership. Such leaders place the welfare of customers and employees above those of shareholders in the corporate hierarchy. Another key value of an authentic leader is to help employees achieve a fair balance between work and family life.[23] In his book *True North*, George says that authentic leaders lead with their hearts, as well as their heads, enabling them to have passion. One example is Howard Schultz, the founder of Starbucks, who wanted to develop an enterprise his father would be proud of. Another authentic leader is Andrea Jung of Avon, who joined the company so she could help women achieve self-sufficiency. In general, authentic leaders stay true to their values, even under pressure. Furthermore, they keep in mind that employees want meaning and significance in their work, not only money.[24]

Providing moral leadership begins with understanding one's own values. Leadership Skill-Building Exercise 4-2 gives you an opportunity to think through your work-related values so that you can better provide moral leadership to others. Also, more will be said about values and ethics in Chapter 6.

**7.** *Being a servant leader.*   Your desire to help others is another important workplace value. A **servant leader** serves constituents by working on their behalf to help them achieve their goals, not the leader's own goals. The idea behind servant leadership, as formulated by Robert K. Greenleaf, is that leadership derives naturally from a commitment to service.[25] Serving others, including employees, customers, and community, is the primary motivation for the servant leader. And true leadership emerges from a deep desire to help others. A servant leader is therefore a moral leader. Servant leadership has been accomplished when group members become wiser, healthier, and more autonomous. The following are key aspects of servant leadership.[26]

- *Place service before self-interest*. A servant leader is more concerned with helping others than with acquiring power, prestige, financial reward, and status. The servant leader seeks to do what is morally right, even if it is not financially rewarding. He or she is conscious of the needs of others and is driven by a desire to satisfy them. (You will recall that wanting to satisfy the needs of others is a basic relationship behavior.)
- *Listen first to express confidence in others*. The servant leader makes a deep commitment to listening in order to get to know the concerns, requirements, and problems of group members. Instead of attempting to impose his or her will on others, the servant leader listens carefully to understand what course of action will help others accomplish their goals. After understanding others, the best course of action can be chosen. Through listening, for example, a servant leader might learn that the group is more concerned about team spirit and

## ◎ Leadership Skill-Building Exercise 4-2

### Clarifying Your Work Values

***Instructions:*** To provide effective value leadership, it is essential that you first understand your own values with respect to dealing with others. Rank from 1 to 12 the importance of the following values to you as a person. The most important value on the list receives a rank of 1; the least important, a rank of 12. Use the space next to "Other" if we have left out an important value in your life.

_____ Having respect for the dignity of others

_____ Ensuring that others have interesting work to perform

_____ Earning the trust of others

_____ Earning the respect of others

_____ Impressing others with how well my group performs

_____ Giving others proper credit for their work

_____ Inspiring continuous learning on the part of each member in our group, myself included

_____ Holding myself and others accountable for delivering on commitments

_____ Helping others grow and develop

_____ Inspiring others to achieve high productivity and quality

_____ Developing the reputation of being a trustworthy person

_____ Other

1. Compare your ranking of these values with that of the person next to you, and discuss.
2. Perhaps your class, assisted by your instructor, might arrive at a class average on each of these values. How does your ranking compare to the class ranking?
3. Look back at your own ranking. Does your ranking surprise you?
4. Are there any surprises in the class ranking? Which values did you think would be highest and lowest?

Clarifying your values for leadership is far more than a pleasant exercise. Many business leaders have fallen into disgrace and brought their companies into bankruptcy because of values that are unacceptable to employees, stockholders, outside investigators, and the legal system. For example, a CEO who valued "developing the reputation of being a trustworthy person" would not borrow $400 million from the company while paying thousands of employees close to the minimum wage.

harmony than striving for companywide recognition. The leader would then concentrate more on building teamwork than searching for ways to increase the visibility of the team.

■  *Inspire trust by being trustworthy*. Being trustworthy is a foundation behavior of the servant leader. He or she is scrupulously honest with others, gives up control, and focuses on the well-being of others. Usually such leaders do not have to work hard at being trustworthy because they are already quite moral. In support of this principle, a survey found that most employees want a boss who is a trusted leader, not a pal.[27]

- *Focus on what is feasible to accomplish.* Even though the servant leader is idealistic, he or she recognizes that one individual cannot accomplish everything. So the leader listens carefully to the array of problems facing group members and then concentrates on a few. The servant leader thus systematically neglects certain problems. A labor union official might carefully listen to all the concerns and complaints of the constituents and then proceed to work on the most pressing issue.
- *Lend a hand.* A servant leader looks for opportunities to play the Good Samaritan. As a supermarket manager, he or she might help out by bagging groceries during a busy period. Or a servant leader might help dig up mud in the company lobby after a hurricane.
- *Provide emotional healing.* A servant leader shows sensitivity to the personal concerns of group members, such as a worker being worried about taking care of a disabled parent. At clothing retailer Men's Warehouse, Inc., servant leadership is in style. A district manager at the Warehouse may want to go home and be with his family, but he will tell a store manager that he will stay and cover the store, so the store manager can spend time with *his* or *her* family at a son's baseball game. The underlying idea is for managers to give top priority to helping others.[28]

In addition to being logically sound, research with 182 workers indicates that servant leadership has a positive relationship with organizational citizenship behavior, job performance, and staying with the organization.[29]

Leadership Skill-Building Exercise 4-3 provides an opportunity for you to practice relationship-oriented and task-oriented behaviors. Combined, these are sometimes referred to as the "nuts and bolts" of leadership.

## 360-DEGREE FEEDBACK FOR FINE-TUNING A LEADERSHIP APPROACH

In most large organizations, leaders not only provide feedback to group members, but they also receive feedback that gives them insight into the effects of their attitudes and behaviors. The feedback is systematically derived from a full sampling of parties who interact with the leader. In particular, **360-degree feedback** is a formal evaluation of superiors based on input from people who work for and with them, sometimes including customers and suppliers. It is also referred to as multisource feedback or multirater feedback. The process is also called 360-degree survey, because the input stems from a survey of a handful of people. The multiple input becomes another way of measuring leadership effectiveness.

One variation of the method is to build a 360-degree feedback system accessed via the Internet and the company's intranet. The Internet systems reduce some of the burdensome amount of paper involved in most 360-degree feedback systems, yet the participants must still fill out electronic forms.

Specialists in the field view 360-degree feedback as more suited for its original purpose of development for a manager or leader than for administrative purposes such as performance evaluation and salary administration. When used for development, 360-degree feedback should emphasize qualitative comments rather than

## ◎ Leadership Skill-Building Exercise 4-3

### Applying Relationship-Oriented and Task-Oriented Attitudes and Behaviors

About six role players who can tolerate brutal outdoor conditions are needed for this exercise. The setting is an oil drilling rig in the Arctic Circle, where deep-underground oil reserves have been discovered, and energy companies are now digging. Today the wind-chill factor is –40 degrees Fahrenheit. The crew of five is uncomfortable and a little confused about how to get the drilling started this morning. The leadership task of the supervisor is to help the crew get the digging accomplished.

Supervisor A attempts to engage in relationship-oriented attitudes and behavior with the group. He or she will use several of the behaviors mentioned in the text. The other five or so role players will react to his or her leadership. Work the role play for about 10 minutes.

After the first scenario is complete, Supervisor B will engage in task-oriented attitudes and behaviors. He or she will use several of the behaviors mentioned in the text. The other five or so role players will react to his or her leadership. Work the role play for about 10 minutes.

Class members not thrown into the frozen tundra will observe the interactions of the supervisor with the workers. Provide feedback as to (a) how well the leadership attitudes and behaviors were carried out, and (b) how likely these attitudes and behaviors were helpful in accomplishing the task of getting the drilling started.

strictly quantitative ratings.[30] For example, being told, "You do not maintain eye contact with me during meetings," is more helpful than simply receiving a low rating on "Makes others feel comfortable." The feedback is communicated to the leader (as well as others receiving 360-degree feedback) and interpreted with the assistance of a human resources professional or an external consultant.

The data from the survey can be used to help leaders fine-tune their attitudes and behavior. For example, if all the interested parties gave the leader low ratings on "empathy toward others," the leader might be prompted to improve his or her ability to empathize, such as by reading about empathy, attending a seminar, and simply making a conscious attempt to empathize when involved in a conflict of opinion with another person.

An example of a 360-degree feedback form is shown in Figure 4-2. The example shows the gaps between the leader's self-perceptions and the perceptions of the group. When such gaps occur, sometimes professionally trained counselors should be involved in 360-degree feedback. Some people feel emotionally crushed when they find a wide discrepancy between their self-perception on an interpersonal skill dimension and the perception of others. A middle manager involved in a 360-degree evaluation prided herself on how well she was liked by others. The feedback that emerged, however, depicted her as intimidating, hostile, and manipulative. Upon receiving the feedback, the woman went into a rage (proving the feedback true!) and then into despondency. Professional counseling can sometimes help a person benefit from critical feedback and place it in perspective.

For best results, it is extremely important that 360-degree surveys reflect those behaviors and attitudes that the organization values most highly. Care should also be taken that the dimensions measured reflect important aspects of leadership functioning. Following are some suggestions for making better use of 360-degree surveys.[31]

**Manager evaluated:** *Bob Germane*
**Ratings** *(10 is highest)*

| Behavior or Attitude | Self Rating | Average Group Rating | Gap |
|---|---|---|---|
| 1. Gives right amount of structure | 9 | 7.5 | -1.5 |
| 2. Considerate of people | 10 | 6.2 | -3.8 |
| 3. Sets a direction | 9 | 3.9 | -5.1 |
| 4. Sets high standards | 7 | 9.0 | +2.0 |
| 5. Gives frequent feedback | 10 | 6.3 | -3.7 |
| 6. Gets people pulling together | 9 | 5.1 | -3.9 |
| 7. Inspires people | 10 | 2.8 | -7.2 |
| 8. Gives emotional support | 8 | 3.7 | -4.3 |
| 9. Is a helpful coach | 10 | 4.5 | -5.5 |
| 10. Encourages people to be self-reliant | 6 | 9.4 | +3.4 |

**FIGURE 4-2** A 360-Degree Feedback Chart.

Note: A negative gap means you rate yourself higher on the behavior or attitude than does your group. A positive gap means the group rates you higher than you rate yourself.

- Focus on business goals and strategy. Feedback should provide leaders and managers with insight into the skills they need to help the organization meet its goals.
- Ensure that the feedback dimensions reflect important aspects of leadership functioning.
- Train workers in giving and receiving feedback. Providing constructive feedback takes coaching, training, and practice.
- Create an action plan for improvement for each leader based on the feedback. For example, a leader rated low on interpersonal skills might benefit from training in emotional intelligence.
- Ensure that the managers rated have full ownership of the feedback information so that they will perceive the feedback as being geared toward personal development rather than administrative control.

## LEADERSHIP STYLES

A leader's combination of attitudes and behaviors leads to a certain regularity and predictability in dealing with group members. **Leadership style** is the relatively consistent pattern of behavior that characterizes a leader. The study of leadership style is an extension of understanding leadership behaviors and attitudes. Most classifications of leadership style are based on the dimensions of consideration and initiating structure. Phrases such as "he's a real command-and-control-type" and "she's a consensus leader" have become commonplace.

Here we describe the participative leadership style, the autocratic leadership style, the Leadership Grid,™ the entrepreneurial leadership style, gender differences in leadership style, and choosing the best style. Chapter 5 continues the exploration of leadership styles by presenting several contingency leadership theories.

## Participative Leadership

Sharing decision making with group members and working with them side by side has become the generally accepted leadership approach in the modern organization. **Participative leaders** share decision making with group members. Participative leadership encompasses so many behaviors that it can be divided into three subtypes: consultative, consensus, and democratic.

**Consultative leaders** confer with group members before making a decision. However, they retain the final authority to make decisions. **Consensus leaders** strive for consensus. They encourage group discussion about an issue and then make a decision that reflects general agreement and that group members will support. All workers who will be involved in the consequences of a decision have an opportunity to provide input. A decision is not considered final until it appears that all parties involved will at least support the decision. **Democratic leaders** confer final authority on the group. They function as collectors of group opinion and take a vote before making a decision.

The participative style is based on management openness because the leader accepts suggestions for managing the operation from group members. Welcoming ideas from below is considered crucial because as technology evolves and organizations decentralize, front-line workers have more independence and responsibility. These workers are closer to the market, closer to seeing how the product is used, and closer to many human resource problems. Front-line knowledge can provide useful input to leaders for such purposes as developing marketing strategy and retaining employees.[32]

The participative style encompasses the teamwork approach. Predominant behaviors of participative leaders include coaching team members, negotiating their demands, and collaborating with others. Often the team member who has the most relevant knowledge for the task at hand slips into a leadership role. Research indicates that poor-performing teams are often dominated by the team leader, whereas high-performing teams are characterized by shared leadership.[33]

The participative style is well suited to managing competent people who are eager to assume responsibility. Such people want to get involved in making decisions and giving feedback to management. Since most graduates from business and professional programs expect to be involved in decision making, participative leadership works well with the new breed of managers and professionals.

Ricardo Semler, the CEO of the Brazilian equipment supplier Semco, makes extreme use of participative leadership and management. The company continues to grow substantially and be profitable. Of the employees' 3,000 votes, Semler gets only one. Working with an educator named Clovis da Silva Boijikian, they took radical steps, including the following:

- Hearing frequent complaints about the company cafeteria, they asked the employees to help improve it and eventually turned it over to them.
- Employees were empowered to set their own compensation. An analyst helped benchmark pay across positions and companies, setting average wage scales, adding 10 percent to make Semco more competitive, and then making salary levels public information.[34]

Participative leadership does have some problems. It often results in extensive and time-consuming team meetings and committee work. Also, consensus and democratic leaders are sometimes accused of providing too little direction, or being *macromanagers*. Sometimes participative leadership is carried to extremes. Team members are consulted about trivial things that management could easily handle independently. Another problem is that many managers still believe that sharing decision making with members reduces their power.

If democrat leadership goes one step further, the result is extreme macromanagement, which is referred to as the *laissez-faire* leadership style. A study conducted with 4,500 Norwegian employees found that employees managed by a laissez-faire leader experienced role ambiguity. The ambiguity led them to anxiously guess what criteria their supervisor would follow when evaluating their performance, and also guess about which tasks should receive the highest priority.[35]

## Autocratic Leadership

In contrast to participative leaders are **autocratic leaders,** who retain most of the authority. They make decisions confidently, assume that group members will comply, and are not overly concerned with group members' attitudes toward a decision. Autocratic leaders are considered task-oriented because they place heavy emphasis on getting tasks accomplished. Typical autocratic behaviors include telling people what to do, asserting themselves, and serving as a model for team members.

The leadership behavior of Jerry Sanders, the flamboyant founder of Advanced Micro Devices (AMD), helps us understand how domineering an autocratic leader can be. During the management committee meetings, Sanders would talk the entire forty-five minutes. Sanders's replacement, Hector Ruiz, speaks for twenty minutes. "Under Jerry, frankly, the company was very autocratic and power-centric," says Ruiz.[36]

In some situations, and in some organizational cultures, autocratic leadership is called for. When Bob Nardelli, formerly of Home Depot, joined Chrysler as the CEO in 2007, a company spokesman said that Nardelli's aggressive style was an asset for Chrysler. "Being a disciplinarian is a good thing because we have a plan, but we really need to execute it, and that's what Bob brings to the table," he said.[37] However, at Home Depot, Nardelli's style seemed ill-suited where his data-driven, in-your-face style grated on many experienced executives. The result was 100 percent turnover among his top 170 managers, many of whom left voluntarily.[38]

To help overcome his hatchet-person, autocratic reputation, Nardelli became more conciliatory and friendly at Chrysler.

Nardelli illustrates the important point that few leaders have a pure style. Although he might be regarded as autocratic, Nardelli readily hires talent to supplement his knowledge and skills. After joining Chrysler he hired several executives from Toyota, and also hired consultants. Relying on the talents of others indicates that he is practicing participative decision making and leadership.

Part of your skill development as a leader involves gaining insight into your own leadership style or potential style. To this end, you can take Leadership Self-Assessment Quiz 4-2.

 ## Leadership Self-Assessment Quiz 4-2

### What Style of Leader Are You or Would You Be?

**Instructions:** Answer the following questions, keeping in mind what you have done, or think you would do, in the scenarios and attitudes described.

| | Mostly True | Mostly False |
|---|:---:|:---:|
| 1. I am more likely to take care of a high-impact assignment myself than turn it over to a group member. | ☒ | ☐ |
| 2. I would prefer the analytical aspects of a manager's job to working directly with group members. | ☐ | ☒ |
| 3. An important part of my approach to managing a group is to keep the members informed almost daily of any information that could affect their work. | ☒ | ☐ |
| 4. It is a good idea to give two people in the group the same problem and then choose what appears to be the best solution. | ☐ | ☒ |
| 5. It makes good sense for the leader or manager to stay somewhat aloof from the group so that you can make a tough decision when necessary. | ☐ | ☒ |
| 6. I look for opportunities to obtain group input before making a decision, even on straightforward issues. | ☐ | ☒ |
| 7. I would reverse a decision if several of the group members presented evidence that I was wrong. | ☒ | ☐ |
| 8. Differences of opinion in the work group are healthy. | ☒ | ☐ |
| 9. I think that activities to build team spirit, like fixing up a poor family's house on a Saturday, are an excellent investment of time. | ☒ | ☐ |
| 10. If my group were hiring a new member, I would like the person to be interviewed by the entire group. | ☐ | ☒ |

## Quiz 4-2 (continued)

|  | Mostly True | Mostly False |
|---|---|---|
| 11. An effective team leader today uses email for about 98 percent of communication with team members. | ☐ | ☒ |
| 12. Some of the best ideas are likely to come from the group members rather than from the manager. | ☒ | ☐ |
| 13. If our group were going to have a banquet, I would get input from each member on what type of food should be served. | ☒ | ☐ |
| 14. I have never seen a statue of a committee in a museum or park, so why bother making decisions by a committee if you want to be recognized? | ☐ | ☒ |
| 15. I dislike it intensely when a group member challenges my position on an issue. | ☒ | ☐ |
| 16. I typically explain to group members how (what method) they should use to accomplish an assigned task. | ☒ | ☐ |
| 17. If I were out of the office for a week, most of the important work in the department would get accomplished anyway. | ☒ | ☐ |
| 18. Delegation of important tasks is something that would be (or is) very difficult for me. | ☐ | ☒ |
| 19. When a group member comes to me with a problem, I tend to jump right in with a proposed solution. | ☒ | ☐ |
| 20. When a group member comes to me with a problem, I typically ask that person something like, "What alternative solutions have you thought of so far?" | ☐ | ☒ |

***Scoring and Interpretation:*** The answers for a participative leader are as follows:

| | | |
|---|---|---|
| 1. Mostly false | 8. Mostly true | 15. Mostly false |
| 2. Mostly false | 9. Mostly true | 16. Mostly false |
| 3. Mostly true | 10. Mostly true | 17. Mostly true |
| 4. Mostly false | 11. Mostly false | 18. Mostly false |
| 5. Mostly false | 12. Mostly true | 19. Mostly false |
| 6. Mostly true | 13. Mostly true | 20. Mostly true |
| 7. Mostly true | 14. Mostly false | |

If your score is 15 or higher, you are most likely (or would be) a participative leader. If your score is 5 or lower, you are most likely (or would be) an authoritarian leader.

**Skill Development:** The quiz you just completed is also an opportunity for skill development. Review the twenty questions and look for implied suggestions for engaging in participative leadership. For example, question 20 suggests that you encourage group members to work through their own solutions to problems. If your goal is to become an authoritarian leader, the questions can also serve as useful guidelines. For example, question 19 suggests that an authoritarian leader looks first to solve problems for group members.

**Knowledge Bank**
Contains a diagram of an earlier version of the Leadership Grid.
**www.cengage.com/ management/dubrin**

## Leadership Grid™ Styles

A classic method of classifying leadership styles suggests that the best way to achieve effective leadership is to integrate the task and relationship orientations. The **Leadership Grid™** is a framework for specifying the extent of a leader's concern for production and people.[39]

Concern for production is rated on the grid's horizontal axis. Concern for production includes results, bottom line, performance, profits, and mission. Concern for people is rated on the vertical axis, and it includes concern for group members and coworkers. Both concerns are leadership attitudes or ways of thinking about leadership. Each of these concerns (or dimensions) exists in varying degrees along a continuum from 1 to 9. A manager's standing on one concern is not supposed to influence his or her standing on the other. As shown in Figure 4-3, the Grid encompasses seven leadership styles. If you are already familiar with the Grid, you will notice that the names of the styles have been changed in this version.

The creators of the Grid argue strongly for the value of 9, 9 sound (contribute and commit). According to their research, the sound management approach pays off. It results in improved performance, low absenteeism and turnover, and high morale. Sound (9, 9) management relies on trust and respect, which help bring about good results.

## Entrepreneurial Leadership

Many entrepreneurs use a similar leadership style that stems from their personality characteristics and circumstances. Although there are different types and definitions of entrepreneurs, in general an entrepreneur is a person who founds and operates an innovative business. Not all business owners, including franchise operators, are therefore entrepreneurial leaders. The general picture that emerges of an entrepreneur is a task-oriented and charismatic person. Entrepreneurs drive themselves and others relentlessly, yet their personalities also inspire others.

This entrepreneurial leadership style often incorporates the behaviors described in the following paragraphs.[40] However, authorities disagree about whether an entrepreneurial personality exists.

**1. *Strong achievement drive and sensible risk taking.*** Entrepreneurs have stronger achievement motives than most leaders (see Chapter 2). Building a business is an excellent vehicle for accomplishment and risk taking. To accomplish what they think needs to be accomplished, entrepreneurs are willing to work extraordinary hours, with twelve-hour days, seven days a week not being unusual. Because entrepreneurs take sensible risks, many do not perceive themselves as being risk takers—just as many tightrope walkers believe they are not taking risks because they are in control. Leadership Self-Assessment Quiz 4-3 gives you the opportunity to think about your risk-taking tendencies.

**2. *High degree of enthusiasm and creativity.*** Entrepreneurs are highly enthusiastic, partially because they are so excited about their achievements. As *Entrepreneur*

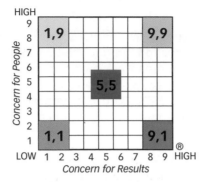

**The Seven Managerial Grid Styles**

**9,1** Controlling (Direct & Dominate)

- I expect results and take control by clearly stating a course of action. I enforce rules that sustain high results and do not permit deviation.

**1,9** Accommodating (Yield & Comply)

- I support results that establish and reinforce harmony. I generate enthusiasm by focusing on positive and pleasing aspects of work.

**5,5** Status Quo (Balance & Compromise)

- I endorse results that are popular but caution against taking unnecessary risk. I test my opinions with others involved to assure ongoing acceptability.

**1,1** Indifferent (Evade & Elude)

- I distance myself from taking active responsibility for results to avoid getting entangled in problems. If forced, I take a passive or supportive position.

**PAT** Paternalistic (Prescribe & Guide)

- I provide leadership by defining initiatives for myself and others. I offer praise and appreciation for support, and discourage challenges to my thinking.

**OPP** Opportunistic (Exploit & Manipulate)

- I persuade others to support results that offer me private benefit. If they also benefit, that's even better in gaining support. I rely on whatever approach is needed to secure an advantage.

**9,9** Sound (Contribute & Commit)

- I initiate team action in a way that invites involvement and commitment. I explore all facts and alternative views to reach a shared understanding of the best solution.

**FIGURE 4-3** The Leadership Grid.™

The Managerial Grid (or the Leadership Grid) is a very simple framework that elegantly defines seven basic styles that characterize workplace behavior and the resulting relationships. The seven Managerial Grid styles are based on how two fundamental concerns (concern for people and concern for results) are manifested at varying levels whenever people interact.

*Source:* © Copyright 2004–2006 Grid International, Inc. (All rights reserved.)

magazine puts it, "Something about being an entrepreneur is, for them, a five-star, butt-kicking, rocket-boosting blast." Entrepreneurs' enthusiasm, in turn, makes them persuasive. As a result, they are often perceived as charismatic. Some entrepreneurs are so emotional that they are regarded as eccentric.

**3.** *Tendency to act quickly when opportunity arises.* Entrepreneurs are noted for seizing upon opportunity. When a deal is on the horizon, they push themselves and those around them extra hard.

**4.** *Constant hurry combined with impatience.* Entrepreneurs are always in a hurry. While engaged in one meeting, their minds typically begin to focus on the next meeting. Their flurry of activity rubs off on group members and those around them. Entrepreneurs often adopt a simple dress style in order to save time, and they typically allow little slack time between appointments.

**5.** *Visionary perspective combined with tenacity.* Entrepreneurs, at their best, are visionaries. As with other types of effective leaders, they see opportunities others fail to observe. Specifically, they have the ability to identify a problem and arrive at a solution. Ted Turner of CNN is a legendary example of an entrepreneurial visionary. Turner picked up on a trend that people wanted—an all-news cable channel that they could access anytime. Not only is CNN a commercial success, but it also revolutionized the way people get their news all over the globe. After the vision is established, the entrepreneur tenaciously implements the vision, working an eighty-hour week if need be. For many entrepreneurs, just to stay in business requires tenacity. Sathvik Krishnamurthys is the founder of Voltage Security, a startup that makes security software. He says that the real name of the entrepreneurial game is slogging it out. "This is an endurance race," he reflects.[41]

**6.** *Dislike of hierarchy and bureaucracy.* Entrepreneurs are not ideally suited by temperament to working within the mainstream of a bureaucracy. Many successful entrepreneurs are people who were frustrated by the constraints of a bureaucratic system. The implication for leadership style is that entrepreneurs deemphasize rules and regulations when managing people.

**7.** *Preference for dealing with external customers.* One reason that entrepreneurs have difficulty with bureaucracy is that they focus their energies on products, services, and customers, rather than on employees. Some entrepreneurs are gracious to customers and moneylenders but brusque with company insiders. A blind spot many entrepreneurs have is that they cannot understand why their employees do not share their passion for work and customer focus. As a result, they may be brusque with employees who do not share their dedication to the firm.

**8.** *Eye on the future.* Entrepreneurs have the pronounced characteristic of thinking about future deals and business opportunities even before a current business is running smoothly. "Where is my next deal coming from?" is the mantra of the true entrepreneur. Even after accumulating great wealth from a current business

**Knowledge Bank**
Contains additional information about the entrepreneurial personality.

**www.cengage.com/
management/dubrin**

activity, the entrepreneurial leader looks toward future opportunities. A good example is Richard Branson, whose empire contains about 250 companies with the Virgin label, yet he continues to look for the next company to start or acquire (as described in Chapter 3).

As explained in the accompanying Knowledge Bank, the entrepreneurial personality, if carried to an extreme, can lead to addictive behavior, including substance abuse. To practice one aspect of entrepreneurial leadership, do Leadership Skill-Building Exercise 4-4.

## Leadership Self-Assessment Quiz 4-3

### What Is Your Propensity for Taking Risks?

**Instructions:** Indicate how well each of the following statements reflects your attitudes or behavior, using this scale: very inaccurately (VI); inaccurately (I); moderately well (MW); accurately (A); very accurately (VA).

| | VI | I | MW | A | VA |
|---|---|---|---|---|---|
| 1. If I had a serious illness, I would purchase generic instead of brand-name drugs. | 1 | 2 | 3 | 4 | 5 |
| 2. I invest (or would invest) much more money in bonds or CDs (certificates of deposit) than in stocks. | 5 | 4 | 3 | 2 | 1 |
| 3. The thought of starting my own business appeals to me. | 1 | 2 | 3 | 4 | 5 |
| 4. I am (or was) willing to go on blind dates frequently. | 1 | 2 | 3 | 4 | 5 |
| 5. My career advice to young people is to pursue a well-established occupation with a high demand for newcomers to the field. | 5 | 4 | 3 | 2 | 1 |
| 6. I would be willing to relocate to a city where I had no family or friends. | 1 | 2 | 3 | 4 | 5 |
| 7. During the last few years, I have taken up a new sport, dance, or foreign language on my own. | 1 | 2 | 3 | 4 | 5 |
| 8. My preference is to have at least 90 percent of my compensation based on guaranteed salary. | 5 | 4 | 3 | 2 | 1 |
| 9. From time to time I buy jewelry, clothing, or food from street vendors. | 1 | 2 | 3 | 4 | 5 |
| 10. The idea of piloting my own single-engine plane over the ocean appeals to me. | 1 | 2 | 3 | 4 | 5 |
| 11. I regularly send text messages while driving at highway speeds. | 1 | 2 | 3 | 4 | 5 |
| 12. Even if it's against the law, I talk on my cell phone while driving in busy traffic. | 1 | 2 | 3 | 4 | 5 |

**Total score:** _____

## Quiz 4-3 (continued)

***Scoring and Interpretation:*** Obtain your score by adding the numbers you have circled.

- **56–60:** You are a heavy risk taker, bordering on reckless at times. You are most likely not assessing risk carefully enough before proceeding.
- **48–55:** You probably are a sensible risk taker and an adventuresome person in a way that enhances your leadership appeal to others.
- **15–47:** You have a propensity to avoid risks. Your conservatism in this regard could detract from an entrepreneurial leadership style.

Risk taking is important for leadership because both charismatic and entrepreneurial leaders are noted for their risk taking. In addition, it is difficult to bring about change (a vital leadership function) if you are averse to taking risks.

## Gender Differences in Leadership Style

Controversy over whether men and women have different leadership styles continues. Several researchers and observers argue that women have certain acquired traits and behaviors that suit them for relations-oriented leadership. Consequently, women leaders frequently exhibit a cooperative, empowering style that includes nurturing team members. According to this same perspective, men are inclined toward a command-and-control, militaristic leadership style. Women find participative management more natural than do men because they feel more comfortable interacting with people. Furthermore, it is argued that women's natural sensitivity to people gives them an edge over men in encouraging group members to participate in decision making. Here we look briefly at some of the evidence and reasoning showing that gender differences do and do not exist between the leadership styles of today's organizational leaders.

As many researchers use the term, *gender* refers to perceptions about the differences among males and females. An example would be to believe that women managers tend to be better listeners than their male peers. Gender differences refer to roles that men and women occupy. Sex differences, however, refer to actual (objective and quantitative) differences, such as the fact that the mean height of men exceeds that of women. Nevertheless, the terms *gender* and *sex* are still used interchangeably in general usage and to some extent in scholarly writings.

***The Argument for Male–Female Differences in Leadership Style***  Judy Rosener concluded that men and women do tend toward opposite styles. Based on self-reports, she found that men tended toward a command-and-control style. In contrast, women tended toward a transformational style, relying heavily on

Leadership Skill-Building Exercise 4-4

### Entrepreneurial Leadership

An important part of the entrepreneurial role is to convince others of the merit of your idea so that they will invest in your company or lend you money. Two students play the role of a team of entrepreneurs who have a new product or service and want to launch a business. (The two entrepreneurs choose the product or service.) About five other students play the role of a group of venture capitalists or bankers listening to the presentation to decide whether to invest or lend money. The entrepreneurs will communicate excitement and commitment about their product, along with a good business plan. (You might want to quickly review the material about persuasive communication in Chapter 12.) The students who are not participating will evaluate how well the two entrepreneurs displayed aspects of the entrepreneurial leadership style.

interpersonal skills.[42] Another perspective on gender differences is that women entrepreneurs are more likely than their male counterparts to perceive their business as a family. As corporate managers, women tend to place greater emphasis on forming caring, nurturing relationships with employees. Women are also more likely than men to praise group members. And when an employee falls short of expectations, women are more likely to buffer criticism by finding something praiseworthy.[43]

One question relating to gender differences is whether men or women are more effective as leaders. Eighteen hundred men and women managers from the United States and Canada were matched on organization level, job function, and management experience. Each manager completed a self-evaluation and was also evaluated by an average of one boss, four peers, and four direct reports who used the observer version of the same questionnaire. Leadership differences between men and women leaders were perceived in a similar way by the four groups (self, boss, peers, and direct reports), as follows:

- Women scored higher on leadership scales measuring orientation toward production and obtaining results, whereas men scored higher on scales assessing an orientation toward strategic planning and organizational vision.
- Women were perceived as functioning with more energy, intensity, and emotional expression and a greater capacity to keeps workers enthused. Men were seen as more likely to maintain a low-key style through the control of emotional expression.
- Women were rated higher on relationship-oriented leadership skills by all groups, whereas men were rated higher on task-oriented leadership skills by superiors and peers, but not by direct reports.

Despite these differences, on the dimension of overall effectiveness, the sexes were perceived the same. Superiors gave equal effectiveness ratings to men and women. However, peers and direct reports perceive women as slightly more effective than men. The researchers recommended that women may benefit from additional training in strategic analysis and men may benefit from additional training in interpersonal skills.[44]

Fundamental differences in the biological and psychological makeup of men and women have also been used as evidence that the two sexes are likely to manifest different leadership styles. Brain researchers Raquel Gur and Ruben Gur uncovered one such set of differences. They found that women may be far more sensitive to emotional cues and verbal nuances than men. Women leaders would therefore be more suited to responding to the feelings of group members and understanding what they really mean by certain statements.[45]

Gender differences in communication also are reflected in leadership style. Above all, women are more likely than men to use spoken communication for building relationships and giving emotional support.[46] Men focus more on disseminating information and demonstrating competence. Women are therefore more likely to choose a relationship-oriented leadership style.

***The Argument Against Gender Differences in Leadership Style***   Based on a literature review, Jan Grant concluded that there are apparently few, if any, personality or behavioral differences between men and women managers. Also, as women move up the corporate ladder, their identification with the male model of managerial success becomes important; they consequently reject even the few managerial feminine traits they may have earlier endorsed.[47]

To what extent the stereotypes of men and women leaders are true is difficult to judge. Even if male and female differences in leadership style do exist, they must be placed in proper perspective. Both men and women leaders differ among themselves in leadership style. Plenty of male leaders are relationship oriented, and plenty of women practice command and control (the extreme task orientation). Many women believe that women managers can be more hostile and vindictive than men managers.

Perhaps the best approach to leadership takes advantage of the positive traits of both men and women. To compete in the global marketplace, companies need a diverse leadership team including men and women.[48] Not recognizing that both male and female styles are needed can lead to confusion for women managers. Alice H. Eagly and Linda L. Carli write that female leaders often struggle to cultivate an appropriate and effective leadership style—one that reconciles the communal qualities that people prefer in women with the harsher qualities people think people need to succeed.[49]

## Selecting the Best Leadership Style

An underlying theme of our discussion of leadership styles, and the next chapter, is that there is no one best or most effective leadership style. A study with 3,000 executives revealed that leaders who get the best results do not rely on one style. Instead, they use several different styles in one week, such as by being autocratic in some situations and democratic in others.[50] Another consideration is the national culture in which the leadership takes place. For example, an effective leadership style for most German workers would be a high performance (task) orientation and a modest amount of compassion (consideration).[51]

The organizational culture also influences which leadership style will be tolerated and effective. A friendly, collaborative culture calls for more of a consensus style of leadership. In contrast, in a perform-or-perish culture, a more directive or autocratic leadership style will be effective. Many insiders believe that one of the reasons Carly Fiorina met with mixed success in her rein at Hewlett-Packard Corp. was because her authoritarian, insensitive leadership style clashed with the collaborative HP culture. (Fiorina strongly disagrees that she was not a huge success at HP, and she regards her critics as people who were reluctant to accept change.)

Thirty-five years ago pioneering researcher Ralph Stogdill made a statement about selecting a leadership style that still holds today: "The most effective leaders appear to exhibit a degree of versatility and flexibility that enables them to adapt their behavior to the changing and contradictory demands made on them."[52]

Leadership Self-Assessment Quiz 4-4 gives you an opportunity to think about your own willingness to adapt to circumstances as a leader. By developing such flexibility, you increase your chances of becoming an effective leader—one who achieves high productivity, quality, and satisfaction. Finally, before moving on to the end-of-chapter activities, do Leadership Skill-Building Exercise 4-5.

 ## Leadership Self-Assessment Quiz 4-4

### How Flexible Are You?

***Instructions:*** To succeed as a managerial leader, a person needs a flexible style: an ability to be open to others and a willingness to listen. Where do you stand on being flexible? Test yourself by answering "often," "sometimes," or "rarely" to the following questions.

1. Do you tend to seek out only those people who agree with your analysis of issues?     _____

2. Do you ignore most of the advice from coworkers about process improvements?     _____

3. Do your team members go along with what you say just to avoid an argument?     _____

## Quiz 4-4 (continued)

4. Have people referred to you as "rigid" or "close minded" on several occasions?    _____

5. When presented with a new method, do you immediately look for a flaw?    _____

6. Do you make up your mind early on with respect to an issue, and then hold firmly to your opinion?    _____

7. When people disagree with you, do you tend to belittle them or become argumentative?    _____

8. Do you often feel you are the only person in the group who really understands the problem?    _____

***Check Your Score:*** If you answered "rarely" to seven or eight questions, you are unusually adaptable. If you answered "sometimes" to at least five questions, you are on the right track, but more flexibility would benefit your leadership. If you answered "often" to more than four questions, you have a long way to go to improve your flexibility and adaptability. You are also brutally honest about your faults, which could be an asset.

 ## Leadership Skill-Building Exercise 4-5

### Contrasting Leadership Styles

One student plays the role of a new associate working for a financial services firm that sells life insurance and other investments. The associate has completed a six-week training program and is now working full-time. Four weeks have passed, and the associate still has not made a sale. The associate's boss is going to meet with him or her today to discuss progress. Another student plays the role of a task-oriented leader. The two people participate in the review session

Before playing (or assuming) the role of the associate or the boss, think for a few minutes how you would behave if you were placed in that role in real life. Empathize with the frustrated associate or the task-oriented leader. A good role player is both a scriptwriter and an actor.

Another two students repeat the same scenario except that this time the manager is a strongly relationship-oriented leader. Two more pairs of students then have their turn at acting out the task-oriented and relationship-oriented performance reviews. Another variation of this role play is for one person to play the roles of both the task-oriented and the relationship-oriented boss. Other class members observe and provide feedback on the effectiveness of the two styles of leadership.

### Reader's Roadmap

So far in this book, we have examined the nature of leadership and the inner qualities of leaders, along with their behaviors, attitudes, and styles. In the next chapter, we describe some of the specific approaches to adapting one's leadership approach to the situation.

## SUMMARY

Effective leadership requires the right behaviors, skills, and attitudes, as emphasized in the classic Ohio State University studies. Two major dimensions of leadership behavior were identified: consideration and initiating structure. Consideration is the degree to which the leader creates an environment of emotional support, warmth, friendliness, and trust. Making connections with people is a current aspect of consideration. Initiating structure is the degree to which the leader organizes and defines relationships in the group by such activities as assigning tasks and specifying procedures. Both consideration and initiating structure are related to important leadership outcomes such as job satisfaction and performance.

Many task-related attitudes and behaviors of effective leaders have been identified. Among them are (1) adaptability to the situation, (2) direction setting, (3) high performance standards, (4) concentrating on strengths of group members, (5) risk taking and execution of plans, (6) hands-on guidance and feedback, and (7) ability to ask tough questions.

Many relationship-oriented attitudes and behaviors of leaders have also been identified. Among them are (1) aligning people, (2) openness to workers' opinions, (3) creating inspiration and visibility, (4) satisfying higher-level needs, (5) giving emotional support and encouragement, (6) promoting principles and values, and (7) being a servant leader.

Servant leaders are committed to serving others rather than achieving their own goals. Aspects of servant leadership include placing service before self-interest, listening to others, inspiring trust by being trustworthy, focusing on what is feasible to accomplish, lending a hand, and emotional healing.

Many leaders receive extensive feedback on their behaviors and attitudes in the form of 360-degree feedback, whereby people who work for or with the leader provide feedback on the leader's performance. Such feedback is likely to be useful when the feedback relates to business goals and strategy and to important aspects of leadership, when training is provided in giving and receiving feedback, when action plans are developed, and when managers own the feedback evaluation.

Understanding leadership style is an extension of understanding leadership attitudes and behavior. Participative leaders share decision making with group members. The participative style can be subdivided into consultative, consensus, and democratic leadership. The participative style is well suited to managing competent people who are eager to assume responsibility. Yet the process can be time-consuming, and some managers perceive it to be a threat to their power. Autocratic leaders retain most of the authority for themselves. The Leadership Grid™ classifies leaders according to their concern for both production (task accomplishment) and people.

Another important style of leader is the entrepreneur. The entrepreneurial style stems from the leader's personal characteristics and the circumstances of self-employment. It includes a strong achievement drive and sensible risk taking; a high degree of enthusiasm and creativity; the tendency to act quickly on opportunities; hurriedness and impatience; a visionary perspective; a dislike of hierarchy and bureaucracy; a preference for dealing with external customers; and an eye on the future.

Male–female differences in leadership style have been observed. Women have a tendency toward relationship-oriented leadership, whereas men tend toward command and control. A major study showed that men and women leaders are perceived to be about equally effective. Some people argue that male–female differences in leadership are inconsistent and not significant.

Rather than searching for the one best style of leadership, managers are advised to diagnose the situation and then choose an appropriate leadership style to match. To be effective, a leader must be able to adapt his or her style to the circumstances.

## KEY TERMS

| | | |
|---|---|---|
| Effective leader | Management openness | Consultative leaders |
| Consideration | Servant leader | Consensus leaders |
| Initiating structure | 360-degree feedback | Democratic leaders |
| Pygmalion effect | Leadership style | Autocratic leaders |
| Tough question | Participative leaders | Leadership Grid™ |

##  GUIDELINES FOR ACTION AND SKILL DEVELOPMENT

Most leadership style classifications are based on the directive (task-oriented) dimension versus the nondirective (relationship-oriented) dimension. In deciding which of these two styles is best, consider the following questions:

1. **What is the structure of your organization and the nature of your work?** You might decide, for example, that stricter control is necessary for some types of work, such as dealing with proprietary information.
2. **Which style suits you best?** Your personality, values, and beliefs influence how readily you can turn over responsibility to others.
3. **Which style suits your boss and the organization culture?** For example, a boss who is highly directive may perceive you as weak if you are too nondirective. In a tough-minded, perform-or-perish culture, you might want to use a highly directive leadership style.
4. **How readily will you be able to change your style if good results are not forthcoming?** Morale can suffer if you grant too much latitude today and have to tighten control in the future.
5. **Is there high potential for conflict in the work unit?** A directive leadership style can trigger conflict with independent, strong-willed people. A more nondirective style allows for more freedom of discussion, which defuses conflict.[53]

### Discussion Questions and Activities

1. How is initiating structure related to the cognitive skills of a leader?
2. Give an example of a high-consideration behavior that a supervisor of yours showed on your behalf. What was your reaction to his or her behavior?
3. Why is direction setting still an important leadership behavior in an era of empowerment?
4. Why is an effective leader supposed to provide emotional support to team members, even when they are mature adults?
5. In what ways might a *personalized charismatic leader* have quite different motives than a servant leader?
6. How might a manager use email to help carry out both task-oriented and relationship-oriented behaviors?
7. What might the manager of an H & R Block or Hewlett Jackson branch do to provide hands-on leadership to the tax preparers?
8. How would you characterize the leadership style of your favorite executive, athletic coach, or television character who plays a boss?
9. Why is the consensus leadership style widely recommended for providing leadership to workers under age 35?
10. What can a man do to overcome the stereotype that people expect him to be a command-and-control style leader?

## Leadership Case Problem A

### Is Margo Too Macro?

Margo Santelli is the director of the municipal bond group of a financial services firm. Santelli has four managers reporting to her, each of whom supervises a unit of the group, including retail sales, institutional sales, customer service, and internal administration.

Laura Gordon, the branch director and company vice president, heard rumblings that the group was not receiving enough supervision, so she decided to investigate. During a dinner meeting requested by Laura, she asked Margo about her approach to leading the group. Margo replied:

> "I am leading my four managers as if they are all responsible professionals. I believe in management by exception. Unless I am aware of a problem, I am hesitant to get involved in how my managers conduct their work. Don't forget that as the head of the municipal bond group, I have some responsibility for spending time with major customers as well as meeting with you and other senior executives.
>
> "I do hold a weekly meeting, and conduct my annual performance reviews as required."

Laura thanked Margo for having attended the dinner, and said that the meeting was informative. With Margo's permission, Laura said that she would be visiting the municipal bond group to have a few casual conversations with the four managers.

When asked about Margo's leadership, the first manager said his nickname for Santelli was Macro Margo because, instead of being a micromanager, she went to the other extreme and was a *macromanager*, who had minimal contact with the group. He added that at times Margo didn't seem to even care what was happening. The manager said, "I recently asked Margo's advice about finding a good contact who could introduce me to the pension fund manager of a hospital. Margo told me that a big part of my job was to develop contacts on my own."

The second manager Laura spoke to said that she enjoyed working with Margo because she was a nice person who didn't get in her hair. "I don't need a boss to remind me to attain my goals or get my work done on time. A little smile of encouragement here and there is all I need," the manager said.

The third manager said to Laura, "I think Margo would be a great manager for me a few years down the road. But right now, I do not want to feel so much on my own. Margo is a talented person who I could learn from. Yet she is more involved with customers and higher-level management than she is her managers. I'm new in the field, so I could use more of a coaching style of manager."

The fourth manager said, "I remember meeting Margo a few times, but I don't remember much about her. You said she is my manager? I don't care if my comments get back, because I'm joining a competitor next month."

### Questions

1. To what extent has Margo Santelli chosen the right approach to leading the managers in her unit of the financial services firm?
2. What advice can you offer Margo to be a more effective leader?
3. What advice can you offer Laura to help Margo be a more effective leader?
4. Explain whether or not you think Laura was justified in asking Margo's direct reports about Margo's approach to leadership.

## Leadership Case Problem B

### Failure Pumps Up Dick Enrico

When Dick Enrico started Scarpelli's Italian restaurant in Minneapolis in the early 1970s, he wanted to give it a 1930s-style gangster atmosphere. But with only $15,000, his budget was too tight for elaborate décor. So he persuaded a local art-school teacher to give her students an unusual assignment: create tommy guns and papier-mâché busts of gangsters for the eatery. To make the menus look authentic, he shot holes in them with a .22-caliber rifle. The restaurant started with a bang, but momentum slipped, and in the end he sold the operation at a loss.

Enrico was never short on ideas, but it has taken a long string of failures for the 64-year-old entrepreneur to learn how to create a lasting success. Throughout his forty-six years as an entrepreneur, he has started twenty businesses that have folded or been sold at fire-sale prices, including a waterbed retailer and a franchise that helped people quit smoking.

But as difficult as Enrico's startup attempts proved to be—they cost him millions of dollars and at one point drove him into depression—his string of failures eventually helped lead to success. Although some of his ideas, Enrico says, were "just ahead of my time," many of the concepts were workable. The failures helped him realize that his biggest problem was not generating new ventures, but running them.

So after Enrico opened an exercise-equipment store in 1992, he took a different route and found a manager to run the day-to-day business while he focused on big-picture ideas to build the company. The result is that 2nd Wind Exercise Equipment, Inc, has expanded into a chain of 100 stores that is now generating $100 million in annual revenue. It has added new equipment from eleven manufacturers and now operates in five midwestern states, and it has plans to expand into two more states.

### Different Paths

In the past, the sting of Enrico's numerous setbacks had been compounded by the success of his younger brother. As Dick Enrico struggled to prop up ailing ventures, Roger Enrico was ascending within the ranks of PepsiCo, Inc., rising to president and then chief executive and chairman. "I probably felt so inferior," Dick Enrico says.

Dick Enrico started his career selling pots and pans door to door, and then he established a cookware sales operation of his own. Many later ventures failed. One business, United Crane, Inc., sold vending machines with tiny cranes that picked up stuffed animals. His waterbed stores, called Aqua Knight, were among his other failures. Enrico attributes his failures largely to poor management, including the need for greater oversight to prevent theft and inventory shortages. Aqua Knight went under because Enrico tried to handle everything from accounting to sales. Besides being too stretched to think, Enrico became bored and impatient with the operational work, which he considered tedious.

### Going "Broke" Again

Enrico says he financed his ventures by borrowing from banks, friends, and credit cards, although he is vague about how he continued to get backing after so many failures. "I just worked at it," he says. "A deal here, a deal there—whatever. But it was tough." He described himself as going "broke" on three separate occasions. His brother invested in two of his ideas.

Brad Krohn, chairman and chief executive of the Business Bank in Minnetonka, says that even after five of Enrico's ideas flopped, he was not hesitant to continue lending him money. "For most people I would be, but it all comes down to character," Krohn says. Enrico always paid him back.

In 1986 Enrico pulled out of a long slump by selling car phones. With cash in his pocket and spirits lifted, in 1992 he began renting and selling used exercise equipment that he found through classified advertisements in newspapers. He sold his 1986 Corvette to finance the venture, which he called 2nd Wind Exercise Equipment, and bought forty used

NordicTrack machines. Demand became so strong that he could not find enough stationary bikes and treadmills to fill his stores. When he asked equipment vendors to supply him with new products, they turned him down, saying he was "an embarrassment to the industry . . . a scratch-and-dent joint," Enrico says.

Finally, though, one supplier agreed to sell him new treadmills, and the business grew more rapidly. Enrico turned to Martin Bruder, a former supervisor for a health-club chain, to take over 2nd Wind's operation. Under his management, the company has boosted earnings and retail outlets. Enrico continues to appear in the company's advertisements and scouts out new locations of new sites, but he stays out of day-today operations. "I realized the importance of quality people" running the operation, says Enrico.

### The Future

Dick and Roger Enrico became closer in the early 1990s when Roger Enrico began making trips to Minneapolis for meetings of Target Corporation's board, on which he serves as a director. When they ate dinner together, they talked mostly about business. Dick Enrico liked to hear about the executives he read about in the newspapers, and Roger Enrico enjoyed listening to his brother's colorful stories and new ideas.

As 2nd Wind grew bigger, Roger Enrico began listening with a more discerning ear. In May 2004 he flew a group of representatives from a private equity firm to Minneapolis to meet Dick Enrico. They wanted to know if 2nd Wind could expand to other major markets, and Enrico ultimately did expand considerably.

"He's the quintessential man of perseverance," Roger Enrico says. "And if you think about what makes really good business leaders—people who can build and grow things—it is that quality to persevere and to stay with it."

### Questions

1. What recommendations can you offer Dick Enrico to improve his chances of staying successful for the rest of his career?
2. What does Enrico's story illustrate about the difference between leadership and management?
3. Identify several entrepreneurial traits and characteristics Dick Enrico possesses, and justify your answer. Base part of your answer on the pitch he delivers on his video, shown on www.2ndwindexercise.com. Comment on Enrico's communication skills.

Source: Adapted from Janet Adamy, "Try, Try, Again," *The Wall Street Journal*, July 12, 2004, p. R9; www.2ndwindexercise.com, accessed December 24, 2007.

## Leadership Skill-Building Exercise 4-6

### My Leadership Portfolio

For this addition to your leadership portfolio, identify four leadership task-oriented behaviors or relationship-oriented behaviors that you have demonstrated this week. Your list can be any combination of the two sets of behaviors. Also jot down the result you achieved by exercising these behaviors. Here is an example:

"Thursday night I applied *direction setting* and it really worked. We have a group assignment in our marketing class with each group consisting of about five people. Our assignment is to analyze how well employee self-service is working in supermarkets and home-improvement stores. The group was hitting a wall because in their Internet searches they were finding mostly advertisements for Home Depot and the like. I suggested that we each visit a supermarket or home-improvement store and make firsthand observations of the customers who were using the automated checkout system. I also suggested we ask a couple of questions of the store associate supervising the activity. The group loved my idea, and the project was a big success. We supplemented written articles with a firsthand field study. I set the group in the right direction."

## Internet Skill-Building Exercise

### Identifying Leadership Behaviors and Attitudes

Select a business or sports leader of interest to you. If you cannot think of a leader offhand, visit web sites of a company or athletic team that might interest you. For example, if you have been a fan of Kellogg Corporation products for a long time, search the Kellogg web site to identify a key company executive. Search the site for any clues to the executive's leadership behaviors and attitudes, as perhaps revealed in statements about employee relations or management philosophy. For example, an executive might make a statement about where the company is headed in the next five years, thereby indicating *direction setting*. You will probably not get enough information on the company web site, so plug your leader's name into a search engine to find two articles about him or her.

After you have gathered your case history information, identify at least four separate leadership behaviors and attitudes practiced by the leader in question. You will have to make inferences because a leader will rarely say, "Here are my leadership behaviors and attitudes."

Apply the chapter concepts! Visit the Web and complete this Internet skill-building exercise to learn more about current leadership topics and trends.

# Contingency and Situational Leadership

## CHAPTER 5

## LEARNING OBJECTIVES

After studying this chapter and doing the exercises, you should be able to

- Describe how the situation influences the choice of leadership objectives.

- Present an overview of the contingency theory of leadership effectiveness.

- Explain the path-goal theory of leadership effectiveness.

- Explain Situational Leadership® II (SLII).

- Use the normative decision model to determine the most appropriate decision-making style in a given situation.

- Explain the cognitive resource theory as a contingency approach.

- Describe an approach to contingency management for leading an entire enterprise.

- Explain the basics of leadership during a crisis.

- Explain how evidence-based leadership can contribute to contingency and situational leadership.

## CHAPTER OUTLINE

redicting a blockbuster, Pfizer introduces the diabetes drug Exubera, a form of insulin inhaled through a tubular device. It's quickly dismissed as a "medicinal bong" by a prominent diabetic blogger. At almost the same time, the president of the American Diabetes Association, citing lung-function risks, says, "I see it as my job to talk people out of it." Pfizer quickly gives up on the product, taking a $2.8 billion write-off. [1]

The incident about making an unanticipated and embarrassing mistake in introducing a new drug illustrates an increasingly important leadership task: leading people through a crisis. Leadership of this type is a special case of the general subject of this chapter—adjusting one's approach to the situation. Contingency and situational leadership further expands the study of leadership styles by adding more specific guidelines about which style to use under which circumstance.

In this chapter we present an overview of the situational perspective on leadership. We then summarize the five best-known contingency theories of leadership: Fiedler's contingency theory, path-goal theory, the situational leadership model, the normative decision model, and cognitive resource theory. We also describe a contingency model that applies mostly to CEOs. In addition, we describe crisis leadership, because leading others through a crisis has become a frequent challenge in recent years. Finally, we describe how evidence-based leadership and management contribute to the contingency approach.

## SITUATIONAL INFLUENCES ON EFFECTIVE LEADERSHIP BEHAVIOR

The situation can influence the leadership behavior or style a leader emphasizes. The essence of a **contingency approach to leadership** is that leaders are most effective when they make their behavior contingent on situational forces, including group member characteristics. Both the internal and the external environment have a significant impact on leader effectiveness. For example, the quality of the work force and the competitiveness of the environment can influence which behaviors the leader emphasizes. A manager who supervises competent employees might be able to practice consensus leadership readily. And a manager who faces a competitive environment might find it easier to align people to pursue a new vision.

A useful perspective on implementing contingency leadership is that the manager must be flexible enough to avoid clinging to old ideas that no longer fit the current circumstances. [2] Being stubborn about what will work in a given situation and clinging to old ideas can result in ineffective leadership. The effective leader adapts to changing circumstances. For example, at one point offering employees generous benefits might not have been motivational. In reality, with many employers having cut back on benefits such as health insurance, these benefits can be helpful in attracting and retaining workers.

As mentioned at several places in this text, the organizational culture is a major situational variable the leader needs to take into account in choosing which approach to leadership will lead to favorable outcomes. A command-and-control leadership style may not be effective in a company with a collaborative, friendly organizational culture. If the culture seems at odds with what a highly placed leader wants to accomplish, he or she may attempt to change the culture. For example, when Jim McNerney was the top executive at 3M, he worked successfully on getting the innovative culture to become more aware of costs and profits.

Victor H. Vroom and Arthur G. Jago have recently identified three conclusions about the role of situations in leadership, and these findings support the model of leadership presented in Figure 1-2, Chapter 1. The conclusions are geared to support the idea that leadership involves motivating others to work collaboratively in the pursuit of a common goal.[3]

**1. *Organizational effectiveness is affected by situational factors not under leader control.*** The leader might be able to influence the situation, yet some situational factors are beyond the leader's complete control. The manager of a prosperous, independent coffee shop might be running her business and leading her employees successfully for ten years. Suddenly a Starbucks opens across the street, thereby seriously affecting her ability to lead a successful enterprise. She might be smart enough to have a contingency plan of offering services Starbucks cannot match, yet staying in business will be a struggle.

**2. *Situations shape how leaders behave.*** Contingency theorists believe that forces in the situation are three times as strong as the leader's personal characteristics in shaping his or her behavior. How the leader behaves is therefore substantially influenced by environmental forces. In the face of competition from Starbucks, our coffee shop owner might now act with a greater sense of urgency, be much more directive in telling her workers what to do, and become much less warm and friendly. Her normal level of enthusiasm might also diminish.

**3. *Situations influence the consequences of leader behavior.*** Popular books about management and leadership assume that certain types of leader behavior work in every situation. Situational theorists disagree strongly with this position. Instead, a specific type of leadership behavior might have different outcomes in different situations. The leader behavior of empowerment illustrates this idea. Perhaps empowerment will work for our coffee shop owner because she has a group of dedicated workers who want their jobs and her enterprise to endure. Yet empowering incompetent workers with a weak work ethic is likely to backfire because the workers will most likely resist additional responsibility.

# FIEDLER'S CONTINGENCY THEORY OF LEADERSHIP EFFECTIVENESS

Fred E. Fiedler developed a widely researched and quoted contingency model more than forty years ago that holds that the best style of leadership is determined by the situation in which the leader is working.[4] Here we examine how the style and situation are evaluated, the overall findings of the theory, and how leaders can modify situations to their advantage.

### Measuring Leadership Style: The Least Preferred Coworker (LPC) Scale

Fiedler's theory classifies a manager's leadership style as relationship motivated or task motivated. Style is therefore based on the extent to which the leader is relationship motivated or task motivated. According to Fiedler, leadership style is a relatively permanent aspect of behavior and thus difficult to modify. He reasons that once leaders understand their particular leadership style, they should work in situations that match that style. Similarly, the organization should help managers match leadership styles and situations.

The least preferred coworker (LPC) scale measures the degree to which a leader describes favorably or unfavorably his or her least preferred coworker—that is, an employee with whom he or she could work the *least well*. A leader who describes the LPC in relatively favorable terms tends to be relationship motivated. In contrast, a person who describes this coworker in an unfavorable manner tends to be task motivated. You can use Leadership Self-Assessment Quiz 5-1 to measure your leadership style.

 **Leadership Self-Assessment Quiz 5-1**

### The Least Preferred Coworker (LPC) Scale for Measuring Leadership Style

Throughout your life, you will work in many groups with a wide variety of people—on your job, in social groups, in religious organizations, in volunteer groups, on athletic teams, and in many other situations. Some of your coworkers may be very easy to work with in attaining the group's goals, while others less so.

Think of all the people with whom you have ever worked, and then think of the person with whom you could work *least well*. He or she may be someone with whom you work now or someone with whom you worked in the past. This does not have to be the person you liked least well, but should be the person with whom you had the most difficulty getting a job done—the *one* individual with whom you could work *least well*.

Describe this person on the scale that follows by placing an X in the appropriate space. Look at the words at both ends of the line before you mark your X. *There are no right or wrong answers*. Work rapidly: Your first answer is likely to be the right one. Do not omit any items, and mark each item only once. Now describe the person with whom you can work least well.

|  |  |  |  |  |  |  |  |  |  | Scoring |
|---|---|---|---|---|---|---|---|---|---|---|
| Pleasant | — 8 | — 7 | — 6 | — 5 | — 4 | — 3 | — 2 | — 1 | Unpleasant | ___ |
| Friendly | — 8 | — 7 | — 6 | — 5 | — 4 | — 3 | — 2 | — 1 | Unfriendly | ___ |
| Rejecting | — 1 | — 2 | — 3 | — 4 | — 5 | — 6 | — 7 | — 8 | Accepting | ___ |
| Tense | — 1 | — 2 | — 3 | — 4 | — 5 | — 6 | — 7 | — 8 | Relaxed | ___ |

## Quiz 5-1 (continued)

**Scoring**

| | 1 | 2 | 3 | 4 | 5 | 6 | 7 | 8 | | Scoring |
|---|---|---|---|---|---|---|---|---|---|---|
| Distant | 1 | 2 | 3 | 4 | 5 | 6 | 7 | 8 | Close | ____ |
| Cold | 1 | 2 | 3 | 4 | 5 | 6 | 7 | 8 | Warm | ____ |
| Supportive | 8 | 7 | 6 | 5 | 4 | 3 | 2 | 1 | Hostile | ____ |
| Boring | 1 | 2 | 3 | 4 | 5 | 6 | 7 | 8 | Interesting | ____ |
| Quarrelsome | 1 | 2 | 3 | 4 | 5 | 6 | 7 | 8 | Harmonious | ____ |
| Gloomy | 1 | 2 | 3 | 4 | 5 | 6 | 7 | 8 | Cheerful | ____ |
| Open | 8 | 7 | 6 | 5 | 4 | 3 | 2 | 1 | Guarded | ____ |
| Backbiting | 1 | 2 | 3 | 4 | 5 | 6 | 7 | 8 | Loyal | ____ |
| Untrust-worthy | 1 | 1 | 1 | 1 | 1 | 1 | 1 | 1 | Trustworthy | ____ |
| Considerate | 8 | 7 | 6 | 5 | 4 | 3 | 2 | 1 | Inconsiderate | ____ |
| Nasty | 1 | 2 | 3 | 4 | 5 | 6 | 7 | 8 | Nice | ____ |
| Agreeable | 8 | 7 | 6 | 5 | 4 | 3 | 2 | 1 | Disagreeable | ____ |
| Insincere | 1 | 2 | 3 | 4 | 5 | 6 | 7 | 8 | Sincere | ____ |
| Kind | 8 | 7 | 6 | 5 | 4 | 3 | 2 | 1 | Unkind | ____ |

**Total score:** _____

***Scoring and Interpretation:*** To calculate your score, add the numbers in the right column. If you scored 73 or higher, you are a high LPC leader, meaning that you are relationship motivated. If you scored 64 or lower, you are a low LPC leader, meaning that you are task motivated. A score of 65 to 72 places you in the intermediate range. Compare your score to your score in Leadership Self-Assessment Quiz 4-1.

## Quiz 5-1 (continued)

In attempting to make sense of your score, recognize that the LPC scale is but one measure of leadership style and that the approach to measurement is indirect and somewhat abstract. The leadership style measure presented in Leadership Self-Assessment Quiz 4-1 is more direct. To repeat, the general idea of the LPC approach is that if you have a positive, charitable attitude toward people you had a difficult time working with, you are probably relationship oriented. In contrast, if you took a dim view of people who gave you a hard time, you are probably task oriented. The message here is that a relationship-oriented leader should be able to work well with a variety of personalities.

*Source:* Adapted from Fred E. Fiedler, Martin M. Chemers, and Linda Mahar, *Improving Leadership Effectiveness.* Copyright © 1976 John Wiley & Sons Inc. Reprinted by permission of John Wiley & Sons Inc.

### Measuring the Leadership Situation

Fiedler's contingency theory classifies situations as high, moderate, and low control. The more control that the leader exercises, the more favorable the situation is for him or her. The control classifications are determined by rating the situation on its three dimensions: (1) *leader–member relations* measure how well the group and the leader get along; (2) *task structure* measures how clearly the procedures, goals, and evaluation of the job are defined; and (3) *position power* measures the leader's authority to hire, fire, discipline, and grant salary increases to group members.

Leader–member relations contribute as much to situation favorability as do task structure and position power combined. The leader therefore has the most control in a situation in which his or her relationships with members are the best.

### Overall Findings

The key points of Fiedler's contingency theory are summarized and simplified in Figure 5-1. The original theory is much more complex. Leadership effectiveness depends on matching leaders to situations in which they can exercise more control. A leader should therefore be placed in a situation that is favorable to, or matches, his or her style. If this cannot be accomplished, the situation might be modified to match the leader's style by manipulating one or more of the three following situational variables.

The theory states that task-motivated leaders perform the best in situations of both high control and low control. Relationship-motivated leaders perform the best in situations of moderate control. The results of many studies indicated that the relationship-motivated leader outperformed the task-motivated leader in three of the eight situations but that the reverse was true in the other five situations. The eight situations result from each of the three situational variables being classified in one of two ways (good or poor, high or low, or strong or weak), as shown in Figure 5-2.

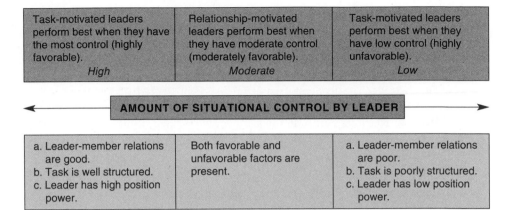

FIGURE 5-1 Summary of Findings from Fiedler's Contingency Theory.

Task-motivated leaders perform better in situations that are highly favorable for exercising control because they do not have to be concerned with the task. Instead, they can work on relationships. In moderately favorable situations, the relationship-motivated leader achieves higher group productivity because he or she can work on relationships and not get involved in overmanaging. In very-low-control situations, the task-motivated leader is able to structure and make sense out of confusion, whereas the relationship-motivated leader wants to give emotional support to group members or call a meeting.

## Making the Situation More Favorable for the Leader

A practical implication of contingency theory is that leaders should modify situations to match their leadership style, thereby enhancing their chances of being effective. Consider a group of leaders who are task motivated and decide that they need to exercise more control over the situation to achieve higher work-unit productivity. To increase control over the situation, they can do one or more of the following:

■ Improve leader–member relations through displaying an interest in the personal welfare of group members, having meals with them, actively listening to their concerns, telling anecdotes, and in general being a "nice person."

### Situational Characteristics

| Situation (Octant) Number → | 1 | 2 | 3 | 4 | 5 | 6 | 7 | 8 |
|---|---|---|---|---|---|---|---|---|
| **Leader–Member Relations** | Good | Good | Good | Good | Poor | Poor | Poor | Poor |
| **Task Structure** | High | High | Low | Low | High | High | Low | Low |
| **Position Power** | Strong | Weak | Strong | Weak | Strong | Weak | Strong | Weak |

FIGURE 5-2 The Eight Different Situations in Fiedler's Contingency Theory.

- Increase task structure by engaging in behaviors related to initiating structure, such as being more specific about expectations, providing deadlines, showing samples of acceptable work, and providing written instructions.
- Exercise more position power by requesting more formal authority from higher management. For example, the leader might let it be known that he or she has the authority to grant bonuses and make strong recommendations for promotion.

Now imagine a relationship-motivated leader who wants to create a situation of moderate favorability so that his or her interests in being needed by the group could be satisfied. The leader might give the group tasks of low structure and de-emphasize his or her position power.

### Evaluation of Fiedler's Contingency Theory

A major contribution of Fiedler's work is that it has prompted others to conduct studies about the contingency nature of leadership. Fiedler's theory has been one of the most widely researched theories in industrial/organizational psychology, and at one time it was used extensively as the basis for leadership training programs. The model has also alerted leaders to the importance of sizing up the situation to gain control. At the same time, Fiedler pioneered in taking into account both traits and the situation to better understand leadership.[5]

Despite its potential advantages, however, the contingency theory is too complicated to have much of an impact on most leaders. A major problem centers on matching the situation to the leader. In most situations, the amount of control the leader exercises varies from time to time. For example, if a relationship-motivated leader were to find the situation becoming too favorable for exercising control, it is doubtful that he or she would be transferred to a less favorable situation or attempt to make the situation less favorable.

## THE PATH-GOAL THEORY OF LEADERSHIP EFFECTIVENESS

The **path-goal theory** of leadership effectiveness, as developed by Robert House, specifies what a leader must do to achieve high productivity and morale in a given situation. In general, a leader attempts to clarify the path to a goal for a group member so that he or she receives personal payoffs. At the same time, this group member's job satisfaction and performance increase.[6] Like the expectancy theory of motivation, on which it is based, path-goal theory is multifaceted and has several versions. Its key features are summarized in Figure 5-3.

The theory is so complex that it is helpful to take an overview before studying more of the details. The major proposition of path-goal theory is that the manager should choose a leadership style that takes into account the characteristics of the group members and the demands of the task. Furthermore, initiating structure will be effective in situations with a low degree of subordinate task structure, but ineffective in highly structured task situations. The rationale is that in the first situation, subordinates welcome initiating structure because it helps to provide

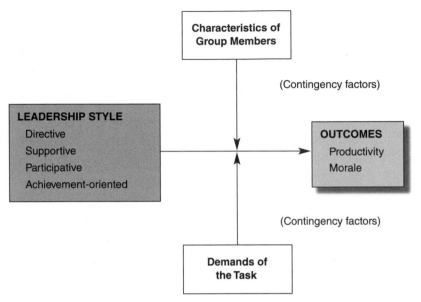

**FIGURE 5-3** The Path-Goal Theory of Leadership.
To achieve the outcomes of productivity and morale, the manager chooses one of
four leadership styles, depending on (a) the characteristics of the situation, and (b) the
demands of the task.

structure to their somewhat ambiguous tasks. Instead of just flailing around, the leader provides guidance. In the situation of highly structured tasks, more structure is seen as unnecessary and associated with overly close supervision.[7]

In his reformulated version of path-goal theory, House offered a meta-proposition, which provides a capsule summary of a dizzying amount of studies and theorizing in relation to the theory. Understanding this meta-proposition would be a good take-away from the theory: For leaders to be effective, they should engage in behaviors that complement subordinates' environments and abilities. They should engage in these behaviors in a manner that compensates for deficiencies, and that enhances subordinate satisfactions as well as individual and work-unit performance.[8] For example, if our coffee shop owner found that one of her workers was fearful of losing his job because of Starbucks competition, she would give him lots of encouragement and explain the survival plan of the coffee shop in detail.

Two key aspects of this theory will be discussed: matching the leadership style to the situation and steps the leader can take to influence performance and satisfaction.

## Matching the Leadership Style to the Situation

Path-goal theory emphasizes that the leader should choose among four leadership styles to achieve optimum results in a given situation. Two important sets of contingency factors are the type of subordinates and the tasks they perform (a key environmental factor). The type of subordinates is determined by how much control they think they have over the environment (locus of control) and by how well they think they can do the assigned task.

Environmental contingency factors are those that are not within the control of group members but influence satisfaction and task accomplishment. Three broad classifications of contingency factors in the environment are (1) the group members' tasks, (2) the authority system within the organization, and (3) the work group.

To use path-goal theory, the leader must first assess the relevant variables in the environment. Then she or he selects the one of the four styles listed next that fits those contingency factors best:

1. ***Directive style.*** The leader who is directive (similar to task motivated) emphasizes formal activities such as planning, organizing, and controlling. When the task is unclear, the directive style improves morale.
2. ***Supportive style.*** The leader who is supportive (similar to relationship motivated) displays concern for group members' well-being and creates an emotionally supportive climate. He or she enhances morale when group members work on dissatisfying, stressful, or frustrating tasks. Group members who are unsure of themselves prefer the supportive leadership style.
3. ***Participative style.*** The leader who is participative consults with group members to gather their suggestions, and then considers these suggestions seriously when making a decision. The participative leader is best suited for improving the morale of well-motivated employees who perform nonrepetitive tasks.
4. ***Achievement-oriented style.*** The leader who is achievement oriented sets challenging goals, pushes for work improvement, and sets high expectations for team members, who are also expected to assume responsibility. This leadership style works well with achievement-oriented team members and with those working on ambiguous and nonrepetitive tasks.

A leader can sometimes successfully combine more than one of the four styles, although this possibility is not specified in path-goal theory. For example, during a crisis, such as a major product recall, the marketing manager might need to be directive to help the group take fast action. After the initial emergency actions have been taken, the leader, recognizing how stressed the workers must be, might shift to a supportive mode.

## Steps Leaders Can Take to Influence Performance and Satisfaction

In addition to recommending the leadership style to fit the situation, the path-goal theory offers other suggestions to leaders. Most of them relate to motivation and satisfaction, including the following:

1. Recognize or activate group members' needs over which the leader has control.
2. Increase the personal payoffs to team members for attaining work goals. The leader might give high-performing employees special recognition.

3. Make the paths to payoffs (rewards) easier by coaching and providing direction. For instance, a manager might help a team member be selected for a high-level project.

4. Help group members clarify their expectations of how effort will lead to good performance and how performance will lead to a reward. The leader might say, "Anyone who has gone through this training in the past came away knowing how to implement an ISO 9000 (quality standards) program. And most people who learn how to meet these standards wind up getting a good raise."

5. Reduce frustrating barriers to reaching goals. For example, the leader might hire a temporary worker to help a group member catch up on paperwork and email.

6. Increase opportunities for personal satisfaction if the group member performs effectively. The "if" is important because it reflects contingent behavior on the leader's part.

7. Be careful not to irritate people by giving them instructions on things they already can do well.

8. To obtain high performance and satisfaction, the leader must provide structure if it is missing and supply rewards contingent on adequate performance. To accomplish this, leaders must clarify the desirability of goals for the group members.[9]

As a leader, you can derive specific benefit from path-goal theory by applying these eight methods of influencing performance. Chemers points out that although research interest in path-goal theory has waned in recent years, the basic tenets of the theory are on target. Any comprehensive theory of leadership must include the idea that the leader's actions have a major impact on the motivation and satisfaction of group members.[10] Despite the potential contributions of path-goal theory, it contains so many nuances and complexities that it has attracted little interest from managers.

## SITUATIONAL LEADERSHIP® II (SLII)

The two contingency approaches to leadership presented so far take into account collectively the task, the authority of the leader, and the nature of the subordinates. Another explanation of contingency leadership places its primary emphasis on the characteristics of group members. **Situational Leadership II (SLII)**, developed by Kenneth H. Blanchard and his colleagues, explains how to match leadership style to the capabilities of group members on a given task.[11] For example, you might need less guidance from a supervisor when you are skilled in a task than when you are performing a new task.

SLII is designed to increase the frequency and quality of conversations about performance and professional development between managers and group members so that competence is developed, commitment takes place, and turnover among talented workers is reduced. Leaders are taught to use the leadership style that matches or responds to the needs of the situation.

Before delving further into the situational leadership model, do Leadership Self-Assessment Quiz 5-2. It will help alert you to the specific behaviors involved in regarding the characteristics of group members as key contingency variables in choosing the most effective leadership style.

 ## Leadership Self-Assessment Quiz 5-2

### Measuring Your Situational Perspective

**Instructions:** Indicate how well you agree with the following statements, using the following scale: DS = disagree strongly; D = disagree; N = neutral; A = agree; AS = agree strongly. Circle the most accurate answer.

| | DS | D | N | A | AS |
|---|---|---|---|---|---|
| 1. Workers need to be carefully trained before you can place high expectations on them. | DS | D | N | A | AS |
| 2. The more knowledgeable the worker is, the less he or she needs a clear statement of objectives. | DS | D | N | A | AS |
| 3. "Hand holding" is an ineffective leadership technique for anxious group members. | DS | D | N | A | AS |
| 4. The same well-delivered pep talk will usually appeal to workers at all levels. | DS | D | N | A | AS |
| 5. As a manager, I would invest the least amount of time supervising the most competent workers. | DS | D | N | A | AS |
| 6. It is best not to put much effort into supervising unenthusiastic staff members. | DS | D | N | A | AS |
| 7. An effective leader delegates equal kinds and amounts of work to group members. | DS | D | N | A | AS |
| 8. Even the most effective workers need frequent reassurance and emotional support. | DS | D | N | A | AS |
| 9. If I noticed that a group member seemed insecure and anxious, I would give him or her especially clear instructions and guidelines. | DS | D | N | A | AS |
| 10. Many competent workers get to the point where they require relatively little leadership and supervision. | DS | D | N | A | AS |

**Total score:** _____

## Quiz 5-2 (continued)

### *Scoring and Interpretation*

1. DS = 1, D = 2, N = 3, A = 4, AS = 5
2. DS = 1, D = 2, N = 3, A = 4, AS = 5
3. DS = 5, D = 4, N = 3, A = 2, AS = 1
4. DS = 5, D = 4, N = 3, A = 2, AS = 1
5. DS = 1, D = 2, N = 3, A = 4, AS = 5
6. DS = 5, D = 4, N = 3, A = 2, AS = 1
7. DS = 5, D = 4, N = 3, A = 2, AS = 1
8. DS = 5, D = 4, N = 3, A = 2, AS = 1
9. DS = 1, D = 2, N = 3, A = 4, AS = 5
10. DS = 1, D = 2, N = 3, A = 4, AS = 5

- **45–50 points:** You have (or would have) a strong situational perspective as a leader and manager.
- **30–44 points:** You have (or would have) an average situational perspective as a leader and manager.
- **10–29 points:** You rarely take (or would take) a situational perspective as a leader and manager.

*Skill Development:* For the vast majority of leadership and management assignments, it pays to sharpen your situational perspective. If you scored lower than you want, sharpen your insights into situations by asking yourself, "What are the key factors in this situation that will influence my effectiveness as a leader-manager?" Study both the people and the task in the situation.

### Basics of SLII

**Knowledge Bank**
Contains a description of the original situational model of leadership.

**www.cengage.com/management/dubrin**

Situational Leadership II stems from the original situational model. The major premise of SLII is that the basis for effective leadership is managing the relationship between a leader and a subordinate on a given task. The major concepts of the SLII model are presented in Figure 5-4. According to SLII, effective leaders adapt their behavior to the level of *commitment* and *competence* of a particular subordinate to complete a given task. For example, team member Tanya might be committed to renting some empty office space by year-end and also highly skilled at such an activity. Or she might feel that the task is drudgery and not have much skill in selling office space. The combination of the subordinate's commitment and competence determines his or her *developmental level,* as follows:

**D1**—Enthusiastic Beginner. The learner has low competence but high commitment.
**D2**—Disillusioned Learner. The individual has gained some competence but has been disappointed after having experienced several setbacks. Commitment at this stage is low.

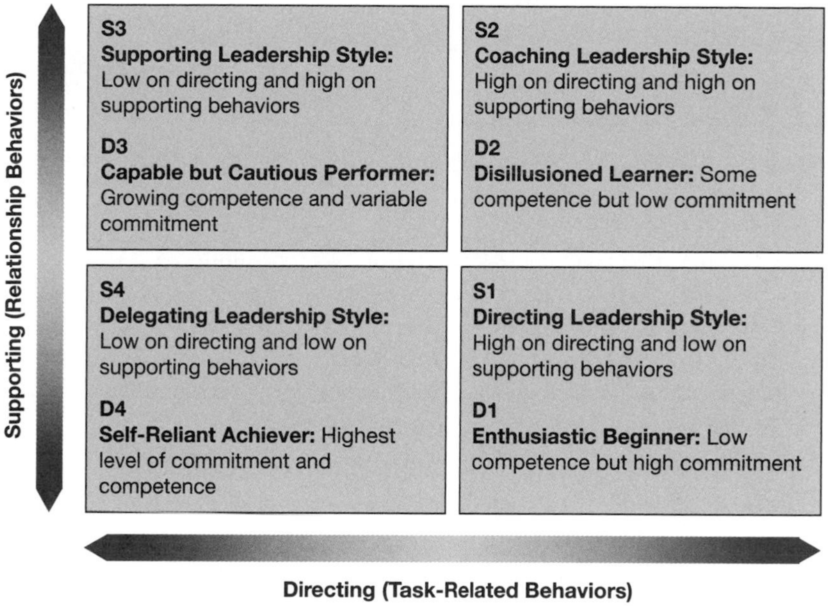

| | |
|---|---|
| **S3**<br>**Supporting Leadership Style:** Low on directing and high on supporting behaviors<br><br>**D3**<br>**Capable but Cautious Performer:** Growing competence and variable commitment | **S2**<br>**Coaching Leadership Style:** High on directing and high on supporting behaviors<br><br>**D2**<br>**Disillusioned Learner:** Some competence but low commitment |
| **S4**<br>**Delegating Leadership Style:** Low on directing and low on supporting behaviors<br><br>**D4**<br>**Self-Reliant Achiever:** Highest level of commitment and competence | **S1**<br>**Directing Leadership Style:** High on directing and low on supporting behaviors<br><br>**D1**<br>**Enthusiastic Beginner:** Low competence but high commitment |

Supporting (Relationship Behaviors)

**Directing (Task-Related Behaviors)**

**FIGURE 5-4** Situational Leadership II (SLII).

**D3**—Capable but Cautious Performer. The learner has growing competence, yet commitment is variable.

**D4**—Self-Reliant Achiever. The learner has high competence and commitment.

SLII explains that effective leadership depends on two independent behaviors: *supporting* and *directing*. (By now, you have read about this dichotomy several times in this chapter as well as in Chapter 4.) Supporting refers to relationship behaviors such as the leader's listening, giving recognition, communicating, and encouraging. Directing refers to task-related behaviors such as the leader's giving careful directions and controlling.

As shown in Figure 5-4, the four basic styles are:

**S1**—Directing. High directive behavior/low supportive behavior.
**S2**—Coaching. High directive behavior/high supportive behavior.
**S3**—Supporting. Low directive behavior/high supportive behavior.
**S4**—Delegating. Low directive behavior/low supportive behavior.

For best results on a given task, the leader is required to match his or her style to the developmental level of the group member. Each quadrant in Figure 5-4 indicates the desired match between leader style and subordinate development level.

A key point of SLII is that no one style is best: an effective leader uses all four styles depending on the subordinate's developmental level on a given task. The most appropriate leadership style among S1 to S4 corresponds to the subordinate developmental levels of D1 to D4, respectively: enthusiastic beginners (D1) require a directing (S1) leader; disillusioned learners (D2) need a coaching (S2) leader;

## ◎ Leadership Skill-Building Exercise 5-1

### Applying Situational Leadership II

You are playing the role of a team leader whose team has been given the responsibility of improving customer service at a consumer electronics megastore. Before jumping into this task, you decide to use SLII. Today you are going to meet with three team members individually to estimate their developmental level with respect to performing the customer-service-improvement task. You will want to estimate both their *competence* and *commitment* to perform the task. (Three different people will play the role of group members whose readiness is being assessed.) After the brief interviews (about five minutes) are conducted, you will announce which leadership style you intend to use with each of the people you interviewed. Class members not directly involved in the role play will offer feedback on how well you assessed the team members' readiness.

capable but cautious performers (D3) need a supporting (S3) style of leader; and self-reliant achievers (D4) need a delegating (S4) style of leader.

### Evaluation of SLII

Situational leadership represents a consensus of thinking about leadership behavior in relation to group members: competent people require less specific direction than do less competent people. The model is also useful because it builds on other explanations of leadership that emphasize the role of task and relationship behaviors. As a result, it has proved to be useful as the basis for leadership training. At least 3 million managers have been trained in situational leadership, covering various stages of the model, so we can assume that situational leadership makes sense to managers and companies. The situational model also corroborates common sense and is therefore intuitively appealing. You can benefit from this model by attempting to diagnose the readiness of group members before choosing the right leadership style.

A challenge in applying SLII is that the leader has to stay tuned into which task a group member is performing at a given time and then implement the correct style. Because assignments can change rapidly and group members are often working on more than one task in a day, the leader may have to keep shifting styles.

SLII presents categories and guidelines so precisely that it gives the impression of infallibility. In reality, leadership situations are less clear-cut than the four quadrants suggest. Also, the prescriptions for leadership will work only some of the time. For example, many supervisors use a coaching style (S2) with a disillusioned learner (D2) and still achieve poor results. A major concern is that there are few leadership situations in which a high-task, high-relationship orientation does not produce the best results.

Leadership Skill-Building Exercise 5-1 provides you with the opportunity to practice implementing the situational leadership model. The same exercise also supports other contingency and situational models.

# THE NORMATIVE DECISION MODEL

Another contingency viewpoint is that leaders must choose a style that elicits the correct degree of group participation when making decisions. Since many of a leader's interactions with group members involve decision making, this perspective is sensible. The **normative decision model** views leadership as a decision-making process in which the leader examines certain factors within the situation to determine which decision-making style will be the most effective. Here we present the latest version of the model that has evolved from the work of Victor Vroom and his associates over thirty years, based on research with more than 100,000 managers.[12] The models have changed but they all include the basic idea of matching decision-making style to situational factors.

## Decision-Making Styles

The normative model (formerly known as the leader-participation model) identifies five decision-making styles, each reflecting a different degree of participation by group members:

1. *Decide.* The leader makes the decision alone and either announces or sells it to the group. The leader might use expertise in collecting information from the group or from others who appear to have information relevant to the problem.
2. *Consult (Individually).* The leader presents the problem to the group members individually, gathers their suggestions, and then makes the decision.
3. *Consult (Group).* The leader presents the problem to group members in a meeting, gathers their suggestions, and then makes the decision.
4. *Facilitate.* The leader presents the problem and then acts as a facilitator, defining the problem to be solved and the boundaries in which the decision must be made. The leader wants concurrence and avoids having his or her ideas receive more weight based on position power.
5. *Delegate.* The leader permits the group to make the decision within prescribed limits. Although the leader does not directly intervene in the group's deliberations unless explicitly asked, he or she works behind the scenes, providing resources and encouragement.

## Contingency Factors and Application of the Model

The leader diagnoses the situation in terms of seven variables, or contingency factors, that contribute to selecting the most appropriate decision-making style. Based on answers to those variables, the leader or manager follows the path through decision matrices to choose one of five decision-making styles. The model has two versions: one when time is critical, and one when a more important consideration is developing group members' decision-making capabilities. When development of group members receives higher priority, the leader or manager relies more on the group to make a decision even if the process is time consuming.

Figure 5-5 depicts the matrix for time-driven group problems, a situation in which a decision must be reached rapidly. The situational factors, or problem variables, are listed at the top of the matrix. Specifying these factors makes the model a contingency approach. The decision-making style chosen depends on these factors, which are defined as follows:

Instructions: The matrix operates like a funnel. You start at the left with a specific decision problem in mind. The column headings denote situational factors which may or may not be present in that problem. You progress by selecting High or Low (H or L) for each relevant situational factor. Proceed down from the funnel, judging only those situational factors for which a judgment is called for, until you reach the recommended process.

| Decision Significance | Importance of Commitment | Leader Expertise | Likelihood of Commitment | Group Support | Group Expertise | Team Competence | |
|---|---|---|---|---|---|---|---|
| H | H | H | H | – | – | – | Decide |
| H | H | H | L | H | H | H | Delegate |
| H | H | H | L | H | H | L | Consult (Group) |
| H | H | H | L | H | L | – | Consult (Group) |
| H | H | H | L | L | – | – | Consult (Group) |
| H | H | L | H | H | H | H | Facilitate |
| H | H | L | H | H | H | L | Consult (Individually) |
| H | H | L | H | H | L | – | Consult (Individually) |
| H | H | L | H | L | – | – | Consult (Individually) |
| H | H | L | L | H | H | H | Facilitate |
| H | H | L | L | H | H | L | Consult (Group) |
| H | H | L | L | H | L | – | Consult (Group) |
| H | H | L | L | L | – | – | Consult (Group) |
| H | L | H | – | – | – | – | Decide |
| H | L | L | – | H | H | H | Facilitate |
| H | L | L | – | H | H | L | Consult (Individually) |
| H | L | L | – | H | L | – | Consult (Individually) |
| H | L | L | – | L | – | – | Consult (Individually) |
| L | H | H | – | – | – | – | Decide |
| L | H | L | – | – | – | H | Delegate |
| L | H | L | – | – | – | L | Facilitate |
| L | L | – | – | – | – | – | Decide |

*(Left margin: PROBLEM STATEMENT)*

**FIGURE 5-5** The Time-Driven Model for Choosing a Decision-Making Style.

*Source:* Victor H. Vroom's Time-Driven Model, reproduced from *A Model of Leadership Style*. Copyright 1998. Reprinted by permission of the author.

***Decision Significance:*** The significance of the decision to the success of the project or organization

***Importance of Commitment:*** The importance of team members' commitment to the decision

***Leader Expertise:*** Your knowledge or expertise in relation to the problem

***Likelihood of Commitment:*** The likelihood that the team will commit itself to a decision you might make on your own

***Group Support:*** The degree to which the team supports the organization's objectives at stake in the problem

***Group Expertise:*** Team members' knowledge or expertise in relation to the problem

***Team Competence:*** The ability of the team members to work together in solving problems

Accurate answers to these seven situational factors can be challenging to obtain. The leader may have to rely heavily on intuition and also minimize distorted thinking, such as believing he or she has some expertise but in fact does not.

To apply the model, visualize yourself as the division head of a medical supplies company. A decision you face is whether to globally outsource the manufacture of knee braces. The industry is booming because so many people twist or severely damage their knees in sports. Yet competition is increasing so manufacturing costs must be reduced. The problem statement for the group is "Shall we outsource the manufacture of our knee braces to a medical supply company in Malaysia?" The company in mind has a fine reputation for its manufacture of other medical products such as crutches and prosthetic devices. You proceed as follows:

1. Begin at the left side of the matrix in Figure 5-5, at the "Problem Statement." At the top of the matrix are the seven situational factors, each of which may be present (H for high) or absent (L for low) in that problem. Keep in mind that you are not allowed to cross a horizontal line as you proceed through the matrix.
2. Ascertaining if the decision is significant, or has a high impact on the success of the project, you select H.
3. Moving to the right, you answer the second question about the importance of commitment. You would certainly need the key members of the team to be committed to an activity as complex as the manufacture of knee braces, so you select H.
4. You move to the right again, this time answering the question about leader experience. You conclude that you don't have much relevant experience about globally outsourcing (or offshoring) a medical product, so you answer L.
5. You move to the right again without crossing a horizontal line, and answer the question of likelihood of commitment. You decide that it is unlikely that that the team will commit itself to a decision you might make on your own, so you go answer L.
6. Moving to the right, and again not crossing the horizontal line, you answer the question about group support. You think that the group does support the organization's objective of lowering costs on the knee brace, so you answer H.
7. You move to the right, don't cross the line, and answer the question about group expertise. You decide that the group can acquire expertise about outsourcing knee braces, so you answer H.

## ⊚ Leadership Skill-Building Exercise 5-2

### Applying the Time-Driven Model

The exercise presented here can be done individually or in small groups.

The bank examiners have just left, having insisted that many of your commercial real estate loans be written off, which will deplete your already low capital. Along with the many other banks in your region, your bank is in serious danger of being closed by the regulators. As the financial problems surfaced, many of the top executives left to pursue other interests, but fortunately you were able to replace them with three highly competent, younger managers. Although they had no prior acquaintance with one another, each is a product of a fine training program with one of the money center banks, in which they rotated through positions in all of the banking functions.

Your extensive experience in the industry leads you to the inevitable conclusion that the only hope is a two-pronged approach involving the reduction of all but the most critical expenses and the sale of assets

to other banks. The task must be accomplished quickly because further deterioration of the quality of the loan portfolio could result in a negative capital position and force regulators to close the bank.

The strategy is clear to you, but you have many details that will need to be worked out. You believe that you know what information will be needed to get the bank on a course for future prosperity. You are fortunate in having three young executives to help you. Although they have had little or no experience in working together, you know that each is dedicated to the survival of the bank. Like you, they know what needs to be done and how to do it.

The suggested path is found in the References section for Chapter 5.

*Source:* Victor H. Vroom's Time-Driven Model, reproduced from *A Model of Leadership Style.* Copyright 1998. Reprinted by permission of the author.

8. Still moving to the right and heading toward the end of the matrix, you answer the question about the team members' ability to work together in solving problems. You know that your team is strong in group problem solving, so you answer H.

9. A little shift to the right and you reach the shaded box labeled "Facilitate." So you use the decision-making style Number 4, Facilitate, and you will act as a facilitator in coming to a decision about whether to outsource the manufacture of knee braces to the Malaysia.

If you make a few practice decisions with the model in Figure 5-5, it becomes much easier to do. If you continue the process without crossing any horizontal line on the matrix, you will arrive at one of the five recommended decision styles. Sometimes a conclusive determination can be made based on two factors, such as L, L. Others require three (such as L, H, H), four (such as H, H, H, H), or as many as seven factors (such as H, H, L, L, H, H, H).

Different people giving different answers to the situational factors will arrive at different conclusions about the recommended decision style in the situation. The leader needs sufficient information to answer each of seven questions accurately. Leadership Skill-Building Exercise 5-2 presents a scenario that Vroom developed to give you another opportunity to apply the model.

The normative model provides a valuable service to practicing managers and leaders. It prompts them to ask questions about contingency variables in decision-making situations. It has been found that for previous versions of the model, managers who follow its procedures are likely to increase their decision-making effectiveness. Furthermore, managers who make decisions consistent with the model (again, based on previous versions) are more likely to be perceived as effective.[13] These same good results are probable for Vroom's later model because it incorporates most of the concepts in the previous models but is easier to follow. As with other contingency approaches, however, the model does not deal with the charismatic and inspirational aspects of leadership.

# COGNITIVE RESOURCE THEORY: HOW INTELLIGENCE, EXPERIENCE, AND STRESS INFLUENCE LEADERSHIP

Another contingency theory describes how a leader's intelligence and experience can influence performance when the stress level of the people is considered. The general thrust of **cognitive resource theory** is that stress plays a key role in determining how a leader's intelligence is related to group performance.[14] The theory, as developed by Fiedler and his colleagues, also explains how directive behavior is tied in with intelligence. Several of the many predictions made by cognitive resource theory are as follows:

**1.** Because experienced leaders have a larger variety of behaviors to fall back on, those with greater experience but lower intelligence are likely to have higher-performing groups under high-stress conditions. The veteran leader-manager has acquired the necessary skills and knowledge to guide the group through a difficult situation, such as dealing with a competitive threat. Under low-stress conditions, leader experience is less relevant.

**2.** Because experience leads to habitual behavior patterns, highly experienced leaders often use traditional solutions to problems when instead a creative approach is necessary. Leaders with high intelligence are more valuable than experienced leaders when innovation is needed and stress levels are low. The highly intelligent leader relies on intellectual ability to analyze the problem and find an optimal solution. (Leader experience helps under high-stress conditions but is not a significant factor when stress levels are low.)

**3.** The intellectual abilities of a leader who is experiencing stress will be diverted from the task at hand. As a result, measures of leader intelligence and competence do not correlate with group performance when the leader is stressed.

**4.** The intellectual abilities of directive leaders will correlate more highly with group performance than will the intellectual abilities of nondirective leaders. This is true because the directive leader provides more ideas and suggestions to the group.[15] The nondirective leader is more likely to urge the group member to be more self-reliant.

**5.** A leader's intellectual abilities will be related to group performance to the degree that the task requires the use of intellectual ability.[16] Cognitive resource theory assumes that intelligent leaders devise better plans for doing the work than less intelligent leaders, especially when the plan is complex. (How does this finding fit your observations about the role of intelligence in problem solving?)

Cognitive resource theory highlights how intelligence, experience, and stress can influence both leader and group performance. However, it neglects the utility of a combination of an experienced *and* intelligent leader in low-stress and high-stress situations. In reality, leaders who are both intelligent and experienced will perform the best in most situations.

# CONTINGENCY LEADERSHIP IN THE EXECUTIVE SUITE

An investigation of how top-level executives lead their organizations provides additional insight into contingency leadership.[17] The approach these leaders take lies on the borderline between style and strategy. We include the information here under contingency leadership because each approach is chosen based on an analysis of the requirements of the situation. A leadership approach is defined as a coherent, explicit style of management, not a personal style. However, the style of management centers on leadership behaviors.

Charles M. Farkas, Philippe DeBacker, and Suzy Wetlaufer interviewed 163 top executives on six continents to learn how these leaders delivered consistently extraordinary results. After scrutinizing 12,000 pages of interview transcripts, they identified five distinct approaches that were revealed by the analysis: strategic, human assets, expertise, box, and change agent. The overriding conclusion from the study is that successful CEOs assess their companies' needs, then adapt their leadership style to fit the particular situation. We will summarize each approach, including its associated contingency factors and leadership behaviors. Table 5-1 provides an outline of the approaches and accompanying contingency factors.

The *strategic approach* is a systematic, dispassionate, and structured analysis of a company's strengths and weaknesses and of its mission. CEOs using this approach perceive their major contribution as creating, testing, and designing the implementation of a long-term business strategy. Much of their workday is devoted to activities intended to analyze their organization's current situation and the most advantageous business position in the future. CEOs using this approach devote about 80 percent of their time to external factors such as customers, competitors, technological advances, and market trends.

CEOs should use the strategic approach in unstable environments in which the volume and pace of change are high. Significant complexity in terms of technology, geography, or functions is another contingency factor calling for the strategic approach. For example, the CEO of Coca-Cola uses a strategic approach because the company has 32,000 employees in approximately 200 countries worldwide. CEOs who must frequently make decisions of enormous consequence often choose the strategic approach.

**TABLE 5-1** Contingency Factors for Five Approaches to CEO Leadership

| CEO LEADERSHIP APPROACH | CONTINGENCY FACTORS |
| --- | --- |
| Strategic (create, test, and design long-term strategy) | Unstable environment, high rate of change, complexity. |
| Human assets (add value through hiring, retention, and development programs) | Business units are better positioned than headquarters to make strategy. |
| Expertise (design and implement programs around significant specific expertise such as technology) | Certain expertise can be the source of competitive advantage. |
| Box (add value through controls that set boundaries for employee performance) | Presence of government examiners who insist on strict controls to protect consumer and company. |
| Change agent (create an environment of continual reinvention) | Company wants to remain a leader in the field, and status quo is unacceptable. |

*Source*: From Charles M. Farkas and Suzy Wetlaufer, "The Ways Chief Executive Officers Lead," *Harvard Business Review*, May–June 1996, pp.110–122; Farkas and Philippe DeBacker, *Maximum Leadership: The World's Leading CEOs Share Their Five Strategies for Success* (New York: Holt, 1996).

In the *human assets approach*, the CEO and the corporate staff add value to the organization through hiring, retention, and development programs. CEOs using this approach believe that strategy formulation belongs in the business units. They see their most important job as imparting selected values, behaviors, and attitudes by managing the growth and development of individuals. To implement this approach, they travel extensively and spend most of their time in human resource activities such as recruiting, performance evaluation, and career planning. An important goal of the human assets approach is to develop business unit managers to the point at which they act and make decisions the way the CEO would. The human assets CEO believes that good employees should do things the *company way*. Herb Kelleher, the former CEO of Southwest Airlines, said, "We hire great attitudes, and we'll teach them any functionality they need."[18] (We hope this hiring strategy does not apply to airline pilots.)

The human assets approach is most frequently used when a company has such far-flung operations that managers in the business units are better equipped than those in the corporate group to formulate strategy. Consistency in running the geographically remote businesses is achieved by the CEO's imparting corporate values to employees worldwide. Consistency in values is also enhanced when the CEO is involved in hiring key people. Another contingency factor favoring the human assets approach is if key executives strongly believe that the company values and standards of behavior are necessary for the success of the business.

Executives who use the *expertise approach* believe that the CEO's key responsibility is selecting and disseminating throughout the organization an area of expertise that will give the firm a competitive advantage. The majority of their working time is devoted to activities that foster the cultivation and continual improvement of this expertise. Among these activities are studying new technological research, analyzing competitors' products, and meeting with engineers and customers. Areas of expertise include marketing, manufacturing, technology, and distribution.

Organizational members who have good technical expertise and share it across organizational units are rewarded. A key contingency factor for favoring the expertise approach is if a certain expertise can give the firm a significant competitive advantage. An example is Chrysler recently hiring Deborah Wahl Meyer as the new chief marketing officer and vice president so she could apply the same marketing expertise she had used in promoting the Lexus for Toyota.

A *box approach* occurs when the corporate group adds value by creating, communicating, and overseeing an explicit set of controls. The controls can take a variety of forms, including financial measures, rules, procedures, and values that define boundaries for the performance of all employees. The purpose of these controls is to ensure uniform and predictable experiences for employees and customers, and to lower risk. CEOs who use the box approach devote much of their workday to attending to deviations from standard, such as quarterly results that are below forecast. They also devote time to rewarding employees whose behavior and performance match the control standards.

The key contingency factor favoring the box approach is a regulated environment such as banking or nuclear power plants in which the government insists on strict controls to protect employees and customers. The purpose of the controls is to strive for consistency. A pharmaceutical executive is likely to implement the box approach because of the need for consistency in testing new drugs.

CEOs who use the *change agent approach* believe that their most critical role is to create an environment of continual reinvention, even if such an emphasis on change creates short-term disturbances such as anxiety, confusion, and poorer financial results. Change agent CEOs spend up to 75 percent of their time using speeches, meetings, and other forms of communication to motivate members to embrace change. They meet regularly with a variety of stakeholders to beat the drums for change. Change agent executives regularly visit factories, create and answer email, and attend company picnics. (It is a good thing these CEOs have a strong internal staff to run the business!) Employees who embrace change receive the biggest rewards. At the investment bank Goldman Sachs, a talented young banker was promoted to partner two years ahead of others in his class because he was willing to accept an assignment in Asia at a time when few U.S. employees were willing to work abroad.

The change agent approach appears to be triggered when the CEO believes that the status quo will lead to the company's undoing, such as when a software development company is content with its current lineup of products. The contingency factor is not obvious, such as a troubled organization needing change; rather, the CEO has the vision to recognize that trouble lies ahead unless changes are made now.

These five leadership approaches are not mutually exclusive, and sometimes a CEO will emphasize more than one approach. For example, the change agent approach might be needed to implement a radical business strategy. Yet in the most effectively run organizations, the CEO usually has a dominant approach or style that serves as a compass and rudder for all corporate decisions. In general, emphasizing one of these approaches, at least for a period in a firm's history, can help a CEO lead with clarity, consistency, and commitment.

The Leader in Action profile describes a deal maker who emphasizes the five leadership approaches just described.

## Leader in Action

### Big Eddie Knows How to Deal

Few people would be surprised that security is tight at Eddie Lampert's office: in 2003 he was kidnapped at gunpoint while leaving work and held for ransom for two days before talking his way free. In fact, there is no sign on the low-rise building in Greenwich, Connecticut, that his $9 billion private investment fund, ESL Investments, Inc., is even there at all. There is also no sign on ESL's door upstairs—and certainly no indication that the man sitting there might be the next Warren E. Buffett. He is so focused on his goals that he was back at work negotiating a big deal two days after his kidnappers released him.

### Lampert's Investment Strategy and Deals

Lampert has built his success on companies that are seriously undervalued. He will even risk jumping into ones that are reeling from bad management or poor strategies because the potential returns are far greater.

In November 2004, Lampert swooped in and launched an $11 billion purchase of Sears. The new company, called Sears Holding Corp., owned Sears and Kmart after the merger. After the deal, many investors bought Kmart and Sears stock, because they saw Kmart not as a retailer trying to move product but as a springboard for lucrative deals. Lampert has made it clear that more than superior returns on investment are riding on Kmart. He also wants to earn respect as a businessman who provides expertise in how a company is run. Like Buffett, he wants chief executives to open their arms and partner with him. Dressed in a hand-tailored suit with a subtle pinstripe and an open-collared blue-striped shirt, he acknowledges that his role model is a tough comparison.

Kmart is a classic example of how Lampert works. He seized control of a $23 billion retail chain, the nation's third-largest discounter, for less than $1 billion in bankruptcy court. He emerged as the largest shareholder and became chairman as part of a reorganization in which virtually all of its debt was converted into shares.

Before the merger, Lampert was milking Kmart for cash. He imposed a program of keeping the lid on capital spending, holding inventory down, and stopping the endless clearance sales. He sold sixty-eight stores to Home Depot and Sears, raising almost $850 million in cash. With the help of outside advisers, Lampert added four upmarket brands to Kmart's clothing line and also broadened its consumer electronics selection. These moves resulted in a stock market capitalization of $8.6 billion, on a par with Federated Department Stores. Robert Miller said the increased valuation occurred "because Lampert is a smart cookie. Essentially he is transforming the assets into a more valuable state" (*Business Week*, November 22, 2004, p. 147).

Several years later, Sears stock was faltering, and selling beyond what its retail business was worth. Some analysts believed that the price of the Sears stock would not go too low because of the "Lampert premium," or investor confidence that the chairman would spin gold from Sears's threads. In 2007 when ESL was headed for losses, including a decline in the price of Sears stock, and deteriorating store sales, Lampert still had a contingency plan. He could sell the chain's real estate for a large profit. The large cash reserves that Lampert helped conserve were thought to be another safeguard to getting Sears and Kmart though difficult times in the retail industry.

By 2008, Sears had yet to be a winner from the standpoint of profit and market share. Cash flows were dwindling, and profit was declining, including a second-quarter loss. To help deal with the decline, and revitalize the company, Sears was divided into a five-unit holding company, and parts of the business no longer reported to Lampert. Part of the reorganization was to dismiss CEO Aylwin B. Lewis, and search for an experienced retailer as a replacement.

Lampert is obsessed with making sure that every dollar he invests in a company earns the highest return. That means his companies have often used cash to buy back shares rather than boost capital spending. The CEOs of his companies say a big part

## Action (continued)

of their conversations with Lampert focuses on how best to allocate the capital.

A major part of Lampert's business strategy at Sears has been to slash spending in order to raise cash. Lampert has been accused of under-investing in stores in order to focus on complex investment schemes. Nevertheless, Lampert and his managers launched an advertising campaign to get consumers back into the stores at both Sears and Kmart.

To ultimately strengthen the finances of ESL Investments, Lampert decided in 2008 to gamble on a U.S. housing recovery. He bought stakes in battered home builders, mortgage lenders, and home-improvement retailer Home Depot. The housing investments fit Lampert's interest in out-of-favor companies and industries because of their potential for substantial gains in the long run.

### Lampert the Manager and Leader

Lampert can be quite assertive with management. He played rough at AutoZone, where he started amassing shares in 1997. After his stake reached 15.7 percent, he obtained a board seat in 1999. Lampert runs a tight ship at ESL too. Not a penny gets invested without his approval, say former employees. Gavin Abrams, a former ESL analyst, says Lampert has an uncanny ability to see how the pieces of an investment fit together. Once ESL has invested, it stays in close touch with the company. Lampert is sometimes in daily touch with the top executive in the company in which ESL holds a stake.

Lampert runs his fund with just fifteen employees, mostly research analysts. As he walks the floor, ESL president William C. Crowley is locked on the phone in his office. Lampert's is next door, a corner suite whose central focus is a dual set of black, flat-paneled computer screens perched on his desk. He spends much more time analyzing his investments and dealing with company outsiders than in working with the analysts on his own staff.

Whatever he does next, Lampert is full of surprises. When he was kidnapped, he managed to talk his way out of captivity by offering a small fraction of the $1 million his captors wanted. Investors are betting these deal-making skills will keep making him—and them—lots of money.

### Questions

1. Explain which one or two of the five CEO leadership approaches Eddie Lampert emphasizes.
2. How would you characterize Lampert's leadership style?
3. Based on evidence presented in this profile, how would you rate Lampert's charisma?

*Source:* Robert Berner, "Eddie's Master Stroke," *Business Week*, November 29, 2004, pp. 034–036; Berner, "The Next Warren Buffet," *Business Week*, November 22, 2004, pp.144–154; Robert Berner, "Hold the Tears for Eddie Lampert," *Business Week*, December 24, 2007, pp. 060–061. A few facts are from "Retail Value – 'Lampert Premium' = Sear's Stock?" *The Wall Street Journal*, July 18, 2007, p. C1, and Peter Eavis, "Sears' Till Stirs Concern," *The Wall Street Journal*, February 8, 2008, pp. C1, C8.

Recent support for the importance of contingency leadership in the executive suite comes from the study of 1,000 great U.S. business leaders of the twentieth century. The authors of the study, Anthony J. Mayo and Nitin Nohria, concluded that when it came to long-term success, the ability to understand and adapt to changing conditions equals in importance the executive's personality traits or other competency. Understanding the context, or the spirit of the times, was a major contingency factor in applying the right leadership to achieve success. Here is one example: One of the defining characteristics of the 1990s was Internet opportunities. In stepped

Meg Whitman to build eBay from a fledgling Internet retail model into a vibrant and passionately loyal community.[19]

# LEADERSHIP DURING A CRISIS

Among the potential crises facing organizations are a drastic revenue decline; pending bankruptcy; homicide in the workplace; scandalous or criminal behavior by executives; natural disasters, such as hurricanes, floods, or earthquakes; and bombings and other terrorist attacks. Leading during a crisis can be regarded as contingency leadership because the situation demands that the leader emphasize certain behaviors, attitudes, and traits. **Crisis leadership** is the process of leading group members through a sudden and largely unanticipated, intensely negative, and emotionally draining circumstance. Here we describe eight leadership attributes and behaviors associated with successfully leading an organization or organizational unit through a crisis.

*Be Decisive*   The best-accepted principle of crisis leadership is that the leader should take decisive action to remedy the situation. After the plan is formulated, it should be widely communicated to help reassure group members that something concrete is being done about the predicament. After their physical facilities were destroyed in the terrorist attacks on the World Trade Center on September 11, 2001, several leaders announced the next day that their firms would move to nearby backup locations. Communicating plans helps reduce uncertainty about what is happening to the firm and the people in it. A leader who takes highly visible action to deal with a crisis is likely to be viewed as competent.[20]

A corollary of being decisive during a crisis is not to be indecisive, or to hide from the crisis in its midst. The investment bank Bear Stearns Cos. was facing a crisis during the summer of 2007 when its hedge funds (exotic, complicated investments) were hemorrhaging value. Many investors wanted refunds, and lenders to the fund were demanding more collateral. During ten critical days of this crisis, Bear's chief executive James Cayne was playing in a bridge tournament in Nashville, Tennessee, without a cell phone or email hookup. Later that year during a mortgage-market and credit panic, Cayne missed many key company events because he was playing golf. Some observers believed that with an income the previous year of $36 million, Cayne should have provided more decisive leadership during the crises. Yet several company insiders defended Cayne's action, saying that he was still exerting leadership during the crisis.[21]

*Lead with Compassion*   Displaying compassion with the concerns, anxieties, and frustrations of group members is a key interpersonal skill for crisis leadership. The type of compassionate leadership that brings about organizational healing involves taking some form of public action that eases pain and inspires others to act as well. Compassionate leadership encompasses two related sets of actions. The first is to create an environment in which affected workers can freely discuss how they feel, such as a group meeting to talk about the crisis or disaster. The second is to create an environment in which the workers who experience or witness pain can find a method to alleviate their own suffering and that of others. The leader might establish a special fund to help the families of workers who were victims of the disaster or give workers the opportunity to receive grief counseling.

The two-pronged approach to leading with compassion is illustrated by TJX Companies, Inc., president and CEO Edmond English, who lost seven employees aboard one of the airplanes that struck the World Trade Center. He assembled his staff members together shortly after the attacks to confirm the names of the victims, encouraging his workers to express their feelings. English called in grief counselors that same day and chartered a plane to fly in victims' relatives from Europe and Canada to company headquarters in Massachusetts.[22]

***Reestablish the Usual Work Routine***   Although it may appear callous and counterintuitive, an effective way of helping people deal with a workplace crisis is to encourage them to return to their regular work. It is important for workers to express their feelings about the crisis before refocusing on work, but once they have, returning to work helps ground them in reality and restores purpose to their lives. Randall Marshall, director of trauma studies for the New York State Office of Mental Health, said after 9/11, "A healthy response to this type of situation is to get back into a routine."[23]

***Avoid a Circle-the-Wagons Mentality***   One of the worst ways to lead a group through a crisis is to strongly defend yourself against your critics or deny wrongdoing. The same denial approach is referred to as maintaining a bunker mentality or stonewalling the problem. Instead of cooperating with other stakeholders in the crisis, the leader takes a defensive posture. A case in point is Yoichiro Kaizaki, the former chairman of Bridgestone Corporation, the Japanese owner of Firestone tires. Rather than act promptly to control the damage when the news of faulty Firestone tires on Ford Explorers first surfaced, he refused to face critics until the controversy was raging. His stubborn behavior appears to have worsened the publicity for Firestone and Bridgestone.[24]

***Display Optimism***   Pessimists abound in every crisis, so an optimistic leader can help energize group members to overcome the bad times. The effective crisis leader draws action plans that give people hope for a better future. Barbara Baker Clark contends that the role of a leader during a crisis is to encourage hopefulness. She states:

> I'm not saying that you have to plaster a stupid grin on your face even if the bottom line is tanking or people are dying in battle. I am saying don't wallow in pessimism. Believe it or not, it matters to your employees that you remain reasonably optimistic. It will reduce anxiety and keep everyone motivated. That's the power of leadership.[25]

***Prevent the Crisis Through Disaster Planning***   The ideal form of crisis leadership is to prevent a crisis through disaster planning. A key part of planning for a physical disaster, for example, is to anticipate where you would go, how you would get in touch with employees, and where you might set up a temporary workplace. Having a list of backup vendors in case they are hit by a physical disaster is also important.

Small business owners should be networking with other business owners and agree to assist each other if a crisis strikes. Arranging in advance for support groups, such as grief counselors, is another key element of disaster planning. Even the fact of letting employees know that a disaster plan is in place can be an effective leadership act because it may lower worker anxiety.[26]

***Provide Stable Performance***    Effective leaders are steady performers, even under heavy workloads and uncertain conditions. Remaining steady under crisis conditions contributes to effectiveness because it helps team members cope with the situation. When the leader remains calm, group members are reassured that things will work out. Stability also helps the managerial leader appear professional and cool under pressure. Richard Stuckey was one of three managers appointed to help Citigroup cope with the writedown of $111 billion in bad mortgage loans. He had previously established a reputation as a Wall Street turnaround specialist. A colleague described Stuckey in these terms: "He's a very methodical, calm, cool, collected kind of guy. If there's a lot of pressure on him internally or externally, that's not going to sway what he's doing."[27]

***Be a Transformational Leader***    During times of large and enduring crisis, transformational leadership may be the intervention of choice. The transformational leader can often lead the organization out of its misery. Transformational leadership is likely to benefit the troubled organization both in dealing with the immediate crisis and in performing better in the long run. Rick Stuckey, just mentioned, is a transformational leader who avoids drastic cost-cutting when turning around a troubled company. David Novak, the CEO of Yum Brands (which includes KFC, Taco Bell, Pizza Hut, and Long John Silver's), has seen his share of crisis, including vermin infestation in a restaurant that was broadcast on television and YouTube. He says that honesty, consistency, and continuity of communication is the key to managing through these issues, and that the transformation may take six to nine months.[28]

Another way in which a transformational leader helps a company or work unit cope with crisis is to have established a climate of trust long before the crisis struck,[29] as implied in the statement about Rick Stuckey. If workers and other shareholders trust the leader, they will take more seriously his or her directives during the crisis. Leadership at both Wal-Mart and McDonald's did a notable job of holding their work force together after Hurricane Katrina. Executives and store managers alike scrambled to get in touch with employees to assure them that they would all have their jobs back as soon as operations were up and running. In general, workers in the Gulf Coast area had trusted leadership at the two companies.

# EVIDENCE-BASED LEADERSHIP FOR THE CONTINGENCY AND SITUATIONAL APPROACH

A leading-edge way for a person to practice contingency leadership would be to look for research-based evidence about the best way to deal with a given situation. Before taking action, the leader would ask, "What does the research literature tell me is most likely to work in this situation?" **Evidence-based leadership or management** is an approach whereby managers translate principles based on best evidence into organizational practices.[30] Quite often the best evidence is empirical (based on experience) and recent, yet old principles can still be useful. The alternative to evidence-based leadership is to rely heavily on common sense and adopting practices used by other companies whether or not they fit a particular situation. Many of the principles and suggestions presented throughout this text would help a manager practice evidence-based leadership.

An example of using evidence-based leadership follows: Research indicates that empowerment is more likely to be successful with group members whose cultural values favor a manager or leader sharing power. In contrast, empowerment is less likely to be successful when the group members expect the leader to retain most of the power. (See Chapter 14 for the evidence.) In this example, a *principle* (empowerment works best when cultural values are compatible) is translated into *practice* (using empowerment to motivate and satisfy workers when the cultural values of the workers are compatible with empowerment).

Evidence-based leadership and management is not yet widely practiced, but taking the study of leadership and management seriously will move managers and organizations toward basing their practices and decisions on valid evidence. The result is likely to be more precise contingency leadership.

### Reader's Roadmap

So far in this book, we have examined the nature of leadership, the inner qualities of leaders, and leadership styles, including contingency leadership. In the next chapter, we focus on a topic that incorporates many of these ideas: leadership ethics and social responsibility.

## SUMMARY

Theories of contingency and situational leadership build on the study of leadership style by adding more specific guidelines about which style to use under which circumstances. Leaders are most effective when they make their behavior contingent on situational forces, including group member characteristics. Organizational effectiveness is affected by situational factors not under the leader's control. Situations shape how leaders behave, and also influence the consequences of leader behavior.

Fiedler's contingency theory states that the best style of leadership is determined by the situation in which the leader is working. Style, in Fiedler's theory, is measured by the least preferred coworker (LPC) scale. If you have a reasonably positive attitude toward your least preferred coworker, you are relationship motivated. You are task motivated if your attitude is negative. Situational control, or favorability, is measured by a combination of the quality of leader–member relations, the degree of task structure, and the leader's position power.

The key proposition of Fiedler's theory is that in situations of high control or low control, leaders with a task-motivated style are more effective.

In a situation of moderate control, a relationship-motivated style works better. Leaders can improve situational control by modifying leader–member relations, task structure, and position power.

The path-goal theory of leadership effectiveness specifies what the leader must do to achieve high productivity and morale in a given situation. The major proposition of the theory is that the manager should choose a leadership style that takes into account the characteristics of the group members and the demands of the task. Initiating structure by the leader works best when the group faces an ambiguous task. Effective leaders clarify the paths to attaining goals, help group members progress along these paths, and remove barriers to goal attainment. Leaders must choose a style that best fits the two sets of contingency factors—the characteristics of the subordinates and the tasks. The four styles in path-goal theory are directive, supportive, participative, and achievement oriented.

Situational Leadership II (SLII), developed by Blanchard, explains how to match leadership style to the capabilities of group members on a given task. The combination of the subordinate's commitment and competence determines the four developmental levels: enthusiastic beginner, disillusioned learner, capable but cautious performer, and self-reliant achiever. The model classifies leadership style according to the relative amounts of supporting and directing the leader engages in. The four styles are different combinations of task and relationship behavior, both rated as high versus low: directing, coaching, supporting, and delegating. The most appropriate leadership style corresponds to the subordinate developmental levels. For example, enthusiastic beginners require a directing leader.

The normative decision model explains that leadership is a decision-making process. A leader examines certain contingency factors in the situation to determine which decision-making style will be the most effective in either a time-driven or developmental situation. The model defines five decision-making styles: two individual and three group. By answering a series of seven diagnostic questions in a matrix, the manager follows the path to a recommended decision style.

Cognitive resource theory describes how a leader's intelligence and experience can influence performance under conditions of stress. A major prediction of the theory is that leaders with high intelligence are more valuable than experienced leaders when innovation is needed and stress levels are low. The highly intelligent leader relies on intellectual ability to analyze the problem and find an optimal solution. Also, the intellectual abilities of directive leaders will correlate more highly with group performance than will the intellectual abilities of nondirective leaders.

CEOs who are successful assess their companies' needs, then adapt their leadership style to fit the situation. The five approaches or styles are strategic, human assets, expertise, box (emphasis on controls), and change agent. Each approach is emphasized under different circumstances; for example, the human assets approach is used when business units are better positioned than headquarters to make strategy. A study of 1,000 great business leaders found that for long-term success, the ability to adapt to changing conditions equals in importance the executive's personality traits or other competencies.

Leading others through a crisis can be considered a form of contingency leadership because the leader adapts his or her style to the situation. In a crisis, leaders should (a) be decisive, (b) lead with compassion, (c) reestablish the usual work routine, (d) avoid a circle-the-wagons mentality, (e) display optimism, (f) prevent the crisis through disaster planning, (g) provide stable performance, and (h) be a transformational leader.

A leading-edge way for a person to practice contingency leadership would be to look for research-based evidence about the best way to deal with a given situation. This approach means using evidence-based leadership or management.

## KEY TERMS

Contingency approach to
    leadership
Path-goal theory

Situational Leadership II (SLII)
Normative decision model
Cognitive resource theory

Crisis leadership
Evidence-based leadership or
    management

## ✔ GUIDELINES FOR ACTION AND SKILL DEVELOPMENT

1. A major contingency factor for a team or group leader is the talent and motivation of the individual being led. Although talented and well-motivated workers may not require close monitoring of their efforts, they still require encouragement and recognition to sustain high performance. Otherwise, the leader has very little impact on their performance or their intention to stay a member of the team or group.

2. Consider four factors as a shortcut to deciding whether a decision is best made by a group, thereby practicing participative leadership. The stronger the need for *buy-in* or *commitment,* the more important group participation is. When a *creative solution* is important, group input is valuable because varied viewpoints ordinarily enhance creativity. When *time is scarce,* it is better for the leader to make the decision. When a decision is needed that *reflects the bigger picture,* the leader is often in the best position to make it.

3. A subtle way of practicing contingency leadership is to adapt to times that may have changed in terms of the demands of your leadership position.[31] You have to fine-tune your leadership approach to meet the new circumstances. Assume that hospital administrator Maggie has held her position for ten years. According to her perception of her role, the focus of her leadership would be to inspire her staff toward doing what is best for patient care. Yet her role has now changed. Focusing on what is good for patients still receives high priority, yet Maggie has to emotionally accept the reality that finding ways to inspire her group to reduce the cost of operating the hospital has become a key part of her leadership and management role.

### Discussion Questions and Activities

1. Visualize yourself preparing a job résumé with the intent of finding a leadership position in business. Explain whether or not you would include on your résumé the fact that you practice contingency leadership.

2. Describe how it might be possible for a manager to be charismatic yet also practice contingency leadership.

3. Identify a personality trait you think would help a manager function as a contingency leader. Also identify a trait you think might detract from a manager's ability to function as a contingency leader.

4. Assume that the CFO of a big company takes on the responsibility of coaching a youth league soccer team. In what way should he or she practice contingency leadership?

5. How would a manager know which variables in a given situation should influence which approach to leadership he or she should take?

6. Which of the four path-goal styles do you think would be the best for managing a professional football or professional soccer team? Justify your answer.

7. Suppose that you are a first-level supervisor with responsibility for the physical relocation of your company's office. How would you assess the developmental level of your group members?

8. According to the situational model of leadership, which style is likely to be the most effective for leading a strongly motivated group of ecommerce specialists?

9. Why might a transformational leader be helpful in a crisis?

10. To what extent do you think most business leaders will ever use experience-based leadership or management?

## Leadership Case Problem A

### Keeping the Cloud Computing Mastermind Happy

One simple question. That's all it took for Christophe Bisciglia to bewilder confident job applicants at Google. Bisciglia, an angular 27-year-old senior software engineer with long wavy hair, wanted to see if these undergrads were ready to think like Googlers. "Tell me," he says, "what would you do if you had 1,000 times more data?"

What a strange idea. If they returned to their school projects and were foolish enough to cram formulas with a thousand times more details about shopping or maps or—heaven forbid—with video files, they'd slow their college servers to a crawl.

At that point in the interview, Bisciglia would explain his question. To thrive at Google, he told them, they would have to learn to work—and to dream—on a vastly larger scale. He described Google's globe-spanning network of computers. Yes, they answered search queries instantly. But together they also blitzed through mountains of data, looking for answers or intelligence faster than any other machine on earth. Most of this hardware wasn't on the Google campus. It was just out there, somewhere on earth, whirring away in big refrigerated data centers. But at Google it was called "the cloud." And one challenge of programming at Google was to leverage that cloud—to push it to do things that would overwhelm lesser machines.

New hires at Google, Bisciglia says, usually take a few months to get used to this scale. "Then one day, you see someone suggest a wild job that needs a few thousand machines, and you say: '"Hey, he gets it."'"

What recruits needed, Bisciglia eventually decided, was advance training. So one autumn when he ran into Google CEO Eric E. Schmidt between meetings, he floated in idea. He would use his 20 percent time, the allotment Googlers have for independent projects, to launch a course. He would introduce students at his alma mater, the University of Washington, to programming at the scale of a cloud. Call it Google 101. Schmidt liked the plan. Over the following months, Bisciglia's Google 101 would evolve and grow. It would eventually lead to an ambitious partnership with IBM to plug universities around the world into Google-like computing clouds.

"I had originally thought Bisciglia was going to work on education, which was fine," Schmidt said late one recent afternoon at Google headquarters. "Nine months later, he comes out with this new cloud strategy, which was completely unexpected." The idea, as it developed, was to deliver to students, researchers, and entrepreneurs the immense power of Google-style computing, either via Google's machines or others offering the same service. In Bisciglia's words: "Just as people are social animals, computers are social machines—the more the merrier. . . . One computer just won't hack it; these days, to support a new paradigm of massively parallel systems architecture, we need to break the machine out of its bunker and give it some friends" (www.blogs.computerworld, p. 2).

The Google cloud is a network made of hundreds of thousands—by some estimates, 1 million—of cheap servers, each having not much more power than the PCs we have in our homes. The cloud stores staggering amounts of data, including numerous copies of the World Wide Web. This makes search faster, helping ferret out answers to billions of queries in a fraction of a second. When individual pieces die, engineers pluck them out, and replace them with faster boxes. Cloud computing, with Google's machinery at the center, fits neatly into the company's grand vision from the beginning: "to organize the world's information and make it universally accessible."

Changing the nature of computing and scientific research wasn't at the top of Bisciglia's agenda the day he collared Schmidt. What he really wanted, he says, was to go back to school. Unlike many of his colleagues at Google, a place teeming with Ph.D.s, Bisciglia was snatched up by the company as soon as he graduated from the University of Washington. He'd never been a grad student. He ached for a break from his daily routines at Google—the 10-hour workdays building search algorithms in his cube in Building 44, the long commutes on Google buses from the apartment he shared with three roomies in San Francisco. He wanted to return to Seattle, if only one day a week, and work with his professor and mentor, Ed Lazowska. "I had an itch to teach," he says.

In late 2006, as he shuttled between the Googleplex and Seattle preparing for Google 101, Bisciglia used his entrepreneurial skills to piece together a sprawling team of volunteers. He worked with college interns to develop the curriculum, and he dragooned a couple of Google colleagues from a nearby facility to use some of their 20 percent time to help him teach it. Following Schmidt's advice, Bisciglia worked to focus Google 101 on something students could learn quickly. "I was, like, what's the one thing I could teach them in two months that would be useful and really important?" he recalls. His answer was MapReduce, the software at the heart of Google computing.

## Questions

1. What approach to or style of leadership should managers at Google use to keep Bisciglia happy and therefore staying with the company? (Google Christophe Bisciglia to see if he is still a Googler.)
2. What has this case got to do with contingency and situational leadership?
3. To what extent do you think the accomplishments of Bisciglia help him be perceived as charismatic?

Excerpted from Stephen Baker, "Google and the Wisdom of Clouds," *Business Week*, December 24, 2007, pp. 048–055; "And Here's the Mastermind: Christophe Bisciglia," blogs .computerworld.com/node/6326/print, October 9, 2007.

# Leadership Case Problem B

## Oh Rats, What a Problem

A pack of a dozen or more rats scurrying around a closed KFC/Taco Bell restaurant in New York City's Greenwich Village on an early Friday morning in 2007 prompted shrieks from onlookers and fodder for morning television talk shows, which aired video of the infestation. A TV crew discovered the rat infestation and began filming through a window of the building. About a dozen rats were filmed racing around the restaurant's floors, playing with each other and sniffing for food as they dashed around tables and children's high chairs.

The restaurant on Sixth Avenue near New York University had been cited as recently as December 2006 for a number of health code violations, including evidence of rodents and live cockroaches. KFC/Taco Bell is owned by Yum Brands, a publicly held corporation based in Louisville, Kentucky. The two restaurants often operate in the same retail space.

A company spokesperson said in a written statement that the restaurant was inspected as recently as one day before the incident and tried to address the problem by mentioning construction in the basement. Ironically, it said that construction work might have temporarily worsened the infestation problem.

"Nothing is more important to us than the health and safety of our customers. This is completely unacceptable and in absolute violation of our high standards" (usatoday.com, March 1, 2007, p. 1). "We've talked with the franchisee, who is actively addressing this issue, as is evident by the preventative construction in the basement yesterday that temporarily escalated the situation. This store will remain closed until this issue is completely resolved. The health department inspected the restaurant yesterday and we will ask them to return when work is complete to give the restaurant a clean bill of health." (cnn.money.com, February 23, 2007, p. 1)

Although it passed its health inspections, the restaurant had been cited for evidence of rodents several times in the last three years, among other violations. In its most recent inspection, the restaurant had scored a ten on the city Department of Health's inspection meter. A score of twenty-eight or more indicates that the restaurant poses a public health record. The restaurant's scores had improved from a sixteen in 2004 and a fourteen in March of 2006.

Still the Department of Health had cited the restaurant for evidence of rodents and live rodents and insects in each of three previous years before the latest incident. Spokeswoman Sara Markt said if there is an "imminent risk to health" —a "critical violation that can't be corrected" —closure could be a possibility.

The Taco Bell chairs suffered an enormous public relations setback in the fall of 2006 when dozens of people were sickened by E. coli bacteria, which the Centers for Disease Control and Prevention traced back to the chain's supplier of lettuce. The outbreak prompted the closure of many Taco Bell restaurants throughout the Northeast.

Rats have long been a problem in New York City, with such a dense population and such a large and readily available food supply for the rodents. They are frequently seen scampering through subway tunnels, rooting through trash, dashing across parks and burrowing into the walls of apartment buildings.

## Questions

1. How would you advise leadership at Yum to deal with the problem of adverse publicity about the rats in the restaurant?
2. What is your evaluation of the crisis management skill of a franchise owner who refuses to speak to a reporter?
3. What would you think of Yum leadership if they had used the following excuse: "We're not the only enterprise in New York to have a rat problem. Give us a break."?

*Source:* Caleb Silver, "Taco Bell Rats Are Stars for a Day," cnnmoney.com, February 23, 2007; "KFC, Taco Bell Parent: Rat Appearance 'Completely Unacceptable,'" usatoday.com, March 1, 2007.

 ## Leadership Skill-Building Exercise 5-3

### My Leadership Portfolio

For this chapter entry in your leadership portfolio, visualize two different leadership scenarios that you witnessed directly, read about, or saw on television or in a movie. Think through how you would have used a different leadership approach for each one if you had been the leader. To illustrate, suppose you had passed a construction site for a skyscraper and noticed that the crane operator seemed confident and competent. You might conclude, "In this situation, I would have used a *delegating* style of leadership with the crane operator because she was so self-sufficient. Yet I would still have given her some recognition for a job well done at the end of her shift."

Another scenario might be that you witnessed a bloody fight at a professional hockey match. You might conclude, "In this situation, I would be as directive as possible. I would suspend and fine the players, with no room for negotiation. Decisive action must be taken to help quell violence in professional sports."

## Internet Skill-Building Exercise

### Crisis Management

The state of Maine regards managing crises in the workplace as one aspect of employee wellness. The "Wellness Tips" presented in www.state.me.us/beh/EAP/leadership.htm provide several suggestions to help leaders manage, motivate, and lead their employees in a drastically changed work environment.

Apply the chapter concepts! Visit the Web and complete this Internet skill-building exercise to learn more about current leadership topics and trends.

1. How does this crisis management advice compare to what you learned in this chapter?
2. Which of these ideas would you be the most likely to use if you were the leader facing a workplace crisis?

## CHAPTER 6

# Leadership Ethics and Social Responsibility

## LEARNING OBJECTIVES

After studying this chapter and doing the exercises, you should be able to

- Specify key principles of ethical and moral leadership.
- Apply a guide to ethical decision making.
- Present representative examples of unethical behavior by business leaders.
- Describe what leaders can do to foster an ethical and socially responsible organization.
- Explain the link between business ethics and organizational performance.

## CHAPTER OUTLINE

**Principles and Practices of Ethical and Moral Leadership**

Five Ethical Leadership Behaviors
Factors Contributing to Ethical Differences
The Ethical Mind for Leaders

**Guidelines for Evaluating the Ethics of a Decision**

**A Sampling of Unethical Leadership Behaviors**

**Leadership, Social Responsibility, and Creating an Ethical Organizational Culture**

Providing Strategic Leadership of Ethics and Social Responsibility
Creating a Pleasant Workplace
Helping Build a Sustainable Environment
Engaging in Philanthropy
Working with Suppliers to Improve Working Conditions
Establishing Written Codes of Ethical Conduct
Developing Formal Mechanisms for Dealing with Ethical Problems
Accepting Whistleblowers
Providing Training in Ethics and Social Responsibility
Placing Company Interests over Personal Interests

**Ethical Behavior and Organizational Performance**

**Summary**

British multibillionaire and Virgin Group founder Richard Branson says he will invest an estimated $3 billion (U.S.) over ten years in renewable energy projects and technologies that help crack down on global warming. Ironically, the money is the anticipated profits of his emissions-spewing travel businesses, such as airline Virgin Atlantic and railway operator Virgin Trains, both heavy users of fossil fuels.

Branson announced the financial commitment in New York on the second day of the annual Clinton Global Initiative summit, hosted by former U.S. President Bill Clinton. The money will be managed through a new investment company called Virgin Fuels. "I really do believe the world is facing a catastrophe and there are scientists who say we are already too late, but I don't believe this is the case," said the 56-year-old entrepreneur.

"We have to wean ourselves off our dependence on coal and fossil fuels. Our generation has the knowledge, it has the financial resources, and as importantly, it has the willpower to do so." In a statement, he described the contribution as a "small way to enable our children to enjoy this beautiful world." In the next ten years, Branson said, Virgin Fuels will invest in renewable energy projects within the Virgin Group and make outside investments in biofuel research and development, production, and distribution.

Nicholas Parker, chairman of the Cleantech Venture Network, which organized the conference, said, "People are saying that it's time to stop mucking around on climate change, and that we're going to give leadership on this."[1]

Sir Richard Branson illustrates the generosity, thoughtfulness, ethical behavior, and social consciousness shown by many business leaders whether or not you believe the world is facing a catastrophic climate change. However, the "good side" of business leaders rarely receives as much publicity as the "bad side." In this chapter, we examine leadership ethics and social responsibility from several major perspectives: principles of ethical and moral leadership, an ethical decision-making guide, examples of ethical violations, examples how leaders develop an ethical and socially responsible culture, and the link between business ethics and organizational performance.

## PRINCIPLES AND PRACTICES OF ETHICAL AND MORAL LEADERSHIP

Enough attention has been paid to what leaders at all levels *should* do that some principles of ethical and moral leadership have emerged. Because terms dealing with the ideal behavior of leaders are used so loosely, it is helpful to define what these terms have generally come to mean in the business community. **Ethics** is the study of moral obligations, or of separating right from wrong. *Ethics* can also be a plural noun meaning the accepted guidelines of behavior for groups or institutions.[2] In this sense it means much the same as **morals**, which are an individual's determination of what is right or wrong; morals are influenced by a person's values. Values are tied closely to ethics because ethics become the vehicle for converting values into action. A leader who values fairness will evaluate group members on the basis of their performance, not personal friendships. And a moral leader will practice good ethics.

Edwin H. Locke, the goal theorist, argues that ethics is at the center of leadership because the goal of a rational leader is to merge the interests of all parties so that everyone benefits and the organization prospers.[3] The ethics link is that if everyone benefits, all people are being treated ethically.

In this section, we present a sampling of ethical and moral behaviors, all centering on the idea that a leader should do the *right* thing, as perceived by a consensus of reasonable people. None of these terms can be pinned down with great precision. We also present a brief explanation of why the ethical and moral behavior of leaders differs so widely, and pay separate attention to the importance of an ethical mind. Before studying these principles, do Leadership Self-Assessment Quiz 6-1 to think through your work-related ethics and morality.

 Leadership Self-Assessment Quiz 6-1

**The Leader Integrity Scale**

*Instructions:* Circle the numbers to indicate how well each item describes your current attitudes and behavior or how you would behave in a group situation. Response choices: 1 = not at all; 2 = somewhat; 3 = very much; 4 = exactly.

1. I use other people's mistakes to attack them personally.          1    2    3    4

2. I always get even.          1    2    3    4

3. As a leader, I would give special favors to my favorite employees.          1    2    3    4

4. I lie to group members if it fits my purposes.          1    2    3    4

5. I would let a group member take the blame to protect myself.          1    2    3    4

6. I would deliberately fuel conflict among group members.          1    2    3    4

7. People who know me well consider me to be ruthless.          1    2    3    4

8. I would use a performance evaluation to criticize an individual as a person.          1    2    3    4

9. I hold grudges against people.          1    2    3    4

## Quiz 6-1 (continued)

10. I would allow coworkers to be blamed for my mistakes.                               1   2   3   4

11. I would falsify records to help my work situation.                                  1   2   3   4

12. My morals are low.                                                                  1   2   3   4

13. I would make fun of someone's mistakes rather than coach the person on how to do the job better.   1   2   3   4

14. I would exaggerate someone's mistakes to make him or her look bad to my superiors.   1   2   3   4

15. I get revenge on people when possible.                                              1   2   3   4

16. I would blame a group member for my mistakes.                                       1   2   3   4

17. I would avoid coaching an employee so that he or she could fail.                     1   2   3   4

18. A person's ethnic group influences how I treat him or her.                          1   2   3   4

19. I would deliberately distort what another person said to make me look good.          1   2   3   4

20. I would deliberately make employees angry with each other.                          1   2   3   4

21. I am a hypocrite.                                                                   1   2   3   4

22. I would limit the training opportunities of others to prevent them from advancing.  1   2   3   4

23. I would blackmail an employee if I thought I could get away with it.                1   2   3   4

24. I enjoy turning down the requests of group members.                                 1   2   3   4

25. If an employee were to get on my bad side, I would make trouble for him or her.     1   2   3   4

26. I would take credit for the ideas of others.                                       1   2   3   4

27. I would steal from the organization.                                               1   2   3   4

28. I would engage in sabotage against the organization just to get even.               1   2   3   4

29. I would fire a person I did not like if I could get away with it.                    1   2   3   4

30. I would do things that violate organizational policy, and then expect employees to cover for me.   1   2   3   4

## Quiz 6-1 (continued)

*Scoring and Interpretation:* Add up your responses to all thirty items. The interpretation of the score is shown here. In interpreting your score, recognize that people tend to overrate themselves on ethical behavior because it is painful to admit to being devious and unethical.

- **30–35 very ethical:** If you scored in this range, your self-image is that you are trustworthy and highly principled. If your answers are accurate, it could mean that your high ethics could be an asset to you as a leader.

- **36–61 moderately ethical:** Scores in this range mean that your impression is that you sometimes engage in slightly unethical behavior. You might strive to be more consistently ethical.

- **62–120 very unethical:** This range describes leaders who may be perceived as engaging in practices that are unethical, dishonest, unfair, and unprincipled. Although many unethical leaders are successful for a while, your unethical attitudes and behavior could be career-limiting factors. It is time to reflect on your values and start taking corrective action. Studying ethics can also help.

*Source*: Adapted from S. B. Craig and S. B. Gustafson, "Perceived Leader Integrity Scale: An Instrument for Assessing Employee Perceptions of Leader Integrity," *Leadership Quarterly*, vol. 9 (2), 1998, pp. 143–144.

### Five Ethical Leadership Behaviors

***Be Honest and Trustworthy and Have Integrity in Dealing with Others***    Survey evidence supports the belief that ethical leadership is important for the welfare of a company, particularly for attracting, retaining, and ensuring productivity among employees. According to an LRN Ethics study conducted in the United States:

- A majority of full-time workers say it is critical to work for an ethical company.
- More than one in three workers left a job because of poor ethics by company leaders.
- Eighty-two percent of workers would be willing to receive less pay to work for an ethical company.
- Only 11 percent of workers claim not to be affected by unethical behavior.[4]

Despite the importance of leaders who are trustworthy, evidence suggests that trust in business leaders is now low. As part of an ongoing study of employee attitudes and opinions, 1,200 workers were surveyed across a variety of industries. Only 60 percent said they believed that coworkers acted with integrity, with only 56 percent indicating that top management acted with integrity. Nevertheless, 72 percent believed their immediate boss behaved with honesty and integrity.[5]

Furthermore, two studies found that most Asian employees have a low level of trust and confidence in their business leaders and that business leaders have too much power.[6]

An ethical leader is honest and trustworthy and therefore has integrity. According to ethics researcher Thomas E. Becker, this quality goes beyond honesty and conscientiousness. **Integrity** refers to loyalty to rational principles; it means practicing what one preaches regardless of emotional or social pressure.[7] For example, a leader with integrity would believe that employees should be treated fairly, and the pressure to cut costs would not prompt him or her to renege on a commitment to reimburse an employee for relocation expenses. As another example, a leader who preaches cultural diversity would assemble a diverse team.

***Pay Attention to All Stakeholders***   An ethical and moral leader strives to treat fairly all interested parties affected by his or her decision. To do otherwise creates winners and losers after many decisions are made. The widely held belief that a CEO's primary responsibility is to maximize shareholder wealth conflicts with the principle of paying attention to all stakeholders. A team of management scholars observes, "We used to recognize corporations as both economic and social institutions—as organizations that were designed to serve a balanced set of stakeholders, not just the narrow interests of the shareholder."[8] A leader interested in maximizing shareholder wealth might attempt to cut costs and increase profits in such ways as (1) laying off valuable employees to reduce payroll costs, (2) overstating profits to impress investors, (3) overcharging customers, and (4) reducing health benefits for retirees. Although these practices may be standard, they all violate the rights of stakeholders.

Jim Goodnight, the CEO of software company SAS, is among the business leaders who contend that there is a strong link between employee satisfaction and increased productivity and profits. He explains, "Because we put employee-oriented measures in place long ago, we have the benefit of years of experience to show that the long-term benefits far outweigh the short-term costs. Most companies don't know how to represent that kind of return in their annual reports."[9]

Another behavior of *authentic leaders* is to perceive their role to include having an ethical responsibility to all of their shareholders. The welfare of others takes precedence over their own personal welfare (as in servant leadership). Authentic leaders have a deep commitment to their personal growth as well as to the growth of other stakeholders.[10]

***Build Community***   A corollary of taking into account the needs of all stakeholders is that the leader helps people achieve a common goal. Leadership researcher Peter G. Northouse explains that leaders need to take into account their own and their followers' purposes and search for goals that are compatible to all.[11] When many people work toward the same constructive goal, they build community. A business leader who works with many people to help poor schoolchildren is an ideal example of someone who builds community.

The Global Compact, an initiative of the United Nations to ensure that business practices conform with human rights, labor, and environmental standards, seeks to build community on an international scale. The common goal is equitable treatment of workers. More than 1,700 multinational companies have joined, and the pact has become the world's largest voluntary corporate citizenship group. Among the goals of the Global Compact is to get companies to make explicit statements about human rights in their policies.[12]

*Respect the Individual*    Respecting individuals is a principle of ethical and moral leadership that incorporates other aspects of morality. If you tell the truth, you respect others well enough to be honest. If you keep promises, you also show respect. And if you treat others fairly, you show respect.[13] Showing respect for the individual also means that you recognize that everybody has some inner worth and should be treated with courtesy and kindness. An office supervisor demonstrated respect in front of his department when he asked a custodian who entered the office, "What can we do in this department to make your job easier?"

*Accomplish Silent Victories*    According to Joseph L. Badaracco Jr., modesty and restraint are largely responsible for the achievements of the most effective moral leaders in business. The ethical and moral leader works silently and somewhat behind the scenes, to accomplish moral victories regularly. Instead of being perceived as a hero or heroine, the moral leader quietly works on an ethical agenda. Quite often he or she will work out a compromise to ensure that a decision in process will have an ethical outcome.

A case in point is the middle manager at a telecommunications company whose senior managers decided to outsource the manufacture of a product line to China. As a result the small U.S. community was to lose about 200 jobs. The middle manager lobbied for months for the company to establish its new call center in the same town, thereby enabling about sixty-five of the workers to continue employment with the company.[14]

## Factors Contributing to Ethical Differences

There are many reasons for differences in ethics and morality among leaders. One is the leader's *level of greed, gluttony, and avarice*. Many people seek to maximize personal returns, even at the expense of others. Former Federal Reserve chairman Alan Greenspan commented publicly on the problem of executive greed. He said that "an infectious greed" had contaminated the business community in the late 1990s, as one executive after another manipulated earnings or resorted to fraudulent accounting to capitalize on soaring stock prices.[15] Table 6-1 presents a sampling of executive compensation that could be interpreted as signs of greed and avarice. Instead of taking so much money for themselves, how about sharing more of the money with employees and stockholders, and offering lower prices for customers? The counterargument is that supply and demand rules, with a limited supply of capable CEOs.

So you have to pay talented executives loads of money to stay competitive, even if the compensation exceeds $100 million per year.

Timothy P. Flynn, chairman of the global accounting firm KPGM, has identified reasons why good people choose the wrong path. One reason is rationalization, leading people to focus on the intent of the action, not the action itself. For example, people might say they are doing something wrong (such as exaggerating profits) to help a client, or boost the stock price to help investors. Another reason is implied permission—"Nobody is telling me to stop, so it must be okay."[16] For example, a manager might continue to place only personal friends and relatives in key jobs because he or she was not told to stop.

A fourth key contributor to a leader's ethics and morality is his or her *level of moral development*. Some leaders are morally advanced, while others are morally challenged—a mental condition that often develops early in life. People progress through three developmental levels in their moral reasoning. At the *preconventional level*, a person is concerned primarily with receiving external rewards and avoiding punishment. A leader at this level of development might falsify earnings statements for the primary purpose of gaining a large bonus. At the *conventional level*, people learn to conform to the expectations of good behavior as defined by key people in their environment and societal norms. A leader at this level might be moral enough just to look good, such as being fair with salary increases and encouraging contributions to the United Way campaign. At the *postconventional level*, people are guided by an internalized set of universal principles that may even transcend the laws of a particular society. A leader at the postconventional level of moral behavior would be concerned with doing the most good for the most people, without regard for whether such behavior brought him or her recognition and fortune.[17] The servant leader described in Chapter 4 would be at this advanced level of moral development.

A fifth factor contributing to the moral excesses of business leaders is that many of them have developed a sense of **entitlement**. In the opinion of several psychiatrists and corporate governance experts, some CEOs lose their sense of reality and feel entitled to whatever they can get away with or steal. For example, Conrad Black, the CEO of Hollinger International Inc., felt entitled to have the company

**TABLE 6-1** A Sampling of Extraordinary Business Executive Compensation

| EXECUTIVE AND COMPANY | RECENT ANNUAL SALARY AND BONUS |
| --- | --- |
| Larry Ellison, CEO, Oracle | $9,369, 000 |
| Angelo R. Mozilio, CEO, Countrywide Financial | $23,328,000 |
| Daniel P. Amos, Aflac | $4,102,000 |
| Lloyd C. Blankfein, Goldman Sachs Group | $27,585,000 |
| David C. Novak, Yum Brands | $ 6,055,000 |
| Bob R. Simpson, XTO Energy | $32,208,000 |

*Source*: Gathered from facts in "What the Boss Makes," *Forbes*, May 19, 2008, p. 136.

pay for his personal servants. Also, many executives feel entitled to healthy compensation. The average CEO pay at major corporations is now 364 times higher than the lowest-paid employees.[18]

A sixth factor contributing to unethical and immoral leadership behavior is the *situation*, particularly the organizational culture. If leaders at the top of the organization take imprudent, quasi-legal risks, other leaders throughout the firm might be prompted to behave similarly. The risk-taking culture at Enron Corporation is said to have contributed to firm leaders' engaging in questionable financial transactions such as creating false profit statements. The imprudent risks in subprime mortgages taken with investor money by investment banks in recent years might also reflect an aggressive culture. Financial executives were pushed to maximize profits, sometimes not taking into account investor welfare.[19]

*A person's character* is a seventh factor that contributes to ethical differences. The higher the quality of a person's character, the more likely he or she will behave ethically and morally. For example, a leader who is honest and cooperative will tend to behave more ethically than a leader who is dishonest and uncooperative. Leadership Self-Assessment Quiz 6-2 digs into the behavioral specifics of good character as perceived by the U.S. Air Force.

 ## Leadership Self-Assessment Quiz 6-2

### The Air Force Character Attributes Checklist

*Instructions:* Listed and defined next are character attributes the U.S. Air Force wants to see among the ranks of its leaders. For each attribute, note your standing as being high (H), average (A), or low (L). A checklist of this nature lends itself to self-serving bias, so work extra hard to be objective. When applicable, visualize an example of how you have exhibited, or have not exhibited, a particular character attribute.

|  |  | My Standing | | |
|---|---|---|---|---|
| Factor | Description | H | A | L |
| Integrity | Consistently adhering to a moral or ethical code or standard. A person who consistently chooses to do the right thing when faced with alternative choices. | ☐ | ☐ | ☐ |
| Honesty | Consistently being truthful with others. | ☐ | ☐ | ☐ |
| Loyalty | Being devoted and committed to one's organization, supervisors, coworkers, and subordinates. | ☐ | ☐ | ☐ |
| Selflessness | Genuine concern about the welfare of others and a willingness to sacrifice one's personal interest for others and the organization. | ☐ | ☐ | ☐ |
| Compassion | Concern for the suffering or welfare of others and providing aid or showing mercy for others. | ☐ | ☐ | ☐ |

## Quiz 6-2 (continued)

| Factor | Description | My Standing | | |
|---|---|---|---|---|
| | | **H** | **A** | **L** |
| Competency | Capable of excelling at all tasks assigned. Is effective and efficient. | ☐ | ☐ | ☐ |
| Respectfulness | Shows esteem for and consideration and appreciation of other people. | ☐ | ☐ | ☐ |
| Fairness | Treats everyone in an equitable, impartial, and just manner. | ☐ | ☐ | ☐ |
| Responsibility and self-discipline | Can be depended on to make rational and logical decisions and to do tasks assigned. Can perform tasks assigned without supervision. | ☐ | ☐ | ☐ |
| Decisiveness | Capable of making logical and effective decisions in a timely manner. Makes good decisions promptly after considering data appropriate to the decision. | ☐ | ☐ | ☐ |
| Spiritual appreciation | Values the spiritual diversity among individuals with different backgrounds and cultures and respects all individuals' rights to differ from others in their beliefs. | ☐ | ☐ | ☐ |
| Cooperativeness | Willing to work or act together with others in accomplishing a task toward a common end or purpose. | ☐ | ☐ | ☐ |

**Interpretation:** The more of the attributes you rated as "high," the more likely it is that others perceive you as having good character. The list may provide some clues to leadership development. For example, if you are perceived to be low on integrity and cooperativeness, you are less likely to be able to influence others.

**Note:** Although competency and decisiveness are not ordinarily considered character traits, being competent and decisive contributes to having good character.

*Source:* U.S. Air Force, as reprinted in Cassie B. Barlow, Mark Jordan, and William H. Hendrix, "Character Assessment: An Examination of Leadership Levels," *Journal of Business and Psychology*, Summer 2003, p. 568.

### The Ethical Mind for Leaders

Cognitive and educational psychologist Howard Gardner believes that for a leader to stay ethical, he or she must develop an **ethical mind,** or a point of view that helps the individual aspire to good work that matters to their colleagues, companies, and society in general.[20] Developing an ethical mind begins with the belief that retaining an ethical compass is essential to the health of the organization. Early life influences, such as encouragement not to cheat on exams or plagiarize when writing papers, are a good start. Next, the leader must state his or her ethical beliefs and stick to them. (The ethical beliefs already mentioned in this chapter are relevant, such as being convinced that attention must be paid to all stakeholders.) The leader must also make a rigorous self-test to make sure values are being adhered to, such as checking to see if merit instead of favoritism is a key criterion for promotion. Taking the time to reflect on beliefs can help the leader stay focused on ethical behavior. Asking mentors to comment on the ethics of your behavior can be a useful reality check. Finally, to stay ethical, the leader should act quickly on strongly unethical behavior of others, such as confronting a colleague who is using the corporate jet for a family vacation.

So which leader has an ethical mind? You will probably find many of them as hard-working middle managers. A famous business leader with an ethical mind might be Warren Buffett, the investment sage. He has consistently been one of the world's richest people, yet maintains high ethical standards for himself and his investment firm, Berkshire Hathaway. Buffett sends memos regularly to the companies owned by his firm, advising them to stay ethical. And he is widely quoted for stating that the rationale "everyone else is doing it" is not acceptable.[21]

## GUIDELINES FOR EVALUATING THE ETHICS OF A DECISION

Several guidelines, or ethical screens, have been developed to help leaders or other influence agents decide whether a given act is ethical or unethical. The Center for Business Ethics at Bentley College has developed six questions to evaluate the ethics of a specific decision:[22]

- *Is it right?* This question is based on the deontological theory of ethics that there are certainly universally accepted guiding principles of rightness and wrongness, such as "thou shall not steal."
- *Is it fair?* This question is based on the deontological theory of justice that certain actions are inherently just or unjust. For example, it is unjust to fire a high-performing employee to make room for a less competent person who is a relative by marriage.
- *Who gets hurt?* This question is based on the utilitarian notion of attempting to do the greatest good for the greatest number of people.
- *Would you be comfortable if the details of your decision or actions were made public in the media or through email?* This question is based on the universalist principle of disclosure.
- *What would you tell your child, sibling, or young relative to do?* This question is based on the deontological principle of reversibility, which evaluates the ethics of a decision by reversing the decision maker.
- *How does it smell?* This question is based on a person's intuition and common sense. For example, counting a product inquiry over the Internet as a sale would "smell" bad to a sensible person.

Ethical issues that require a run through the guide are usually subtle rather than blatant, or a decision that falls into the gray zone. An example is the financial transactions of a small group of traders at the investment bank Goldman Sachs

## ⊙ Leadership Skill-Building Exercise 6-1

### The Best Buy In-Store Web Site

Imagine that you and several other classmates are Best Buy executives and that you are reviewing the following case history related to your retail stores:

In Connecticut it was discovered that a Best Buy store had a special version of its web site for in-store use that was really an intranet that did not display the sales and special offers on the web site accessed by the public. The result was a bait-and-switch operation that worked in this way: Customers would visit the store thinking they could get a deal that they found on the Best Buy web site, only to be told (and shown) that whatever deal they saw was no longer being offered. The in-store computer was used to access what customers thought was the Best Buy web site, but it was actually an intranet site with prices modified from the real web site.

Your assignment as part of the Best Buy team is to first decide whether using a fake company web site is ethical by running the decision through the ethical decision-making guide presented in this chapter. Second, decide what Best Buy should do with the intranet. Also, think through how the company should deal with the negative publicity associated with the phony web site.

This exercise is important because it helps alert you to consider the ethics of contemplated decisions. In the current climate, many companies are seeking to promote into leadership positions at any level those individuals with a track record of making ethical decisions.

*Source:* Based on facts in "Best Buy's Secret 'Employee Only' In-Store Website Shows Different Prices than Public Website," Consumerist.com, December 29, 2007; "Connecticut AG Sues Best Buy over Phony Version of Company Website," www.techdirt.com, May 24, 2007.

Group Inc. during the subprime mortgage crisis. The group's gamble that securities backed by risky home loans would fall in value generated nearly $4 billion in profits in a year. (This practice is referred to as *selling short*.) At the same time, subprime mortgages were being generated at a rapid pace and being sold to Goldman Sachs clients. So, the firm was making loads of money by hoping that investments sold to their own clients would lose value rapidly. The ethical question asked is why Goldman continued to sell collateral debt obligations to customers while its own traders were betting that the value of these investments would fall? [23] Also, should Goldman brokers have told clients that the smart money believed that they were being sold investments destined to decline in value rapidly? How would you like to purchase a house from a real estate broker who was making side bets that houses in the area were going to drop in value?

Leaders regularly face the necessity of running a contemplated decision through an ethics test. Leadership Skill-Building Exercise 6-1 provides an opportunity to think through the ethics of a decision made by a consumer electronics store.

The question of ethics arises when a person conducts a job search. The job seeker might want to size up the ethical climate established by company leaders. The wave of corporate scandals that took place a few years ago prompted more job seekers than in the past to examine prospective employers' ethical standards and practices.[24] Table 6-2 presents a list of ethics-related questions a job seeker might ask before joining a firm. In this way, the prospective leader would have a chance of finding an ethical and moral climate compatible with his or her values.

**TABLE 6-2** A Job Seeker's Ethics Audit

**SOME PROBING QUESTIONS TO ASK ABOUT A PROSPECTIVE EMPLOYER:**

☐ Is there a formal code of ethics? How widely is it distributed? Is it reinforced in other formal ways such as through decision-making systems?

☐ Are workers at all levels trained in ethical decision making? Are they also encouraged to take responsibility for their behavior or to question authority when asked to do something they consider wrong?

☐ Do employees have formal channels available to make their concerns known confidentially? Is there a formal committee high in the organization that considers ethical issues?

☐ Is misconduct disciplined swiftly and justly within the organization?

☐ Is integrity emphasized to new employees?

☐ How are senior managers perceived by subordinates in terms of their integrity? How do such leaders serve as models for ethics-related behavior?

*Source*: Linda K. Treviño, chair of the Department of Management and Organization, Smeal College of Business, Pennsylvania State University (as reprinted in Kris Maher, "Wanted: Ethical Employer," *The Wall Street Journal*, July 9, 2002, p. B1).

## A SAMPLING OF UNETHICAL LEADERSHIP BEHAVIORS

We have been alluding to unethical behavior in this and previous chapters. Here we present a sampling of unethical behaviors from the past and present. A statement often made is that about 95 percent of business leaders are ethical and that the 5 percent of bad apples (mostly senior executives) get all the publicity. However, the impact of unethical leadership has been enormous. Unethical behavior has thrown companies into bankruptcy, led to the layoffs of thousands of workers, diminished trust in stock investments, and discouraged many talented young people from embarking on a business career.

Table 6-3 presents some unethical, immoral, and often illegal behaviors engaged in by business leaders whose acts have been publicly reported. Thousands of other unethical acts go unreported, such as a business owner who places a family member, friend, or lover on the payroll at an inflated salary for work of limited value to the firm.

## LEADERSHIP, SOCIAL RESPONSIBILITY, AND CREATING AN ETHICAL ORGANIZATIONAL CULTURE

One way of being ethical and moral is to guide the firm, or a unit within, toward doing good deeds. **Corporate social responsibility** is having obligations to society beyond the company's economic obligations to owners or stockholders and also beyond those prescribed by law or contract. Both ethics and social responsibility relate to the goodness or morality of organizations, but social responsibility relates to an organization's impact on society and goes beyond doing what is ethical.

**TABLE 6-3** Examples of Unethical Behavior by Business Leaders

The sampling of unethical behaviors presented here includes behaviors that resulted in criminal prosecutions, and those that resulted in only embarrassment and negative press.

| LEADER AND COMPANY | OFFENSE AND OUTCOME |
| --- | --- |
| Dennis Kozlowski, former CEO of Tyco International LTD | Did not pay back large sums of money borrowed from company; avoided paying sales tax on art; padded earnings growth. Sent to prison in 2004 for eight to twenty-five years, and paid $70 million in restitution. |
| Bernie Ebbers of MCI/WorldCom | Misclassified about $9 billion in expenses; borrowed $408 million from company to pay margin calls on stocks; overcharged customers. In July 2005, sentenced to twenty-five years in prison for fraud. |
| Patrician Dunn, non-executive chairman of Hewlett-Packard | Spied on other board members to uncover who leaked sensitive information to the press. Nine reporters covering HP were also spied on. Spies were paid more than $325,000 to pose as journalists and board members (referred to as *pretexting*) to obtain phone records, and also used fake email addresses and installed spyware on a board member's computer. Dunn resigned her post at HP. In 2007 the State of California dropped the criminal charges. |
| Frank P. Quattrone, former investment banker at Crédit Suisse First Boston | Accused of handing out hot initial public offering shares to friends; pressuring analysts to write favorable reports on clients; and destroying documents under investigation. In 2006 freed from charges after a conviction that was later reversed, and a hung jury. |
| Steven P. Jobs, CEO of Apple Corp. and Pixar | Accused in 2006 of backdating stock options so a favored few employees could be guaranteed a profit from their options. Also, Jobs was accused of receiving stock options in 2001 without approval of the board, and that falsified documents were used to indicate board approval. About 100 other companies were involved in similar backdating, so no charges were filed against Jobs or Apple. |
| Chung Mong-koo, chairman of Hyundai Motor Co. | Suspected of embezzling $110 million of company money to build a slush fund for private purposes, including payments to lobbyists for government favors. Convicted in 2007 of embezzlement and sentenced to three-year prison term, with the decision under appeal. |
| Martha Stewart, chairwoman and CEO of Martha Stewart Living Omnimedia | Charged with conspiracy and obstruction of justice and intentionally making false statements in connection with sale of ImClone stock. Convicted in 2004, and spent five months in prison and five months of house arrest including wearing an electronic ankle bracelet. Stewart returned to her company and television show after serving her sentence. |

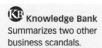
**Knowledge Bank** Summarizes two other business scandals.

**www.cengage.com/ management/dubrin**

*Source:* The facts in the table have been widely circulated in the media. Representative sources for the facts include the following: "High Profiles in Hot Water," *The Wall Street Journal*, June 28, 2002, p. B1; James S. Granelli, Kim Christensen and Jim Puzzanghera, "HP Spied on More Than Phone Calls," www.latimes.com/business, September 21, 2006; Barbara Kiviat, "The One that Got Away," *Time*, September 4, 2006, pp. 38–39; Ian King and Connie Gugliemo, "Report: Jobs Got Options Without OK," *Bloomberg News*, December 29, 2006; Nick Wingfield, "Apple Probe Spotlights Two," *The Wall Street Journal*, January 2, 2007, p. B11; Bo-Mi Lim, "Hyundai Chief Convicted of Embezzlement," The Associated Press, February 5, 2007; "Executives on Trial," *The Wall Street Journal*, May 26, 2006, p. A9.

The idea of corporate social responsibility continues to evolve, and has recently been explained as the process by which managers within an organization think about and discuss relationships with stakeholders, and how they will work toward attaining the common good. To analyze a firm's corporate social responsibility, it is therefore necessary to understand what it thinks, says, and tends to do in relation to others.[25] According to ethics professor R. Edward Freeman, corporate social responsibility is no longer an add-on, but is built into the core purpose of a business.[26]

Being socially responsible fits into the "Thou Shalt" approach, or finding out better ways for leaders to make a positive contribution to society. In contrast, the "Thou Shalt Not" approach focuses on avoiding the kind of wrongdoing depicted in Table 6-3.[27] Our focus here is illustrative actions that leaders can take to enhance social responsibility, as well as create an organizational culture that encourages ethical behavior, as outlined in Figure 6-1.

## Providing Strategic Leadership of Ethics and Social Responsibility

The most effective route to an ethical and socially responsible organization is for senior management to provide strategic leadership in that direction. In this way, senior managers become ethics leaders: their policies and actions set the ethical and

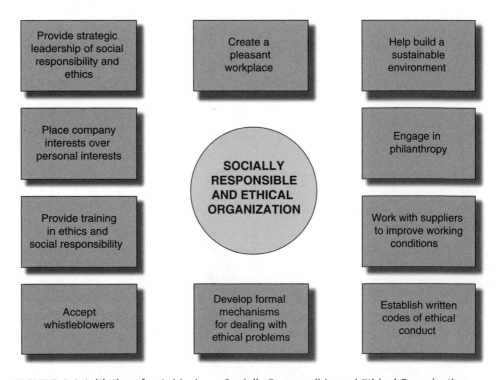

**FIGURE 6-1** Initiatives for Achieving a Socially Responsible and Ethical Organization.

social responsibility tone for the organization. If high ethics receive top priority, workers at all levels are more likely to behave ethically. When Paul O'Neil became CEO and chairperson at Alcoa years ago, he believed that plant safety was an ethical obligation. He visited Alcoa plants, communicating with managers and workers about the necessity of workplace safety. O'Neil tied promotions, evaluations, and firing to workplace safety. After twelve years of this safety climate, the annual lost workday rate was reduced from 1.87 to .014 (a reduction of 99.3 percent).[28]

Strategic leadership of ethics and social responsibility includes leading by example. If workers throughout the firm believe that behaving ethically is "in" and behaving unethically is "out," ethical behavior will prevail. Ethical behavior that is rewarded is likely to endure. Linda Klebe Treviño and Michael E. Brown observe that ethical behavior can be rewarded by promoting and compensating people who perform well and have developed a reputation of integrity with managers, coworkers, and customers. In addition, workers who perform unethically should not be rewarded, and perhaps disciplined.[29] A sales manager who uses a "35-day month" might not be rewarded for sales booked during those five days borrowed from the next month just to look good in the previous months.

## Creating a Pleasant Workplace

A social responsibility initiative that directly affects employees' well-being is to create a comfortable, pleasant, and intellectually stimulating work environment. Because many people invest about one-third of their time at work, a pleasant work environment increases the chances that their life will be enriched. Robert Levering and Milton Moskowitz, of the Great Place to Work® Institute, in cooperation with *Fortune,* have institutionalized the idea of being a "best company to work for." Employers nominate themselves, and two-thirds of the score is based on how randomly selected employees respond to the Great Place to Work Trust Index,© a survey measuring organizational culture. An evaluation of the Culture Audit by staff members at the Great Place to Work Institute determines the rest of the score. The focus is on employee satisfaction, yet the firms that fall into the "the 100 best companies to work for" are also typically profitable. Among the benefits these companies offer are flexible working hours; on-site day care; concierge services, such as dry cleaning pickup; domestic-partner benefits to same-sex couples; and fully paid sabbaticals. Following are the three most highly rated companies:[30]

> *Google, Mountain View, California:* The company whose name has become a verb sets the standard for Silicon Valley. Among its perks are free gourmet meals, a swimming spa, and free medical services on-site. Engineers are empowered to spend 20 percent of their time on independent projects. Google receives 1,300 unsolicited job résumés per day. Hiring standards are tough, emphasizing brilliance, good team-player skills, and diverse interests. Salary data are not made public, but many Google employees become wealthy through the exercise of legitimate stock options. Ninety percent of employees receive stock options.
>
> *Quicken Loans, Livonia, Michigan:* This mortgage lender has a reputation for being ethically driven. Quicken avoided the subprime mortgage crisis by restricting itself to

traditional mortgages. The average annual pay for salaried staff is $75,765, and $41,780 for the hourly staff.

*Wegmans Food Markets, Inc., Rochester, New York:* The foundation belief of this privately held 71-store grocery chain is "Employees first, customers second." The Wegman family believes that when employees are happy, customers will be too. This private grocery chain receives thousands of letters every day from consumers who would like a Wegmans store in their neighborhood. The average annual pay for the salaried staff is $49,411, and $27, 414 for the hourly staff. Wegmans was named the nation's top supermarket by the Food Network in 2007.

The employee programs that qualify a company as a best place to work focus on employee benefits. However, the leaders of these companies also emphasize stimulating work.

## Helping Build a Sustainable Environment

Socially responsible leaders influence others to sustain and preserve the external environment through a variety of actions that go beyond mandatory environmental controls such as managing toxic waste. Helping build a sustainable environment can involve hundreds of different actions such as making packaging smaller, making more extensive use of fluorescent lighting, and when feasible using energy from solar panels and wind turbines to replace burning of fossil fuels. Furthermore, many companies sponsor team-building events in which participants build a playground or refurbish an old house in a declining neighborhood. Preserving an old building uses less energy than constructing a new one, and the same act enhances the aesthetics of the environment. Three specific examples of representative leadership initiatives for helping create a sustainable environment follow:

- Several tire companies, including Bridgestone Corp. and Michelin SA, are manufacturing tires with less rolling resistance, or the force a tire must overcome to move a vehicle. Less fuel is consumed by a vehicle when it has less rolling resistance, yet there are concerns that the tire will not last as long and may have longer stopping distances on wet surfaces.[31]
- Katrina Markoff, the owner and founder of Vosgtes-Haut Chocolat (a variety of truffles), runs her Chicago headquarters with 100 percent renewable energies. "But we're shooting for LEED platinum-level certification, which means we'll basically have no waste and be almost 70 percent off the grid (power supply)," explains Markoff.[32]
- Spearheaded by CEO Lee Scott, Wal-Mart has taken major initiatives to become the greenest retailer, including opening several "green" supercenters. Among Scott's goals are to (a) increase the efficiency of its energy fleet by 25 percent in three years, and double efficiency in ten years, (b) reduce solid waste from U.S. stores by 25 percent, (c) invest $500 in sustainability projects, (d) work with suppliers to figure out ways to cut down on packaging waste, as well as new ways to decrease energy use, and (e) encourage customers to shift to the modern, energy-efficient fluorescent bulbs.[33]

**Knowledge Bank**
Contains an example of green goals established by a well-known business organization.

**www.cengage.com/ management/dubrin**

Whether or not you believe that the three examples just presented are publicity stunts to be perceived as an environmentally friendly company, the environment most likely benefits. Another way for a leader to help the environment is to be directly in the recycling business. Electronic recycling is particularly important because electronics are the fastest-growing solid waste stream in the world, and contain toxins such as mercury and chromium. A sizable company in this field is Electronic Recyclers International in Fresno, California. ERI chief executive John S. Shegerian takes performing a social good one step further: One-third of the 200 full- and part-time employees are part of its "second chance" program, which includes primarily ex-cons and former addicts.[34] The social-good aspect is that being employed facilitates a person's not lapsing back into criminal behavior and drug addiction. Leadership Skill-Building Exercise 6-2 provides an opportunity for you to practice conducting an environmental audit.

## Engaging in Philanthropy

A standard organizational leadership approach to social responsibility is to donate money to charity and various other causes. Most charities are heavily dependent on corporate support. Colleges, universities, and career schools also benefit from corporate donations. Many of the leading philanthropists donate money during their lifetime rather than giving through their estates. The most striking example is Bill and Melinda Gates of Microsoft, who formed their own foundation whose primary aims globally are to reduce extreme poverty, combat AIDS, and vaccinate children against illnesses. In the United States the focus is more on educational opportunities and access to information technology. In 2007 the foundation had an endowment of $37.3 billion, with Warren Buffet having doubled the endowment in 2006. Furthermore, Bill Gates has called for a revision of capitalism in which poor people receive more benefits. Gates said he is troubled because advances in technology, health care, and education tend to help the rich and neglect the poor.[35]

Many corporate donors want their charitable investments to benefit the end consumer, not get lost in red tape and overhead, and show measurable results. The new breed of philanthropist studies each charitable cause as he or she would a potential business investment, seeking maximum return in terms of social impact. This philanthropist might also seek follow-up data, for example, on how many children were taught to read or by what percentage new cases of AIDS declined.

Another approach to getting a rapid turnaround on charitable giving is for a company to respond directly to immediate needs, thereby displaying decisive leadership. When wildfires destroyed thousands of homes in California in October 2007, employees at six Bloomingdale's Inc. stores in the area donated quickly hundreds of blankets and household items. Within a month the chain initiated a program to raise funds for a San Diego disaster rebuilding fund. Shoppers were encouraged to donate to the charity, and the company's charitable foundation matched cash donations of $50 or more.[36]

As the accompanying Leader in Action profile illustrates, philanthropy can take a form other than donating money to causes. It can involve influencing others to make the donations.

## ◉ Leadership Skill-Building Exercise 6-2

### Conducting an Environmental Audit

To create an environmentally friendly workplace, somebody has to take the initiative to spot opportunities for change, thereby exercising leadership. Organize the class into groups of about five, with one person being appointed the team leader. You might have to do the work outside of class because your assignment is to do an environmental audit of a workplace including a nonprofit setting such as a place of worship, a school, or an athletic facility. If the audit is done during class time, evaluate a portion of the school, such as a classroom, an athletic facility, or the cafeteria. Your task is to conduct an environmental audit with respect to the energy efficiency and healthfulness of the workplace. Make judgments, perhaps on a 1-to-10 scale, plus comments about the following factors:

1. How energy efficient is the workplace in terms of such factors as building insulation, use of fluorescent lighting, heating and cooling, and use of solar panels?
2. How safe is the environment in terms of pollutants, and steps to prevent physical accidents?
3. How aesthetic is the environment in terms of protecting against sight and sound pollution?

Summarize your findings and suggestions in a bulleted list of less than one page. Present your findings to classmates, and perhaps to a manager of the workplace. Classmates might comment on whether your findings will really improve the planet from an ecological standpoint.

### Working with Suppliers to Improve Working Conditions

An opportunity for practicing social responsibility is for company leaders to work with suppliers to improve physical and mental working conditions. Instead of refusing to deal with a supplier who operates a sweatshop, management might work with the supplier to improve plant working conditions. The justification for helping the supplier improve conditions is that the supplier's employees are often in dire need of a paying job. Almost any job is better than no job to a person facing extreme poverty or who is dependent on modest wages for food and shelter. Helping suppliers to improve working conditions has been conceptualized as corporations being vehicles for positive social change—yet another way of demonstrating corporate social responsibility.[37]

Gap Inc. took a major initiative to begin improving working conditions at suppliers. Company leadership issued a report conceding that working conditions are far from perfect at many of the 3,000 factories worldwide that manufacture clothing for Gap. Among the working-condition violations were that between 10 and 25 percent of its Chinese factories used psychological coercion or verbal abuse. More than 50 percent of the factories visited in sub-Saharan Africa operated machinery without proper safety devices. Gap representatives now invest more time in training and helping factories develop programs for compliance with working-condition codes.[38]

## Leader in Action

### Joe Crosby of Coach's Low Country Brands Helps the Community

Joe Crosby, cofounder of a small Seneca, South Carolina, company that sells seasonings and other foods, donates to charity in various ways. But instead of writing checks to high-profile national or international organizations, he supports and gets involved with causes close to home.

His company, Coach's Low Country Brands, hosts a charity golf tournament every August to raise money to help elementary-school teachers buy classroom supplies—something teachers must typically pay for themselves. In one year the tournament raised $40,000 through corporate sponsorships and a raffle. The company later gave each of 400 teachers in the county a $106 gift card to Staples. "I will always take care of my county and my state first," says Crosby, "because my business started in South Carolina."

Crosby raises money for seventeen colleges and universities in the Southeast by putting the schools' logos on some bottles of his seasoning and donating $2 from each sale of the $16 bottles to the schools' scholarship funds. "Some people buy it because they see I'm donating money to their local schools," he says. About 8,000 such bottles were sold within the first two months of the initiative.

### Questions

1. What is your evaluation of the usefulness of the type of philanthropy Joe Crosby practices?
2. To what extent do you think donating a portion of the sale of seasonings is just a marketing gimmick?
3. In what way is Coach's Low Country Brands "doing well by doing good"?

*Source*: Kelly K. Spors, "Cause and Effect: Though Small Firms May Lack the Cash to Make Major Gifts, They Can Still Make a Difference in Their Communities," *The Wall Street Journal*, December 10, 2007, p. R8.

### Establishing Written Codes of Ethical Conduct

Many organizations use written codes of conduct as guidelines for ethical and socially responsible behavior. Such guidelines continue to grow in importance because workers in self-managing teams have less leadership than previously. Regardless of the industry, most codes deal with quite similar issues. Patricia Breeding, integrity compliance officer for Covenant Health, in Knoxville, Tennessee, says, "They all address conflicts of interest, gifts and things like vendor relationships. They use the word 'customer' in one and 'patient' in another but they're all about doing the right thing."[39] Prohibition against bribery of government or corporate officials is being incorporated more frequently into ethical codes to combat potential major problems. For example, the German company Siemens AG paid a $280 million U.S. fine for having paid bribes in Nigeria, Russia, and Libya to help receive large contracts.[40] The Sarbanes-Oxley Act, triggered by the financial scandals around the year 2000, requires public companies to disclose whether they have adopted a code of ethics for senior financial officers. In some firms, such as Boeing Company, workers at all levels are required to sign the code of conduct.

A written code of conduct is more likely to influence behavior when both formal and informal leaders throughout the firm refer to it frequently. Furthermore, adherence to the code must be rewarded, and violation of the code should be punished.

## Developing Formal Mechanisms for Dealing with Ethical Problems

Many large employers have ethics programs of various types. Large organizations frequently establish ethics committees to help ensure ethical and socially responsible behavior. Top-level leadership participation in these formal mechanisms gives them more clout. Committee members include a top management representative plus other managers throughout the organization. An ethics and social responsibility specialist from the human resources department might also join the group. The committee establishes policies about ethics and social responsibility and may conduct an ethical audit of the firm's activities. In addition, committee members might review complaints about ethical problems.

The U.S. federal government has a unit called the Pentagon's Standards of Conduct Office for dealing with ethical problems. Its most potent weapon is an Encyclopedia of Ethical Failure, a listing of ethical failures within the government that is published on the Internet by Pentagon lawyer Stephen Epstein. Brief case histories are presented of shenanigans and shockingly poor judgment that have derailed the careers of fellow public servants in various governmental bureaus. One example is the case of a Customs and Border protection officer who landed a government helicopter on his daughter's grade-school playground. Despite having a supervisor's off-the-wall clearance to fly there, the officer was fired for misusing government property. In another case, an Army official was caught channeling bogus business to himself and his girlfriend's daughter. Epstein reported the episode under the headline, "One Happy Family Spends Time Together in Jail."[41]

The takeaway point here is that unethical behavior within a large organization might be made public, resulting in considerable embarrassment and a career setback for the accused.

## Accepting Whistleblowers

A **whistleblower** is an employee who discloses organizational wrongdoing to parties who can take action. It was a whistleblower who began the process of exposing the scandalous financial practices at Enron Corporation, such as hiding losses. Sherron Watkins, a vice president, wrote a one-page anonymous letter exposing unsound, if not dishonest, financial reporting: Enron had booked profits for two entities that had no assets. She dropped the letter off at company headquarters the next day.

Whistleblowers often go directly to a federal government bureau to report what they consider to be fraud and poor ethics by their employer. The single largest settlement was $920 million, against Tenet Healthcare Corp., the nation's second-largest hospital chain. Following allegations by six whistleblowers, prosecutors accused Tenet of overbilling the government by $806 million in Medicare payments and paying $49 million in kickbacks to physicians who referred patients to the health care organization.[42]

Whistleblowers are often ostracized and humiliated by the companies they hope to improve. For example, they may receive no further promotions or poor performance evaluations. Also, many whistleblowers are fired or demoted, even for high-profile tips that proved true.[43] The Sarbanes-Oxley Act includes some protection for whistleblowers. Employees who report fraud related to corporate accounting, internal accounting controls, and auditing have a way of gaining reinstatement, as well as back pay and legal expenses. Nevertheless, more than half of the pleas of whistleblowers are ignored. So it is important for leaders at all levels to create a comfortable climate for legitimate whistleblowing. The leader needs to sort out the difference between a troublemaker and a true whistleblower.

Being a whistleblower requires a small act of leadership, in the sense of taking the initiative to bring about change. However, the organization turned in might not think the change is constructive.

## Providing Training in Ethics and Social Responsibility

Forms of ethics training include messages about ethics and social responsibility from company leadership, classes on ethics at colleges, and exercises in ethics. These training programs reinforce the idea that ethically and socially responsible behavior is both morally right and good for business. Much of the content of this chapter reflects the type of information communicated in such programs. Training programs in ethics and social responsibility are most likely to be effective when the organizational culture encourages ethical behavior.

Caterpillar, the manufacturer of construction and mining equipment, exemplifies a modern approach to training in ethics. During the annual training, all 95,000 employees ponder a series of questions presented to them either via the Internet or on paper. The scenarios, written in-house, encourage workers to consider the best way to behave in a particular situation. Employees are able to consult the code of ethics as they reflect on the scenarios. One scenario involves a plant-floor employee adding a cleansing agent used by other employees to the agent the employee is presently using. One of the alternatives is "Check with an environmental health and safety group to ensure the combination is safe."[44]

Leadership Skill-Building Exercise 6-3 gives you the opportunity to engage in a small amount of ethics training.

## Placing Company Interests over Personal Interests

Many ethical violations, such as senior managers' voting themselves outrageous compensation, stem from managers' placing their personal interests over the welfare of the company and other employees. Jonathan M. Tish, the chairman and CEO of Loews Hotels, says that success in today's interdependent world demands "We" leaders, or people who look beyond self-interest to build partnerships in pursuit of a greater good. "We" leaders unify rather than divide, collaborate rather than compete, and believe that it is possible to "do well" and "do good" at the same time. A major requirement for building a partnership is fairness. Everyone must benefit from a partnership.[45]

## ◎ Leadership Skill-Building Exercise 6-3

### Dealing with Defining Moments

The toughest ethical choices for many people occur when they have to choose between two rights. The result is a defining moment, because we are challenged to think in a deeper way by choosing between two or more ideals. Working individually or in teams, reach a decision about the two following defining moments. Explain why these scenarios could require choosing between two rights, and explain the reasoning behind your decisions.

1. You are the manager of a department in a business firm that assigns each department a fixed amount of money for salary increases each year. An average-performing member of the department asks you in advance for an above-average increase. He explains that his mother has developed multiple sclerosis and requires the services of a paid helper from time to time. You are concerned that if you give this man an above-average increase, somebody else in the department will have to receive a below-average increase.

2. You are the team leader of a group of packaging scientists at a large consumer products company. Two years ago, top management decided that

any employee who is late to work more than 10 percent of the time over the course of a year should be fired. At about the same time, top management began incorporating a measure of *diversity success* into managers' performance evaluations. Managers who hired and retained targeted groups would receive a high rating on *diversity success*. Poor hiring and retention of targeted groups would result in a low performance rating. It is now mid-December, and Tim, the only employee over age 60, has been late 11 percent of the time. Several former employees have recently charged your company with age discrimination. Firing Tim will enable you to comply with the lateness policy, yet your diversity performance will suffer. Also, top management does not want to deal with any more employment discrimination suits.

Getting started dealing with defining moments is useful practice because so many leadership issues are in the gray zone—neither completely right nor completely wrong. Part of dealing with defining moments is doing some soul searching.

## ETHICAL BEHAVIOR AND ORGANIZATIONAL PERFORMANCE

High ethics and social responsibility are sometimes related to good financial performance. A recently developed model of the relationship between corporate social performance and profits emphasizes the role of supply and demand. The model states that when demand for social responsibility investments increases, value-maximizing managers will find it in their self-interest to make these investments even if cash flow is reduced. Also, despite spending money, the market value of the firm might increase when the demand for these investment opportunities is greater than the supply. An example might be that investing in programs to improve literacy among poor children might have a payoff because there is a big demand for this type of investment.[46] However, investing money to help preserve reptiles in the Arizona desert might not have a good return because of low demand. Also, donating money to a symphony orchestra might not have a big profit return because in some communities there is a big supply of corporate money to help fund orchestras.

The relationship between social responsibility and profits can also work in two directions: more profitable firms can better afford to invest in social responsibility initiatives, and these initiatives can lead to more profits. Sandra A. Waddock and Samuel B. Graves analyzed the relationship between corporate social performance and corporate financial performance for 469 firms, spanning thirteen industries, for a two-year period. They used many different measures of social and financial performance. An example of social performance would be helping to redevelop a poor community.

The researchers found that financial success creates enough money left over to invest in corporate social performance. The study also found that good corporate social performance contributes to improved financial performance as measured by return on assets and return on sales. Waddock and Graves concluded that the relationship between social and financial performance may be a **virtuous circle**, meaning that corporate social performance and corporate financial performance feed and reinforce each other.[47]

Corporate social responsibility can sometimes increase profits because the socially responsible action is cost-effective. Texas Instruments built a LEED-certified manufacturing facility in Richardson, Texas, that is predicted to save the company $4 million in energy costs annually from environmentally friendly innovations designed into the building. LEED refers to the Leadership in Energy and Environmental Design Green Building Rating System,™ and includes such diverse measures as water savings and energy efficiency.[48]

Being ethical also helps avoid the costs of paying huge fines for being unethical, including charges of discrimination and class-action lawsuits because of improper financial reporting. The enormous fine imposed on Siemens, as mentioned earlier, illustrates the potential cost of being unethical. Being accused of unethical and illegal behavior can also result in a sudden drop in customers and clients, as well as extreme difficulty in obtaining new customers and clients.

In short, a leader who is successful at establishing a climate of high ethics and social responsibility can earn and save the company a lot of money. Yet there are times when being socially responsible can eat into profits. A small company called Earth Mama Angel Baby uses recycled materials for packaging its organic, preservative-free lotions, shampoos, and other products for pre- and postnatal women and infants. Owner Melinda Olsen says that her ideals come at a high price, with the cost of organic ingredients lowering her gross margins to about 13 percent in comparison to the competition.[49] Yet as a leader she places a higher value on her ideals than maximizing profit.

### Reader's Roadmap

So far in this book, we have examined the nature of leadership, the inner qualities of leaders, and leadership styles, contingency leadership, and the leader's ethical behavior and social responsibility. In the next chapter, we focus on how leaders acquire and maintain power, and their use of organizational politics.

## SUMMARY

Principles of ethical and moral leadership all center on the idea that a leader should do the right thing, as perceived by a consensus of reasonable people. Key principles of ethical and moral leadership are as follows: (1) be honest and trustworthy and have integrity in dealing with others, (2) pay attention to all stakeholders, (3) build community, (4) respect the individual, and (5) accomplish silent victories. Differences in ethics and morality can be traced to seven factors: (1) the leader's level of greed, gluttony, and avarice; (2) rationalization; (3) implied permission to engage in unethical acts; (4) the leader's level of moral development; (5) a sense of entitlement; (6) situational influences; and (7) a person's character. It has been proposed that to stay ethical a leader must develop an ethical mind focused on good work.

Before reaching a decision about an issue that is not obviously ethical or blatantly unethical, a leader or manager should seek answers to questions such as: Is it right? Is it fair? Who gets hurt? Before joining a company, a job seeker should search for answers to ethics-related questions, such as "Is there a formal code of ethics?"

Unethical behavior has brought companies into bankruptcy, led to layoffs of thousands of workers, diminished trust in stock investments, and discouraged many talented young people from embarking on a business career.

Another way a leader can be ethical and moral is to spearhead the firm, or a unit within it, toward doing good deeds—toward being socially responsible and creating an ethical organizational culture. Among the many possible socially responsible and ethical acts are (1) providing strategic leadership of social responsibility and ethics, (2) creating a pleasant workplace, (3) helping build a sustainable environment, (4) engaging in philanthropy, (5) working with suppliers to improve working conditions, (6) establishing written codes of conduct, (7) developing formal mechanisms for dealing with ethical problems, (8) accepting whistleblowers, (9) providing training in ethics, and (10) placing company interests over personal interests.

High ethics and social responsibility are sometimes related to good financial performance, according to research evidence and opinion. Causes in big demand are more likely to have a financial payoff. More profitable firms have the funds to invest in good social programs. Being ethical helps avoid big fines for being unethical, and ethical organizations attract more employees. Socially responsible behavior can be cost-effective. However, being socially responsible can sometimes lower profit margins, yet the leader's ideals are important.

## KEY TERMS

| | | |
|---|---|---|
| **Ethics** | **Entitlement** | **Whistleblower** |
| **Morals** | **Ethical mind** | **Virtuous circle** |
| **Integrity** | **Corporate social responsibility** | |

## ✔ GUIDELINES FOR ACTION AND SKILL DEVELOPMENT

A provocative explanation of the causes of unethical behavior emphasizes the strength of relationships among people. Assume that two people have close ties to each other—they may have worked together for a long time or have known each other both on and off the job. As a consequence, they are likely to behave ethically toward one another on the job. In contrast, if a weak relationship exists between two people, either party is more likely to treat the other badly. In the work environment, the people involved may be your work associates, your contacts, or your internal and external customers.[50] The message is for you as a leader to build strong relationships with others in order to increase the frequency of ethical behavior.

## Discussion Questions and Activities

1. If President George W. Bush engaged in questionable ethical behavior while he was an energy company executive, why should you worry about being ethical?

2. The majority of business executives accused of unethical behavior have studied ethics either as a subject in a business course or as an entire course. So what do you think went wrong?

3. The Humane Society is trying to block Amazon .com from selling magazines like *The Feathered Warrior* and *The Gamecock* because the magazines encourage cockfighting and run advertisements for blades that attach to the legs of birds. The Humane Society emphasizes that cockfighting is illegal in all states, and is also unethical. How should Amazon respond to the Humane Society?

4. CityWatcher.com, a company that provides surveillance security services, implanted radio frequency identification (RFID) chips into the arms of two willing employees to help control access to secure areas. What ethical issues might be involved in planting RFID chips in employees, even if the workers consent?

5. How can consumers use the Internet to help control the ethical behavior of business leaders?

6. In what ways are many retail customers quite unethical?

7. What is your position on the ethics of a business leader's receiving $100 million or more in annual compensation?

8. Should leaders of companies that produce fattening food that can lead to cardiac problems and obesity be targeted for being socially irresponsible?

9. A study by Liberty Mutual Research Institute found that approximately 2,600 deaths and 330,000 injuries annually in the United States stem from speaking on cell phones while driving. What social responsibility obligations should cell phone manufacturers and cell phone service providers have for dealing with this problem?

10. Explain whether you would be willing to accept a 10 percent smaller salary increase or bonus so your employer could invest in a socially responsible cause such as providing shelter for homeless people or Internet access for poor children.

## Leadership Case Problem A

### Rent-Way Slides Away

Near midnight on a Friday in 2000, William E. Morgenstern, the chief executive of Rent-Way, one of the nation's largest rent-to-own retailers, received a call from a woman who warned him that the company he had built from scratch was about to fall apart. In the days before that call, Morgenstern had been scrambling to reconcile discrepancies he had discovered in Rent-Way's books. Since its founding in 1981 in Erie, Pennsylvania, Rent-Way had grown into a national powerhouse by renting furniture and electronics to low-income consumers through more than 1,100 stores. The stock price had tripled since its initial offering in 1993, propelling dozens of Erie families who had invested in the company to sudden wealth.

When he discovered the accounting problems, Morgenstern initially hoped for a quick explanation. But interviews with executives led to more questions. Then came the midnight phone call: a weeping employee told him that, for three years, Morgenstern's top deputies had forced her to cook Rent-Way's books. Morgenstern then called the company's lawyer in panic. What, he asked, should they do?

"It was the darkest moment of my life," said Morgenstern, who stepped down as Rent-Way's chief executive in 2005, retaining the chairman's post. "I started this company at 22 after three years of college. It represented all of my wealth. I tried to make the right decision at every juncture, but we had to pay a terrific price."

Rent-Way's board made a decision within days of detecting the fraud—Morgenstern called the Securities and Exchange Commission and revealed everything. The company would turn over documents typically protected by attorney–client privilege, he said. He then invited the SEC to conduct an on-site investigation. "There was a stunned silence from the regulators," said one participant in the call.

At Rent-Way, executives hoped that openness would contain the damage. The company had experience confronting criticism. For years, consumer advocates had attacked the rent-to-own industry as predatory, complaining that the business's rough-and-tumble practices focused on low-income, unsophisticated customers and included exorbitant fees to rent appliances.

"We were committed to not letting this company be brought down by a small group of people engaged in criminal activity," said William Lerner, a Rent-Way director and former SEC official. "We were determined to do everything as morally and ethically as we could."

A financial restatement turned a cumulative $45 million profit from 1998 to 2000 into a $35 million loss. The news pushed Rent-Way's stock price into a free fall, down from $30 to $3.25 in two months. Some board members raised the possibility of declaring bankruptcy. Others suggested selling the company to a private equity group.

Anger mounted in Erie toward Rent-Way. Walking through a local supermarket, a shopper confronted Morgenstern and shouted that he could not afford groceries because his portfolio had disappeared. Anonymous callers made threatening phone calls to Morgenstern's home. His children asked to stay home from school because teachers told them

that their father was a crook. Morgenstern fought suggestions to sell. "Our employees had invested their entire life savings and would have been wiped out," he said. "If I ran away, I would have regretted it for the rest of my life." At Rent-Way's annual convention in Las Vegas, four months after the fraud was revealed, Morgenstern promised that the company would survive, and would emerge stronger than ever. A year after the fraud emerged, revenue had rebounded, increasing by 10 percent. However, Rent-Way had to refinance because of the fraud. Even as revenue grew, the company had to pay interest on debt at a high interest rate because of the scandal.

The United States attorney's office in Erie, which successfully prosecuted three Rent-Way executives for criminal fraud, commended Morgenstern's openness as "a good example of how a company can alleviate the consequences of misconduct by fully and openly cooperating with the government." Nevertheless, Rent-Way's stock price refused to budge and interest payments commanded more and more cash. Some argued that Morgenstern was responsible for allowing a culture of fraud to flourish, regardless of his lack of involvement. He wondered if his staff construed his relentless cheerleading about beating stock market expectations as encouragement to break the law.

To help with the credit crunch, almost 300 stores were sold to Rent-A-Center, its biggest rival. Four years later Rent-Way opened fifty-four new stores; income grew, and the stock began to inch higher. Soon, hurricane damage closed 25 percent of Rent-Way stores in the Southeast. An increase in gas prices made it harder for low-income people to spend money on televisions and sofas.

Despite increasing its operating revenue by more than 300 percent since the fraud was revealed, Rent-Way was sold to Rent-A-Center for $567 million. A stock owned one day before the fraud broke was worth 35 cents on the dollar six years later. After the sale, Morgenstern said: "I did everything that I thought was right, but in some ways it didn't matter. This wasn't a broken company. And when I found illegal activity, I exposed it. But that shouldn't have ended a great company. I don't know what else I could have done."

## Questions

1. What do you think of the ethics of Rent-Way's basic business model of rent-to-own that focuses on low-income people?
2. What might leadership at Rent-Way have done to prevent the accounting irregularities that brought the company into disfavor?
3. What else might Morgenstern have done to help his company recover from the scandal?
4. Should the company have gone to the expense of an annual convention in Las Vegas when it was facing major financial problems?

# Leadership Case Problem B

## "GE, Can't You Just Shut Up and Sell Us Stuff?"

Several years ago, General Electric Co. chairman Jeffrey Immelt vowed to make GE a corporate leader in addressing climate change. Since then, Immelt says, he's heard a refrain from some big GE customers: "Can't you just shut up and sell us stuff?" That would be a paraphrase, maybe with a few blanks in between.

Customer grumbling isn't the only hurdle facing the effort to bring earth-friendly policies to a $163-billion-a-year conglomerate that sells everything from airplane engines to light bulbs. Some of Immelt's underlings have questioned whether carbon-dioxide emissions are a proven cause of climate change.

And he himself is willing to push GE only so far. "I don't want to change the economic flow of the company," Immelt says. So GE continues to sell coal-fired steam turbines and is delving deeper into oil-and-gas production. Meanwhile, its finance unit seeks out coal-related investments including power plants, which are a leading cause of carbon-dioxide emissions in the United States.

Yet these limitations haven't stopped GE from making a big marketing to-do of its commitment to the environment. Indeed, the primary focus of the conglomerate's marketing efforts these days is a $1-million-a-year campaign to publicize its search for "innovative solutions to environmental challenges."

GE has dubbed its campaign "ecoimagination" and Immelt calls it a success. GE was on track to sell $17 billion of its self-described environmentally friendly products in 2010. GE says it reduced its own greenhouse-gas emissions by 4 percent between 2004 and 2006, even as revenue grew 21 percent.

In January 2007, Immelt backed a proposal to cap industrial carbon-dioxide emissions in the United States. A government-imposed cap would likely limit $CO_2$ emissions by big manufacturers and power plants, both of which are important customers.

His own lieutenants acknowledge that Immelt is creating friction. "Is there a tension there? Of course there is," says Lorraine Bolsinger, who runs the eco-imagination program. "This is a big tough issue. The whole world is moving in a new direction. We've got to try to keep pace."

Immelt's environmental outlook was shaped in part by GE's long struggle with regulators and advocacy groups over New York's Hudson River, where GE had legally discharged toxic polychlorinated biphenyls in the 1960s and 1970s. Shortly after taking over as chairman in 2001, Immelt agreed with the Environmental Protection Agency to develop a cleanup plan for the Hudson.

Immelt says global warming isn't a moral issue for him. "I never put it in right versus wrong," he says. Rather he believes that making changes to address potential climate change is a political necessity. GE works with GreenOrder, an environmentally focused marketing consulting firm, to certify the products' environmental benefits, then wraps them in its ecoimagination label. How much credibility GreenOrder certification carries with environmental groups isn't clear.

Immelt stresses that GE's environmental projects must make economic sense. "We invest in the basic strategies that we think are going to fit into the program, but make money for our investors at the same time."

In January 2007, Immelt was among nine CEOs to join environmentalists in asking the U.S. government to limit carbon-dioxide emissions. Some business executives were unhappy. Immelt fielded an angry call from John Wilder, the chairman of a company called TXU, who was worried about the potential impact of carbon limits on the proposed coal-fired plants. (Wilder had recently agreed to purchase $600 million in steam turbines from GE to build 11 new coal-fired plants.) Wilder also circulated a letter among utility executives questioning Immelt's position—and sent it to GE.

## Questions

1. What do you advise leaders at GE to do about satisfying customers who are not so environmentally conscious?
2. What is your opinion of the ethics of GE leadership, which is engaging in environmentally friendly activities while at the same time selling products that are environmentally unfriendly?
3. How should Immelt deal with GE managers who do not agree with his concern about reducing $CO_2$ emissions?
4. What is your opinion of the level of social responsibility shown by Immelt and most likely his executive team at GE?

*Source*: Kathryn Kranhold, "GE's Environment Push Hits Business Realities: CEO's Quest to Reduce Emissions Irks Clients; the Battle of the Bulbs," *The Wall Street Journal (Central Edition)*, September 14, 2007, pp. A1, A10. Copyright 2007 by Dow Jones & Company, Inc. Reproduced with permission of Dow Jones & Company, Inc. In the format Textbook via Copyright Clearance Center.

 ## Leadership Skill-Building Exercise 6-4

## My Leadership Portfolio

For this chapter's entry into your leadership journal, reflect on any scenario you have encountered recently that would have given you the opportunity to practice ethical or socially responsible behavior. The scenario could have taken place in relation to employment, an interaction with fellow students, or being a customer of some type. Write down the scenario, and how you responded to it. Indicate what you learned about yourself. An example follows:

I had been thinking of purchasing advanced software to manage and edit photos on my computer. The software I needed would cost several hundred dollars. The other day, while going through my email, I came upon an advertisement offering the

exact photo software I wanted for $50. At first, I thought this would be a real money saver. After thinking through the ethical issues, I came to realize that the person selling this software was probably a pirate. If I purchased from this character, I would be supporting a software pirate. Besides, buying stolen goods might even be a crime. I learned from this incident that there are many opportunities in everyday life to practice good—or bad—ethics. I want to become a moral leader, so practicing good ethics will help me.

P.S.: By being ethical I probably avoided buying some virus-infected software that could have played havoc with my computer.

## Internet Skill-Building Exercise

### Career Consequences of Unethical Leadership Behavior

In this chapter and at other places in the text, you have read about business executives accused of unethical, illegal, or socially irresponsible behavior. An important issue is to understand the career consequences to these individuals stemming from their misbehavior. Use the Internet to find the current status of four executives whose unethical behavior has been cited in this chapter. Verify this status, looking for potential consequences such as (1) new employment in a corporation, (2) self-employment, (3) loss of employment, (4) working as a consultant, (5) elected as a public official, or (6) incarceration. Based on your findings, draw a conclusion about the career consequences of unethical leadership behavior.

**Apply the chapter concepts! Visit the Web and complete this Internet skill-building exercise to learn more about current leadership topics and trends.**

## CHAPTER 7

# Power, Politics, and Leadership

## LEARNING OBJECTIVES

After studying this chapter and doing the exercises, you should be able to

- Recognize the various types of power.
- Identify tactics used for becoming an empowering leader.
- Know how to use delegation to support empowerment.
- Pinpoint factors contributing to organizational politics.
- Describe both ethical and unethical political behaviors.
- Explain how a leader can control dysfunctional politics.

## CHAPTER OUTLINE

Emmitt Smith had a long and unforgettable career as a running back for the Dallas Cowboys of the National Football League, gaining more yards than any other running back in NFL history. Well mannered and well spoken, with a gracious smile, Smith accumulated an extraordinary fan base—admired by many people who otherwise did not have much interest in professional football. Smith contributed substantially to the nation-wide popularity of the Dallas Cowboys during has playing days with the team.

On a winter day in Dallas, Smith is being noticed at every turn:

> As [he] climbs into his silver Hummer and heads to lunch, a young woman pulls alongside, powers open her passenger-side window, and . . . yells, "I'm soooo proud of you."
>
> Minutes later in the restaurant, women of all ages greet him like a favorite son, and men shake his hand with Texas pride . . . "You sure did do some dancin'!" bellows one . . .

This adulation is not only a result of Smith's achievements during his fifteen-year career with the Dallas Cowboys. In the fall of 2006, he gained more admirers when he was a victor on the popular reality television show *Dancing With the Stars*.

Emmitt Smith is now focused on his long-time major ambition beyond football: becoming a real-estate tycoon.

In rushing for an NFL-record 18,355 yards with Dallas and the Arizona Cardinals, Smith covered a lot of real estate. He also invested in the sector, and he has profited by buying and selling properties in and around Dallas and his hometown, Pensacola, Florida, since he was a rookie.

While still early in his professional playing career, Smith wanted to learn the real estate business. So he spent time during the off season at the office of another Cowboy legend, Roger Staubach, and recently became a developer. The real estate development enterprise he formed with Staubach specializes "in transforming underutilized parcels in densely populated areas into commercially viable properties". Some of the value enhancement in the properties stemmed from attracting nationally known retail giants as tenants. While a player, Smith also took the opportunity to closely observe the Cowboys' owner Jerry Jones manage his real estate business.

Smith brings more than star power to the job. "He has the leadership skills to build a real business," Staubach says.[1]

The story about a popular football player who parlayed his fame into winning a dance contest and becoming a successful businessperson tells us a lot about how developing expertise in one domain can help us be successful in another domain. Smith also capitalized on his football success to make contacts with two powerful people who helped him accelerate his career. This chapter covers the nature of power, the ways leaders acquire power and empower others, and the use and control of organizational politics. Chapter 8 continues the discussion of organizational (or office) politics by examining influence tactics.

# SOURCES AND TYPES OF POWER

To exercise influence, a leader must have **power**, the potential or ability to influence decisions and control resources. Organizational power can be derived from many sources. How a person obtains power depends to a large extent on the type of power he or she seeks. Therefore, to understand the mechanics of acquiring power, one must also understand what types of power exist and the sources and origins of these types of power. Seven types or sources of power, including some of their subtypes, are described in the following sections.

## Position Power

Power is frequently classified according to whether it stems from the organization or the individual.[2] Four bases of power—legitimate power, reward power, coercive power, and information power—stem from the person's position in the organization.

*Legitimate Power*   The lawful right to make a decision and expect compliance is called **legitimate power**. People at the highest levels in the organization have more power than do people below them. However, organizational culture helps establish the limits to anyone's power. Newly appointed executives, for example, are often frustrated with how long it takes to effect major change. A chief financial officer (CFO) recruited to improve the profitability of a telecommunications firm noted, "The company has been downsizing for three years. We have more office space and manufacturing capacity than we need. Yet whenever I introduce the topic of selling off real estate to cut costs, I get a cold reception."

At the top of the organization, a leader's legitimate power is strengthened when he or she carries the titles of both chief executive officer and chairman or chairwoman. For example, Edward Johnson III has filled the chairman and chief executive roles at Fidelity Investments for over 30 years, giving him considerable power. Speculation arose that when Johnson III retired, his successor would have less power because the roles would be divided between two people, with perhaps his daughter Abigail Johnson occupying one of the posts.[3]

*Reward Power*   The authority to give employees rewards for compliance is referred to as **reward power**. If a vice president of operations can directly reward supervisors with cash bonuses for achieving productivity targets, this manager will exert considerable power.

*Coercive Power*   **Coercive power** is the power to punish for noncompliance; it is based on fear. A common coercive tactic is for an executive to demote a subordinate manager if he or she does not comply with the executive's plans for change. Coercive power is limited, in that punishment and fear achieve mixed results as motivators. The leader who relies heavily on coercive power runs the constant threat of being ousted from power. Nevertheless, coercive power is widely practiced. The former chief executive of Merrill Lynch & Co., E. Stanley O'Neal, exercised considerable coercive power. He has presided over one of the most intense restructurings in Wall Street history, eliminating more than 23,000 jobs, closing more than 300 offices, and ousting 19 senior executives. In the process he has purged an entire generation of key people to strengthen his own power grip. Several years later when the firm lost billions of dollars on investments linked to subprime mortgages, O'Neal was ousted immediately.[4]

*Information Power*   **Information power** is power stemming from formal control over the information people need to do their work. A sales manager who controls the leads from customer inquiries holds considerable power. As the branch manager of a real estate agency put it: "Ever since the leads were sent directly to me, I get oodles of cooperation from my agents. Before that, they would treat me as if I were simply the office manager." The Web part of the Internet has weakened information as a source of power to some extent because more people have access to more information, especially in a field such as real estate.

## Personal Power

Three sources of power stem from characteristics or behaviors of the power actor: expert power, referent power, and prestige power. All are classified as **personal power** because they are derived from the person rather than the organization. Expert power and referent power contribute to charisma. Referent power is the ability to influence others through one's desirable traits and characteristics (see Chapter 3). Expert power is the ability to influence others through specialized knowledge, skills, or abilities. An example of a leader with substantial expert power is automotive executive Bob Lutz. For many years he had spearheaded new car development at Chrysler Corporation. At age 69 he was recruited to General Motors as vice chairman for product development. His mission was to work with designers and engineers to give new GM models sex appeal. Lutz has achieved some successes since his appointment, and is credited with helping GM produce several innovative models, such as the refreshed Chevrolet Malibu, the CTS Cadillac, and the Chevrolet Volt.[5]

Another important form of personal power is **prestige power**, the power stemming from a person's status and reputation.[6] A manager who has accumulated important business successes acquires prestige power. Managers have visibility, including a middle manager who has been successful at reducing turnover in the restaurant or hotel industry. Integrity is another contributor to prestige power because it enhances a leader's reputation. Executive recruiters identify executives who can readily be placed in senior positions because of their excellent track records (or prestige).

Manager Assessment Quiz 7-1 provides a sampling of the specific behaviors associated with five of the sources of power—three kinds of position power and two kinds of personal power.

Manager Assessment Quiz 7-1

## Rating a Manager's Power

**Instructions:** If you currently have a supervisor or can clearly recall one from the past, rate him or her. Circle the appropriate number of your answer, using the following scale: 5 = strongly agree; 4 = agree; 3 = neither agree nor disagree; 2 = disagree; 1 = strongly disagree. (The actual scale presents the items in random order. They are classified here according to the power source for your convenience.)

|  | Strongly Agree | | | Strongly Disagree | |
|---|---|---|---|---|---|
| **My manager can (or former manager could) . . .** | | | | | |
| **Reward Power** | | | | | |
| 1. increase my pay level. | 5 | 4 | 3 | 2 | 1 |
| 2. influence my getting a pay raise. | 5 | 4 | 3 | 2 | 1 |
| 3. provide me with specific benefits. | 5 | 4 | 3 | 2 | 1 |
| 4. influence my getting a promotion. | 5 | 4 | 3 | 2 | 1 |
| **Coercive Power** | | | | | |
| 5. give me undesirable job assignments. | 5 | 4 | 3 | 2 | 1 |
| 6. make my work difficult for me. | 5 | 4 | 3 | 2 | 1 |
| 7. make things unpleasant here. | 5 | 4 | 3 | 2 | 1 |
| 8. make being at work distasteful. | 5 | 4 | 3 | 2 | 1 |
| **Legitimate Power** | | | | | |
| 9. make me feel that I have commitments to meet. | 5 | 4 | 3 | 2 | 1 |
| 10. make me feel like I should satisfy my job requirements. | 5 | 4 | 3 | 2 | 1 |
| 11. make me feel I have responsibilities to fulfill. | 5 | 4 | 3 | 2 | 1 |
| 12. make me recognize that I have tasks to accomplish. | 5 | 4 | 3 | 2 | 1 |
| **Expert Power** | | | | | |
| 13. give me good technical suggestions. | 5 | 4 | 3 | 2 | 1 |
| 14. share with me his or her considerable experience and/or training. | 5 | 4 | 3 | 2 | 1 |
| 15. provide me with sound job-related advice. | 5 | 4 | 3 | 2 | 1 |
| 16. provide me with needed technical knowledge. | 5 | 4 | 3 | 2 | 1 |
| **Referent Power** | | | | | |
| 17. make me feel valued. | 5 | 4 | 3 | 2 | 1 |
| 18. make me feel that he or she approves of me. | 5 | 4 | 3 | 2 | 1 |
| 19. make me feel personally accepted. | 5 | 4 | 3 | 2 | 1 |
| 20. make me feel important. | 5 | 4 | 3 | 2 | 1 |

**Total score:** _____

***Scoring and Interpretation:*** Add all the circled numbers to calculate your total score. You can make a tentative interpretation of the score as follows:

- **90+:** High power
- **70–89:** Moderate power
- **below 70:** Low power

Also, see if you rated your manager much higher in one of the categories.

***Skill Development:*** This skill development rating can help you as a leader because it points to specific behaviors you can use to be perceived as high or low on a type of power. For example, a behavior specific for establishing referent power is to "make people feel important" (No. 20).

*Source:* Adapted from "Development and Application of New Scales to Measure the French and Raven (1959) Bases of Social Power," by Timothy R. Hinkin and Chester A. Schriescheim, *Journal of Applied Psychology*, August 1989, p. 567. Copyright © 1989 by the American Psychological Association. Adapted with permission of the American Psychological Association and Timothy R. Hinkin.

### Power Stemming from Ownership

Executive leaders accrue power in their capacity as agents acting on behalf of shareholders. The strength of ownership power depends on how closely the leader is linked to shareholders and board members. A leader's ownership power is also associated with how much money he or she has invested in the firm.[7] An executive who is a major shareholder is much less likely to be fired by the board than one without an equity stake. The CEOs of high-technology firms are typically company founders who later convert their firm into a publicly held company by selling stock. After the public offering, many of these CEOs own several hundred million dollars' worth of stock, making their position quite secure. The New Golden Rule applies: The person who holds the gold, rules.

### Power Stemming from Dependencies

According to the **dependence perspective,** a person accrues power by others being dependent on him or her for things they value. Figure 7-1 depicts this basic model of sources of power. Because the things valued could be physical resources or a personal relationship, dependence power can be positional or personal. Richard M. Emerson noted that power resides implicitly in the other's dependence.[8] A leader–group member example would be that the group member who needs considerable recognition to survive becomes dependent on the leader who is a regular source of such recognition. An organizational example is that the health care system in the United States is becoming more dependent on information technology to help streamline the system. Health care information technology specialists therefore have more power. In the words of Lee Scott, the CEO of Wal-Mart, whose company is developing in-store clinics, "Health IT is perhaps the single largest opportunity to drive costs out of the health care system."[9]

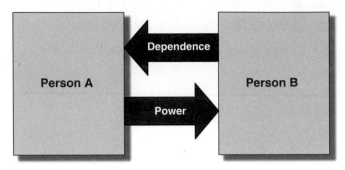

**FIGURE 7-1** The Dependence Theory of Power

*Source: Adapted from* Wilf H. Ratsburg, "Power Defined," www.geocities.com/Athens/Forum/1650/htmlpower.html, accessed January 4, 2008.

An extension of the dependence theory is the **resource dependence perspective.** According to this perspective, the organization requires a continuing flow of human resources, money, customers and clients, technological inputs, and materials to continue to function. Organizational subunits or individuals who can provide these key resources accrue power.[10]

When leaders start losing their power to control resources, their power declines. A case in point is Donald Trump. When his vast holdings were generating a positive cash flow and his image was one of extraordinary power, he found many willing investors. The name *Trump* on a property escalated its value. As his cash-flow position worsened, however, Trump found it difficult to find investment groups willing to buy his properties at near the asking price. However, by mid-1993, Trump's cash-flow position had improved again and investors showed renewed interest. A few years later Trump had regained all of his power to control resources, and money from investors flowed freely in his direction. In 2004, the Trump casino business filed for bankruptcy, mostly to refinance debt. Yet Trump has so much equity built into the Trump name that it is a resource that makes many developers dependent on him. Many condominium developers, for example, give "The Donald" an equity stake in the business just because the Trump name is on the business. Trump, after all, claims that he is "the hottest brand on the planet."[11] (The point of this seemingly contradictory example is that when you lose control of resources your power might decline, but if you are super-powerful you will recover quickly.)

## Power Derived from Capitalizing on Opportunity

Power can be derived from being in the right place at the right time and taking the appropriate action. It pays to be "where the action is." For example, the best opportunities in a diversified company lie in one of its growth divisions. Also, many small recycling firms moved from junkyard status to ecology firms as the interest in environmental sustainability surged in the late 2000s. A person or a firm also needs to have the right resources to capitalize on an opportunity, such as having the capacity to recycle on a larger scale.

### Power Stemming from Managing Critical Problems

The **strategic contingency theory** of power suggests that units best able to cope with the firm's critical problems and uncertainties acquire relatively large amounts of power.[12] The theory implies, for example, that when an organization faces substantial lawsuits, the legal department will gain power and influence over organizational decisions. Another important aspect of the strategic contingency theory concerns the power a subunit acquires by virtue of its centrality. **Centrality** is the extent to which a unit's activities are linked into the system of organizational activities. A unit has high centrality when it is an important and integral part of the work done by another unit. The second unit is therefore dependent on the first subunit. A sales department would have high centrality, whereas an employee credit union would have low centrality.

### Power Stemming from Being Close to Power

The closer a person is to power, the greater the power he or she exerts. Likewise, the higher a unit reports in a firm's hierarchy, the more power it possesses. In practice, this means that a leader in charge of a department reporting to the CEO has more power than one in charge of a department reporting to a vice president. Leaders in search of more power typically maneuver toward a higher-reporting position in the organization.

Historian Robert A. Caro reminds us that acquiring power alone does not make for great leadership. It takes an ambitious person to acquire power, and sometimes the approach to acquiring power may not be highly ethical, such as hoarding vital information or making others dependent on you. The person who then uses the accumulated power to create and implement a useful vision qualifies as an excellent leader.[13] The accompanying Leader in Action profile provides a brief description of a powerful and ethical leader.

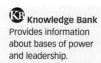

**Knowledge Bank**
Provides information about bases of power and leadership.
**www.cengage.com/ management/dubrin**

## TACTICS FOR BECOMING AN EMPOWERING LEADER

A leader's power and influence increase when he or she shares power with others. As team members receive more power, they can accomplish more—they become more productive. And because the manager shares credit for their accomplishments, he or she becomes more powerful. A truly powerful leader makes team members feel powerful and able to accomplish tasks on their own. A similar rationale for empowerment is that in a competitive environment that is increasingly dependent on knowledge, judgment, and information, the most successful organizations will be those that effectively use the talents of all players on the team.[14] As Stephen Covey notes, empowerment and leadership distribution are happening among progressive companies throughout the world. Also, the more trusting the culture is, the more likely it is that employees will be empowered.[15]

An advantage of empowerment from a cost perspective is that empowering workers to assume more managerial responsibility enables the organization to get

## Leader in Action

### A. G. Lafley, the Widely Admired Big Company Executive

Since taking charge in 2000, when Procter & Gamble was sinking under the weight of too many new products and organizational changes, A. G. Lafley has refocused on consumers and rejuvenated core businesses. P&G now boasts twenty-three billion-dollar brands, including Tide, Crest, Pampers, Gillette, Olay, Pantene, and the latest edition, Gain laundry detergent.

By denouncing insularity and demanding innovation in everything that P&G does, this company lifer has pushed P&G toward higher-margin areas like health, beauty, and personal care. The payback: Profits have tripled on his watch, to more than $10 billion on $76.5 billion in revenues. Lafley gathers ideas and listens carefully to company insiders as well as the full range of stakeholders, including customers, suppliers, and outside packaging experts.

Of course, Lafley has bought some of that growth: The acquisition of Gillette for $54 billion in 2005 was the largest in company history. But it is the record of organic growth—an average of 6 percent a year—that has made P&G a stock market standout and Lafley a role model for other CEOS.

#### Questions

1. Based on this brief description, which sources of power does Lafley appear to display?
2. Why has organic growth earned Lafley more admiration than if most of the growth came from acquisitions?
3. Why would a CEO of one of the world's best-known companies want to denounce *insularity?*

*Source:* Patricia Sellers, "Power 25: A. G. Lafley, Chairman and CEO, Procter & Gamble," *Fortune*, December 10, 2007, p. 122.

by with fewer bosses. Research in Europe suggests that a manager's span of control (number of direct reports) can be over 30 employees, in part because of using technology to communicate and help monitor work. The leader/manager who empowers workers can focus less on controlling workers and more on helping them overcome obstacles or capitalize on opportunities, such as pursuing innovative ideas.[16]

Here we look briefly at the nature of empowerment before describing a number of empowering practices and two cautions about empowerment.

### The Nature of Empowerment

In its basic meaning, **empowerment** refers to passing decision-making authority and responsibility from managers to group members. Almost any form of participative management, shared decision making, and delegation can be regarded as empowerment. Gretchen M. Spreitzer conducted research in several work settings to develop a psychological definition of empowerment.[17] Four components of empowerment were identified: meaning, competence, self-determination, and impact. Full-fledged empowerment includes all four dimensions, along with a fifth one, internal commitment.

*Meaning* is the value of a work goal, evaluated in relation to a person's ideals or standards. Work has meaning when there is a fit between the requirements of a work role and a person's beliefs, values, and behaviors. A person who is doing meaningful work is likely to feel empowered. *Competence,* or *self-efficacy,* is an individual's belief in his or her capability to perform a particular task well. The person who feels competent feels that he or she has the capability to meet the performance requirements in a given situation, such as a credit analyst saying, "I've been given the authority to evaluate credit risks up to $10,000 and I know I can do it well."

*Self-determination* is an individual's feeling of having a choice in initiating and regulating actions. A high-level form of self-determination occurs when a worker feels that he or she can choose the best method to solve a particular problem. Self-determination also involves such considerations as choosing the work pace and work site. A highly empowered worker might choose to perform the required work while on a cruise rather than remain in the office. *Impact* is the degree to which the worker can influence strategic, administrative, or operating outcomes on the job. Instead of feeling there is no choice but to follow the company's course, he or she might have a say in the future of the company. A middle manager might say, "Here's an opportunity for recruiting minority employees that we should exploit. And here's my action plan for doing so."

Another dimension of true empowerment is for the group member to develop an *internal commitment* toward work goals. Internal commitment takes place when workers are committed to a particular project, person, or program for individual motives. An example would be a production technician in a lawn mower plant who believes he is helping create a more beautiful world.

The focus of empowerment as just described is on the changes taking place within the individual. However, groups can also be empowered so the group climate contributes to these attitudes and feelings. An example of a statement reflecting an empowering climate would be "People in our organization get information about the organization's performance in a timely fashion."[18] Being part of an empowered group can help a group member become committed to achieving group goals.

## Empowering Practices

The practices that foster empowerment supplement standard approaches to participative management, such as conferring with team members before reaching a decision. The practices, as outlined in Figure 7-2, are based on direct observations of successful leaders and experimental evidence. Before reading about these practices, do Leadership Self-Assessment Quiz 7-1.

**Foster Initiative and Responsibility** A leader can empower team members simply by fostering greater initiative and responsibility in their assignments. For example, one bank executive transformed what had been a constricted branch manager's job into a branch "president" role. Managers were then evaluated on the basis of deposits because they had control over them. After the transformation, branch managers were allowed to stay with one branch rather than being rotated every three years.[19]

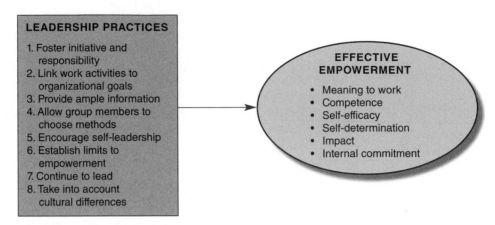

**FIGURE 7-2** Effective Empowering Practices.
Certain leadership and managerial practices lead to effective empowerment, which in turn often leads to higher motivation and productivity.

***Link Work Activities to Organizational Goals*** Empowerment works better when the empowered activities are aligned with the strategic goals of the organization. Empowered workers who have responsibility to carry out activities that support the major goals of the organization will identify more with the company. At the same time, they will develop a feeling of being a partner in the business.[20] Imagine a scenario in which a company auditor is authorized to spend large sums of travel money to accomplish her job. She is given this authority because a strategic goal of top-level management is to become a company admired for its honest business practices.

***Provide Ample Information*** For empowerment to be effective, employees should have ample information about everything that affects their work. Especially important is for workers to fully understand the impact of their actions on the company's costs and profits. Armed with such information, employees are more likely to make decisions that have a positive influence on the bottom line. When employees have such information, they are more likely to use empowerment to make decisions that contribute to business success. As an example, an empowered sales representative, armed with cost information, is less likely to grant discounts that lose money for the company.

***Allow Group Members to Choose Methods*** Under ideal conditions the leader or manager explains to the individual or group what needs to be done (sets a direction) and lets the people involved choose the method. Explaining why the tasks need to be performed is also important. One of the roles of a true professional is to choose the method for accomplishing a task, such as a tax consultant deciding how to prepare the taxes for a business owner. Norman Bodek explains: "What irks people the most is to be told how to do something. Allowing people to determine the most efficient work technique is the essence of empowerment."[21]

**Leadership Self-Assessment Quiz 7-1**

## Becoming an Empowering Manager

***Instructions:*** To empower employees successfully, the leader has to convey appropriate attitudes and develop effective interpersonal skills. To the best of your ability, indicate which skills and attitudes you now have, and which ones require further development.

|  | Can Do Now | Would Need to Develop |
|---|---|---|
| **Empowering Attitude or Behavior** | _____ | _____ |
| 1. Believe in team members' ability to be successful | _____ | _____ |
| 2. Have patience with people and give them time to learn | _____ | _____ |
| 3. Provide team members with direction and structure | _____ | _____ |
| 4. Teach team members new skills in small, incremental steps so they can easily learn those skills | _____ | _____ |
| 5. Ask team members questions that challenge them to think in new ways | _____ | _____ |
| 6. Share information with team members, sometimes just to build rapport | _____ | _____ |
| 7. Give team members timely feedback and encourage them throughout the learning process | _____ | _____ |
| 8. Offer team members alternative ways of doing things | _____ | _____ |
| 9. Exhibit a sense of humor and demonstrate care for workers as people | _____ | _____ |
| 10. Focus on team members' results and acknowledge their personal improvement | _____ | _____ |

***Skill Development:*** If, as a leader or manager, you already have most of these attitudes and have engaged in most of these behaviors, you will be good at empowerment. Most of these attitudes and practices can be developed without transforming your personality.

*Source: Supervisory Management* by Stone, Florence. Copyright 1991 by *American Management Association* (J). Reproduced with permission of *American Management Association* (J) in the format Textbook via Copyright Clearance Center.

***Encourage Self-Leadership***   Encouraging team members to lead themselves is the heart of empowerment. The basic idea of **self-leadership** is that all organizational members are capable of leading themselves at least to some extent. Complete self-leadership would involve workers deciding what should be done, why it should be done, and how to accomplish the task. Google engineers practice self-leadership to some extent because they can devote 20 percent of their working hours to projects of their own choosing, as mentioned earlier.

When employees practice self-leadership, they feel empowered. At W. L. Gore & Associates, Inc., a manufacturer of insulated material including GORE-TEX,® there are no bosses or managers but many leaders. Every employee is regarded as a knowledge worker who has the ability to identify profitable new products. An example of self-leadership takes place during salary reviews. A compensation team drawn from individuals at the associate's work site periodically reviews each associate's (employee's) salary. Each associate has a sponsor who acts as his or her advocate during the reviews. The sponsor gathers data about the associate's performance by speaking to internal and external customers.[22]

***Establish Limits to Empowerment***   One of the major situations in which empowerment creates disharmony and dysfunction is when workers lack a clear perception of the boundaries of empowerment. Empowered group members may feel that they can now make decisions unilaterally, without conferring with managers, team leaders, or other team members.[23] Limits to empowerment might mean explaining to employees that they have more authority than before, but still they cannot engage in such activities as the following:

- Set their own wages and those of top management
- Make downsizing decisions
- Hire mostly friends and relatives
- Work fewer than forty hours for full pay

Many employees justify dysfunctional actions by saying, "I'm empowered to do what I want." It is management's responsibility to guide employment activities that support the organization.

***Continue to Lead***   Although leaders empower group members, they should still provide guidance, emotional support, and recognition. Mark Samuel helps companies organize into teams to enhance accountability for results, yet at the same time he emphasizes the leader's role: "Empowerment often becomes an abdication of leadership. In other words, if I empower you, I don't have to guide you. People need guidance. Leadership cannot abdicate the role of providing guidance."[24] Because employees are empowered does not mean that they should be abandoned.

***Take into Account Cultural Differences***   All empowering practices can be influenced by cross-cultural factors. A group member's cultural values might lead to either an easy acceptance of empowerment or reluctance to be empowered. Americans are stereotyped as individualists. Nevertheless, they are so accustomed to working in teams (sports included) that being part of an empowered team would seem natural.

But not all cultures support empowerment. In one study, data from employees of a single firm with operations in the United States, Mexico, Poland, and India were used to test the fit of empowerment and continuous improvement practices with national culture. The company was engaged in light manufacturing, and data were collected from about forty sites. Empowerment was negatively associated with job satisfaction in the Indian plants but positively associated in the other three samples. The underlying cultural reason is that Indians (at least those working in India) expect the leader or manager to make most of the decisions.[25] Continuous improvement was positively related to satisfaction in all four samples.

Empowerment is an integral part of leadership and management, and therefore presumed to contribute to individual and organizational effectiveness. A study of management teams in 102 hotel properties demonstrated that empowerment is beneficial, yet works indirectly. Empowering leadership was positively related to workers sharing knowledge and team efficacy. The latter refers to self-confidence about attaining goals, measured by such perceptions as "We are confident of achieving the occupancy goal of our hotel." Both knowledge sharing and efficacy were positively associated with team performance, as measured by the hotel's occupancy rate.[26] A study with M.B.A. students engaged in consulting projects showed that when leadership was shared between team leaders and group members, clients tended to rate the consulting teams more favorably. Business faculty advisers were the team leaders. The tie-in with empowerment is that shared leadership is a form of empowerment.[27]

## Effective Delegation and Empowerment

A major contributor to empowerment is **delegation**, the assignment of formal authority and responsibility for accomplishing a specific task to another person. Delegation is narrower than empowerment because it deals with a specific task, whereas empowerment covers a broad range of activities and a mental set about assuming more responsibility. Delegation, like empowerment, is motivational because it offers group members the opportunity to develop their skills and demonstrate their competence. When delegation is poor, conflict often erupts between the person who thought he or she was responsible for a task, and the delegator.

A classic example of this type of conflict took place during the brief reign of William Perez as CEO of Nike, reporting to founder Phil Knight. Perez thought he had been delegated considerable responsibility from chairman Knight, but the delegation was limited. For example, Perez though he would have free rein to revamp marketing strategy. He proposed increasing direct sales to consumers through Web and Nike stores. However, Knight jumped in and favored the existing practice of selling through third-party retailers. Perez lasted only fourteen months in the position.[28]

You are invited to gain some practice in the realities of empowerment by doing Leadership Skill-Building Exercise 7-1. Keep in mind the importance of delegation when doing the exercise.

**Knowledge Bank**
Describes guidelines
for effective delegation.

www.cengage.com/
management/dubrin

Leadership Skill-Building Exercise 7-1

### Conducting an Empowerment Session

The description of empowering practices has given you some useful ideas to get started empowering others if you are already a manager. The role-assuming exercise described here gives you a chance to practice your empowering skills. One person plays the role of a leader, and six other people play the role of group members. You are meeting with your group today to get them started on the road toward empowerment. You will need to engage in dialogue with the group to begin the empowerment process. The empowerment scenarios described next should be staffed by different groups of students:

### Information Technology Customer-Service Center

You are in charge of an information technology call center whose primary activity is to respond to telephone inquiries from around the country from customers who are having problems in using the company's software. The workers who answer the phone are full-time professionals, many of whom are recent college graduates. A major goal of yours is to empower your workers to do as much as they can to satisfy the demands of the callers. You want your staff to take more personal responsibility for customer problems.

### Vision-Care Proprietors

You are the CEO of a nationwide chain of vision-care stores that sell both eyeglasses and contact lenses. You believe strongly that one of the constraining forces in your business is that your store managers, as well as franchise owners, do not take enough responsibility for running their operations. They rely too heavily on the corporate group for guidance and problem resolution. Today you are holding an empowerment meeting with the seven vision-care proprietors in your region. If your approach to empowerment works well, you will expand to other regions. Six other students play the role of store managers and franchise owners who generally believe that the corporate group should take the initiative to lead the stores toward greater prosperity. After all, why be a manager within a corporation or a franchise owner? Without corporate assistance, you might as well open your own vision-care store.

Doing this exercise is useful because it helps you develop the right mental set for a leader who empowers group members. Another advantage is that it sensitizes you to the importance of looking for signs of hesitation and ambivalence when you attempt to empower group members.

## FACTORS THAT CONTRIBUTE TO ORGANIZATIONAL POLITICS

As used here, the term **organizational politics** refers to informal approaches to gaining power through means other than merit or luck. Politics are played to achieve power, either directly or indirectly. For example, a person seeking to enhance his or her legitimate power might use a variety of tactics to be favorably perceived by top-level decision makers in the company. Power may be achieved in such diverse ways as by being promoted, by receiving a larger budget or other resources, by obtaining more resources for one's work group, or by being exempt from undesirable assignments. The meaning of *organizational politics* continues to shift in a positive, constructive direction. A group of researchers concluded: "Political skill is an interpersonal style that combines social awareness with the ability to communicate well."[29] Nevertheless, many writers still regard organizational politics as emphasizing self-interest at the expense of others, engaging in mysterious activities, or "kissing up."

People want power for many different reasons, which is why political behavior is so widespread in organizations. By definition, politics is used to acquire power. A number of individual and organizational factors contribute to political behavior, as described next.

## Pyramid-Shaped Organization Structure

The very shape of large organizations is the most fundamental reason why organizational members are motivated toward political behavior. A pyramid concentrates power at the top. Only so much power is therefore available to distribute among the many people who would like more of it. Each successive layer on the organization chart has less power than the layer above. At the very bottom of the organization, workers have limited power except for their legal rights. Also, an entry-level worker with a valuable skill in a tight labor market has some usable power. Since most organizations today have fewer layers than they previously had, the competition for power has become more intense. Although empowerment may be motivational for many workers, it is unlikely to satisfy the quest to hold a formal position of power. Workers still struggle to obtain a corner office or cubicle.

## Subjective Standards of Performance

People often resort to organizational politics because they do not believe that the organization has an objective and fair way of judging their performance and suitability for promotion. Similarly, when managers have no objective way of differentiating effective people from the less effective, they will resort to favoritism. The adage "It's not what you know but who you know" applies to organizations that lack clear-cut standards of performance.

## Environmental Uncertainty and Turbulence

When people operate in an unstable and unpredictable environment, they tend to behave politically. They rely on organizational politics to create a favorable impression because uncertainty makes it difficult to determine what they should really be accomplishing.

The uncertainty, turbulence, and insecurity created by corporate downsizings are a major contributor to office politics. Many people believe intuitively that favoritism plays a major role in deciding who will survive the downsizing. In response to this perception, organizational members attempt to ingratiate themselves with influential people.

## Emotional Insecurity

Some people resort to political maneuvers to ingratiate themselves with superiors because they lack confidence in their talents and skills. A pension fund manager who has directed the firm toward investments with an annualized 15 percent return does not have to be overly political because he or she will have confidence in his or her capabilities. A person's choice of political strategy may indicate emotional insecurity. For instance, an insecure person might laugh loudly at every humorous comment the boss makes.

### Machiavellian Tendencies

Some people engage in political behavior because they want to manipulate others, sometimes for their own personal advantage. The term *Machiavellianism* traces back to Niccolo Machiavelli (1469–1527), an Italian political philosopher and statesman. His most famous work, *The Prince*, describes how a leader may acquire and maintain power. Machiavelli's ideal prince was an amoral, manipulating tyrant who would restore the Italian city-state of Florence to its former glory. Three hundred and sixty years later, a study by Gerald Biberman showed a positive relationship between Machiavellianism and political behavior, based on questionnaires that measured these tendencies.[30]

### Encouraging Admiration from Subordinates

Most organizational leaders say they do not encourage kissing up and that they prefer honest feedback from subordinates. Yet without meaning to, these same managers and leaders encourage flattery and servile praise. Managers, as well as other workers, send out subtle signals that they want to be praised, such as smiling after receiving a compliment and frowning when receiving negative feedback. Also, admirers are more likely to receive good assignments and high performance evaluations. Executive coach Marshall Goldsmith explains that, without meaning to, many managers create an environment where people learn to reward others with accolades that are not completely warranted. People generally see this tendency in others but not in themselves.[31]

## POLITICAL TACTICS AND STRATEGIES

To make effective use of organizational politics, leaders must be aware of specific political tactics and strategies. To identify and explain the majority of political tactics would require years of study and observation. Leaders so frequently need support for their programs that they search for innovative types of political behaviors. Furthermore, new tactics continue to emerge as the workplace becomes increasingly competitive. Here we look at a representative group of political tactics and strategies categorized as to whether they are ethical or unethical. (Several of the influence tactics described in Chapter 8, such as ingratiation, might also be considered political behaviors.)

### Ethical Political Tactics and Strategies

So far we have discussed organizational politics without pinpointing specific tactics and strategies. This section describes a sampling of ethical political behaviors, divided into three related groups: tactics and strategies aimed at (1) gaining power,

(2) building relationships with superiors and coworkers, and (3) avoiding political blunders. All of these political approaches help the leader gain or retain power. Using them can also help the leader succeed in and manage stressful work environments. As defined by a group of researchers, political skill is a constructive force. It is an interpersonal style that manifests itself in being socially astute and engaging in behaviors that lead to feelings of confidence, trust, and sincerity.[32] For example, a middle manager with political skill might be able to defend her group against an angry CEO looking for a scapegoat.

   Leadership Self-Assessment Quiz 7-2 gives you an opportunity to measure your tendencies toward engaging in positive political tactics and strategies.

 ## Leadership Self-Assessment Quiz 7-2

### The Positive Organizational Politics Questionnaire

*Instructions:* Answer each question "mostly agree" or "mostly disagree," even if it is difficult for you to decide which alternative best describes your opinion.

| | Mostly Agree | Mostly Disagree |
|---|---|---|
| 1. Pleasing my boss is a major goal of mine. | _____ | _____ |
| 2. I go out of my way to flatter important people. | _____ | _____ |
| 3. I am most likely to do favors for people who can help me in return. | _____ | _____ |
| 4. Given the opportunity, I would cultivate friendships with powerful people. | _____ | _____ |
| 5. I will compliment a coworker even if I have to think hard about what might be praiseworthy. | _____ | _____ |
| 6. If I thought my boss needed the help, and I had the expertise, I would show him or her how to use an electronic gadget for personal life. | _____ | _____ |
| 7. I laugh heartily at my boss's humor, so long as I think he or she is at least a little funny. | _____ | _____ |
| 8. I would not be too concerned about following a company dress code, so long as I looked neat. | _____ | _____ |
| 9. If a customer sent me a compliment through email, I would forward a copy to my boss or another influential person. | _____ | _____ |
| 10. I smile only at people in the workplace whom I genuinely like. | _____ | _____ |
| 11. An effective way to impress people is to tell them what they want to hear. | _____ | _____ |

## Quiz 7-2 (continued)

| | Mostly Agree | Mostly Disagree |
|---|---|---|
| **12.** I would never publicly correct mistakes made by the boss. | _____ | _____ |
| **13.** I would be willing to use my personal contacts to gain a promotion or desirable transfer. | _____ | _____ |
| **14.** I think it is a good idea to send a congratulatory note to someone in the company who receives a promotion to an executive position. | _____ | _____ |
| **15.** I think "office politics" is only for losers. | _____ | _____ |
| **16.** I have already started to develop a network of useful contacts. | _____ | _____ |

***Scoring and Interpretation:*** Give yourself a plus 1 for each answer that agrees with the keyed answer. Each question that receives a score of plus 1 shows a tendency toward playing positive organizational politics. The scoring key is as follows:

| | | |
|---|---|---|
| **1.** Mostly agree | **6.** Mostly agree | **11.** Mostly agree |
| **2.** Mostly agree | **7.** Mostly agree | **12.** Mostly agree |
| **3.** Mostly agree | **8.** Mostly disagree | **13.** Mostly agree |
| **4.** Mostly agree | **9.** Mostly agree | **14.** Mostly disagree |
| **5.** Mostly agree | **10.** Mostly disagree | **15.** Mostly disagree |

- **1–6:** Below-average tendency to play office politics
- **7–11:** Average tendency to play office politics
- **12 and above:** Above-average tendency to play office politics; strong need for power

***Skill Development:*** Thinking about your political tendencies in the workplace is important for your career because most successful leaders are moderately political. The ability to use politics effectively and ethically increases with importance in the executive suite. Most top players are effective office politicians. Yet being overly and blatantly political can lead to distrust, thereby damaging your career

***Strategies Aimed at Gaining Power***    All political tactics are aimed at acquiring and maintaining power, even the power to avoid a difficult assignment. Tom Peters says that although power can often be abused, it can also be used to benefit many people. "And as a career building tool, the slow and steady (and subtle) amassing of power is the surest road to success."[33] Here are nine techniques aimed directly at gaining power.

**1. *Develop power contacts.*** Cultivating friendly, cooperative relationships with powerful organizational members and outsiders can make the leader's cause much easier to advance. Developing power contacts is a focused type of social networking. These contacts can benefit a person by supporting his or her ideas in meetings and other public forums. One way to develop these contacts is to be more social, for example, by throwing parties and inviting powerful people and their guests. Some organizations and some bosses frown on social familiarity, however. And power holders receive many invitations, so they might not be available. Considerable networking for the development of power contacts now takes place through social networking web sites geared toward professionals, such as LinkedIn, and specialty sites such as those geared toward special industry groups. An example of the latter is INmobile.org for the wireless industry.

**2. *Control vital information.*** Power accrues to those who control vital information, as indicated in the discussion of personal power. Many former government or military officials have found power niches for themselves in industry after leaving the public payroll. Frequently such an individual will be hired as the Washington representative of a firm that does business with the government. The vital information they control is knowledge of who to contact to shorten some of the complicated procedures in getting government contracts approved.

To facilitate controlling vital information, it is politically important to stay informed. Successful leaders develop a pipeline to help them keep abreast, or ahead, of developments within the firm. For this reason, a politically astute individual befriends the president's assistant. No other source offers the potential for obtaining as much information as the executive administrative assistant.

**3. *Control lines of communication.*** Related to controlling information is controlling the lines of communication, particularly access to key people. Administrative assistants and staff assistants frequently control an executive's calendar. Both insiders and outsiders must curry favor with the conduit in order to see an important executive. Although many people attempt to contact executives directly through email, some executives delegate the responsibility of screening email messages to an assistant. The assistant will also screen telephone calls, thus being selective about who can communicate directly with the executive.

**4. *Do what the political environment demands.*** A high-level political strategy is to do whatever the political environment demands to attain your goals. In this way you gain the support of decision makers. Ralph D. Crosby is the CEO of EADS North America—the U.S. defense arm of the giant European Aeronautic Defence & Space Co., whose divisions include Airbus. To facilitate obtaining orders from the U.S. government, one of Crosby's first moves was establishing stateside final production factories for helicopters. The move brought 645 high-paying assembly jobs to Texas, Mississippi, and Alabama. Crosby also partnered with big U.S. contractors to help cultivate senators who make defense-spending decisions.[34]

**5. *Bring in outside experts.*** To help legitimate their positions, executives will often hire a consultant to conduct a study or cast an opinion. Consciously or unconsciously, many consultants are hesitant to "bite the hand that feeds them."

A consultant will therefore often support the executive's position. In turn, the executive will use the consultant's findings to prove that he or she is right. This tactic might be considered ethical because the executive believes he or she is obtaining an objective opinion.

**6. *Make a quick showing.*** A display of dramatic results can help gain acceptance for one's efforts or those of the group. Once a person has impressed management with his or her ability to solve that first problem, that person can look forward to working on problems that will bring greater power. A staff professional might volunteer to spruce up a company web site to make it more appealing. After accomplishing that feat, the person might be invited to join the e-commerce team. On the flip side, *not* making a quick showing will sometimes result in a manager being fired in less than a year. Two of dozens of possible examples in recent years are that Adobe Systems Inc. and Sears Holdings Corp. both fired chief financial officers within six months because the officers were unable to attain outstanding results quickly.[35] (However, we do not know what political blunders these executives made.)

**7. *Remember that everyone expects to be paid back.*** According to the Law of Reciprocity, everybody in the world expects to be paid back.[36] If you do not find some way to reimburse people for the good deeds they have done for you, your supply of people to perform good deeds will run short. Because many of these good deeds bring you power, such as by supporting your initiative, your power base will soon erode. As a way of paying back the person who supported your initiative, you might mention publicly how the person in question provided you with expert advice on the technical aspects of your proposal.

Leadership Skill-Building Exercise 7-2 gives you an opportunity to develop practical solutions to the challenge of reciprocating for favors granted you by network members.

**8. *Be politically correct.*** Political correctness involves being careful not to offend or slight anyone, and being extra civil and respectful.[37] The politically correct person therefore avoids creating some enemies. An effective use of political correctness would be to say that "We need a ladder in our department because we have workers of different heights who need access to the top shelves." It would be politically incorrect to say, "We need ladders because we have some short workers who cannot reach the top shelves."

**9. *Be the first to accept reasonable changes.*** A natural inclination for most people is to resist change, so the person who steps forward first to accept reasonable changes will acquire some political capital. The team member who welcomes the changes exerts a positive influence on group members who may be dragging their heels about the change. An example might be that the company is attempting to shift to an online system of performance evaluation, thereby eliminating paper filing. It is politically wise to be an early adopter of the new system.

***Strategies and Tactics Aimed at Building Relationships***    Much of organizational politics involves building positive relationships with network members who can be helpful now or later. This network includes superiors, subordinates, other

**Leadership Skill-Building Exercise 7-2**

### Paying Back Favors from Network Members

Most readers are aware that effective networkers find some way to pay back those people in their network who have done them favors. For example, if a store owner refers you to a contact that might lead to a job interview, you might refer a customer to his or her store. However, finding useful ways to reciprocate favors by network members is not so easy. Your assignment is to brainstorm in groups to develop alternative solutions to the problem, "How can we reciprocate when a network member does us a favor?" The network members can be physical as well as those you have developed virtually, such as

FaceBook members. Aim for at least a dozen suggestions. After first compiling the suggestions, refine the list for duplication and precision. Perhaps reduce your list to the six most effective suggestions. If feasible, a team leader from each group presents the suggestions to the rest of the class.

Class members might then discuss answers to these questions: (1) Which several suggestions were the most frequently offered across the groups? (2) Which suggestions do I think are good enough to use now or in the future?

lower-ranking people, coworkers, external customers, and suppliers. The following are several representative strategies and tactics:

**1. *Display loyalty.*** A loyal worker is valued because organizations prosper more with loyal than with disloyal employees. Blind loyalty—the belief that the organization cannot make a mistake—is not called for; most rational organizations welcome constructive criticism. An obvious form of loyalty to the organization is longevity. Although job-hopping is more acceptable today than in the past, tenure with the company is still an asset for promotion. Tenure tends to contribute more to eligibility for promotion in a traditional industry such as food processing than in high-technology firms.

**2. *Manage your impression.*** Impression management includes behaviors directed at enhancing one's image by drawing attention to oneself. Often the attention of others is directed toward superficial aspects of the self, such as clothing and grooming. Yet impression management also deals with deeper aspects of behavior, such as speaking well and presenting one's ideas coherently. Bad speech habits are recognized as a deterrent to advancement in organizations.[38]

Another part of impression management is telling people about your success or implying that you are an "insider." Email is used extensively today to send messages to others for the purpose of impressing them with one's good deeds. Displaying good business etiquette has received renewed attention as a key part of impression management, with companies sending staff members to etiquette classes to learn how to create favorable impressions on key people. Many management scholars take a dim view of impression management, yet the topic has been carefully researched.[39]

**3. *Ask satisfied customers to contact your boss.*** A favorable comment by a customer receives considerable weight because customer satisfaction is a top corporate priority. If a customer says something nice, the comment will carry more weight than one from a coworker or subordinate. The reason is that coworkers and subordinates might praise a person for political reasons. Customers' motivation is assumed to be pure because they have little concern about pleasing suppliers.

**4. *Be courteous, pleasant, and positive.*** Courteous, pleasant, and positive people are the first to be hired and the last to be fired (assuming they also have other important qualifications). Polite behavior provides an advantage because many people believe that civility has become a rare quality.

**5. *Ask advice.*** Asking advice on work-related topics builds relationships with other employees. Asking another person for advice—someone whose job does not require giving it—will usually be perceived as a compliment. Asking advice transmits a message of trust in the other person's judgment.

**6. *Send thank-you notes to large numbers of people.*** One of the most basic political tactics, sending thank-you notes profusely, is simply an application of sound human relations. Many successful people take the time to send handwritten notes to employees and customers to help create a bond with those people. Handwritten notes have gained in currency because they are a refreshing change from electronic communication.

**7. *Flatter others sensibly.*** Flattery in the form of sincere praise can be an effective relationship builder. By being judicious in your praise, you can lower the defenses of work associates and make them more receptive to your ideas. A survey of 760 directors found that ingratiatory behavior toward the chief executive plays a bigger role in receiving a board appointment than does having attended an elite school or having elite social connections. James D. Westphal and Ithai Stern concluded that the most efficient way to get more board appointments is to engage in ingratiating behavior (a form of politics). The type of political behavior focused on flattery. Providing advice and information to CEOs frequently was advantageous. Furthermore, not monitoring the strategic decisions of board members too closely was also effective in receiving nominations to other boards. Caucasian males appeared to gain more advantage from ingratiating themselves to peer directors than did ethnic minorities and women.[40]

An effective, general-purpose piece of flattery is to tell another person that you are impressed by something he or she has accomplished. Leadership Skill-Building Exercise 7-3 will help you enhance your skills in flattery.

**Strategies Aimed at Avoiding Political Blunders**    A strategy for retaining power is to refrain from making power-eroding blunders. Committing these politically insensitive acts can also prevent one from attaining power. Several leading blunders are described next.

**1. *Criticizing the boss in a public forum.*** The oldest saw in human relations is to "praise in public and criticize in private." Yet in the passion of the moment, we may still surrender to an irresistible impulse to criticize the boss publicly.

**2. *Bypassing the boss.*** Protocol is still highly valued in a hierarchical organization. Going around the boss to resolve a problem is therefore hazardous. You might be able to accomplish the bypass, but your career could be damaged and

Leadership Skill-Building Exercise 7-3

### Flattery Role Play

One student plays the role of a team leader who wants to build alliances with important people in the organization. The company is a major player in consumer electronics, including plasma-screen television receivers. One day the team leader is waiting in line to board an airplane, and he or she figures the wait will be about ten minutes. Another student plays the role of the corporate vice president of marketing, who unexpectedly is standing next to the team leader in the boarding line.

The marketing vice president is middle age, a family person, and has been with the company for twenty-five years. The alliance-building team leader figures he or she has about seven minutes available to make an initial contact with the senior executive and perhaps start a good working relationship. So the team leader decides to engage in appropriate flattery. The marketing vice president seems at least willing to converse with the team leader. Run the scenario for about six minutes in front of the class. The rest of the class members will observe and provide some feedback on the effectiveness of the flattery techniques.

The potential contribution of this exercise is that it may help raise your awareness of the opportunity to engage in constructive political behavior. Recognizing opportunities to gain political advantage can be helpful to a leader's career.

your recourses limited. Except in cases of outrageous misconduct such as blatant sexual harassment or criminal misconduct, your boss's boss will probably side with your boss.

**3. *Declining an offer from top management*.** Turning down top management, especially more than once, is a political blunder. You thus have to balance sensibly managing your time against the blunder of refusing a request from top management. Today, an increasing number of managers and corporate professionals decline opportunities for promotion when the new job requires geographic relocation. For these people, family and lifestyle preferences are more important than gaining political advantage on the job.

**4. *Putting your foot in your mouth* (being needlessly tactless).** To avoid hurting your career, it is important to avoid—or at least minimize—being blatantly tactless toward influential people. An example would be telling the CEO that he should delegate speech making to another person because he or she is such a poor speaker. "You don't get to be a senior person if you are repeatedly tactless," advises the head of a New York recruiting firm.[41] When you feel you are on the verge of being critical, delay your response, and perhaps reword it for later delivery. Use your emotional intelligence! If you are needlessly tactless, compensate the best you can by offering a full apology later.

**5. *Not conforming to the company dress code*.** Although some degree of independence and free thinking is welcome in many organizations, violating the dress code can block you from acquiring more power. Conforming to the dress code suggests that you are part of the team and you understand what is expected. Dress codes can be violated by dressing too informally *or* formally, and by wearing clothing that symbolizes a cultural identity.[42]

**6.** *Writing embarrassing or incriminating email messages.* A political blunder committed frequently is to use company email to send messages that if discovered would embarrass you or place you at risk for being fired. Hundreds of workers have sent messages to the effect, "The CEO is an idiot," only to be confronted with the evidence later. (Almost any email message can be retrieved by IT specialists.) A celebrated case was the firing of Julie Roehm from her senior vice president of marketing position at Wal-Mart. The company uncovered the following *private* email she sent to a subordinate, Sean Womack: "I think about us together all the time. Little moments like watching your face when you kiss me." Womack's estranged wife helped Wal-Mart find the love message. Roehm was also being questioned about other blunders such as possibly accepting gifts from an ad agency, and not being a good cultural fit at Wal-Mart.[43]

## Unethical Political Tactics and Strategies

Any technique of gaining power can be devious if practiced in the extreme. A person who supports a boss by feeding him or her insider information that could affect the price of company stock is being devious. Some approaches are unequivocally unethical, such as those described next. In the long run they erode a leader's effectiveness by lowering his or her credibility. Devious tactics might even result in lawsuits against the leader, the organization, or both.

*Backstabbing*   The ubiquitous back stab requires that you pretend to be nice but all the while plan someone's demise. A frequent form of backstabbing is to initiate a conversation with a rival about the weaknesses of a common boss, encouraging negative commentary and making careful mental notes of what the person says. When these comments are passed along to the boss, the rival appears disloyal and foolish. Email has become a medium for the back stab. The sender of the message documents a mistake made by another individual and includes key people on the distribution list. A sample message sent by one manager to a rival began as follows, "Hi, Ted. I'm sorry you couldn't make our important meeting. I guess you had some other important priorities. But we need your input on the following major agenda item we tackled. . . ."

*Embrace or Demolish*   The ancient strategy of "embrace or demolish" suggests that you remove from the premises rivals who suffered past hurts through your efforts; otherwise, the wounded rivals might retaliate at a vulnerable moment. This kind of strategy is common after a hostile takeover; many executives lose their jobs because they opposed the takeover. A variation of embrace or demolish is to terminate managers from the acquired organization who oppose adapting to the culture of the new firm. For example, a free-wheeling manager who opposes the bureaucratic culture of the acquiring firm might be terminated as "not able to identify with our mission."

*Setting a Person Up for Failure*   The object of a setup is to place a person in a position where he or she will either fail outright or look ineffective. For example, an executive whom the CEO dislikes might be given responsibility for a troubled division whose market is rapidly collapsing. The newly assigned division president cannot stop the decline and is then fired for poor performance.

***Divide and Rule***   An ancient military and governmental strategy, this tactic is sometimes used in business. The object is to have subordinates fight among themselves, therefore yielding the balance of power to another person. If team members are not aligned with one another, there is an improved chance that they will align with a common superior. One way of getting subordinates to fight with one another is to place them in intense competition for resources. An example would be asking them to prove data explaining why their budget is more worthy than the budget requested by rivals.

***Playing Territorial Games***   Also referred to as turf wars, **territorial games** involve protecting and hoarding resources that give one power, such as information, relationships, and decision-making authority. Territorial behavior, according to Annette Simmons, is based on a hidden force that limits peoples' desire to give full cooperation. People are biologically programmed to be greedy for whatever they think it takes to survive in the corporate environment.

The purpose of territorial games is to vie for the three kinds of *territory* in the modern corporate survival game: information, relationships, or authority. A relationship is "hoarded" through such tactics as not encouraging others to visit a key customer or blocking a high performer from getting a promotion or transfer.[44] For example, the manager might tell others that his star performer is mediocre to prevent the person from being considered for a valuable transfer possibility. Other examples of territorial games include monopolizing time with clients, scheduling meetings so someone cannot attend, and shutting out coworkers from joining you on an important assignment.

A review of research and theory suggests that territoriality can sometimes help the organization by increasing the commitment of workers and reducing conflict. Commitment might increase because workers might feel a sense of ownership, such as feeling at home in a personally decorated cubicle. Conflict might be reduced because people stay out of each other's territory. However, a major negative consequence of territoriality is that employees become self-focused, which detracts from their ability to focus on the organization. Territoriality can create isolation among workers, leading to less connectedness with others in the organization.[45] As one marketing manager said, "Why do we bother inviting finance types to our meetings?"

***Creating and Then Resolving a False Catastrophe***   An advanced devious tactic is for a manager to pretend a catastrophe exists and then proceed to "rescue" others from the catastrophe, thereby appearing to be a superhero.[46] The political player rushes in and declares that everything is a mess and the situation is almost hopeless; shortly thereafter, he or she resolves the problem. An example would be for a newly appointed information technology manager to inform top management that the system he inherited is antiquated and approaching the point of severely damaging the company's operations. One week later, he claims to have miraculously overhauled the information system, such as by ordering new equipment and hiring a few key personnel.

# EXERCISING CONTROL OVER DYSFUNCTIONAL POLITICS

Carried to excess, organizational politics can hurt an organization and its members. Too much politicking can result in wasted time and effort, thereby lowering productivity. A study of 1,370 employees in four organizations investigated how the perception of political behavior was related to certain outcomes. Among the many findings were the following:

- Perceptions of political behavior taking place in the work group were associated with less commitment to the organization and a stronger turnover intention (planning to leave the firm voluntarily).
- Perceptions of political behavior taking place throughout the organization were also associated with less commitment to the organization and a stronger turnover intention.[47]

The human consequences of excessive negative and unethical politics can also be substantial. Examples include lowered morale and loss of people who intensely dislike office politics. To avoid these negative consequences, leaders are advised to combat political behavior when it is excessive and dysfunctional. Table 7-1 presents some symptoms of dysfunctional office politics.

In a comprehensive strategy to control politics, *organizational leaders must be aware of its causes and techniques.* For example, during a downsizing the CEO can be on the alert for instances of backstabbing and transparent attempts to please

**TABLE 7-1** Symptoms of Dysfunctional Office Politics (the DOOP Scale)

The ten statements below concern ethics in interpersonal relationships on the job. The more frequently any of these actions take place, the more likely the organization or organizational unit is beset with dysfunctional office politics.

1. A conflict between two or more persons or groups was resolved on the basis of who held the most power rather than on what would have made sense and would have worked better.
2. A person or group "got even" in some way with another person or group.
3. Information about what was going on at work was withheld from a person or group.
4. Information was reported about a person or group that was intentionally exaggerated, misconstrued, and/or made mostly untrue by some other person or group.
5. A person or group was led to believe one thing, when the other was clearly true.
6. A person or group agreed with another person or group solely to "keep the boat from rocking."
7. A person or group's worthwhile efforts or initiatives were intentionally undermined.
8. A person reported confidential or unfavorable information about a person or group in order to gain a special advantage.
9. A person or group who looked at things differently and had different points of view was punished and/or silenced by another person or group.
10. An organizational decision was based on self-interest rather than on what made sense and would have worked better.

*Source:* From Thomas P. Anderson, "Creating Measures of Dysfunctional Office and Organizational Politics: The DOOP and Short Form DEEP Scales," *Psychology: A Journal of Human Behavior,* vol. 31, no. 2, 1994, p. 34. Reprinted by permission of the author.

him or her. Open communication also can constrain the impact of political behavior. For instance, open communication can let everyone know the basis for allocating resources, thus reducing the amount of politicking. If people know in advance how resources are allocated, the effectiveness of attempting to curry favor with the boss will be reduced. When communication is open, it also makes it more difficult for some people to control information and pass along gossip as a political weapon.

*Avoiding favoritism and cronyism*—avoiding giving the best rewards to the group members you like the most or to old friends—is a potent way of minimizing politics within a work group. If group members believe that getting the boss to like them is much less important than good job performance in obtaining rewards, they will kiss up to the boss less frequently. In an attempt to minimize favoritism, the manager must reward workers who impress him or her through task-related activities.

*Setting good examples at the top of the organization* can help reduce the frequency and intensity of organizational politics. When leaders are nonpolitical in their actions, they demonstrate in subtle ways that political behavior is not welcome. It may be helpful for the leader to announce during a staff meeting that devious political behavior is undesirable and unprofessional.

Another way of reducing the extent of political behavior is for *individuals and the organization to share the same goals*, a situation described as *goal congruence*. If political behavior will interfere with the company and individuals achieving their goals, workers with goal congruence are less likely to play office politics excessively. A project leader is less likely to falsely declare that the boss's idea is good just to please the boss if the project leader wants the company to succeed.

L. A. Witt conducted a study with 1,200 workers in five organizations that lends support to the importance of goal congruence in combating politics. Witt concluded that one way to approach the negative impact of organizational politics is for the manager to ensure that group members hold the appropriate goal priorities. In this way they will have a greater sense of control over and understanding of the workplace and thus be less affected by organizational politics.[48]

Politics can sometimes be constrained by a *threat to discuss questionable information in a public forum*. People who practice devious politics usually want to operate secretly and privately. They are willing to drop hints and innuendoes and make direct derogatory comments about someone else, provided they will not be identified as the source. An effective way of stopping the discrediting of others is to offer to discuss the topic publicly.[49] The person attempting to pass on the questionable information will usually back down and make a statement closer to the truth.

Finally, *hiring people with integrity* will help reduce the number of dysfunctional political players. References should be checked carefully with respect to the candidate's integrity and honesty.[50] Say to the reference, "Tell me about _____'s approach to playing politics." Leadership Skill-Building Exercise 7-4 provides an opportunity to practice the subtle art of discouraging excessive political behavior on the job.

Leadership Skill-Building Exercise 7-4

## Controlling Office Politics

One student plays the role of a corporate executive visiting one of the key divisions. Six other students play the roles of managers within the division, each of whom wants to impress the boss during their meeting. The corporate executive gets the meeting started by asking the managers in turn to discuss their recent activities and accomplishments. Each

division-level manager will attempt to create a very positive impression on the corporate executive. After about nine minutes of observing them fawning over him or her, the executive decides to take action against such excessive politicking. Review the information on political tactics and their control before carrying out this role-assuming exercise.

### Reader's Roadmap

 So far in this book, we have examined the nature of leaders, their ethics, and how they acquire power. The next chapter explains influence tactics, or ways of converting power into action.

## SUMMARY

Organizational power is derived from many sources, including position power (legitimate, reward, coercive, and information) and personal power (expert, reference, and prestige). Power also stems from ownership, dependencies, capitalizing on opportunity, managing critical problems, and being close to power.

Full-fledged empowerment includes the dimensions of meaning, self-determination, competence, impact, and internal commitment. Actions that can be taken to become an empowering leader include the following: foster initiative and responsibility, link work activities to the goals of the organization, provide ample information, allow group members to choose methods, encourage self-leadership, establish limits to empowerment, and continue to lead. Also, take into account cultural differences in how empowerment is accepted. Delegation is another important part of empowerment.

To acquire and retain power, a leader must skillfully use organizational politics. The meaning of *politics* continues to shift in a positive, constructive

direction. Contributing factors to organizational politics include the pyramidal shape of organizations, subjective performance standards, environmental uncertainty, emotional insecurity, Machiavellian tendencies, and encouraging admiration from subordinates.

To make effective use of organizational politics, leaders must be aware of specific political tactics and strategies. Ethical methods can be divided into those aimed directly at gaining power, those aimed at building relationships, and those aimed at avoiding political blunders. Unethical and devious tactics, such as the embrace-or-demolish strategy, constitute another category of political behavior.

Carried to extremes, organizational politics can hurt an organization and its members. Being aware of the causes and types of political behavior can help leaders deal with the problem. Setting good examples of nonpolitical behavior is helpful, as is achieving goal congruence and threatening to publicly expose devious politicking. It is also good to hire people who have integrity.

## KEY TERMS

| | | |
|---|---|---|
| **Power** | **Prestige power** | **Centrality** |
| **Legitimate power** | **Dependence perspective** | **Empowerment** |
| **Reward power** | **Resource dependence** | **Self-leadership** |
| **Coercive power** | **perspective** | **Delegation** |
| **Information power** | **Strategic contingency** | **Organizational politics** |
| **Personal power** | **theory** | **Territorial games** |

## ✔ GUIDELINES FOR ACTION AND SKILL DEVELOPMENT

To enhance your interpersonal effectiveness at the outset of joining a firm, it is helpful to size up the political climate. Even if you are new to the firm, it will often be helpful to ask the following eight diagnostic questions during meetings:

1. What method do people use here to offer new ideas?
2. How do staff members offer opposing ideas or disagreement?
3. How much evidence is required, and what type of evidence is required, to persuade other staff members?
4. What responses does assertive behavior elicit? What facial expressions do you see around the table when someone presents a strong idea? Whose words elicit nods from the meeting leader? Whose words prompt the reaction "Let's move on"?
5. How much personal reference is tolerated?
6. How much display of emotional intensity is tolerated?
7. Who gets heard? Promoted? Passed over?[51]
8. What is the appropriate use of electronic devices like laptop computers and BlackBerrys during meetings?

### Discussion Questions and Activities

1. Why do so many people think that possessing power is a good thing?
2. How can a leader occupy a top-level executive position and still have relatively little power?
3. Contrary to popular opinion, CEOs of major U.S. companies come from a wide variety of private universities and state universities, not just a handful of well-publicized M.B.A. programs. What does this fact tell you about sources of power and organizational politics?
4. What can you do this week to enhance your power?
5. Many business leaders say something to the effect of, "We practice empowerment because we don't expect our employees to leave their brains at the door." What are these leaders talking about?
6. Empowerment has been criticized because it leaves no one in particular accountable for results. What is your opinion of this criticism?
7. Why are entrepreneurial leaders often poor delegators?
8. Many people have asked the question "Isn't office politics just for incompetents?" What is your answer to this question?
9. A woman who is a CEO fires thousands of people and closes many units of the organization. Which is the best label for her in terms of political correctness: hatchet man, hatchet woman, or hatchet person? Explain your position.
10. Ask an experienced worker to give you an example of the successful application of organizational politics. Which tactic was used, and what was the outcome?

## Leadership Case Problem A

### Kimberly Davis Dances Around Mergers

Kimberly Davis, senior vice president, Global Philanthropy, JPMorgan Chase and president of the JPMorgan Chase Foundation, age 47, was interviewed by a reporter from *Black Enterprise* about her career. The interview transcript follows.

*BE:* Describe the mergers you've experienced and how you were able to position yourself for success.

*KD:* Let me start with the first: I was with a small bank in Bridgeport, Connecticut, called City Trust Bank with about 2,400 employees. In August 1991, it was acquired by Chase Manhattan. By January of 1992, I realized that to be successful in the new organization, I was going to have to figure out a way to move my job prospects to the headquarters in New York. They were consolidating all of the back-office capabilities at City Trust into the new Chase organization, and many of the profit-and-loss roles were being integrated into New York. I figured that I had eighteen months before most of the jobs in Connecticut would be eliminated. Within the next two years, the organization went from 2,400 down to 200.

*BE:* And you were one of the 200?

*KD:* I was one of the 200. One of the things that's important in a career is having a strong expertise. For me, it was finance and marketing. I had been in a position where I had held two very substantial roles in finance and marketing, so when the new people came in I was able to quickly show my competence. And because of my ability to build relationships with them, I became someone they embraced as part of the new management structure. Part of it is luck. I would be remiss if I believed that all of it had to do with competence.

*BE:* And the mergers continued?

*KD:* In 1995, Chase and Chemical Bank merged. Chemical and Manufacturer's Hanover had just merged, and those two organizations hadn't really been integrated when Chase and Manhattan merged—so it was really three mergers—Manufacturer's Hanover, Chemical, and Chase. That was very ugly and the cultures were very different. There was a lot of infighting. But I met the head of human resources at an event a year before the merger. When the merger happened, I got a call from him saying he was impressed with me, and I took the initiative to build a relationship with him. He later had a big opportunity in human resources and asked me if I'd be willing to do a two-year stint. People thought I was crazy to leave a profit-and-loss position and move to human resources but strategically, it was a wonderful way for me to learn the new organization from the top. Being in that staff role in corporate, I was able to see all of the businesses as opposed to being in the one narrow business pre-merger.

*BE:* How should a professional prepare once a merger is on the horizon?

*KD:* Identify where the growth opportunities are, and what the new business model is going to be. Who's in power; who's out of power? Align yourself with those who are in power and show your ability to deliver results very quickly. Don't be afraid to take the risk of knocking on doors, getting to know people, letting people know your intentions about your career. Many times after a merger we lay low and want to let the dust settle. All of the good opportunities are being divvied up while we're laying low. It takes a long time even after a merger is announced for things to become integrated—almost two years. There's a lot that you can deliver and produce during that period of time.

### Questions

1. Identify several political tactics Davis used to come out ahead after mergers.
2. Identify the sources of power Davis used to advance her career.

3. What is your evaluation of the ethics Davis displays?
4. What career advice might you offer Kimberly Davis?

*Source:* Adapted slightly from Laura Egodigwe, "Survivor Instinct: How a Strategic Executive Read All the Corporate Signs—and Played Her Vantage Points," *Black Enterprise*, March 2007, p. 63. Copyright 2007 by Black Enterprise Magazine. Reproduced with permission of Black Enterprise Magazine in the format Textbook via Copyright Clearance Center.

## Leadership Case Problem B

### Yo-Yo Empowerment at Direct Mail Inc.

Business has been great for Direct Mail Inc., a company that designs a variety of direct marketing campaigns for its customers. Despite the increase in online advertising, direct mail has been a growth industry in recent years. Among the services of Direct Mail are personalized advertising flyers gearing products to the interests of the recipients, with flyers being mailed to both homes and offices. For example, a person who had ordered fine wines online or by telephone might receive a brochure about wine racks or wine storage cabinets. Another service Direct Mail offers is "transactional promotions," or bills that arrive with advertising on the same page.

Dennis Parker, the founder and CEO of Direct Mail, says that he is astonished by the growth of his industry. When he started his company, Parker was warned that going into the junk mail business was a high-risk venture. Yet recently, advertisers have come to realize that people act on flyers directed to their interest at a higher rate than they respond to Internet advertising or general advertisements in newspapers and magazines.

Parker says that he is passionate about his business for many reasons. He enjoys keeping up with the technology of digital presses, and seeing so much new business coming to Direct Mail based on its reputation. Parker says also that he enjoys the leadership and management challenge of running a growing business. "I'm especially good at motivating my workers through empowerment," he says.

Audrey Valentine, the director of marketing, was having a dinner meeting with Parker at her initiative to talk about his empowering style of leadership. With a gentle laugh, Valentine said to Parker, "I'm not telling you anything this evening I haven't hinted at least six times before. The management team knows you are a sharp businessperson, and a kind manager, but you are also a *yo-yo delegator*."

"What do you mean, I'm a yo-yo delegator?" asked Parker.

"I'll explain what I mean, Dennis. You do the same thing to me, the head of finance, and our operations guy. Remember when you told me something like, 'We haven't done much business yet in the home furnishing field. Why don't you see what new business you can generate in that field?' I put my best effort into drumming up a lead with a home furnishing executive. When I told you of my progress, you asked me to turn over the lead to you so you could wrap up the deal. The yo-yo here is that you give me something to do, and then you take it back when it looks good. What you send out comes back quickly to you."

After listening to Valentine's feedback about the yo-yo delegation, Parker calmly explained: "In this business, high-level contacts and relationships are important. Empowerment can only go so far. A big customer would prefer to deal directly with the CEO, so that's why I step in to help you."

**Questions**

1. What advice can you offer Parker about his approach to empowerment?
2. To what extent is Valentine committing a political blunder in telling her boss that he is a yo-yo delegator?

3. What is your evaluation of the corporate social responsibility of a direct mail business, considering that probably over 95 percent of recipients of the mailings throw them away immediately?

 **Leadership Skill-Building Exercise 7-5**

### My Leadership Portfolio

For this insert into your leadership portfolio, think through all the recent opportunities you might have had to use political tactics. How did you deal with the situation? Did you capitalize on any opportunities? Did you use an ethical approach? Did you use any unethical tactics? Did you commit any political blunders? Here would be an example:

I saw a flyer indicating that our Business Management Association was having a guest speaker, an executive from Merrill Lynch. I had been pretty

busy with studies, my job, and social life, yet I decided to invest the time and attend. As it worked out, the meeting was a wonderful opportunity to make a couple of good contacts. After the talk, I spoke to the speaker and complimented her. We had a brief conversation about how I was looking for a career in investment banking, and she gave me her business card. I sent her an email message the next day, thanking her for the time she gave me. I also met a couple of important people at the meeting, and got their cards also.

## Internet Skill-Building Exercise

### Advice About Office Politics

Here is an opportunity to get some free advice about a problem of office politics. Go to www.office-politics.com and post an office politics problem you might be facing, and then receive an answer from a panel of experts about how to deal with the problem. The site also presents updated references on organizational politics. Or, you might simply want to ask about a problem of office politics. Here are several examples of problems other people have submitted to www.office-politics.com:

Apply the chapter concepts! Visit the Web and complete this Internet skill-building exercise to learn more about current leadership topics and trends.

- "We recently lost a highly intelligent, highly motivated executive to another firm."
- "People in the office are making off-the-wall comments like 'What does she do all day' or 'She does nothing.'"
- "I have just learned that I am the most 'hated' person in my office."

# Influence Tactics
## of **Leaders**

## LEARNING OBJECTIVES

After studying this chapter and doing the exercises, you should be able to

- Describe the relationship between power and influence.

- Identify a set of honest and ethical influence tactics.

- Identify a set of less honest and ethical influence tactics.

- Summarize some empirical research about the effectiveness and sequencing of influence tactics.

- Describe how implicit leadership theories are related to a leader's ability to influence group members.

## CHAPTER OUTLINE

**A Model of Power and Influence**

**Description and Explanation of Influence Tactics**

    Essentially Ethical and Honest Tactics
    Essentially Dishonest and Unethical Tactics

**Leadership Influence for Organizational Change**

**Relative Effectiveness and Sequencing of Influence Tactics**

    Relative Effectiveness of Influence Tactics
    Sequencing of Influence Tactics

**Implicit Leadership Theories and Leadership Influence**

**Summary**

When Bill Amelio joined Lenovo a few years ago, he faced the challenge of bringing together the organizational cultures of a Chinese computer maker and the struggling PC division of an iconic American brand. Lenovo had just swallowed IBM's Think-Pad business for $1.75 billion, creating overnight the third-largest PC maker in the world after HP and Dell. Amelio had previously run Asian operations for Dell, and had also spent eighteen years at IBM. His biggest initial challenge in merging the two firms was simply where to locate the united company. ThinkPad operations were based in Raleigh, North Carolina, while Lenovo was headquartered in Beijing. Instead of picking one place, Amelio decided to go with no headquarters at all. He works out of Singapore; Lenovo chairman Yang Yuanqing relocated to Raleigh; and top executives hold meetings in a different location every month. Based on financial results, the method appears to be working.

Shortly after the merger, Lenovo came under fire when lawmakers said the U.S. State Department shouldn't be purchasing laptops from a Chinese maker. Amelio invited the critics to send inspectors and explained to them that most PC companies source through China. Lenovo worked to reassure old ThinkPad customers that the brand's reputation for high-quality manufacturing would stay intact. Amelio says there's been a minimal drop-off in loyalty.[1]

Bill Amelio did some heavy thinking to devise influence tactics to pull off a merger between two companies with different organizational and national cultures. Avoiding the disruption of having a new company headquarters was persuasive, as was his argument that a Lenovo PC wasn't really much more Chinese than the PCs made by other American manufacturers. Without effective influence tactics, a leader is similar to a soccer player who has not learned to kick a soccer ball, or a newscaster who is unable to speak.

Leadership, as oft repeated, is an influence process. To become an effective leader, a person must be aware of the specific tactics leaders use to influence others. Here we discuss a number of specific influence tactics, but other aspects of leadership also concern influence. Being charismatic, as described in Chapter 3, influences many people. Leaders influence others through power and politics, as described in Chapter 7. Furthermore, motivating and coaching skills, as described in Chapter 10, involve influencing others toward worthwhile ends.

The terms *influence* and *power* are sometimes used interchangeably, whereas at other times power is said to create influence, and vice versa. In this book, we distinguish between power and influence as follows: **Influence** is the ability to affect the behavior of others in a particular direction,[2] whereas power is the potential or capacity to influence. Leaders are influential only when they exercise power. A leader therefore must acquire power to influence others.

Influence tactics have grown in importance because so often a leader or corporate professional has to influence others without having formal authority over them. IBM refers to this skill as *collaborative influence*, meaning that various groups team up informally depending on the task at hand, to accomplish the work. For example, helping a customer needing assistance in setting up an online distribution system for novel T-shirts might require the project leader to coordinate the efforts of people from various departments.[3]

A similar example is that a vice president at Google needed to lobby Gmail engineers who did not work for him to modify software for potential corporate customers. He likens his efforts to a Peace Corps mission: all heart but with little power to enforce his will.[4]

Another factor contributing to the importance of influence tactics is that employees often doubt that the leader, particularly a CEO, will be around for long. As a result, employees will wait out the boss rather than comply with unpopular orders. Therefore the most reliable way for managers to be effective is to get employees on their side.[5]

This chapter presents a model of power and influence, a description and explanation of influence tactics (both ethical and less ethical), a description of how leaders influence large-scale change, and a summary of the research about the relative effectiveness and sequencing of influence tactics. We also present a theory about the characteristics group members expect in a leader in order to be influenced by him or her.

## A MODEL OF POWER AND INFLUENCE

The model shown in Figure 8-1 illustrates that the end results of a leader's influence (the outcomes) are a function of the tactics he or she uses. The influence tactics are in turn moderated, or affected by, the leader's traits, the leader's behaviors, and the situation.

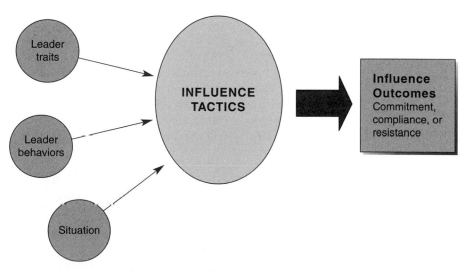

**FIGURE 8-1** A Model of Power and Influence.

Looking at the right side of the model, the three possible outcomes are commitment, compliance, and resistance. **Commitment** is the most successful outcome: the target of the influence attempt is enthusiastic about carrying out the request and makes a full effort. Commitment is particularly important for complex, difficult tasks because these require full concentration and effort. If you were influencing a technician to upgrade your operating system software, you would need his or her commitment. **Compliance** means that the influence attempt is partially successful: the target person is apathetic (not overjoyed) about carrying out the request and makes only a modest effort. The influence agent has changed the person's behavior but not his or her attitude. A long-distance truck driver might comply with demands that he sleep certain hours between hauls, but he is not enthusiastic about losing road time. Compliance for routine tasks—such as wearing a hard hat on a construction site—is usually good enough. Resistance is an unsuccessful influence attempt: the target is opposed to carrying out the request and finds ways to either not comply or do a poor job. **Resistance** includes making excuses for why the task cannot be carried out, procrastinating, and outright refusing to do the task.[6]

Going to the left side of the model, the leader's personality traits affect the outcome of influence tactics. An extroverted and warm leader who has charisma can more readily use some influence tactics than a leader who is introverted and cold. For example, he or she can make an inspirational appeal. A highly intelligent leader would be able to influence others because he or she has built a reputation as a subject matter expert. Whichever influence tactics a leader chooses, the goal is to get group members on his or her side.

The leader's behaviors also affect the outcome of influence tactics in a variety of ways, particularly because influence tactics *are* actions or behaviors. For example, setting high standards facilitates making an inspirational appeal. As another example, the leader who performs well consistently is better able to lead by example because he or she is a good role model.

Finally, the situation partly determines which influence tactic will be effective. The organizational culture or subculture is one such key situational factor. For example, in a high-technology environment, inspirational appeal and emotional display are less likely to be effective than rational persuasion and being a subject matter expert, because high-tech workers are more likely to be impressed by facts than by feeling.

The rest of this chapter identifies and describes influence tactics, including some mention of situational variables. Leader traits and power have been described in previous chapters. Leadership Self-Assessment Quiz 8-1 will give you an opportunity to think about which influence tactics you tend to use.

## DESCRIPTION AND EXPLANATION OF INFLUENCE TACTICS

Influence tactics are often viewed from an ethical perspective. Following this perspective, the influence tactics described here are classified into those that are essentially ethical and honest and those that are essentially manipulative and dishonest. The categorization presented here is far from absolute. Except for the extremes, most of the tactics could conceivably be placed in either category,

## Leadership Self-Assessment Quiz 8-1

### Survey of Influence Tactics

**Instructions:** Indicate how frequently you use the influence tactics listed here: VI = very infrequently or never; I = infrequently; S = sometimes; F = frequently; VF = very frequently. The VI to VF categories correspond to a 1-to-5 scale.

|  | 1<br>VI | 2<br>I | 3<br>S | 4<br>F | 5<br>VF |
|---|---|---|---|---|---|
| 1. I lead by demonstrating the right behavior myself. | ☐ | ☐ | ☐ | ☐ | ☐ |
| 2. I rely on facts and logic to persuade others. | ☐ | ☐ | ☐ | ☐ | ☐ |
| 3. People often listen to me because of my expertise. | ☐ | ☐ | ☐ | ☐ | ☐ |
| 4. If I want something done, I stand ready to do a favor in return. | ☐ | ☐ | ☐ | ☐ | ☐ |
| 5. I enjoy negotiating a price or an offer. | ☐ | ☐ | ☐ | ☐ | ☐ |
| 6. I am assertive (open and forthright in my demands). | ☐ | ☐ | ☐ | ☐ | ☐ |
| 7. I joke with or kid other people to make a point. | ☐ | ☐ | ☐ | ☐ | ☐ |
| 8. I will sometimes get quite emotional to make a point. | ☐ | ☐ | ☐ | ☐ | ☐ |
| 9. I promise to reward the person to get what I want. | ☐ | ☐ | ☐ | ☐ | ☐ |
| 10. I attempt to get other people on my side in order to win my point. | ☐ | ☐ | ☐ | ☐ | ☐ |
| 11. I cooperate with others in order to influence them. | ☐ | ☐ | ☐ | ☐ | ☐ |
| 12. As a leader, I participate heavily in the task of the group. | ☐ | ☐ | ☐ | ☐ | ☐ |
| 13. I form an alliance with the other person. | ☐ | ☐ | ☐ | ☐ | ☐ |
| 14. I threaten to go over the person's head to the boss. | ☐ | ☐ | ☐ | ☐ | ☐ |
| 15. I compliment the other person. | ☐ | ☐ | ☐ | ☐ | ☐ |
| 16. I use as much charm as possible to get my way. | ☐ | ☐ | ☐ | ☐ | ☐ |

**Scoring and Interpretation:** The more of these tactics you use frequently or very frequently, the more influential you probably are. Experience is a factor, because you could be potentially influential but have not yet had the opportunity to use many of these tactics.

**Skill Development:** The Survey of Influence Tactics might give you some clues for development. Look for influence tactics that appear to represent a good idea, but where you need skill development. Next, take the opportunity to practice the tactic. For example, take statement 15, "I compliment the other person." Perhaps you neglect to compliment others when you want to influence them. Using the guidelines for flattery given in the previous chapter, practice complimenting another person when you want to influence him or her.

depending on how they are used. For example, one can use the tactic "joking and kidding" in either a well-meaning or mean-spirited way. Joking and kidding could therefore be classified as "essentially ethical" or "essentially manipulative."

**TABLE 8-1** Essentially Ethical and Honest Influence Tactics

1. Leading by example and respect
2. Using rational persuasion
3. Developing a reputation as a subject matter expert (SME)
4. Exchanging favors and bargaining
5. Legitimating a request
6. Making an inspirational appeal, being charming, and emotional display
7. Consulting
8. Forming coalitions
9. Being a team player
10. Practicing hands-on leadership

## Essentially Ethical and Honest Tactics

This section describes essentially ethical and honest tactics and strategies for influencing others, as outlined in Table 8-1. Used with tact, diplomacy, and good intent, these strategies can help you get others to join you in accomplishing a worthwhile objective. Because these influence tactics vary in complexity, they also vary with respect to how much time is required to develop them.

*Leading by Example and Respect*     A simple but effective way of influencing group members is by **leading by example,** or acting as a positive role model. The ideal approach is to be a "do as I say and do" manager—that is, one whose actions and words are consistent. Actions and words confirm, support, and often clarify each other. Being respected facilitates leading by example because group members are more likely to follow the example of leaders they respect.

Leading by example is often interpreted to mean that the leader works long and hard, and expects others to do the same, with this type of behavior being prevalent among entrepreneurs who hire a staff. A case in point is Steven A. Cohen, who built a highly successful financial services and hedge fund firm, SAC Capital. He spends weekends working at his trading desk.[7]

*Using Rational Persuasion*     Rational persuasion is an important tactic for influencing people. It involves using logical arguments and factual evidence to convince another person that a proposal or request is workable and likely to achieve the goal.[8] Assertiveness combined with careful research is necessary to make rational persuasion an effective tactic. It is likely to be most effective with people who are intelligent and rational. Chief executive officers typically use rational persuasion to convince their boards that an undertaking, such as product diversification, is mandatory. A major moderating variable in rational persuasion is the credibility of the influence agent. Credibility helps an individual be more persuasive in two ways. First, it makes a person more convincing. Second, it contributes to a person's perceived power, and the more power one is perceived to have, the more targets will be influenced.[9]

Leaders who emphasize the rational decision-making model favor rational persuasion. For example, a leader favoring this model might say, "Don't tell me what you feel, give me the facts," in response to a subordinate who said, "I have the feeling that morale is down."

***Developing a Reputation as a Subject Matter Expert***   Becoming a subject matter expert (SME) on a topic of importance to the organization is an effective strategy for gaining influence. Being an SME can be considered a subset of rational persuasion. Managers who possess expert knowledge in a relevant field and who continually build on that knowledge can get others to help them get work accomplished. Many of the leaders described throughout this text use expert knowledge to influence others. Small-business owners, in particular, rely on being subject matter experts because they founded the business on the basis of their product or technical knowledge. For example, the leader of a software company is usually an expert in software development.

Steve Jobs is an extraordinary example of a subject matter expert because of his heavy involvement in many product developments at Apple Corp. and Pixar over the years. His influence is also based on his vision and his extraordinary self-confidence.[10]

***Exchanging Favors and Bargaining***   Offering to exchange favors if another person will help you achieve a work goal is another standard influence tactic. By making an exchange, you strike a bargain with the other party. The exchange often translates into being willing to reciprocate at a later date. It might also be promising a share of the benefits if the other person helps you accomplish a task. For example, you might promise to place a person's name on a report to top management if that person will help you analyze the data and prepare the tables.

A recommended approach to asking for a favor is to give the other person as much time as feasible to accomplish the task, such as by saying, "Could you find ten minutes between now and the end of the month to help me?" Not pressing for immediate assistance will tend to lower resistance to the request. Giving a menu of options for different levels of assistance also helps lower resistance. For example, you might ask another manager if you can borrow a technician for a one-month assignment; then, as a second option, you might ask if the technician could work ten hours per week on the project.[11] To ensure that the request is perceived as an exchange, you might explain what reciprocity you have in mind: that you will mention your coworker's helpfulness to his or her manager.

***Legitimating a Request***   To legitimate is to verify that an influence attempt is within your scope of authority. Another aspect of legitimating is showing that your request is consistent with the organizational policies, practices, and expectations of professional people. Making legitimate requests is an effective influence tactic because most workers are willing to comply with regulations. A team leader can thus exert influence with a statement such as this one: "Top management wants a 25 percent reduction in customer complaints by next year. I'm therefore urging everybody to patch up any customer problems he or she can find." According to research conducted by Gary Yukl, behavior intended to establish the legitimacy of a request includes the following:

Providing evidence of prior precedent

Showing consistency with the organizational policies that are involved in the type of request being made

Showing consistency with the duties and responsibilities of the person's position or role expectations

Indicating that the request has been endorsed by higher management or by the person's boss[12]

Legitimating sometimes takes the form of subtle organizational politics. A worker might push for the acceptance of his or her initiative because it conforms to the philosophy or strategy of higher management. At Wal-Mart, for example, it is well known that Chairman Lee Scott is "green" in the sense of wanting to preserve the external environment. A store manager might then encourage workers to put all plastic bottles in recycling bins because "It's something 'Lee' would want us to do."

***Making an Inspirational Appeal, Being Charming, and Emotional Display***    A leader is supposed to inspire others, so it follows that making an inspirational appeal is an important influence tactic. As Jeffrey Pfeffer notes, "Executives and others seeking to exercise influence in organizations often develop skill in displaying, or not displaying, their feelings in a strategic fashion."[13] An inspirational appeal usually involves displaying emotion and appealing to group members' emotions. A moderating variable in the effectiveness of an inspirational appeal or emotional display is the influence agent's **personal magnetism,** or the quality of being captivating, charming, and charismatic. Possessing personal magnetism makes it easier for the leader to inspire people.

Powerful people sometimes combine personal magnetism, including charm, with having tougher qualities. Steve Schwarzman is the CEO of the successful buyout firm, The Blackstone Group, which controls forty-seven companies. A business reporter noted, "With personal riches estimated at more than $3 billion and undisputed control over Wall Street's hottest firm, Schwarzman can afford to be soft-spoken, even charming, despite his reputation as one of the Street's most aggressive, demanding bosses."[14]

For an emotional appeal to be effective, the influence agent must understand the values, motives, and goals of the target. Often this means that the leader must explain how the group efforts will have an impact outside the company. A study concluded: "Business leaders tend to think in terms of bottom-line goals, like boosting revenues or profits. But they need to speak about their goals in terms of how they will make a positive difference in the world. If you can see a goal—if you can touch, feel, and smell it—it seems more doable."[15]

***Consultation with Others***    Consultation with others before making a decision is both a leadership style and an influence technique. The influence target becomes more motivated to follow the agent's request because the target is involved in the decision-making process. Consultation is most effective as an influence tactic when the objectives of the person being influenced are consistent with those of the leader.[16] An example of such goal congruity took place in a major U.S. corporation. The company had decided to shrink its pool of suppliers to form closer partnerships with a smaller number of high-quality vendors. As a way of influencing others to follow this direction, a manufacturing vice president told his staff, "Our strategy is to reduce dealing with so many suppliers to improve quality and reduce costs. Let me know how we should implement this strategy." The vice president's influence attempt met with excellent reception, partially because the staff members also wanted a more streamlined set of vendor relationships.

*Forming Coalitions*    At times it is difficult to influence an individual or group by acting alone. A leader will then have to form coalitions, or alliances, with others to create the necessary clout. A **coalition** is a specific arrangement of parties working together to combine their power. Coalition formation works as an influence tactic because, to quote an old adage, "there is power in numbers." Coalitions in business are a numbers game—the more people you can get on your side, the better. However, the more powerful the leader is, the less he or she needs to create a coalition. As mentioned at the start of the chapter, *collaborative influence* is one of IBM's ten new leadership traits and behaviors. The company emphasizes forming coalitions with other members of the company community.

*Being a Team Player*    Influencing others by being a good team player is an important strategy for getting work accomplished. A leader might be a team player by doing such things as pitching in during peak workloads. An example would be an information technology team leader working through the night with team members to combat a virus attack on the company's computer network.

Being a team player is a more effective influence tactic in an organizational culture that emphasizes collaboration than one in which being tough-minded and decisive is more in vogue. A study of CEO leadership profiles among buyout firms found that teamwork was less associated with success than traits such as persistence and efficiency. Leaders in buyout firms are strongly financially oriented and are much more concerned with making deals than building relationships.[17]

*Practicing Hands-On Leadership*    A **hands-on leader** is one who gets directly involved in the details and processes of operations. Such a leader has expertise, is task oriented, and leads by example. By getting directly involved in the group's work activities, the leader influences subordinates to hold certain beliefs and to follow certain procedures and processes. For example, the manager who gets directly involved in fixing customer problems demonstrates to other workers how he or she thinks such problems should be resolved.

Hands-on leadership is usually expected at levels below the executive suite, yet many high-level executives are also hands-on leaders. A strong example is Bo I. Andersson, the purchasing czar of General Motors Corp. A former Swedish Army officer who rose through the ranks of GM, he is regarded as a seriously hands-on individual. He has the reputation of tracking down every quality glitch, delay, and problem on his BlackBerry, and then proceeds to call the supplier to discover the nature of the problem. Andersson also pays relentless attention to detail.[18] The downside of being a hands-on leader is that if you do it to excess, you become a micromanager.

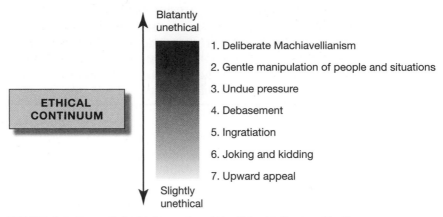

FIGURE 8-2 Essentially Dishonest and Unethical Influence Tactics.

## Essentially Dishonest and Unethical Tactics

The tactics described in this section are less than forthright and ethical, yet they vary in intensity with respect to dishonesty. Most people would consider the first four strategies presented here as unethical and devious, yet they might regard the last three tactics as still within the bounds of acceptable ethics, even though less than fully candid. Also, some people would regard upward appeal as being entirely ethical. The tactics in question are outlined in Figure 8-2.

*Deliberate Machiavellianism*    Niccolo Machiavelli advised that princes must be strong, ruthless, and cynical leaders because people are self-centered and self-serving. People in the workplace who ruthlessly manipulate others have therefore come to be called **Machiavellians**. They tend to initiate actions with others and control the interactions. Machiavellians regularly practice deception, bluffing, and other manipulative tactics.[19] A modern example of deliberate Machiavellianism is the practice of forcing managerial and professional employees into working many extra hours of uncompensated overtime. The employees are told that if they refuse to work extra hours, they will not be considered worthy of promotion or as good team players. Even when positions in other companies are readily available, most career-minded people will stay because they want to preserve a good reputation.

*Gentle Manipulation of People and Situations*    Some people who attempt to influence others are manipulative, but to a lesser extent than an outright Machiavellian. They gain the compliance of another person by making untrue statements or faking certain behaviors. For example, a leader might imply that if a colleague supports his position in an intergroup conflict, the person *might* be recommended for promotion. Another manipulative approach is to imply dire consequences to innocent people if the influence target does not comply with demands of the influence agent, such as, "Even if you don't want to put in extra effort for me, think of the people with families who will be laid off if we don't make our targets."

A widely used manipulative approach is the **bandwagon technique,** in which one does something simply because others are doing likewise. An example is a manager who informs the vice president that she wants an enlarged budget for attendance at the latest technology seminars because "all other companies are doing it."

The bandwagon technique can be combined with peer pressure to influence a group member. If one person is not stepping forward to work well as a team member, the manager will say, "Bob, everyone in the department is committed to developing a team atmosphere and we'd like you to be a part of it."[20]

***Undue Pressure*** Effective leaders regularly use motivational techniques such as rewards and mild punishments. Yet when rewards become bribes for compliance and threats of punishment become severe, the target person is subjected to undue pressure or coercion. An example of a bribe by a manager might be, "If you can work eighty hours on this project this week, I'll recommend you for the highest pay grade." Two specific behaviors labeled coercive in a research study were as follows: "I demand that she do it," and "I threaten her with something if she doesn't do it."[21]

***Debasement*** A subtle manipulative tactic is **debasement,** demeaning or insulting oneself to control the behavior of another person. Richard Parsons, former chief executive and chairman of AOL Time Warner Inc., the media giant, uses debasement to disarm people. A long-time friend says of Parsons, "Richard's ability to get people to underestimate him is a great skill. If you are obvious, they know where to hit you. Who wins between the bull and matador?"[22] Specific debasing tactics revealed by research include the following: "I lower myself so she'll do it," and "I act humble so she'll do it."[23]

***Ingratiation*** Getting somebody else to like you can be considered a mildly manipulative influence tactic—particularly if you do not like the other person. Frank P. Quattrone, the high-tech investment banker whose conviction for obstructing justice was later overturned, is a master of ingratiation. More than 300 high-tech executives and venture capitalists received shares in hot IPOs (initial public offerings), allegedly for giving investment-banking business to Quattrone's firm, Credit Suisse First Boston. Quattrone also invited his high-tech pals to play golf with him at exclusive courses, and he entertained them lavishly in his palatial home.[24] Ingratiating tactics identified in a study about influence tactics included the following:

Made him or her feel important (for example, "Only you have the brains and talent to do this")
Acted very humbly toward him or her while making my request
Praised him or her
Asked in a polite way
Pretended I was letting him or her decide to do what I wanted (acted in a pseudo-democratic manner)[25]

Leaders who ordinarily are the opposite of ingratiating will sometimes go out of their way to be humble and agreeable to fit an important purpose. A case in point is Bill Gates, who is often sarcastic and cutting. When Gates and Microsoft Corporation were being sued by the U.S. Department of Justice for possible monopolistic practices, Gates went on a goodwill tour, an events-packed trip around San Francisco and Silicon Valley. During his meetings with the public, Gates was modest and at times self-deprecating, even praising the competition. He shook hands, signed autographs, and smiled frequently. Gates was so convincing that a schoolgirl said, "You can tell he's not in it for the money. He wants to make software better."[26] (Later on in life, Gates and his wife became major philanthropists, helping poor children throughout the world, so maybe the schoolgirl was insightful!)

Leadership Self-Assessment Quiz 8-2 provides you an opportunity to measure your own ingratiating tendencies and to think through further what ingratiating yourself to your boss means in practice. Remember that being liked helps you get promoted, receive more compensation, and avoid being downsized, yet you should avoid being dishonest.

 ## Leadership Self-Assessment Quiz 8-2

### Measure of Ingratiating Behavior in Organizational Settings (MIBOS)

***Instructions:*** Indicate how frequently you use (or would use) the tactics for pleasing your boss listed here. N = never do it; S = seldom do it; Oc = occasionally do it; Of = often do it; A = almost always do it. The N-to-A categories correspond to a 1-to-5 scale.

|  | 1 N | 2 S | 3 Oc | 4 Of | 5 A |
|---|---|---|---|---|---|
| 1. Impress upon your supervisor that only he or she can help you in a given situation mainly to make him or her feel good. | ☐ | ☐ | ☐ | ☐ | ☐ |
| 2. Show your supervisor that you share enthusiasm about his or her new idea even when you may not actually like it. | ☐ | ☐ | ☐ | ☐ | ☐ |
| 3. Try to let your supervisor know that you have a reputation for being liked. | ☐ | ☐ | ☐ | ☐ | ☐ |
| 4. Try to make sure that your supervisor is aware of your success. | ☐ | ☐ | ☐ | ☐ | ☐ |
| 5. Highlight the achievements made under your supervisor's leadership in a meeting he or she does not attend. | ☐ | ☐ | ☐ | ☐ | ☐ |
| 6. Give frequent smiles to express enthusiasm and interest about something your supervisor is interested in even if you do not like it. | ☐ | ☐ | ☐ | ☐ | ☐ |
| 7. Express work attitudes that are similar to your supervisor's as a way of letting him or her know that the two of you are alike. | ☐ | ☐ | ☐ | ☐ | ☐ |
| 8. Tell your supervisor that you can learn a lot from his or her experience. | ☐ | ☐ | ☐ | ☐ | ☐ |
| 9. Exaggerate your supervisor's admirable qualities to convey the impression that you think highly of him or her. | ☐ | ☐ | ☐ | ☐ | ☐ |

## Quiz 8-2 (continued)

|  | 1 | 2 | 3 | 4 | 5 |
|---|---|---|---|---|---|
|  | N | S | Oc | Of | A |
| 10. Disagree on trivial or unimportant issues but agree on those issues in which he or she expects support from you. | ☐ | ☐ | ☐ | ☐ | ☐ |
| 11. Try to imitate such work behaviors of your supervisor as working late or occasionally working on weekends. | ☐ | ☐ | ☐ | ☐ | ☐ |
| 12. Look for opportunities to let your supervisor know your virtues and strengths. | ☐ | ☐ | ☐ | ☐ | ☐ |
| 13. Ask your supervisor for advice in areas in which he or she thinks he or she is smart to let him or her feel that you admire his or her talent. | ☐ | ☐ | ☐ | ☐ | ☐ |
| 14. Try to do things for your supervisor that show your selfless generosity. | ☐ | ☐ | ☐ | ☐ | ☐ |
| 15. Look out for opportunities to admire your supervisor. | ☐ | ☐ | ☐ | ☐ | ☐ |
| 16. Let your supervisor know the attitudes you share with him or her. | ☐ | ☐ | ☐ | ☐ | ☐ |
| 17. Compliment your supervisor on his or her achievement, however it may appeal to you personally. | ☐ | ☐ | ☐ | ☐ | ☐ |
| 18. Laugh heartily at your supervisor's jokes even when they are really not funny. | ☐ | ☐ | ☐ | ☐ | ☐ |
| 19. Go out of your way to run an errand for your supervisor. | ☐ | ☐ | ☐ | ☐ | ☐ |
| 20. Offer to help your supervisor by using your personal contacts. | ☐ | ☐ | ☐ | ☐ | ☐ |
| 21. Try to persuasively present your own qualities when attempting to convince your supervisor about your abilities. | ☐ | ☐ | ☐ | ☐ | ☐ |
| 22. Volunteer to be of help to your supervisor in matters like locating a good apartment, finding a good insurance agent, etc. | ☐ | ☐ | ☐ | ☐ | ☐ |
| 23. Spend time listening to your supervisor's personal problems even if you have no interest in them. | ☐ | ☐ | ☐ | ☐ | ☐ |
| 24. Volunteer to help your supervisor in his or her work even if it means extra work for you. | ☐ | ☐ | ☐ | ☐ | ☐ |

***Scoring and Interpretation:*** The more of these ingratiating behaviors you use frequently or almost always, the more ingratiating you are. A score of 40 or less suggests that you do not put much effort into pleasing your manager, and you may need to be a little more ingratiating to achieve a good relationship with your supervisor. A score between 41 and 99 suggests a moderate degree of ingratiating behavior. A score of 100 or more suggests that you are too ingratiating and might be perceived as being too political or insincere. So some honesty is called for, providing you are tactful.

***Skill Development:*** Leaders or future leaders should remember that a moderate amount of ingratiating behavior is the norm in relationships with superiors. Ingratiating yourself to people who report to you can also be a useful influence tactic.

*Source:* Adapted from Kamalesh Kumar and Michael Beyerlein, "Construction and Validation of an Instrument for Measuring Ingratiatory Behaviors in Organizational Settings," *Journal of Applied Psychology,* October 1991, p. 623. Copyright © by the American Psychological Association. Adapted with permission.

***Joking and Kidding***    Good-natured kidding is especially effective when a straight-forward statement might be interpreted as harsh criticism. Joking or kidding can thus get the message across and lower the risk that the influence target will be angry with the influence agent. Joking and kidding might be interpreted either as dishonest or as extraordinarily tactful because the criticizer softens the full blow of the criticism. A small-business owner successfully used joking and kidding to help the receptionist wear clothing more appropriate for the position. As the owner entered the office, he noticed that the receptionist was wearing a tank top and very large, circular earrings. The owner said, "Melissa, you look great, but I think you have your dates confused. You are dressed for the company picnic, and it takes place tomorrow." Melissa smiled, and then dressed more professionally in the future.

***Upward Appeal***    In **upward appeal,** the leader exerts influence on a team member by getting a person with more formal authority to do the influencing. Some managers and researchers regard upward appeal as an ethical and standard practice, yet it does contain an element of manipulation and heavy-handedness. An example: "I sent the guy to my boss when he wouldn't listen to me. That fixed him." More than occasional use of upward appeal weakens the leader's stature in the eyes of group members and superiors, thus eroding his or her effectiveness. Leaders can apply upward appeal in other ways. A leader might attempt to persuade another staff member that higher management approved his or her request. The target of the influence event is thus supposed to grant acceptance automatically. Or the leader can request higher management's assistance in gaining another person's compliance with the request. The influence target thus feels pressured.[27]

In studying the most severe unethical influence (and political) tactics, it is important to recognize that the use of these influence approaches can bring about human suffering. For example, bullying and intimidating tactics may not be illegal, but they are unethical. Cruelty in the organization creates many problems. As one observer notes, "Cruelty is blatantly unethical and erodes the organizational character through intellectual, emotional, moral, and social vices that reduce the readiness of groups to act ethically."[28] Examples of cruelty include insulting a group member's physical appearance or belittling him or her.

Leadership Skill-Building Exercise 8-1 gives you an opportunity to practice influence tactics in a high-stakes business situation.

Leadership Skill-Building Exercise 8-2 will help you recognize several of the influence tactics described in this chapter. Another tactic mentioned in the exercise, assertiveness, was described in Chapter 2.

**KB** **Knowledge Bank**
Presents two more mildly unethical influence tactics: game playing and the silent treatment.

**www.cengage.com/management/dubrin**

## LEADERSHIP INFLUENCE FOR ORGANIZATIONAL CHANGE

Most of the discussion so far relates to the leader/manager influencing people one at a time or in small groups. Top-level leaders exert many of their influence attempts in the direction of bringing about changes throughout the entire organization, often by attempting to overhaul the organizational culture. One such change would be attempting to influence a culture that was too collaborative to make

**Leadership Skill-Building Exercise 8-1**

### Ethical Influence Tactics

One student plays the role of an Air Force procurement officer. Another student plays the role of an aerospace company chief financial officer. The two are discussing at lunch a possible $23 billion deal for the aerospace company. The chief financial officer desperately wants the contract for the aerospace company, and the Air Force procurement officer sees this as an opportunity to gain some personal advantage from the deal: She might advance her career and help her daughter's boyfriend get a job at the aerospace company. But despite the procurement officer's hints about gaining some personal advantage, the company financial officer decides to use ethical influence tactics to win the contract. The two role players conduct the interview for about ten minutes. Later, the class observers will provide feedback about the effectiveness of the influence tactics used by both players.

**Leadership Skill-Building Exercise 8-2**

### Identifying Influence Tactics

***Instructions:*** After reading each tactic listed here, label it as being mostly an example of one of the following: I = ingratiation; E = exchange of favors; R = rationality; A = assertiveness; U = upward appeal.

**Tactic Code**

1. I sympathized with the person about the added problems that my request caused. _____
2. I offered to help if the person would do what I wanted. _____
3. I set a time deadline for the person to do what I asked. _____
4. I obtained the informal support of higher-ups. _____
5. I used logic to convince him or her. _____
6. I made a formal appeal to higher levels to back up my request. _____
7. I had a showdown in which I confronted the person head-on. _____
8. I offered to make a personal sacrifice if the person would do what I wanted (for example, work late or harder). _____
9. I made him or her feel good about me before making my request. _____
10. I explained the reasons for my request. _____

**Answers:**

| | | |
|---|---|---|
| 1. I | 5. R | 9. I |
| 2. E | 6. U | 10. R |
| 3. A | 7. A | |
| 4. U | 8. E | |

***Skill Development:*** Being able to identify influence tactics raises your awareness of how to influence others and which tactics others are using to influence you.

*Source:* Based on information in Chester A. Schriescheim and Timothy R. Hinkin, "Influence Tactics Used by Subordinates: A Theoretical and Empirical Analysis and Refinement of the Kipnis, Schmidt, and Wilkinson Subscales," *Journal of Applied Psychology*, June 1990, p. 246. Copyright © 1990 American Psychological Association. Adapted with permission.

decisions more quickly and independently, or the reverse. Another change would be to make the culture more focused on products the market wanted, and less focused on innovation for its own sake. Yet another cultural change facing a CEO would be to make a risk-averse workforce more entrepreneurial and risk taking.

Before plunging ahead with attempts at massive cultural change, the leader needs to study the old culture and understand why it contributed to the prosperity and growth of the organization. When John Thain took over as CEO at Merrill Lynch in 2007, Win Smith, a former Merrill director and son of one of the founders, was quite pleased. Smith said, "He understands the power of culture, which Stan (O'Neal, the CEO Thain replaced) did not. He'll take time to understand the old culture and what made it so good."[29]

After a new CEO is appointed, the person typically makes a public statement to the effect that: "My number-one job is to change the culture." A leader might do the following to bring about change as well ensuring that a healthy corporate culture is maintained.

- Serve as a role model for the desired attitudes and behaviors. Leaders must behave in ways consistent with the values and practices they wish to see imitated throughout the organization. If the change the leader wants is a stronger focus on customer service, leaders must treat employees as customers, thereby acting as role models for the way customers should be treated.[30] The leaders must also talk in positive terms about customer service, with statement such as, "The real joy in our work is helping customers solve their problems."

- Impose a new approach through executive edict. From the time he started his position as chairman and CEO of General Electric, Jeff Immelt was on a mission to transform the hard-driving process-oriented company into an organization steeped in creativity and wired for business growth. In addition to outstanding efficiency in operations, Immelt presented new imperatives for risk taking, sophisticated marketing, and, of utmost importance, innovation.[31]

- Establish a reward system that reinforces the culture, such as giving huge suggestion awards to promote an innovative culture. At Boeing Co., CEO W. James McNerney Jr. wants to create a common culture and work toward a shared goal. So to discourage negative internal competition and the hoarding of information, part of executive compensation is based on how well managers share information with other units across the company.[32]

- Select candidates for positions at all levels whose values mesh with the values of the desired culture. Many firms hire only those candidates whose work and school experience suggest that they might be good team players—a cultural value.

- Sponsor new training and development programs that support the desired cultural values. Among many examples, top management might sponsor diversity training to support the importance of cultural diversity, or training in quality to support the value of quality. Edward W. Lampert, the chairman of Sears Holding Company (a merger of Sears and Kmart), wanted to create a culture based on selling, including improving teamwork and customer service. One of his techniques to achieve this goal was a training session for 500 managers in which he showed clips from *Miracle on Ice*, about the U.S. hockey team that won the gold medal in the 1980 Winter Olympics.[33]

## ▶ Leader in Action

### Starbucks' Developer Attempts to Perk Up the Place

A couple of years ago, Starbucks Corp. chairman Howard Schultz swooped in to fix his struggling coffee empire by returning as the company's chief executive, taking over for a CEO who had been there three years. Schultz, although he arrived after the company started, nurtured it from a small Seattle bean seller into the world's largest coffee chain, with more than 15,000 locations. In 2008, Schultz planned to slow the number of stores built in the United States and close struggling locations. He said he also planned to improve the customer experience at U.S. stores, streamline management, and accelerate expansion overseas.

In a letter to employees, Schultz said, "The reality we face is both challenging and exciting. It's challenging because there are no overnight fixes." Starbucks' stock was on the decline and the company faced increased competition from McDonald's Corp., which planned to install coffee bars selling espresso drinks at its nearly 14,000 locations.

The question was raised whether Schultz's fixes were drastic enough to improve Starbucks' results. Starbucks had been talking about making some of these changes for several months. Some of his objectives, such as "re-igniting the emotional attachment to customers," are so intangible that it is difficult for investors to know whether they are happening.

But Schultz is highly respected for turning Starbucks into one of the hottest growth stocks in the 1990s and creating a retail powerhouse with an unusual combination of brand cachet and mass appeal. He's known for having tough standards and fighting passionately to make his company successful. In recent years, as chairman, he remained deeply involved in the business, sometimes focusing on side projects like Starbucks' effort to expand into music and film.

"Given what the board believes needs to be done, there is no better person to drive change and ensure that Starbucks is positioned to innovate, execute, and relentlessly focus the entire organization on the customer," Craig Weatherup, chairman of the Starbucks board's nominating and corporate governance committee, said. Schultz, who was CEO from 1987 to 2000, told employees that the board decided he should lead the transformation.

Schultz emphasized that he wanted to improve the company's U.S. business, which had more than 10,000 locations at the time and accounted for the largest portion of Starbucks' profit. In his letter to employees, he said he wanted to do that by giving employees better training and tools, launching products—"some of which will have an impact as significant as Frappucino products and the Starbucks Card"—and introducing new concepts in store design. He said that slowing the pace of store openings and closing weak stores will help improve store-level economics and help the company focus on execution. Executives blamed the soft economy for slower traffic in Starbucks stores, pointing to other retailers who have seen their sales slow. But analysts say part of the reason for traffic declines and slower sales growth is that Starbucks has built so many stores in the United States that new ones no longer generate the same strong returns and eat into sales at older locations. During 2008, Starbuck management closed 600 stores worldwide, as consumers became less willing to spend so much money on luxury coffee.

### Questions

1. Which influence tactics is Schultz attempting to use to rejuvenate Starbucks?
2. To what extent is it feasible to change an organization the size of Starbucks?
3. Write a bulleted memo to Howard Schultz telling him what changes you think Starbucks should make.
4. Think back to a recent time when you visited a Starbucks coffee shop. Did the person behind the counter form an emotional attachment with you? If you are not a Starbucks patron, ask the same question of somebody who is.

*Source:* Excerpted from Janet Adamy, "Schultz Takes Over to Try to Perk Up Starbucks," *The Wall Street Journal (Central Edition),* January 8, 2008, pp. B1, B2. Copyright 2007 by Dow Jones & Company, Inc. Reproduced with permission of Dow Jones & Company, Inc. In the format Textbook via Copyright Clearance Center. Adamy, "Schultz's Second Act Jolts Starbucks," *The Wall Street Journal,* May 19, 2008, pp. A1, A11.

A leader who exhibited all of these behaviors would qualify as a transformational leader because of all the positive changes. The accompanying Leader in Action profile on page 245 describes a CEO who is attempting to bring about some changes you will be able to experience with the investment of the price of a latte.

# RELATIVE EFFECTIVENESS AND SEQUENCING OF INFLUENCE TACTICS

Although we have described influence tactics separately, they must also be understood in relation to one another. Two ways of comparing influence tactics are to examine their relative effectiveness and to study the order in which they might be used to achieve the best result.

## Relative Effectiveness of Influence Tactics

Since influence tactics are a major component of leadership, research about their relative effectiveness is worth noting. A study by Gary Yukl and J. Bruce Tracey provides insights into the relative effectiveness of influence tactics.[34] One hundred and twenty managers participated in the study, along with 526 subordinates, 543 peers, and 128 superiors, who also rated the managers' use of influence tactics. Half the managers worked for manufacturing companies, and half worked for service companies.

The people who worked with the managers completed a questionnaire to identify which of nine influence tactics the managers used. As defined for the participants, the tactics were as follows:

1. Rational persuasion
2. Inspirational appeal
3. Consultation
4. Ingratiation
5. Exchange
6. Personal appeal
7. Coalition
8. Legitimating
9. Pressure

Another question asked how many influence attempts by the agent resulted in complete commitment by the target respondent. Respondents were also asked to rate the overall effectiveness of the manager in carrying out his or her job responsibilities. The item had nine response choices, ranging from "the least effective manager I have ever known" to "the most effective manager."

The results suggested that the most effective tactics were rational persuasion, inspirational appeal, and consultation. (An effective tactic was one that led to task commitment and that was used by managers who were perceived to be effective by the various raters.) In contrast, the least effective were pressure, coalition, and appealing to legitimate authority (legitimating). Ingratiation and exchange were moderately effective for influencing team members and peers. The same tactics, however, were not effective for influencing superiors. A related interpretation of the data would be that noncoercive tactics that provide a rational and justifiable basis for attitude change are more effective in gaining compliance than are threatening or manipulative attempts.[35]

Inspirational appeal, ingratiation, and pressure were used primarily in a downward direction, that is, toward a lower-ranking person. Personal appeal, exchange, and legitimating were used primarily in a lateral direction. It was also found that coalitions were used most in lateral and upward directions and that rational persuasion was used most in an upward direction.

The researchers concluded that some tactics are more likely to be successful. Yet they caution that the results do not imply that these tactics will always result in task commitment. The outcome of a specific influence attempt is also determined by other factors, such as the target's motivation and the organizational culture. Also, any tactic can trigger target resistance if it is not appropriate for the situation or if it is applied unskillfully. Tact, diplomacy, and insight are required for effective application of influence tactics.

Which influence tactic a manager might consider effective, and therefore choose, depends to some extent on how much group members are trusted. When we distrust people, we are likely to attempt to control their actions. Carole V. Wells and David Kipnis conducted a survey about trust involving 275 managers and 267 employees. The managers answered questions about subordinates, and subordinates answered questions about their managers. The two groups, however, were not describing each other. A key finding was that both managers and employees used strong tactics of influence when they distrusted the other party—either a manager or a subordinate. The strong influence tactics studied were appeals to higher authority, assertiveness, coalition building, and sanctions.[36]

Another perspective on the relative effectiveness of influence tactics comes from a study of territory managers and their service-center managers who worked for a distribution company. A major finding was that the quality of the relationship with the leader (leader–member exchange, or LMX) had an impact on the effectiveness of influence tactics. When group members perceived a poor relationship with their leader, the leader's use of inspirational appeal and exchange resulted in less helping of coworkers by members. However, the leaders' consultation tactics were positively associated with the members helping work associates. When group members perceived their relationship with the leader as positive, exchange tactics by the leaders positively related to helping behavior.

An interpretation offered for these interactions has a lesson for leaders. Members in low-quality relationships may interpret appeals to their values, goals, and aspirations or exchange offers as empty. As a result, the members did not engage in more helping behaviors based on inspirational appeals. Yet consultation is more effective and may prompt members to become more helpful.[37]

## Sequencing of Influence Tactics

Another important consideration in using influence tactics is the sequence or order in which they should be applied. In general, you should begin with the

## ⊙ Leadership Skill-Building Exercise 8-3

### Applying Influence Tactics

Divide the class into small teams. Each group assigns one leadership influence tactic to each team member. During the next week or so, each team member takes the opportunity to practice the assigned influence tactic in a work or personal setting. Hold a group discussion with the same class teams after the influence attempts have been practiced. Report the following information: (1) under what circumstances the influence tactic was attempted; (2) how the influence target reacted; and (3) what results, both positive and negative, were achieved.

Practicing influence tactics directly contributes to your leadership effectiveness because leadership centers on influence. If you want to exert leadership as a nonmanager, you will have to be particularly adept at using influence tactics because your formal authority will be quite limited.

most positive, or least abrasive, tactic. If you do not gain the advantage you seek, proceed to a stronger tactic. For example, if you want a larger salary increase than that initially assigned you, try rational persuasion. If persuasion does not work, move on to exchanging favors. Use a more abrasive tactic such as upward appeal only as a last resort. The reason is that abrasive tactics trigger revenge and retaliation. Many people who have taken their complaints to an outside agency such as a governmental office have found themselves with a limited future in their organization. Although the appeal is legally justified, it is politically unwise.

The sequencing of tactics can also be considered in terms of cost and risk. A sensible approach is to begin with low-cost, low-risk tactics. If the outcome is important enough to the influence agent, he or she can then proceed to higher-cost and higher-risk influence tactics. An example of a low-cost, low-risk tactic would be joking and kidding. An accounting manager who was disappointed with the budget offered her group might say to her boss, "Does the new budget mean that our group will have to pay for our own CDs and green eyeshades?" It would be much more costly in terms of time and potential retaliation to form a coalition with another underbudgeted group to ask for an enlarged budget.

In addition to the sequencing of tactics, the influence agent must also consider the direction of the influence attempt as a contingency factor. In general, the more position power an individual exerts over another, the less the need for being cautious in the use of influence tactics. For example, a vice president can more readily use undue pressure against a supervisor than vice versa. When you have more power, there are likely to be fewer negative consequences from using more powerful tactics.

Leadership Skill-Building Exercise 8-3 provides an opportunity to practice implementing various influence tactics. As with any other skill, influence skills need to be practiced under field conditions.

# IMPLICIT LEADERSHIP THEORIES AND LEADERSHIP INFLUENCE

A final perspective on influence tactics is that people are more likely to be influenced by leaders who match their expectations of what a leader should be. **Implicit leadership theories** are personal assumptions about the traits and abilities that characterize an ideal organizational leader. These assumptions, both stated and unstated, develop through socialization and past experiences with leaders. The assumptions are stored in memory and activated when group members interact with a person in a leadership position. Our assumptions about leaders help us make sense of what takes place on the job. Assume that Reggie was raised in a household and neighborhood in which business leaders are highly respected and thought to be dedicated and intelligent. When Reggie later works in a full-time professional job, he is most likely to be influenced by a supervisor he perceives to be dedicated and intelligent because this person fits Reggie's preconceived notion of how a leader should behave.

According to implicit leadership theory, as part of making assumptions and expectations of leader traits and behaviors, people develop leadership prototypes and antiprototypes. *Prototypes* are positive characterizations of a leader, whereas *antiprototypes* are traits and behaviors people do not want to see in a leader. People have different expectations of what they want in a leader, yet research conducted with 939 subordinates in two different samples in British companies shows there is some consistency in implicit leadership theories. The study showed that these theories are consistent across different employee groups and are also stable trait-based stereotypes of leadership.[38] Another study in England showed that if the leader matches employee assumptions about having the right traits, the LMX will be more positive. In turn, the group member will be more readily influenced by the leader.[39]

Table 8-2 lists the six traits group members want to see in a leader (prototypes), as well as the two traits they do not want to see in a leader (antiprototypes). Your study of leadership traits in Chapters 2 and 3 will reinforce these leadership attributes. The antiprototype of *masculinity* suggests that followers prefer a compassionate and relationship-oriented leader to a command-and-control leader. An implication of these data is that a leader who fits group members' prototypes is more likely to influence them than a leader who fits their antiprototype.

**TABLE 8-2** Implicit Leadership Theory Dimensions

| LEADERSHIP PROTOTYPE | LEADERSHIP ANTIPROTOTYPE |
| --- | --- |
| 1. Sensitivity (compassion, sensitive) | 1. Tyranny (dominant, selfish, manipulative) |
| 2. Intelligence (intelligent, clever) | 2. Masculinity (male, masculine) |
| 3. Dedication (dedicated, motivated) | |
| 4. Charisma (charismatic, dynamic) | |
| 5. Strength (strong, bold) | |
| 6. Attractiveness (well dressed, classy) | |

*Source:* Gathered from information in Olga Epitropaki and Robin Martin, "Implicit Leadership Theories in Applied Settings: Factor Structure, Generalizability, and Stability over Time," *Journal of Applied Psychology*, April 2004, pp. 297–299.

### Reader's Roadmap

So far we have studied considerable information about the nature of leadership; the attributes, behaviors, and styles of leaders; the ethics and social responsibility of leaders; and how leaders exert power and use politics and influence. The next chapter explains a variety of techniques for developing teamwork.

## SUMMARY

To become an effective leader, a person must be aware of specific influence tactics. Influence is the ability to affect the behaviors of others in a particular direction. Power, in contrast, is the potential or capacity to influence. A model presented here indicates that a leader's influence outcomes are a function of the influence tactics he or she uses. The influence tactics are, in turn, moderated, or affected by, the leader's traits and behaviors and also by the situation. The outcomes of influence attempts are commitment, compliance, or resistance, all of which influence end results such as group success or failure.

Influence tactics are often viewed from an ethical perspective. Some tactics are clearly ethical, but others are clearly unethical. Used with tact, diplomacy, and good intent, ethical influence tactics can be quite effective. The essentially ethical tactics described here are leading by example and respect, using rational persuasion, being a subject matter expert, exchanging favors and bargaining, legitimating a request, making an inspirational appeal and emotional display, consulting, forming coalitions, being a team player, and practicing hands-on leadership.

Essentially dishonest and unethical tactics presented here were divided into two groups: clearly unethical and borderline. The more clearly unethical and devious tactics are deliberate Machiavellianism, gentle manipulation of people and situations, undue pressure, and debasement. The three borderline influence tactics are ingratiation, joking and kidding, and upward appeal (hardly devious at all).

Top-level leaders exert many of their influence attempts toward bringing about changes throughout the entire organization, often by attempting to overhaul the organizational culture. The leader should first study the old culture to search for its merits. Tactics for cultural change by the leader include serving as a role model, executive edict, giving rewards to reinforce the culture, selecting candidates who fit the culture, and establishing training and development programs to support the culture.

A study of influence tactics concluded that the most effective were rational persuasion, inspirational appeal, and consultation. The least effective were pressure, coalition, and appealing to legitimate authority. The quality of the leader–member (LMX) relationship has an impact on the effectiveness of influence tactics, with a poor relationship lowering the effectiveness of inspirational appeal and exchange.

Certain tactics are more effective for exerting influence upward, whereas others are better suited for downward influence. For example, inspirational appeal, ingratiation, and exchange are moderately effective for influencing subordinates and peers. Yet the same tactics are not effective for influencing superiors. When we distrust people, we tend to think that stronger influence tactics, such as an appeal to higher authority, will be effective.

Sequencing of influence tactics is another important consideration. In general, begin with the most positive, or least abrasive, tactic. If you do not gain the advantage you seek, proceed to a stronger tactic. Also, begin with low-cost, low-risk tactics.

Implicit leadership theories are personal assumptions about the traits and abilities that characterize an ideal organizational leader. Prototypes are positive characterizations of a leader, whereas antiprototypes are negative. Subordinates are more likely to be influenced by leaders who fit their prototype, and do not fit their antiprototype, of a leader.

## KEY TERMS

| | | |
|---|---|---|
| Influence | Personal magnetism | Debasement |
| Commitment | Coalition | Upward appeal |
| Compliance | Hands-on leader | Implicit leadership theories |
| Resistance | Machiavellians | |
| Leading by example | Bandwagon technique | |

## ✔ GUIDELINES FOR ACTION AND SKILL DEVELOPMENT

A recent study provides some clues as to the circumstances in which more heavy-handed influence tactics will work with a subordinate. Managers tended to use hard (tough) follow-up tactics when a subordinate's refusal is related to work expected in his or her role, and when the subordinate was seen as malingering. (An example here would be saying to a specialist in accounts receivable, "You've been goofing off too long. If you don't chase after those customers overdue on their accounts, you might not get a raise for next year.") Harder tactics were also used more frequently when exchanges between the leader and member were not positive. Managers withdrew their request when the request was seen as outside the subordinate's role, or the request was ambiguous. When the leader–member exchange was less positive, managers were also more likely to withdraw the request.[40]

### Discussion Questions and Activities

1. Explain the following analogy: Influence is to leadership as eggs are to an omelet.
2. Which influence tactic described in this chapter do you think would work the best for you? Why?
3. Which influence tactic do you think would work the most poorly for you? Why?
4. What differences have you observed among the influence tactics used by technically oriented versus people-oriented people?
5. Identify two exchanges of favor you have seen or can envision on the job.
6. In what way is being a subject matter expert (SME) a source of power as well as an influence tactic?
7. How might a business owner use the bandwagon technique to get his or her employees to lead a healthier lifestyle?
8. Which influence tactics have been the most effective in influencing you? Support your answer with an anecdote.
9. Why should a top-level executive worry about respecting the existing organizational culture when trying to influence an organization to change in a particular direction?
10. Get the opinion of an experienced leader as to the most effective influence tactics. Share your findings with class members.

## Leadership Case Problem A

### Be Fit or Be Out of Favor at CFI Westgate

Employees at CFI Westgate Resorts, an Orlando, Florida–based vacation properties company, have an incentive to get healthy. If they join in the company-wide weight-loss contest and succeed in reaching their goals, they could win cash prizes or a luxury vacation.

Inspiration for the contest, now in its second year, came from CEO David Siegel, who himself recently lost more than 20 pounds. "He put it on the radar," says Mark Waltrip, chief operating office at Westgate, adding that in the contest's first year, some employees lost up to 60 pounds.

Westgate was one of the first companies to take a hard line on smoking several years ago. Peter Cappelli, director of the Center for Human Resources at Wharton, was asked to comment on the anti-smoking campaign. He said that crackdowns on employees who smoke on or off the job were the "thin edge of a wedge. . . . It has become socially acceptable to attack smoking and smokers. Will we see the same thing around obesity? The time is probably ripe for that."

In 2002, Siegel announced that all Westgate employees would have one year to quit smoking completely or else face termination. The company offered smoking cessation classes, nicotine patches, and other support, according to Waltrip, who said Siegel decided on the policy after a close friend died of lung cancer—and after he learned that Florida state law does not protect smokers. Another concern was the fact that smokers drive up health care premiums.

"If someone wants to smoke, that is their [he means his or her] choice, but when their choices impact their employer and fellow employees, then, frankly, we're not going to take it," says Waltrip. Since the ban on smoking was finally enacted in 2003, health premiums have increased at an average of 5 percent at Westgate, much lower than increases at other companies.

Siegel found himself at the center of controversy when he told a Florida TV station that Westgate would take every legal step to insist on healthy employees. "If you are an alcoholic and we have the right to fire you, we will do that, too," he said. Bloggers and online commentators attacked Siegel for discriminating unfairly against overweight people and stepping too far into employees' private lives. A pregnant woman said, "Last time I was pregnant, I gained 40 pounds. How much time would I have to lose that weight before getting canned?"

According to Waltrip, however, Westgate is approaching the obesity issue more gingerly than Siegel's comment would imply. "Weight [he means being overweight] is complicated—it can be caused by disease—so before we go down that path of penalizing employees who are overweight, we need to understand and build a consensus around it." He says the company does not currently penalize overweight or obese workers.

### Questions

1. Which influence tactics does David Siegel appear to be using in his attempt to combat employee smoking and obesity?
2. What suggestions might you offer Siegel to help him be more successful in his attempts at influencing employee weight control?
3. What is your evaluation of the ethics of a CEO attempting to influence employees to avoid obesity?

*Source:* Adapted and excerpted from "From Incentives to Penalties: How Far Should Employers Go to Reduce Workplace Obesity?" *Knowledge@Wharton* (http://knowledge .wharton.upenn), January 9, 2008.

## Leadership Case Problem B

### The Chief Avon Lady Attempts a Makeover

A few years back, the success story of Avon Products Inc. turned ugly. After six straight years of 10 percent–plus growth and a tripling of earnings under CEO Andrea Jung, the company suddenly began losing sales across the globe. Developing markets such as Central Europe and Russian, the engine of Avon's amazing run, stumbled just as sales in the United States and Mexico stalled. The global diversity that had long propped up the company's performance suddenly began to weight it down.

By September 2007, problems in China, Eastern Europe, and Russia were mounting, and Jung was backpedaling at full speed. Angry shareholders bailed out, and the stock price plummeted. For an eighteen-month period, Jung tried to figure out what went wrong and how to fix it, and the company began to emerge from Wall Street's doghouse. Avon sells Skin So Soft and ANEW skin-care products as well as makeup and other items through a network of 5 million independent representatives. Avon signed up 399,000 new salespeople in China. Renewed growth in Central Europe is helping, too.

An expert in building brands, Jung had no turnaround experience when she arrived in her job. At times she doubted she could make the deep cuts necessary to right the company. "I'd never done anything like that before," said the 48-year-old Jung. "My first reaction was: 'I get it. I see the numbers, but I don't know if I, or we, have the stomach for it.'"

One of Jung's most important moves has been forcing managers to make decisions based on fact rather than intuition. During a twelve-month period, Jung has reorganized Avon's management structure, taking away much of the autonomy from country managers, in favor of globalized manufacturing and marketing. Previously, Avon managers from Poland to Mexico ran their own plants, developed new products, and created their own ads, often relying as much on gut as numbers. In Jung's words, they were "king or queen of every decision."

Jung trimmed out seven layers of management, bringing the total from fifteen down to eight, and finally launched the kind of numbers-heavy return-on-investment analysis that most large consumer products companies have been doing for decades. That analysis is directed from New York headquarters by an executive team stocked with more people from the outside.

"When she speaks about what we have to do to achieve our goals, she is much closer to the operations now," said a board member. "She has her hands directly on the levers that have to be moved."

Upon the advice of a consultant, Jung flew around the globe on a CEO road show, addressing audiences of her top 1,000 global managers. Her message: By the end of the year, one-quarter of you will be gone. "I put a lot of people in those jobs," said Jung. "You can imagine it was the toughest time to walk the halls." In January 2008, Jung cut another 2,400 jobs, eliminated some product lines, and restricted business trips.

Avon's new executives and their new data were on display at an analysts' conference in February 2007. In four hour's worth of PowerPoint slides, the company presented a detailed explanation of what had gone wrong in many of its 114 worldwide markets. One revelation: The roster of products for sale in Mexico had ballooned to 13,000. Another: Decreasing the payoffs for adding new representatives had stalled the U.S. business.

Jung's No. 1 role continues to be communicating the company's new strategy. Before the analysts' conference, Jung visited Bangkok, Hong Kong, London, São Palo, Shanghai, and Warsaw. All that travel comes at a sacrifice. In 2007, Jung's daughter was a high school senior, and she had a son who was nine. Jung says she has reprioritized her life, skipping business dinners and formal evening affairs to be sure she sees her children when she's in New York. But she also told them that she loves the company and the work, even if the work has been grueling during the previous months. "I think it's important they know that," she said. "Otherwise why would you do this?"

## Questions

1. How convinced is Jung that she is turning around Avon Products?
2. In what direction should Jung be influencing Avon sales representatives?
3. How effective do you think Jung's pitch to her children was in terms of getting them to accept her heavy travel schedule and time away from home?
4. Have you purchased an Avon product for yourself or as a gift in the past twenty-four months? If not, what would an Avon rep have to do to influence you to make such a purchase?

*Source:* Excerpted from Nanette Byrnes, "Avon: More Than Cosmetic Changes," *Business Week*, March 12, 2007, pp. 062–063. A few updated facts are from Andria Cheng, "Avon Products to Slash 2,400 Jobs," www.marketwatch.com, January 8, 2008.

 Leadership Skill-Building Exercise 8-4

## My Leadership Portfolio

Influence is to leadership as an egg is to an omelet, so you need to practice your influence tactics to enhance your leadership effectiveness. In this chapter's entry to your leadership journal, describe any influence tactic you implemented recently. Describe what you did, and how the influence target reacted. Comment on how you might use the tactic differently in your next influence attempt. Also describe which influence tactic or combination of tactics you plan to use in the upcoming week. Here might be an example:

I coach a youth basketball team called the "West Side Indians." The kids are great, and I am enjoying the experience. Yet the name "Indians" really bothers me because it is so behind the times, and a lot of people think using the term "Indian" for sport is racist. So I tried to influence the league director that we needed a name change. I presented my argument using a bunch of facts about how "Indian" has become passé for sports team. (My technique was rational persuasion.) I did get a listen, but I didn't get approval for the name change. So next, I combined my logical argument with an inspirational appeal. I asked the league directors how they would like it if our team were called "The West Side Chinese" or the "West Side Jews." Finally, my influence tactics worked, and for next season my team will be the "West Side Rattlers."

## Internet Skill-Building Exercise

## How Machiavellian Are You?

Go to www.humanlinks.com/personal/power_orientation.htm, and follow the instructions for taking the Power Orientation Test. Your score will be compared to a national average. Compare your score on this test with the Positive Organizational Politics Questionnaire you took in Chapter 7.

*Apply the chapter concepts! Visit the Web and complete this Internet skill-building exercise to learn more about current leadership topics and trends.*

1. Do you think the two tests measure similar tendencies?
2. If the range of your scores on the two tests is quite different, such as high on the Power Orientation Test and low on the Positive Organizational Politics Questionnaire, how do you explain these differences?
3. How does your score on the Power Orientation Test compare with your score on the Leader Integrity Scale from Chapter 6? What do you see as the relationship between ethical behavior and Machiavellianism?

# Developing Teamwork

## LEARNING OBJECTIVES

After studying this chapter and doing the exercises, you should be able to

- Understand the leader's role in a team-based organization.

- Describe leader actions that foster teamwork.

- Explain the potential contribution of outdoor training to the development of team leadership.

- Describe how the leader–member exchange model contributes to an understanding of leadership.

## CHAPTER OUTLINE

International Business Machines Corp. programmer Rob Nicholson has never met most of the fifty colleagues, on three continents, with whom he collaborates on writing software. But Nicholson feels part of a team from the moment he logs on each morning in Hursley, England.

Colleagues in India, alerted that Nicholson is online, fire questions. Then Nicholson checks notes on interactive bulletin boards, or wikis, that his team shares. One recent day, he found notes from teammates in India, suggesting changes to a proposed software design that he had posted the previous night; he revised the design that day. Nicholson says the constant communication helps him feel there are "lots of people attacking the same hill."

IBM uses high-tech tools to grapple with an increasingly common problem: making far-flung teams work well together. One key to smooth teamwork is dividing projects into small pieces. Nicholson says the team of fifty, charged with making IBM's WebSphere software with code written in other programming languages, breaks projects into two-week chunks. Each chunk is further split into tasks designed to take one programmer a day or two to complete. That means mistakes or miscommunications are caught quickly, and there is little waiting for others to finish work. Nicholson says that openness is essential in order to keep the information—and work—flowing. "Don't lock stuff up," he says.[1]

The IBM anecdote illustrates the importance business firms attach to building better teamwork, even when team members make their contributions from different parts of the globe. Also illustrated is the fact that leaders have to find ways to build teamwork to meet the demands of a high-tech work environment. Developing teamwork is such an important leadership role that team building is said to differentiate successful from unsuccessful leaders.[2] Furthermore, leaders with a reputation as teamwork builders are often in demand, such as Mark Hurd, the chairman and CEO of Hewlett-Packard, who heavily emphasizes teamwork as the path to corporate success. At one time, he often refused to be photographed alone because he claimed his success was dependent on the team.

A difficulty in understanding teams is that the words *teams* and *teamwork* are often overused and applied loosely. For some people, *team* is simply another term for *group*. As used here, a **team** is a work group that must rely on collaboration if each member is to experience the optimum success and achievement.[3] **Teamwork** is work done with an understanding and commitment to group goals on the part of all team members. All teams are groups, but not all groups are teams. Jon R. Katzenbach and Douglas K. Smith, on the basis of extensive research in the workplace, make a clear differentiation between teams and groups.[4] A team is characterized by a common commitment, whereas the commitment within a group might not be as strong. A team accomplishes many collective work products, whereas group members sometimes work slightly more independently. A team has shared leadership roles, whereas members of a group have a strong leader. In a team there is individual and mutual accountability; in contrast, a group emphasizes individual accountability.

Team members produce a collective work product, whereas group members sometimes produce individual work products. A team leader is likely to encourage open-ended discussion and active problem-solving meetings, whereas a group leader is more likely to run an efficient meeting. Also, teams discuss, decide, and do real work together, whereas a group is more likely to discuss, decide, and delegate.

Although the distinction between a group and a team may be valid, it is difficult to cast aside the practice of using the terms *group* and *team* interchangeably. For example, a customer service team is still a team even if its teamwork is poor.

The central focus of this chapter is a description of specific leader actions that foster teamwork. We also describe outdoor training, a widely used method of teamwork development. In addition, we summarize a leadership theory that provides insight into how teamwork emerges within a work group.

To evaluate how well any work team or group familiar to you is functioning as a team, do Leadership Self-Assessment Quiz 9-1. The quiz will help sensitize you to important dimensions of team effectiveness.

 **Knowledge Bank**
To provide background information on team functioning, the Knowledge Bank describes some of the advantages and disadvantages of group activity.

**www.cengage.com/ management/dubrin**

---

## Leadership Self-Assessment Quiz 9-1

### The Teamwork Checklist

**Instructions:** This checklist serves as an informal guide to diagnosing teamwork. Base your answers on the experiences you have in leading a team, at work or outside work. Indicate whether your team has (or had) the following characteristics:

| | Mostly Yes | Mostly No |
|---|---|---|
| 1. Definite goals each member knows and understands | | |
| 2. Clearly established roles and responsibilities | | |
| 3. Members who work together very well without strong egos or personalities that create problems | | |
| 4. Well-documented guidelines for behavior and ground rules | | |
| 5. After a consensus is reached, support from every team member | | |
| 6. Awareness of team members that they have achieved success | | |
| 7. Open communication in an atmosphere of trust | | |
| 8. Continuous learning and training in appropriate skills | | |
| 9. Flexible, open-minded, and dependable team members | | |
| 10. Patient and supportive higher management | | |
| 11. Individual member pride in own work | | |
| 12. Rewards tied to individual as well as team results | | |
| 13. Team members who automatically provide backup and support for one another without the team leader's stepping in | | |

## Quiz 9-1 (continued)

*Scoring and Interpretation:* The more statements are answered "mostly yes," the more likely it is that good teamwork is present. The answers will serve as discussion points among team members for improving teamwork and group effectiveness. Negative responses to the statements can be used as suggestions for taking action to improve teamwork in your group.

*Source:* Based on material gathered from Mark Kelly, *The Adventures of a Self-Managing Team* (San Diego, Calif.: Pfeiffer, 1991); "Team Leadership: How to Inspire Commitment, Teamwork and Cooperation," brochure, Seminars International, Olathe, Kans., 1996.

## THE LEADER'S ROLE IN THE TEAM-BASED ORGANIZATION

Although an important goal of a team-based organization is for group members to participate in leadership and management activities, leaders still play an important role. In fact, they learn to lead in new ways. Team-based organizations need leaders who are knowledgeable in the team process and can help with the interpersonal demands of teams, for example, by giving feedback and resolving conflict. Quite often the leader is a facilitator who works with two or three teams at a time. He or she helps them stay focused when personality and work-style differences create problems. Without effective leadership, teams can get off course, go too far or not far enough, lose sight of their mission, and become blocked by interpersonal conflict. Effective leadership is particularly important early in the history of a group to help it reach its potential. Key roles of a leader in a team-based organization include the following:

- Building trust and inspiring teamwork
- Coaching team members and group members toward higher levels of performance
- Facilitating and supporting the team's decisions
- Expanding the team's capabilities
- Creating a team identity
- Anticipating and influencing change
- Inspiring the team toward higher levels of performance
- Enabling and empowering group members to accomplish their work
- Encouraging team members to eliminate low-value work[5]

Several of these roles have already been noted in this book, and several others, such as building trust and coaching, are described later. All of these roles contribute to effective leadership in general. The enabling role, for example, centers on empowerment. Yet properly motivating team members also enables, or facilitates, work accomplishment. The empowering processes described in Chapter 7 are a major part of enabling. Group members who are empowered are enabled to accomplish their work. The leader behavior and attitudes that foster teamwork, described in the next section, might also be interpreted as part of the leader's role in a team-based organization.

When the leader is not a member of the team, he or she is classified as an *external leader*. A study conducted in three different industrial workplaces with self-managing teams offers some understanding of the external leader's role. (A self-managing team has considerable autonomy.) It was found that under ordinary work conditions, when the leaders were too actively involved in coaching the team and in sense making, satisfaction with leadership declined. *Sense making* refers to identifying important environmental events, and offering interpretations of these events to the team. An example would be identifying increases in the price of natural gas, and then explaining to the facilities maintenance team how price increases will affect their work. When the team faced disruptive conditions, such as an unusually heavy work overload or a rapid change in technology, coaching and sense making by the leader increased satisfaction with leadership.[6]

# LEADER ACTIONS THAT FOSTER TEAMWORK

Sometimes a leader's inspiring personality alone can foster teamwork. An experiment with Dutch business students showed that leaders who were perceived as charismatic and fair facilitated cooperation among group members.[7] Yet inspirational leaders, as well as less charismatic ones, can also encourage teamwork through their attitudes and what they do. Table 9-1 lists the teamwork-enhancing actions that are described

**TABLE 9–1** Leader Actions That Foster Teamwork

| ACTIONS LEADERS CAN TAKE USING THEIR OWN RESOURCES | ACTIONS GENERALLY REQUIRING ORGANIZATION STRUCTURE OR POLICY |
|---|---|
| 1. Defining the team's mission and tasks | 1. Designing physical structures that facilitate communication |
| 2. Establishing a climate of trust | 2. Emphasizing group recognition and rewards |
| 3. Developing a norm of teamwork, including emotional intelligence | 3. Initiating ritual and ceremony |
| 4. Emphasizing pride in being outstanding | 4. Practicing open-book management |
| 5. Serving as a model of teamwork, including power sharing | 5. Selecting team-oriented members |
| 6. Using a consensus leadership style | 6. Using technology that facilitates teamwork |
| 7. Establishing urgency, demanding performance standards, and providing direction | |
| 8. Encouraging competition with another group | |
| 9. Encouraging the use of jargon | |
| 10. Minimizing micromanagement | |
| 11. Practicing e-leadership for virtual teams | |

in the following pages. For convenience, the actions are divided into two types: actions leaders can take using their own resources (informal techniques) and actions that generally require organization structure or policy (formal techniques).

## Actions Leaders Can Take Using Their Own Resources

***Defining the Team's Mission***    A starting point in developing teamwork is to specify the team's mission. Commitment to a clear mission is a key practice of a highly effective team. The mission statement for the group helps answer the question, "Why are we doing this?" To answer this question, the mission statement should set out a specific goal, purpose, and philosophical tone. Any goal contained within the mission statement should be congruent with organizational objectives. If a team wants to cut back on its number of suppliers, the organization should have the same intent also. Here are two examples of team mission statements:

- To plan and implement new manufacturing approaches to enhance our high-performance image and bolster our competitive edge
- To enhance our web site development capability so we can provide decision makers throughout the organization with assistance in developing web sites that exceed the state of the art

The leader can specify the mission when the team is formed or at any other time. Developing a mission for a long-standing team breathes new life into its activities. Being committed to a mission improves teamwork, as does the process of formulating a mission. The dialogue necessary for developing a clearly articulated mission establishes a climate in which team members can express feelings, ideas, and opinions. Participative leadership is required in developing a mission, as in most other ways of enhancing teamwork.

To help implement the mission, it is quite helpful for the leader to define the team tasks, or to work with the group in defining these tasks. Team members can then identify the subtasks for which each member has responsibility.[8] For example, a dental office might want to understand why so many patients have left the practice. One team member might be assigned the task of contacting former patients, and another team member might be assigned the task of asking current patients if they are experiencing any problem with the dental practice.

***Establishing a Climate of Trust***    If team members do not trust each other or the leader, it is unlikely that they will work cooperatively together. As Kouzes and Posner note, trust is at the heart of collaboration. Unless team members trust each other, they will not be dependent on each other and therefore will not work well as a team.[9] A starting point in establishing a climate of trust is for the leader to be credible and engage in the many other trustworthy behaviors described in Chapter 2. Encouraging open communication about problems and sharing information are two specific ways the leader can help promote a climate of trust.

***Developing a Norm of Teamwork, Including Emotional Intelligence***    A major strategy of teamwork development is to promote the attitude among group members that working together effectively is expected. Developing a norm of teamwork is difficult for a leader when a strong culture of individualism exists within a firm. Nokia Inc., the telecommunications firm based in Finland, illustrates the teamwork type of organizational culture. Part of the culture of collegiality can be traced to the Finnish character. It is natural for Nokia employees to work together and iron out differences of opinion.[10]

A belief in cooperation and collaboration rather than competitiveness as a strategy for building teamwork has been referred to as **cooperation theory.**[11] Individuals who are accustomed to competing with one another for recognition, salary increases, and resources must now collaborate. Despite the challenge of making a culture shift, the leader can make progress toward establishing a teamwork norm by doing the following:

- Encourage team members to treat one another as if they were customers, thus fostering cooperative behavior and politeness.
- Explicitly state the desirability of teamwork on a regular basis both orally and in writing.
- Communicate the norm of teamwork by frequently using words and phrases that support teamwork. Emphasizing the words *team members* or *teammate*, and deemphasizing the words *subordinates* and *employees*, helps communicate the norm of teamwork.
- Work with the group to establish a code of conduct that everyone agrees to follow. Aspects of the code might include "never abandon a teammate," "never humiliate anyone," and "keep all agreements."

Normative statements about teamwork by influential team members are also useful in reinforcing the norm of teamwork. A team member might take a leadership role by saying to coworkers: "I'm glad this project is a joint effort. I know that's what earns us merit points here."

The leader's role in developing teamwork can also be described as helping the group develop emotional intelligence. The leader contributes to the group's emotional intelligence by creating norms that establish mutual trust among members. It is also important for members to have a sense of group identity as defined in their mission statement. Group efficacy, or feeling competent to complete the group task, also contributes to emotional intelligence. Ensuring that the group has the right skills can enhance such efficacy. These three conditions—mutual trust, group identity, and group efficacy—are the foundation of cooperation and collaboration.

The leader can also promote group emotional intelligence by bringing emotions to the surface in both group and one-on-one meetings. The leader then discusses how these emotions might be affecting the group's work.[12] For example, team members might discuss how they feel about their perceived importance to the organization. One maintenance group said that they felt entirely unappreciated until a key piece of equipment broke down, and this underappreciation was adversely affecting their morale. The team leader helped the group develop an internal public relations campaign about their contribution to productivity.

Another example of dealing with emotions is encouraging group members to speak up when they feel the group is being either unproductive or highly productive. Expressing positive emotion can be an energizer.

**KB Knowledge Bank**
To provide additional rules and thoughts that are likely to bring about cooperation within the group, see the Knowledge Bank. Additional insights about cooperation are important because teamwork and cooperation are almost synonymous.

**www.cengage.com/management/dubrin**

## Leadership Skill-Building Exercise 9-1

### Shelters for the Homeless

This exercise should take about thirty-five minutes; it can be done inside or outside class. Organize the class into teams of about six people. Each team takes on the assignment of formulating plans for building temporary shelters for the homeless. The dwellings you plan to build, for example, might be two-room cottages with electricity and indoor plumbing. During the time allotted to the task, formulate plans for going ahead with Shelters for the Homeless. Consider dividing up work by assigning certain roles to each team member. Sketch out tentative answers to the following questions: (1) How will you obtain funding for your venture? (2) Which homeless people will you help? (3) Where will your shelters be? (4) Who will do the construction?

After your plan is completed, evaluate the quality of the teamwork that took place within the group. Review the chapter for techniques you might have used to improve it.

The same kind of teamwork skills you use in this exercise can be readily applied to most teamwork assignments on the job. Note carefully that although some types of teams call for members to be generalists, dividing up the tasks is still a basic principle of collective effort.

*Emphasizing Pride in Being Outstanding*    A standard way to build team spirit, if not teamwork, is to help the group realize why it should be proud of its accomplishments. Most groups are particularly good at some task. The leader should help the group identify that task or characteristic and promote it as a key strength. A shipping department, for example, might have the best on-time shipping record in the region. Or a claims-processing unit might have the fewest overpayments in an insurance company.[13]

To try your hand at being part of an outstanding team, do Leadership Skill-Building Exercise 9-1.

*Serving as a Model of Teamwork, Including Power Sharing*    A powerful way for a leader to foster teamwork is to be a positive model of team play. And one way to exemplify teamwork is to reveal important information about ideas and attitudes relevant to the group's work. As a result of this behavior, team members may follow suit. A leader's self-disclosure fosters teamwork because it leads to shared perceptions and concerns.[14]

Interacting extensively with team members serves as a model of teamwork because it illustrates the mechanism by which team development takes place—frequent informal communication. While interacting with team members, the team leader can emphasize that he or she is a team member. For example, he or she might say, "Remember the deadline. We must all have the proposal in the mail by Thursday." A less team-member-oriented statement would be, "Remember the deadline. I need the proposals in the mail by Thursday."[15]

Another way of being a model of teamwork is to share power with group members because a good team player avoids hogging power and making all of the decisions. As each team member takes the opportunity to exert power, he or she feels more like a major contributor to team effort. Jon Gruden, the youngest coach in NFL history to win a Super Bowl, uses power sharing to build teamwork. He says he realizes the players "get a little sick of hearing from me all the time," so he breaks up the monotony by letting one assistant coach address the team before each week's game. Each coach is required to develop a metaphor and the keys to winning that game. For one game, the defensive line coach began by talking about a rock: "That rock is your opponent and you've got to keep pounding on it with a hammer."[16] As a result of sharing power, the coaches feel even more strongly that they are an integral part of Gruden's team.

To be a model of team play as a leader, you need the attitudes of a team player. Leadership Self-Assessment Quiz 9-2 gives you an opportunity to measure such attitudes.

 ## Leadership Self-Assessment Quiz 9-2

### Team Player Attitudes

**Instructions:** Describe how well you agree with each of the following statements, using the following scale: disagree strongly (DS); disagree (D); neutral (N); agree (A); agree strongly (AS).

|  | DS | D | N | A | AS |
|---|---|---|---|---|---|
| 1. I am at my best when working alone. | 5 | 4 | 3 | 2 | 1 |
| 2. I have belonged to clubs and teams since I was a child. | 1 | 2 | 3 | 4 | 5 |
| 3. It takes far too long to get work accomplished with a group. | 5 | 4 | 3 | 2 | 1 |
| 4. I like the friendship of working in a group. | 1 | 2 | 3 | 4 | 5 |
| 5. I would prefer to run a one-person business than to be a member of a large firm. | 5 | 4 | 3 | 2 | 1 |
| 6. It is difficult to trust others in the group on key assignments. | 5 | 4 | 3 | 2 | 1 |
| 7. Encouraging others comes to me naturally. | 1 | 2 | 3 | 4 | 5 |
| 8. I like the give-and-take of ideas that is possible in a group. | 1 | 2 | 3 | 4 | 5 |
| 9. It is fun to share responsibility with others in the group. | 1 | 2 | 3 | 4 | 5 |
| 10. Much more can be accomplished by a team than by the same number of people working alone. | 1 | 2 | 3 | 4 | 5 |

Total score: _____

**Scoring and Interpretation:** Add the numbers you circled to obtain your total score.

- **41–50:** You have strong positive attitudes toward being a team member and working cooperatively with other members.
- **30–40:** You have moderately favorable attitudes toward being a team member and working cooperatively with other members.
- **10–29:** You much prefer working by yourself to being a team member. To work effectively in a company that emphasizes teamwork, you may need to develop more positive attitudes toward working jointly with others.

***Using a Consensus Leadership Style***   Teamwork is enhanced when a leader practices consensus decision making. Contributing to important decisions helps group members feel that they are valuable to the team. Consensus decision making also leads to an exchange of ideas within the group, with group members supporting and refining each other's suggestions. As a result, the feeling of working jointly on problems is enhanced. Generation X managers (those who were born in 1965 or later) are likely to practice consensus leadership. Part of the reason is that many of these people have taken leadership courses. Bonnie Stedt, who holds the job title of senior relationship leader and executive vice president for American Express in New York City, made this analysis of Gen-X managers that still holds today:

> I look at them as a very promising generation. They bring so much to the work force especially as managers. Xers tend to be flexible, good at collaboration and consensus building and mature beyond their years. They are also capable of multitasking. Gen-X managers are very team oriented, and they absolutely want everyone on the team to get credit.[17]

Another way of framing the consensus leadership style is saying that it reflects a belief in shared governance and partnerships instead of patriarchal caretaking.[18] (This is essentially the same idea as power sharing.) The team, rather than hierarchical departments, becomes the focus of organizational activity. As with the other tactics and techniques for enhancing teamwork, people have to participate in a cultural shift to fully accept shared governance.

Striving for consensus does not mean that all conflict is submerged to make people agree. Disagreements over issues are healthy, and team members are more likely to be committed to the consensus decision if their voice has been heard. An example of a conflict over an issue would be the marketing team of an automotive company debating whether dealer discounts improve sales in the long run.

***Establishing Urgency, Demanding Performance Standards, and Providing Direction***
Team members need to believe that the team has urgent, constructive purposes. They also want a list of explicit expectations. The more urgent and relevant the rationale is, the more likely it is that the team will achieve its potential. A customer service team was told that further growth for the corporation would be impossible without major improvements in providing service to customers. Energized by this information, the team met the challenge.

To help establish urgency, it is helpful for the leader to challenge the group regularly. Teamwork is enhanced when the leader provides the team valid facts and information that motivate them to work together to modify the status quo. New information prompts the team to redefine and enrich its understanding of the challenge it is facing. As a result, the team is likely to focus on a common purpose, set clearer goals, and work together more smoothly.[19]

***Encouraging Competition with Another Group***   One of the best-known methods of encouraging teamwork is rallying the support of the group against a real or imagined threat from the outside. Beating the competition makes more sense when the competition is outside your organization. When the enemy is within, the team spirit within may become detrimental to the overall organization, and we–they problems may arise. While encouraging competition with another group, the leader should encourage rivalry, not intense competition that might lead to unethical business practices, such as making false charges against them. An example of ethical competition against another group would be a product development group at Research in Motion (producer of the BlackBerry) competing to produce a cell phone to compete against the iPhone of Apple Corp.

***Encouraging the Use of Jargon***   Lee G. Bolman and Terrence E. Deal contend that the symbolic and ritualistic framework of a group contributes heavily to teamwork. An important part of this framework is a specialized language that fosters cohesion and commitment. In essence, this specialized language is in-group jargon that creates a bond among team members; sets the group apart from outsiders; reinforces unique values and beliefs, thus contributing to corporate culture; and allows team members to communicate easily, with few misunderstandings.[20] Examples of in-group jargon at Microsoft Corporation are to label an intelligent person as having "bandwidth," and a serious person as being "hardcore."

***Minimizing Micromanagement***   A strategic perspective on encouraging teamwork is for the leader to minimize **micromanagement,** the close monitoring of most aspects of group member activities. To be a good team leader, the manager must give group members ample opportunity to manage their own activities. Avoiding micromanagement is a core ingredient of employee empowerment because empowered workers are given considerable latitude to manage their own activities. An example of heavy micromanagement follows:

> When Scott Olsen was an investment banker, his department head reviewed the big presentations he and his colleagues worked on and reacted first and foremost to the documents' formatting. "We are showing him financial analysis that has our clients making or losing hundreds of millions of dollars, and he is commenting on whether this font is a size larger—or perhaps bolded?—than this other font," says Olsen. The formatting critique ate up time that could have been used to refine the analysis.[21]

The contingency leader recognizes the fine line between avoiding micromanagement and not providing the guidance and accountability that team members may need to function well as a unit. Consultant Bruce Tulgan reports, "When we asked employees what they want from the people above them, the first thing they mention is never a raise. It's always more coaching, more guidance, clearer goals, more constructive criticism, and more recognition for achievement."[22] An implication is that a manager tinged with a little micromanagement is likely to engage in these constructive behaviors.

Leadership Self-Assessment Quiz 9-3 provides some assistance in helping you avoid becoming a micromanager. This skill is important because in most leadership situations, being perceived as a micromanager is a liability.

***Practicing E-Leadership for Virtual Teams***   As suggested in the chapter opener, the Internet, including email, influences a leader's work to some extent. If team leader Jennifer based in Seattle sends a note of congratulations to team member Surinda based in Mumbai, she is practicing e-leadership. Jennifer and Surinda are part of a

Leadership Self-Assessment Quiz 9-3

## Overcoming Micromanagement

This brief self-quiz and accompanying suggestions provide some useful insights into avoiding micromanagement. Keeping micromanagement tendencies under control is important because the team is likely to feel more empowered, and the most capable team members will feel less like quitting. Furthermore, holding on to unimportant tasks cuts dramatically into a leader's productivity and that of staff. Is micromanagement impeding your progress?

*Instructions:* Ask yourself these four questions, and circle the appropriate answer:

| | | |
|---|---|---|
| 1. I sign off on all projects, from large to small. | YES | NO |
| 2. Most decisions end up in my lap. | YES | NO |
| 3. I feel overwhelmed by administrative tasks. | YES | NO |
| 4. Staff turnover is high and morale is low. | YES | NO |

*Interpretation:* If you answered "Yes" two or more times, you need to learn how to modify your death-grip management style.

*Skill Development:* The following three steps can help you feel more comfortable delegating and also encourage employee growth.

1. **Establish a trust level for each staffer.** For example, Helen has excellent judgment, so give her project authority. Although Tim is an excellent worker, you need to supervise him closely.
2. **Make sure staffers understand your instructions.** Ask them to repeat assignments verbally and confirm complex tasks with a follow-up email message.
3. **Open multiple avenues of communication.** Establish check-in, interim, and deadline dates. Follow up faithfully. Tell employees that your door is always open, but give them a good sense of how much authority they have and when they should consult you. Ask staffers, "How's it going?" occasionally. Then let them get on with their work.

*Source:* From "Power Productivity: Stop Micromanaging and Spur Productivity," in *Manager's Edge*, July 2002, p. 6. Adapted from *The Organized Executive*, Briefings Publishing Group, (800) 722-9221.

virtual team: they work with each other yet do not share the same physical facility. **E-leadership** is a form of leadership practiced in a context where work is mediated by information technology. The focus of leadership shifts from individuals to networks of relationships because the Internet facilitates connecting so many people.[23] E-leadership could, therefore, encompass any activity undertaken by a leader when the Internet connects people. Our concern here is how e-leadership facilitates building teamwork, especially in a virtual team.

When team members are geographically dispersed, a leader's communication with team members takes place using information technology, including the dissemination of information needed for task accomplishment. A participative leader may establish chat rooms to solicit opinions from members of a cross-border virtual team before reaching a final decision. The leader might also conduct an electronic poll to attain consensus on a controversial issue. The leader can foster team spirit (and therefore teamwork) by sending congratulatory email messages for a job well done. In short, the e-leader improves teamwork by staying connected electronically to team members—although not to the point of blitzing them with so many messages that he or she becomes an annoyance.

Based on observations, interviews, and survey data, two intensive studies have identified leadership practices of effective leaders of virtual teams. The purpose of these practices is to overcome the unique challenges of managing virtual teams, such as not being able to see in-person when the team needs focus and direction. The conclusions of the researchers dealing mostly with building teamwork are presented next.[24]

**1. *When building a virtual team, solicit volunteers when feasible.*** As the experiences at Wikipedia and Linux have shown, virtual teams appear to thrive when they include volunteers with valuable skills. A team of volunteers has an elite status that contributes to team spirit. In addition to being volunteers, it is helpful for the virtual team to include members who already know each other. In this way a component of camaraderie already exists.

**2. *Ensure that the task is meaningful to the team and the company.*** Ideally the team task should resonate with the values of each member and the team collectively. Team members working on a relevant task are more likely to be spirited and cooperative. A relevant example was a virtual team at BP called Ignite that explored the idea of shifting more energy production to sustainable resources, such as solar power and wind. It was this team's energy and focus that resulted in the company's push toward sustainable energy. (Several critics have said that BP's efforts were just a publicity stunt, with no real help to the environment. Nevertheless, a spirited team produced a good result.)

**3. *Establish and maintain trust through the use of communication technology.*** A major hurdle in working with a virtual team is deciding on what information gets communicated and to whom. In some instances a norm might be established that restricts members from conveying negative information to anyone outside the team. It is also useful to ensure that all team members are equally inconvenienced by time zone differences, such as having a meeting at 3 A.M. their time. Meeting times would be rotated so team members in one time zone would not suffer.

**4. *Ensure that diversity in the team is understood, appreciated, and leveraged.*** Diversity within the team can take many forms, such as experiences, skills, and interests. To ensure that diversity is understood and appreciated, leaders frequently develop an *expertise directory* when the team first forms. The directory can include a photo of each member along with details about his or her training, experience, and previous assignments. A skills matrix of team members can serve the same purpose.

**5. *Maintain frequent communications, including virtual meetings.*** The majority of team leaders in the study reported that regular audio-conferences involving all members were the lifeblood of the team, even when tasks were distributed among the team members. The virtual meetings are used to keep members engaged, excited about the work, and aligned with each other. At the beginning of the meeting, it is helpful to have the team member reconnect with the human side of each team member. Exchanging personal stories helps build closeness.

Other forms of communication besides audio-conferences can serve the function of developing teamwork. At Nokia, for example, the favored communication tool is text messaging, while at other companies email or voice mail was more effective. Most importantly, communication should be frequent and rapid.

**6. *Monitor team progress through the use of technology.*** An example of monitoring would be checking to see who is using the team's online knowledge repository regularly and who is not. The leader can also check to see if some members are not doing their fair share of work, and then coach the underperformer. This approach might improve teamwork because loafers drag down a team.

**7. *Enhance external visibility of the team and its members*** Virtual team members may have at least two bosses (the virtual team leader and the on-site boss) so it is important that the work of the virtual team gets reported externally. A virtual team in the electronics testing industry was required to report the team's results to a steering committee. The link to teamwork is that receiving rewards and recognition helps build team spirit.

**8. *Ensure that individuals benefit from participating in virtual teams.*** Even if the members are good team players, they need personal benefits to experience team spirit. One approach is to have virtual reward ceremonies, such as having gifts delivered to each team member and then having a virtual party. (No need for designated drivers here because the party takes place at the homes of team members!) The team leader can also encourage executives at the team members' work environment to thank the team members. Offering opportunities for personal growth, such as mini-lectures by an expert, can also be helpful.

You will observe that the eight suggestions for leading virtual teams include both actions leaders can take on their own, plus the use of company technology.

**Knowledge Bank**
Contains two additional suggestions for improving teamwork through actions the leader can take on his or her own.

**www.cengage.com/ management/dubrin**

## Actions Generally Requiring Organization Structure or Policy

***Designing Physical Structures That Facilitate Communication*** Group cohesiveness, and therefore teamwork, is fostered when team members are located close together and can interact frequently and easily. In contrast, people who spend most of their time in their private offices or cubicles are less likely to interact. Frequent interaction often leads to camaraderie and a feeling of belongingness. A useful tactic for achieving physical proximity is to establish a shared physical facility, such as a conference room, research library, or beverage lounge. This area should be decorated differently from other areas in the building, and a few amenities should be added, such as a coffeepot, microwave oven, and refrigerator. Team members can then use this area for refreshments and group interaction.

An extreme approach to encouraging team members to talk to each other is to have a day in which sending messages back and forth to each other through email or instant messaging is prohibited. Sara Roberts, the president of a consulting firm, says that too much email makes building rapport difficult. "People hide behind email. For just one day a week, I want us to pick up the phone or talk face to face."[25] For most offices, the disadvantages of restricted communication that would result from not exchanging emails, including attached files, would probably outweigh the benefit of more personal interactions.

Recognizing the contribution of a shared physical facility to promoting teamwork, many organizations have incorporated more open working space into the workplace, often eliminating private offices. Many people express dissatisfaction with this lack of privacy, but it is difficult to assess the productivity loss and morale problems stemming from limited opportunity for quiet reflection on the job.

***Emphasizing Group Recognition and Rewards*** Giving rewards for group accomplishment reinforces teamwork because people receive rewards for what they have achieved collaboratively. The recognition accompanying the reward should emphasize the team's value to the organization rather than that of the individual. Recognition promotes team identity by enabling the team to take pride in its contributions and progress. The following are examples of team recognition:

- A display wall for team activities such as certificates of accomplishment, schedules, and miscellaneous announcements
- Team logos on items such as identifying T-shirts, athletic caps, mugs, jackets, key rings, and business cards
- Celebrations to mark milestones such as first-time activities, cost savings, and safety records
- Equipment painted in team colors
- Athletic team events such as softball, volleyball, and bowling
- Team-of-the-Month award, with gifts from the organization to team members or to the entire team

A warning is that many employees may view switching to a team-based pay plan that places much of their pay at risk as an unnerving proposition.

***Initiating Ritual and Ceremony*** Another way to enhance teamwork is to initiate ritual and ceremony.[26] Ritual and ceremony afford opportunities for reinforcing values, revitalizing spirit, and bonding workers to one another and to the team. An example is holding a team dinner whenever the group achieves a major milestone, such as making a winning bid on a major contract. Another formal ritual is to send a team on a retreat to develop its mission and goals and to build camaraderie. When the team is working and socializing closely together during the retreat— even one long day—teamwork is reinforced.

***Practicing Open-Book Management*** A method of getting the company working together as a team is to share information about company finances and strategy with large numbers of employees. In **open-book management** every employee is trained, empowered, and motivated to understand and pursue the company's business goals. In this way employees become business partners and perceive themselves to be members of the same team. In a full form of open-book management, workers share strategic and financial information as well as responsibility. The company also shares risks and rewards based on results, so workers are likely to pull together as a team so that the company can succeed.[27] The idea is to have a well-informed, partner-oriented, high-performance company. Part of keeping workers well informed is for company leaders to host roundtable discussions about company financial information. Another approach is to regularly disseminate by email information about the company's financial progress.

***Selecting Team-Oriented Members***   A heavy-impact method of building teamwork is to select team members who are interested in and capable of teamwork. A starting point is self-selection. It is best for the team leader to choose workers who ask to be members of a team. A person's record of past team activity can also help one determine whether that person is an effective team player. Many managers believe that those who participate in team sports now or in the past are likely to be good team players on the job. Many female executives contend that the sports they played while growing up helped prepare them for the team aspects of corporate life. In one study, 81 percent of the 401 businesswomen surveyed agreed that sports helped them function better on a team. In addition, 69 percent said that sports promoted the leadership skills that contributed to professional success.[28]

***Using Technology That Enhances Teamwork***   Workers can collaborate better when they use information technology that fosters collaboration, often referred to as *groupware*. For example, the straightforward act of exchanging frequent email messages and instant messages can facilitate cooperation. Electronic brainstorming is another example of groupware. Virtual teams by their nature rely on information technology to enhance teamwork.

Another development is web sites where workers can collaborate to save time and money on activities as varied as product design and mergers. Companies can now make products more cheaply and quickly by using the Web to synchronize the various aspects of design with suppliers. For example, by using a system of collaborative software at General Motors Corporation factories, management has cut the time it takes to complete a vehicle mockup from twelve weeks to two weeks.[29] The link to teamwork is that members of different groups work more smoothly as a team with members outside the group. This is somewhat different from the emphasis in this chapter on teamwork *within* the group.

## OFFSITE TRAINING AND TEAM DEVELOPMENT

Cognitive information about strategies and tactics for improving teamwork is potentially valuable. The person reading such information can selectively apply the concepts, observe the consequences, and then fine-tune his or her approach. Another approach to developing teamwork is to participate in experiential activities (several are presented throughout this text).

The most popular experiential approach to building teamwork and leadership skills is offsite outdoor training, also referred to as outdoor training. Wilderness training is closely associated with outdoor training, except that the setting is likely to be much rougher—perhaps in the frozen plains of northernmost Minnesota. Some forms of outdoor training take place in city parks, as well as in the city itself to rehabilitate or build a house.

Both outdoor and wilderness training are forms of learning by doing. Participants are supposed to acquire leadership and teamwork skills by confronting physical challenges and exceeding their self-imposed limitations. The goals of outdoor training are reasonably consistent across different training groups. The Big Rock Creek Camp, which offers team building and leadership training, specifies these representative goals:

- Discover your strengths and weaknesses.
- Test your limits (they are far broader than you imagine).
- Work together as a team.
- Have fun.
- Face the essence of who you are and what you are made of.

## Features of Outdoor and Offsite Training Programs

Program participants are placed in a demanding outdoor environment, where they rely on skills they did not realize they had and on one another to complete the program. The emphasis is on building not only teamwork but also self-confidence for leadership. Sometimes lectures on leadership, self-confidence, and teamwork precede the activity. The list of what constitutes a team-building activity continues to grow and now includes tightrope walking, gourmet cooking as a team, paintballing, and scavenger hunts. Building or repairing houses for people in need is popular, as described in the accompanying Leader in Action profile. Another novel approach is for participants to work with horses in a stable to simulate the role of the boss and employee (played by the horse). In one of these team-building activities, blindfolded individuals mount the horses and rely on coworkers to guide them through an obstacle course.[30]

Outward Bound is the best-known and largest outdoor training program. It offers more than 500 courses in wilderness areas in twenty states and provinces. The courses typically run from three days to four weeks. Worldwide, Outward Bound runs about forty-eight schools on five continents. The Outward Bound Professional Development Program, geared toward organizational leaders, emphasizes teamwork, leadership, and risk taking. The wilderness is the classroom, and the instructors draw analogies between each outdoor activity and the workplace. Among the courses offered are dog-sledding, skiing and winter camping, desert backpacking, canoe expeditions, sailing, sea kayaking, alpine mountaineering, mountain backpacking and horsetrailing, and cycling.

Rope activities are typical of outdoor training. Participants are attached to a secure pulley with ropes; then they climb up a ladder and jump off to another spot. Sometimes the rope is extended between two trees. Another activity is a "trust fall," in which each person takes a turn standing on a platform and falling backward into the arms of coworkers. The trust fall can also be done on ground level. Many readers of this book have already participated in a trust fall. Leadership Skill Building Exercises 9-2 and 9-3 present representative offsite activities.

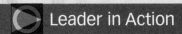

## Leader in Action

### Developing the Leadership Team at Molson Coors by Helping Habitat for Humanity

When the breweries at Molson and Coors merged a few years back, the new leadership team wanted to start things off on the right foot with a team-building exercise.

"We quickly got past the idea of a ropes course or golf outing; we really wanted something where we would give back to one of the communities where we do business," said Samuel D. Walker, chief legal officer for Molson Coors. As a result, the eleven-member executive team spent a full day of their Las Vegas meeting that year helping build a house under the tutelage of Habitat for Humanity.

"We had to unload this truck full of cement roof tiles," Walker said. "We actually had to figure out how to have kind of a bucket line, handing these very heavy tiles from one person to the next. That's the ultimate team-building exercise."

Other members of the team said that these activities helped them forge bonds that remained even after they returned to the office.

Guy Amato, president and chief executive of Habitat for Humanity's Las Vegas affiliate, said the number of requests for groups who want to participate in building a home while in town has more than doubled in recent years.

### Questions

1. Why do you think the team-building experience offered by Habitat for Humanity is so popular with managers?
2. Why would one of the world's largest breweries care if its team-building exercises do any good for the community?
3. Give an example of several teamwork skills that might be practiced or enhanced by helping build a house.

*Source:* Excerpted from Martha C. White, "Doing Good on Company Time," *The New York Times* (nytimes.com), May 8, 2007.

Outdoor training enhances teamwork by helping participants examine the process of getting things done through working with people. Participants practice their communication skills in exercises such as rappelling down a cliff by issuing precise instructions to one another about how to scale the cliff safely. At the same time, they have to learn to trust one another because their survival appears to depend on trust.

One of the most intensive and extensive examples of team building through outdoor training is conducted annually at Seagate Technology, the leading manufacturer of hard drives. About 200 employees from around the world spend a week in Queenstown, New Zealand, located at the bottom of the world. The activities include hiking, kayaking, adventure racing, and breaking boards with the goal of building a more collaborative, team-oriented company. (Adventure racing is about running and biking through an unfamiliar course, such as at the bottom of a glacier.) Participants frequently shout to each other, "You're awesome," throughout many of the activities. A major rationale for the extensive team-building activity is that when people are placed in unfamiliar situations, especially when fatigued, they are more likely to ask for help and work as a team.[31]

## Leadership Skill-Building Exercise 9-2

### The Newspaper Shelter

The objective of this exercise is to allow for observation of team interaction while exploring communication skills, cooperation, planning, and having fun. Organize the class into teams of about seven to ten people. The materials required are newspapers and masking tape or duct tape.

Imagine that you are stuck in the desert or on a deserted island. Your assignment is to build a structure that is free-standing and will protect the entire group from the sun. (If weather and time permit, this activity might be conducted outdoors.) You have about fifteen minutes to plan how you are going to build the structure. After the fifteen minutes, you will have twenty minutes to build the structure, but you are not allowed to talk to each other during the building phase.

After the activity is completed, answer the following questions about team process:

1. What worked during the process? What hindered the process?
2. How did the planning take place?
3. Did everyone have an active role?
4. How did it feel to not be able to talk during the building phase?
5. Did you work as a team? How did you know?
6. What did you learn about yourself and your teammates during this exercise?

*Source:* Adapted from the Leadership Center at Washington State University.

## Leadership Skill-Building Exercise 9-3

### Trust Me

Part of trusting team members is to trust them with your physical safety. The trust builder described here has been incorporated into many team-building programs. Proceed as follows:

- *Step 1:* Each group member takes a turn being blindfolded, perhaps using a bandanna.
- *Step 2:* The remaining team members arrange between five and eight chairs into a formation of their choosing, using a different formation for each blindfolded member.
- *Step 3:* At the appropriate signal from a team member, the blindfolded person starts to walk. The rest of the team gives instructions that will enable the blindfolded person to get past the formation of chairs without a collision.
- *Step 4:* At the end of the blindfolded person's experience, he or she immediately answers the following questions: (a) How did you feel when blindfolded in this exercise? (b) Explain why you either trusted or did not trust your team members. (c) What did you need from your team members while you were blindfolded?
- *Step 5:* After each person has taken a turn, discuss in your team (a) the impact of this exercise on the development of trust in teams and (b) what you learned about teamwork from the exercise.

### Evaluation of Outdoor Training for Team Development

Many outdoor trainers and participants believe strongly that they derived substantial personal benefits from outdoor training. Among the most important are greater self-confidence, appreciating hidden strengths, and learning to work better with others. Strong proponents of outdoor training believe that those who do not appreciate the training simply do not understand it. Many training directors also have positive attitudes toward outdoor training. They believe that a work team that experiences outdoor training will work more cooperatively back at the office. For example, Ron Roberts, the president of Action Centered Training, points out that paintball may have little to do with a job but it can have a powerful effect. Winning demands teamwork, including forceful communication. Roberts says, "If they don't work as a team, they get shot and experience pain. It's not for everybody. But the principles of communication, teamwork, leadership and strategic planning are there."[32]

Many people have legitimate reservations about outdoor training, however. Although outdoor trainers claim that almost no accidents occur, a threat to health and life does exist, and groin injuries are frequent. (To help minimize casualties, participants usually need medical clearance.) Another concern is that the teamwork learned in outdoor training does not spill over into the job environment. As Jay Conger explains, the workplace is a different environment from the wilderness. And real workplace teams tend to gain and lose their members rapidly as teammates are transferred, promoted, terminated, or quit. This mobility often negates all the team-building efforts that take place during the experience. Another problem is that when teams return to work, they often revert to noncollaborative behavior.[33] Based on his research, management professor Chris Neck concludes that there is little compelling evidence of long-term benefits for entire teams, but there is evidence that individuals' attitudes and teamwork skills improve immediately after the exercises.[34]

One way to facilitate the transfer of training from outdoors to the office is to hold debriefing and follow-up sessions. Debriefing takes place at the end of outdoor training. The participants review what they learned and discuss how they will apply their lessons to the job. Follow-up sessions can then be held periodically to describe progress in applying the insights learned during outdoor training. Melissa Williams, practice manager at Specialists in Pain Management in Chattanooga, Tenn., makes this observation about the effectiveness of offsite team building:

> The activities were great. But the most helpful part of the daylong workshop was reviewing what we had learned. The facilitated sessions made us aware of some conflicting areas we hadn't recognized or addressed before. But by the time we finished, we had fixed a number of issues without people even realizing it.[35]

## THE LEADER–MEMBER EXCHANGE MODEL AND TEAMWORK

Research and theory about the development of teamwork lag research and theory about many other aspects of leadership. Nevertheless, the leader–member exchange model, developed by George Graen and associates, helps explain why one subgroup in

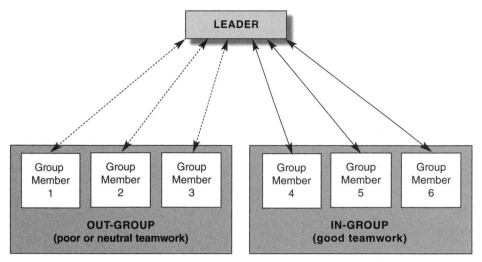

**FIGURE 9-1** The Leader–Member Exchange Model.

*Source:* From Gregory Moorhead and Ricky W. Griffin, *Organizational Behavior: Managing People and Organizations*, 4th ed., p. 314. Copyright © 1995 by Houghton Mifflin Company. Reprinted by permission of Houghton Mifflin Company.

a unit is part of a cohesive team but another group is excluded.[36] The theory, already mentioned several times in this text, deals with the relationship between a leader and a team member. However, the same theory tells us a lot about teamwork.

The **leader–member exchange model (LMX)** proposes that leaders develop unique working relationships with group members. One subset of employees, the in-group, is given additional rewards, responsibility, and trust in exchange for their loyalty and performance. The in-group becomes part of a smoothly functioning team headed by the formal leader. In contrast, the out-group employees are treated in accordance with a more formal understanding of leader–group member relations. Out-group members are less likely to experience good teamwork.

Figure 9-1 depicts the major concept of the leader–member exchange model. Here we look at several aspects of LMX as it relates most closely to teamwork. Leader–member exchange has also been researched in relationship to many other aspects of workplace behavior.

## Different-Quality Relationships

Leaders do not typically use the same leadership style in dealing with all group members. Instead, they treat each member somewhat differently. The linkages (relationships) that exist between the leader and each individual team member probably differ in quality. In theory, the differences lie on a continuum of low quality to high quality. With group members on the top half of the continuum, the leader has a good relationship; with those on the lower half of the continuum, the leader has a poor relationship. Each of these pairs of relationships, or dyads, must be judged in terms of whether a group member is "in" or "out" with the leader. The positive regard that leaders and members have for each other is a major contributor to the quality of their relationship.[37]

Members of the in-group are invited to participate in important decision making, are given added responsibility, and are privy to interesting gossip. Members of the out-group are managed according to the requirements of their employment contract. They receive little warmth, inspiration, or encouragement. Robert Vecchio explains that an in-group member is elevated to the unofficial role of trusted assistant.[38] An out-group member is treated much like a hired hand. In-group members tend to achieve a higher level of performance, commitment, and satisfaction than do out-group members. Furthermore, they are less likely to quit. A study conducted in a retail setting found that when the quality of the leader–member exchange is high, group members are more strongly committed to company goals.[39] In turn, this commitment leads to stronger teamwork because the workers pull together to pursue goals.

The in-group versus out-group status also includes an element of reciprocity or exchange. The leader grants more favors to the in-group member, who in response works harder to please the leader, a contributor to being a good team player. Two studies provide more specific information about the consequences of a positive exchange between a supervisor and group members. In a hospital setting, positive exchanges involved group members' engaging in increased good citizenship behavior and in-group role behaviors such as putting extra effort into performing their duties.[40] As a result, the leader would feel justified in granting the in-group members more resources, such as a larger salary increase or a larger budget.

A study conducted in diverse industrial settings also found that high-quality exchanges between supervisors and employees contribute to employees' engaging in extra-role behavior, or being cooperative in ways that were not expected of them. Supervisory ratings of employee altruism were used to measure helping behaviors, as when an accountant helps a sales representative prepare a sales forecast. The researchers concluded that through the development of high-quality relationships with group members, supervisors are able to motivate the group members and enable them to engage in helping behaviors that benefit them as well as their coworkers.[41]

One contribution of positive LMXs is that they facilitate good safety performance, an important aspect of teamwork in many work environments. Sixty-four group leaders in a manufacturing plant participated in a study. A major finding of the study was that positive leader–member exchanges were associated with more communication about safety. The enhanced communication led to more commitment to safety, which in turn led to fewer accidents on the job.[42]

Another of the many consequences of positive leader–member exchanges is that they it may facilitate the leader having a transformational effect. A study of 283 individuals from a broad cross-section of job types indicated that transformational relationships were significantly stronger for followers who perceived high-quality relationships with their supervisors. An example of a transformational relationship would be inspiring the subordinate to seek different perspectives when solving problems, or bringing about change.[43] Transformational effects also tie in with teamwork because the workers become energized to jointly accomplish goals.

## First Impressions

The leader's first impression of a group member's competency plays an important role in placing the group member in the in-group or the out-group. Another key linking factor is whether the leader and team member have positive or negative chemistry. We can assume that group members who make effective use of influence and political tactics increase their chances of becoming members of the in-group.

A field study seems to confirm that first impressions make a difference. The researchers gathered ratings of six aspects of the manager–group member dyad. One measure was the group members' perceived similarity with the leader. For example, "My supervisor and I are alike in a number of ways." A second measure was feelings about the manager, such as, "I like my supervisor very much as a friend." A third rating dealt directly with the member's view of the LMX. For example, "I can count on my supervisor to 'bail me out,' even at his or her expense, when I really need it."

A fourth rating measured the leader expectation of the member, such as, "I think my new employee will be an excellent employee." A fifth rating measured leader liking of the member, such as, "I like my subordinate very much as a person." A sixth rating was the leader's view of the LMX, including a rating of the statement, "I would be willing to 'bail out' my subordinate, even at my own expense, if he or she really needed it."

Results showed that the initial leader expectations of members and member expectations of the leader were good predictors of the leader–member exchanges at two weeks and at six weeks. Member expectations of the leader also accurately predicted member assessments of the quality of the leader–member exchange at six months. An important interpretation of these results is that the leader–member exchange is formed in the first days of the relationship.[44] As the adage states, "You have only one chance to make a good first impression."

In summary, the leader–member exchange model provides a partial explanation of teamwork development. Members of the in-group work smoothly together and with the leader because they feel privileged. Being a member of the out-group may not diminish teamwork, but it certainly does not make a positive contribution.

## Reader's Roadmap

So far we have studied considerable information about the nature of leadership; the attributes, behaviors, and styles of leaders; the ethics and social responsibility of leaders; and how leaders exert power and use politics and influence. The techniques for developing teamwork are part of a leader's relationship with the group, as is the subject of the next chapter, motivational skills.

## SUMMARY

Leaders are required to build teamwork because it is needed for such key activities as group problem solving and achieving high quality. Teamwork is an understanding of and commitment to group goals on the part of all group members.

Leaders still play an important role in a team-based organization, such as being expert in the team process, being facilitators, building trust and inspiring teamwork, and enabling and empowering group members to accomplish their work. The enabling role centers on empowerment. The external leader of a self-managing team plays a key role when the team faces disruptive conditions.

A wide range of leader actions fosters teamwork. Measures leaders can take using their own resources include (1) defining the team's mission; (2) establishing a climate of trust; (3) developing a norm of teamwork, including emotional intelligence; (4) emphasizing pride in being outstanding; (5) serving as a model of teamwork, including power sharing; (6) using a consensus leadership style; (7) establishing urgency, demanding performance standards, and providing direction; (8) encouraging competition with another group; (9) encouraging the use of jargon; (10) minimizing micromanagement; and (11) practicing e-leadership for virtual teams.

Techniques to foster teamwork that require relying on organization structure or policy include the following: (1) designing physical structures that facilitate communication; (2) emphasizing group recognition and rewards; (3) initiating ritual and ceremony; (4) practicing open-book management; (5) selecting team-oriented members; and (6) using technology that facilitates teamwork.

In outdoor (or offsite) training, a popular experiential approach to building teamwork and leadership skills, building self-confidence is the focus. Outdoor training enhances teamwork by helping participants examine the process of collaboration. The Outward Bound Professional Development Program is geared toward organization leaders. Opinion about the effectiveness of outdoor training for developing teamwork and leadership skills is mixed. Concern has been expressed that the skills learned in the field do not carry over to the workplace.

The leader–exchange model helps explain why one subgroup in a work unit is part of a cohesive team and another unit is excluded. According to the model, leaders develop unique working relationships with subordinates. As a result, in-groups and out-groups are created. Members of the in-group tend to perform better, have higher satisfaction, and exhibit more teamwork than members of the out-group. The leader's first impression of a group member's competency plays an important role in placing that person into the in-group or the out-group.

## KEY TERMS

| | | |
|---|---|---|
| Team | Micromanagement | Leader–member exchange |
| Teamwork | E-leadership | model (LMX) |
| Cooperation theory | Open-book management | |

## ✔ GUIDELINES FOR ACTION AND SKILL DEVELOPMENT

Improving teamwork through the design of offices is receiving considerable attention. Texas Professional Training Associates explains how to customize your (you being the leader/manager) space to promote teamwork:

1. **Create common areas.** Have ample space, accessible from throughout your office, for the team to meet formally and informally. Leave your team-meeting tools—flip charts,

whiteboards—in place even when the team is not meeting. Along these lines Global Crossing, the telecommunications network company, had a new building constructed recently. The building enables employees to collaborate more in a single, one-story space designed to encourage creative interaction and teamwork.

2. **Put yourself in the center.** Instead of reserving the back office, try to put yourself in the middle. You can be close to day-to-day action and more accessible to your team.

3. **Set up multipurpose rooms.** The back office can be used as a well-equipped workroom or library whenever team members—individually or in groups—feel they would be more productive away from their desks.

4. **Insert "activity generators."** Lively activity depends on having "generators" to draw traffic and bring people together. In your office, this could be the coffeepot, the mailboxes, or the reception desk. Turn these areas into places for team members to gather and interact comfortably and productively.[45]

### Discussion Questions and Activities

1. What would be the potential disadvantages of selecting a team leader who is highly charismatic and visionary?

2. Identify several collective work products from any group in which you have worked.

3. Imagine yourself as the team leader, and the gang invites you to join them for an after-hours drink at a bar. From the standpoint of enhancing teamwork, explain whether joining the team would be effective.

4. Is there a role for independent-thinking, decisive, and creative leaders in a team-based organization? Explain.

5. What forces for and against being a good team player are embedded in American culture?

6. As the team leader, should you dress in about the same fashion as the rest of the team? Or should you dress a little fancier? Explain your reasoning.

7. What can a team leader, who is a telecommuter, do to enhance teamwork among his or her team—who also are telecommuters?

8. What is your opinion of the value of experience in team sports for becoming a good team player in the workplace?

9. Why would the team-building activity of preparing a gourmet meal lead to enhanced teamwork back on the job?

10. How can political skill help a person avoid being adversely affected by the leader–member exchange model?

## Leadership Case Problem A

### Why Can't We Work Like a Real Team?

Crystal Motors is a new car dealer representing two U.S.-made luxury vehicles. Following the traditional organization structure of an automobile dealership, the company is divided into three segments: sales, service, and the office. The credit department is considered part of the office. Charlie Ventura is the president and owner of Crystal Motors, Marcie Magellan is manager of the service department, and Rob Waters is the office manager.

Crystal Motors has been profitable for ten consecutive years despite heavy competition from luxury foreign vehicles. About 10 percent of the company's profits stem directly from the sale of vehicles, 5 percent from commissions on financing, and about 85 percent from the service department. When asked about this imbalance in profits, Ventura explained, "It's the nature of the beast. When consumers see the sticker price on our vehicles, they think we're making a bundle on each one that we sell. The truth nationwide is that it is very difficult to make money on car sales alone. Commissions on vehicles financed through us help a little with profits, but our real margins come from service."

Ventura is looking to boost profits for the upcoming year. He thinks that it will be difficult to squeeze much more profit from sales. Ventura notes that his marketing budget is already quite high and that his sales staff is well trained and effective. He worries that the escalating cost of fuel and all the publicity about the negative impact of large vehicles on the environment will constrain sales for the next few years. As a consequence, Ventura thinks that his best chance for improving profit margins is to increase the efficiency of the service department. "Marcie and I agree that we have a long way to go to get our service department to get its act together," says Ventura.

The service department is divided into teams, each assigned a different color: green, blue, red, orange, and purple. After a customer purchases a vehicle, he or she is assigned to one of the color-coded teams. Magellan explains that each team is assigned a team leader who represents the face to the public and is also responsible for making sure the vehicle in question is serviced properly. All of the teams use the same centralized body shop.

When asked about the inefficiencies in the service department, Magellan's eyebrows rose. "My take is that a team is supposed to work together," she said. "Our technicians and general helpers work on their own without acting as if they are part of a true team. Just last week I got this ticked-off customer screaming at me. She told me that she found grease stains on the white leather seats of her $50,000 convertible. I asked Jason, the Green Team leader, what happened. He said it wasn't the team's fault because the person who is supposed to put protective paper inside the car before the vehicle is serviced didn't show up for work that day.

"I remember several times that a car wasn't cleaned and polished in time for the scheduled customer pickup. It's not too cool when you pick up a new $40,000 vehicle when there is caked mud on the bottom of the fenders. That time the Red Team leader told me that the car wash gal was overloaded the day the car was to be picked up by the customer."

Ventura commented that he has heard about instances in which poor cooperation has resulted in lost opportunities to generate revenues from repairs. "Here, let me show you a customer complaint card," said Ventura:

> Last week I had my car in for a lube, oil change, and tire rotation. I assumed that when I picked up my car, everything was okay. But two days later, I had this terrible vibration when I stepped on the brakes. I was so angry with Crystal Motors for not having found this problem that I went to Midas to get the brake work done.

"We found out later that the person who switched the tires on the car in question did see a bent rod under the car, but figured that the team leader was responsible for finding problems. So he didn't report the problem."

Magellan agreed that teamwork could stand improvement in the service department. She said, "I guess we need to work more like a pit crew, and less like a bunch of guys and gals just coming to work and doing their jobs."

## Questions

1. What do you recommend that leadership at Crystal Motors do to enhance teamwork in the service department?
2. What different contributions might Ventura and Magellan make in enhancing teamwork in the service department?
3. What do you recommend that the team leaders do to get the service technicians and general workers to cooperate better with each other?
4. In what way is a pit crew an effective team?

## Leadership Case Problem B

### Over the Top at Bell ExpressVu

Fran Boutilier and Alison Green kicked butt when they went to work for Bell ExpressVu. The first female senior executives at the satellite TV delivery service, they surpassed the performance of their male predecessors, posting better results and earning shares and praise respectively from Bell Canada's top boss, Michael Sabia, the two say in sworn court documents.

But one day, at an executive retreat, the two women refused to kick or be kicked. In documents filed in a civil lawsuit alleging gender discrimination in the workplace by their former employers, the women say they had to put up with a macho corporate culture that included sexist, vulgar language and being frozen out of drinking sessions with the "boy's club." The company denies that the women were subjected to discrimination.

A July 2005 offsite retreat, organized around a martial arts theme, was "over the top," Green said in an interview. They were assigned *The Art of War* to read. "War music" was playing. "We had to wear war paraphernalia . . . bandannas, costumes, and props," Boutilier said. And they were expected to participate in a judo class.

"I'm from New York," says Green. "I'm used to crazy things. What shocked me was Fran and I were both in business attire. We both wore high heels, stockings, and skirts." Boutilier paired off with a third woman who was there from a different arm of Bell Canada. Green says she refused to pair off with a man to practice kicks, punches, and chokeholds.

"It was full body contact," she says. "There was no way. . . . I kind of feigned injury and said that I couldn't do it. I mean that's rule 101. No bodily contact between male and female employees."

Not long after that, the two women separately earned the dubious distinction of being the company's first two female VPs to be fired. In a statement of defense filed in the civil suit, the company says that "Bell Canada actively promotes diversity in its work force, including the equal treatment of employees regardless of gender, and does not tolerate discrimination in the workplace based on sex." The company says the women were not subject to discrimination, but were fired because of concerns about their management performance.

The company counters the concerns about the martial arts retreat, saying a woman organized it, and that it included a poster-painting exercise to express creativity. Boutilier, the company claims, did not address call volume problems in her area. Bell notes that Boutilier was not replaced by a man, but by a woman. The company says Green was overly aggressive in dealing with subordinates and resisted offers of coaching.

### Questions

1. What does this story about the fired executives have to do with team building?
2. Based on the descriptions provided by Boutilier and Green, how professionally was the retreat conducted?
3. What recommendations might you offer management at Bell ExpressVu for offsite, team-building activities?

*Source:* Excerpted from Tonda MacCharles, "Ex-Bell Execs Allege Sexism," *The Toronto Star* (thestar.com), January 14, 2008.

Leadership Skill-Building Exercise 9-4

## My Leadership Portfolio

Now that you have studied a basketful of ideas about enhancing teamwork, you can add to your skill repertoire by implementing a few of these tactics. The next time you are involved in group activity, as either the leader or a group member, attempt to enhance cooperation and teamwork within the group. Make specific use of at least two of the recommended tactics for improving teamwork. Make an entry in your journal after your first attempts to enhance teamwork. Here is an example:

I am the head of the Hispanic Business Club at our college. Attendance hasn't been too great in recent meetings, and the club seems headed nowhere. So at our last meeting, I suggested that we devote the entire meeting to building a mission statement. I explained that if we knew what our purpose was, maybe we would pull together better. We are still working on the mission, but so far it has to do with enhancing the impact and reputation of Hispanic business leaders. I also suggested that we invest in T-shirts with a logo we could be proud of. This idea may sound hokey, but the group really rallied around the idea of building unity through new T-shirts.

## Internet Skill-Building Exercise

### Are Team Leadership Skills or Teamwork Skills in Demand?

Here is a reality check about the demand for team leadership skills and teamwork skills. Visit www.hotjobs.yahoo.com and search under various job categories of potential interest to you, such as operations, or sales, or advertising. Continue until you locate the actual jobs and job descriptions. This will take a little digging because not every employer provides a description of the qualifications needed for the position. Your specific assignment is to locate two jobs that mention the requirement of "team leadership skills," or "teamwork skills." A particular qualification might imply such skills, such as "the ability to coordinate the efforts of others."

After you complete your search, reflect on whether employers are explicit about wanting team leadership skills and teamwork skills. Even if this assignment does not proceed smoothly, you will attain the side benefit of seeing what kind of *hot jobs* exist that fit your qualifications.

Apply the chapter concepts! Visit the Web, and complete this Internet skill-building exercise to learn more about current leadership topics and trends.

## CHAPTER 10

# Motivation and Coaching Skills

## LEARNING OBJECTIVES

After studying this chapter and doing the exercises, you should be able to

- Identify and describe leadership skills linked to expectancy theory.
- Describe goal theory.
- Describe how leaders can motivate others through recognition.
- Describe how leaders can motivate using social equity theory.
- Understand the characteristics of coaching and how to practice coaching skills and techniques.
- Describe how executive coaches help enhance leadership skills.

## CHAPTER OUTLINE

**Expectancy Theory and Motivational Skills**
Basic Components of Expectancy Theory
Leadership Skills and Behaviors Associated with Expectancy Theory

**Goal Theory**
Basic Findings of Goal Theory
Underlying Mechanisms and Concerns

**Using Recognition and Pride to Motivate Others**
Appealing to the Recognition Need of Others
Appealing to Pride
Equity Theory and Social Comparison

**Coaching as an Approach to Motivation**
Key Characteristics of Coaching
Fallacies About Coaching

**Coaching Skills and Techniques**

**Executive Coaching and Leadership Effectiveness**
Specific Forms of Assistance Provided by Executive Coaches
Contributions of and Concerns About Executive Coaching

**Summary**

On a warm night in early October, David Brandon stepped into a brightly lit Domino's Pizza franchise in Olive Branch, Mississippi, a little town just south of the Tennessee state line. The CEO of the Ann Arbor, Michigan–based pizza giant fished a $100 bill from his wallet, stuck it above the pepperoni and cheese, stepped back and grinned. His challenge: The C-note for the employee who could make a large pizza with the company-prescribed amount of pepperoni—forty to fifty pieces—the fastest.

With stopwatch in hand and his dark blue suit within reach of the floury cloud of pizza making, Brandon's competitive nature, accessible personality, and hands-on approach to running Domino's Pizza Inc. were on full display. Nearly eight years after the former University of Michigan backup quarterback took the helm, Brandon has unleashed Domino's once hidebound patriarchal culture and created an energized, fast-growing company.

Watching him in action, Brandon appears every bit a business leader hitting his stride—high energy, goal oriented and, above all, people focused. On the flight down, he personally served Sprite, orange juice, and salad to passengers on the company jet. Nearly every New Year's Eve—one of pizza's busiest nights—he works a Domino's, stretching dough and spreading cheese.

Brandon is being touted as a possible candidate to run for governor of Michigan, and he is also a front-line player in the effort to rejuvenate southeast Michigan.[1]

This story about a well-known business executive illustrates how a motivational leader can help move an organization forward. Some people might think that giving a $100 reward to the fastest pizza maker is a little hokey, but the technique does have the effect of showing that the CEO cares about revving up performance. Effective leaders are outstanding motivators and coaches. They influence others in many of the ways previously described. In addition, they often use specific motivational and coaching skills. These techniques are important because not all leaders can influence others through formal authority or charisma and inspirational leadership alone. Face-to-face, day-by-day motivational skills are also important. Good coaching is a related essential feature of management because motivating workers is an important part of coaching them. During a coaching session, the leader will often attempt to motivate the person being coached.

In this chapter we approach motivation and coaching skills from various perspectives. We examine first how leaders make effective use of expectancy theory, recognition, goal setting, and equity theory to motivate group members. Second, we describe coaching, including a description of specific coaching skills and the role of the executive coach. Most readers of this book have already studied motivation, so here we describe how it is possible to apply a few popular motivation theories rather than repeat a discussion of theories you have already studied, such as reinforcement theory or Maslow's need hierarchy.

Before reading about several approaches to worker motivation, you are invited to take Leadership Self-Assessment Quiz 10-1, which deals with your understanding of motivation.

**Leadership Self-Assessment Quiz 10-1**

## My Approach to Motivating Others

*Instructions:* Describe how often you act or think in the way indicated by the following statements when you are attempting to motivate another person. Scale: very infrequently (VI); infrequently (I); sometimes (S); frequently (F); very frequently (VF).

|  | VI | I | S | F | VF |
|---|---|---|---|---|---|
| 1. I ask the other person what he or she is hoping to achieve in the situation. | 1 | 2 | 3 | 4 | 5 |
| 2. I attempt to figure out if the person has the ability to do what I need done. | 1 | 2 | 3 | 4 | 5 |
| 3. When another person is heel dragging, it usually means he or she is lazy. | 5 | 4 | 3 | 2 | 1 |
| 4. I explain exactly what I want to the person I am trying to motivate. | 1 | 2 | 3 | 4 | 5 |
| 5. I like to give the other person a reward up front so he or she will be motivated. | 5 | 4 | 3 | 2 | 1 |
| 6. I give lots of feedback when another person is performing a task for me. | 1 | 2 | 3 | 4 | 5 |
| 7. I like to belittle another person enough so that he or she will be intimidated into doing what I need done. | 5 | 4 | 3 | 2 | 1 |
| 8. I make sure that the other person feels fairly treated. | 1 | 2 | 3 | 4 | 5 |
| 9. I figure that if I smile nicely, I can get the other person to work as hard as I do. | 5 | 4 | 3 | 2 | 1 |
| 10. I attempt to get what I need done by instilling fear in the other person. | 5 | 4 | 3 | 2 | 1 |
| 11. I specify exactly what needs to be accomplished. | 1 | 2 | 3 | 4 | 5 |
| 12. I generously praise people who help me get my work accomplished. | 1 | 2 | 3 | 4 | 5 |
| 13. A job well done is its own reward. I therefore keep praise to a minimum. | 5 | 4 | 3 | 2 | 1 |
| 14. I make sure to let people know how well they have done in meeting my expectations on a task. | 1 | 2 | 3 | 4 | 5 |
| 15. To be fair, I attempt to reward people similarly no matter how well they have performed. | 5 | 4 | 3 | 2 | 1 |
| 16. When somebody doing work for me performs well, I recognize his or her accomplishments promptly. | 1 | 2 | 3 | 4 | 5 |
| 17. Before giving somebody a reward, I attempt to find out what would appeal to that person. | 1 | 2 | 3 | 4 | 5 |

## Quiz 10-1 (continued)

| | VI | I | S | F | VF |
|---|---|---|---|---|---|
| **18.** I make it a policy not to thank somebody for doing a job he or she is paid to do. | 5 | 4 | 3 | 2 | 1 |
| **19.** If people do not know how to perform a task, motivation will suffer. | 1 | 2 | 3 | 4 | 5 |
| **20.** If properly laid out, many jobs can be self-rewarding. | 1 | 2 | 3 | 4 | 5 |

Total score: _____

*Scoring and Interpretation:* Add the circled numbers to obtain your total score.

- **90–100:** You have advanced knowledge and skill with respect to motivating others in a work environment. Continue to build on the solid base you have established.

- **50–89:** You have average knowledge and skill with respect to motivating others. With additional study and experience, you will probably develop advanced motivational skills.

- **20–49:** To effectively motivate others in a work environment, you will need to greatly expand your knowledge of motivation theory and techniques.

*Source:* The general idea for this quiz comes from David Whetton and Kim Cameron, *Developing Management Skills,* 5th ed. (Upper Saddle River, N.J.: Prentice Hall, 2002), pp. 302–303.

## EXPECTANCY THEORY AND MOTIVATIONAL SKILLS

Expectancy theory is a good starting point in learning how leaders can apply systematic explanations of motivation, for two major reasons. First, the theory is comprehensive: it incorporates and integrates features of other motivation theories, including goal theory and behavior modification. Second, it offers the leader many guidelines for triggering and sustaining constructive effort from group members.

The **expectancy theory** of motivation is based on the premise that the amount of effort people expend depends on how much reward they expect to get in return. In addition to being broad, the theory deals with cognition and process. Expectancy theory is cognitive because it emphasizes the thoughts, judgments, and desires of the person being motivated. It is a process theory because it attempts to explain how motivation takes place.

The theory is really a group of theories based on a rational, economic view of people.[2] In any given situation, people want to maximize gain and minimize loss. The theory assumes that they choose among alternatives by selecting the one they think they have the best chance of attaining. Furthermore, they choose the alternative that appears to have the biggest personal payoff. Given a choice, people will select the assignment they think they can handle the best and will benefit them the most.

## Basic Components of Expectancy Theory

Expectancy theory contains three basic components: valence, instrumentality, and expectancy. Because of these three components, the theory is often referred to as VIE theory. Figure 10-1 presents a basic version of expectancy theory. All three elements must be present for motivation to take place. To be motivated, people must value the reward, think they can perform, and have reasonable assurance that their performance will lead to a reward.

*Valence*   The worth or attractiveness of an outcome is referred to as **valence**. As shown in Figure 10-1, each work situation has multiple outcomes. An **outcome** is anything that might stem from performance, such as a reward. Each outcome has a valence of its own. And each outcome can lead to other outcomes or consequences, referred to as *second-level outcomes*. A person who receives an outstanding performance evaluation (a first-level outcome) becomes eligible for a promotion (a second-level outcome). Second-level outcomes also have valences. The sum of all the valences must be positive if the person is to work hard. If the sum of all of the valences is negative, the person might work hard to avoid the outcome.

Valences range from –100 to +100 in the version of expectancy theory presented here. (The usual method of placing valences on a –1.00 to +1.00 scale does not do justice to the true differences in preferences.) A valence of 100 means that a person intensely desires an outcome. A valence of –100 means that a person is strongly motivated to avoid an outcome such as being fired or declaring bankruptcy. A valence of zero signifies indifference to an outcome and is therefore of no use as a motivator.

An example of using negative and positive valence at the same time would be for the CEO to use data to point out how bleak the company will become if it does not change, and how wonderful the company will become if it does change. Jack and Suzy Welch recommend, "Contrast plant closings with growth opportunities at home and abroad, lost jobs with more interesting work, and flat or shrinking wages with more money for everyone."[3]

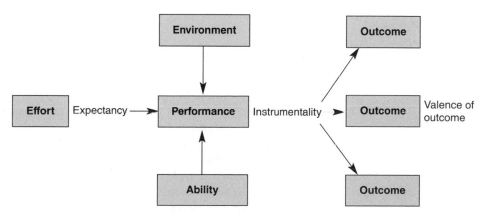

**FIGURE 10-1** The Expectancy Theory of Motivation.

***Instrumentality***   An individual's assessment of the probability that performance will lead to certain outcomes is referred to as **instrumentality.** (An instrumentality is also referred to as a *performance-to-outcome expectancy* because it relates to the outcome people expect from performing in a certain way.) When people engage in a particular behavior, they do so with the intention of achieving a desired outcome or reward. Instrumentalities range from 0 to 1.0, where 0 is no chance of receiving the desired reward and 1.0 is a belief that the reward is certain to follow. For example, an hourly worker might say, "I know for sure that if I work overtime, I will receive overtime pay."

***Expectancy***   An individual's assessment of the probability that effort will lead to correct performance of the task is referred to as **expectancy.** (The same concept is also referred to as *effort-to-performance expectancy*.) An important question people ask themselves before putting forth effort to accomplish a task is, "If I put in all this work, will I really get the job done properly?" Expectancies range from 0 to 1.0, where 0 is no expectation of performing the tasks correctly, and 1.0 signifies absolute faith in being able to perform the task properly. Expectancies thus influence whether a person will even strive to earn a reward. Self-confident people have higher expectancies than do less self-confident people. Being well trained increases a person's subjective sense that he or she can perform the task.

The importance of having high expectancies for motivation meshes well with a current thrust in work motivation that emphasizes the contribution of **self-efficacy**, the confidence in your ability to carry out a specific task. If you have high self-efficacy about the task, your motivation will be high. Low self-efficacy leads to low motivation. Some people are poorly motivated to skydive because they doubt they will be able to pull the ripcord while free-falling at 120 mph.

In short, if you are confident about your task-related skills, you will get your act together to do the task. This is one reason that you should give people the skills and confidence they need to put forth effort.

An apparent contradiction in expectancy theory requires explanation. Some people will engage in behaviors with low expectancies, such as trying to invent a successful new product or become the CEO of a major corporation. The compensating factor is the large valences attached to the second-level outcomes associated with these accomplishments. The payoffs from introducing a successful new product or becoming a CEO are so great that people are willing to take a long shot.

***A Brief Look at the Evidence***   The application of expectancy theory, especially the VIE version, to work motivation has been the subject of research for close to forty years. Two researchers performed a meta-analysis of seventy-seven studies examining how well various aspects of expectancy theory were related to workplace criteria such as performance and effort. Although the results were not consistent, the general conclusion reached was that the three components of expectancy theory are positively related to workplace criteria. For example, job performance showed a positive correlation with valence, instrumentality, expectancy, and the total VIE model. The total VIE model typically refers to a multiplication of the values for valence, instrumentality, and expectancy. Another finding was that effort expended on the job was positively correlated with valence, instrumentality, expectancy, the VIE model, and performance.[4] The last correlation helps verify the justification for leaders' and managers' concern about motivating employees: People who try harder perform better!

## Leadership Skills and Behaviors Associated with Expectancy Theory

Expectancy theory has many implications for leaders and managers with respect to motivating others.[5] Some of these implications also stem from other motivational theories, and they fit good management practice in general. As you read each implication, reflect on how you might apply the skill or behavior during a leadership assignment.

**1. *Determine what levels and kinds of performance are needed to achieve organizational goals.*** Motivating others proceeds best when workers have a clear understanding of what needs to be accomplished. At the same time, the leader should make sure that the desired levels of performance are possible. For example, sales quotas might be set too high because the market is already saturated with a particular product or service.

**2. *Make the performance level attainable by the individuals being motivated.*** If the group members believe that they are being asked to perform extraordinarily difficult tasks, most of them will suffer from low motivation. A task must generally be perceived as attainable to be motivational.

**3. *Train and encourage people.*** Leaders should give group members the necessary training and encouragement to be confident they can perform the required task. Some group members who appear to be poorly motivated simply lack the right skills and self-confidence.

**4. *Make explicit the link between rewards and performance.*** Group members should be reassured that if they perform the job to standard, they will receive the promised reward.

**5. *Make sure the rewards are large enough.*** Some rewards that are the right kind fail to motivate people because they are not in the right amount. The promise of a large salary increase might be motivational, but a 1 percent increase will probably have little motivational thrust for most workers.

**6. *Analyze what factors work in opposition to the effectiveness of the reward.*** Conflicts between the leader's package of rewards and other influences in the work group may require the leader to modify the reward. For example, if the work group favors the status quo, a large reward may be required to encourage innovative thinking.

**7. *Explain the meaning and implications of second-level outcomes.*** It is helpful for employees to understand the value of certain outcomes, such as receiving a favorable performance evaluation. (For example, it could lead to a salary increase, assignment to a high-status task force, or promotion.)

8. *Understand individual differences in valences.* To motivate group members effectively, leaders must recognize individual differences or preferences for rewards. An attempt should be made to offer workers rewards to which they attach a high valence. One employee might value a high-adventure assignment; another might attach a high valence to a routine, tranquil assignment. Cross-cultural differences in valences may also occur. For example, many (but not all) Asian workers prefer not to be singled out for recognition in front of the group. According to their cultural values, receiving recognition in front of the group is insensitive and embarrassing. Another example is that gift certificates for stores might have more valence in the United States than in Italy, where workers may prefer a small fashion boutique. Leadership Skill-Building Exercise 10-1 deals with the challenge of estimating valences.

9. *Recognize that when workers are in a positive mood, high valences, instrumentalities, and expectancies are more likely to lead to good performance.* An experiment with college students indicated that participants in a positive mood performed better, were more persistent, tried harder, and reported higher levels of motivation than those in a neutral mood. The positive affect made awards appear more attractive (higher valence). Being in a good mood also strengthened the link between performance and outcome (instrumentality), as well as between effort and performance (expectancy).[6] A note of caution is that the mood elevator in this experiment was a bag of candy. A manager might need more sustainable methods of increasing positive affect. Being able to keep employees in a good mood is an advanced application of emotional intelligence.

# GOAL THEORY

Goal setting is a basic process that is directly or indirectly part of all major theories of work motivation. Leaders and managers widely accept goal setting as a means to improve and sustain performance. A vision, for example, is really an exalted goal. To inspire his workers, Doug Ducey, the founder of the ice cream chain Cold Stone Creamery, formulated the vision "The world will know us as the ultimate ice cream experience." Ducey believes that the vision helped his company grow to from 74 stores to 1,000 stores during a five-year period.[7]

The core finding of goal theory is that individuals who are provided with specific hard goals perform better than those who are given easy, nonspecific, "do your best" goals or no goals. At the same time, however, the individuals must have sufficient ability, accept the goals, and receive feedback related to the task.[8] Our overview of goal theory elaborates on this basic finding.

## Basic Findings of Goal Theory

The premise underlying goal theory (or goal-setting theory) is that behavior is regulated by values and goals. A **goal** is what a person is trying to accomplish. Our values create within us a desire to behave in a way that is consistent with

⊙ Leadership Skill-Building Exercise 10-1

## Estimating Valences for Applying Expectancy Theory

***Instructions:*** A major challenge in applying expectancy theory is estimating what valence attaches to possible outcomes. A leader or manager also has to be aware of the potential rewards or punishment in a given work situation. Listed are a group of rewards and punishments, along with a space for rating the reward or punishment on a scale of –100 to +100. Work with about six teammates, with each person rating all of the rewards and punishments.

| Potential Outcome | Rating (–100 to +100) |
|---|---|
| 1. Promotion to vice president | _____ |
| 2. One-step promotion | _____ |
| 3. Above-average performance evaluation | _____ |
| 4. Top-category performance evaluation | _____ |
| 5. $7,000 performance bonus | _____ |
| 6. $3,000 performance bonus | _____ |
| 7. $100 gift certificate | _____ |
| 8. Employee-of-the-month plaque | _____ |
| 9. Note of appreciation sent by email and placed in file | _____ |
| 10. Lunch with boss at good restaurant | _____ |
| 11. Lunch with boss in company cafeteria | _____ |
| 12. Challenging new assignment | _____ |
| 13. Allowed to accumulate frequent flyer miles for own use | _____ |
| 14. Allowed to purchase software of choice | _____ |
| 15. Assigned new equipment for own use | _____ |
| 16. Private corner office with great view | _____ |
| 17. Assigned a full-time administrative assistant | _____ |
| 18. Documentation of poor performance | _____ |
| 19. Being fired | _____ |
| 20. Being fired and put on industry "bad list" | _____ |
| 21. Demoted one step | _____ |
| 22. Demoted to entry-level position | _____ |
| 23. Being ridiculed in front of others | _____ |
| 24. Being suspended without pay | _____ |
| 25. Being transferred to undesirable location | _____ |

After completing the ratings, discuss the following issues:

1. Which rewards and punishments received the most varied ratings?
2. Which rewards and punishments received similar ratings?

Another analytical approach would be to compute the means and standard deviations of the valences for each outcome. Each class member could then compare his or her own valence ratings with the class norm. To add to the database, each student might bring back two sets of ratings from employed people who are not in the class.

To apply this technique to the job, modify this form to fit the outcomes available in your situation. Explain to team members that you are attempting to do a better job of rewarding and disciplining and that you need their thoughts. The ratings made by team members might provide fruitful discussion for a staff meeting.

them. For example, a leader who values honesty will establish a goal of hiring only honest employees. The leader would therefore have to make extensive use of reference checks and honesty testing. Edwin A. Locke and Gary P. Latham have incorporated hundreds of studies about goals into a theory of goal setting and task performance.[9] Figure 10-2 summarizes some of the more consistent findings, and the information that follows describes them. A leader should keep these points in mind when motivating people through goal setting.

To begin, remember that *specific goals lead to higher performance than do generalized goals*. Telling someone to "do your best" is a generalized goal. A specific goal would be, "Increase the number of new hires to our management training program to fifteen for this summer." Another key point is that *performance generally improves in direct proportion to goal difficulty*. The harder one's goal is, the more one accomplishes. An important exception is that when goals are too difficult, they may lower performance. Difficulty in reaching the goal leads to frustration, which in turn leads to lowered performance (as explained in relation to expectancy theory).

The finding about effective goals being realistic has an important exception for the accomplishment of high-level complex tasks. Effective leaders often inspire constituents by framing goals in terms of a noble cause or something heroic. The

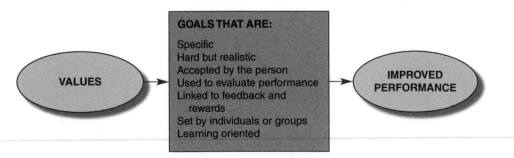

**FIGURE 10-2** Goal Theory.

manager of a group that made photo printers, for example, might explain that making high-quality printers enables people to preserve their memories.[10] Here are two suggestions for developing noble powerful goals:

- Create a big, comprehensive goal: an ideal accomplishment for your group.
- Break the goal down into smaller steps, such as hiring two top-notch workers for the group. Regard each step (or subgoal) as a project designed to get you to your destination.[11] The same approach has been referred to as "running sprints rather than marathons."

*For goals to improve performance, the group member must accept them.* If a group member rejects a goal, he or she will not incorporate it into planning. This is why it is often helpful to discuss goals with group members rather than impose goals on them. More recent research, however, suggests that the importance of goal commitment may be overrated. A meta-analysis of mostly laboratory studies about the effect of goal commitment on performance concluded that commitment had a small impact on performance. Goals appeared to improve performance whether or not people participating in the studies felt committed to them.[12] Despite these recent findings, many managers and leaders think employee commitment to goals is important.

Participating in goal setting has no major effect on the level of job performance except when it improves goal acceptance. Yet the leader should recognize that participation is valuable because it can lead to higher satisfaction with the goal-setting process. *Goals are more effective when they are used to evaluate performance.* When workers know that their performance will be evaluated in terms of how well they attain their goals, the impact of goals increases.

Keep in mind the key principle that *goals should be linked to feedback and rewards*. Rewarding people for reaching goals is the most widely accepted principle of management. Another goal-setting principle is that *group goal setting is as important as individual goal setting*. Having employees work as teams with a specific team goal, rather than as individuals with only individual goals, increases productivity. Furthermore, a combination of compatible group and individual goals is more effective than either individual or group goals alone.

A final goal-setting principle is that a *learning goal orientation* improves performance more than a *performance goal orientation* does. A person with a learning (or mastery) goal orientation wants to develop competence by acquiring new skills and mastering new situations. In contrast, the person with a performance goal orientation wants to demonstrate and validate his or her competence by seeking favorable judgments and avoiding negative judgments. In support of the distinction being made, a study with medical supply sales representatives found that a learning goal orientation had a positive relationship with sales performance. In contrast, a performance goal orientation was unrelated to sales performance.[13]

## Underlying Mechanisms and Concerns

Despite their contribution to performance, goals are not motivational in themselves. Rather, the discrepancies created by what individuals do and what they aspire to

**Leadership Skill-Building Exercise 10-2**

### The Application of Goal Theory

In a group of about five to six people, visualize your group as a task force whose mission is to make and implement suggestions for reducing water consumption in your company, a manufacturer of camping equipment. Water is a major company expense, and there is a distinct possibility that the county in which you are located will soon be rationing water. One of the group members plays the role of the task force leader. The leader must help the group establish goals that are likely to be motivational, following the principles of goal theory.

The goal of today's meeting is to establish four goals that are likely to lead to high performance. After each team has established its goals, present them to other class members. Students listening to the goals of the other groups should be willing to offer constructive feedback.

Practice in setting effective goals is useful because leaders and managers are frequently expected to set goals. When the goal follows at least some of the major findings of goal theory, there is a greater likelihood that productivity will increase.

creates self-dissatisfaction, which in turn creates a desire to reduce the discrepancy between the real and the ideal.[14] A person who has a desire to attain something is in a state of arousal. The tension created by not having already achieved a goal spurs the person to reach the goal. As a leader, you can sometimes create this tension by suggesting possibilities that group members might strive for.

A major concern about using goals to motivate performance is that leaders, as well as other workers, will take unethical and dysfunctional shortcuts to attain their goals. For example, a CEO might drastically reduce investment in research and development and lay off too many valuable workers to meet a profit goal such as earnings per share. Also, managers have been known to engage in unethical behavior such as shipping unfinished products to reach sales goals.[15]

Goal setting is widely practiced by leaders and managers, but they typically do not give careful consideration to goal-setting theory. Leadership Skill-Building Exercise 10-2 gives you an opportunity to apply what you have learned about goal setting.

**⊗ Knowledge Bank**
Describes how behavior modification is used to motivate workers. Many of you who have studied organizational behavior, human relations, or the first course in psychology have some knowledge of behavior modification.
**www.cengage.com/ management/dubrin**

## USING RECOGNITION AND PRIDE TO MOTIVATE OTHERS

Motivating others by giving them recognition and praise can be considered a direct application of positive reinforcement, that is, reinforcing the right behavior by giving a reward. Nevertheless, recognition is such a potentially powerful motivator that it merits separate attention. Also, recognition programs to reward and motivate employees are a standard practice in business and nonprofit firms. An example is rewarding high-performing employees with a crystal vase (company logo inscribed) or designating them "employee of the month." Pride, as described next, is related to recognition. People who are proud of their work want to be recognized for their good deeds.

Recognition is a strong motivator because it is a normal human need. To think through the strength of your own need for recognition, take Leadership Self-Assessment Quiz 10-2. Recognition is also effective because most workers feel they do not receive enough recognition. Several studies conducted over a fifty-five-year time span have indicated that employees welcome praise for a job well done as

 **Leadership Self-Assessment Quiz 10-2**

### How Much Do I Crave Recognition?

***Instructions:*** Respond to the following statements on the following scale: disagree strongly (DS), disagree (D), neutral (N), agree (A), and agree strongly (AS).

| | DS | D | N | A | AS |
|---|---|---|---|---|---|
| 1. I keep (or would keep) almost every plaque, medal, or trophy I have ever received on display in my living quarters. | 1 | 2 | 3 | 4 | 5 |
| 2. I feel a nice warm glow each time somebody praises my efforts. | 1 | 2 | 3 | 4 | 5 |
| 3. When somebody tells me "nice job," it makes my day. | 1 | 2 | 3 | 4 | 5 |
| 4. When I compliment someone, I am really looking for a compliment in return. | 1 | 2 | 3 | 4 | 5 |
| 5. I would rather win an "employee-of-the-month" award than receive a $50 bonus for my good work. | 1 | 2 | 3 | 4 | 5 |
| 6. If I had the resources to make a large donation to charity, I would never make the donation anonymously. | 1 | 2 | 3 | 4 | 5 |
| 7. Thinking back to my childhood, I adored receiving a gold star or similar acknowledgment from my teacher for my good work. | 1 | 2 | 3 | 4 | 5 |
| 8. I would rather be designated as *Time* magazine's Person of the Year than be one of the world's richest people. | 1 | 2 | 3 | 4 | 5 |
| 9. I love to see my name in print. | 1 | 2 | 3 | 4 | 5 |
| 10. I do not receive all the respect I deserve. | 1 | 2 | 3 | 4 | 5 |

**Total score:** _____

***Scoring and Interpretation:*** Add the circled numbers to obtain your total score.

- **45–50:** You have an above-average recognition need. Recognition is therefore a strong motivator for you. You will be happiest in a job where you can be recognized for your good deeds.
- **25–44**: You have an average need for recognition and do not require constant reminders that you have done a good job.
- **10–24:** You have a below-average need for recognition and like to have your good deeds speak for themselves. When you do receive recognition, you would prefer that it be quite specific to what you have done, and not too lavish. You would feel comfortable in a work setting with mostly technical people.

much as they welcome a regular paycheck. For example, in one study it was found that 66 percent of employees named appreciation as their most important motivator.[16] This finding should not be interpreted to mean that praise is an adequate substitute for salary. Employees tend to regard compensation as an entitlement, whereas recognition is perceived as a gift.[17] Workers, including your coworkers, want to know that their output is useful to somebody.

## Appealing to the Recognition Need of Others

To appeal to the recognition need of others, identify a meritorious behavior, and then recognize that behavior with an oral, written, or material reward. Three examples of using recognition to sustain desired behavior (a key aspect of motivation) follow:

- As the team leader, you receive a glowing letter from a customer about Kent, one of your team members, who solved the customer's problem. You have the letter laminated and present it as a gift to Kent. (The behavior you are reinforcing is good customer service.)
- One member of your department, Jason, is a mechanical engineer. While at a department lunch taking place during National Engineers Week, you stand up and say, "I want to toast Jason in celebration of National Engineers Week. I certainly would not want to be sitting in this office building today if a mechanical engineer had not assisted in its construction." (Here, the only behavior you are reinforcing is the goodwill of Jason, so your motivational approach is general, not specific.)
- A sales manager of a real estate firm in Florida distributes to employees a file folder labeled "Success File." Whenever employees accomplish something special, she writes them a letter of appreciation and suggests that they file it in their Success File. Later, if they encounter rough spots in their work, they can reread the letters to remind themselves how much they are appreciated. (Recognition here is being used to both reward people for what they have accomplished and to reenergize people based on previous recognition.)[18]

An outstanding advantage of recognition, including praise, as a motivator is that it is no cost or low cost yet powerful. Reward expert Bob Nelson reminds us that while money is important to employees, thoughtful recognition motivates them to elevate their performance.[19] Recognition thus has an enormous return on investment in comparison to a cash bonus.

A challenge in using recognition effectively is that not everyone responds well to the same form of recognition. An example is that highly technical people tend not to like general praise like "Great job" or "Awesome, baby." Instead, they prefer a laid-back, factual statement of how their work made a contribution. According to one study, the more highly a person sees himself or herself as having a technical orientation, the more the person wants praise to be quite specific and task oriented.[20] The tech center worker who just conquered a virus on your desktop would prefer a compliment such as, "I appreciated your having disabled the virus and restored my computer to full functioning." This type of compliment would be preferable to, "Fantastic, you are a world-class virus fighter."

To maximize its motivational impact, recognition should be linked to corporate values and should also help workers attain personal goals. Visualize a security guard whose outside passion is sustaining the environment who becomes recognized with the new title of Security and Energy Conservation Monitor. The title combines his interest in saving energy with the company's interest in keeping outside doors closed and unusual lights turned off.[21]

Executive coach Marshall Goldsmith offers this advice to leaders who choose to use positive recognition as a motivator:

1. Compose a list of all of the important people in your life.
2. Write down the name of every important person within each group.
3. Review the list twice a week and ask, "Did someone on this page do something that I should recognize?"
4. For each affirmative answer, give quick recognition either by email, text messaging, voice mail, or a paper note. If the answer is negative, do nothing.

Within one year, you will have developed a reputation for giving positive recognition.[22] At the same time, you will have motivated many people in the process.

## Appealing to Pride

Wanting to feel proud motivates many workers, and giving recognition for a job well done helps satisfy this desire to feel proud. Being proud of what you accomplish is more of an internal (intrinsic) motivator than an external (extrinsic) motivator such as receiving a gift. Giving workers an opportunity to experience pride can therefore be a strong internal motivator yet they simultaneously receive recognition.

Imagine that you are the assistant service manager at a company that customizes recreational vehicles to meet the requirements of individual clients. Your manager asks you to prepare a PowerPoint presentation of trends in customization for people who live most of the year in their RVs. You make your presentation to top management, the group applauds, executives shake your hand, and later you receive several congratulatory email messages. One of the many emotions you experience is likely to be pride in having performed well. You are motivated to keep up the good work.

Workers can also experience pride in relation to recognition symbols. For example, a worker might receive a floor clock for having saved the company thousands of dollars in shipping costs. The clock might be more valuable to the worker as a symbol of accomplishment than as a household decoration. The feeling of pride stems from having accomplished a worthwhile activity (saving the company money) rather than from being awarded a floor clock.

According to consultant Jon R. Katzenbach, managers and leaders can take steps to motivate through pride. A key tactic is for the manager to set his or her compass on pride, not money. It is more important for workers to be proud of what they are doing day by day than for them to be proud of reaching a major goal. The manager should celebrate "steps" (or attaining small goals) as much as the "landings" (the major goal). The most effective pride builders are masters at identifying and recognizing the small achievements that will instill pride in their people.[23]

## Equity Theory and Social Comparison

Expectancy theory, as described earlier, emphasizes the rational and thinking side of people. Similarly, another theory focuses on how fairly people think they are being treated in comparison to certain reference groups. According to **equity theory**, employee satisfaction and motivation depend on how fairly the employees believe they are treated in comparison to peers. The theory contends that employees hold certain beliefs about the outcomes they receive from their jobs, as well as the inputs they invest to obtain these outcomes.

The outcomes of employment include pay, benefits, status, recognition, intrinsic job factors, and anything else stemming from the job that workers perceive as useful. The inputs include all the factors that employees perceive as being their investment in the job or anything of value that they bring to the job. These inputs include job qualifications, skills, education level, effort, trust in the company, support of coworkers, and cooperative behavior.

The core of equity theory is that employees compare their inputs and outcomes (making social comparisons) with others in the workplace.[24] If employees believe that they receive equitable outcomes in relation to their inputs, they are generally satisfied and motivated. When workers believe that they are being treated equitably, they are more willing to work hard. Conversely, when employees believe that they give too much as compared to what they receive from the organization, a state of tension, dissatisfaction, and demotivation ensues. The people used for reference are those whom the employee perceives as relevant for comparison. For example, an industrial sales representative would make comparisons with other industrial sales reps in the same industry about whom he has information.

There are two kinds of comparisons. People consider their own inputs in relation to outcomes received, and they also evaluate what others receive for the same inputs. Equity is said to exist when an individual concludes that his or her own outcome/input ratio is equal to that of other people. Inequity exists if the person's ratio is not the same as that of other people. All these comparisons are similar to those judgments made by people according to expectancy theory—they are subjective hunches that may or may not be valid. Inequity can be in either direction and of varying magnitude. The equity ratio is often expressed as follows:

$$\frac{\text{Outcomes of Individual}}{\text{Inputs of Individual}} \quad \text{compared to} \quad \frac{\text{Outcomes of Others}}{\text{Inputs of Others}}$$

According to equity theory, the highest level of motivation occurs when a person has ratios equal to those of the comparison person. When people perceive an inequity, they are likely to engage in one or more of the three following actions that lead to a negative outcome for the employer.

1. *Alter the outcome.* The person who feels mistreated might ask for more salary or a bonus, promotional opportunities, or more vacation time. Some people might even steal from the company to obtain the money they feel they deserve. Others might attempt to convince management to give less to others.

Leadership Skill-Building Exercise 10-3

## The Application of Equity Theory

The object of this skill-building exercise is to apply equity theory to yourself, so you can then apply the theory to motivating others. The focus of the exercise is to search for values for the two ratios.

1. *Outcomes of Individual/Inputs of Individual*
   Reflect on a job you hold now or held in the past. First, list all the outcomes you received or are receiving on that job. Information in the text will give you some ideas. List factors such as salary, bonuses, friendships with coworkers, vacations, and new learning. Next, list all your inputs, such as education, prior training, money invested in education, and cooperative behavior.

2. *Outcomes of Others/Inputs of Others*
   To obtain data for this ratio, you will have to do some research. Perhaps you can send emails to current or past coworkers. To find out what others doing this type of work are earning, you might consult www.salary.com or similar web sites. Reach any conclusion you can about whether you were, or are, being treated equitably.

   Next, reflect on how your evaluation of equity might affect your past or current motivation. Ask several of your classmates about their results for this exercise. Based on your analysis, does it appear that equity theory offers any promise as a motivational theory for leaders to apply?

**2. *Alter the input.*** A person who feels treated inequitably might decrease effort or time devoted to work. The person who feels underpaid might engage in such self-defeating behavior by faking sick days to take care of personal business. Another extreme would be to encourage others to decrease their inputs so they will earn less money.

**3. *Leave the situation.*** As an extreme move, the person who feels treated inequitably might quit a job. He or she would then be free to pursue greater equity in another position.

Equity theory has several direct implications for the leader who is attempting to motivate subordinates. First, no matter how well designed a program of productivity or cost-cutting might be, it must still provide equitable pay. Otherwise, the negative perceptions of workers might lead to less effort to accomplish the goals of management. Second, the leader should attempt to see that subordinates perceive themselves to be getting a fair deal in terms of what they are giving to and receiving from the company. For example, a discussion with a given worker might reveal that the worker feels underutilized in terms of his or her education, training, and experience. Giving the worker a new, challenging assignment might lead to higher motivation on the part of the worker. Another approach to enhancing motivation would be to place the worker in a job with a higher pay grade, so he or she would feel more equitably treated. (Of course, there are often constraints on how much a leader can manipulate pay and job assignments.)

Leadership Skill-Building Exercise 10-3 will help you personalize equity theory.

# COACHING AS AN APPROACH TO MOTIVATION

Effective leaders are good coaches, and good coaches are effective motivators. The coaching demands are much less rigorous for leaders who have little face-to-face contact with organization members, such as financial deal makers, CEOs, and chairpersons of the board. Nevertheless, there is a coaching component at all levels of leadership. David Novak, the chief executive of Yum Brands Inc., sees himself more as a coach and cheerleader than as The Boss. Part of his being a coach includes careful listening to the ideas of staff members.[25] Studies conducted by Rainmaker Thinking, Inc., indicate that many managers are falling down by failing to coach employees, particularly in the form of specific feedback on performance with guidance for improvement.[26]

Coaching is a way of enabling others to act and build on their strengths. To coach is to care enough about people to invest time in building personal relationships with them. The organization also benefits from coaching because of the elevated productivity of many of the workers who are coached. Coaching is also seen as a key vehicle for engaging (or motivating) workers. James Harter, chief scientist for Gallup's international management practice, contends that the majority of engaged employees work for managers who devote substantial time to helping their subordinates succeed.[27]

## Key Characteristics of Coaching

Coaching in the workplace might ordinarily be explained as the art of management. Because of the uniqueness of a coaching relationship, the person being coached is better motivated to accomplish goals for the good of the organization. Coaching is an interaction between two people, usually the manager and an employee. The purpose of the interaction is to help the employee learn from the job in order to help his or her development.[28] The interaction of the two personalities influences the coaching outcome. Some leaders, for example, can successfully coach certain people, but not others.

Coaching requires a high degree of interpersonal risk and trust on the part of both people in the relationship. The coach might give the person being coached wrong advice. Or the person being coached might reject the coach's encouragement. Think of the risk involved when a basketball player asks the coach for advice on how to correct a shot that is not working well. As a result of the coaching, the player might shoot more poorly, to the embarrassment of both. Similarly, an organizational leader might coach a team member in a direction that backfires—for example, that results in even fewer sales than before.

Research at the Center for Creative Leadership found that managers too often perceive coaching as simply telling people what to do. In contrast, effective coaching focuses on the growth and development of individuals rather than telling direct reports what to do in a given situation. To help subordinates grow and develop, the leader as coach should give subordinates the resources they need to make their own decisions. The people being coached should be challenged to find the right solution, and then provided feedback on how well they have performed.

Assume that a manager wants the accident rate on the construction of skyscrapers reduced substantially. Instead of telling a direct report exactly how to accomplish this goal, the manager might point to new sources of help for accident reduction. In the process, the direct report might find solutions the manager did not already know about.[29]

A key advantage of coaching is that it generates new possibilities for action and facilitates breakthroughs in performance. A vice president might say to a lower-ranking manager, "Have you thought of getting your people more involved in setting objectives? If you did, you might find greater commitment and follow-through." The middle manager begins to involve managers more in setting objectives, and performance increases. Coaching in this situation has achieved substantial results.

At its best, coaching offers some concrete contributions, including higher motivation. An effective coach keeps up the spirit and offers praise and recognition frequently. Good coaching also leads to personal development. Group members are encouraged to cross-train and serve as backups for each other. Good coaching also improves group performance. The effective coach makes team members aware of one another's skills and how these skills can contribute to attaining the group's goals.[30]

## Fallacies About Coaching

Another approach to understanding the coaching function of leadership is to examine certain common misperceptions about coaching, as explained by Ian Cunningham and Linda Honold.[31] One false belief is that *coaching applies only in one-to-one work*. In reality, the team or other group can also be coached. As a team leader, you might make a suggestion to the group, such as, "Why are you rushing through such an important issue?" A major misperception is that *coaching is mostly about providing new knowledge and skills*. The truth is that people often need more help with underlying habits than with knowledge and skills. A good example is coaching another person about work habits and time management. You can provide the individual with loads of useful knowledge and techniques; however, if the person is a procrastinator, he or she must reduce procrastination before time management skills will help.

Another stereotype deals with an important ethical issue: *if coaches go beyond giving instruction in knowledge and skills, they are in danger of getting into psychotherapy*. The counterargument is that coaches should simply follow the model of effective parents: listening to the other person, attempting to understand his or her real concerns, and offering support and encouragement. Another stereotype particularly resistant to extinction is that *coaches need to be expert in something in order to coach*. To use a sports analogy, a good coach does not have to be or have been an outstanding athlete. An important role for the coach is to ask pertinent questions and listen. Questioning and listening can help the other person set realistic learning goals.

An understandable stereotype is that *coaching has to be done face-to-face*. The face-to-face approach facilitates coaching. Nevertheless, telephone and email are

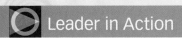
**Leader in Action**

## Doug Conant of Campbell Soup Demands Talent Development

Doug Conant, the CEO of Campbell Soup, rates managers on how well they develop talent. He rewards managers who unleash talent and get high performance from their staffs. Lisa Walker, the business director of the wellness team at Campbell USA, is an example of a talent developer. She knew she needed an energized team to lead the company's launch of low-sodium soups. She strengthened her ranks by giving equal attention to the star performers and to those needing help. "When someone is struggling, it's a huge drain on everyone else who must pick up the slack—so it's in my and the company's interests to help that struggling person," she says.

She feels buoyed when her coaching advice enables someone talented to advance. Walker taught one employee who liked to "charge ahead with projects" how to confer more with other colleagues—a skill he needed to master if he wanted to move up.

The employee later told Walker, "It's clear that you and the company really care about my success," she recalls. "That's about the best feedback I can ever get as a manager."

### Questions

1. What does this brief description tell you about Lisa Walker's understanding of the purpose of coaching subordinates?
2. Why does Walker think that the appreciative feedback she received from her subordinate was so wonderful?

*Source:* Excerpted from Carol Hymowitz, "Managers Lose Talent When They Neglect to Coach Their Staffs," *The Wall Street Journal*, March 19, 2007, p. B1.

---

useful alternatives when time and distance create barriers. A worker on a field trip, for example, might send his manager an email message, asking, "The customer says that if I make a mistake with this installation, he'll never do business with us again. Any suggestions?"

The accompanying Leader in Action profile describes the importance the CEO of a famous company attaches to talent development through coaching.

## COACHING SKILLS AND TECHNIQUES

Leaders and managers have varied aptitudes for coaching. One way to acquire coaching skill is to study basic principles and suggestions and then practice them. Another is to attend a training program for coaching that involves modeling (learning by imitation) and role playing. Here we examine a number of suggestions for coaching, all of which might also apply to coaching a group or a team as well as an individual. The typical scenario for a leader to coach a team would take place in a meeting with all most of the group. If implemented with skill, the suggestions will improve the chances that coaching will lead to improved performance of individuals and groups.

1. ***Communicate clear expectations to group members***. For people to perform well and to continue to learn and grow, they need a clear perception of what

is expected of them. The expectations of a position become the standards by which performance will be judged, thus serving as a base point for coaching. If a team member is supposed to contribute three new ideas each month for improving operations, coaching is justified when an average of only one idea per month is forthcoming.

**2. *Build relationships.*** Effective coaches build personal relationships with team members and work to improve their interpersonal skills.[32] Having established rapport with team members facilitates entering into a coaching relationship with them. The suggestions that follow about active listening and giving emotional support are part of relationship building.

**3. *Give feedback on areas that require specific improvement.*** To coach a group member toward higher levels of performance, the leader pinpoints what specific behavior, attitude, or skills require improvement. An effective coach might say, "I read the product-expansion proposal you submitted. It's okay, but it falls short of your usual level of creativity. Our competitors are already carrying each product you mentioned. Have you thought about . . . ?" Another important factor in giving specific feedback is to avoid generalities and exaggerations, such as, "You never come up with a good product idea" or "You are the most unimaginative product development specialist I have ever known." To give good feedback, the leader or manager has to observe performance and behavior directly and frequently, such as by watching a supervisor dealing with a safety problem.

To make the feedback process less intimidating, it is helpful to ask permission before you start coaching, indicate your purposes, and explain your positive intentions: for example, "Jack, do you have a few minutes for me to share my thoughts with you?" (permission); "I'd like to talk to you about the presentation you just made to the venture capitalists" (purpose); "I liked your creativity, yet I have some ideas you might use in your next presentation" (positive intentions).[33] Feedback is also likely to be less intimidating when the coach explains which behaviors should decrease and which should increase. This approach is a variation of combining compliments with criticism to avoid insulting the person being coached. You might say, "Tanya, I need you to place more emphasis on quality and less on speed."

**4. *Listen actively.*** Listening is an essential ingredient in any coaching session. An active listener tries to grasp both facts and feelings. Observing the group member's nonverbal communication is another part of active listening. The leader must also be patient and not poised for a rebuttal of any difference of opinion between him or her and the group member. Beginning each coaching session with a question helps set the stage for active listening. The question will also spark the employee's thinking and frame the discussion: for example, "How might we use the new computer system to help our staff generate more sales?"

Part of being a good listener is encouraging the person being coached to talk about his or her performance. Asking open-ended questions facilitates a flow of conversation: for example, ask, "How did you feel about the way you handled conflict with the marketing group yesterday?" A close-ended question covering the same issue would be, "Do you think you could have done a better job of handling conflict with the marketing group yesterday?"

**5. *Help remove obstacles.*** To perform at anywhere near top capacity, individuals may need help in removing obstacles such as a maze of rules and regulations and rigid budgeting. An important role for the leader of an organizational unit is thus to be a "barrier buster." A leader or manager is often in a better position than a group member to gain approval from a higher-level manager, find money from another budget line, expedite a purchase order, or authorize hiring a temporary worker to provide assistance. Yet if the coach is too quick to remove obstacles for the group member, the latter may not develop enough self-reliance.

**6. *Give emotional support.*** By being helpful and constructive, the leader provides much-needed emotional support to the group member who is not performing at his or her best. A coaching session should not be an interrogation. An effective way of giving emotional support is to use positive rather than negative motivators. For example, the leader might say, "I liked some things you did yesterday, and I have a few suggestions that might bring you closer to peak performance."

Displaying empathy is an effective way to give emotional support. Indicate with words that you understand the challenge the group member faces with a statement such as, "I understand that working with a reduced staff has placed you under heavy time pressures." The genuine concern you show will help establish the rapport useful in working out the problem together.

**7. *Reflect content or meaning.*** An effective way of reflecting meaning is to re-phrase and summarize concisely what the group member is saying. A substandard performer might say, "The reason I've fallen so far behind is that our company has turned into a bureaucratic nightmare. We're being hit right and left with forms to fill out for customer satisfaction. I have fifty email messages that I haven't read yet." You might respond, "You're falling so far behind because you have so many forms and messages that require attention." The group member might then respond with something like, "That's exactly what I mean. I'm glad you understand my problem." (Notice that the leader is also giving the group member an opportunity to express the feelings behind his or her problem.)

**8. *Give some gentle advice and guidance.*** Too much advice giving interferes with two-way communication, yet some advice can elevate performance. The manager should assist the group member in answering the question "What can I do about this problem?"[34] Advice in the form of a question or suppositional statement is often effective. One example is, "Could the root of your problem be insufficient planning?" A direct statement, such as, "The root of your problem is obviously insufficient plan-ning," often makes people resentful and defensive. By responding to a question, the person being coached is likely to feel more involved in making improvements.

Part of giving gentle guidance for improvement is to use the word *could* instead of *should*. To say, "You should do this," implies that the person is currently doing some-thing wrong, which can trigger defensiveness. Saying, "You could do this," leaves the person with a choice: accept or reject your input and weigh the consequences.[35] (You *could* accept this advice to become a better coach!)

**9. *Allow for modeling of desired performance and behavior.*** An effective coaching technique is to show the group member by example what constitutes the desired behavior. Assume that a manager has been making statements to customers that stretch the truth, such as falsely saying that the product met a zero-defects standard. In coaching him, the manager's boss might allow the manager to observe how she handles a similar situation with a customer. The manager's boss might telephone a customer and say, "You have been inquiring about whether we have adopted a zero-defects standard for our laser printers. Right now, we are doing our best to produce error-free products. Yet so far we do not have a formal zero-defects program. We stand by our printers and will fix any defect at no cost to you."

**10.** *Gain a commitment to change.* Unless the leader receives a commitment from the team member to carry through with the proposed solution to a problem, the team member may not attain higher performance. An experienced manager develops an intuitive sense for when employees are serious about performance improvement. Two clues that commitment to change is lacking are (1) overagreeing about the need for change and (2) agreeing to change without display of emotion.

**11.** *Applaud good results.* Effective coaches on the playing field and in the workplace are cheerleaders. They give encouragement and positive reinforcement by applauding good results. Some effective coaches shout in joy when an individual or team achieves outstanding results; others clap their hands in applause.

Leadership Self-Assessment Quiz 10-3 will help you think through the development you need to be an effective coach. If you are already an effective coach, look for ways to improve. Leadership Skill-Building Exercise 10-4 gives you a chance to practice coaching.

 ## Leadership Self-Assessment Quiz 10-3

### Characteristics of an Effective Coach

*Instructions:* Following is a list of traits, attitudes, and behaviors characteristic of effective coaches. Place a check mark next to each trait, attitude, or behavior that you need to develop along those lines (for example, whether you need to become more patient). On a separate sheet of paper, design an action plan for improvement for each trait, attitude, or behavior that you need to develop. An example of an action plan for improving patience might be, "I'll ask people to tell me when I appear too impatient. I'll also try to develop self-control about my impatience."

**Trait, Attitude, or Behavior**

1. Empathy (putting self in other person's shoes) ☐
2. Listening skill ☐
3. Insight into people ☐
4. Diplomacy and tact ☐
5. Patience toward people ☐
6. Concern for welfare of people ☐
7. Low hostility toward people ☐
8. Self-confidence and emotional security ☐

## Quiz 10-3 (continued)

**9.** Noncompetitiveness with group members ☐

**10.** Enthusiasm for people ☐

**11.** Satisfaction in helping others grow ☐

**12.** Interest in development of group members ☐

**13.** High expectations for each group member ☐

**14.** Ability to give authentic feedback ☐

**15.** Interest in people's potential ☐

**16.** Honesty and integrity (or trustworthiness) ☐

**17.** Friendliness ☐

**18.** Develops trust and respect ☐

*Source:* Items 1–10 adapted with permission from Andrew J. DuBrin, *Participant Guide to Module 10: Development of Subordinates*, p. 11. Copyright © 1985. Items 11–15 gathered from information in William D. Hitt, *The Leader–Manager: Guidelines for Action* (Columbus, OH.: Battelle Press, 1988), pp. 183–186.

## EXECUTIVE COACHING AND LEADERSHIP EFFECTIVENESS

A form of coaching in vogue is for managers to consult professional coaches to help them become more effective leaders and to guide them in their careers. **Executive coaching** is "A one-on-one development process formally contracted between a coach and a management-level client to help achieve goals related to professional development and/or business performance."[36]

In the past, management psychologists were typically hired as outside coaches to help managers become more effective leaders. Today, people from a wide variety of backgrounds become executive coaches, as well as career coaches and life coaches. Many executive coaches are former executives themselves.

### Specific Forms of Assistance Provided by Executive Coaches

Executive coaches help managers become more effective leaders by helping them in a variety of ways, such as those described next. However, it is unlikely that one coach would provide all these services, or that one manager would want or need all of them.

- Helping corporate stars attain peak performance, much like an athletic coach working with an outstanding athlete. One approach to heightened performance is to help the leader uncover personal assets and strengths he or she may not have known existed. An example would be discovering that the leader has untapped creativity and imagination.[37]

## ⊙ Leadership Skill-Building Exercise 10-4

### Coaching for Improved Performance

Jennifer is a financial consultant (stockbroker) at a branch office of an established financial services firm. Her manager, Derek, is concerned that Jennifer is 25 percent below quota in sales of a new commodities mutual fund offered by the company. Derek schedules a late-afternoon meeting in his office to attempt to help Jennifer make quota. He has told Jennifer, "I want to talk about your sales performance on the new commodities fund and see if I can be helpful." Jennifer is concerned that the meeting might be a discipline session in disguise.

Have one member of the class assume the role of Derek, and another the role of Jennifer. Derek, of course, will attempt to implement recommended coaching techniques. Other class members will watch and then provide constructive feedback.

This exercise is a key skill builder because so much of face-to-face leadership involves working out performance problems with group members. If every employee were an outstanding, independent performer, we would have less need for managers and leaders.

- Counseling the leader about weaknesses that could interfere with effectiveness, such as being too hostile and impatient. The coach will also solicit feedback by interviewing coworkers and subordinates, and then distilling the feedback to help the executive.
- Serving as a sounding board when the leader faces a complex decision about strategy, operations, or human resource issues.
- Making specific suggestions about self-promotion and image enhancement, including suggestions about appearance and mannerisms.
- Helping the leader achieve a better balance between work and family life, thereby having more focused energy for the leadership role.
- Serving as a trusted confidante to discuss issues the leader might feel uncomfortable talking about with others: for example, talking about feeling insecure in his or her position.
- Giving advice about career management, such as developing a career path.
- Strengthening the executive's strategic decision-making skills by helping him or her think more broadly about issues and appreciate how his or her actions will affect the organizational system. The coach might point out a blind spot in the leader's decision making, such as neglecting part of the human consequences of a decision.
- Assisting an executive in selecting direct reports by looking for compatibility between the candidate and the executive, as well as reviewing other qualifications.[38]

Note that the coach works as an adviser about behavior but does not explicitly help the leader with functional details of the job, such as how to develop a new product strategy or design an organization.

The leader/manager's employer usually hires the executive coach. The purpose of engaging the coach could be to accelerate the development of a star player or assist an executive who is having soft-skill problems. For example, the direct reports of a manager at a consulting firm referred to her as a "weed whacker," so an executive coach was hired to help the executive develop more emotional intelligence. The executive soon learned that employees perceived in her tone and body language that she was attacking them. Coaching helped her soften her approach and work better with others.[39]

A refinement of individual coaching is for the coach to work with both the individual and his or her work associates. The coach solicits feedback from the group members and involves them in helping the manager improve. For example, the coach might tell team members to assert their rights when the manager throws a temper tantrum or makes unreasonable demands. The coach might also work with the superiors or peers of the person being coached. Coach Marshall Goldsmith says, "My success rate as a coach has improved dramatically as I've realized that people's getting better is not a function of me; it's a function of the person and the people around the person."[40]

## Contributions of and Concerns About Executive Coaching

Executive coaching may frequently accomplish several of the ends specified in the previous list. Company evidence about the contribution of business coaching is sometimes impressive. A huge global services company offered coaching to 127 senior managers and then observed the results. The coached executives scored higher than a contrast group of executives on a long list of measures, including "results obtained," "builds relationships," and "applies integrative thinking."[41]

Executive coaching, however, has some potential drawbacks for the leader. A major problem is that a coach may give advice that backfires because he or she does not understand the particular work setting. A coach told a manager in an information technology firm that she should become more decisive in her decision making and less dependent on consensus. The advice backfired because the culture of the firm emphasized consensus decision making. Furthermore, many people who present themselves as executive coaches may not be professionally qualified or may not have much knowledge about business.[42] To help establish who is qualified to coach, the coaching industry has established the International Coaching Federation. The Federation certifies various levels of coaching based on training and experience, and establishes ethical standards such as client privacy.[43]

An ethical problem is that many coaches delve into personal and emotional issues that should be reserved for mental health professionals. Psychotherapist Steven Berglas contends that executive coaches can make a bad situation worse when they ignore psychological problems they do not understand.[44] The leader who is performing poorly because of a deep-rooted problem such as hostility toward others is given superficial advice about "making nice." Another potential ethical problem is that the leader/manager may become too dependent on the coach, checking with him or her before making any consequential decision.

### Reader's Roadmap

So far we have studied considerable information about the nature of leadership; the attributes, behaviors, and styles of leaders; the ethics and social responsibility of leaders; and how leaders exert power and use politics and influence. The techniques for developing teamwork are part of a leader's relationship with the group, as is the subject of this chapter: motivation and coaching skills. In the next chapter, we describe creativity and innovation as part of leadership.

## SUMMARY

Effective leaders are outstanding motivators and coaches, and the role of the leader and manager today emphasizes coaching. The expectancy theory of motivation is useful for developing motivational skills because it is comprehensive, building on other explanations of motivation.

Expectancy theory has three major components: valence, instrumentality, and expectancy. *Valence* is the worth or attractiveness of an outcome. Each work situation has multiple outcomes, and each outcome has a valence of its own. Valences range from –100 to +100 in the version of expectancy theory presented here. Zero valences reflect indifference and therefore are not motivational. Very high valences help explain why some people persist in efforts despite a low probability of payoff. *Instrumentality* is the individual's assessment of the probability that performance will lead to certain outcomes. (An outcome is anything that might stem from performance, such as a reward.) *Expectancy* is an individual's assessment of the probability that effort will lead to performing the task correctly.

Expectancy theory has implications and provides guidelines for leaders, including the following: (1) determine necessary performance levels; (2) make the performance level attainable; (3) train and encourage people; (4) make explicit the link between rewards and performance; (5) make sure the rewards are large enough; (6) analyze factors that oppose the effectiveness of the reward; (7) explain the meaning and implications of second-level

outcomes; (8) understand individual differences in valences; and (9) recognize that when workers are in a good mood, valences, instrumentalities, and expectancies will more likely enhance performance.

Goal setting is a basic process that is directly or indirectly part of all major theories of motivation. Goal theory includes the following ideas: (1) specific and difficult goals result in high performance (yet outrageous goals can inspire); (2) goals must be accepted by group members; (3) goals are more effective when they are linked to feedback and rewards; (4) the combination of individual and group goals is very effective; and (5) a learning goal orientation is effective.

Motivating others by giving them recognition and praise can be considered a direct application of positive reinforcement. Recognition programs to reward and motivate employees are standard practice. Recognition is a strong motivator because it is a normal human need to crave recognition, and workers often do not feel they receive enough recognition. To appeal to the recognition need, identify a meritorious behavior and then recognize that behavior with an oral, written, or material reward. To maximize its motivational impact, recognition should be linked to corporate values and personal goals. Recognition and praise are no-cost or low-cost motivators that are powerful.

Giving workers an opportunity to experience pride can be a strong internal motivator, yet workers still receive recognition. To motivate through pride, it is best for the manager to set the compass on pride, not money, and for workers to be proud of daily accomplishments.

Equity theory can be applied to employee motivation. The core of the theory is that employees compare their inputs and outcomes with others in the workplace. When employees believe that they are being treated equitably, they are more willing to work hard. Then the leader should attempt to see that subordinates see themselves as getting a fair deal in terms of what they are giving to and getting from the company.

A major purpose of coaching is to achieve enthusiasm and high performance in a team setting. Several characteristics of coaching contribute to its close relationship with leadership. Coaching is a two-way process, suggesting that being a great coach requires having a talented team. Coaching requires a high degree of interpersonal risk and trust on the part of both sides in the relationship. Effective coaching focuses on the growth and development of people rather than telling them how to deal with a given situation.

The coaching function can also be understood by recognizing several common misperceptions: (1) coaching applies only to one-on-one work; (2) coaching is mostly about providing new knowledge and skills; (3) coaching easily falls into psychotherapy; (4) coaches need to be experts in what they are coaching; and (5) coaching has to be done face-to-face.

Suggestions for improving coaching are as follows: (1) communicate clear expectations, (2) build relationships, (3) give feedback on areas that require specific improvement, (4) listen actively, (5) help remove obstacles, (6) give emotional support including empathy, (7) reflect content or meaning, (8) give gentle advice and guidance, (9) allow for modeling of desired performance and behavior, (10) gain a commitment to change, and (11) applaud good results.

Managers frequently consult executive coaches to help them be more effective leaders. Such coaches provide a variety of services, including helping attain peak performance, counseling about weaknesses, helping achieve balance in life, helping the leader uncover hidden assets, and giving career advice. Studies show that executive coaching is effective, yet there are potential problems: executive coaches can give bad advice, the coach might be unqualified in general or to deal with mental health issues, and the leader may become too dependent on the coach.

## KEY TERMS

| | | |
|---|---|---|
| **Expectancy theory** | **Instrumentality** | **Goal** |
| **Valence** | **Expectancy** | **Equity theory** |
| **Outcome** | **Self-efficacy** | **Executive coaching** |

## GUIDELINES FOR ACTION AND SKILL DEVELOPMENT

Given that recognition can be such a relatively low-cost yet highly effective motivator, the leader/manager should keep in mind available forms of recognition. In addition to considering those in the following list, use your imagination to think of other forms of recognition. For the recognition technique to work well, it should have high valence for the person or group under consideration.

- Compliments, such as "You help us accomplish our mission," or "Our customers love what you are doing for them"

- Encouragement for a job well done
- Comradeship with the boss
- A pat on the back or a handshake
- Public expression of appreciation
- A meeting of appreciation with the executive
- Team uniforms, hats, T-shirts, or mugs
- A note of thanks to the individual (handwritten, email, or text message)
- A flattering letter from a customer distributed over email
- Employee-of-month award
- A wall plaque indicating accomplishment
- A special commendation placed in employee file
- A gift from the company recognition program, such as a watch, a clock, or a pin

Approaches to recognition may pack an extra punch when they do not take the same form every time. For a job well done, the worker might receive a warm email one week, a gift certificate the next, and perhaps an employee-of-the month designation in the future.

### Discussion Questions and Activities

1. Identify several outcomes you expect from occupying a leadership position. What valences do you attach to them?

2. How can the influence exerted by a charismatic leader tie in with expectancy theory?
3. Explain how valence, instrumentality, and expectancy could relate to job performance.
4. What is a potential second-level outcome a person could gain from receiving an A in this course? From receiving an F?
5. What is an example of a noble cause a leader at Domino's Pizza might use to motivate a store manager? What about a noble cause for workers in the Tata Motors division that is manufacturing a car to sell for $2,500?
6. In what way might giving group members frequent recognition contribute to a leader's being perceived as charismatic?
7. How would a leader/manager be aware of a given group member's input/output ratio so the leader/manager could apply equity theory?
8. In what ways is coaching related to hands-on leadership?
9. How might a leader use coaching to help increase ethical behavior among group members?
10. Ask a manager or coach to describe the amount of coaching he or she does on the job. Be prepared to bring your findings back to class.

## Leadership Case Problem A

### Justin Salisbury Tries a Little Recognition

Justin Salisbury is a super-franchiser for a large chain of soup-and-sandwich shops. He owns twelve shops in the same region, having invested $2 million to own these stores. One-half the investment in the stores came from inheritance and investments Justin had made prior to becoming a franchisor. The other half of the money was borrowed, so Justin feels considerable pressure to earn enough gross profit from the stores to make his debt payments and earn a living.

Justin concluded that he needed to increase revenues from his stores about 15 percent in order to net enough profit for a comfortable living. He believed

that his business processes were good enough to make a profit, and that the company was giving his franchise operations enough marketing and advertising support. Justin also thought that his managers were running efficient operations. He was concerned, however, that they weren't trying hard enough to achieve good customer service by encouraging the order takers at the stores to pay more attention to customers. For example, when Justin visited the stores (or sent a family member in his place), the order takers didn't smile enough or ask frequently enough, "What else would you like with your order?"

## Leadership Case Problem A (continued)

Justin decided that he shouldn't micromanage by telling the store managers how to motivate their staffs. Yet he decided to discuss with his managers what he wanted—more profit by doing a better job of motivating the order takers and cashiers. He also pointed out to his twelve store managers that he would be rewarding and recognizing their accomplishments in boosting store revenues. After consulting with the managers, Justin established the goal of a 15 percent increases in revenues within twelve months.

Two weeks after the goal-setting discussions with the twelve store managers, Justin announced that he would be recognizing and rewarding attaining a 15 percent or better increase in revenue with two of the following forms of recognition:

- A wall plaque designating the manager as a "Store Manager of the Year"
- A year's membership in an athletic club for the manager and a spouse or partner
- A bonus equivalent to 2 percent of annual salary
- An iPod
- An expense-paid trip for the manager and his or her family to one day at an amusement park or theme park

Justin waited for responses from his managers to the proposed recognition plan. He received several email messages acknowledging an appreciation of his program, yet no burst of enthusiasm. Justin thought to himself, "I guess the managers don't understand yet how great it feels to be recognized for making a tough financial target. I think that when they earn their recognition awards, I will see a lot more enthusiasm."

### Questions

1. What advice can you give Justin Salisbury about the most likely motivational consequences of his recognition program?
2. What other form of recognition should Justin offer the store managers?
3. Would it be better for Justin to have a recognition program aimed directly at the order takers and cashiers than at their managers? Explain your reasoning.

## Leadership Case Problem B

### Coach Sally Gorman

Sally Gorman is the manager of the mortgage department of a suburban bank branch. She has six direct reports, including three mortgage consultants. Although the consultants work full-time at the bank, they are considered subcontractors who work only on commission—without any salary and benefits. A consequence of this compensation arrangement is that the mortgage consultants are under considerable pressure to sell home mortgages to bank customers. Until a mortgage is approved, the consultant receives zero financial compensation.

Tony Costello, a 28-year-old mortgage consultant, asked for an appointment to speak to Sally about his recent problems in nailing down mortgages. Sally was eager to meet with Tony because she was also under pressure for the mortgage department to place more mortgages. A partial transcript of their meeting follows:

*Tony:* Sally, I've come to you for help. For several months, I haven't been closing enough mortgages to make a living. My wife and I have two children, and we can't make ends meet on her salary alone. Is there

## Leadership Case Problem B (continued)

any way the bank can put me on salary? Or maybe give me a few months' advance? I've been a great producer in the past.

*Sally:* Grow up, Tony. When you took this job, you knew it did not include a salary, and that the bank does not allow advances. We need you to produce, but we can't change the bank rules. We are not a mom-and-pop operation.

*Tony:* Do you know how brutal it is out there? Home sales are down 20 percent in our area. I don't have enough warm leads coming into the bank to shop for a mortgage. Besides that, our approval committee has been shooting down too many deals on me lately.

*Sally:* Wake up, Tony. The mortgage business has changed recently. We can't add any more high-risk loans to our portfolio. It's very difficult to resell those mortgages to other institutions.

*Tony:* Okay, then, what do you propose I do to generate more mortgage applications that the mortgage committee will approve?

*Sally:* Do what you do best. You're a professional. Just bear down harder on good mortgage possibilities who visit your desk. Be persuasive. Turn up the heat. Do something good or be gone.

*Tony:* I am trying. I want my commissions as much as the bank wants its mortgages.

*Sally:* Just keep trying harder, and get back to me with results, not excuses.

*Tony:* I guess that the bank and I are in the same boat. I'll talk to you later, Sally.

### Questions

1. What advice can you offer Sally Gorman to do a better job of coaching Tony Costello?
2. What advice can you offer Tony Costello to get more out of the coaching session?
3. What is the most positive thing Sally did as a coach?
4. What is the most negative thing Sally did as a coach?

 ## Leadership Skill-Building Exercise 10-5

### My Leadership Portfolio

One of the easiest and most powerful ways of motivating people is to recognize their efforts, as described in this chapter. Like any other interpersonal skill, being effective at giving recognition takes practice. During the next week, find three people to recognize, and observe how they react to your recognition. For example, if a server gives you fine service, after the meal explain how much you enjoyed the service and leave a larger-than-average tip. If your hair stylist does a fine job, similarly provide a compliment and a good tip. Or find some helper to recognize with a compliment but without a tip. Observe the responses of these people—both their facial expressions and what they say. Of even more importance, observe if any of these people appear eager to serve you the next time you interact with them.

As with other parts of your leadership portfolio, keep a written record of what happened to you and how much skill you think you have developed.

## Internet Skill-Building Exercise

### Dream Job Coaching

Visit www.dreamjobcoaching.com and find answers to the following questions:

1. According to Dream Job Coaching, what does coaching entail?
2. How does Dream Job Coaching help you find an ideal position?
3. How could the principles of Dream Job Coaching help you be a more effective coach?

Apply the chapter concepts! Visit the Web and complete this Internet skill-building exercise to learn more about current leadership topics and trends.

# Creativity, Innovation, and Leadership

## LEARNING OBJECTIVES

After studying this chapter and doing the exercises, you should be able to

- Identify the steps in the creative process.

- Identify characteristics of creative problem solvers.

- Be prepared to overcome traditional thinking in order to become more creative.

- Describe both organizational and individual approaches to enhance creative problem solving.

- Explain how the leader and the organization can establish a climate that fosters creativity.

- Identify several leadership practices that contribute to organizational innovation.

## CHAPTER OUTLINE

**Steps in the Creative Process**

**Characteristics of Creative Leaders**
Knowledge
Cognitive Abilities
Personality
Passion for the Task and the Experience of Flow
The Componential Theory of Individual Creativity

**Overcoming Traditional Thinking as a Creativity Strategy**

**Organizational Methods to Enhance Creativity**
Systematically Collecting Fresh Ideas
Brainstorming
Using the Pet-Peeve Technique
Equipping a Kitchen for the Mind

**Self-Help Techniques to Enhance Creative Problem Solving**
Practicing Creativity-Enhancing Exercises
Staying Alert to Opportunities
Maintaining an Enthusiastic Attitude, Including Being Happy
Maintaining and Using a Systematic Place
    for Recording Your Ideas
Playing the Roles of Explorer, Artist, Judge, and Lawyer
Engaging in Appropriate Physical Exercise

**Establishing a Climate and Culture for Creative Thinking**
Leadership Practices for Enhancing Creativity
Methods of Managing Creative Workers

**Additional Leadership Practices That Enhance Innovation**

**Summary**

315

According to legend, it was melting ice cream that helped launch Fudgie the Whale and Cookie Puss. In 1934, Thomas Carvel was a young Greek immigrant in the New York suburbs who sold ice cream created in the back of a truck. On Memorial Day weekend, the truck broke down and the ice cream softened, and people loved it. Mr. Carvel soon invented equipment to produce soft ice cream and designed a glass-fronted building to sell it from.

He started franchising in 1947 and quickly sold 100 franchises.

The franchise network grew to over 800 stores. In addition to making their own ice cream, franchises also reproduced Mr. Carvel's novelty cakes, of which Fudgie the Whale and Cookie Puss were kids' birthday-party favorites. Even after selling his company to international investment group Investcorp in 1989, Mr. Carvel, then in his 80s, remained active until his death a year later.[1]

The story about the birth of American icon Carvel tells us a lot about creativity applied to business. The creative leader recognizes a good opportunity that others might miss. Instead of saying, "I'm ruined, my ice cream is melting," Carvel probably said, "Wow, there are marketing possibilities in soft ice cream." By thinking creatively (such as by developing a new product based on a mishap), a person can form a new enterprise that can keep many people engaged in productive activity. However, the creative idea has to be executed properly for innovation to take place. Although the terms *creativity* and *innovation* are often used interchangeably, **innovation** refers to the creation of new ideas and *their implementation* or *commercialization*. A major focus of innovation is taking organizations built for efficiency and rewiring them for creativity and growth.[2]

Long-time leadership authority Warren Bennis regards creativity as an essential characteristic of leaders.[3] Creative thinking enables leaders to contribute novel insights that can open up new opportunities or alternatives for the group or the organization. The role of a creative leader is to bring into existence ideas and things that did not exist previously or that existed in a different form. Leaders are not bound by current solutions to problems. Instead, they create images of other possibilities. Leaders often move a firm into an additional business or start a new department that offers another service. Such activity is of high priority because many business forecasters predict that employee creativity and innovation will be the most important factors in establishing and maintaining a competitive advantage.[4]

This chapter emphasizes the development of creativity in the leader. It also explains the nature of creativity and creative people and examines the leader's role in establishing an atmosphere that helps group members become more creative, along with leadership practices conducive to innovation.

## STEPS IN THE CREATIVE PROCESS

An important part of becoming more creative involves understanding the stages involved in **creativity**, which is generally defined as the production of novel and useful ideas. A well-accepted model of creativity can be applied to organizations.

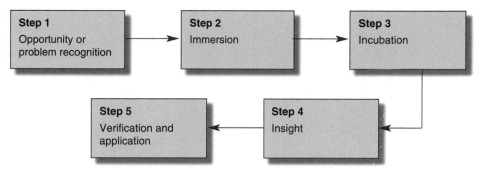

**FIGURE 11-1** Steps in the Creative Process.

Creative problem solvers often go through these steps below the level of conscious awareness. Yet being aware of these steps (such as immersing yourself in knowledge) when faced with a challenging problem will often increase the probability of finding a creative solution.

This model divides creative thinking into five stages,[5] as shown in Figure 11-1. Step 1 is *opportunity or problem recognition:* a person discovers that a new opportunity exists or a problem needs to be resolved. Many years ago an entrepreneurial leader, Robert Cowan, recognized a new opportunity and asked, "Why do business meetings have to be conducted in person? Why can't they connect through television images?"[6]

Step 2 is *immersion.* The individual concentrates on the problem and becomes immersed in it. He or she will recall and collect information that seems relevant, dreaming up alternatives without refining or evaluating them. Cowan grabbed every fact he could about teleconferencing. At one point he helped NASA and the University of Alaska produce the first videoconference by satellite. He then synthesized all his information into a book about teleconferencing.

Step 3 is *incubation.* The person keeps the assembled information in mind for a while. He or she does not appear to be working on the problem actively, but the subconscious mind is still engaged. While the information is simmering, it is being arranged into meaningful new patterns. Cowan did not actively pursue his business videoconferencing idea for several years.

Step 4 is *insight.* The problem-conquering solution flashes into the person's mind at an unexpected time, such as on the verge of sleep, during a shower, or while running. Insight is also called the *Aha! experience:* all of a sudden something clicks. At one point Cowan suddenly thought of forming a teleconferencing business to exploit the potential of his idea. The "aha" moment usually arrives after hours of thought and study, as indicated by Step 2, immersion. Also, the solution that flashes into mind is usually based on previous useful ideas.[7] Cowan had been thinking about business meetings for a long time.

Step 5 is *verification and application.* The individual sets out to prove that the creative solution has merit. Verification procedures include gathering supporting evidence, using logical persuasion, and experimenting with new ideas. Application requires tenacity because most novel ideas are first rejected as being impractical. When banks refused to finance Cowan's startup business, Cowan and his wife raised $45,000 from friends and obtained a second mortgage on their house. Cowan did start his business, but he faced financial trouble. When Cowan's company was on the verge of folding, Charles Schwab, the brokerage firm, hired it to connect its 100 branch offices.

Cowan's opportunity-spotting has evolved into a small industry, serving the needs of millions of workers in the era of global business. The end product of Cowan's creative thinking was a business possibility rather than an invention. Nevertheless, businesspeople typically follow the same five steps of creative thought as do inventors. Even though creativity usually follows the same steps, it is not a mechanical process that can be turned on and off. Much of creativity is intricately woven into a person's intellect and personality.

# CHARACTERISTICS OF CREATIVE LEADERS

Creative leaders, like creative workers of all types, are different in many ways from their less creative counterparts. They are devoted to their fields and enjoy intellectual stimulation, and they challenge the status quo, which leads them to seek improvements. For example, someone questioned why affluent people needed to own their vacation homes full-time instead of part of the time—resulting in the time-share industry. Above all, creative people are mentally flexible and can see past the traditional ways of looking at problems.

As described next, the specific characteristics of creative people, including creative leaders, can be grouped into four areas: knowledge, cognitive abilities, personality, and passion for the task and the experience of flow.[8] These characteristics are highlighted in Figure 11-2. In addition, we present a theory of creativity that helps explain how these characteristics lead to creative output. Before studying this information, compare your thinking to that of a creative person by doing Leadership Self-Assessment Quiz 11-1.

## Knowledge

Creative problem solving requires a broad background of information, including facts and observations. Knowledge provides the building blocks for generating and combining ideas. Most creative leaders are knowledgeable, and their knowledge contributes to their charisma. A well-known case in point is Steven P. Jobs, the chief executive of Apple Inc. and Pixar Animation Studios. He contributes design and marketing decisions to most of Apple's key products, and he played a major role in the development of the popular iPhone. A contributor to Jobs's creativity is his in-depth technical knowledge of computer hardware and software. Another example is the cross-breeding of the iPod nano with a Nike running shoe. A chip inserted into the shoe turns the shoe into a step counter that is wirelessly connected to a receiver in the iPod nano. The iPod then displays such information as the number of miles run and calories burned.[9] As with most creative people, Jobs has had his share of failed innovations, including the cube-shaped Mac. However, a few failures along the way rarely discourage a creative person.

Knowledge
Knowledgeable about
wide range of information

Personality
Nonconformist
Self-confident
Thrill-seeking
Energetic
Persistent

**Cognitive Abilities**
Highly intelligent
Intellectually curious
Able to think divergently

**Passion for the Task
and Flow**

**FIGURE 11-2** Characteristics of Creative Leaders.
Having the right characteristics improves the chances of a person being a creative problem solver and
a creative leader.

 Leadership Self-Assessment Quiz 11-1

**The Creative Personality Test**

*Instructions:* Describe each of the following statements as "mostly true" or "mostly false."

|  | Mostly True | Mostly False |
|---|---|---|
| 1. It is generally a waste of time to read magazine articles, Internet articles, and books outside my immediate field of interest. | ☐ | ☐ |
| 2. I frequently have the urge to suggest ways of improving products and services I use. | ☐ | ☐ |
| 3. Reading fiction and visiting art museums are time wasters. | ☐ | ☐ |
| 4. I am a person of very strong convictions. What is right is right; what is wrong is wrong. | ☐ | ☐ |
| 5. I enjoy it when my boss hands me vague instructions. | ☐ | ☐ |
| 6. Making order out of chaos is actually fun. | ☐ | ☐ |
| 7. Only under extraordinary circumstances would I deviate from my To-Do list (or other ways in which I plan my day). | ☐ | ☐ |
| 8. Taking a different route to work is fun, even if it takes longer. | ☐ | ☐ |
| 9. Rules and regulations should not be taken too seriously. Most rules can be broken under unusual circumstances. | ☐ | ☐ |

## Quiz 11-1 (continued)

10. Playing with a new idea is fun even if it does not benefit me in the end.     ☐     ☐

11. Some of my best ideas have come from building on the ideas of others.     ☐     ☐

12. In writing, I try to avoid the use of unusual words and word combinations.     ☐     ☐

13. I frequently jot down improvements in the job I would like to make in the future.     ☐     ☐

14. I prefer to stay with technology devices I know well rather than frequently updating my equipment or software.     ☐     ☐

15. I prefer writing personal notes or poems to loved ones rather than relying on greeting cards.     ☐     ☐

16. At one time or another in my life I have enjoyed doing puzzles.     ☐     ☐

17. If your thinking is clear, you will find the one best solution to a problem.     ☐     ☐

18. It is best to interact with coworkers who think much like you.     ☐     ☐

19. Detective work would have some appeal to me.     ☐     ☐

20. Tight controls over people and money are necessary to run a successful organization.     ☐     ☐

**Scoring and Interpretation:** Give yourself a score of 1 for each answer that matches the answer key:

| | | |
|---|---|---|
| 1. Mostly false | 8. Mostly true | 15. Mostly true |
| 2. Mostly true | 9. Mostly true | 16. Mostly true |
| 3. Mostly false | 10. Mostly true | 17. Mostly false |
| 4. Mostly false | 11. Mostly true | 18. Mostly false |
| 5. Mostly true | 12. Mostly false | 19. Mostly true |
| 6. Mostly true | 13. Mostly true | 20. Mostly false |
| 7. Mostly false | 14. Mostly false | |

**Total score:** _____

Extremely high or low scores are the most meaningful. A score of 15 or more suggests that your personality and attitudes are similar to those of creative people, including creative leaders. A score of 8 or less suggests that you are more of an intellectual conformist at present. Do not be discouraged. Most people can develop in the direction of becoming more creative.

How does your score compare to your self-evaluation of your creativity? We suggest you also obtain feedback on your creativity from somebody familiar with your thinking and your work.

## Cognitive Abilities

Intellectual abilities comprise such abilities as general intelligence and abstract reasoning. Creative problem solvers, particularly in business, tend to be bright but are not at the absolute top end of the brilliance scale. Extraordinarily high intelligence is not required to be creative, although creative people are facile at generating creative solutions to problems in a short period of time. Creative people also maintain a youthful curiosity throughout their lives, and the curiosity is not centered just on their own field of expertise. Instead, their range of interests encompasses many areas of knowledge, and they are enthusiastic about puzzling problems. These mental workouts help sharpen a person's intelligence.

Creative people show an identifiable intellectual style: being able to think divergently. They are able to expand the number of alternatives to a problem, thus moving away from a single solution. Yet the creative thinker also knows when it is time to narrow the number of useful solutions. For example, the divergent thinker might think of twenty-seven ways to reduce costs, but at some point he or she will have to move toward choosing the best of several cost-cutting approaches. In recent years several business firms have included design school graduates in their product development teams because designers tend to think flexibly. The idea is to search for new options that do not already exist. An example is that Intel works with design students to work on new products for aging baby boomers' future homes.[10]

As already shown in the Carvel and videoconference examples, a hallmark of a creative businessperson's intellect is to spot opportunities that others might overlook. Many a creative developer has seen the opportunities in abandoned factories and converted them into loft apartments and offices for small businesses that wanted to operate in an aesthetic environment.

## Personality

The noncognitive aspects of a person heavily influence creative problem solving. Creative people tend to have a positive self-image without being blindly self-confident. Because they are self-confident, they are able to cope with criticism of their ideas, and they can tolerate the isolation necessary for developing ideas. Part of the self-confidence of a creative worker focuses on the belief that he or she can solve problems creatively. Talking to others is a good way to get ideas, yet at some point the creative problem solver has to work alone and concentrate.

Creative people are frequently nonconformists and do not need strong approval from the group. Nonconformity can also mean being a maverick. Richard E. Cheverton observes: "The maverick is really the person who is the focus of creativity in a company, but a lot of people perceive them as jerks because they like to stir the pot. But these are just people driven to accomplish things anonymously. They just want to get things done, and they do not care about office politics or organizational charts. They like to spread the credit around."[11] A maverick personality who is not granted the freedom to develop new ideas is likely to join another firm or start a business.

Many creative problem solvers are thrill seekers who find that developing imaginative solutions to problems is a source of thrills. Creative people are also persistent, which is especially important for the verification and application stage of creative thinking. Selling a creative idea to the right people requires considerable follow-up. Finally, creative people enjoy dealing with ambiguity and chaos. Less creative people become quickly frustrated when task descriptions are unclear and disorder exists.

### Passion for the Task and the Experience of Flow

A dominant characteristic of creative people that is closely related to personality is a passion for the work. More than twenty years of research in industry conducted by Teresa M. Amabile and her associates led to the *intrinsic motivation principle of creativity:* people will be at their creative best when they feel motivated primarily by the interest, satisfaction, and challenge of the work itself—and not by external pressures.[12]

Passion for the task and high intrinsic motivation contribute in turn to a total absorption in the work and intense concentration, or **the experience of flow.** It is an experience so engrossing and enjoyable that the task becomes worth doing for its own sake regardless of the external consequences.[13] Perhaps you have had this experience when completely absorbed in a hobby or some analytical work, or when you were at your best in a sport or dance. (Flow also means *being in the zone.*) The highly creative leader, such as a business owner developing a plan for worldwide distribution of a product, will often achieve the experience of flow.

One of the problems with attempting to be creative under high-pressure conditions is that the pressure may interfere with the intense concentration required for high creativity. Based on her analysis of nearly 12,000 journal entries of workers engaged in creative tasks, Amabile discovered that time pressures may block people from deeply engaging with the problem. People can be creative when they are under heavy time pressures, but only when they can focus on the work.[14]

To fully understand the contribution of personal characteristics to creativity, we note the basic formula of human behavior: $B = f(P \times E)$ (behavior is a function of a person interacting with the environment). In this context, certain personal characteristics may facilitate a leader's being creative, but the right environment is necessary to trigger creative behavior. As will be described later, the right environment includes the leader encouraging creative thinking.

### The Componential Theory of Individual Creativity

The *componential theory of individual creativity* developed by Amabile integrates some of the information presented so far about the contribution of personal characteristics to creativity. According to this theory, creativity takes place when three components join together: expertise, creative-thinking skill, and task motivation.[15]

*Expertise* refers to the necessary knowledge to put facts together (the knowledge required for creativity, as already explained). *Creative-thinking skill* refers to the ability to imaginatively approach problems. If you know how to keep digging for alternatives and to avoid getting stuck in the status quo, your chances of being creative multiply. The exercises to be presented in this chapter foster this type of mental flexibility. Finally, *task motivation* refers to persevering, or sticking with a problem to a conclusion, which is essential for finding creative solutions. A few rest breaks to gain a fresh perspective may be helpful, but the creative person keeps coming back until a solution emerges.

The combined forces of the three factors lead to individual creativity as follows: expertise × creative-thinking skill × task motivation = creativity. Because there are substantial individual differences for each factor, such as wide variation in domain-relevant expertise, not all leaders are equally creative.

# OVERCOMING TRADITIONAL THINKING AS A CREATIVITY STRATEGY

A unifying theme runs through all forms of creativity training and suggestions for creativity improvement: creative problem solving requires an ability to overcome traditional thinking. The concept of *traditional thinking* is relative, but it generally refers to a standard and frequent way of finding a solution to a problem. A traditional solution to a problem is thus a modal or most frequent solution. For example, traditional thinking suggests that to increase revenue, a retail store should conduct a sale. Creative thinking would point toward other solutions. As an example, a retail store might increase sales by delivering goods for a small fee, or providing for online shopping (of the store's products) in the store.

The creative person looks at problems in a new light and transcends conventional thinking about them. A historically significant example is Henry Ford, who was known for his creative problem-solving ability. A meatpacking executive invited Ford to visit his Chicago plant and observe how employees processed beef. The automotive executive noticed that at one end of the plant whole carcasses of steers were placed on a giant conveyor belt. As the meat traveled through the plant, workers carved it into various cuts until the carcass was consumed. A flash of whimsical insight hit Ford: What if the process were reversed, and all the pieces would become a whole steer again? Ford asked himself, "Why can't an automobile be built that way?" He took his creative idea back to the Ford Motor Company in Detroit and constructed the world's first manufacturing assembly line.[16]

The central task in becoming creative is to break down rigid thinking that blocks new ideas. At the same time, the problem solver must unlearn the conventional approach.[17] Henry Ford unlearned the custom approach to building autos so he could use an assembly line. (In the current era, people who have unlearned the assembly-line approach and switched to customization are considered to be creative!)

**KB** Knowledge Bank
Provides more depth on the topic of creative thinking.

**www.cengage.com/ management/dubrin**

Overcoming traditional thinking is so important to creative thinking that the process has been characterized in several different ways. The most familiar is that *a creative person thinks outside the box*. A box in this sense is a category that confines and restricts thinking. Because you are confined to a box, you do not see opportunities outside the box. For example, if an insurance executive thinks that health insurance is only for people, he or she might miss out on the growing market for domestic animal health insurance. Inside the accompanying box insert, you will find several business examples of thinking outside the box.

## Modern Business Examples of Thinking Outside the Box

- Conventional wisdom says that sidewalks have to be made out of cement or concrete, and that when tree roots damage the sidewalks, the trees have to go. Lindsay Smith noted that twenty-six trees in her neighborhood in Gardena, California, were being cut down because their roots were damaging the sidewalk. With guidance from U.S. Rubber Recycling, she founded Rubbersidewalks, a company that has installed footpaths made of recycled tires in sixty cities in the United States and Canada. Each square piece can be removed for repairs, thereby saving the destruction of trees. Also rubber is more compatible with tree roots than is concrete.

- Conventional wisdom says that to rent videos or DVDs you have to visit a physical video or DVD store. Netflix shot out of nowhere to create a new segment in the movie rental business with a simple business model that allows consumers to rent popular DVDs online and have the movies arrive quickly in the mail, all for a monthly fee. Netflix's success spawned competitors, but so far the company still has about a 95 percent market share.

- Conventional wisdom says that for-sale homes have to be displayed in a dignified way, such

as the agent driving an interested party in a car or making online visits. Cesar Dias, a real estate agent in Stockton, California, challenged that idea. His Repo Home Tour fills two brightly colored, eighteen-seat buses with prospective buyers with an interest in viewing foreclosed houses that can be purchased at rock-bottom prices. At the time, Stockton was leading the country in the foreclosure rate, making his Repo Home Tour all the more useful—and therefore innovative.

- Conventional wisdom says that ATM monitors are used only to display bank-statement-related information. Not Bank of America: they started a program of selling advertising space on ATMs.

- Conventional wisdom says that banks cannot make home loans to devout Muslims because, according to the Koran (Islam's sacred book), Muslims are forbidden to pay or receive interest. As a consequence, a potential segment of the market was shut out from receiving home mortgages. The University Bank of Ann Arbor, Michigan, developed a unique interest-free program designed for people whose religious beliefs forbid paying interest. The bank developed a mortgage alternative loan transaction (MALT) program that replaces a traditional home loan with a redeemable lease. The bank holds the home in trust, and the customer makes monthly payments to that trust. Each rent payment includes a set amount of savings that builds equity in the property. After the savings account equals the home's original price, the customer owns the home free and clear.

*Source:* Stacy Perman, "Concrete Decision," *BusinessWeek SmallBiz,* February/March 2007, p. 034;

Christopher Stern, "Netflix Braces for Amazon: DVD Rental Company Cuts Fees to Compete," *Washington Post,* October 16, 2004, p. 1E; Steve Chawkins, "Stockton's Magical Misery Tours," *Los Angeles Times* (latimes.com), December 13, 2007; Sally Beatty, "Bank of America Puts Ads in ATMs," *Wall Street Journal,* July 25, 2002, p. B8; Karen Dybis, "Banks Offer No-Interest Options for Muslims," *Detroit News,* December 21, 2004 (detnews.com).

# ORGANIZATIONAL METHODS TO ENHANCE CREATIVITY

**Knowledge Bank**
Provides more information on brainstorming and other creativity-enhancing methods.

**www.cengage.com/ management/dubrin**

To enhance creative problem solving, most organizations regularly engage in brainstorming. We focus here on new developments in brainstorming and other creativity-enhancing methods. Programs of this nature are applied to actual problems, while at the same time they provide an opportunity to improve creative thinking.

The leader has a dual role in implementing creative problem-solving techniques: he or she facilitates group interaction and also provides a fair share of creative output. The four creativity-enhancing, problem-solving techniques described here are (1) systematically collecting fresh ideas; (2) brainstorming; (3) using the pet-peeve technique; and (4) equipping a kitchen for the mind. The Knowledge Bank presents a fifth method. A notable point about creativity-enhancing methods is that no one method is likely to be consistently better than any other method. The underlying mechanism is that each creativity-enhancing method helps bring new ideas to the surface. Danny Strickland, the chief innovator at Coca-Cola, points out that all of these creativity tools have one simple thing at the heart. "They try to bring in new information that will help change your perspective. If you change the way you think about something, then suddenly new ideas come to mind." [18]

## Systematically Collecting Fresh Ideas

Creativity is often referred to as a numbers game, because the more ideas you try, the greater the probability of finding one that works. A notable way of collecting fresh ideas is for employees to furnish them to a company database so that when somebody needs a fresh idea it can be accessed through a company search engine. Google, the search-engine company, uses an internal web site to collect and retrieve ideas. Many of the ideas are used to improve the company's enormously popular search engine. Google's idea search begins with a company-use-only web page. Using a program called Sparrow, Google employees can readily create a page of ideas. This enables company leaders (such as a product manager) to cast a net across the company's 300 employees. Using this method, every Google staff member invests a fraction of the workday on research and development. Employees are encouraged to invest 20 percent of their time working on whatever they think will have the biggest payoff for the company.[19]

To facilitate having fresh ideas, the leader or manager can establish idea quotas, such as by asking staff members to bring one new idea to each meeting. Although the vast majority of these ideas may not lead to innovation, a few good ones will emerge. One reason idea quotas work is that they are a goal. Another is that an environmental need (in this case, the idea quota) is an excellent creativity stimulant.

A major leadership accomplishment is to obtain widespread participation in contributing innovative thinking. A. G. Lafley, the Procter & Gamble CEO, explains this approach:

> The P&G of five years or six years ago depended on 8,000 scientists and engineers for the vast majority of innovation. The P&G we're trying to unleash today asks all 100,000-plus of us to be innovators. We actively solicit good ideas, and if the concept is promising we put it into development. For example, we are now selling a line of hair care for women of color called Pantene Pro-V Relaxed and Natural. A few African-American employees came to me and said we're missing out: The stuff that's on the market really doesn't work, and we can do better.[20] [The line is doing well.]

## Brainstorming

**KB** **Knowledge Bank**
Contains rules for
brainstorming.

**www.cengage.com/
management/dubrin**

The best-known method for creativity improvement is brainstorming, which most of you have already done. Although brainstorming is often condemned as being superficial, it remains a key idea-generation method for even the most advanced technology companies. A notable example is the firm Intellectual Ventures, whose primary mission is to develop inventions, cofounded by Nathan P. Myhrvold, the former chief technology officer at Microsoft. Myhrvold assembles groups of doctors, engineers, and scientists known for their brilliance, along with in-house inventors and lawyers, for day-long brainstorming sessions. The Intellectual Ventures staff takes ideas from the brainstorming sessions and turns them into patents. Inventors get a share of any eventual royalties.[21]

The Intellectual Ventures application of brainstorming emphasizes the observation that goals are an essential part of the process. The Ventures team focuses on the goal of attaining ideas worthy of a patent. According to the theorizing of Robert C. Litchfield, the various rules of brainstorming can be regarded as goals, including (a) generate quantity, (b) avoid criticism, (c) combine and improve on previous ideas, and (d) combine and improve on previous ideas.[22]

As a refresher, do Leadership Skill-Building Exercise 11-1. Because the vast majority of employers use brainstorming, it is helpful to have some advanced knowledge of the topic other than that it is simply shouting out ideas.

A key aspect of brainstorming is that all ideas can be steppingstones and triggers for new and more useful ideas. Any idea might lead to other associations and connections. Thus, during the idea-generating part of brainstorming, potential

## ◉ Leadership Skill-Building Exercise 11-1

### Choose an Effective Domain Name

To refresh your memory, first study the rules for brainstorming presented in the Knowledge Bank. Then do the brainstorming exercise.

Organize into groups to play *Choose an Effective Domain Name*. Your task is to develop original domain names for several products or services. An effective domain name is typically one that is easy to remember and will capture potential customers in an uncomplicated Web search. One reason this exercise is difficult is that "cybersquatters" grab unclaimed names they think business owners might want, and then sell these names later. For example, a cybersquatter (or domain name exploiter) might develop or buy the domain name www.catfood.com, hoping that an etailer of cat food will want this name in the future. The owner of catfood.com would charge a company like PetSmart every time a surfer looking to purchase cat food over the Internet entered www.catfood.com and was then linked to PetSmart.

After your team has brainstormed a few possible domain names, search the Internet to see if your domain name is already in use. Simply enter "www" plus the name you have chosen into your browser. Or visit the site of a company like DomainCollection.com. After you have developed your list of domain names not already in use, the team leader will present your findings to the rest of the class.

- Hair salons
- Replacement parts for antique or classic autos
- A used-car chain
- Alzheimer's disease treatment centers
- Personal loans for people with poor (subprime) credit ratings
- Recycled steel for manufacturers
- You choose one of your own

solutions are not criticized or evaluated in any way, so that spontaneity is encouraged. The idea for an antitheft device for automobiles, The Club, is reported to have stemmed from brainstorming. One marketing person suggested that cars should have a portable steering wheel that the driver could remove after the car is parked. Somebody else suggested that the steering wheel be made inoperative, which led to the idea of an ultrastrong bar to lock the steering wheel in place. The Club and its imitators have become highly successful products; a version of The Club has been developed for securing doors.

Brainstorming continues to evolve as a method of creative problem solving. Another variation is the *6-3-5 method*. Six people take five minutes to write down three ideas each on a sheet of paper or large index card. After five minutes, the participants pass their papers or cards clockwise and add their own ideas to each new sheet. They continue passing along and writing down ideas until the sheets or cards get back to the people who originated them. Next, they hold a group discussion of the merits of the various ideas.[23] During the discussion, it is likely that some members will modify their ideas or think of new ones because they will be stimulated by the list of eighteen ideas. Often, however, the list will contain many duplicate or similar ideas.

Another variation of brainstorming is to encourage *extreme thinking*. Participants are asked to contribute ideas that would probably work but are so outrageous they could get the group fired. Later the group figures out a way to narrow the potential solutions.[24] Here would be two examples of extreme thinking during brainstorming about product development:

- At Starbucks, somebody suggests that the average price of Starbucks coffee should be lowered to 50 cents per cup so as to compete better with McDonald's and Dunkin' Donuts.
- At GM, somebody suggests that GM get out of selling vehicles in North America because it is so difficult to sell GM vehicles profitably there.

Brainstorming, much like other creative problem-solving techniques, works best in an organizational culture that fosters innovation. It is an integral part of the famous design firm IDEO, Inc., whose employees believe passionately in innovation. As a result they are able to argue about alternative solutions to problems yet still unite to produce an effective design.[25]

### Using the Pet-Peeve Technique

An important part of leadership is for organizational units to find ways to continuously improve their service to external and internal customers. The **pet-peeve technique** is a method of brainstorming in which a group identifies all the possible complaints others might have about the group's organizational unit.[26] Through brainstorming, group members develop a list of complaints from any people who interact with their group. Sources of complaints include inside customers, outside customers, competitors, and suppliers.

Group members can prepare for the meeting by soliciting feedback on themselves from the various target groups. In keeping with the informal, breezy style of the pet-peeve group, feedback should be gathered informally. Rather than approach target groups with a survey, members might tell others about the upcoming pet-peeve session and then ask, "What complaints can you contribute?"

During the no-holds-barred brainstorming session, group members throw in some imaginary and some humorous complaints. Humorous complaints are especially important, for humor requires creative thinking. After all complaints have been aired, the group can process the information during a later session, when they can draw up action plans to remedy the most serious problems.

A pet-peeve session in the human resources department of a manufacturer of small electronic appliances generated many complaints, including the following:

"A lot of people wonder what we are doing. They think we just fill out forms and create work for ourselves."

"Some line managers think our job is to find good reasons why they shouldn't hire their best job candidates."

"Job candidates from the outside think our job is to shred résumés. They think we throw away or delete 90 percent of the résumés that arrive at the company."

As a result of these penetrating, albeit exaggerated, self-criticisms, the human resources department developed an effective action plan. The department leader arranged brief meetings with units throughout the organization to discuss the department's role and to answer questions.

**The Pet-Peeve Technique**

Review the description of the pet-peeve technique given in the text. Break into groups of about five contributors each. Each group assumes the role of an organizational unit. (Pick one that is familiar to the group, either through direct contact or through secondhand knowledge. For example, you might assume the role of the auditing group of an accounting firm, the financial aid office at your school, or the service department of an automobile dealer.) Generate a number of real and imagined criticisms of your group. Take the two most serious criticisms and develop an action plan to move your group to a higher plane.

The pet-peeve technique is potentially valuable for a leader because it can help the group improve its work processes. Because it has a good-spirited touch, it is not likely to be perceived as threatening. Leadership Skill-Building Exercise 11-2 presents an opportunity to practice the pet-peeve technique.

### Equipping a Kitchen for the Mind

According to Mike Vance, every business needs a **kitchen for the mind,** a space designed to nurture creativity. The supplies can be ordinary items such as a chalkboard, flip charts, a coffeepot, a refrigerator, a pencil sharpener, and a personal computer with graphics software. Creativity rooms are also sometimes supplied with children's toys, such as dart guns, Frisbees, Nerf balls, and stuffed animals. The purpose of the toys is to help people loosen up intellectually and emotionally, thus stimulating creative thinking. Many large corporations, including General Electric and Motorola, have established creative kitchens, which they often supply with VCRs, DVD players, and multimedia computers.

More important than the equipment within the kitchen for the mind is the existence of a communal meeting place where people can get together to think creatively. Vance contends that even when people's resources are limited, they can still use their ingenuity to produce creative ideas.[27]

**Knowledge Bank**
Physical activities are yet another way of enhancing creativity, as presented in the Knowledge Bank.

**www.cengage.com/ management/dubrin**

## SELF-HELP TECHNIQUES TO ENHANCE CREATIVE PROBLEM SOLVING

Leaders and others who want to solve problems more creatively can find hundreds of methods at their disposal, all of them aiming to increase mental flexibility. Six strategies and specific techniques for enhancing creative problem solving are presented next and are outlined in Table 11-1. These strategies and techniques support and supplement the organizational programs described previously. An underlying contribution of these techniques is that they facilitate flexible thinking, or viewing the world with open and curious eyes.[28] With such a mental stance, almost

**TABLE 11-1** Self-Help Techniques for Creativity Improvement

1. Practicing creativity-enhancing exercises
2. Staying alert to opportunities
3. Maintaining an enthusiastic attitude, including being happy
4. Maintaining and using a systematic place for recording your ideas
5. Playing the roles of explorer, artist, judge, and lawyer
6. Engaging in appropriate physical exercise

anything can spark a new idea. As a warehouse manager you might observe young people rollerblading in the park. With a creative attitude, you might conclude that your logistic specialists would be more efficient if they used Rollerblades rather than walked.

## Practicing Creativity-Enhancing Exercises

An established way to sharpen creative thinking is to regularly engage in activities that encourage flexible thinking. If you enjoy photography, put yourself on assignment to take a photograph illustrating a theme. You might, for example, take photographs illustrating the proper use of your company's product. Puzzles of all types are useful in stretching your imagination; many creative people regularly do crossword puzzles. Another mind stretcher is to force yourself to write jokes around a given theme. Can you create a joke about the creativity of a leader?

Learning a second language, including sign language, can facilitate creativity because you are forced to shift mental sets. For example, your second language may require you to remember the gender of every noun and to match the spelling of each adjective to the gender and number (singular versus plural) of the noun.

Leadership Skill-Building Exercise 11-3 gives you an opportunity to practice creative thinking. Doing exercises of this nature enhances creative problem solving.

## Staying Alert to Opportunities

A characteristic of creative leaders is that they can spot opportunities that other people overlook. Opportunity seeking is associated with entrepreneurial leadership because the entrepreneur might build an organization around an unmet consumer need. The idea behind the international chain of Starbucks coffee shops began when Howard Schultz, the director of a four-store retail operation called Starbucks Coffee, Tea, and Spice, was attending a housewares convention in Milan, Italy. Schultz noticed the coffee-bar phenomenon. Milan alone had 1,500 of them, all serving trendy beverages such as espresso. Believing that coffee bars would also prosper in the United States, Schultz convinced Starbucks to open one. Schultz left the company to form his own small chain of coffee bars, and then he bought out Starbucks's two founding partners and merged Starbucks with his firm.[29] (What unmet consumer need did Schultz identify?)

## ⊙ Leadership Skill-Building Exercise 11-3

### Word Hints to Creativity

Find a fourth word that is related to the other three words in each row.

Example: poke      go      molasses      _____

The answer is *slow:* slowpoke, go slow, and slow as molasses. Now try these words:

1. surprise     line      birthday      _____
2. base         snow      dance         _____
3. rat          blue      cottage       _____
4. nap          litter    call          _____
5. golf         foot      country       _____
6. house        tired     leash         _____

7. tiger        plate     news          _____
8. painting     bowl      nail          _____
9. jump         sea       priest        _____
10. maple       beet      loaf          _____
11. oak         show      plan          _____
12. light       village   golf          _____
13. merry       out       up            _____
14. jelly       green     kidney        _____
15. bulb        house     lamp          _____
16. You come up with three words to really stretch your mind _____ _____ _____

***Scoring and Interpretation*** Answers appear on page 000. If you were able to think of the "correct" word, or another plausible one, for ten or more of these words, your score compares favorably to that of creative individuals. More important than the score is the fact that you acquired some practice in making remote associations—a characteristic talent of creative people.

*Source:* Updated and adapted from "Ideas: Test Your Creativity," by Eugene Raudsepp, *Nation's Business* (June 1965), p. 80.

### Maintaining an Enthusiastic Attitude, Including Being Happy

The managerial leader faces a major hurdle in becoming a creative problem solver. He or she must resolve the conflict between being judicial and being imaginative. In many work situations, being judicial (or judgmental) is necessary. Situations calling for judicial thinking include reviewing proposed expenditures and inspecting products for quality or safety defects. Imaginative thinking is involved when searching for creative alternatives. Alex F. Osburn, a former advertising executive and the originator of brainstorming, notes how judgment and imagination are often in conflict:

> The fact that moods won't mix largely explains why the judicial and the creative tend to clash. The right mood for judicial thinking is largely negative. "What's wrong with this? . . . No this won't work." Such reflexes are right and proper when trying to judge.

In contrast, our creative thinking calls for a positive attitude. We have to be hopeful. We need enthusiasm. We have to encourage ourselves to the point of self-confidence. We have to beware of perfectionism lest it be abortive.[30]

The action step is therefore to project oneself into a positive frame of mind when attempting to be creative. The same principle applies when attempting to be creative about a judicial task. For instance, a leader might be faced with the task of looking for creative ways to cut costs. The manager would then have to think positively about thinking negatively!

Closely related to enthusiasm as a contributor to creativity is the finding that being in a good mood facilitates creativity. The finding comes from an analysis of diaries or journals, as described earlier. The journal entries showed that people are happiest when they come up with a creative idea. However, they are more likely to have a breakthrough idea if they were happy the day before. One day's happiness is often a predictor of the next day's creative idea.[31]

## Maintaining and Using a Systematic Place for Recording Your Ideas

It is difficult to capitalize on creative ideas unless you keep a careful record of them. A creative idea trusted to memory may be forgotten in the press of everyday business. An important suggestion kept on your daily planner may become obscured. Creative ideas can lead to breakthroughs for your group and your career, so they deserve the dignity of a separate notebook, or computer file, or any other storage device that works for you. Recording tools include notebooks or journals, personal digital assistants, index cards, audio recorders, voice mail and email messages sent to you, flip charts, pocket-size notepads, and an idea file/database such as a storage box for index cards.[32] A cautious or forgetful person is advised to keep two copies of the ideas: one at home and one in the office.

## Playing the Roles of Explorer, Artist, Judge, and Lawyer

Another creativity-improvement method incorporates many of the preceding methods. Say you want to enhance your creativity on the job. This method calls for you to adopt four roles in your thinking.[33] First, be an *explorer*. Speak to people in different fields and get ideas that can bring about innovations for your group. For example, if you manage a telecommunications group, speak to salespeople and manufacturing specialists.

Second, be an artist by stretching your imagination. Strive to spend about 5 percent of your day asking what-if questions. For example, the leader of a telecommunications group might ask, "What if some new research suggests that the extensive use of telecommunications devices is associated with high rates of cancer?" Also remember to challenge the commonly perceived rules in your field. A bank manager, for example, asked why customers needed canceled checks returned each month. The questioning led to a new bank practice: returning canceled checks only if the customer pays an additional fee.

Third, know when to be a *judge*. After developing some imaginative ideas, at some point you have to evaluate them. Do not be so critical that you discourage your own imaginative thinking. Be critical enough, however, so that you do not try to implement weak ideas. A managing partner in an established law firm formulated a plan for opening two storefront branches that would offer legal services to the public at low prices. The branches would advertise on radio, on television, and in newspapers. After thinking through her plan for several weeks, however, she dropped the idea. She decided that the storefront branches would most likely divert clients away from the parent firm, rather than create a new market.

Fourth, achieve results with your creative thinking by playing the role of lawyer. Negotiate and find ways to implement your ideas within your field or place of work. The explorer, artist, and judge stages of creative thought might take only a short time to develop a creative idea. Yet you may spend months or even years getting your breakthrough idea implemented. For example, many tax-preparation firms now loan clients instant refunds in the amount of their anticipated tax refunds. It took a manager in a large tax-preparation firm a long time to convince top management of the merits of the idea.

### Engaging in Appropriate Physical Exercise

A well-accepted method of stimulating creativity is to engage in physical exercise. Stephen Ramocki, a marketing professor at Rhode Island College, found that a single aerobic workout is sufficient to trigger the brains of students into high gear—and that the benefit lasted for a minimum of two hours. Gary Kasparov, the chess champion, is a gym fanatic and an extraordinary intellect. He has credited his physical fitness with boosting his skill in chess.

🅚🅑 **Knowledge Bank**
Two more self-help techniques to enhance creative problem solving are described in the Knowledge Bank.

**www.cengage.com/ management/dubrin**

The fact that creative insights often arise during physical exercise fits the steps on the creative process referred to as immersion and incubation. Another explanation of why exercise facilitates creativity is that exercising pumps more blood and oxygen into the brain. Exercise also enhances activity in the frontal lobe, the region of the brain involved in abstract reasoning and attention.[34] The fact that physical exercise can boost creative thinking should not be interpreted in isolation. Without other factors going for a leader, such as a storehouse of knowledge and passion for the task, physical exercise will not lead to creative breakthroughs.

## ESTABLISHING A CLIMATE AND CULTURE FOR CREATIVE THINKING

Leaders need to develop creative ideas of their own to improve productivity and satisfaction. Establishing a climate, or culture, conducive to creative problem solving is another requirement of effective leadership. A foundation step in fostering organizational creativity is to establish a vision and mission that include creativity, such as "We will become the most innovative provider of automobile care (mufflers, brakes, etc.) products and services in North America" (Monro Muffler Brake, Inc.). Vision statements and mission statements set the pace, but they must be supported by the right climate, or organizational culture, and extensive use of the techniques described throughout this chapter.

Information about establishing a climate for creativity can be divided into (1) leadership and managerial practices for enhancing creativity and (2) methods for managing creative workers. To become sensitized to this vast amount of information, do Leadership Diagnostic Activity 11-1. The instrument gives you an opportunity to ponder many of the management and leadership practices that encourage or discourage creative problem solving.

 ## Leadership Diagnostic Activity 11-1

### Assessing the Climate for Innovation

***Instructions:*** Respond "mostly yes" or "mostly no" as to how well each of the following characteristics fits an organization familiar to you. If you are currently not familiar with an outside organization, respond to these statements in regard to your school.

|  | Mostly Yes | Mostly No |
|---|:---:|:---:|
| 1. Creativity is encouraged here. | ☐ | ☐ |
| 2. Our ability to function creatively is respected by the leadership. | ☐ | ☐ |
| 3. Around here, people are allowed to try to solve the same problems in different ways. | ☐ | ☐ |
| 4. The main function of members of this organization is to follow orders that come down through channels. | ☐ | ☐ |
| 5. Around here, a person can get into a lot of trouble by being different. | ☐ | ☐ |
| 6. This organization can be described as flexible and continually adapting to change. | ☐ | ☐ |
| 7. A person cannot do things that are too different around here without provoking anger. | ☐ | ☐ |
| 8. The best way to get along in this organization is to think the way the rest of the group does. | ☐ | ☐ |
| 9. People around here are expected to deal with problems in the same way. | ☐ | ☐ |
| 10. This organization is open and responsive to change. | ☐ | ☐ |
| 11. The people in charge around here usually get credit for others' ideas. | ☐ | ☐ |
| 12. In this organization, we tend to stick to tried and true ways. | ☐ | ☐ |
| 13. This place seems to be more concerned with the status quo than with change. | ☐ | ☐ |
| 14. Assistance in developing new ideas is readily available. | ☐ | ☐ |

## Activity 11-1 (continued)

|  | Mostly Yes | Mostly No |
|---|---|---|
| **15.** There are adequate resources devoted to innovation in this organization. | ☐ | ☐ |
| **16.** There is adequate time available to pursue creative ideas here. | ☐ | ☐ |
| **17.** Lack of funding to pursue creative ideas is a problem in this organization. | ☐ | ☐ |
| **18.** Personnel shortages inhibit innovation in this organization. | ☐ | ☐ |
| **19.** This organization gives me free time to pursue creative ideas during the workday. | ☐ | ☐ |
| **20.** The reward system here encourages innovation. | ☐ | ☐ |
| **21.** This organization publicly recognizes those who are innovative. | ☐ | ☐ |
| **22.** The reward system here benefits mainly those who do not rock the boat. | ☐ | ☐ |

***Scoring and Interpretation:*** The score in the direction of a climate for innovation is "mostly yes" for statements 1, 2, 3, 6, 10, 14, 15, 16, 19, 20, and 21, and "mostly no" for statements 4, 5, 7, 8, 9, 11, 12, 13, 17, 18, and 22. A score of 16 or higher suggests a climate well suited for innovation, 9 to 15 is about average, and 8 or below suggests a climate that inhibits innovation.

*Source:* From Susanne G. Scott and Reginald Bruce, "Determinants of Innovative Behavior: A Path Model of Individual Innovation in the Workplace," *Academy of Management Journal,* by Hitt, Michael A., June 1994, p. 593. Copyright 1994 by Academy of Management. Reproduced with permission of Academy of Management in the format Textbook via Copyright Clearance Center.

## Leadership Practices for Enhancing Creativity

Eight leadership and managerial practices are particularly helpful in fostering creative thinking, as revealed by the work of many researchers and observers.[35] The organizational methods already described for enhancing creativity might also be interpreted as leadership practices.

**1. *Hire creative people from the outside and identify creative people from within.*** The most robust leadership and management practice for enhancing creativity is to hire people with the aptitude for, or track record in, being creative. Creativity training is helpful, yet starting with creative people enhances the potential of training. Dave Ditzel, the founder of Transmeta and a Bell Labs alumnus, says you need talent spotters. He believes that it is a lot more productive to find ten superinnovative workers than to subject 10,000 creatively challenged employees to training.[36] Part of the same argument is that hiring innovative people helps foster an innovative environment. Arthur D. Levinson, chairman and chief executive of Genentech, the heralded biotechnology firm, says, "If you want an innovative environment, hire innovative people, listen to them tell you want they want, and do it."[37]

**2. *Intellectual challenge.*** Matching people with the right assignments enhances creativity because it supports expertise and intrinsic motivation. The amount of stretch is consistent with goal theory; too little challenge leads to boredom, but too much challenge leads to feelings of being overwhelmed and loss of control. The leader or manager must understand his or her group members well to offer them the right amount of challenge. Moderate time pressures can sometimes bring about the right amount of challenge.

**3. *Freedom to choose the method.*** Workers tend to be more creative when they are granted the freedom to choose which method is best for attaining a work goal (as described in our study of empowerment in Chapter 7). Stable goals are important because it is difficult to work creatively toward a moving target.

**4. *Ample supply of the right resources.*** Time and money are the most important resources for enhancing creativity. Deciding how much time and money to give to a team or project is a tough judgment call that can either support or stifle creativity. Under some circumstances setting a time deadline will trigger creative thinking because it represents a favorable challenge. An example would be hurrying to be first to market with a new product. False deadlines or impossibly tight ones can create distrust and burnout. To be creative, groups also need to be adequately funded.

**5. *Effective design of work groups.*** Work groups are the most likely to be creative when they are mutually supportive and when they have a diversity of backgrounds and perspectives. Blends of gender, race, and ethnicity are recognized today as contributing to creative thought, similar to cross-functional teams with their mix of perspectives from different disciplines. The various points of view often combine to achieve creative solutions to problems. Homogeneous teams argue less, but they are often less creative. Putting together a team with the right chemistry—just the right level of diversity and supportiveness—requires experience and intuition on the leader's part.

**6. *Supervisory encouragement.*** The most influential step a leader can take to bring about creative problem solving is to develop a permissive atmosphere that encourages people to think freely. Praising creative work is important because, for most people to sustain their passion, they must feel that their work matters to the organization. Creative ideas should be evaluated quickly rather than put through a painfully slow review process.

**7. *Organizational support.*** The entire organization as well as the immediate manager should support creative effort if creativity is to be enhanced on a large scale. The company-wide reward system should support creativity, including recognition and financial incentives. Organizational leaders should encourage information sharing and collaboration, which lead to the development of the expertise so necessary for creativity and to more opportunities for intrinsic motivation. Executives who combat excessive politics can help creative people focus on work instead of fighting political battles. In a highly political environment, a worker would be hesitant to suggest a creative idea that was a political blunder, such as replacing a product particularly liked by the CEO.

**8. *Have favorable exchanges with creative workers.*** Another insight into encouraging a creative climate is for leaders to have favorable exchanges with group members, as defined by LMX theory (see Chapter 9). A study with 191 research and development specialists found a positive relationship between LMX ratings and creativity of workers as measured by supervisory ratings.[38] When group members have positive relationships with their manager, they may have a more relaxed mental attitude that allows the imagination to flow. A useful strategy for enhancing creativity throughout the organization is to emphasize the importance of working with a sense of heightened awareness, of being alert to new possibilities.

The Leader in Action profile on the next page describes an entrepreneur who deliberately attempts to create an organizational culture that fosters creativity.

## Methods of Managing Creative Workers

Closely related to establishing organizational conditions favoring creativity is choosing effective methods for managing creative workers. The suggestions that follow supplement effective leadership and management practices in general.[39]

**1. *Give creative people tools and resources that allow their work to stand out.*** Creative workers have a high degree of self-motivation and therefore want to achieve high-quality output. To achieve such high quality, they usually need adequate resources, such as state-of-the-art equipment and an ample travel budget for such purposes as conducting research.

**2. *Give creative people flexibility and a minimum amount of structure.*** Many creative workers regard heavy structure as the death knell of creativity. "Structure" for these workers means rules and regulations, many layers of approval, strict dress codes, fixed office hours, rigid assignments, and fill-in-the-blank Web forms or paperwork. (Typically, the leader/manager will have to achieve a workable compromise in this area that stays within the framework of organizational policy. Regular office hours, for example, are a must for team assignments. Also, creative people may need help with meeting deadlines because many creative people do not manage time well.)

Although structure should be minimized, some constraints will foster creativity such as the leader presenting demands about the cost of the product or service, and the time the innovation will be needed. Marissa Ann Mayer, the vice president for search products and user experience at Google, offers this example: When the company develops a new toolbar, it must work for all users, and it must be fast to download, even over a modem. Toolbar developers are required to work within these constraints, and the constraints have been found to speed development. Time constraints have also proved useful because failures can be discovered fast and abandoned quickly.[40]

**3. *Give gentle feedback when turning down an idea.*** Creative employees are emotionally involved with their work. As a result, they are likely to interpret criticism as a personal attack on their self-worth. (Students often feel the same way about their term papers and projects.)

## Leader in Action

### CEO Josh Linkner Builds a Culture of Creativity at ePrize

Josh Linkner, age 36, is the founder and CEO of ePrize, LLC, located in Pleasant Ridge, Michigan. An excerpt of his secrets for success follows:

> At ePrize we work hard to create an atmosphere that encourages creativity and empowers people to reach personal greatness. Our culture is based on respect and trust. We want to hear everyone's ideas.
>
> Our facility is another example. Because we produce interactive promotions, games, sweepstakes and more for many of the world's largest companies, I want it to be a vibrant, fun, crazy place. We have a 1,300-square-foot rooftop patio that seats 30, with couches and coffee tables. I can't understand how companies ask their people to do creative work and then stick them in cube farms.
>
> I believe leaders are here to serve. Our job is to empower others to reach personal greatness. My job is to maximize the potential of our organization and to make a difference. I am a life-long learner, and I try to create a learning organization. The toughest decisions are when we have a great person who is no longer right for the company. I always want to put the best interest of the company ahead of anything personal.
>
> I really want to continue to create an amazing place for our team to work, a place that empowers people to do extraordinary things. It all gets back to our culture for me.
>
> Like too many people, I'm a self-professed workaholic. I don't always keep traditional office hours and work a lot from home and on the weekends. I average 60 to 70 hours per week. I like to see my kids in the morning, and then I'm pretty focused and intense from there on out.
>
> I have an assistant who helps with scheduling and keeping things moving at warp speed. I use a Black-Berry and in my case it's truly a "Crack-berry." I received about 350 e-mails per day and send about 150. I can't imagine an executive in the Digital Age who doesn't use e-mail.
>
> I meet once a week with my core team and also have weekly one-on-ones with key people. We hold a full-company "huddle" once a month, when we rent an auditorium and bring everybody together. We share our successes, take our challenges head-on and have a great time. It really keeps us working in lockstep. Meeting with people is the lifeblood of most companies.
>
> To keep up, I check out several web sites, including Harvard Business Review, Yahoo!, Google, Click Z, the "Wall Street Journal," and Weather.com. And, of course, I monitor ePrize.com and CaffeineNow.com. In print, I read *Harvard Business Review*, *Crain's Detroit Business*, *The Detroit News*, and *BusinessWeek*. I don't read cover to cover, but I give them a good skimming, at the least. I'm currently reading a book called *Mavericks at Work* that talks about the importance of being bold and taking risks.
>
> During the day, I rarely go out for lunch, and only do so for lunch meetings. I do pause during the day to walk around, visit with people or play a few jazz guitar riffs to loosen up.
>
> I have a fully colored office that is warm and inviting. I keep a jazz guitar on hand to blow off steam and ignite creativity. I have a gigantic computer screen that people who visit always make fun of. And then, about two weeks later, they tell me they bought one for themselves.
>
> No matter what's going on, I'm always trying to make sure I'm having fun, learning, and making a difference.

### Questions

1. What does Linkner do at his company that contributes to a creative organizational culture?
2. Which creativity-enhancing activities does Linkner engage in himself?
3. So what is wrong with working in a "cube farm" from the standpoint of being creative?

*Source:* Adapted and excerpted from "ePrize CEO Builds Culture of Creativity," detnews.com, March 19, 2007. Reprinted courtesy of ePrize, LLC.

**4. *Employ creative people to manage and evaluate creative workers.*** Managers of creative workers should have some creative ability of their own so that they can understand creativity and be credible as leaders. Understanding the creative process is important for evaluating the creative contribution of others. What constitutes creative output is somewhat subjective, but the output can be tied to objective criteria. At Hallmark Cards, Inc., for example, creativity is measured by such factors as how well the creative work sold and how well it performed in a consumer preference test. In general, a manager's intuition about the potential contribution of a creative idea or product still weighs heavily in the evaluation.

# ADDITIONAL LEADERSHIP PRACTICES THAT ENHANCE INNOVATION

Creativity in organizations leads to innovations in products, services, and processes (such as a billing system or safety improvement). All leadership and management practices that enhance creative problem solving therefore also enhance innovation. Here we describe eight additional leadership initiatives that enhance innovation.

**1. *Continually pursue innovation.*** A major characteristic of the Most Admired Companies, as compiled by the Hay Group consultancy for *Fortune*, is constant innovation. Translated into practice, this means that company leaders stay alert to innovative possibilities. Innovation is important because a new technology can make an industry obsolete or place it in grave danger. What will happen to petroleum refineries when (and if) the fuel cell takes hold?

**2. *Take risks and encourage risk taking.*** "No risk, no reward" is a rule of life that applies equally well to the leadership of innovation. Even in a slow-growth economy, companies cannot win big in the marketplace by doing things just a teeny bit better than the competition. It is necessary to gamble intelligently, shrewdly, and selectively even during a period of insecurity and instability.[41] Because most new ideas fail, part of taking risks is being willing to go down blind alleys.

**3. *Emphasize collaboration among employees.*** A recent analysis suggests that most innovations stem from networks, or groups of people working in concert. The workers needed for the innovation are often dispersed throughout the organization. Choosing the right leader for a project can be the key to collaboration. The workers chosen to develop new ideas are often top performers in individual areas. However, they may be lacking the connections within the company that are vital for accomplishing the innovation task. For instance, an outstanding engineer might be selected to lead a major project. But a lower-ranking engineer who has worked in more divisions of the company might be a wiser choice because he or she could tap broader knowledge and connections inside the company. A consumer products company intentionally placed workers together on a project who had developed friendships during a business conference. One result was customized packaging and designs for candy that commanded much higher prices than the company's traditional offerings.[42]

Leaders in multiunit organizations are at an advantage for innovation because workers from the various units can share ideas that would be useful for many different products. For example, if one unit of a medical company developed a patch for delivering medicine to the body, other units might be able to profit from the same technology. The topic of encouraging idea sharing will be reintroduced in Chapter 13.

**4. *Acquire innovative companies.*** The innovation process takes a long time as it proceeds from a creative idea, through initial experimentation, to feasibility determination, and then to final application. To shorten the process and reduce the risk of a failed innovation, many companies acquire smaller companies that have the innovation they seek. Cisco Systems, Inc., spearheaded by chief executive John Chambers, has been a model of innovation through acquisition. During an eight-year period, Cisco gobbled up more than seventy companies, mostly because each one offered a technology Cisco needed for its product mix. For example, it would buy a company that produced a specialty router.[43] Although Cisco continues to acquire other companies (ten acquisitions in 2007 alone), it still develops innovations internally.

**5. *Avoid innovation for its own sake.*** Leaders also have to exercise good judgment: innovation just because it is innovation is not always valuable. Many gadgets are scientific marvels, yet they have limited market appeal. An example is the robot lawnmower, which arouses the curiosity of many people but does not appeal much to consumers. Most companies have loads of interesting ideas floating to the surface, but very few will even translate into a profitable product or service. A survey of 1,090 executives in 63 countries indicated that only 48 percent were satisfied with their return on investments from innovation.[44]

The information presented earlier about playing the role of a judge in creativity is particularly relevant here. One of the problems with too many products being developed is that they can create a logjam. Such a blockage took place at Avery Dennison Corp., the adhesive label maker. A consultant found that the company was jamming too many new ideas into its product pipeline, resulting in insufficient slack time to keep critical tasks on schedule. The remedy was to shrink the number of product rollouts, which resulted in a net number of more successful product introductions.[45]

**6. *Loose-tight leadership enhances creativity and innovation.*** *Looseness* refers to granting space for new ideas and exploration, whereas the tight approach means finally making a choice among the alternatives. When the Gillette Company was exploring various alternatives for a breakthrough razor, many potentially useful ideas surfaced. The management group in charge said, "Let's go for it," when the idea to add flexible blades to the Trac II razor was presented (it became the Sensor razor).[46] Innovation is also enhanced when workers throughout the organization are able to pursue absurd ideas without penalty for being wrong or for having wasted some resources. An axiom of creativity is that many ideas typically have to be tried before a commercially successful one emerges.

**7. *Integrate development and production.*** Innovation may suffer when the people who develop ideas do not work closely with the people responsible for their production or manufacture. For many years, Japanese companies had moved manufacturing to low-cost countries to save money. Leadership at Canon, Inc., however, has found that the key to creating new products quickly is for the production team to physically work close to the product developers. The result is more input and communication. Although the cost of the product, such as an advanced digital camera, may be higher, its high quality leads to higher consumer demand.[47]

**8. *Recognize the hidden opportunities when products and ideas flop.*** Many product innovations had their origins in flops and failures because somebody was perceptive enough to recognize the new possibilities that emerged from the setback. Success emerged from the ashes of the products that appeared to be drastic mistakes. Two famous examples follow:

- In 1983, Apple produced Lisa, the first commercial personal computer featuring a graphical user interface (GUI). Lisa sold poorly because it was sluggish and highly priced. However, the GUI of Lisa helped to inspire Apple's user-friendly product line including the iMac, the iPod, and the iPhone.
- In 1962, McDonald's tested the Hula Burger, a cheese-topped grilled pineapple on a bun for Chicago residents who chose not to eat meat on Friday (a Christian tradition at the time). Consumers shunned the Hula Burger, and the company learned that meatless didn't have to mean wacky. The next year, a franchise owner developed a tastier alternative for "meatless Fridays"—the Filet-O-Fish, which became a McDonald's classic.

Not all product failures lead to profitable innovations. One of the most useless flops was the CueCat. Launched in 2000, the device scanned bar codes from magazines and newspaper ads to direct readers to web sites so they wouldn't have to trouble themselves with typing in the URL.[48] In instances of total failure, the leader might have to study what went wrong and encourage the product developers involved to do better in the future.

### Reader's Roadmap

So far, we have studied considerable information about the nature of leadership; the attributes, behaviors, and styles of leaders; the ethics and social responsibility of leaders; and how leaders exert power and use politics and influence. We then studied techniques for developing teamwork as well as motivation and coaching skills. After having studied creativity and innovation as part of leadership, we focus next on communication skills as they relate to leadership.

## SUMMARY

A creative idea becomes an innovation when it is implemented or commercialized. Creativity is an essential characteristic of leaders. A creative leader brings forth ideas or things that did not exist previously or that existed in a different form. The creative process has been divided into five steps: opportunity or problem recognition; immersion (the individual becomes immersed in the idea); incubation (the idea simmers); insight (a solution surfaces); and verification and application (the person supports and implements the idea).

Distinguishing characteristics of creative people fall into five areas: knowledge, cognitive abilities, personality, passion for the task, and the experience of flow. Creative people possess extensive knowledge, good intellectual skills, intellectual curiosity, and a wide range of interests. Personality attributes of creative people include a positive self-image, tolerance for isolation, nonconformity, and the ability to tolerate ambiguity and chaos. Passion for the work and flow are related to intense intrinsic motivation. Creative people also enjoy interacting with others. The right personal characteristics must interact with the right environment to produce creative problem solving. The componential theory of creativity focuses on the expertise, creative-thinking skills, and task motivation of creative people.

A major strategy for becoming creative is to overcome traditional thinking, or a traditional mental set. Also, it is necessary to break down rigid thinking that blocks new ideas.

Creative thinking can be enhanced by systematically collecting fresh ideas and brainstorming. Goals are an important part of brainstorming. Two variations of brainstorming are the 6-3-5 method and extreme thinking. A spin off of brainstorming is the pet-peeve technique, in which a group thinks of all the possible complaints others might have about their unit. Some organizations also equip a kitchen for the mind, or a space designed for creativity.

Self-help techniques to enhance creative problem solving include (1) practicing creativity-enhancing exercises, (2) staying alert to opportunities, (3) maintaining enthusiasm and being happy, (4) maintaining and using a systematic place for recording ideas, (5) playing the roles of explorer, artist, judge, and lawyer, and (6) engaging in appropriate physical exercise.

Establishing a climate conducive to creative problem solving is another requirement of effective leadership. A foundation step is to establish a vision statement and mission that include creativity. Specifically, leaders should (1) hire creative people from the outside and identify creative people from within, (2) provide intellectual challenge, (3) allow workers freedom to choose their own method, (4) supply the right resources, (5) design work groups effectively, (6) have supervisors encourage creative workers, (7) give organizational support for creativity, and (8) have favorable exchanges with creative workers.

Special attention should be paid to managing creative workers. One should provide excellent tools and resources, give creative people flexibility, turn down ideas gently, and employ creative people to manage and evaluate creative workers.

Eight additional leadership initiatives that enhance innovation are the following: continually pursue innovation; take risks and encourage risk taking; emphasize collaboration; acquire innovative companies; avoid innovation for its own sake; use loose-tight leadership; integrate development and production; and recognize hidden opportunities in flops.

## KEY TERMS

| | | |
|---|---|---|
| **Innovation** | **Experience of flow** | **Kitchen for the mind** |
| **Creativity** | **Pet-peeve technique** | |

## ✔ GUIDELINES FOR ACTION AND SKILL DEVELOPMENT

Tom Freston has a long career of being a creative leader and managing creative people. His current assignment is the chief executive of the part of Viacom that is home to cable networks such as MTV and VH-I, as well as movie studio Paramount Pictures. Freston offers five tips for managing a creative organization that reinforce several ideas already presented in this chapter.[49]

1. Put great creative people at the top.
2. Ensure that ideas flow from the bottom up with a minimum of hierarchy.
3. Maniacally know your audience.
4. Hire passionate, diverse people.
5. Have a lot of fun.

### Discussion Questions and Activities

1. Give an example of creativity in business that does *not* relate to the development or marketing of a product or service.
2. Is it important for the leader to be creative and innovative? Or, should he or she simply hire creative and innovative group members?
3. In many companies, it is expected for managerial and professional workers to wear formal business attire to work (such as suits and high heels). What effect do you think this dress code has on creativity?
4. In what way does your current program of study contribute to your ability to solve problems creatively?
5. The opinion has often been expressed that too much emphasis on teamwork inhibits creativity. What do you think of this argument?
6. What is the underlying process by which creativity-building exercises, such as the pet-peeve technique, are supposed to increase creativity?
7. How might a manager physically lay out an office to improve the chances that creative problem solving will take place?
8. Why do many people believe that if you emphasize being efficient, such as using the quality-improvement process Six Sigma, creativity and innovation are likely to suffer?
9. Critics of Dell Computer claim that the company is not innovative, even calling Dell the Wal-Mart of technology companies. In what way do you think Dell is innovative, or not innovative?
10. Speak to the most creative person you know in any field, and find out if he or she uses any specific creativity-enhancing technique. Be prepared to bring your findings back to class.

## Leadership Case Problem A

### Hitting Paydirt

Contractors who used to make dozens of phone calls to find dirt or a place to dump it can instead make a single call to DirtMaker. The 35-employee, $20 million company matches dirt buyers and sellers, and tests and transports the soil. "We're like a dating service for dirt," says Dave Rossi, who cofounded the Los Gatos (Calif.) dirt broker with his wife, Lesley Matheson.

Rossi, now 37, was working as a manager for a commercial construction company in 1999 when he realized how much time and effort went into handling dirt. "Getting rid of dirt was a difficult task that required calling a lot of different people, many of whom weren't the most scrupulous," says Rossi. He thought a web site would be a good way to match the players and mentioned the idea to Matheson, who has a Ph.D. in computer science from Princeton and an M.B.A. from the Wharton School at the University of Pennsylvania. Matheson, 47, went to work building a local search engine that linked dirt buyers and sellers based mostly on location—years before Google and Yahoo! rolled out their own local search capabilities. Says Matheson, "In some respects, we were ahead of our time."

The couple tapped their savings and pooled funds from eight investors, raising $1.7 million to launch DirtMarket.com. But contractors didn't embrace the site. "Most didn't even have email," says Rossi. Undeterred, they used the technology Matheson developed to become dirt brokers, directly matching contractors who pay them to remove dirt with those who pay them to find it. DirtMarket takes a cut on both sides of the transaction, with profit margins averaging around 25 percent.

In 2004, the company spotted another niche. When a project involves a lot of excavation, a construction company typically hires an engineering firm to remove dirt from the site, which can account for as much as 75 percent of a project's cost. "We always thought the process was backwards," says Rossi. So DirtMarket started an engineering contracting division that oversees a project, including hiring an engineering firm, handling the digging, and removing the dirt. About 80 percent of the company's revenues now comes from this division, which it markets primarily by word of mouth. Says Rossi, "We have a lot of repeat customers."

The couple, who met on a blind date, has divided the tasks of running the company according to their complementary strengths. Matheson, the company's president, manages operations. "I'm happy working in an office, surrounded by computers," she says. "Dave's the gregarious, hand-shaking guy." As CEO,

Rossi handles business development, including a new partnership with Home Depot. Landscapers, homeowners, and other customers at sixty Home Depot stores can place orders in the store and get soil, bark, or rock delivered through DirtMarket. Rossi expects the service to be in 500 stores, primarily in the West, in the next three years.

An outsider commented, "It seems Rossi and Matheson have hit pay dirt."

## Questions

1. In what way have Rossi and Matheson shown an ability to identify an opportunity?
2. In what way have the operators of DirtMarket overcome traditional mental sets, or thought outside the box?
3. To what extent do you think that Matheson's having a Ph.D. in computer science and an M.B.A. helped her become a leader in the dirt business?
4. What might be a possible threat from the external environment that could hurt the business model of DirtMarket?
5. To try out your creative thinking today, make up a joke about DirtMarket. (In this case, dirty jokes are welcome.)

*Source:* Excerpted from Sarah Max, "The Good Earth: Dirt Market Finds Riches in All Things Dirt," *BusinessWeek SmallBiz*, December 2007/January 2008, p. 022.

## Leadership Case Problem B

### Sparking Innovation at Gap

When Robert Fisher was the interim CEO of Gap Inc., he said that the apparel retailer needed to make faster decisions and cut through the bureaucracy if it hoped to hire and retain creative talent to turn the company around. Fisher also said the San Francisco company had relied too heavily on customer research and focus groups, which he said provide helpful feedback but can't forecast what Gap should produce next.

"Designers need to be in a position where they can think creatively," said Fisher, a Gap director since 1990, and chairman since 2004. "We almost tried to institutionalize creativity." He said that the problem wasn't apparent until he took over as interim CEO in January 2007. Fisher reiterated that he didn't intend to be a candidate for the permanent CEO job, declining to explain why. "This is a board decision," he said. "I'm working really hard to fix this business as much as I can" (*Wall Street Journal*, March 6, 2007, p. B2).

Fisher had to address the high turnover in key positions that plagued the 3,100-store company during 2006 under previous CEO Paul Pressler. Fisher said he would examine whether the company has too many management layers at headquarters. He also said the retailer would return more decision-making power to leaders of the Gap, Old Navy, and Banana Republic brands. "We've become too bureaucratic and overly analytical," he said. "That's not appealing to the people in merchandising and design" (*Wall Street Journal*, March 6, 2007, p. B2).

Fisher also has to grapple with long-standing problems at the brands that former CEO Pressler took over in 2002, but has never recaptured the excitement of its peak in the late 1990s, when offices were move to casual dress and commercials such as "Khakis Swing" were hits.

"We've got to have a clear point of view about who we are," Fisher said. He said the "clean" department in Gap stores that stocks classic work basics is a good reflection of Gap's style, and "we're going to be grounded in khaki and denim, as that's where the roots of this business are" (*Wall Street Journal*, March 6, 2007, p. B2).

The Old Navy brand, with 1,008 stores, hasn't kept up with the relentless progress made by discounters such as Target Corp. that have grabbed market share by making their clothes more stylish while holding down prices. Target adds excitement by hiring high-end designers to create products for its stores that are available for only a short time.

In July 2007, Gap surprised Wall Street by naming Glenn Murphy, a Canadian drugstore executive, as its new CEO. Murphy had been chairman and chief executive of Shoppers Drug Mart. Many observers had assumed the company would recruit someone from the apparel sector, especially given Gap's long string of fashion missteps.

"One of their key criteria was apparel experience and Murphy doesn't seem to have that," said Mark Montagna, vice president of specialty retail for C. L. King & Associates. "He's walking into a really tough job because here's the biggest fish in specialty apparel, and he's got to turn around all three divisions,"

says Montagna. "I think the fact that Murphy has worked for mature retailers is a big help because certainly Gap is mature. He has a track record of success so hopefully he can do the same again" (*TheStreet.com*, pp. 1, 2).

With more than 20 years of retail experience, Murphy has been credited for reinvigorating retail brands in food, health and beauty, and books. "Glenn is known for being a decisive leader with great retail instincts who understands his customers," Fisher said. "He has revitalized major retail brands by offering new products and significantly improving the store experience. He's well qualified to return Gap Inc. to the level of sustained performance we all expect" (*TheStreet.com*, p. 1).

Howard Davidowitz, chairman of a New York–based retail consulting and investment banking firm, says he is puzzled by Gap's choice of leadership. "The people who drive companies are fashion geniuses—the people who fall on their face are people who are not," Davidowitz says (*TheStreet.com*, p. 2). Other observers mentioned that Gap has strong merchants heading its three divisions.

## Questions

1. What steps do you think CEO Murphy should take to enhance innovation at Gap?
2. Is Fisher thinking too narrowly by insisting that Gap should stick to being grounded in khaki and denim? Explain your reasoning.
3. What is your opinion of the wisdom of hiring a non-fashion executive to revitalize Gap?
4. What is your opinion of the statement that being too analytical and bureaucratic might have interfered with the creativity of Gap?
5. How is Gap doing these days? Does the financial performance of the firm justify having brought Murphy on board? Or is Murphy still around?

*Source:* Amy Merrick, "Gap Aims to Unleash Creativity for Revival," *Wall Street Journal*, March 6, 2007, p. B2; Suzanne Kapner, "Surprise Greets Gap's CEO Choice," *New York Post* (nypost.com), July 27, 2008; Pia Sarkar, "Gap's CEO Pick Surprises," *TheStreet.com*, July 26, 2007.

## Leadership Skill-Building Exercise 11-4

### My Leadership Portfolio

You guessed it. For this chapter's entry into your leadership portfolio, record any creative or innovative idea you have had lately in relation to organizational activity, including school. After recording the idea, ask yourself what prompted you to develop it. If you have not contributed a creative idea recently, your assignment is to develop a creative idea within the next ten days. If possible, make plans to implement the idea; otherwise, it will not lead to innovation. Here is an example of a creative community initiative taken by Alexis, a marketing major:

> In my neighborhood, there is a ten-story high-rise building, with practically all of the tenants being senior citizens who live on limited pensions. Some of the folks in the building are in their eighties, and even nineties. The building is old, and not particularly warm, especially for people with poor blood circulation. I've often heard friends and family members say that we should do something to help the seniors in the high rise, but nobody seems to go beyond expressing a little sympathy.
>
> Then I got a brainstorm. I thought, "Why not organize a 'Socks for Seniors' program?" My friends and I would buy dozens of pairs of socks that usually sell for about $3.00 a pair from deep discounters like dollar stores. We could raise some of the money by returning bottles and cans with deposits. A few friends of mine made a bunch of telephone calls, and we raised $175 in no time for our project. Then one cold night, we visited the high rise, rang a few doorbells, and told the residents what we were up to. We were allowed in to start distributing the socks. The smiles and words of appreciation we received were enormous. My idea is soooo good, I plan to do it every year. My friends are with me, and we think that if we post this idea on a web site, it might spread around the country.

## Internet Skill-Building Exercise

### Creativity in Business

Here is an opportunity to interact with the work of creativity guru Michael Ray of Stanford University. Visit www.michael-ray.com. Look over the site, and then go to "take our survey." The survey gives you the opportunity to examine your creative process and the type of work that brings meaning to your life. Your questionnaire will be scored, and you will be provided with comparative results from work done at Stanford. After you have completed the experience, reflect on these questions:

1. What did you learn about your creative process?
2. How does the feedback about your creativity that you acquired on this site compare to the feedback you received from the exercises in this chapter?

Apply the chapter concepts! Visit the Web and complete this Internet skill-building exercise to learn more about current leadership topics and trends.

# Communication and Conflict Resolution Skills

## LEARNING OBJECTIVES

After studying this chapter and doing the exercises, you should be able to

- Explain why good communication skills contribute to effective leadership.

- Describe the basics of inspirational and emotion-provoking communication.

- Describe key features of a power-oriented linguistic style.

- Describe the six basic principles of persuasion.

- Describe the challenge of selective listening, and the basics of making the rounds.

- Be sensitive to the importance of overcoming cross-cultural barriers to communication.

- Identify basic approaches to resolving conflict and negotiating.

## CHAPTER OUTLINE

**Inspirational and Powerful Communication**
Speaking and Writing
The Six Basic Principles of Persuasion
Nonverbal Communication Including Videoconferencing

**Listening as a Leadership Skill**
Selective Listening to Problems
Making the Rounds

**Overcoming Cross-Cultural Communication Barriers**

**The Leader's Role in Resolving Conflict and Negotiating**
Conflict Management Styles
Resolving Conflict Between Two Group Members
Negotiating and Bargaining

**Summary**

"I've heard so many executives tell employees to be candid and then jump down their throats if they bring up a problem or ask a critical question," says Yogesh Gupta, president and CEO of FatWire, a software company that helps businesses manage their web sites.

Gupta was determined not to do that when he was recruited to FatWire from CA (Computer Associates). Since then he has spent hours talking with his 200 employees and seeking the advice of his nine senior managers—all but one of whom are veterans of the company. He has frequent private meetings with each member of the management team so they will feel freer to be candid with him. In that way, he can ask the important questions: What am I doing wrong?

What would you do differently if you were running the company? What's the biggest thing getting in the way of you doing your job well?

Already he has learned from these talks that FatWire should beef up its staff in marketing and in product development. Others have counseled him to improve FatWire's customer-support processes. Every time Gupta has gotten good advice privately, he has found a way to publicly praise the manager so others will come forward with suggestions.

"I know I have to say, 'You did the right thing to speak up' again and again because employees fear they'll get blamed if they say anything negative," says Gupta.[1]

The executive leader just described acts on an obvious truth that many leaders ignore—open communication between company leaders and group members helps an organization overcome problems and attain success. Effective managers and leaders listen to employees, and open communications contribute to leadership effectiveness. Peter de la Billiere reminds us that no leader is effective unless he or she is skillful at communication, which includes being able to transmit and receive messages.[2] Along the same lines, John Hamm notes that effective communication is a leader's most essential tool for executing the essential job of leadership: inspiring organizational members to take responsibility for creating a better future.[3]

Effective communication skills contribute to inspirational leadership. Chapter 3 describes how charismatic leaders are masterful oral communicators. This chapter expands on this theme and also covers the contribution of nonverbal, written, and supportive communication. In addition, it describes how the ability to overcome cross-cultural communication barriers enhances leadership effectiveness. Finally, because leaders spend a substantial amount of time resolving conflicts, the chapter also discusses conflict resolution skills.

To focus your thinking on your communication effectiveness, complete Leadership Self-Assessment Quiz 12-1.

**KB Knowledge Bank**
Provides some evidence supporting the conclusion that many companies are not communicating their mission, vision, and values as well as they might.

www.cengage.com/management/dubrin

Leadership Self-Assessment Quiz 12-1

### A Self-Portrait of My Communication Effectiveness

**Instructions:** The following statements relate to various aspects of communication effectiveness. Indicate whether each of the statements is mostly true or mostly false, even if the most accurate answer would depend somewhat on the situation. Asking another person who is familiar with your communication behavior to help you answer the questions may improve the accuracy of your answers.

| | Mostly True | Mostly False |
|---|---|---|
| 1. When I begin to speak in a group, most people stop talking, turn toward me, and listen. | ☐ | ☐ |
| 2. I receive compliments on the quality of my writing. | ☐ | ☐ |
| 3. The reaction to the outgoing message on my voicemail has been favorable. | ☐ | ☐ |
| 4. I welcome the opportunity to speak in front of a group. | ☐ | ☐ |
| 5. I have published something, including a letter to the editor, an article for the school newspaper, or a comment in a company newsletter. | ☐ | ☐ |
| 6. I have my own web site. | ☐ | ☐ |
| 7. The vast majority of my written projects in school have received a grade of B or A. | ☐ | ☐ |
| 8. People generally laugh when I tell a joke or make what I think is a witty comment. | ☐ | ☐ |
| 9. I stay informed by reading newspapers, watching news on television, or reading news web sites. | ☐ | ☐ |
| 10. I have heard such terms as *enthusiastic, animated, colorful,* or *dynamic* applied to me. | ☐ | ☐ |

**Total score:** _____

**Scoring and Interpretation:** If eight or more of these statements are true in relation to you, it is most likely that you are an effective communicator. If three or fewer statements are true, you may need substantial improvement in your communication skills. Your scores are probably highly correlated with charisma.

**Skill Development:** The behaviors indicated by the ten statements in the self-assessment exercise are significant for leaders because much of a leader's impact is determined by his or her communication style. Although effective leaders vary considerably in their communication style, they usually create a positive impact if they can communicate well. Observe some current business leaders on CNBC news or a similar channel to develop a feel for the communication style of successful business leaders.

# INSPIRATIONAL AND POWERFUL COMMUNICATION

Information about communicating persuasively and effectively is extensive. Here we focus on suggestions for creating the high-impact communication that contributes to effective leadership. Effective communication is frequently a criterion for being promoted to a leadership position. In this section, suggestions for becoming an inspirational and emotion-provoking communicator are divided into the following two categories: (1) speaking and writing, and (2) nonverbal communication. We also discuss six basic principles of persuasion.

## Speaking and Writing

You are already familiar with the basics of effective spoken and written communication. Yet the basics—such as writing and speaking clearly, maintaining eye contact, and not mumbling—are only starting points. The majority of effective leaders have an extra snap or panache in their communication style, both in day-by-day conversations and when addressing a group. The same energy and excitement is reflected in both speaking and writing. Suggestions for dynamic and persuasive oral and written communication are presented next and outlined in Table 12-1.

*Be Credible*    Attempts at persuasion, including inspirational speaking and writing, begin with the credibility of the message sender. If the speaker is perceived as highly credible, the attempt at persuasive communication is more likely to be successful. The perception of credibility is influenced by many factors, including those covered in this entire section. Being trustworthy heavily influences being perceived as credible. A leader with a reputation for lying will have a difficult time convincing people about the merits of a new initiative such as outsourcing. Being perceived as intelligent and knowledgeable is another major factor contributing to credibility.

**TABLE 12-1** Suggestions for Inspirational Speaking and Writing

**A. A VARIETY OF INSPIRATIONAL TACTICS**
1. Be credible.
2. Gear your message to the listener.
3. Sell group members on the benefits of your suggestions.
4. Use heavy-impact and emotion-provoking words.
5. Use anecdotes to communicate meaning.
6. Back up conclusions with data (to a point).
7. Minimize language errors, junk words, and vocalized pauses.
8. Write crisp, clear memos, letters, and reports, including a front-loaded message.
9. Use business jargon in appropriate doses.

**B. THE POWER-ORIENTED LINGUISTIC STYLE**
Included here are a variety of factors such as downplaying uncertainty, emphasizing direct rather than indirect talk, and choosing an effective communication frame.

***Gear Your Message to the Listener***   An axiom of persuasive communication is that a speaker must adapt the message to the listener's interests and motivations. The company CEO visiting a manufacturing plant will receive careful attention—and build support—when he says that jobs will not be outsourced to another country. The same CEO will receive the support of stockholders when he emphasizes how cost reductions will boost earnings per share and enlarge dividends. The average intelligence level of the group is a key contingency factor in designing a persuasive message. People with high intelligence tend to be more influenced by messages based on strong, logical arguments. Bright people are also more likely to reject messages based on flawed logic.[4]

***Sell Group Members on the Benefits of Your Suggestions***   A leader is constrained by the willingness of group members to take action on the leader's suggestions and initiatives. As a consequence, the leader must explain to group members how they can benefit from what he or she proposes. For example, a plant manager attempting to sell employees on the benefits of recycling supplies as much as possible might say, "If we can cut down enough on the cost of supplies, we might be able to save one or two jobs."

Selling group members is quite often done more effectively when the persuader takes the time to build consensus. Instead of inspiring the group in a flash, the leader wins the people over gradually. One caution is that this deliberate method of persuasion through consensus is poorly suited to crises and other urgent situations.

***Use Heavy-Impact and Emotion-Provoking Words***   Certain words used in the proper context give power and force to your speech. Used comfortably, naturally, and sincerely, these words will project the image of a self-confident person with leadership ability or potential. Two examples of heavy-impact phrases are "We will be outsourcing those portions of our knowledge work that are not mission critical," and "We will be innovational in both product development and business processes." However, too much of this type of language will make the leader appear that he or she is imitating a Dilbert cartoon (a long-running cartoon satire about managers and businesspeople).

Closely related to heavy-impact language is the use of emotion-provoking words. An expert persuasive tactic is to sprinkle your speech with emotion-provoking— and therefore inspiring  words. Emotion-provoking words bring forth images of exciting events. Examples of emotion-provoking and powerful words include "*outclassing* the competition," "*bonding* with customers," "*surpassing* previous profits," "*capturing* customer loyalty," and "*rebounding* from a downturn." It also helps to use words and phrases that connote power. Those now in vogue include *virtual organization*, *transparent organization*, and *knowledge management*.

A large vocabulary assists using both heavy-impact and emotion-provoking words. When you need to persuade somebody on the spot, it is difficult to search for the right words in a dictionary or thesaurus. Also, you need to practice a word a few times to use it comfortably for an important occasion.

***Use Anecdotes to Communicate Meaning*** Anecdotes are a powerful part of a leader's kit of persuasive and influence tactics, as already mentioned in this chapter and in Chapter 3 about charismatic leadership. A carefully chosen anecdote is also useful in persuading group members about the importance of organizational values. So long as the anecdote is not repeated too frequently, it can communicate an important message.

Teresa Lever-Pollary is the CEO of Nighttime Pediatric Clinics Inc. in Midvale, Utah. She noticed that as the company grew to four clinics and seventy employees, it was losing touch with the values that helped make it such a successful provider of after-hours pediatric care. Lever-Pollary collected more than eighty stories from her employees and printed them in a book that she distributes to stakeholders. One of her favorite anecdotes was a nurse's recollection of the manner in which a pediatrician lured an ant from inside a child's ear using a morsel of cake frosting. The ant crawled out, and the doctor gently released it outdoors. The story precisely illustrates Nighttime's focus on carefully and professionally caring for small living organisms.[5]

***Back Up Conclusions with Data*** You will be more persuasive if you support your spoken and written presentations with solid data. One approach to obtaining data is to collect them yourself—for example, by conducting an email survey of your customers or group members. The sales manager of an office supply company wanted to begin a delivery service for his many small customers, such as dental and real estate offices. He sent email messages to a generous sampling of these accounts and found they would be willing to pay a premium price if delivery were included. By using these data to support his argument, he convinced the company owner to approve the plan. He thus exercised leadership in providing a new service.

Published sources also provide convincing data for arguments. Supporting data for hundreds of arguments can be found in the business pages of newspapers, in business magazines and newspapers, and on the Internet. The *Statistical Abstract of the United States*, published annually, is an inexpensive yet trusted reference for thousands of arguments.

Relying too much on research has a potential disadvantage, though. Being too dependent on data could suggest that you have little faith in your intuition. For example, you might convey a weak impression if, when asked your opinion, you respond, "I can't answer until I collect some data." Leaders are generally decisive. An important issue, then, is for the leader to find the right balance between relying on data and using intuition alone when communicating an important point.

***Minimize Language Errors, Junk Words, and Vocalized Pauses*** Using colorful, powerful words enhances the perception that you are self-confident and have leadership qualities. Also, minimize the use of words and phrases that dilute the impact of your speech, such as "like," "y' know," "you know what I mean," "he goes" (to mean "he says"), and "uhhhhhhh." Such junk words and vocalized pauses convey the impression of low self-confidence, especially in a professional setting, and detract from a sharp communication image.

An effective way to decrease the use of these extraneous words is to tape-record or video-record your side of a phone conversation and then play it back. Many people are not aware that they use extraneous words until they hear recordings of their speech.

A good leader should be sure always to write and speak with grammatical precision to give the impression of being articulate and well informed, thereby enhancing his or her leadership stature. Here are two examples of common language errors: "Just between you and I" is wrong; "just between you and me" is correct. "Him and I," or "Her and I," are incorrect phrases despite how frequently they creep into social and business language. "He and I" and "She and I" are correct.

Another very common error is using the plural pronoun *they* to refer to a singular antecedent. For example, "The systems analyst said that *they* cannot help us" is incorrect. "The systems analyst said *she* cannot help us" is correct. Using *they* to refer to a singular antecedent has become so common in the English language that many people no longer make the distinction between singular and plural. Some of these errors are subtle and are made so frequently that many people do not realize they are wrong, but again, avoiding grammatical errors may enhance a person's leadership stature.[6]

When in doubt about a potential language error, consult a large dictionary. An authoritative guide for the leader (and anyone else) who chooses to use English accurately is *The Elements of Style* by William Strunk, Jr., and E. B. White.[7]

***Use Business Jargon in Appropriate Doses*** Business and government executives and professionals make frequent use of jargon. Often the jargon is used automatically without deliberate thought, and at other times jargon words and phrases are chosen to help establish rapport with the receiver. A vastly overused phrase these days is "at the end of the day," with "buckets" fighting for second place. "The end of the day" has come to replace "in the final analysis," and "buckets" replace "categories." Many businesspeople say "at the end of the day" twice in the same paragraph. Here is a typical use of "buckets" as a category: Cingular (now AT&T) boasted that its new rate plan in South Florida enables customers to "dig into their big bucket of night and weekend minutes" earlier than before.[8]

Sprinkling business talk with jargon does indeed help establish rapport, and adds to a person's popularity. But too much jargon makes a person seem stereotyped in thinking, and perhaps even unwilling to express an original thought—and therefore lacking power.

***Write Crisp, Clear Memos, Letters, and Reports, Including a Front-Loaded Message*** Business leaders characteristically write easy-to-read, well-organized messages both in email and more formal reports. Writing, in addition to speaking, is more persuasive when key ideas are placed at the beginning of a conversation, email message, paragraph, or sentence.[9] Front-loaded messages (those placed at the beginning of a sentence) are particularly important for leaders because people expect leaders to be forceful communicators. A front-loaded and powerful message might be "Cost reduction must be our immediate priority," which emphasizes that cost reduction is the major subject. It is clearly much more to the point than, for example, "All of us must reduce costs immediately."

One way to make sure messages are front-loaded is to use the active voice, making sure the subject of the sentence is doing the acting, not being acted upon. Compare the active (and front-loaded) message "Loyal workers should not take vacations during a company crisis" to the passive (non-front-loaded) message "Vacations should not be taken by loyal company workers during a crisis." Recognize, however, that less emphasis is placed on the active voice today than several years ago.

***Use a Power-Oriented Linguistic Style***   A major part of being persuasive involves choosing the correct **linguistic style**, a person's characteristic speaking pattern. According to Deborah Tannen, linguistic style involves such aspects as amount of directness, pacing and pausing, word choice, and the use of such communication devices as jokes, figures of speech, anecdotes, questions, and apologies.[10]

Linguistic style is complex because it includes the culturally learned signals by which people communicate what they mean, along with how they interpret what others say and how they evaluate others. The complexity of linguistic style makes it difficult to offer specific prescriptions for using one that is power oriented. Many of the elements of a power-oriented linguistic style are included in other suggestions made in this section of the chapter. Nevertheless, here are several components of a linguistic style that would give power and authority to the message sender in many situations, as observed by Deborah Tannen and other language specialists:[11]

- Speak loud enough to be heard by the majority of people with at least average hearing ability. Speaking too softly projects an image of low self-confidence.
- Downplay uncertainty. If you are not confident of your opinion or prediction, make a positive statement anyway, such as saying, "I know this new system will cure our inventory problems."
- Use the pronoun *I* to receive more credit for your ideas. (Of course, this could backfire in a team-based organization.)
- Minimize the number of questions you ask that imply that you lack information on a topic, such as, "What do you mean by an IPO?"
- Minimize self-deprecation with phrases such as "This will probably sound stupid, but . . ." Apologize infrequently, and particularly minimize saying, "I'm sorry."
- Offer negative feedback directly, rather than softening the feedback by first giving praise and then moving to the areas of criticism.
- Make your point quickly. You know you are taking too long to reach a conclusion when others look bored or finish your sentences for you.
- Emphasize direct rather than indirect talk: say, "I need your report by noon tomorrow," rather than, "I'm wondering if your report will be available by noon tomorrow."
- Weed out wimpy words. Speak up without qualifying or giving other indices of uncertainty. It is better to give dates for the completion of a project rather than say "Soon" or "It shouldn't be a problem." Instead, make a statement like "I will have my portion of the strategic plan shortly before Thanksgiving. I need to collect input from my team and sift through the information."
- Know exactly what you want. Your chances of selling an idea increase to the extent that you have clarified the idea in your own mind. The clearer and

more committed you are at the outset of a session, the stronger you are as a persuader and the more powerful your language becomes.

■ Speak at length, set the agenda for a conversation, make jokes, and laugh. Be ready to offer solutions to problems, as well as to suggest a program or plan. All of these points are more likely to create a sense of confidence in listeners.

■ Strive to be bold in your statements. As a rule of thumb, be bold about ideas, but tentative about people. If you say something like "I have a plan that I think will solve these problems," you are presenting an idea, not attacking a person.

■ Frame your comments in a way that increases your listener's receptivity. The *frame* is built around the best context for responding to the needs of others. An example would be to use the frame "let's dig a little deeper" when the other people present know something is wrong but cannot pinpoint the problem. Your purpose is to enlist the help of others in finding the underlying nature of the problem.

Despite these suggestions for having a power-oriented linguistic style, Tannen cautions that there is no one best way to communicate. How you project your power and authority is often dependent on the people involved, the organizational culture, the relative rank of the speakers, and other situational factors. The power-oriented linguistic style should be interpreted as a general guideline.

**Knowledge Bank**
Contains information about using a combination of influence tactics to persuade others.

www.cengage.com/ management/dubrin

## The Six Basic Principles of Persuasion

Persuasion is a major form of influence, so it has gained in importance in the modern organization because of the reason described in Chapter 8: Managers must often influence people for whom they have no formal responsibility. The trend stems from leaner corporate hierarchies and the breaking down of division walls. Managers must persuade peers in situations where lines of authority are unclear or do not exist.[12] One way to be persuasive is to capitalize on scientific evidence about how to persuade people. Robert B. Cialdini has synthesized knowledge from experimental and social psychology about methods for getting people to concede, comply, or change. These principles can also be framed as influence principles, but with a focus on persuasion.[13] The six principles described next have accompanying tactics that can be used to supplement the other approaches to persuasion described in this chapter.

**1.** *Liking: People like those who like them.* As a leader, you have a better chance of persuading and influencing group members who like you. Emphasizing similarities between you and the other person and offering praise are the two most reliable techniques for getting another person to like you. The leader should therefore emphasize similarities, such as common interests with group members. Praising others is a powerful influence technique and can be used effectively even when the leader finds something relatively small to compliment. Genuine praise is the most effective.

**2.** *Reciprocity: People repay in kind.* Managers can often influence group members to behave in a particular way by displaying the behavior first. The leader might therefore serve as a model of trust, good ethics, or strong commitment to company goals. In short, give what you want to receive.

**3.** *Social proof: People follow the lead of similar others.* Persuasion can have high impact when it comes from peers. If you as the leader want to influence a group to convert to a new procedure, such as virtually eliminating paper records in the office, ask a believer to speak up in a meeting or send his or her statement of support via email. (But do not send around paper documents.)

**4.** *Consistency: People align with their clear commitments.* People need to feel committed to what you want them to do. After people take a stand or go on record in favor of a position, they prefer to stay with that commitment. Suppose you are the team leader and you want team members to become more active in the community as a way of creating a favorable image for the firm. If the team members talk about their plans to get involved and also put their plans in writing, they are more likely to follow through. If the people involved read their action plans to each other, the commitment will be even stronger.

**5.** *Authority: People defer to experts.* As explained in our study of expert power and credibility, people really do defer to experts. The action plan here is to make constituents aware of your expertise to enhance the probability that your plan will persuade them. A leader might mention certification in the technical area that is the subject of influence. For example, a leader attempting to persuade team members to use statistical data to improve quality might mention that he or she is certified in the quality process Six Sigma (is a Six Sigma Black Belt).

**6.** *Scarcity: People want more of what they can have less of.* An application of this principle is that the leader can persuade group members to act in a particular direction if the members believe that the resource at issue is shrinking rapidly. They might be influenced to enroll in a course in outsourcing knowledge work, for example, if they are told that the course may not be offered again for a long time. Another way to apply this principle is to persuade group members by using information not readily available to others. The leader might say, "I have some preliminary sales data. If we can increase our sales by just 10 percent in the last month of this quarter, we might be the highest performing unit in the company."

The developer of these principles explains that they should be applied in combination to multiply their impact. For example, while establishing your expertise you might simultaneously praise people for their accomplishments. It is also important to be ethical, such as by not fabricating data to influence others.[14]

## Nonverbal Communication Including Videoconferencing

Effective leaders are masterful nonverbal as well as verbal communicators. Nonverbal communication is important because leadership involves emotion, which words alone cannot communicate convincingly. A major component of the emotional impact of a message is communicated nonverbally.

A self-confident leader not only speaks and writes with assurance but also projects confidence through body position, gestures, and manner of speech. Not everybody interprets the same body language and other nonverbal signals in the same way, but some aspects of nonverbal behavior project a self-confident, leadership image in many situations.[15]

- Using an erect posture when walking, standing, or sitting. Slouching and slumping are almost universally interpreted as an indicator of low self-confidence.
- Standing up straight during a confrontation. Cowering is interpreted as a sign of low self-confidence and poor leadership qualities.
- Patting other people on the back while nodding slightly.
- Standing with toes pointing outward rather than inward. Outward-pointing toes are usually perceived as indicators of superior status, whereas inward-pointing toes are perceived to indicate inferiority.
- Speaking at a moderate pace, with a loud, confident tone. People lacking in self-confidence tend to speak too rapidly or very slowly.
- Smiling frequently in a relaxed, natural-appearing manner.
- Maintaining eye contact with those around you.
- Gesturing in a relaxed, nonmechanical way, including pointing toward others in a way that welcomes rather than accuses, such as using a gesture to indicate, "You're right," or "It's your turn to comment."

A general approach to using nonverbal behavior that projects confidence is to have a goal of appearing self-confident and powerful. This type of autosuggestion makes many of the behaviors seem automatic. For example, if you say, "I am going to display leadership qualities in this meeting," you will have taken an important step toward appearing confident.

Your external image also plays an important role in communicating messages to others. People pay more respect and grant more privileges to those they perceive as being well dressed and neatly groomed. Even on casual dress days, most effective leaders will choose clothing that gives them an edge over others. Appearance includes more than the choice of clothing. Self-confidence is projected by such small items as the following:

- Neatly pressed and sparkling clean clothing
- Freshly polished shoes
- Impeccable fingernails
- Clean jewelry in mint condition
- Well-maintained hair
- Good-looking teeth with a white or antique-white color

What constitutes a powerful and self-confident external image is often influenced by the organizational culture. At a software development company, for example, powerful people might dress more casually than at an investment banking firm. Leadership at many law firms is moving back toward formal business attire for the professional staff. Your verbal behavior and the forms of nonverbal behavior previously discussed contribute more to your leadership image than your clothing, providing you dress acceptably.

A subtle mode of nonverbal communication is the use of time. Guarding time as a precious resource will help you project an image of self-confidence and leadership. A statement such as "I can devote fifteen minutes to your problem this Thursday at 4:00 P.M." connotes confidence and being in control. (Too many of these statements, however, might make a person appear unapproachable and inconsiderate.) Other ways of projecting power through the use of time include such behaviors as being prompt for meetings and starting and stopping meetings on time. It may also be helpful to make references to dates one year into the future and beyond, such as, "By 2013 we should have a 25 percent market share."

Videoconferencing places extra demands on the nonverbal communication skills of leaders, managers, and other participants. Jeffrey Schwartz, chief executive officer of an industrial real estate investment trust, explains that videoconferences represent a powerful tool for far-flung managers to make a name for themselves back at corporate headquarters.[16] The opposite is also true: if your verbal and nonverbal communication skills are poor, you will create a poor impression. The camera magnifies everything such as scratching your head, biting your lip, inserting your finger in your ear, and checking your BlackBerry. Etiquette tips for making a strong nonverbal presence during a videoconference include the following (and are similar to nonverbal communication suggestions in general):

- Choose what you wear carefully, remembering that busy (confusing and complex) patterns look poor on video. Also do not wear formal attire mixed with running shoes because you might move into full camera view.
- Speak in crisp conversational tones and pay attention. (The tone and paying attention are the nonverbal aspects of communication.)
- Never forget the video camera's powerful reach such as catching you rolling your eyes when you disagree with a subordinate.
- Avoid culturally insensitive gestures including large hand and body gestures that make many Asians feel uncomfortable. Asians believe that you should have long-term relationships before being demonstrative.[17]

An effective way of sharpening your videoconferencing nonverbal skills, as well as other nonverbal skills, is to be videotaped several times. Make adjustments for anything you don't like, and repeat what you do like. Feedback on your behavior from another observer can be quite helpful.

Now that you have refreshed your thoughts on effective verbal and nonverbal communication, do Leadership Skill-Building Exercise 12-1.

## LISTENING AS A LEADERSHIP SKILL

Listening is a fundamental management and leadership skill. Listening also provides the opportunity for dialogue, in which people understand each other better by taking turns having their point of view understood. For a leader to support and encourage a subordinate, active listening (as described in the discussion of coaching) is required. Also, effective leader–member exchanges require that each party listen to one another. The relationship between two parties cannot be enhanced unless each one listens to the other. Furthermore, leaders cannot identify problems unless they listen carefully to group members. According to Richard M. Harris, in today's complex, fast-paced organization, effective communication—including listening—is essential. But all too frequently, messages are misinterpreted, ignored, or missed altogether. As a result, creativity is stifled, morale is lowered, and goals may go unmet.[18]

Leadership Skill-Building Exercise 12-1

## Feedback on Verbal and Nonverbal Behavior

Ten volunteers have one week to prepare a three-minute presentation on a course-related subject of their choice. The topics of these presentations could be as far-reaching as "The Importance of the North American Free Trade Agreement" or "My Goals and Dreams." The class members who observe the presentations prepare feedback slips on 3 × 5 cards, describing how well the speakers communicated powerfully and inspirationally. One card per speaker is usually sufficient. Notations should be made for both verbal and nonverbal feedback.

Emphasis should be placed on positive feedback and constructive suggestions. Students pass the feedback cards along to the speakers. The cards can be anonymous to encourage frankness, but they should not be mean spirited.

Persuading and inspiring others is one of the main vehicles for practicing leadership. Knowing how others perceive you helps you polish and refine your impact.

---

Two major impediments face the leader who wants to be an effective listener. First, the leader is so often overloaded with responsibilities, including analytical work, that it is difficult to take the time to carefully listen to subordinates. Second is the speed difference between speaking and listening. The average rate of speaking is between 110 and 200 words per minute, yet people can listen in the range of 400 to 3,000 words per minute. So the leader, as well as anybody else, will often let his or her mind wander.

Here we look at two leadership aspects of listening to supplement your general knowledge of listening, acquired most likely in other courses: selective listening to problems, and making the rounds.

### Selective Listening to Problems

Organizational leaders are so often bombarded with demands and information that it is difficult to be attentive to a full range of problems. So the leader makes an intentional or unintentional decision to listen to just certain problems. Erika H. James notes that despite how our brains ordinarily work, success is dependent on staying open to all incoming information.[19] The busy leader must avoid listening to limited categories of information such as good news, bad news, or financial news. A CEO with a propensity to listen only to financial results might ignore any word of problems so long as the company is earning a profit. For example, the CEO of an energy company was so happy with financial results that he ignored pleas from the director of human resources about problems brewing. The problems related to discrimination and sexual harassment lawsuits that would be forthcoming if certain behaviors of some line managers were not stopped immediately. Without intervention by top-level leadership, the problems continued, and the company eventually faced expensive and embarrassing lawsuits.

## Making the Rounds

A robust communication channel for the leader/manager is to engage in face-to-face communication with direct reports and others, with an emphasis on listening. **Making the rounds** refers to the leader casually dropping by constituents to listen to their accomplishments, concerns, and problems and to share information. *Rounding* is a well-established concept from health care in which the physician talks to patients and other health care workers to observe problems and progress firsthand.[20] Through rounding, vital information is gathered if the physician or manager listens carefully. Making the rounds is also referred to as *management by walking around*, yet "rounding" seems more focused and systematic.

From the perspective of listening, the leader stays alert to potential problems. Assume that a subordinate is asked, "How are things going?" and she replies, "Not too terrible." This response begs a little digging, such as, "What is happening that is a little terrible?"

Table 12-2 offers you a few suggestions for doing an effective job of dropping by to exchange information with employees. Leadership Skill-Building Exercise 12-2 gives you an opportunity to try out the fundamental leadership skill of communication.

The accompanying Leader in Action profile illustrates a leader who makes communicating—both sending and receiving messages—an important part of his job.

**TABLE 12-2** How to Succeed in Management by Making the Rounds

Here's a checklist of walk-around tips a manager can start using today, as provided by communications consultant Linda Duyle:

- *Get out of the office.* Dedicate some time each week to get out and talk with your work force.
- *Leave behind your cell phone and BlackBerry.* Minimize distractions that can tug on your attention and block effective listening. You want to demonstrate courtesy and respect during your time on the floor.
- *Start slowly.* Don't feel the need to dive right into your discussion even if you have prepared an agenda. Effective listening requires you to focus on the person with whom you are speaking. Clear your mind of distractions.
- *Make eye contact.* Look directly at the people with whom you are speaking.
- *Make it two-way communication.* When you're asked a question that you can't answer, tell the employee that you don't have the answer but will get back to him or her.
- *Be honest.* If times are tough, don't sugarcoat reality. For example, if the company lost a big contract, bring it up in your casual conversation.
- *Process information.* You may want to bring a small notepad with you to write down questions or comments that you'd like to remember or that require follow-up. You will learn some great new things about your people and operations.
- *Show appreciation.* Thank the person for his or her time and comments.
- *Never quit.* People may not be comfortable during the early months of the walk-around process. But as they see you more frequently and your willingness to be visible, comfort in the process will improve.

*Source:* Adapted and abridged from Linda Dulye, "Get Out of Your Office," *HR Magazine*, July 2006, pp. 100–101. Copyright 2006 by Society for Human Resource Management (SHRM). Reproduced with permission of SHRM in the format Textbook via Copyright Clearance Center.

## Leadership Skill-Building Exercise 12-2

### Leadership Listening

Six or seven students gather for a team meeting to discuss an important operational problem, such as finding new ways to reduce the cycle time required to complete their tasks, or deciding how to convince top management to expand the team budget. One person plays the role of the team leader. All of the group members take turns at making both useful and apparently not-useful suggestions. The team leader, along with team members, displays careful listening whenever ideas surface. Students not directly involved in the group role play will take note of the listening skills they observe so that they can provide feedback later. Be particularly observant of selective listening. If class time allows, another team of six or seven students can repeat the group role play.

 ## Leader in Action

### Automotive Systems Leader Engages in Two-Way Communication

Carlos Mazzorin is one business leader who understands the importance of two-way communication and staying accessible to his employees. As chairman and CEO of automotive systems manufacturer Magna Donnelly, he makes time to hold regular town hall meetings at the company's various plants and factories. And each time he visits a site—which is often—he spends at least an hour out on the floor, talking "off the cuff" with employees.

And that's not all he does. He has also created two communication vehicles that employees *love*.

- *Carlos' Chatline*. In this monthly publication, Mazzorin brings employees up to speed on what's happening with Magna Donnelly operations around the world, explains recent product innovations, and keeps employees up to date on any important news facing the company—internally and externally.

- *Comments to Carlos*. This is a chance for *any* employee to ask Mazzorin a question. Office workers can email the questions directly to him; plant and factory workers can submit them through a submission box (the communications department forwards the contents to Mazzorin).

Unlike some CEOs, Mazzorin doesn't duck the tough questions. He handles inquires about possible mergers, bad news, and anything else that comes in from employees and the grapevine. And it's no surprise that employee focus groups reveal that Mazzorin gets very high marks for credibility, believability, and communication skills.

### Questions

1. In what way does Mazzorin engage in two-way communication?
2. Why might the focus groups conclude that Mazzorin has good communication skills?
3. What evidence is implied that Mazzorin emphasizes listening?

*Source:* "Communication Works Only If You're Willing to Listen at Least as Much as You Talk . . . or Write," *Communications Solutions* (Ragan's Management Resources, 11 East Wacker Drive, Suite 500, Chicago, IL 60601, www.managementresources.com, Sample Issue, distributed 2008). Reprinted courtesy of Ragan Communications.

# OVERCOMING CROSS-CULTURAL COMMUNICATION BARRIERS

 **Knowledge Bank**
Describes a few mental processes that contribute to communication barriers with people of other cultures.

**www.cengage.com/ management/dubrin**

Another communication challenge facing leaders and managers is overcoming communication barriers created by dealing with people from different cultures and subcultures. In today's workplace, leaders communicate with people from other countries and with a more diverse group of people in their own country. Because of this workplace diversity, leaders who can manage a multicultural and cross-cultural work force are in strong demand. Here we give some guidelines for overcoming some cross-cultural communication barriers. Implementing these guidelines will help overcome and prevent many communication problems. A useful starting point here is to take Leadership Self-Assessment Quiz 12-2 to help you think through your cross-cultural skills and attitudes.

## Leadership Self-Assessment Quiz 12-2

### Cross-Cultural Skills and Attitudes

***Instructions:*** Listed here are various skills and attitudes that various employers and cross-cultural experts think are important for relating effectively to coworkers in a culturally diverse environment. Indicate whether or not each statement applies to you.

| | Applies to Me Now | Not There Yet |
|---|---|---|
| 1. I have spent some time in another country. | ☐ | ☐ |
| 2. At least one of my friends is deaf, blind, or uses a wheelchair. | ☐ | ☐ |
| 3. Currency from other countries is as real as the currency from my own country. | ☐ | ☐ |
| 4. I can read in a language other than my own. | ☐ | ☐ |
| 5. I can speak in a language other than my own. | ☐ | ☐ |
| 6. I can write in a language other than my own. | ☐ | ☐ |
| 7. I can understand people speaking in a language other than my own. | ☐ | ☐ |
| 8. I use my second language regularly. | ☐ | ☐ |
| 9. My friends include people of races different from my own. | ☐ | ☐ |
| 10. My friends include people of different ages. | ☐ | ☐ |
| 11. I feel (or would feel) comfortable having a friend with a sexual orientation different from mine. | ☐ | ☐ |
| 12. My attitude is that although another culture may be very different from mine, that culture is equally good. | ☐ | ☐ |
| 13. I would be willing to (or already do) hang art from different countries in my home. | ☐ | ☐ |
| 14. I would accept (or have already accepted) a work assignment of more than several months in another country. | ☐ | ☐ |
| 15. I have a passport. | ☐ | ☐ |

## Quiz 12-2 (continued)

*Scoring and Interpretation:* If you answered "Applies to Me Now" to 10 or more questions, you most likely function well in a multicultural work environment. If you answered "Not There Yet" to 10 or more questions, you need to develop more cross-cultural awareness and skills to work effectively in a multicultural work environment. You will notice that being bilingual gives you at least 5 points on this quiz.

*Source:* Several ideas for statements on this quiz are derived from Ruthann Dirks and Janet Buzzard, "What CEOs Expect of Employees Hired for International Work," *Business Education Forum*, April 1997, pp. 3–7; Gunnar Beeth, "Multicultural Managers Wanted," *Management Review*, May 1997, pp. 17–21.

**1.** *Be sensitive to the fact that cross-cultural communication barriers exist.* Awareness of these potential barriers is the first step in dealing with them. When dealing with a person of a different cultural background, solicit feedback to minimize cross-cultural barriers to communication. For example, investigate which types of praise or other rewards might be ineffective for a particular cultural group. In many instances, Asians newly arrived in the United States feel uncomfortable being praised in front of others, because in Asian cultures group performance is valued more than individual performance.

Being alert to cultural differences in values, attitudes, and etiquette will help you communicate more effectively with people from different cultures. Observe carefully the cultural mistakes listed in Table 12-3. At the same time, recognize that these *mistakes* are based on cultural stereotypes and reflect typical or average behavior of members of a particular cultural group.

**2.** *Challenge your cultural assumptions.* The assumptions we make about cultural groups can create communication barriers. The assumption you make about another group may not necessarily be incorrect, but stopping to challenge the assumptions may facilitate communication. An American leader, for example, might assume that the norms of independence and autonomy are valued by all groups in the workplace. Trudy Milburn notes that even the concept of equality can be phrased to alienate cultural groups. A sentence from the Johnson & Johnson mission statement reads, "Everyone must be considered as an individual." However, the word *individual* does not have positive connotations for all groups. Among many Latino cultural groups, the term *individual* is derogatory because it may connote the separation of one person from the rest of the community.[21]

**3.** *Show respect for all workers.* The same behavior that promotes good cross-cultural relations in general helps overcome communication barriers. A widely used comment that implies disrespect is to say to a person from another culture, "You have a funny accent." Should you be transposed to that person's culture, you too might have a "funny accent." The attitude of highest respect is to communicate your belief that although another person's culture is different from yours, it is not inferior to your culture. Showing respect for another culture can be more important than being bilingual in overcoming communication barriers.[22]

**TABLE 12-3** Cultural Mistakes to Avoid with Selected Cultural Groups

**EUROPE**

| | |
|---|---|
| Great Britain | ■ Asking personal questions. The British protect their privacy.<br>■ Thinking that a businessperson from England is unenthusiastic when he or she says, "Not bad at all." English people understate positive emotion.<br>■ Gossiping about royalty. |
| France | ■ Expecting to complete work during the French two-hour lunch.<br>■ Attempting to conduct significant business during August—*les vacances* (vacation time).<br>■ Greeting a French person for the first time and not using a title such as *sir* or *madam* (or *monsieur, madame,* or *mademoiselle*). |
| Italy | ■ Eating too much pasta, as it is not the main course.<br>■ Handing out business cards freely. Italians use them infrequently. |
| Spain | ■ Expecting punctuality. Your appointments will usually arrive twenty to thirty minutes late.<br>■ Making the American sign for "okay" with your thumb and forefinger. In Spain (and many other countries) this is vulgar. |
| Scandinavia, Denmark, Sweden, Norway | ■ Being overly rank-conscious in these countries. Scandinavians pay relatively little attention to a person's place in the hierarchy. |

**ASIA**

| | |
|---|---|
| All Asian Countries | ■ Pressuring an Asian job applicant or employee to brag about his or her accomplishments. Asians feel self-conscious when boasting about individual accomplishments and prefer to let the record speak for itself. In addition, they prefer to talk about group rather than individual accomplishment. |
| Japan | ■ Shaking hands or hugging Japanese (as well as other Asians) in public. Japanese consider the practices offensive.<br>■ Not interpreting "We'll consider it" as a "no" when spoken by a Japanese businessperson. Japanese negotiators mean "no" when they say, "We'll consider it."<br>■ Not giving small gifts to Japanese when conducting business. Japanese are offended by not receiving these gifts.<br>■ Giving your business card to a Japanese businessperson more than once. Japanese prefer to give and receive business cards only once. |
| China | ■ Using black borders on stationery and business cards. Black is associated with death.<br>■ Giving small gifts to Chinese when conducting business. Chinese are offended by these gifts.<br>■ Making cold calls on Chinese business executives. An appropriate introduction is required for a first-time meeting with a Chinese official. |
| Korea | ■ Saying "no." Koreans feel it is important to have visitors leave with good feelings. |
| India | ■ Telling Indians you prefer not to eat with your hands. If the Indians are not using cutlery when eating, they expect you to do likewise. |

**MEXICO AND LATIN AMERICA**

| | |
|---|---|
| Mexico | ■ Flying into a Mexican city in the morning and expecting to close a deal by lunch. Mexicans build business relationships slowly. |
| Brazil | ■ Attempting to impress Brazilians by speaking a few words of Spanish. Portuguese is the official language of Brazil. |
| Most Latin American Countries | ■ Wearing elegant and expensive jewelry during a business meeting. Most Latin Americans think American people should appear more conservative during a business meeting. |

Note: A cultural mistake for Americans to avoid when conducting business in most countries outside the United States and Canada is to insist on getting down to business too quickly. North Americans in small towns also like to build a relationship before getting down to business.

**4. *Use straightforward language, and speak slowly and clearly.*** When working with people who do not speak your language fluently, speak in an easy-to-understand manner. Minimize the use of idioms and analogies specific to your language. A systems analyst from New Delhi, India, left confused after a performance review with her manager. The manager said, "I will be giving you more important assignments because I notice some good chemistry between us." The woman did not understand that *good chemistry* means *rapport*, and she did not ask for clarification because she did not want to appear uninformed.

Speaking slowly is also important because even people who read and write a second language at an expert level may have difficulty catching some nuances of conversation. Facing the person from another culture directly also improves communication because your facial expressions and lips contribute to comprehension. And remember, there is no need to speak much louder.

**5. *Look for signs of misunderstanding when your language is not the listener's native language.*** Signs of misunderstanding may include nods and smiles not directly connected to what you are saying, a lack of questions, inappropriate laughter, and a blank expression. If these signs are present, work harder to apply the suggestions in point 4.[23]

**6. *When the situation is appropriate, speak in the language of the people from another culture.*** Americans who can speak another language are at a competitive advantage when dealing with businesspeople who speak that language. The language skill, however, must be more advanced than speaking a few basic words and phrases. Speaking the local language will often bring a person more insight and prevent misunderstandings. Equally important, being bilingual helps bring a person the respect that a leader needs to be fully credible.[24]

As more deaf people have been integrated into the work force, knowing American Sign Language can be a real advantage to a leader when some of his or her constituents are deaf.

**7. *Observe cross-cultural differences in etiquette.*** Violating rules of etiquette without explanation can erect immediate communication barriers. A major rule of business etiquette in most countries is that the participants conducting serious business together should first share a meal. So if you are invited to a banquet that takes place the night before discussions about a major business deal, regard the banquet as a major opportunity to build a relationship. To avoid the banquet is a serious *faux pas*.

**8. *Do not be diverted by style, accent, grammar, or personal appearance.*** Although these superficial factors are all related to business success, they are difficult to interpret when judging a person from another culture. It is therefore better to judge the merits of the statement or behavior. A highly intelligent worker from another culture may still be learning English and thus make basic mistakes. He or she might also not yet have developed a sensitivity to dress style in your culture.

**9. *Avoid racial or ethnic identification except when it is essential to communication.*** Using a person's race or ethnicity as an adjective or other descriptor often suggests a negative stereotype.[25] For example, suppose a leader says,

"I am proud of André. He is a very responsible (*member of his race*) customer service rep." One possible interpretation of this statement is that most customer service reps of André's race are not so responsible. Or, a leader might say, "We are happy to have Martha on our team. She is an easy-to-get-along-with (*mention of ethnicity*) lady." A possible implication is that women from Martha's particular country are usually not too easy to work with.

**10.** ***Be sensitive to differences in nonverbal communication.*** A person from another culture may misinterpret nonverbal signals. To use positive reinforcement, some managers will give a sideways hug to an employee or will touch the employee's arm. People from some cultures resent touching from workmates and will be offended. Koreans in particular dislike being touched or touching others in a work setting.

**11.** ***Be attentive to individual differences in appearance.*** A major cross-cultural insult is to confuse the identity of people because they are members of the same race or ethnic group. An older economics professor reared in China and teaching in the United States had difficulty communicating with students because he was unable to learn their names. The professor's defense was that "so many of these Americans look alike to me." A study suggests that people have difficulty seeing individual differences among people of another race because they see so-called racial differences first; they might think, "He has the nose of a Chinese person." However, people can learn to search for more distinguishing features, such as a dimple or eye color, and expression (serious or not so serious).[26]

# THE LEADER'S ROLE IN RESOLVING CONFLICT AND NEGOTIATING

Leaders and managers spend considerable time resolving conflicts and negotiating. A frequent estimate is that they devote about 20 percent of their time to dealing with conflict. Conflict arises frequently among top executives, and it can have enormous consequences for the organization. If this conflict is ignored, the result can be an enterprise that competes more passionately with itself that with the competition.[27] An example of such competition would be two business units competing for resources. Departmental competition has been regarded as the "ugly underbelly" of all sizes of companies, often resulting in product delays, increased costs, and dwindling market shares as departments fight each other for domination behind the scenes. Frequent conflict is found also between off-line and online units.[28] Until conflict between or among the groups is resolved, collaboration is unlikely.[29] For example, if the operations group is in conflict with the human resources group, it will be difficult for the two groups to collaborate on a diversity training program.

An extensive description of conflict resolution is more appropriate for the study of managerial skills than for the study of leadership skills. The reason is because conflict resolution has more to do with establishing equilibrium than with helping the firm or organizational unit reach new heights. Here we focus on a basic framework for understanding conflict resolution styles, resolving conflict between two group members, and a few suggestions for negotiating and bargaining.

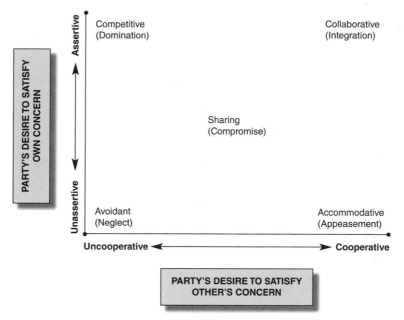

**FIGURE 12-1** Conflict-Handling Styles According to the Degree of Cooperation and Assertiveness.

*Source:* Kenneth W. Thomas, "Organizational Conflict," in Marvin D. Dunnette, ed., *Handbook of Industrial and Organizational Psychology*, p. 900 (Rand McNally). Copyright © 1976, Marvin D. Dunnette. Used by permission of Marvin D. Dunnette.

## Conflict Management Styles

As shown in Figure 12-1, Kenneth W. Thomas has identified five major styles of conflict management: competitive, accommodative, sharing, collaborative, and avoidant. Each style is based on a combination of satisfying one's own concerns (assertiveness) and satisfying the concerns of others (cooperativeness).[30] Leadership Self-Assessment Quiz 12-3 gives you an opportunity to think about your conflict management style.

*Competitive Style*    The competitive style is a desire to achieve one's own goals at the expense of the other party, or to dominate. A person with a competitive orientation is likely to engage in win–lose power struggles.

*Accommodative Style*    The accommodative style favors appeasement, or satisfying the other's concerns without taking care of one's own. People with this orientation may be generous or self-sacrificing just to maintain a relationship. An irate customer might be accommodated with a full refund, "just to shut him (or her) up." The intent of such accommodation might also be to retain the customer's loyalty.

*Sharing Style*    The sharing style is halfway between domination and appeasement. Sharers prefer moderate but incomplete satisfaction for both parties, which results in a compromise. The term *splitting the difference* reflects this orientation, which is commonly used in such activities as purchasing a house or car.

Leadership Self-Assessment Quiz 12-3

## My Conflict Resolution Style

*Instructions:* Answer each of the following statements "mostly true" or "mostly false" with respect to how you have dealt with the situation, would deal with the situation, or how much you agree with the attitude expressed.

|  | Mostly True | Mostly False |
|---|---|---|
| 1. I see myself as a "smash-mouth" negotiator. | ☐ | ☐ |
| 2. The best way to resolve conflict is to overwhelm the other side. | ☐ | ☐ |
| 3. When negotiating a price, I like to make sure that the other side walks away with at least some profit. | ☐ | ☐ |
| 4. When negotiating a price, I like to start with an outrageous demand or offer so I can eventually get the price I really wanted. | ☐ | ☐ |
| 5. After a successful negotiation, one side wins and one side loses. | ☐ | ☐ |
| 6. After a successful negotiation, both sides walk away with something of value. | ☐ | ☐ |
| 7. When I am in conflict with somebody else, I try to listen carefully to understand his or her point of view. | ☐ | ☐ |
| 8. Face it: business is war, so why grant concessions when in a dispute? | ☐ | ☐ |
| 9. When working out a disagreement with a workmate, I keep in mind the fact that we will have to work together in the future. | ☐ | ☐ |
| 10. Nice people finish last when it comes to resolving disputes. | ☐ | ☐ |

**Total score:** _____

*Scoring and Interpretation:* Give yourself a score of 1 for each answer that matches the scoring key:

| | | | |
|---|---|---|---|
| 1. Mostly false | 4. Mostly false | 7. Mostly true | 9. Mostly true |
| 2. Mostly false | 5. Mostly false | 8. Mostly false | 10. Mostly false |
| 3. Mostly true | 6. Mostly true | | |

If your score is 8, 9, or 10, you most likely use the collaborative (win–win) approach to resolving conflict and negotiating. If your score is 7 or less, you most likely use the competitive (win–lose) approach to resolving conflict and negotiating. The collaborative approach is more likely to enhance your leadership effectiveness in the long run.

*Collaborative Style*    In contrast to the other styles, the collaborative style reflects a desire to fully satisfy the desires of both parties. It is based on the underlying philosophy of the **win–win approach to conflict resolution**, the belief that after conflict has been resolved, both sides should gain something of value. The user of win–win approaches is genuinely concerned about arriving at a settlement that meets the needs of both parties, or at least does not badly damage the welfare of the other side. When collaborative approaches to resolving conflict are used, the relationships among the parties are built on and improved.

The collaborative style of conflict management has many variations, one of which is to agree with the person criticizing you. When you agree with a critic, you show that you seek a solution, not a way to demonstrate that you are right. If you agree with the substance of the criticism, you show that you are aware of the situation and ready to do what is best to solve the problem.[31]

To illustrate, if a group member criticizes you for having been too harsh in your evaluation of him or her, you might say: "I agree that my evaluation was harsh, but I was harsh for a purpose. I want to be candid with you so you will be motivated to make what I think are necessary improvements." Your agreement is likely to spark further discussion about how the group member can improve. The collaborative style is the approach an effective leader is most likely to use because the outcome leads to increased productivity and satisfaction.

Another form of agreeing with criticism is for the leader to apologize when he or she has truly made a mistake. An apology often reduces conflict because the other side becomes less hostile, and the scene is set for cooperation. Visualize a scenario in which members of the executive team vote themselves large financial bonuses during a period of financial losses to the company and layoffs of employees. Saying, "We're sorry, and we goofed" to the union and/or employees can help soften the sting. Giving back some of the bonuses would be even more helpful. In general, a good apology must be perceived as genuine, with an honest appeal for forgiveness.[32]

***Avoidant Style***    The avoider combines lack of cooperation and unassertiveness. He or she is indifferent to the concerns of either party. The person may actually be withdrawing from the conflict or be relying upon fate. An example of an avoider is a manager who stays out of a conflict between two team members, leaving them to resolve their own differences.

People engaged in conflict resolution typically combine several of the five resolution styles to accomplish their purpose. For example, a generally effective approach to resolving conflict is to be competitive with regard to a cost that is important to oneself but unimportant to the opponent, and at the same time use accommodation for a cost that is unimportant to oneself but important to the opponent.[33]

Which mode or modes of conflict handling to use depends upon a number of variables, as presented in detail in Table 12-4. The major contingency factors are the importance of the conflict issue and the relative power of the opposing parties. An issue may be so important to a leader, such as preventing his or her organizational unit from being outsourced, that domination may be the most effective mode. At other times a leader may use the accommodating mode of conflict management when the opposing side has much more power, and he or she may want to save domination for a more important issue in the future.

## Resolving Conflict Between Two Group Members

A high-level managerial skill is to help two or more group members resolve conflict between or among them. Much of the time a manager or leader invests in conflict resolution is geared toward assisting others to resolve their conflict. Often

**TABLE 12-4** Appropriate Situations for Using the Five Modes of Conflict Resolution

| CONFLICT-HANDLING MODE | APPROPRIATE SITUATION |
| --- | --- |
| Competing | 1. When quick, decisive action is vital, such as in an emergency<br>2. On important issues when unpopular actions need implementing, such as cost-cutting, enforcing unpopular rules, or discipline<br>3. On issues vital to organization welfare when you know you are right<br>4. Against people who take advantage of noncompetitive behavior |
| Collaborating | 1. To find an integrative solution when both sets of concerns are too important to be compromised<br>2. When your objective is to learn<br>3. To merge insights from people with different perspectives<br>4. To gain commitment by incorporating concerns into a consensus<br>5. To work through feelings that have interfered with a relationship |
| Sharing (Compromising) | 1. When goals are important but not worth the effort or potential disruption of more assertive modes<br>2. When opponents with equal power are committed to mutually exclusive goals<br>3. To achieve temporary settlements of complex issues<br>4. To arrive at expedient solutions under time pressure<br>5. As a backup when collaboration or competition is unsuccessful |
| Avoiding | 1. When an issue is trivial or more important issues are pressing<br>2. When you perceive no chance of satisfying your concern<br>3. When the potential disruption outweighs the benefits of a resolution<br>4. To let people cool down and regain perspective<br>5. When gathering information supersedes making an immediate decision<br>6. When others can resolve the conflict more effectively |
| Accommodating | 1. When you find you are wrong—to allow a better position to be heard, to learn, and to show your reasonableness<br>2. When issues are more important to others than to yourself—to satisfy others and maintain cooperation<br>3. To build social credits for later issues<br>4. To minimize the loss when you are outmatched and losing<br>5. When harmony and stability are especially important<br>6. To allow group members to develop by learning from mistakes |

*Source:* Slightly adapted from Kenneth W. Thomas, "Toward Multidimensional Values in Teaching: The Example of Conflict Behaviors," *Academy of Management Review* by Klimoski, Richard J., April 1977, p. 487. *Academy of Management Review* by Kenneth W. Thomas. Copyright 1997 by the Academy of Management. Reproduced with permission of the Academy of Management in the format Textbook via Copyright Clearance Center.

the conflict is between the heads of two different departments or divisions. The most useful approach is to get the parties in conflict to engage in confrontation and problem solving. (*Confrontation* refers to discussing the true problem, and *problem solving* refers to finding a way to resolve the conflict.) The manager sits down with the two sides and encourages them to talk to each other about the problem, not talk directly to him or her. This approach is preferable to inviting each side to speak with the manager or leader alone, because then each side might attempt to convince the manager that he or she is right. An abbreviated example follows:

*Leader:* I've brought you two together to see if you can overcome the problems you have about sharing the workload during a period in which one of you is overloaded.

*Stephanie:* I'm glad you did. Josh never wants to help me, even when I'm drowning in customer requests.

*Josh:* I would be glad to help Stephanie if she ever agreed to help me. If she has any downtime, she runs to the break room so she can chat on her cell phone.

*Stephanie:* Look who's talking. I have seen you napping in your SUV when you have a little downtime.

*Leader:* I'm beginning to see what's going on here. Both of you are antagonistic toward each other, and you look for little faults to pick. With a little more respect on both sides, I think you would be more willing to help each other out.

*Josh:* Actually, Stephanie's not too bad. And I know she can perform well when she wants to. Next time I see her needing help, I'll pitch in.

*Stephanie:* I know that the name "Josh" is related to joking around, but our Josh really has a warm heart. I'm open to starting with a fresh slate. Maybe Josh can ask me politely the next time he needs help.

Conflict specialist Patrick S. Nugent believes that being able to intervene in the conflicts of group members is a management skill that grows in importance. Such competencies are useful in an emerging form of management based less on traditional hierarchy and more on developing self-managing subordinates and teams. When the conflict is between two different groups, such as online versus off-line marketing, a major goal of conflict resolution is to get the two sides to see the company's big picture.[34]

## Negotiating and Bargaining

As mentioned in Chapter 1, negotiation is a basic leadership role. In support of this idea, Michael Watkins says it is not enough for leaders to be visionaries; they also need to be capable negotiators. One reason is that younger people are less prone to accept power and authority. Another reason is that the trend toward flatter organizations and the use of matrix structures require leaders to be negotiating continuously. (A matrix structure is a project team superimposed on a functional structure.) People often accept orders only after negotiation.[35]

Conflicts can be considered situations that call for negotiating and bargaining, or conferring with another person to resolve a problem. When you are trying to negotiate a fair salary for yourself, you are simultaneously trying to resolve a conflict. At first the demands of the two parties may seem incompatible, but through negotiation a salary may emerge that satisfies both parties. Here we review a handful of practical negotiating tactics a leader will find helpful. The approaches to negotiation presented here emphasize a strategy of integration or collaboration, with a philosophy of win–win.

***Listen First to Investigate What the Other Side Wants***    Listening skills are part of leadership effectiveness in negotiation also. Bobby Covie says, "There's a saying among negotiators that whoever talks the most during a negotiation loses." Being the first to listen helps establish trust. Listening also involves paying attention to what the other side is saying.[36] A person might begin a negotiating session claiming to want a bigger share of the division budget. Yet careful listening might indicate that he really is looking for his department to receive more respect and attention. So the issue is not financial.

As shown in the example just presented, listening helps the negotiator dig for information as to why the other side wants what it does.[37] If the other side wants a bigger budget just to have more respect, there are less expensive ways to grant respect than grant a bigger share of the budget. Perhaps the leader can give the person a classier job title, rename the department, or appoint the person to head a task force. For example, the head of marketing is renamed "chief of brands," and her department, "brand development."

***Begin with a Plausible Demand or Offer***    Most people believe that compromise and allowing room for negotiation include beginning with an extreme demand or offer. The theory is that the final compromise will be closer to the true demand or offer than if the negotiation were opened more realistically. But a plausible demand is better because it reflects good-faith bargaining. Also, if a third party has to resolve the conflict, a plausible demand or offer will receive more sympathy than an implausible one.

***Focus on Interests, Not Positions***    Rather than clinging to specific negotiating points, one should keep overall interests in mind and try to satisfy them. Remember that the true object of negotiation is to satisfy the underlying interests of both sides. As professional mediator John Heister explains, when you focus on interests, all of the disputants get on the same side of the table and say, "We have a problem to solve. Based on our common interests, we need to find a solution that meets the needs of each of the stakeholders."[38]

Here is how the strategy works: Your manager asks you to submit a proposal for increasing sales volume. You see it as an important opportunity to link up with another distributor. When you submit your ideas, you learn that management wants to venture further into ecommerce, not to expand the dealer network. Instead of insisting on linking with another dealer, be flexible. Ask to be included in the decision making for additional involvement in ecommerce. You will increase your sales volume (your true interest), and you may enjoy such secondary benefits as having helped the company develop a stronger ecommerce presence.

***Search for the Value in Differences Between the Two Sides***    Negotiation researcher and practitioner James K. Sebenius explains that according to conventional wisdom we negotiate to overcome the differences dividing the two sides. So we hope to find win–win agreements by searching for common ground. However, many sources of value in negotiation arise from differences among the parties. The differences may suggest useful ideas for breaking a deadlock and reaching a constructive agreement. Framed differently, the differences might suggest what solution will work for both sides. Here is an example:

A small technology company and its investors were stuck in a difficult negotiation with a large acquiring company insistent on paying much less than the asking price. Exploring the differences, it turned out that the acquirer was actually willing to pay the higher price but was concerned about elevating price expectations for further companies it might purchase in the same sector. The solution was for the two sides to agree on a moderate, well-publicized purchase price. The deal contained complex contingencies that almost guaranteed a much higher price later.[39]

(So, in the end, searching for values in differences functions like win–win.)

***Be Sensitive to International Differences in Negotiating Style***   A challenge facing the multicultural leader is how to negotiate successfully with people from other cultures. Frank L. Acuff notes that Americans often have a no-nonsense approach to negotiation. Key attitudes underlying the American approach to negotiation include:

"Tell it like it is."
"What's the bottom line?"
"Let's get it out."

A problem with this type of frankness and seeming impatience is that people from other cultures may interpret such remarks as rudeness. The adverse interpretation, in turn, may lead to a failed negotiation. Acuff gives a case example: "It is unlikely in Mexico or Japan that the other side is going to answer 'yes' or 'no' to any question. You will have to discern answers to questions through the context of what is being said rather than from the more obvious direct cues that U.S. negotiators use."[40] By sizing up what constitutes an effective negotiating style, the negotiator stands a reasonable chance of achieving a collaborative solution. Other cross-cultural differences in negotiation style include these tendencies: Japanese avoid direct confrontation and prefer an exchange of information. Russians crave combat; Koreans are team players; Nigerians prefer the spoken word; and Indians the written one.[41] (We caution again, that cultural stereotypes are true much of the time, but not all of the time.)

When asked to describe the essence of good negotiating in a few sentences, master negotiator Roger Fisher replied, "Be firm and friendly. Hard on the problem, soft on the people. Find out what the other side views as important and negotiate on that. Let the other side make the deal better from its point of view, at the same time that you gain what you are looking for."[42] Adding to Fisher's comments, it is important to recognize that you might want to make another deal, another day, with the same party. As a result, you want to conduct yourself in a dignified way and not attempt to maximize gain for you, and minimize gain for the other side.

Negotiating and bargaining, as with any other leadership and management skill, require conceptual knowledge and practice. Leadership Skill-Building Exercise 12-3 gives you an opportunity to practice collaboration, the most integrative form of negotiating and bargaining, as well as conflict resolution. Practice in finding options for mutual gains is helpful for the leader because negotiating is a high-impact part of his or her job.

**Ⓚ Knowledge Bank**
Describes an experiment about how culture can influence negotiation.

**www.cengage.com/ management/dubrin**

## Leadership Skill-Building Exercise 12-3

### Integrative Bargaining

The class is organized into groups of six, with each group being divided into two negotiating teams of three each. The members of the negotiating teams would like to find an integrative (win–win) solution to the issue separating the two sides. The team members are free to invent their own pressing issue, or they can choose one of the following:

■ Management wants to control costs by not giving cost-of-living adjustments in the upcoming year. The employee group believes that a cost-of-living adjustment is absolutely necessary for its welfare.

■ The marketing team claims it could sell 250,000 units of a toaster wide enough to toast bagels if the toasters could be produced at $10 per unit.

The manufacturing group says it would not be feasible to get the manufacturing cost below $15 per unit.

■ Blockbuster Video would like to build in a new location that is adjacent to a historic district in one of the oldest cities in North America. The members of the town planning board would like the tax revenue and jobs that the Blockbuster store would bring, but they do not want a Blockbuster store adjacent to the historic district.

After the teams have arrived at their solutions through high-level negotiating techniques, the creative solutions can be shared with teammates.

### Reader's Roadmap

So far we have studied considerable information about the nature of leadership; the attributes, behaviors, and styles of leaders; the ethics and social responsibility of leaders; and how leaders exert power and use politics and influence. We then studied techniques for developing teamwork, as well as motivation and coaching skills. After studying creativity and innovation as part of leadership, we focused on communication skills as they relate to leadership. Next, we shift our study to direction setting at the organizational level: strategic leadership.

## SUMMARY

Open communication between company leaders and employees helps an organization overcome problems and attain success. Effective communication skills contribute to inspirational leadership. Nonverbal skills are also important for leadership effectiveness.

Inspirational and powerful communication helps leaders carry out their roles. Suggestions for

inspirational and powerful speaking and writing include the following: (1) be credible; (2) gear your message to your listener; (3) sell group members on the benefits of your suggestions; (4) use heavy-impact and emotion-provoking words; (5) use anecdotes to communicate meaning; (6) back up conclusions with data; (7) minimize language errors, junk words, and vocalized pauses; (8) use business jargon in appropriate doses, and (9) write crisp, clear memos, letters, and reports, including a front-loaded message.

Using a power-oriented linguistic style is another way to communicate with inspiration and power. The style includes a variety of techniques, such as downplaying uncertainty, emphasizing direct rather than indirect talks, and choosing an effective communication frame. Leaders can also improve their communication skills by following the six principles of persuasion: liking, reciprocity, social proof, consistency, authority, and scarcity.

Skill can also be developed in using nonverbal communication that connotes power, being in control, forcefulness, and self-confidence. Videoconferencing places heavy demands on nonverbal communication. Among the suggestions for nonverbal communication are to stand erect; speak at a moderate pace with a loud, clear tone; and smile frequently in a relaxed manner. A person's external image also plays an important part in communicating messages to others. People pay more respect and grant more privileges to those they perceive as being well dressed and neatly groomed.

Listening is a fundamental management and leadership skill. Two impediments for the leaders who wants to listen well are (1) leaders are already overloaded, and (2) people can listen to more words per minute than others can speak. Leaders have to be careful about listening selectively. A robust communication channel for the leader/manager is to engage in face-to-face communication with direct reports by making the rounds.

Overcoming communication barriers created by dealing with people from different cultures is another leadership and management challenge. Guidelines for overcoming cross-cultural barriers include the following: (1) be sensitive to the existence of cross-cultural communication barriers; (2) challenge your cultural assumptions; (3) show respect for all workers; (4) use straightforward language, and speak slowly and clearly; (5) look for signs of misunderstanding when your language is not the listener's native language; (6) when appropriate, speak in the language of the people from another culture; (7) observe cross-cultural differences in etiquette; (8) do not be diverted by style, accent, grammar, or personal appearance; (9) avoid racial or ethnic identification except when it is essential to communication; (10) be sensitive to differences in nonverbal communication; and (11) be attentive to individual differences in appearance.

Leaders and managers spend considerable time managing conflict. Resolving conflict facilitates collaboration. Five major styles of conflict management are as follows: competitive, accommodative, sharing, collaborative (win–win), and avoidant. Each style is based on a combination of satisfying one's own concerns (assertiveness) and satisfying the concerns of others (cooperativeness). The collaborative style of conflict management includes agreeing with the criticizer, and apologizing. When resolving conflict, people typically combine several of the five resolution styles to accomplish their purpose, such as dominating and accommodating. Which modes of conflict handling to use depends upon a number of variables, as presented in detail in Table 12-4.

A high-level managerial skill is to help two or more group members resolve conflict between or among them. The most useful approach is to get the parties in conflict to engage in confrontation and problem solving.

Conflicts can be considered situations calling for negotiating and bargaining. Specific negotiating techniques include the following: (1) listen first to investigate what the other side wants; (2) begin with a plausible demand or offer; (3) focus on interests, not positions; (4) search for the value in differences between the two sides; and (5) be sensitive to international differences in negotiating style.

## KEY TERMS

| Linguistic style | Making the rounds | Win–win approach to conflict resolution |

# GUIDELINES FOR ACTION AND SKILL DEVELOPMENT

A subtle part of being an effective communicator is to avoid language that discourages another person from expressing his or her opinion, or worse, shuts the person up. At times you may feel like putting the lid on a subordinate. However, in the long run silencing your team will backfire because you will lose valuable input. Here are three examples of statements leaders and managers frequently use that clamp down on communication: "I already know that," "Why would you want to change that? It's not broken," and, "Well it's my decision and I say no."[43]

Another technique for curtailing communication is to react to a comment with a blank stare and no comment of your own. Such behavior implies that you either don't care or are denying the reality of what the person is saying.

## Discussion Questions and Activities

1. Now that you have studied this chapter, what are you going to do differently to improve your communication effectiveness as a leader?
2. Find an example of a powerful written or spoken message by a leader. Bring the information back to class to share with others.
3. Identify a leader who you think has a power-oriented linguistic style. How did you arrive at your conclusion?
4. What do you see as a potential downside to using a power-oriented linguistic style?
5. Why is persuasion considered to be one of the leader's essential tools?
6. Given that people really do defer to experts, how might the leader establish his or her expertise?
7. Should a manager be willing to negotiate a performance standard, such as output per month, with a group member?
8. Would a powerful leader like Donald Trump ever have to negotiate anything in the workplace?
9. What concrete steps can a leader take to demonstrate that he or she respects a group member from another culture?
10. Assume that during a meeting, a middle manager is told by a subordinate that he or she is not fit for the position and should resign. What approach do you recommend that the leader take to resolve this conflict?

# Leadership Case Problem A

## Jason Makes the Rounds

Jason Caleb is the general manager of Eco Technologies, a business firm that recycles information technology electronic devices, including PCs, computer monitors, VCRs, DVD players, and cell phones. Some devices are refurbished and resold, while those that cannot be overhauled are broken down into usable parts. Most of the usable refurbished products are sold through brokers or eBay. The leftover scrap is sent to refineries for recycling.

As the interest in environmental sustainability has grown, along with restrictions on placing electronic products in landfills, Eco Technologies has grown substantially. In four years, the company has grown from five to sixty-three employees. Despite the growth in size and volume, Eco Technologies barely ekes out a profit.

With profit margins being so small, Caleb likes to stay in close touch with his supervisors to learn

## Problem A (continued)

of any potential problems, and also to maintain a personal relationship with his hard-working supervisors. "Without my gang of good guys and gals, Technologies would sink faster than a canoe filled to the brim with old PCs and TVs," said Caleb.

To help improve communications with his staff, Caleb decided to make the rounds of the warehouse and office every ten days or so. Last Thursday morning Caleb made his rounds, first stopping to chat with Luke Buscalia, the warehouse supervisor.

"Good morning, Luke," said Jason. "How is everything going at the warehouse? Any problems?

"The biggest problem we face," replied Luke, "is that we are running short on space. My team just doesn't know where to stuff all the old PCs and printers."

Jason said with a laugh, "Have you ever thought of asking all the warehouse technicians to donate the trunks of their vehicles to store some of the PCs and printers? I bet each of those SUVs I see in the lot could store at least five PCs behind the back seat. I know that you can find a solution to the problem. We will be in touch soon."

"Thanks for dropping by the warehouse," said Luke.

Jason moved from the warehouse to refurbishing operations, headed by Sonya Alberto. "What's up in refurbishing?" asked Jason.

Sonya replied, "What's up is that things are mostly down. We urgently need three more refurbishing technicians who know what they are doing. I've drawn blanks in finding any qualified candidates. I'm actually taking on a few small refurbishing projects myself after hours."

"Keep up the good work, Sonya," said Jason. "I'm glad to see that you are a hands-on manager. Just keep trying. You will find a few good technicians."

Sonya thought to herself, "Maybe I didn't get across to Jason how serious my problem is."

Jason next visited Chuck Quinn, the head of scrap operations. Jason asked, "Are things going pretty well for you in salvage?" asked Jason.

"We certainly are busy," replied Chuck. "Yet, I am worried if we can make a profit this year. With all the restrictions on landfills, the refinery operators are getting overloaded. The refineries are paying us less and less. I can see the day coming soon when the refineries will be charging us to accept the scrap, rather than the reverse."

"So long as the day hasn't arrived yet," responded Jason, "I wouldn't worry. Just keep shipping whatever we can to the refineries. It was good chatting with you."

Jason completed his rounds for the day by stopping to see Nancy Greene, the office manager. "Nancy, I hope you are having a good day," he said. "I'm tired of hearing about problems."

"If you are looking for good news, I can give you some," said Nancy. "The bookkeeper said we should make a little profit this month, our turnover is low, and we paid all our bills on time."

"Just what I wanted to hear," responded Jason. "I am willing to listen to problems, but good news is better."

### Questions

1. How effective is Jason Caleb in using "making the rounds" as a communication tool?
2. What recommendations would you make to Jason to use the rounds more effectively?
3. What recommendations would you make to Jason's direct reports to help him use the rounds more effectively?

## Leadership Case Problem B

### West Coast Wellness on the Go

Heather Wyoming was feeling great because she believed that today would be a turning point. As the director of marketing for West Coast Wellness, she was to meet with the executive committee, which included her boss, the CEO. Heather's purpose was to get approval to hire three new sales and marketing representatives. The meeting to discuss her plans took place at 8:30 A.M. A partial transcript of the meeting follows:

*Heather:* Thanks so much for meeting with me this morning. In appreciation, you can see that we have snacks that will make you well. All the pastries, donuts, and bagels are made without trans-fats. And all the juices served are freshly squeezed.

I am glad to see that you are looking well, because today we are celebrating wellness. West Coast Wellness is on the go. We have signed up six new companies and three HMOs in the last few months to use our services. We have also broken the ground by offering individual memberships.

I need your approval to hire three new sales and marketing representatives so we can keep the momentum rolling on our expansion.

*CEO:* How much will these new hires *cost* West Coast?

*Heather:* No cost at all. We will be investing about $25,000 per year for each rep. They will be working on mostly commission. I estimate that each successful rep will bring in a net of about $150,000 in revenue. So there is really no *cost* involved.

*Exec Committee Member 1:* Yet, Heather, we cannot overlook the fact that you want to bring three new employees on board, a situation that creates an immediate financial liability for West Coast Wellness.

*Heather:* I understand your point of view. If the reps produce nothing, we lose a lot of money. However, by hiring the right reps we will turn this potential liability into a great asset. I understand the need for prudent financial management, but I think I am asking to take a prudent risk.

*Exec Committee Member 2:* The regional economy has cooled down considerably, and there are many layoffs. Heather, what makes you so optimistic that we can expand the market for wellness services?

*Heather:* I share your concern about the economy. However, keeping employees well is a fabulous investment. We can demonstrate to potential clients that helping employees stay well increases productivity. When employees lose fewer days to absenteeism and less time to tardiness, they are more productive. Another great selling point we have is that when employers use our services, their medical insurance premiums typically go down.

*Exec Committee Member 3:* Heather, we all share your enthusiasm for wellness—otherwise, we wouldn't be members of the executive committee. But I am a little concerned that the market for our services is saturating. Hiring three more reps might be too optimistic.

*Heather:* You make a great point, yet awareness of wellness is on the rise. Companies are even giving workers financial rewards to get in shape. Obesity is being attacked on all fronts, and smokers are treated like criminals. Wellness is on the move, and we can get a bigger share of the market.

*CEO:* Heather, I am proposing to you and the committee that you begin by hiring one new sales and marketing rep. If that person proves to be a good investment, we will authorize you to hire another rep.

*Heather:* I can buy that logic. Just give me a chance to prove how much I can expand our market. I just want to get started on the path to success. One rep it is for now.

### Questions

1. How successful has Heather been at negotiating her demands?
2. Did Heather leave anything on the table?
3. What leadership characteristics has Heather displayed?

## ⊙ Leadership Skill-Building Exercise 12-4

### My Leadership Portfolio

For this chapter's entry into your leadership portfolio, think through how you have dealt with your opportunities to come across as a leader in your experiences. Did you have an opportunity to attempt to persuade an individual or group? Did you have an opportunity to be supportive toward another person? Did you have an opportunity to make a presentation on the job or in class? During these communication opportunities, how well did you come across as a leader? Did you impress anybody with persuasive skill or warmth? Carlos, an assistant restaurant manager, made this entry in his portfolio:

> I help manage an upscale restaurant. The wait staff has to be on top of its game when in the dining room. Without superior service, nobody is going to pay our prices even if the food and wine are good. Late one afternoon, in dragged Rick, looking in no shape to give good service to our guests. He looked worried and distracted. Instead of telling Rick to go home, I took him aside in the office. I asked him to give me a full explanation of whatever problem he was facing. We both sat down, and I poured Rick a cup of coffee. After a minute or so, Rick opened up to tell me about how he rammed the back of his car into a two-foot-high guardrail in a parking lot. His fiberglass bumper split, and he figures it will cost him $650 to replace it. I listened to his whole story without being judgmental. I said I would check with the manager to see if we could give him extra hours this month to earn more money to apply toward his repair. Rick said, "Thanks for listening," and he left our one-on-one session feeling better and looking well enough to face the guests.
>
> I give myself a gold star for having been a supportive leader. Ha! Ha!

## Internet Skill-Building Exercise

### What Is Your Influence Quotient?

Visit www.influenceatwork.com and take the NQ test, which measures knowledge of a certain type of influence tactic. After taking the test, compare the type of influence tactic measured by the test with (a) the influence tactics mentioned in this chapter about communications and conflict, and (b) the leadership influence tactics described in Chapter 8. In a few words, how might the type of influence tactic described in the test help you be a more effective leader?

**Apply the chapter concepts! Visit the Web and complete this Internet skill-building exercise to learn more about current leadership topics and trends.**

# Strategic Leadership and Knowledge Management

## LEARNING OBJECTIVES

After studying this chapter and doing the exercises, you should be able to

- Describe the nature of strategic leadership.

- Explain how to use the SWOT model to assist in strategic planning.

- Identify a number of current business strategies.

- Describe how leaders contribute to the management of knowledge and the learning organization.

Afew years back, Jim Skinner huddled with a handful of other McDonald's Corp. executives to tackle a big problem: The company, by most measures, was doing terribly. Skinner had jut been named vice chairman and was part of a new management team charged with helping reverse the company's sliding profit.

Three days later the company emerged with a new strategy, named Plan to Win. Instead of continuing to build lots of restaurants, the company would focus on improving existing locations. The goals: faster, friendlier service; tastier food; more appealing ambience; better value; and sharper marketing.

Sticking to that strategy has helped usher in one of the most successful streaks in McDonald's history—and guided it through some tough times. Skinner moved up to the chief executive spot in 2004, after CEO Jim Cantalupo died and his successor as CEO, Charlie Bell, relinquished his post to fight what proved to be a losing battle against cancer. McDonald's has endured a deluge of negative publicity thanks to movies like *Super Size Me* and books like *Fast Food Nation* that criticize the quality of its food and blame it for the nation's obesity epidemic.

Despite that, during the first two years since Skinner took over, the stock climbed 45 percent, and same-store sales and profits have risen steadily. Today, 50 million customers walk through McDonald's doors each day, a gain of 4 million over a three-and-one-half-year period.[1]

The story about the McDonald's comeback illustrates how leaders must continually think through the very nature of their business and the direction in which the firm is headed. A key leadership role is to form a **strategy,** an integrated, overall concept of how the firm will achieve its objectives.[2] In this chapter we approach strategic leadership by emphasizing the leader's role rather than presenting extensive information about business strategy. First, we examine the nature of strategic leadership and describe a frequently used tool for development strategy, SWOT analysis. We then examine the strategies that leaders most frequently use to bring about success. Following that is a description of a leader's contribution to a continuing thrust in strategy, knowledge management, and developing a learning organization.

## THE NATURE OF STRATEGIC LEADERSHIP

Strategic leadership deals with the major purposes of an organization or an organizational unit, and therefore has a different focus than leadership in general: Strategic leadership emphasizes balancing the short-term and long-term needs of the organization to ensure the enduring success of the organization. Leaders engage in strategic leadership when they act, think, and influence in ways that promote the competitive advantage of their organization.[3] For our purposes, **strategic leadership** is the process of providing the direction and inspiration necessary to create or sustain an organization. The founder of Netflix provided strategic leadership because he developed a concept for an organization, developed the organization, and inspired large numbers of people to help him achieve his purpose.

We study strategic leadership separately because in practice it is the province of top-level executives, but not only the chief executive. Craig Mundie, the chief research and strategy officer of Microsoft Corp., is an example of an executive who is not a CEO, yet whose work primarily involves strategy. His key challenge is to position the company to survive and thrive in the post–Bill Gates era. One of his primary tasks is to bring home golden long-term business opportunities.[4]

Strategic leadership is a complex of personal characteristics, thinking patterns, and effective management, all centering on the ability to think strategically. Do Leadership Self-Assessment Quiz 13-1 to explore your orientation toward thinking strategically. Our approach to understanding the nature of strategic leadership will be to describe certain associated characteristics, behaviors, and practices, as outlined in Figure 13-1. The information about transformational leadership presented in Chapter 3 is also relevant here.

## High-Level Cognitive Activity of the Leader

Thinking strategically requires high-level cognitive skills, such as the ability to think conceptually, absorb and make sense of multiple trends, and condense all of this information into a straightforward plan of action. The ability to process information and understand its consequences for the organization in its inter-action with the environment is often referred to as *systems thinking*. Long-term thinking is a key part of strategy. A CEO might work with a twenty-five-year perspective regardless of whether he or she would be with the same firm in twenty-five years.

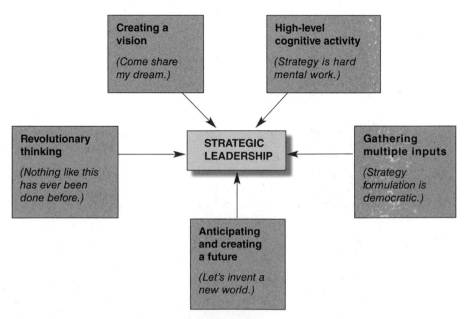

**FIGURE 13-1** Components of Strategic Leadership.

## Leadership Self-Assessment Quiz 13-1

### Are You a Strategic Thinker?

**Instructions:** Indicate your strength of agreement with each of the following statements:
SD = strongly disagree, D = disagree, N = neutral, A = agree, SA = strongly agree.

|    |  | SD | D | N | A | SA |
|----|----|----|----|----|----|----|
| 1. | Every action I take on my job should add value for our customers, our clients, or the public. | 1 | 2 | 3 | 4 | 5 |
| 2. | Let top management ponder the future; I have my own job to get done. | 5 | 4 | 3 | 2 | 1 |
| 3. | Strategic thinking is fluff. Somebody down the organization has to get the job done. | 5 | 4 | 3 | 2 | 1 |
| 4. | A company cannot become great without an exciting vision. | 1 | 2 | 3 | 4 | 5 |
| 5. | What I do on the job each day can affect the performance of the company many years into the future. | 1 | 2 | 3 | 4 | 5 |
| 6. | It is rather pointless to develop skills or acquire knowledge that cannot help you on the job within the next month. | 5 | 4 | 3 | 2 | 1 |
| 7. | Strategic planning should be carried out in a separate department rather than involve people throughout the organization. | 5 | 4 | 3 | 2 | 1 |
| 8. | It makes good sense for top management to frequently ask itself the question, "What business are we really in?" | 1 | 2 | 3 | 4 | 5 |
| 9. | If a company does an outstanding job of satisfying its customers, there is little need to worry about changing its mix of goods or services. | 5 | 4 | 3 | 2 | 1 |
| 10. | Organizational visions remind me of pipe dreams and hallucinations. | 5 | 4 | 3 | 2 | 1 |

**Scoring and Interpretation:** Find your total score by summing the point values for each question. A score of 42 to 50 suggests that you already think strategically, which should help you provide strategic leadership to others. Scores of 20 to 41 suggest a somewhat neutral, detached attitude toward thinking strategically. Scores of 10 to 19 suggest thinking that emphasizes the here and now and the short term. People scoring in this category are not yet ready to provide strategic leadership to group members.

**Skill Development:** Reflecting on your ability to think strategically is useful because leaders at all levels are expected to see the big picture and point people in a useful direction.

Emphasizing the cognitive activity of the leader helps emphasize that the leader plays a major role in strategy formulation. The leader must think through what makes the organization distinct, and define its purpose. Creativity and insight are required to achieve these profound conclusions. Most great companies start with great purposes formulated by the founder. A sterling example is IKEA's intent to offer customers "a wide range of well-designed, functional home furnishing products at prices so low that as many people as possible can afford them."[5] Typically the purpose comes from intuition rather than from extensive analysis, but there are exceptions. Jeff Bezos founded Amazon.com after an extensive analysis of what type of retail business would make sense being based on the Internet. As we all now know, Amazon.com began as a bookseller.

As one moves up the hierarchy, more problem-solving ability and imagination are required to handle the task environment effectively. To engage in strategic management and leadership, a person must have conceptual prowess. An organization will be successful when the cognitive abilities of its leaders are a good fit with the nature of the work. This is one of many reasons that tests of problem-solving ability correlate positively with success in managerial work.[6]

Creative problem solving is also important because the strategic leader has to develop alternative courses of action for shaping the organization. Furthermore, asking what-if questions requires imagination. To help revive the sagging fortunes of Kellogg Corporation several years ago, CEO Carlos Gutierrez asked why the company placed so much emphasis on sales volume. His new strategy, labeled Volume to Value, increased sales by shifting resources to higher-margin products such as Special K and Nutri-Grain bars.[7] Gutierrez essentially asked, "What if we shift our strategy to focusing on high-margin products instead of sales volume?" This strategic thinking set the company off on a positive direction that endured long after Gutierrez left his post to become U.S. Secretary of Commerce.

## Gathering Multiple Inputs to Formulate Strategy

Many strategic leaders arrive at their ideas for the organization's future by consulting with a wide range of interested parties, in a process similar to conducting research to create a vision. Strategy theorist Gary Hamel reasons that imagination is scarcer than resources. As a consequence, "We have to involve hundreds, if not thousands, of new voices in the strategy process if we want to increase the odds of seeing the future."[8]

Jeff Bezos, the CEO of Amazon.com, explains that even though he developed the original concept for his company, many others now contribute to the strategic direction of the company. Amazon has a group called the S Team (S meaning senior) that keeps current on what the company is working on and digs into strategy issues. The team meets for about four hours every Tuesday, along with a twice-a-year two-day meeting to explore new directions for Amazon.[9] As a result of this type of collective strategy formulation, the company continues to use new business models such as letting competitors offer their wares on the Amazon site.

Gathering multiple inputs has the added benefit of building morale. Whirlpool Corporation earns the support of line workers by placing volunteers on strategic teams with midlevel managers and senior executives. The production workers contribute to decisions that affect Whirlpool facilities in the United States. They travel to other countries with executives to new manufacturing facilities to help top management gain a better perspective on production and workforce issues.[10] As a result, Whirlpool leadership can make crisper strategic decisions about production and work force issues.

## Anticipating and Creating a Future

A major component of leadership is direction setting, which involves anticipating and sometimes creating a future for the enterprise or organizational unit. To set a direction is also to tell the organization what it should be doing. To set a productive direction for the future, the leader must accurately forecast or anticipate that future. Insight into tomorrow can take many forms, such as a leader's making accurate forecasts about consumer preferences, customer demands, and the skill mix needed to operate tomorrow's organization. A truly visionary leader anticipates a future that many people do not think will come to pass. A classic example is that in the early days of xerography, market research indicated that most people polled saw no need for a product to replace carbon paper.

The idea of anticipating and creating a future underscores the contribution of strategy in getting a stalled business firm moving forward. Quite often the emergency measure of shrinking a firm is done to rescue the company from financial trouble. When Alcatel-Lucent, the telecom company, was in financial trouble in 2007, Chief Executive Patricia Russo responded by getting rid of the chief financial officer along with 4,000 other employees—a typical maneuver during difficult times. A business analyst commented, "Job cuts alone can't substitute for a thorough strategic re-think. It's not clear what Ms. Russo has in mind besides waiting for better times that may never come. Alcatel has both market and product problems."[11] Russo's inability to derive a turnaround strategy led to her leaving Alcatel in 2008.

Creating the future is a more forceful approach than anticipating the future. The leader, assisted by widespread participation of team members, creates conditions that do not already exist. He or she must ask questions about the shape of the industry in five to ten years and decide how to ensure that the industry evolves in a way that is highly advantageous to the company. Furthermore, the leader must recognize the skills and capabilities that must be acquired now if the company is to occupy the industry high ground in the future.

Creating the future has been conceptualized as reinventing an industry. Entrepreneurial leaders frequently engage in such activity. A classic example is in order. C. K. Prahalad explains that the shoe industry is a good example of reinvention. Nike and Reebok have fundamentally reinvented their industry and consequently are fast-growing businesses in a mature industry. One factor is that they have changed the price-performance relationship in the industry. Both companies have introduced high technology, new materials, large-scale advertising, and global brands. None of these factors was so pronounced previously in the shoe industry.[12]

## Revolutionary and Contrarian Thinking

Using even stronger terms than *reinventing an industry*, Gary Hamel characterizes strategy as being revolutionary. According to Hamel, corporations are reaching the limits of incrementalism. Incremental improvements include squeezing costs, introducing a new product a few weeks earlier, enhancing quality a notch, and capturing another point of market share. These continual improvements enhance an organization's efficiency and are therefore vital to a firm's success, but they are not strategic breakthroughs or radical innovations.[13]

Before an organization can reinvent itself, it may be necessary to admit that a strategy successful in the past no longer fits the time. Ford Motor Company launched a new plan of cutting back on the number of models and deals, and centralizing many, only after Bill Ford admitted something was drastically wrong with the company. In an email to all of Ford Motor's employees, he stated, "The business model that has sustained us for decades is no longer sufficient to sustain profitability."[14]

To be an industry leader, a company's leaders must think in revolutionary terms. Revolutionary companies such as Amazon.com and Netflix create the rules for others to follow. According to Hamel, any strategy that does not seriously challenge the status quo is not actually a strategy. What passes for strategy in most companies is often sterile and unimaginative.

Strategy expert Michael Porter agrees with the revolutionary aspect of business strategy by insisting that a key component of strategy is deliberately choosing to be different.[15] Being different sometimes refers to having an expansive and elegant concept of the future of a business. AT&T Chairman Edward E. Whitacre, Jr., sees his company as embarking on a digital video revolution. His company has launched an all-Internet network, encompassing 40,000 miles of newly laid fiber-optic lines. Part of the revolutionary plan rested on using copper phone wires, already laid, to transport video the last few thousand feet into homes, thereby saving substantial money.[16]

A variation of choosing to be different is to engage in contrarian thinking in which the leader rejects conventional wisdom, much like the investor who trolls for hidden value in out-of-favor stocks. Jim Lanzone is the former CEO of Ask.com. Lanzone rejects the wisdom that success involves striving to be an industry leader. "You can be the fourth-ranked search engine, like we are, and still be doing very, very well," says Lanzone. He says his guiding principle (or strategy) is to stay focused on improving search results rather than on distractions such as email or blog services.[17]

## Creating a Vision

We have already mentioned vision in this book, including the description in Chapter 3 of the vision component of charismatic leadership. Here we examine the concept of vision in more depth, because visions are an integral part of strategic leadership.

The final vision statement is relatively short. James R. Lucas, a specialist in vision formulation, writes that a carefully considered and articulated vision helps us know who we are and who we are not. The vision also points to what we do successfully and what we do not, which activities we should take on and which we should avoid.[18] (A few more specifics about developing a vision statement are presented in the Guidelines for Action and Skill Development section of this chapter.)

Articulating a clear vision helped get several great companies off the ground when the company founders were seeking funding from venture capitalists. When Sergey Brin and Larry Page were planning to launch a company, they had no business experience and no track record, yet they had a powerful one-line vision. They told investors at Sequoia Capital, "We deliver the world's information in one click." The investors liked the vision statement, and invested in the company called Google. When Sandy Lerner and Len Bosack walked into Sequoia seeking venture funds for a new company called Cisco Systems, they used the vision statement, "We network networks."[19] Both the Google and Cisco statements might be classified as dealing with a *mission* because they are related to the present, not the future. However, even the smartest minds in business often use *mission* and *vision* interchangeably.

In companies that believe strongly in visions and strategic goals, all activities throughout the company are supposed to support the vision and goals. For example, before any manager is authorized to launch a project in the business services division at Watson Wyatt in Reigate, England, he or she must demonstrate how the initiative will contribute to the company's strategic goals. For example, one of the company's strategic pillars is to deliver high-quality advice and services to clients. An information technology project that linked directly to this pillar would stand a good chance of being approved.[20]

# CONDUCTING A SWOT ANALYSIS

Strategic planning helps a manager lead strategically. **Strategic planning** encompasses those activities that lead to the statement of goals and objectives and the choice of strategy. Under ideal circumstances, a firm arrives at its strategy after completing strategic planning. In practice, many executive leaders choose a strategy prior to strategic planning. Once the firm has the strategy, such as forming strategic alliances, a plan is developed to implement it.

Quite often strategic planning takes the form of a **SWOT analysis**, a method of considering internal strengths and weaknesses, and external opportunities and threats in a particular situation. A SWOT analysis represents an effort to examine the interaction between the particular characteristics of your organization or organizational unit and the external environment, or marketplace, in which you compete.[21] The framework, or technique, is useful in identifying a niche the company has not already exploited. The four components of a basic version of SWOT are described next.

### Internal Strengths

The emphasis in this step is assessing factors within the organization that will have a positive impact on implementing the plan. (In some versions of SWOT analysis, an analysis of the external environment is included in this step.) What are the good points about a particular alternative? What are your advantages? What do you do well? Use your own judgment and intuition, and also ask knowledgeable people. As a business owner, you may have a favorable geographic location that makes you more accessible to customers than your competitor is. Another strength is that you may have invested in state-of-the art equipment that became available only recently.

A successful example of capitalizing on internal strengths took place when Hewlett-Packard Corp. regained the lead over Dell Inc. in PC sales. Within weeks after arriving at HP to run the company's PC business, Todd Bradley concluded that HP was fighting Dell on the wrong battlefield. HP was mobilizing its resources to compete with Dell where Dell was strong, in direct sales via the Internet and phone. Instead, Bradley decided that HP should capitalize on its strength—retail stores where Dell had no presence at the time. Bradley worked on better distribution of the PCs along with building better relations with retailers. (An effective leader never neglects relations.) As a result of capitalizing on the retail strengths, HP reclaimed its number 1 position in the sale of personal computers.[22]

### Internal Weaknesses

Here the strategy developer takes a candid look at factors within the firm that could have a negative impact on the proposed plan. Consider the risks of pursuing a particular course of action, such as subcontracting work to a low-wage country (outsourcing). What could be improved? What is done badly? What should be avoided? Examine weaknesses from internal and external perspectives. Do outsiders perceive weaknesses that you do not see? (You may have to ask several outsiders to help you identify these weaknesses.) Are there products, services, or work processes your competitors perform better than you do? You are advised to be realistic now and face any unpleasant truths as soon as possible. Again, use your judgment, and ask knowledgeable people. As a manager or business owner, you may have problems managing your inventory, or you may have employees who are not up to the task of implementing a new plan or venture.

### External Opportunities

The purpose of this step is to assess socioeconomic, political, environmental, and demographic factors among others to estimate what benefits they may bring to the organization. Think of the opportunities that await you if you choose a promising strategic alternative, such as creating a culturally diverse customer base. Use your imagination, and visualize the possibilities. Look for interesting trends. Useful opportunities can derive from such events as the following:

- Changes in technology and markets on both a broad and narrow scale
- Changes in government policy related to your field
- Changes in social patterns, population profiles, lifestyles, and so forth.

### External Threats

The purpose of this step is to assess what possible negative impact socioeconomic, political, environmental, and demographic factors may have on the organization. There is a downside to every alternative, so think ahead, and do contingency

## ◉ Leadership Skill-Building Exercise 13-1

### Conducting a SWOT Analysis

In small groups, develop a scenario for a SWOT analysis, such as the group starting a chain of coffee shops, pet-care service centers, or treatment centers for online addictions. Since you will probably have mostly hypothetical data to work with, you will have to rely heavily on your imagination. Group leaders might share the results of the SWOT analysis with the rest of the class. Conducting a SWOT analysis reinforces the skill of thinking strategically about a course of action. A key challenge in preparing this hypothetical SWOT analysis is to make a distinction between internal and external forces.

planning. Ask people who may have tried in the past what you are attempting now. Answer questions such as:

- What obstacles do you face?
- What is your competition doing?
- Are the required specifications for your job, products, or services changing?
- Is changing technology changing your ability to compete successfully?

Despite a careful analysis of threats, do not be dissuaded by the naysayers, heel-draggers, and pessimists. To quote Nike, "Just do it."

Carrying out a SWOT analysis is often illuminating in terms of both pointing out what needs to be done and putting problems into perspective. Although much more complex schemes have been developed for strategic planning, they all include some analysis of strengths, weaknesses, and opportunities.[23] Leadership Skill-Building Exercise 13-1 gives you an opportunity to conduct a SWOT analysis.

## A SAMPLING OF BUSINESS STRATEGIES FORMULATED BY LEADERS

We have been focusing on the process by which leaders and managers make strategic decisions. Also of interest to leaders and potential leaders is the content of such decisions. Business strategies are often classified according to their focus of impact: corporate level, business level, or functional level. Corporate-level strategy asks, "What business are we in?" Business-level strategy asks, "How do we compete?" And functional-level strategy asks, "How do we support the business-level strategy?" Some of the business strategies listed next might cut across more than one of these three levels. The first three of these strategies are the generic strategies espoused by Michael Porter.[24]

**1. *Differentiation.*** A differentiation strategy seeks to offer a product or service that the customer perceives as being different from available alternatives. The organization may use advertising, distinctive features, exceptional service, or new technology to gain this perception of uniqueness. The mammoth size and rugged appearance of the Hummer SUVs is part of the company's (a division of GM) differentiation strategy, despite the fact that several Hummer models are now smaller. What differentiates one of your favorite products?

**2. *Cost leadership.*** A basic strategy is to produce a product or service at a low cost in order to lower the selling price and gain market share. Wal-Mart is a master at cost leadership because the company's massive buying power enables it to receive huge price concessions from suppliers. A variety of general merchandise stores, such as Dollar General, implement the cost leadership strategy even more extremely than does Wal-Mart.

**3. *Focus or niche.*** In a focus strategy, the organization concentrates on a specific regional market or buyer group. To gain market share, the company will use either a differentiation or a cost leadership approach in a targeted market. The focus strategy is a natural, common-sense approach to business because it is difficult to serve every customer well. A focus strategy is about the same thing as finding a *niche*, or your place in the market. Almost every successful business venture was found by locating a niche, including Enterprise Auto, which began its road to prominence by supplying rental autos to people whose vehicles were under repair at a body shop. Two examples of successful, well-planned focus marketing strategies are as follows:

- Instead of competing directly with eBay, several smaller online auctions stick to a narrow, successful niche, giving them an identity that facilitates sales. An example is StubHub, Inc., which competes with eBay as a middleman for ticket sales to sporting events, concerts, and other spectator activities.[25]
- Jack DeBoer is known as the father of the extended-stay hotel concept, and has recently developed another successful niche. Value Place is an extended-stay hotel aimed at delivering low prices, guaranteed cleanliness, and safety to the business traveler on a modest budget. The typical guest is a self-employed business traveler needing to economize, or a traveler who is on a strict per diem limit.[26]

**4. *High quality.*** A basic business strategy is to offer goods or services of higher quality than the competition does. Leaders continue to emphasize quality, even if there is less explicit emphasis today on formal quality programs than in the past. Important exceptions are the Six Sigma programs that emphasize statistical approaches to attaining quality. Leaders at GE and 3M, for example, emphasize Six Sigma. One reason that quality is classified as a strategy is that it contributes to competitive advantage in cost and differentiation. Because many customers now expect high quality, a quality strategy must be supplemented with other points of differentiation, such as supplying customized features and services that customers desire. How about Tiffany & Co. and the Swiss Army knife for a quality strategy?

**5. *Imitation.*** If you cannot be imaginative, why not imitate the best? Manufacturers of popular digital devices such as digital cameras and cell phones use an imitation strategy. The company waits for the right time to introduce a lower-priced competitor. Benchmarking is a form of learning by watching. One company emulates the best practices of another company, usually without outright stealing the product or service ideas of another company. The automotive industry is rampant with one company imitating another. Next time you are in a busy parking lot or driving on the highway, see how many hoods and auto grilles you can find that resemble a Mercedes.

**6. *Strategic alliances.*** A modern business strategy is to form alliances, or share resources, with other companies to exploit a market opportunity. A strategic alliance is also known as a *virtual corporation*. Strategic alliances have become more common as the high-tech industry struggles with needed yet expensive innovation. Sometimes the alliances are between rivals. Microsoft and Novell reached an agreement that bridges different approaches to software development including document format compatibility, resulting in easier sharing of documents. As a result, the two companies became partners for some products and competitors in others.[27]

Strategic alliances sometimes take the form of marketing partnerships in which the two parties benefit considerably when the products or services go well together—hence, the strategic alliance between Papa John's pizza restaurants and Six Flags theme parks. The partnership requires that only Papa John's pizza be sold on Six Flags properties, and helps Six Flags make contact with consumers at approximately 1,100 Papa John's restaurants located within a 100-mile radius of a Six Flags theme park.[28]

**7. *Growth through acquisition.*** A standard strategy for growth is for one company to purchase others. Growth in size is important, but companies may also purchase other companies to acquire a new technology or complete a product line. Buying a new technology is often less expensive than investing huge sums in R&D that might not yield a marketable product. Cisco Systems, Inc., achieved much of its growth by purchasing smaller companies, and much of General Electric's growth over the years can be attributed to acquiring other companies.

**8. *High speed and first-mover strategy.*** High-speed managers focus on speed in all of their business activities, including product development, sales response, and customer service. Knowing that "time is money," they choose time as a competitive resource. It is important to get products to market quickly because the competition might get there first or might deliver a product or service more rapidly. Getting to market first is also referred to as the first-mover strategy. Starbucks was the first national chain of coffee bars. The many storefronts served as marketing devices to acquire more customers.

Moving in after a product or service in already successful will sometimes best the first-mover strategy. A classic example is that Visicalc, the first desktop computer spreadsheet program, lost ground as Lotus took over the field with the 1-2-3. Soon Microsoft's Excel dominated the field.[29]

**9. *Product and global diversification.*** A natural business strategy is to offer a variety of products and services and to sell across borders to enhance market opportunities. Coca-Cola Co. exemplifies a company that thrives on both global and product diversification. Coke now generates 75 percent of its revenue and operating profit from countries outside the United States. Despite the company's reputation for relying too heavily on Coke, it has acquired many smaller brands of beverages in recent years, including the $4.1 billion purchase in 2007 of Glaceau, which sells Vitaminwater and Smartwater.[30]

John Chambers, the charismatic leader of Cisco Systems, Inc., declared recently that he wanted to "be more than a plumber," meaning that he wanted to go beyond building the infrastructure for the Internet. His plans were to turn Cisco into a consumer tech company by acquiring companies such as Scientific Atlanta, Inc., which makes set-top boxes.[31]

Sometimes a company with a strong reputation for delivering one product or service will branch out to capitalize on the allure of its brand. Montblanc, the century-old maker of luxury fountain pens, began marketing its own deluxe watches. The watches are the centerpiece of a bold effort to transform Montblanc, a division of Switzerland-based Richmont SA, into a leading global luxury brand. Aside from pens, the Montblanc trademark now appears on many items, from fragrances and pocket knives to sunglasses. "Watches are clearly the strategic growth area," says Jan-Patrick Schmitz, the head of U.S. operations for Montblanc.[32]

Global diversification is such a widely accepted strategy that the burden of proof would be on a business leader who shunned globalization.

**10. *Sticking to core competencies.*** Many firms of all sizes believe they will prosper if they confine their efforts to the activities they perform best—their core competencies. Corporate strategist Jim Collins calls this the *Hedgehog concept:* becoming very good at one thing in a world of companies that spread themselves into many areas where they lack depth.[33] Many firms that expanded through diversification later trimmed back operations to activities on which they had built their reputation. A representative example is aluminum giant Alcoa, which exited the plastic-wrap and some automotive businesses to respecialize on aluminum mining and production. Part of the reason given was that Alcoa could compete better if it eliminated the distraction of plastic wraps.[34]

**11. *Brand leadership.*** As obvious as it may appear, succeeding through developing the reputation of a brand name can be considered a business strategy. The opposite strategy is to build components for others, build products that others market under their names, or be a commodity like cinder blocks. Jeffrey Bezos of Amazon has implemented a relentless brand leadership strategy to the point that his company has become almost synonymous with etailing. The ultimate goal of the brand leadership strategy is to make Amazon the best-known destination for purchasing anything that might be for sale on the Internet.

According to *BusinessWeek*, the world's ten leading brands in order of strength of brand are (1) Coca-Cola, (2) Microsoft, (3) IBM, (4) GE, (5) Nokia, (6) Toyota, (7) Intel, (8) McDonald's, (9) Disney, and (10) Mercedes-Benz.[35] By building the reputation of their brands, senior management (assisted by countless thousands of workers) has helped these companies succeed financially.

**12.** *Create demand by solving problems.* The simple idea that the best way to sell is to offer to solve a problem has become a business strategy. Cardinal Health, Inc. leadership uses its unique access to drug manufacturers to identify problems in the pharmaceutical business. It then creates new products and services to solve those problems and save customers money. For example, Cardinal workers noticed a problem of delivering medicine to patients in hospitals for such reasons as messy, handwritten prescriptions and a nurse shortage. Cardinal CEO Robert Walter detected an opportunity to deliver drugs better. His solution was to purchase a company that produced an ATM-like machine for dispensing drugs after a prescription is inserted. About 90 percent of U.S. hospitals use these machines.[36] (Note the combination of two strategies here: growth through acquisition and creating demand by solving problems.)

**13.** *Competitive advantage through hiring talented people.* A powerful strategy for gaining competitive advantage is to build the organization with talented, well-motivated people at every level. The most urgent need in building great companies is to find and keep great people. Microsoft and Amazon.com, along with elite business consulting firms, are examples of firms that explicitly use the hiring-talented-people strategy. Talented people may need some leadership direction, but they will think of new products and services and develop effective work processes.

All of these impressive strategies have limited impact unless they are implemented properly, meaning that effective management must support strategic leadership. In Chapter 4, we noted that visions must be followed up with execution. Based on case research in many companies, Michael Beer and Russell A. Eisenstat found that strategies are sometimes not implemented correctly because top management is not aware of problems that threaten the business. In many organizations, it is difficult for leadership to hear the unfiltered truth from managers down below. Beer and Eisenstat developed a method whereby a task force of the most effective managers collects data about strategic and organizational problems. Task force members present their findings to senior managers in the format of an honest conversation. As a result of these discussions, senior managers can make the right moves to adjust strategy.[37] For example, the task force might discover that the true reason a strategy is not working well is that the top management team is not granting enough decision-making authority to the business units. If the business unit leaders were empowered more fully, they could perform better.

The Leader in Action profile illustrates how a company can thrive by modifying its marketing strategy, as well as other aspects of strategy.

**Knowledge Bank** contains information about the Internet and business strategy.

**www.cengage.com/ management/dubrin**

## KNOWLEDGE MANAGEMENT AND THE LEARNING ORGANIZATION

Another thrust of leaders is to help their organizations better adapt to the environment by assisting workers and the organization to become better learners. To accomplish this, the leader manages knowledge and cultivates a learning

Leader in Action

## Julia Stewart, Queen of IHOP and Applebee's International

Glendale, California–based IHOP announced in June 2007 it would acquire Applebee's International for $2.1 billion, with the plan being approved, and the transaction going through later that year. Zane Tankel, who operates twenty-six Applebee's in New York's five boroughs, said that when Julia Stewart was running Applebee's, "She took us straight from print to broadcast, and it made a world of difference," referring to Stewart's four-year stint in the late 1990s at the Overland, Kansas–based chain. "She was always a brilliant marketer."

Such high praise typically attaches itself to Stewart's efforts, most recently in the case of the once-beleaguered IHOP itself. The 52-year-old executive arrived at IHOP in December 2001, a year after she departed Applebee's. Since then, she has led a dramatic turnaround that has changed the franchise model, updated the menu, and boosted morale among franchisees.

"Without question, she has reinvigorated franchisees," declares Natchez, Mississippi–based franchisee David Paradise, who operates twelve IHOPs and eleven Applebee's. "She is very strong on visualizing where we need to go and then aggressively getting us there."

Stewart seems keenly aware of her strengths. Asked who might play her if a movie were made of her life, Stewart answers Renee Russo. "She's a strong, smart, sassy leading lady and she's genuine," she says of the 53-year-old actress and former model. The adjectives fit Stewart like a glove, acknowledge friends and former associates, and they help explain her string of successful ventures in the restaurant business after graduating from San Diego State University in 1977.

Stewart came to national attention in the mid-1980s after spiking the sales needle at then-moribund Stuart Anderson's Black Angus, a chain of mid-priced steakhouses. Her modus operandi: a return-to-basics strategy that featured an endearing spokesman and focused on beef. "We had gotten away from what made us famous," Stewart recalls, adding she got plenty of leeway from Charlie Lynch,

CEO of parent company, Saga. "He told me, 'Go do what needs to be done.'"

When Stewart was at Taco Bell, Bill Floyd, the chain's vice president for operations and Stewart's immediate supervisor, spotted her leadership skills. "We used to say than an important determinant of success [in the Management Recruits program] was whether the crew adopted these people and saw them as someone who connected with them and empathized," he explains. "Julia fit that to a T."

Karen Eadon, senior vice president of marketing at Applebee's during Stewart's tenure there as president, remembers her boss as a "strong leader" who often invited opinions before making strategic decisions. "Julia was very open to divergent points of view and to vigorous discussion that would allow her to see all sides," says Eadon.

Eadon adds that Stewart wanted to improve the entire Applebee's system and focused her efforts on improving food quality and marketing, which went from tactical to strategic. A new tagline—"Eating Good in the Neighborhood"—neatly captured the brand's essence.

After becoming CEO of IHOP, Stewart's boldest move was changing the franchise model, which allowed franchisees to use their own equity to open an IHOP restaurant. "The franchisees today develop their own units. They have a greater investment in it. The have greater opportunity to make more money," offers Bob Leonard, a veteran franchisee and chairman of IHOP's advisory board.

Tankel, the major franchisee from New York, comments: "I'm not sure I would be happy with the merger if it weren't Julia Stewart in charge. I am really happy about Julia."

### Questions

1. Has Julia Stewart really developed corporate strategy or has she simply modified sales and marketing plans?

## Action (continued)

**2.** What hints does this story give that being an excellent leader makes it easier to have your strategy implemented?

**3.** How would being "strong, smart, and sassy" help a leader be a good strategic thinker?

**4.** What major grammatical error do you find in Applebee's tag line? Would the error have any impact on your propensity to dine at Applebee's?

*Source:* Excerpted and adapted slightly from David Farkas, "Full Circle: IHOP CEO Julia Stewart's Rapid Rise Through the Ranks Has Prepared Her to Take On Applebee's," *Chain Leader* (www.chainleader.com), November 1, 2007. Reprinted by permission.

organization. **Knowledge management (KM)** is a concerted effort to improve how knowledge is created, delivered, and applied.[38] When knowledge is managed effectively, information is shared as needed, whether it be printed, stored electronically, or rests in the brains of workers. Managing knowledge helps create a **learning organization**—one that is skilled at creating, acquiring, and transferring knowledge and at modifying behavior to reflect new knowledge and insights.[39] To develop a sensitivity toward some of the key ideas in knowledge management and the learning organization, take Leadership Self-Assessment Quiz 13-2.

### Knowledge Management

Knowledge management (KM) deals with a cultural focus on knowledge sharing. Managing knowledge is an important leadership role because so few organizations make systematic use of the collective wisdom of employees. As illustrated in Figure 13-2, most knowledge in the organization resides in the brains of employees or in documents not readily accessible to others. Here we look at the general format of KM programs, and then potential pitfalls.

Knowledge management has three components, as revealed by the research and observations of Thomas H. Davenport, Laurence Prusak, and Bruce Strong.[40] *Knowledge creation* is used to spur innovation. Programs for creating knowledge solicit ideas, insights, and innovations from many sources, including rank and file workers, customers, and business partners, instead of relying exclusively on the research and development staff. For example, more than 40 percent of Procter & Gamble products have a component from external sources, up from 10 percent six years ago.

*Knowledge dissemination* through information technology is the most frequent activity within knowledge management. Methods of sharing knowledge include company intranets, web portals, and databases. Information is consolidated in one place so it is more accessible to potential users. An example is to make an intranet a one-stop information shop designed to support critical jobs and work processes. For example, Intel places on one web site all of the information workers need to make a capital purchase. *Knowledge application* is the process of getting workers better at what they do. Many organizations have discovered that the most effective way of encouraging workers to apply knowledge is through basic practices such as mentoring, on-the-job training, and workshops.

**Leadership Self-Assessment Quiz 13-2**

### Do You Work for a Learning Organization?

***Instructions:*** Indicate for each of the following statements whether it is mostly true or mostly false in relation to your current, or most recent, place of work. Indicate a question mark when the statement is either not applicable or you are not in a position to judge.

| | Mostly True | Mostly False | ? |
|---|:---:|:---:|:---:|
| 1. Company employees often visit other locations or departments to share new information or skills they have learned. | ☐ | ☐ | ☐ |
| 2. Our company frequently repeats mistakes. | ☐ | ☐ | ☐ |
| 3. We get most of our market share by competing on price. | ☐ | ☐ | ☐ |
| 4. Loads of people in our organization are aware of and believe in our vision. | ☐ | ☐ | ☐ |
| 5. Top management assumes the majority of employees are experts at what they do. | ☐ | ☐ | ☐ |
| 6. Almost all of our learning takes place individually rather than in groups or teams. | ☐ | ☐ | ☐ |
| 7. In our company, after you have mastered your job, you do not have to bother with additional learning such as training programs or self-study. | ☐ | ☐ | ☐ |
| 8. Our firm shies away from inviting outsiders into our company to discuss our business because few outsiders could understand our uniqueness. | ☐ | ☐ | ☐ |
| 9. If it were not for a few key individuals in our company, we would be in big trouble. | ☐ | ☐ | ☐ |
| 10. Our new product launches go smoothly and quickly. | ☐ | ☐ | ☐ |
| 11. Our company creates a lot of opportunities for employees to get together and share information, such as conferences and meetings. | ☐ | ☐ | ☐ |
| 12. We are effective at pricing the service we provide to customers. | ☐ | ☐ | ☐ |
| 13. Very few of our employees have any idea about company sales and profits. | ☐ | ☐ | ☐ |
| 14. I often hear employees asking questions about why the company has taken certain major actions. | ☐ | ☐ | ☐ |

## Quiz 13-2 (continued)

|  | Mostly True | Mostly False | ? |
|---|:---:|:---:|:---:|
| 15. The company maintains a current database about the knowledge and skills of almost all of our employees. | ☐ | ☐ | ☐ |
| 16. Having specialized knowledge brings you some status in our company. | ☐ | ☐ | ☐ |
| 17. It would be stretching the truth to say that many of our employees are passionate about what our organization is attempting to accomplish. | ☐ | ☐ | ☐ |
| 18. Our performance evaluation system makes a big contribution to helping employees learn and improve. | ☐ | ☐ | ☐ |
| 19. Following established rules and procedures is important in our company, so creativity and imagination are not encouraged. | ☐ | ☐ | ☐ |
| 20. Most of our employees believe that if you do your own job well, you do not have to worry about what goes on in the rest of the organization. | ☐ | ☐ | ☐ |
| 21. We get loads of useful new ideas from our customers. | ☐ | ☐ | ☐ |
| 22. I have frequently heard our managers talk about how what goes on in the outside world has an impact on our company. | ☐ | ☐ | ☐ |
| 23. We treat customer suggestions with a good deal of skepticism. | ☐ | ☐ | ☐ |
| 24. During breaks, you sometimes hear employees discussing the meaning and implication of the work they are doing. | ☐ | ☐ | ☐ |
| 25. Employees at every level tend to rely on facts when making important decisions. | ☐ | ☐ | ☐ |
| 26. If a process or procedure works well in our company, we are hesitant to experiment with other approaches to a problem. | ☐ | ☐ | ☐ |
| 27. Our company treats mistakes as a valuable learning experience about what not to do in the future. | ☐ | ☐ | ☐ |
| 28. Our company rarely copies ideas from the successful practices of other companies. | ☐ | ☐ | ☐ |

## Quiz 13-2 (continued)

|  | Mostly True | Mostly False | ? |
|---|:---:|:---:|:---:|
| **29.** Each time we face a significant problem, our company seems to start all over to find a solution. | ☐ | ☐ | ☐ |
| **30.** It is a waste of time to be reading about a learning organization, when my real interest is in learning how to prevent problems. | ☐ | ☐ | ☐ |

***Scoring and Interpretation:*** (1) Record the number of "mostly true" answers you gave to the following questions: 1, 4, 5, 10, 11, 12, 14, 15, 16, 18, 21, 22, 24, 25, 27. (2) Record the number of "mostly false" answers you gave to the following questions: 2, 3, 6, 7, 8, 9, 13, 17, 19, 20, 23, 26, 28, 29, 30. (3) Add the numbers for **1** and **2**. (4) Add half of your (?) responses to **1** and half to **2**.

- **25 or higher:** You are most likely a member of a learning organization. This tendency is so pronounced that it should contribute heavily to your company's success.

- **3–24:** Your company has an average tendency toward being a learning organization, suggesting an average degree of success in profiting from mistakes and changing in response to a changing environment.

*Source:* From A. J. DuBrin, *Looking Around Corners: The Art of Problem Prevention* (Worcester, Mass.: Chandler House Press, 1999), pp. 181–183. Reprinted by permission of Chandler House Press.

***General Format of KM Programs***   Knowledge management systems sometimes take the form of a computer-based system for collecting and organizing potentially useful information. Yet many effective systems rely on person-to-person exchange of information. A study of 800 managers by eePulse, Inc. found that 78 percent share information through personal and informal channels, compared to 19 percent that have technology-driven systems. (Three percent pay no formal attention to knowledge sharing.) Of the companies using technology, the most frequent methods were basic, such as email, telephone, and web-based communication. In one company, employees were not making optimum use of reports placed online by the research department, so the company made the site interactive. Employees can now ask precise questions of the scientists, and knowledge sharing is more successful.[41]

We have emphasized how important it is for leaders to use anecdotes to communicate meaning. Narratives also play a major role in knowledge sharing, as Thomas Davenport illustrates in this anecdote:

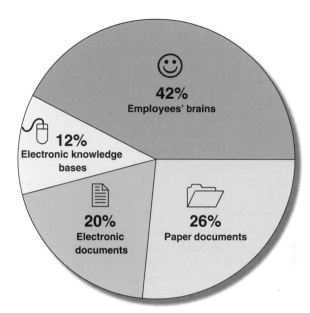

**FIGURE 13-2** Where Corporate Knowledge Lives.
A study of more than 700 U.S. companies shows that only a small portion of corporate knowledge is in a form that can be shared readily. The majority of knowledge resides in the brains of employees and in documents not readily shared.

*Source:* "Knowledge Management: User Survey 97," Copyright © 1997 by *American Management Association (J).* Adaptcd and published in Michael Hickins, "Xerox Shares Its Knowledge," Management Review, September 1999, p. 42. Reproduced with permission of *American Management Association (J)* in the format Textbook via Copyright Clearance Center.

As part of its knowledge management initiative, British Petroleum rolled out some videoconferencing technology for rapidly sharing ideas. Soon after, one of their gas drills broke down in the North Slope of Alaska. BP's leading expert in gas turbines was working in the North Sea; it would have taken him twenty hours to fly to Alaska. Instead of putting him on a plane, BP patched him into the North Slope via videoconferencing, and he worked with on-site technicians to pinpoint the problem and get the drill back on-stream. They finished the job in just thirty minutes. That story quickly circulated throughout BP. In time, it found its way into other organizations. Because it gave real-world evidence of a dramatic improvement, the story became part of knowledge-sharing lore.[42] [Note that the human touch was helpful in selling a technology-based method of knowledge sharing.]

An advance in knowledge management is to deliver information just in time, or at the point at which it is most needed. For example, Partners HealthCare System, Inc., embeds knowledge into the technology that physicians use so that retrieving the knowledge is no longer a separate activity. When a staff physician orders medicine or a lab test, the order-entry system automatically checks his or her decision against a huge clinical database as well as the patient's own medical record. Just-in-time delivery of knowledge is also useful in business. Customer service representatives at Hewlett-Packard and Dell work with computer systems that give them immediate access to information to help them respond to customer problems.[43] In this way, the representative does not have to have reams of information in his or her head.

Whatever advanced technology is used to implement knowledge management, it works best in an organizational culture that values knowledge and encourages its dissemination. A study conducted in 121 new-product development teams and 41 subsidiaries of a high-technology company quantified another factor that influences knowledge sharing. Professional workers are less likely to hoard knowledge when there is less competition across the organizational units.[44]

The organizational subculture shapes our assumptions about what constitutes knowledge, and which knowledge is worth managing.[45] Professional workers in the finance division of Gap Inc. might think that watching MTV on company time or surfing the Net is a waste of company time. In the merchandising division, however, watching MTV and surfing the Net might be perceived as a valuable way of understanding clothing trends.

***Potential Pitfalls of KM Programs*** A major challenge a leader faces in advancing knowledge sharing is the human tendency to want to keep our best ideas secret, so we can receive full credit for them. (The earlier comment about hoarding knowledge also applies here.) Another human factor to keep in mind is that people prefer to share information face-to-face rather than to enter their ideas into a database. Much of what is useful information cannot be neatly categorized. Moreover, the mere act of entering information into a database frequently robs it of the intuitive spark generated by face-to-face communication. Despite the marvels of technology, it cannot combine two bits of data stored in separate memory banks into a new insight, as can face-to-face communication.[46]

Think through your attitudes toward sharing knowledge by taking Leadership Self-Assessment Quiz 13-3.

Knowledge management programs often get off to a good start, and then fizzle. One reason for the later failure is that the first knowledge management team squeezes out all the useful knowledge. Another reason is that knowledge workers become too dependent on the database developed in knowledge management for solving problems. Alton Y. K. Chua did a case analysis of several knowledge management projects that started out well but then folded. The same researcher also investigated how the problems could be prevented. Here we look briefly at one of the projects.

One of the knowledge management projects took place at a consumer bank in Hong Kong. The program markedly improved customer service. The KM system was a web-based database whose contents were developed and maintained by 800 call-center workers. Included in the database were such items as additional information about important customers, useful telephone numbers, and

Leadership Self-Assessment Quiz 13-3

### My Attitudes Toward Sharing Knowledge

*Instructions:* Indicate how much you agree with the following statements: disagree strongly (DA); disagree (D); neutral (N); agree (A); and agree strongly (AS).

| | DA | D | N | A | AS |
|---|---|---|---|---|---|
| 1. I have often helped other students with their homework. | 1 | 2 | 3 | 4 | 5 |
| 2. In brainstorming sessions, I usually hold back giving my best ideas because I do not want them stolen. | 5 | 4 | 3 | 2 | 1 |
| 3. I enjoy helping another person with a work or school problem. | 1 | 2 | 3 | 4 | 5 |
| 4. I would be willing to submit some of my best ideas to a company database, such as an intranet. | 1 | 2 | 3 | 4 | 5 |
| 5. I am concerned about submitting my most creative ideas on a term paper because these ideas could be stolen. | 5 | 4 | 3 | 2 | 1 |
| 6. I enjoy working as part of a team and sharing ideas. | 5 | 4 | 3 | 2 | 1 |
| 7. I get a little suspicious when a coworker or fellow student attempts to pick my brain. | 1 | 2 | 3 | 4 | 5 |
| 8. It upsets me if I do not receive full credit for my ideas. | 5 | 4 | 3 | 2 | 1 |
| 9. If I had a great idea for a screenplay or novel, I would not tell anyone about it before I was finished with the idea. | 5 | 4 | 3 | 2 | 1 |
| 10. I have often let other people know about a good method I developed to improve work efficiency. | 1 | 2 | 3 | 4 | 5 |

Total score: _____

*Scoring and Interpretation:* Tally your score by adding the numbers you circled or checked.

- **40 or higher:** You are generous with respect to knowledge sharing and would probably fit well in an organization that practices knowledge management.
- **20–39:** You have average attitudes toward sharing knowledge, with a mixture of enthusiasm and skepticism about knowledge sharing.
- **1–19:** You are quite cautious and guarded about sharing ideas. Unless you become more willing to share your ideas, you would not fit well in an organization that emphasized knowledge management.

Note: *You are authorized to share this quiz with as many people as you would like.*

advice on procedures for dealing with a problem such as a stolen credit card. Six months after implementation, the call-center agents gave it a very high rating. Turnaround times for phone calls were reduced to twelve minutes from twenty-three minutes.

Based on the success of the pilot program, management decided to replicate the same type of KM system for five other bank departments: marketing, business intelligence, human resources, legal, and procurements. The system proved to be too complicated to develop from a technical standpoint. Also, the culture of sharing that took place in the call center proved difficult to replicate. The lesson learned was that management should resist using a cookie-cutter approach to other parts of the organization after the initial success of a pilot project. The leaders in the project did not stop to figure out why the first project was a success.[47]

## The Learning Organization

According to Peter Senge, a learning organization can be viewed as a group of people working together to enhance their capacities to create the results they value.[48] Organizational leadership, however, must usually take the initiative to create the conditions whereby such enhancement of capacities, or learning, takes place. Toward this end, several firms have created a position labeled chief knowledge officer (CKO), or its equivalent. The major justification for creating such a position is that in many companies, human skills, intuition, and wisdom are replacing capital as the most precious resource. Chief knowledge officers seek to disperse those assets throughout the firm and convert them into innovations. They are in charge of systematically collecting information and connecting people with others who might have valuable information.[49]

In order to manage organizational learning, the most effective strategic leaders function in both the transformational and transactional modes. Acting as a transformational leader, the manager might inspire workers with a vision of knowledge sharing and learning from mistakes. Acting as a transactional leader, he or she might reward workers for sharing knowledge.[50]

Here we identify major leadership initiatives that create and enhance a learning organization. Understanding them will help you grasp the concept of what a leader might do to enhance organizational learning.[51]

To begin, a top-level leader should *create a strategic intent to learn*. Organizational learning then becomes a vehicle for gaining competitive advantage. *Creating a shared vision* enhances learning as organization members develop a common purpose and commitment to having the organization keep learning. If workers at all levels believe that the company is headed toward greatness, they will be motivated to learn to help deliver greatness.

In a learning organization, *employees are empowered to make decisions and seek continuous improvement*. The idea is to develop a community of learning in which every worker believes that he or she can contribute to a smarter, more effective organization.

*Systems thinking* is almost synonymous with organizational learning. The leader helps organization members regard the organization as a system in which everybody's work affects the activities of everybody else. Systems thinking also means keeping the big picture foremost in everybody's mind and being keenly aware of the external environment. In addition to the big picture of systems thinking, the leader must encourage the little picture of *personal mastery of the job*. As team members gain personal mastery of their jobs, they contribute to *team learning,* an essential part of a learning organization. Team learning centers on collective problem solving in which members freely share information and opinions to facilitate problem solving.

*Action learning,* or learning while working on real problems, is a fundamental part of a learning organization. Participants in action learning are asked to work in teams to attack a significant organizational problem, such as decreasing the cycle time on a project. In the process of resolving an actual work problem, the participants acquire and use new skills, tools, or concepts. As the project progresses, new skills are applied while working with the problem. For example, if the team learned how to eliminate duplication of effort in one aspect of the work process, it would look to eliminate duplication at other points in the cycle.

*Learning from failure* contributes immensely to a learning organization. A company that diversified into an area unsuccessfully might analyze why it failed and then not repeat the same mistake. *Encouraging continuous experimentation* is another important practice for crafting a learning strategy. The leader encourages workers to learn from competitors, customers, suppliers, and other units within the organization.

For organizational learning to proceed smoothly, workers throughout the organization must have the *political skills to make connections with and influence others*. For example, if a production technician discovers an effective method of reducing water consumption, he or she must have the skill to sell an influential person on the merits of this idea.

A final perspective on creating the learning organization is that the leader must encourage organizational members to think creatively—to imagine possibilities that do not already exist. Instead of merely adapting to the environment, the organization engages in the type of breakthrough thinking described in our previous discussions of creativity and strategic leadership. Organizations cannot rely on CKOs alone to manage knowledge. The entire knowledge process must be embedded in the position of line manager.[52]

## Reader's Roadmap

So far we have studied the nature of leadership; the attributes, behaviors, and styles of leaders; the ethics and social responsibility of leaders; and how leaders exert power and use politics and influence. We then studied techniques for developing teamwork as well as motivation and coaching skills. After having studied creativity and innovation as part of leadership, we focused on communication skills as they relate to leadership. We then shifted to strategic leadership. Next, we examine another broad challenge facing leaders: dealing with cultural diversity within the organization and across borders.

## SUMMARY

Strategic leadership deals with the major purposes of an organization or organizational unit and provides the direction and inspiration necessary to create, provide direction to, or sustain an organization. Strategic leadership has five important components: (1) the high-level cognitive activity by the leader, (2) gathering multiple inputs to formulate strategy, (3) anticipating and creating a future, (4) revolutionary and contrarian thinking, and (5) creating a vision.

Creating a vision is an integral part of strategic leadership. The final vision statement is relatively short. After formulating a vision, the leader should be involved in its communication and implementation. A carefully considered and articulated vision helps us know who we are and who we are not. The vision also points to what we do successfully and what we do not, which activities we should take on and which to avoid. In companies that believe in visions and strategic goals, all activities throughout the company are supposed to support the vision and goals.

Strategic planning quite often takes the form of a SWOT analysis, taking into account internal strengths and weaknesses and external opportunities and threats in a given situation. A SWOT analysis examines the interaction between the organization and the environment.

Strategic leaders use many different types of business strategies, including the following: (1) differentiation, (2) cost leadership, (3) focus or niche, (4) high quality, (5) imitation, (6) strategic alliances, (7) growth through acquisition, (8) high speed and first-mover strategy, (9) product and global diversification, (10) sticking to core competencies, (11) brand leadership, (12) creating demand by solving problems, and (13) gaining competitive advantage through hiring talented people.

Another strategic thrust of leaders is to help their organizations adapt to the environment by assisting workers and the organization to become better learners. To accomplish this feat, the leader manages knowledge and cultivates a learning organziation. Knowledge management focuses on the systematic sharing of information, including being able to deliver information just in time. Knowledge management consists of knowledge creation, dissemination, and application. A major challenge to knowledge management is the human tendency to want to keep our best ideas secret, so we can receive full credit for them. Knowledge management programs often get off to a good start, and then fizzle. One of the problems is that management might attempt to replicate the same approach to KM used in one part of the organization without studying the new situation.

Major leadership initiatives for creating a learning organization include creating a strategic intent to learn, creating a shared vision, and empowering employees to make decisions and seek continuous improvements. Also important is encouraging systems thinking, encouraging personal mastery of the job, and team learning. Action learning, or learning while working on real problems, learning from failures, and encouraging continuous experimentation are also part of the learning organization. Workers must have the political skills to make connections and influence others. Encouraging creative thinking is also part of the learning organization.

## KEY TERMS

Strategy

Strategic leadership

Strategic planning

SWOT analysis

Knowledge management (KM)

Learning organization

## ✔ GUIDELINES FOR ACTION AND SKILL DEVELOPMENT

To make sure that all workers understand the company's vision of where it wants to go, the vision statement should have certain key characteristics:[53]

1. **Brief.** The statement should be short enough so employees can recall it with ease. In its early days, Starbucks maintained the vision "2,000 stores by 2000."
2. **Verifiable.** A verifiable vision is one that ten people could agree that an organization has achieved. By the year 2008, Starbucks had attained approximately 15,000 cafés.
3. **Focused.** Vision statements often contain too many ideas. It is better to focus on a major goal such as the vision of Ford Motor Company: "Employee involvement is our way of life." (Notice that this vision is about human resource management, not about a product or brand.)
4. **Understandable.** A major purpose of the vision statement is that employees will know where the organization wants to go and how to help it get there. Being understandable is therefore a key quality of the vision statement. Terms such as "world class" and "leading edge" might be subject to wide interpretation. The following component of the H&R Block vision statement would be understandable by most company employees: "Quality products, excellent service, reasonable fees."
5. **Inspirational.** To inspire, a vision statement should make employees feel good about working for the organization and should focus them on measurable business goals.

### Discussion Questions and Activities

1. How might a business strategy deal with a topic other than products or services?
2. In what way can a business strategy motivate and inspire employees?
3. How could you adapt a business strategy to guide you in your own career as a leader?
4. Many top-level managers say that they want lower-ranking managers to think strategically. How can a middle manager or a first-level manager think strategically?
5. Why might finding a niche for the organization be the most important activity of a strategic leader?
6. Working alone or with several team members, provide a recent example of revolutionary thinking by a company.
7. The average age of Cadillac owners, across the various models, was about 65 until the Escalade (a luxury SUV) was introduced to the market. It had an immediate appeal to affluent rappers, professional athletes, and a variety of other young, wealthy entertainers. What is the business strategy lesson here?
8. In what way might doing a good job of knowledge management give a company a competitive advantage?
9. Why is it that even IT professionals believe that the interpersonal aspects of knowledge sharing are more important than the software systems for collecting and sharing ideas?
10. Why do you think it has been so difficult for researchers to prove that knowledge management pays dividends to an organization?

## Leadership Case Problem A

### Samsung Sings a Different Tune

Samsung Electronics Co. Ltd. of South Korea manufactures and sells high-tech consumer products like cell phones that are voice activated and play MP3 tunes. Like many other Samsung devices, the phone combines cutting-edge technology with award-winning design at premium prices. Yet nine years ago, the

## Problem A (continued)

company was known as a mass marketer of cheap TVs and VCRs. On the industrial products side, Samsung had become the world's largest maker of memory chips. Samsung Electronics employs approximately 75,000 people in eighty-nine offices in forty-seven countries.

For much of the past three decades, Samsung and South Korea's other massive conglomerates, known as *chaebols*, were looked down on abroad as low-end makers of refrigerators, VCRs, and sedans. Samsung ran the risk of becoming a faceless supplier of computer monitors and semiconductors to more powerful multinationals. Even that niche was under threat from low-cost producers springing up in China. So leadership at the Samsung Electronics unit agreed on a key strategic move.

### Samsung's Changing Image

Since 1997 Samsung has rubbed shoulders with the market leaders in high-end cell phones, DVD players, elegant flat plasma TVs, and a wide range of other consumer products. These electronic devices are sometimes less expensive than those of Japanese and Finnish competitors but not inferior in quality. Samsung has attained global recognition and has a $500 million annual advertising budget to promote its brand. The company successfully shifted from semiconductors to branded products like mobile phones.

All this favorable attention to Samsung products prompted Eric Kim, 49, former executive vice president for marketing, to assert that he hoped to surpass Sony Corporation in brand recognition. In 2004, Kim joined Intel Corporation as general manager of the Digital Home Group. At Samsung Electronics, many executives express a near obsession with outperforming Sony. According to the consultancy Interbrand, Samsung has the second most recognizable consumer electronics brand in the world. A researcher for the Nomura Securities Co. Ltd. says Samsung is no longer making poor equivalents of Sony products. Instead it is making products that people want.

During a period when most of the world's high-technology companies were shutting plants and trimming research and development to cope with the global economic slump, Samsung was extending its reach. Bolstered by the resurgent Korean economy, Samsung Electronics' worldwide revenues are running more than $80 billion per year. The company is growing fast and is the best performer in the family-controlled conglomerate that spawned it, the Samsung Group.

In addition to developing its own brand, Samsung remains an important supplier of components for other companies. During a product showcase meeting in New York City, Jong-Yong Yun, vice chairman and CEO of Samsung Electronics Co. Ltd., revealed new plans to achieve the company's vision of becoming the leader in the digital convergence revolution. (Digital convergence is about digital devices linking with each other, such as retrieving a desktop computer file with your cell phone while sitting on a park bench.) Key changes to help achieve this convergence include home networking and wireless network products.

Yun also noted that Samsung would continue to invest in people and technology as needed to transform the company. "Business entities cannot survive without innovation as they face numerous changes and uncertainty. Samsung will continue to create solutions that vitalize and enrich your lifestyle," said Yun. "Technology spawns the future; people are key to technology" (*Clari News*, p. 2).

### Kim Takes Action

Much of this success is attributable to Eric Kim, and his impact was still felt after he left the firm. After being recruited to Samsung as executive vice president for marketing, the former Lotus Development Corporation executive overhauled Samsung Electronics' marketing arm. He consolidated fifty-five advertising agencies into one to create a global brand image for the company.

## Problem A (continued)

Kim started developing relationships with American's top retail chains. He explains that his company has exploited an opening created by new digital technology. Consumers are now more open to consider different brands. "That transition, and our strategy to move upmarket very aggressively, are the main reasons why our brand improved rapidly," Kim says (*BusinessWeek Online*, p. 2).

The consumer electronics chain Best Buy has become a major distributor of Samsung products. CompUSA is another strong partner. Samsung dropped Wal-Mart, perceiving the mammoth retailer as incompatible with its upscale image. Kim noted that during the 1980s and 1990s, Japanese and Europeans companies dominated the electronics industry. Yet while still with the company, he believed that Samsung could dominate any market, including the U.S. market.

### Questions

1. Identify at least three business (or marketing) strategies Samsung uses now or has used in the past.

2. What suggestions can you offer Samsung leaders so they can become even more successful in building the Samsung brand?
3. What is your opinion of Eric Kim as a strategic leader? Explain your answer.
4. How realistic is Samsung's vision of becoming the leader in the digital convergence revolution?

*Sources:* Frank Gibney, Jr., "Samsung Moves Upmarket," *Time*, March 25, 2002, pp. 49–51; Jay Solomon, "Seoul Survivors: Back from the Brink, Korea Inc. Wants a Little Respect," *Wall Street Journal*, June 13, 2002, pp. A1, A6; Moon Ihlwan, "Samsung: No Longer Unsung," *BusinessWeek Online*, August 6, 2001; "SAMSUNG Announces Major Semicon Achievements," www.samsung.com/PressCenter/PressRelease, 2004; "Samsung Rewords Strategy to Widen Focus," www.channeltimes .com, accessed December 30, 2004; "Samsung Lifts the Veil on Global Performance, Surge in Brand Value, and Corporate Strategy," *Clari News*, http://quickstart.clari.net/qs_se/webnews/ wed/cb/Bny-samsung-electronics.RTG_DSG.h, September 15, 2003; *Intel Executive Biography*, "Eric B. Kim, Senior Vice President, General Manager, Digital Home Group," accessed February 5, 2008; "Samsung Electronics Co., Ltd. Company Profile," *Yahoo! Finance*, accessed February 5, 2008.

## Leadership Case Problem B

### IHOP Wants to Rejuvenate Applebee's

(You have already studied Julia Stewart in the Leader in Action profile in this chapter. You might use that information to help you analyze this case.)

Now that shareholders have approved IHOP Corp.'s approximately $2.1 billion purchase of Applebee's International, Inc., the pancake chain has to overcome skepticism as to whether it can pull off a turnaround of the nation's largest sit-down restaurant chain.

The approval vote capped a contentious process that started when Applebee's first considered a sale in August of 2006, amid a downturn in the midprice-restaurant industry. Applebee's started with

at least twenty-six suitors; however, the weakening credit markets, coupled with the company's soft sales, drove away some bidders and promoted those remaining to lower their offering price.

IHOP Chief Executive Julia Stewart has already started integrating the two chains. She said she plans to do many of the same things at Applebee's that she did to bring around IHOP after she joined the pancake chain in 2001. Stewart plans to sell hundreds of company-owned Applebee's locations to franchisees, and wants to better differentiate Applebee's from the glut of competitors that have copied the chain.

## Problem B (continued)

Although Stewart is well respected by Wall Street for improving sales and profitability at IHOP, reviving Applebee's was thought to be a more difficult task given the size of the chain and the depth of its problems. CIBC World Markets analyst John Glass said that Applebee's profit margins at the restaurant level during the third quarter of 2007 were the worst in the company's history, calling it a "fundamental meltdown."

It was thought that Applebee's franchisees would be reluctant to buy locations from IHOP at a time when consumers are visiting fast-food restaurants instead of sit-down chains and the bar-and-grill sector is suffering from a glut of locations. Some Applebee's franchisees have already begun looking at more promising restaurant concepts as Applebee's has struggled.

"This is going to be a significant challenge," said Ed Nicklin, a portfolio manager at Westport Asset Management, which owns about 1.7 million shares of Applebee's, about a 2 percent stake. Nicklin said he was optimistic that IHOP management can improve Applebee's operations, but said it must first improve Applebee's food offerings and the look of the restaurants in order for the turnaround to succeed.

### Questions

1. What strategic suggestions might you offer Stewart and the IHOP executive team to improve the performance of its Applebee's division?
2. To what extent are Nicklin's suggestions *strategic*?
3. How about visiting an Applebee's restaurant to make some observations about what the chain can do to become more competitive and profitable? As an alternative, interview a few people in your network who have dined or worked at an Applebee's recently.

*Source:* Janet Adamy, "IHOP's Tall Order: Reviving Applebee's," *Wall Street Journal*, October 31, 2007, p. A17.

 ## Leadership Skill-Building Exercise 13-2

### My Leadership Portfolio

A major part of being a strategic leader is to think strategically. Entrapped by the necessities of the small tasks facing us daily, it is easy to "think little" instead of "think big" as required to be a strategic thinker. A "little thinker" might attend a leadership seminar and spend five minutes demanding a $5.00 rebate because he or she was served ill-prepared food at lunch. A "big thinker" might reflect on the same poorly prepared meal as a lesson in the importance of employees' taking care of small details to ensure customer satisfaction. For this installment in your leadership portfolio, enter into your journal how you capitalized—or did not capitalize—on the opportunity to think strategically during the last week, or so. An example follows:

My friend and I visited a large shopping mall on Saturday morning. We noticed a large number of vehicles, both autos and small trucks, circling around within a block of the mall entrance. The drivers were obviously looking for a parking spot close enough so they could avoid walking the block, or so, necessary if they parked farther from the entrance.

My friend is a fitness nut, so he said the parking space chasers could do themselves a favor by parking a long distance from the mall entrance. In this way they could get a little physical exercise. A strategic flash went through my mind. If I, or perhaps the First Lady, could launch a national campaign for parking a distance away from mall entrances, we could make some headway on two of the major problems facing our society. First, physical inactivity is becoming almost as big a killer as smoking. Second, think of all the gas people are wasting. On a national scale, think of all the gas we would save if people would stop circling around looking for spaces. Besides, those little extra blocks of gas consumption add up. My strategic brainstorm could lead to more fitness and less energy consumption in our country.

## Internet Skill-Building Exercise

### Professional Assistance in Implementing Knowledge Management

Visit www.knowledgebase.net to learn about Knowledge Base, a group of engineers, scientists, and entrepreneurs whose aim is to help their clients and partners achieve corporate objectives by unlocking and leveraging the power of intelligent knowledge management. Take the PowerPoint tour (www.knowledgebase.net/tour/tour1.html). After your tour is complete, answer these questions: (1) What are the goals of Knowledge Base? (2) What is your opinion of the value of the service offered by the company?

Apply the chapter concepts! Visit the Web and complete this Internet skill-building exercise to learn more about current leadership topics and trends.

## CHAPTER 14

# International and Culturally Diverse Aspects of Leadership

## LEARNING OBJECTIVES

After studying this chapter and doing the exercises, you should be able to

- Explain the potential ethical and competitive advantage from leading and managing diversity.

- Describe how cultural factors, including values, influence leadership practice.

- Explain the contribution of cultural sensitivity and cultural intelligence to leadership effectiveness.

- Explain how global leadership skills contribute to leadership effectiveness.

- Pinpoint leadership initiatives to enhance the acceptance of cultural diversity.

## CHAPTER OUTLINE

**The Advantages of Managing for Diversity**

**Cultural Factors Influencing Leadership Practice**

Key Dimensions of Differences in Cultural Values
Cultural Values and Leadership Style

**Cultural Sensitivity and Cultural Intelligence**

Cultural Sensitivity
Cultural Intelligence

**Global Leadership Skills**

A Proposed Model for Global Leadership Skills
Success Factors in International Management Positions
Motivating and Inspiring Workers in Other Cultures

**Leadership Initiatives for Achieving Cultural Diversity**

Hold Managers Accountable for Achieving Diversity
Establish Minority Recruitment, Retention, and Mentoring Programs
Conduct Diversity Training
Conduct Cross-Cultural Training
Encourage the Development of Employee Networks
Avoid Group Characteristics When Hiring for Person–Organization Fit
Attain Diversity Among Organizational Leaders

**Summary**

Ron Hyams, a managing partner with the multinational executive coaching firm Praesta in Cape Town, South Africa, says that before honing cross-cultural skills, leaders of global project teams must recognize where and when cultural differences exist. He says, "Until you have awareness, you can't change." Hyams notes the recent example of a female marketing executive who was accustomed to walking around her company's headquarters looking at her BlackBerry mobile communication device—a familiar sight in airports and office buildings across North America and Europe.

But in South Africa, where she was working, the perception was very negative. "People were expecting eye contact and acknowledgement. When they weren't getting it, they felt insulted and not respected," Hyams says. Once the woman realized how her behavior was perceived, she adjusted to fit the culture.[1]

The story about the marketing executive illustrates the importance of achieving better cross-cultural understanding so that managers can work smoothly with cross-border colleagues. What the executive thought was ordinary business behavior (staying tuned in to her BlackBerry while talking to people) was perceived as rude in the context of her current assignment. Working in another country—and thus dealing with cultural groups different from one's own—is becoming a requirement for many senior-level management positions. In addition, corporate success, profit, and growth depend increasingly on the management of a diverse work force both outside and within one's own country.

The various cultural and demographic groups in the workplace want their leaders and coworkers to treat them with respect, dignity, fairness, and sensitivity. At the same time, these groups must work together smoothly to serve a variety of customers and to generate an array of ideas.[2]

Because the focus on diversity is including so many people in an opportunity to participate fully in the organization, the word *inclusion* is often used to replace *diversity*. Not only is the work force becoming more diverse, but business has also become increasingly global. Small and medium-size firms, as well as corporate giants, are increasingly dependent on trade with other countries. Furthermore, most manufactured goods contain components from more than one country, and global outsourcing has become a dominant trend.

The relevance of understanding international and culturally diverse aspects of leadership is underscored by the fact that international experience and its related skills are in strong demand for executive positions. Business firms want to hire executives who can assist them in accomplishing international goals.[3] A case in point is that Muhtar Kent, the long-time head of Coca-Cola's international division, became the company's top executive in 2008. The international division had accounted for 80 percent of the company's profit during his tenure in the international division.[4]

Our approach to cultural diversity both within and across countries emphasizes the leadership perspective. Key topics include the ethical and competitive advantage of managing for diversity, how cultural factors influence leadership practices, and how cultural sensitivity and global leadership skills contribute to leadership effectiveness. This chapter also describes initiatives that enhance the acceptance of cultural diversity. The underlying theme is that effective leadership of diverse people requires a sensitivity to and enjoyment of cultural differences.

# THE ADVANTAGES OF MANAGING FOR DIVERSITY

The ethical and socially responsible goals of leaders and their organizations include providing adequately for members of the diverse work force. Ethical leaders should therefore feel compelled to use merit instead of favoritism or bias as a basis for making human resource decisions. A firm that embraces diversity is also behaving in a socially responsible manner. A leader, for example, who chose to hire five developmentally disabled, unemployed people would be acting in a socially responsible manner. Hiring these people would transfer responsibility for their economic welfare from the state or private charity to the employer. (Some would argue that unless hiring these people is cost effective, the company is neglecting its responsibility to shareholders.)

The many spheres of activity that managing for diversity encompasses are shown in Figure 14-1. According to research and opinion, managing for diversity also brings the firm a competitive advantage. Such an advantage is most likely to accrue when diversity is built into the firm's strategy. Furthermore, according to long-term research conducted by Massachusetts Institute of Technology Professor Thomas A. Kochan, diversity can enhance business performance only if the proper training is provided and the organizational culture supports diversity.[5] In addition, the chief executive of an organization should be the champion for valuing inclusion, and must establish this perspective and associated actions for others throughout the organization.[6] Here we review evidence and opinion about the competitive advantage of demographic and cultural diversity.

1. *Reduction of turnover and absenteeism costs.* As organizations become more diverse, the cost of managing diversity poorly increases. Turnover and absenteeism decrease when minority groups perceive themselves as receiving fair treatment. More effective management of diversity may increase the job satisfaction of diverse groups, thus decreasing turnover and absenteeism and their associated costs. The major initiatives in managing diversity well at Allstate Corporation have substantially reduced turnover among Latinos and African Americans, both in corporate headquarters and in field locations.[7]

2. *Managing diversity well offers a marketing advantage.* A representational work force facilitates the sale of products and services. A key factor is that a multicultural group of decision makers may be at an advantage in reaching a multicultural market. At least one member of the multicultural group may be able to focus a marketing strategy to demonstrate an appreciation of the targeted audience. Pepsi-Cola North America developed a beverage specifically designed for the Latino community, Dole Aguas Frescas, a line of noncarbonated, caffeine-free juice. The idea came from Latino input within Pepsi-Cola, which revealed that Latinos typically

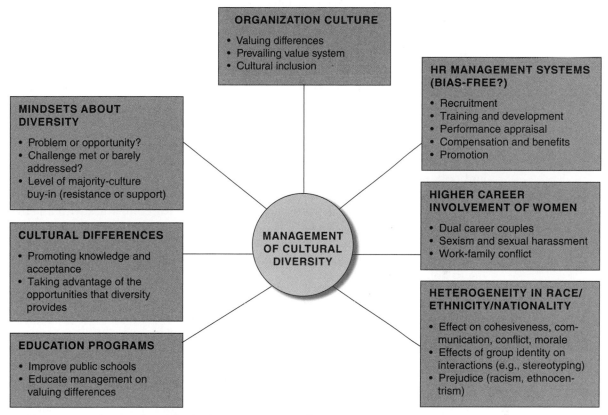

**FIGURE 14-1** Spheres of Activity in the Management of Cultural Diversity.

*Source:* Taylor H. Cox and Stacy Blake, "Managing for Cultural Diversity: Implications for Organizational Competitiveness," *Academy of Management Executive: The Thinking Manager's Source,* August 1991, p. 46. Copyright 1991 by Academy of Management. Reproduced with permission of Academy of Management in the format Textbook via Copyright Clearance Center.

make this type of product in their homes. Tested in the Chicago area, the brand is supported by outdoor advertising, in-store merchandising, and sampling.[8]

A major component of the marketing advantage of diversity is that a work force that matches the diversity of a company's customer base has an edge in appealing to those customers. Sylvia Alston, director of diversity initiatives for the banking giant HSBC–North America, says: "Diversity is absolutely critical, considering that we are so global."[9] On an even broader scale, Bank of America leaders say the banking mammoth fosters a diverse and inclusive workplace because it affords them the business advantage of understanding and satisfying the needs of their associates, customers, clients, and shareholders.[10]

Another marketing advantage is that many people from culturally diverse groups prefer to buy from a company with a good reputation for managing diversity. Allstate Insurance Company, Inc., is well known for its diversity initiatives, and the company has become the nation's leading insurer of African Americans and

Latinos. The large number of agents and customer service representatives from these two groups facilitates attracting and retaining a high percentage of African Americans and Latinos as customers.

**3. *Companies with a favorable record in managing diversity are at a distinct advantage in recruiting and retaining talented people.*** Those companies with a favorable reputation for welcoming diversity attract the strongest job candidates among women and racial and ethnic minorities. Also, a company that does not welcome a diverse work force shrinks its supply of potential candidates.

**4. *Managing diversity well unlocks the potential for excellence.*** When companies hire culturally diverse workers and provide them with all the tools, resources, and opportunities they need to succeed, those companies are more likely to display the full talents of their work force. A man raised in China earned an M.B.A. from an American institute. After carefully searching for companies with an enviable record of managing diversity, he landed a position as a financial analyst with PepsiCo. After one year, his manager complimented his ability to generate ideas and asked why he tried so hard. The analyst said, "In this company, there is nothing to hold me back so long as I am a star performer."

**5. *Heterogeneity in the work force may offer the company a creativity advantage, as well as improve its problem-solving and decision-making capability.*** Creative solutions to problems are more likely to be reached when a diverse group attacks a problem. According to experiments conducted by Scott E. Page, groups of people with diverse perspectives and heuristics (rules of thumb for solving problems) consistently outperformed groups composed of the best individual performers.[11] Of course, there are limits to this conclusion. At times specialized expertise, such as in understanding complex tax regulations or how to perform laser surgery on the retina, is absolutely essential.

It is also possible that a member of a given ethnic group will add a creative touch to product development. Frank Saucedo is director of GM's design studio in North Hollywood. "I grew up in a very automotive family," he says. "My dad worked a lot on cars, and I think Latinos are generally very artistic and expressive. Growing up in this area, you're surrounded by a culture that reveres the car—most people will forgo a meal to buy that set of wheels. Your car says a lot about who you are, and I grew up in that.[12]

Diversity offers both a substantial advantage for organizations and a formidable challenge. Some research suggests that a diverse group is likely to consider a greater range of perspectives and to generate more high-quality solutions than a homogeneous group. Yet the greater the amount of diversity within an organizational subunit, the less cohesive the group. The result may be dissatisfaction and turnover. According to Frances J. Milliken and Luis L. Martins, diversity thus appears to be a double-edge sword: it increases both the opportunity for creativity and the likelihood that group members will be dissatisfied and fail to identify with the group.[13] Another caution is that the leader of the diverse group must help members collaborate; otherwise, the advantages of diverse perspectives will be lost.[14]

Leadership Skill-Building Exercise14-1

**Capitalizing on Diversity**

The class organizes into small groups of about six students, who assume the roles of the top management team of a medium-size manufacturing or service company. Each group has the following assignment: "Being socially aware, ethical, and modern in its thinking, your company already has a highly diverse work force. Yet somehow, your company is not any more profitable than the competition. As the company leaders (yourself a diverse group), today you will work on the problem of how to better capitalize on the cultural diversity within your company. Working for about fifteen minutes, develop a few concrete ideas to enable your company to capitalize on diversity." After the problem solving has been completed, the team leaders might present their ideas to the other groups.

To raise your level of awareness about how to capitalize on the potential advantages of diversity, do Leadership Skill-Building Exercise 14-1, which illustrates that diversity skills are another important subset of interpersonal skills associated with leadership.

## CULTURAL FACTORS INFLUENCING LEADERSHIP PRACTICE

A **multicultural leader** is a leader with the skills and attitudes to relate effectively to and motivate people across race, gender, age, social attitudes, and lifestyles. To influence, motivate, and inspire culturally diverse people, the leader must be aware of overt and subtle cultural differences. Although such culturally based differences are generalizations, they function as starting points in the leader's attempt to lead a person from another culture. For example, many Asians are self-conscious about being praised in front of the group because they feel that individual attention clashes with their desire to maintain group harmony. Therefore, a manager might refrain from praising an Asian group member before the group until he or she understands that group member's preferences. The manager is likely to find that many Asians welcome praise in front of peers, especially when working outside their homeland.

Here we examine two topics that help a leader learn how to manage in a culturally diverse workplace: (1) understanding key dimensions of differences in cultural values and (2) the influence of cultural values on leadership style.

### Key Dimensions of Differences in Cultural Values

One way to understand how national cultures differ is to examine their values or cultural dimensions. The cultural dimensions presented here and outlined in Figure 14-2 are based mostly on those included in GLOBE (Global Leadership and Organizational Behavior Effectiveness), a research program in 62 societal cultures, and builds on previous analyses of cultural dimensions.[15] We also include two other dimensions useful in working with people from other cultures—attitudes

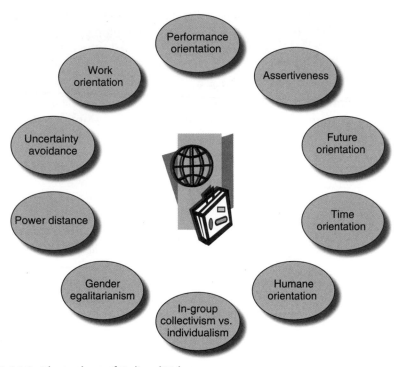

**FIGURE 14-2** Dimensions of Cultural Values.

toward time and work orientation. Keep in mind that these cultural dimensions are stereotypes that apply to a representative person from a particular culture, and are not meant to insult anybody. Individual differences are substantial. For example, many Americans are not assertive, and many French are willing to work 70 hours per week.

**1. Performance orientation** is the degree to which a society encourages (or should encourage) and rewards group members for performance improvement and excellence. Countries high on this dimension are the United States and Singapore, whereas those low on this dimension are Russia and Greece.

**2. Assertiveness** is the degree to which individuals are (and should be) assertive, confrontational, and aggressive in their relationships with one another. Countries scoring high on this dimension are the United States and Austria, whereas those low on this dimension are Sweden and New Zealand. Assertive people enjoy competition in business, in contrast to less assertive cultural groups who prefer harmony, loyalty, and solidarity.

**3. Future orientation** is the extent to which individuals engage (and should engage) in future-oriented behaviors such as delaying gratification, planning, and making investments for the future. Singapore and Switzerland are examples of societies with longer time horizons, whereas Russian and Argentina are less future oriented.

**4. Time orientation** is the importance nations and individuals attach to time. People with an urgent time orientation perceive time as a scarce resource and tend to be impatient. People with a casual time orientation view time as an unlimited and unending resource and tend to be patient. Americans are noted for their urgent time orientation. They frequently impose deadlines and are eager to get started doing business. Asians, Mexicans, and Middle Easterners, in contrast, are patient negotiators.

**5. Humane orientation** is the degree to which a society encourages and rewards, and should encourage and reward, individuals for being fair, altruistic, and caring to others. Egypt and Malaysia rank high on this cultural dimension, and France and Germany rank low.

**6. In-group collectivism** is the degree to which individuals express, and should express, pride, loyalty, and cohesiveness in their organizations and families. Asian societies emphasize collectivism, as do Egypt and Russia. One consequence of collectivism is taking pride in family members and the organizations that employ them.

**7. Gender egalitarianism** is the degree to which a culture minimizes, and should minimize, gender inequality. European countries emphasize gender egalitarianism, and so do the United States and Canada. South Korea is an example of a country that is low on gender egalitarianism and is male dominated.

**8. Power distance** is the degree to which members of a society expect, and should expect, power to be distributed unequally. Individuals who accept power and authority expect the boss to make the major decisions. These same individuals are more formal; however, being formal toward people in positions of authority has decreased substantially throughout the world in recent years. Examples of societies that score high on acceptance of power and authority are Thailand, Brazil, France, and Japan.

**9. Uncertainty avoidance** is the extent to which members of a society rely (and should rely) on social norms, rules, and procedures to lessen the unpredictability of future events. The stronger the desire to avoid uncertainty, the more people seek orderliness, consistency, and laws to cover situations in daily life. Examples of societies with high uncertainty avoidance are Singapore and Switzerland. Societies with low uncertainty avoidance include Russia and Greece.

**10. Work orientation** is the number of hours per week and weeks per year people expect to invest in work versus leisure, or other nonwork activities. American corporate professionals typically work about 55 hours per week, take 45-minute lunch breaks, and two weeks of vacation. Americans tend to have a stronger work orientation than Europeans but a weaker one than Asians. U.S. employees average 1,804 hours of work per year, compared with 1,407 for Norwegian workers and 1,564 for the French. Workers in seven Asian countries including South Korea, Bangladesh, and China work 2,200 hours per year.[16]

How might a manager use information about differences in values to become a more effective leader? A starting point would be to recognize that a person's national values might influence his or her behavior. Assume that a leader wants to influence a person with a low-power-distance orientation to strive for peak performance. The "low-power" person will not spring into action just because the boss makes the suggestion. Instead, the leader needs to patiently explain the personal payoffs of achieving peak performance. Another example is a leader who wants to improve quality and therefore hires people who value collectivism. A backup tactic would be to counsel people who value individualism on the merits of collective action. Leadership Self-Assessment Quiz 14-1 will help you think about how values can moderate (or influence) work performance.

 Leadership Self-Assessment Quiz 14-1

### Charting Your Cultural Value Profile

***Instructions:*** For each of the ten value dimensions, circle the number that most accurately fits your standing on the dimension. For example, if you perceive yourself to have a "high humane orientation," circle the 7 on the fifth dimension.

1. Low performance orientation                                         High performance orientation

     1      2      3      4      5      6      7

2. Low Assertiveness                                                        High Assertiveness

     1      2      3      4      5      6      7

3. Casual time orientation                                                Urgent time orientation

     1      2      3      4      5      6      7

4. Low future orientation                                                 High future orientation

     1      2      3      4      5      6      7

5. Low humane orientation                                               High humane orientation

     1      2      3      4      5      6      7

6. In-group individualism                                                In-group collectivism

     1      2      3      4      5      6      7

7. Low gender egalitarianism                                           High gender egalitarianism

     1      2      3      4      5      6      7

8. Low power distance                                                     High power distance

     1      2      3      4      5      6      7

9. Low uncertainty avoidance                                          High uncertainty avoidance

     1      2      3      4      5      6      7

10. Low work orientation                                                 High work orientation

     1      2      3      4      5      6      7

## Quiz 14-1 (continued)

**Scoring and Interpretation:** After circling one number for each dimension, use a felt-tip pen to connect the circles; this gives you a *profile of cultural values*. Do not be concerned if your marker cuts through the names of the dimensions. Compare your profile to others in class. Should time allow, develop a class profile by computing the class average for each of the ten dimensions and then connecting the points. If the sample size is large enough, compare the cultural value profiles of Westerners and Easterners.

One possible link to leadership development is to hypothesize which type of profile would be the most responsive and which would be the least responsive to your leadership.

### Cultural Values and Leadership Style

The values embedded in a culture influence the behavior of leaders and managers as well as the behavior of other workers. As Geert Hofstede explains, relationships between people in a society are affected by the values programmed in the minds of these people. Because management deals heavily with interpersonal relationships, management and leadership are affected by cultural values. Management and leadership processes may vary from culture to culture, but, being value based, these processes show strong continuity in each society.[17]

*French Managers*   One example of the influence of values on management and leadership style is the behavior of French managers. France has always put a strong emphasis on class. A typical manufacturing plant in France has several classes of workers. Managers and professionals are labeled the *cadres;* first-level supervisors are called the *maîtrise;* and lower-level workers are the *noncadres.* Within each of these classes there are further status distinctions such as higher and lower cadres. French managers who have attended the major business schools (*Grand Écoles*) have the highest status of all. The implication for leadership style is that French managers, particularly in major corporations, are part of an elite class, and they behave in a superior, authoritarian manner. (Of course, not every French manager follows the cultural tradition of being authoritarian.) This style of manager would expect obedience and high respect from group members, and would tend to emphasize bureaucracy.[18]

*German Managers*   Another example of a distinctive leadership style related to culture is the stereotype of the German manager. German managers were studied as part of the GLOBE project. Data were collected on culture and leadership from 457 middle managers in the telecommunications, food processing, and finance industries. A strong performance orientation was found to be the most pronounced German cultural value. German middle managers thus tend to avoid uncertainty, are assertive, and are not terribly considerate of others. They typically show little compassion, and their interpersonal relations are straightforward and stern.[19] And the strong performance they expect must be packed into a short workweek!

***Malaysian Managers***    The characteristic leadership style of Malaysian managers is instructive because other Asian managers use a similar style. Malaysia has become important as a trading partner of both the United States and Europe, particularly because of the outsourcing movement. The following conclusions about the Malaysian leadership style were also based on the GLOBE project.[20] Malaysians emphasize collective well-being (collectivism) and display a strong humane orientation within a society that respects hierarchical differences (high power difference). The culture discourages aggressive, confrontational behavior, preferring harmonious relationships. The preferred organizational leadership style is therefore for managers to show compassion, while at the same time be more autocratic than participative. The Malaysian work group member defers to the boss and in turn is treated with respect and compassion. A Malaysian supervisor might say typically to a worker, "Here is exactly how I want this job done, but I want you to enjoy yourself and learn something valuable while doing the job."

The three highest-ranking leadership dimensions in terms of importance for Malaysian managers were as follows: (1) charismatic/transformational, (2) team oriented, and (3) human oriented. Specifically, the Malaysians emphasized the importance of being willing to act decisively, of using logic and intuition to make decisions firmly and quickly, and of being strong willed, determined, and resolute. Malaysian managers also think it is important for leaders to coordinate activities in a diplomatic style, avoiding conflict and showing consideration for team members.

***Northern U.S. Versus Southern U.S. Managers***    Differences in cultural values between regions of a large country can also have an impact. An example of a cross-regional stereotype is that managers in the southern United States are lower key and more interested in relationship building than are their brusque counterparts in the North. Leaders from the North have a reputation for efficiency and getting tasks accomplished quickly. Leaders from the South perceive such behavior as rude, pushy, and short on relationship building. "If Donald Trump was from the South, he would say, 'You're fired, but bless your heart, you've tried,'" says Joe Hollingsworth, CEO of Hollingsworth Companies in Clinton, Tennessee.[21] The point here is that Southern hospitality has worked its way into leadership style.

However, the stereotype of Southern business leaders being more laid-back and slow moving has been challenged. For one, business in the South may have moved more slowly in the days before air conditioning was widespread. Heat tends to slow people down. John Thompson, CEO of Symantec Corporation and a Florida A&M graduate, says there is nothing regional about attaining business results. "I was raised in the South and spent 27 years working for IBM all over the world. I don't think management style can be localized."[22]

Despite culturally based differences in leadership style, certain leadership practices are likely to work in every culture, including giving people clear directions and administering appropriate rewards for attaining goals. In support of this generalization, a conclusion reached in the GLOBE study was that "in all cultures leader team orientation and the communication of vision, values, and confidence in followers are reported to be highly effective leadership behaviors."[23]

**KB Knowledge Bank**
Describes how a leader might apply the expectancy theory of motivation across cultures.

www.cengage.com/management/dubrin

# CULTURAL SENSITIVITY AND CULTURAL INTELLIGENCE

Some managers are more effective at leading diverse groups than others. The traits and behaviors described in Chapters 2, 3, and 4 should equip a person to lead diverse groups. In addition, cultural sensitivity, cultural intelligence, and certain specific global leadership skills are essential for inspiring people from cultures other than one's own. Although they reinforce each other, here we describe cultural sensitivity and cultural intelligence separately. Global leadership skills encompass so many behaviors that they receive a section of their own.

## Cultural Sensitivity

Leaders, as well as others, who are attempting to influence a person from a foreign country must be alert to possible cultural differences. Thus, the leader must be willing to acquire knowledge about local customs and learn to speak the native language at least passably. The incident about the marketing executive and the BlackBerry described in the chapter opener illustrates the need for cultural sensitivity. A cross-cultural leader must be patient, adaptable, flexible, and willing to listen and learn. All of these characteristics are part of **cultural sensitivity**, an awareness of and a willingness to investigate the reasons why people of another culture act as they do.

A person with cultural sensitivity will recognize certain nuances in customs that will help build better relationships with people in his or her adopted cultures. Refer to Table 12-3 in Chapter 12 for a sampling of appropriate and less appropriate behaviors in a variety of countries. (These are suggestions, not absolute rules.) Another aspect of cultural sensitivity is being tolerant of the subtle differences between cultures. Leadership Self-Assessment Quiz 14-2 gives you an opportunity to reflect on your own tolerance for cross-cultural issues.

 **Leadership Self-Assessment Quiz 14-2**

### My Tolerance for Cultural Differences

**Instructions:** Indicate how comfortable you would feel in the following circumstances: very uncomfortable (VU); uncomfortable (U); neutral (N); comfortable (C); very comfortable (VC).

|  | VU | U | N | C | VC |
|---|---|---|---|---|---|
| 1. Working on a team with both men and women | 1 | 2 | 3 | 4 | 5 |
| 2. Coaching a team or club when all the members are of a different sex than myself | 1 | 2 | 3 | 4 | 5 |
| 3. Having a transsexual person for a boss | 1 | 2 | 3 | 4 | 5 |
| 4. Having a person of a different race for a boss | 1 | 2 | 3 | 4 | 5 |

## Quiz 14-2 (continued)

| | VU | U | N | C | VC |
|---|---|---|---|---|---|
| **5.** Having an opposite-sex person for a boss | 1 | 2 | 3 | 4 | 5 |
| **6.** Answer 6a if you are heterosexual; 6b if you are homosexual: | 1 | 2 | 3 | 4 | 5 |
|    6a. Having a gay or lesbian boss | | | | | |
|    6b. Having a straight boss | | | | | |
| **7.** Having dinner with someone who eats what I consider to be a pet | 1 | 2 | 3 | 4 | 5 |
| **8.** Having dinner with someone who eats what I consider to be a repulsive animal or insect | 1 | 2 | 3 | 4 | 5 |
| **9.** Working alongside a teammate who I know is HIV positive | 1 | 2 | 3 | 4 | 5 |
| **10.** Working alongside a teammate who has served prison time for vehicular homicide | 1 | 2 | 3 | 4 | 5 |

**Total score:** _____

### Scoring and Interpretation:

- **40–50:** You are highly tolerant and flexible in terms of working with a broad spectrum of people. These attitudes should help you be an effective multicultural leader.

- **21–39:** Your tolerance for working with people different from yourself is within the average range. If you learn to become more tolerant of differences, you are more likely to become an effective multicultural leader.

- **10–20:** You may be experiencing difficulties in working with people quite different from yourself. As a consequence, your effectiveness as a multicultural leader might be hampered. If you seek out more diverse cross-cultural experiences, you are likely to become more tolerant of differences.

Cultural sensitivity is also important because it helps a person become a **multicultural worker**. Such an individual is convinced that all cultures are equally good and enjoys learning about other cultures. Multicultural workers and leaders are usually people who have been exposed to more than one culture in childhood. (Refer to Leadership Self-Assessment Exercise 12-2, about cross-cultural relations.) Being multicultural helps one be accepted by a person from another culture. It has been said that a *multilingual* salesperson can explain the advantages of a product in other languages, but it takes a *multicultural* salesperson to motivate foreigners to buy.[24]

Sensitivity is the most important characteristic for leading people from other cultures because cultural stereotypes rarely provide entirely reliable guides for dealing with others. An American manager, for example, might expect Asian group members to accept his or her directives immediately because Asians are known to defer to authority. Nevertheless, an individual Asian might need considerable convincing before accepting authority.

Problems of cultural misunderstanding that leaders should be aware of cluster in five areas.[25] *Language* differences create problems because U.S. workers (most of whom are monolingual) can become frustrated by coworkers' accents and limited English skills. Non–English speakers may feel that they do not fit well into the team. Differences in *religion* are the source of many misunderstandings. In many cultures, religion dominates life in ways that Americans find difficult to comprehend. *Work habits* vary enough across cultures to create friction and frustration. Employees in some cultures are unwilling to spend personal time on work. Problems can also stem from office rituals, such as having coffee or tea together during work breaks, or singing songs together at the start of the workday.

*Women's roles* may differ considerably from those in the United States. Women in many countries may not have the same independence or access to education and higher-level jobs as American women. Workers from various countries may therefore have difficulty accepting the authority of an American manager who is female. *Personal appearance and behavior* vary considerably across cultures. Grooming, office attire, eating habits, and nonverbal communication may deviate significantly from the U.S. standards. Many workers around the world may perceive American workers as overfriendly, aggressive, or rude.

A key item in personal appearance is choosing appropriate attire when working in another culture. Cultural sensitivity helps you detect what type of clothing is appropriate. Many *faux pas* are possible including that many Hindus in India may be offended by a finely tooled leather belt and briefcase because steers have religious significance. In some parts of Asia, white is the color of mourning. A cross-cultural guideline for professionals is that a dark, well-made business suit and conservative accessories such as ties and simple jewelry are acceptable for business around the world.[26]

Cultural sensitivity is enhanced by cultural training, and also by simply listening carefully and observing. A key principle is to be flexible when dealing with people from other cultures. Cultural sensitivity is also enhanced by asking questions, such as whether it is reasonable to expect people to work on Saturday and Sunday. When cross-cultural issues about performance arise, the leader/manager is advised to ask: "My job requires that I manage your performance. Your job is to meet or exceed our performance standards. How can I help you do that?"[27]

Generational differences are another manifestation of cultural differences, quite often within a leader's national culture. For example, young people typically want more frequent recognition and rewards as well as flexible scheduling. Older people might want more deference to their knowledge and experience. The accompanying Leader in Action profile illustrates how cultural sensitivity can facilitate good relationships with both young and old people.

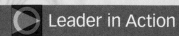

## Leader in Action

### IBM Manager Adapts His Approach to Different Generations

As director of International Business Machine's search and content-discovery software, Aaron Brown supervises a team of six people. Because they include employees who span four decades in age and have work experience of between three and thirty years, he has had to use multiple management styles to direct the small group.

Brown, 31 years old, approaches a 25-year company veteran who was the group's former boss with deference and far more formality than he does the 20-something on his staff, assuring her that her knowledge and loyalty are valued. He motivates a baby boomer with many years of experience at IBM by praising her corporate savvy and willingness to put in long hours and to go the extra mile. And he taps into the technological creativity of a staffer in his twenties while being sure to talk often about his work and praise him almost every day for something he has done.

Brown says he is looking forward to bringing together his staffers of different ages to focus on boosting the company's search-software business. "Managing such a mix of perspectives is challenging—but also fun and helps us to do business," he says. He paired his 20-something employee, recruited from a startup, with a baby boomer for work on a new product. The young employee "has dozens of out-of-the-box ideas and a great sense of, 'Let's change the world right now,'" Brown says. By contrast, the baby boomer is more steadfast "but knows our company's processes and our sales force," he adds.

Encouraged by Brown to pool their strengths rather than to get into a tug of war about whose talents were more vital, the two employees got the product launched in a record three months. Brown thinks that his own close relationships with several older IBM executives have helped him manage across generations. "Listening and communication is key to this," he adds.

### Questions

1. In what way does Brown display cultural sensitivity?
2. To what extent does Brown appear to be thinking in generational stereotypes?
3. What is your opinion about older and younger employees being from different cultures?

*Source:* Excerpted from Carol Hymowitz, "Managers Find Ways to Get Generations to Close Culture Gaps," *Wall Street Journal,* July 9, 2007, p. B1.

### Cultural Intelligence

A refinement and expansion of cultural sensitivity is **cultural intelligence (CQ)**: an outsider's ability to interpret someone's unfamiliar and ambiguous gestures the way that person's compatriots would.[28] For example, an American might be attending a business meeting in Europe. He or she might pick up the clue that the Europeans present prefer to discuss American politics and trade agreements (or current events) for an hour before discussing the business purpose of the meeting. So the cross-border visitor engages in a lively but nonpartisan discussion of politics and trade agreements. Cultural intelligence has three facets or components:

- *Cognitive CQ (head).* The first facet of cultural intelligence is the ability to pick up some factual clues about relevant behavior such as the importance of deadlines.
- *Physical CQ (body).* Your actions and demeanor must prove to your foreign hosts that you have entered their world by adopting people's habits and

mannerisms. You might gently kiss each cheek of a French compatriot (or be kissed), and not shake hands with a Japanese work associate in Tokyo. With the latter, you might bow slightly or smile as a form of greeting.

■ *Emotional/motivational CQ (heart)*. Adapting to a new culture involves overcoming obstacles and setbacks. You need the self-confidence and courage to keep trying even though your first few attempts at adapting your behavior to a group of foreign workers went poorly. You might say to yourself, "Okay, when I stood very close to the Mexican workers, they didn't like it even though they stand close to each other. Maybe I looked a little stiff. I'll practice some more."

To attain the highest level of cultural intelligence, you would need competence in all three facets, and the head, body, and heart would have to work together smoothly. You would need to gather the facts, adapt your mannerism and appearance to fit the culture, and stay motivated to make refinements.

Cultural intelligence is similar to emotional intelligence, yet it goes one step further by enabling a person to distinguish among behaviors that are (a) produced by the culture in question, (b) peculiar to particular individuals, and (c) found in all human beings. Suppose you are making a PowerPoint presentation in Germany and suddenly your presentation is verbally attacked. You ask yourself, "Is this a German trait? Are these people just being hostile? Or are my slides so bad anyone would attack them?" Picking up on the cues, you decide that German corporate professionals find it normal to challenge ideas and that they are not being personal.

# GLOBAL LEADERSHIP SKILLS

In general, **global leadership skills** refer to the ability to exercise effective leadership in a variety of countries. The definition stems from the idea that the essence of global leadership is the ability to influence people who are dissimilar to the leader and stem from different cultural backgrounds.[29] Such skills would therefore include the concepts already reviewed, of cultural sensitivity, being a multicultural worker, and cultural intelligence. Here we look at global leadership skills from several perspectives: a specific model, success factors in international positions, and motivating workers in different cultures.

## A Proposed Model for Global Leadership Skills

*Global leadership skills* are so important that they improve a company's reputation and contribute to a sustainable competitive advantage.[30] Excellent global leaders have a leadership style that generates superior corporate performance in terms of four criteria: (1) profitability and productivity, (2) continuity and efficiency, (3) commitment and morale, and (4) adaptability and innovation. *Behavioral complexity* is the term given to this ability to attain all four criteria of organizational performance. Excellent global leaders are able to understand complex issues from the four perspectives just mentioned and to achieve the right balance. For example, when a company is facing a mature market, it might be necessary to invest more effort into being innovative than into achieving high profits.

The global leader must tap into a deep, universal layer of human motivation to build loyalty, trust, and teamwork in different cultures. Universal needs are found among people in all cultures; for example, both Dominican Republicans and Inuit want to be part of a group. To get at universal needs (such as the desire for affiliation and exploration), the global leader must satisfy three metavalues: community, pleasure, and meaning.

**1. *Community.*** The leaders of successful multinational firms nurture good citizenship behavior, or the desire to serve the common good. In these organizations, teamwork is highly valued and workers are more concerned with the common good than with their individual concerns.

**2. *Pleasure.*** In successful global organizations, fun or intrinsic motivation is an important energizer. Enjoying work by engaging in new activities is an essential part of the organizational culture. The fun, in turn, facilitates productivity and creativity.

**3. *Meaning.*** Meaningful work is another universal motivator. As one CEO said, "People will work for money but die for a cause." Employees prefer to feel that they are contributing something to society through their efforts.[31]

What is a global leader supposed to do to satisfy these three key metavalues? In general, he or she would have to engage in the type of leadership practices and behaviors described throughout this text. A more specific action plan would be to use team development tactics, including empowerment, to promote a sense of community. Pleasure and meaning would derive from job enrichment, with its emphasis on challenging, interesting work.

## Success Factors in International Management Positions

A study was conducted of success factors in international management positions. Two traits were specifically related to success in conducting international business: sensitivity to cultural differences and being culturally adventurous.[32] Cultural sensitivity has already been described. The adventurous aspect refers to a willingness to take chances and experiment with a new culture. A Mexican American from Phoenix, Arizona, who volunteered for a six-month assignment in Johannesburg, South Africa, would be culturally adventurous. Similarly, a set of observations by DDI Inc., specialists in executive behavior, indicated that being a *global explorer* facilitated effective leadership. The global explorer has a passion for the native culture, and will ask questions about how and why things work in the country he or she is visiting for business purposes.

Being a *contextual chameleon* is also quite important, according to DDI. As in cultural sensitivity, effective global leaders are able to adapt to unfamiliar roles and environments. *Handig* is a Dutch term for adaptability; Dutch leaders in their roles as trading mediators between nations have gained a reputation for being flexible, adaptable, and skilled. Another example of responding to the context would be to emphasize consensus-style leadership in Scandinavia because most Scandinavian workers value low power distance.[33]

A study demonstrated that deficits in emotional intelligence contributed to executive failure on assignments in Latin America, Europe, and Japan.[34] Being able to read emotions is particularly helpful when evaluating how well the person from another culture is accepting your propositions.

Tolerance for ambiguity is important for leaders in general, and especially important for developing global leadership skills. Every country he or she works in represents a new way of doing things, so the leadership has to work with only general guidelines. A leader from an American company might be visiting a Korean affiliate. He or she should probably reflect, "Koreans have high respect for authority, and at the same time have a strong work ethic. So how far should I go in asking questions? They might expect me as the leader to have all the answers. Yet at the same time, they probably want to display their knowledge." Asking Korean managers questions before the presentation might be a good idea.[35]

Another area where tolerance for ambiguity is a success factor lies within providing leadership to cross-cultural teams. One of the more pronounced cross-cultural differences is that various members of the team nay have differing attitudes toward hierarchy and authority (or power distance). Team members from some cultures may have difficulty with the flat structure of most teams. If team members defer to a higher-status team member, their behavior will be regarded as appropriate when most of the team derives from a hierarchical culture. In contrast, team members who defer to authority may damage their stature and credibility if most of the team comes from a culture of low power distance (egalitarian). One manager of Mexican heritage who belonged to a cross-cultural team lamented:

> In Mexican culture, you're always supposed to be humble. So whether you understand something or not, you're supposed to put it in the form of a question. You have to keep it open-ended, out of respect. I think that actually worked against me, because the Americans thought I really didn't know what I was talking about. So it made me feel like they thought I was wavering on my answer.[36]

A potential leadership intervention to the problem of status and hierarchy is to talk about the problem in advance, and to encourage behavior that will fit most team members. The team leader might mention several times that the structure is flat, and that all team members have an equal voice. Because cultural values control behavior so strongly, the message will have to be repeated frequently.

A confusing skill issue for many international workers is the importance of having a good command of a second language. Part of the confusion comes from the fact that English has become the standard language of business, technology, engineering, and science. For example, when Europeans from different countries assemble at a business conference, they communicate in English. However, when you are trying to influence a person from another culture, you are more influential if you can speak, read, and write well in his or her language. On the Internet, consumers are four times more likely to purchase from a web site written in their preferred language.[37] A command of a second language also enhances the person's charisma.

## Motivating and Inspiring Workers in Other Cultures

The discussion of expectancy theory in Chapter 10 provided the best general clue to motivating people in other cultures—figure out which rewards have high valence for them. Workers who lack basic necessities in life would rather be rewarded with a scooter or bicycle than a $500 luxury fountain pen or watch. The model for global leadership skills presented earlier dealt with motivation with respect to satisfying human needs. Workers will be motivated and inspired to the extent that need satisfaction will be forthcoming.

Cross-cultural trainer Nancy Settle-Murphy provides another example: Team members from the United States tend to crave popularity and approval. For Germans, the goal is to do an excellent job with great attention to detail. The implication is that German professionals prefer motivation through exciting work, whereas Americans prefer external rewards. Team members from Asian cultures are more motivated by rewards that emphasize group harmony, such as a group reward.[38] (Again we are presented with cultural stereotypes that work much of the time.)

So who is an example of a leader with global leadership skills—one person who has most of the attributes described in this section? A highly visible example is Carlos Ghosn, the chief executive of both Nissan and Renault, known as the "hottest car guy on earth." Several years ago it was even thought that Ghosn might be invited to add General Motors or Ford to his list of responsibilities. He travels around the world in a corporate jet that can fly between Paris and Tokyo nonstop. Ghosn also spends considerable time visiting the U.S. operations of Nissan. He carries two briefcases, one for Renault and another for Nissan. He crosses time zones and cultures with great facility. Born in Brazil to Lebanese parents, and college-educated in Paris, Ghosn speaks several languages and enjoys cuisine from many countries.[39]

# LEADERSHIP INITIATIVES FOR ACHIEVING CULTURAL DIVERSITY

For organizations to value diversity, top management must be committed to it. The commitment is clearest when it is embedded in organizational strategy, as well as in the life and culture of the organization. Diversity initiatives should be deep rather than superficial.[40] A true diversity strategy should encourage all employees to contribute their unique talents, skills, and expertise to the organization's operations, independent of race, gender, ethnic background, and any other definable difference. In addition, leaders should take the initiative to ensure that many activities are implemented to support the diversity strategy. Table 14-1 lists the seven leadership initiatives for encouraging diversity that are discussed in the following text.

**TABLE 14-1** Leadership Initiatives for Achieving Cultural Diversity

1. Hold managers accountable for achieving diversity.
2. Establish minority recruitment, retention, and mentoring programs.
3. Conduct diversity training.
4. Conduct cross-cultural training.
5. Encourage the development of employee networks.
6. Avoid group characteristics when hiring for person–organization fit.
7. Attain diversity among organizational leaders.

## Hold Managers Accountable for Achieving Diversity

A high-impact diversity initiative is for top-level organizational leaders to hold managers accountable for diversity results at all levels. If managers are held accountable for behavior and business changes in the diversity arena, an organizational culture supportive of diversity will begin to develop. Accountability for diversity results when achieving diversity objectives is included in performance evaluations and when compensation is linked in part to achieving diversity results. In response to charges of discrimination, Wal-Mart cut executives' bonuses if they failed to meet diversity goals. CEO Lee Scott holds himself to the same standard.[41]

The Allstate Corporation exemplifies a firm that has worked hard to hold managers accountable for achieving cultural diversity within the firm. The company states that a core component of the diversity strategy at Allstate is effective education and training for all employees. Since its launch, the diversity education program has reached 40,000 employees, delivering a message that focuses on inclusion and maximizing performance at the same time. All employees are required to participate in a classroom and online training program titled "Diversity—Allstate's Competitive Edge." New managers attend a diversity training curriculum, "Creating an Environment for Success." The diversity training for employees helps reinforce the idea for managers that the company is serious about diversity accomplishment.

One of the methods used to gauge leadership effectiveness in managing diversity is an employee feedback survey. All employees of Allstate are surveyed annually through a quarterly leadership measurement system (QLMS). Conducted online, the survey includes measures of satisfaction with both leadership and diversity accomplishment. (Table 14-2 presents the diversity index.) An Allstate human resource specialist has noted that satisfaction with diversity and company leadership are positively correlated.[42]

## Establish Minority Recruitment, Retention, and Mentoring Programs

An essential initiative for building a diverse work force is to recruit and retain members of the targeted minority group. Because recruiting talented members of minority groups and women is competitive, careful human resources planning

---

**TABLE 14-2** The Diversity Index at Allstate

The diversity index at Allstate asks the following questions on employee surveys:

1. To what extent does our company deliver quality service to customers regardless of their ethnic background, etc.?
2. To what extent are you treated with respect and dignity at work?
3. To what extent does your immediate manager/team leader seek out and utilize diverse backgrounds and perspectives?
4. How often do you observe insensitive behavior at work: for example, inappropriate comments or jokes?
5. To what extent do you work in an environment of trust?

*Source*: From Allstate Insurance Company www.allstate.com

is required. At Washington Mutual, Inc., for example, senior regional manager Ming Wong systematically hires employees who reflect the bank's customer base. For example, Ming hires Chinese Americans to work at the bank's San Francisco Chinatown branch.[43]

Efforts at recruiting a culturally diverse work force must be supported by a leadership and management approach that leads to high retention. To increase retention rates, diversity consultants advise employers to strengthen cultural training programs, recognize employees' hidden skills and talents, and give diversity committees clout with top management.[44] Retaining employees is also a function of good leadership and management in general, such as offering workers challenging work, clear-cut goals, feedback, and valuable rewards for goal attainment. Mentoring is a key initiative for retaining minority-group members, as well as for facilitating their advancement.

## Conduct Diversity Training

**Diversity training** has become a widely used method for enhancing diversity within organizations. The purpose of diversity training is to bring about workplace harmony by teaching people how to get along better with diverse work associates. Quite often the program is aimed at minimizing open expressions of racism and sexism. All forms of diversity training center on increasing people's awareness of and empathy for people who are different from themselves in some important way. The subject of diversity training tends to evolve with issues of concern at the time. A growing number of employers now offer training on how to prevent workplace discrimination against gays, lesbians, bisexual, and transgender employees. Even when companies follow antidiscrimination laws, diversity training still plays an important role. Diversity consultant Brian McNaught says, "You need more than policies. You need a culture that on a daily basis feels welcoming, and the only way you change a corporate culture is through education."[45]

Training sessions in valuing differences focus on the ways in which men and women, or people of different races, reflect different values, attitudes, and cultural backgrounds. These sessions can vary from several hours to several days or longer. Sometimes the program is confrontational, sometimes not.

An essential part of relating more effectively to diverse groups is to empathize with their point of view. To help training participants develop empathy, representatives of various groups explain their feelings related to workplace issues. Leadership Skill-Building Exercise 14-2 gives you the opportunity to engage in an effective diversity training exercise. A useful way of framing diversity training is to say that it represents a subset of interpersonal skills: relating effectively to coworkers who are different from you in some meaningful way adds to your interpersonal effectiveness.

An extension of diversity training is helping organizational leaders develop empathy for diverse groups by having them spend time working with demographic groups different from their own. In addition to developing empathy, the executives learn to relate more comfortably with diverse groups. An extreme approach is when Rod Bond, an executive at a food service company, accompanied female colleagues to a meeting of the Women's Food Service Forum, where he was the

## ⊙ Leadership Skill-Building Exercise 14-2

### The Diversity Circle

Some diversity trainers use the *diversity circle* exercise to help workers appreciate diversity and overcome misperceptions. The exercise adapts well for classroom use. Form a group of about ten students. Arrange your chairs into a circle, and put one additional chair in the center of the circle. A "diverse" group member volunteers to sit in the center chair and become the first "awareness subject." Because most people are diverse in some way, most people are eligible to occupy the center chair.

The person in the center tells the others how he or she has felt about being diverse or different and how people have reacted to his or her diversity. For example, an Inuit described how fellow workers were hesitant to ask him out for a beer, worrying whether he could handle alcohol. Another name for this exercise is "How I Felt Different" because each person describes how he or she felt different from others at one point in his or her life.

An equally effective alternative to this procedure is for each class member to come up in front of the class to describe a significant way in which he or she is different. After each class member has presented, a discussion might be held of observations and interpretations.

What lessons did you learn about interpersonal relations from this exercise that will help you be a more effective leader?

only man among 1,500 women. Bond said, "I can begin to feel what it must have felt like to be different." Another example is that Raytheon's missile-systems division once required managers to spend a day in a wheelchair in the office. The goal of the activity was to understand the concerns of the disabled employees. Diversity specialists believe that executives should be asked to engage in activities that relate to their regular work, so they can see how diversity is relevant.[46]

A frequently mentioned concern about diversity training is that it reinforces stereotypes about groups. Participants are informed about group differences, such as cultural values, and tactics might be suggested for coping with these differences—such as using more body language when relating to Latinos.

Leaders of diversity training exercises are cautioned to guard against encouraging participants to be too confrontational and expressing too much hostility. Companies have found that when employees are too blunt during these sessions, it may be difficult to patch up interpersonal relations in the work group later on. Sometimes the diversity trainer encourages group members to engage in outrageous behavior, such as by having women sexually harass men so the men "know what it feels like." Key themes of negative reactions to diversity training are charges of "political correctness" and "white-male bashing."

Even when diversity training is effective in achieving better cross-cultural understanding, and improved cross-cultural relationships, such training may not accelerate the number of minority group members and women into managerial positions. A review of 31 years of data from 830 workplaces suggested that when diversity training was mandatory and aimed at avoiding liability in discrimination lawsuits, the number of women in management, as well as minorities including Latinos and Asians, decreased. In contrast, when diversity training is voluntary and implemented to advance a company's business strategy, the training was associated with increased diversity in management. Another key finding is that diversity training works best when it focuses on organizational skills, such as establishing mentoring relationships and giving women and minorities a chance to prove they can compete successfully in high-profile positions.[47]

## Conduct Cross-Cultural Training

For many years, companies and government agencies have prepared their managers and other workers for overseas assignments. The method frequently chosen is **cross-cultural training**, a set of learning experiences designed to help employees understand the customs, traditions, and beliefs of another language. Foreign language training is often included in cultural training. Table 14-3 illustrates how

**TABLE 14-3** English-to-English Dictionary

| BRITONS SAY . . . | AMERICANS SAY . . . |
|---|---|
| Bank holiday | National holiday |
| Holidays or hols | Vacation |
| Scheme | Plan or program |
| Keen | Enthusiastic |
| To table (an idea) | To put (an idea) out for discussion |
| To put (an idea) aside | To table (an idea) |
| Elevenses | Late morning snack |
| Up to you, really | Do not do it/proceed with caution/have another look at it |
| To ring up | To telephone |
| To knock up* | To visit |
| Fortnight | Two weeks |
| To strike out | To go after something |
| To fail | To strike out |
| Being sent to Coventry | Being ignored |
| Been given the sack, sacked | Fired |
| Aggro | Trouble |
| Pear-shaped | Disaster |
| To throw a wobbly | To have a tantrum |
| Taking the mickey | Making fun of |
| Car park | Parking lot |
| Lift | Elevator |
| Not bad | Very good |
| Not good | Very bad |

*A caution for Britons visiting the United States is that "to knock up" means to impregnate a woman, illustrating that everyday expressions in one language might be perceived as curious or offensive in another country.

*Source:* DeeDee Doke, **"Perfect Strangers,"** *HR Magazine,* December 2004, p. 64. Copyright 2004 by the Society for Human Resource Management. Reproduced with permission of *HR Magazine,* published by the Society for Human Resource Management, Alexandria, VA, in the format Textbook via Copyright Clearance Center.

English can be spoken differently across English-speaking countries. (The information in the table has been included in cultural training.) The multicultural leader needs to know that English is spoken differently in the United States, Great Britain, Australia, and South Africa, among other countries.

Cross-cultural training usually includes the type of information about cross-cultural bloopers included in Chapter 12. Among the hundreds of tidbits included, depending on the target country, are how to handle chopsticks in China (never stick them straight into the rice bowl) and that it is acceptable in Finland to take a sauna with a client (that's the normal way to conduct business there).[48]

The art of facial cheek-kissing is an amusing, yet important aspect of cross-cultural training. Americans favor handshakes for greetings, yet in most countries outside of Asia, light kisses on the cheek of the other person are more acceptable. The kisses are given to people of the same and opposite sex for greeting purposes; however, kissing a business acquaintance of the opposite sex is even more expected and appropriate. Frank Higgins, a global leader of two divisions for Nestlé USA Inc., observes, "I would be rude if I didn't kiss my female colleagues from Mexico." At the company's Zurich headquarters, Higgins triple cheek-kisses.[49]

A recent development in intercultural training is to train global leaders in cultural intelligence. Following the model of cultural intelligence described earlier in this chapter, global managers receive training in the cognitive, physical, and emotional or motivational domains. The training is highly complex, with the leader being expected to learn dozens of different concepts and behaviors, as well as insights. A sampling of what training in cultural intelligence involves is as follows:[50]

> A Canadian manager is attempting to interpret a "Thai smile." First, she needs to observe the various cues provided in addition to the smile gesture itself (for example, other facial or bodily gestures, significance of others who may be in proximity, the source of the original smile gesture) and to assemble them into a meaningful whole and make sense of what is really experienced by the Thai employee. Second, she must have the requisite motivation (directed effort and self-confidence) to persist in the face of confusion, challenge, or apparently mixed signals. Third, she must choose, generate, and execute the right actions to respond appropriately.
>
> If any of these elements is deficient, she is likely to be ineffective in dealing with the Thai employee. A high CQ manager has the capability with all three facets as they act in unison.

Again, cultural intelligence is a refinement of cultural sensitivity. The international leader who remains alert to cues in the environment can go a long way toward building relationships with people from different cultures.

## Encourage the Development of Employee Networks

Another leadership initiative toward recognizing cultural differences is to permit and encourage employees to form **employee network (or affinity) groups**. The network group is composed of employees throughout the company who affiliate on the basis of a group characteristic such as race, ethnicity, sex, sexual orientation, or physical ability status. Group members typically have similar interests and look to the groups as a way of sharing information about succeeding in the organization. Although some human resources specialists are concerned that network groups can lead to divisiveness, others believe they play a positive role.

Bank of America contains affinity groups that take the form of associate groups that share a common identity and meet periodically to network, mentor, and support group members. Among these groups are the Hispanic/Latin Organization for Leadership and Advancement, Black Professional Group, Asian Leadership Network, and Pride Resource Group.[51]

Employee network groups often play a functional role in the organization in addition to the social role. A prime example is The Latino Employee Network (called Adelante) at Frito-Lay, the snack food division of PepsiCo. The group made a major contribution during the development of Doritos Guacamole Flavored Tortilla Chips. Adelante members provided feedback on taste and packaging to help ensure the authenticity of the product in the Latino community. The network members' insight helped make the guacamole-flavored Doritos into one of the most dramatically successful new-product launches in the history of Frito-Lay.[52] Olé!

## Avoid Group Characteristics When Hiring for Person–Organization Fit

An important consideration in employee recruitment and hiring is to find a good *person–organization fit*, the compatibility of the individual with the organization. The compatibility often centers on the extent to which a person's major work-related values and personality traits fit major elements of the organization culture. Following this idea, a person who is adventuresome and prone to risk taking would achieve highest performance and satisfaction where adventuresome behavior and risk taking are valued. Conversely, a methodical and conservative individual should join a slow-moving bureaucracy.

Many business firms today are investing time and effort into recruiting and hiring employees who show a good person–organization fit. A selection strategy of this type can lead to a cohesive and strong organizational culture. The danger, however, is that when employers focus too sharply on cultural fit in the hiring process, they might inadvertently discriminate against protected classes of workers. Specifically, the hiring manager might focus on superficial aspects of conformity to culture, such as physical appearance and which schools the candidates attended. Selecting candidates who look alike and act alike conflicts with a diversity strategy. Elaine Fox, a labor and employment attorney, cautions that "one of the biggest problems that can occur when hiring based on culture is if the culture you're comfortable with doesn't open the way for women and minorities."[53]

Leaders can take the initiative to guard against this problem. The way to circumvent it is to avoid using group characteristics (such as race, sex, ethnicity, or physical status) in assessing person–organization fit. The alternative is to focus on traits and behaviors, such as intelligence or ability to be a team player. Leaders at Microsoft emphasize hiring intelligent people only because bright people fit their culture best. Being intelligent is an individual difference rather than a group characteristic.

### Attain Diversity Among Organizational Leaders

To achieve a multicultural organization, firms must also practice **leadership diversity**—that is, have a culturally heterogeneous group of leaders. Many global firms have already achieved leadership diversity with respect to ethnicity. Sex is another key area for leadership diversity, with many organizations today having women in top executive positions. An organization with true leadership diversity also has a heterogeneous group of leaders in such positions as supervisors, middle managers, and team leaders. McDonald's Corp. and Xerox Corp. are two examples of well-known companies whose C-level executives include minority group members and women. One of the executive positions at McDonald's is chief diversity officer, a practice also followed by several other large business firms including PepsiCo.

Richard D. Parsons, chairman of the board of Time Warner, is one of the highest ranking and most influential African Americans in corporate America. He was recently asked if he was satisfied with the diversification of the management ranks. Parsons' answer provides a balanced understanding of the status of leadership diversity in organizations today:

> No. We've made some progress over the last five or six years, in terms of diversifying the management of our company at all levels. But it's still a work in progress. I think we have most of the infrastructure in place. We have people at all levels who are doing the right thing by virtue of this objective. But we're not where we need to be yet, and we will still need to do more things on the structural side and the human side.[54]

### Reader's Roadmap

So far we have studied the nature of leadership; the attributes, behaviors, and styles of leaders; the ethics and social responsibility of leaders; and how leaders exert power and use politics and influence. We then studied techniques for developing teamwork as well as motivation and coaching skills. After studying creativity and innovation as part of leadership, we focused on communication skills as they relate to leadership. We then shifted our attention to strategic leadership, after which we discussed another broad challenge facing leaders: dealing with cultural diversity within the organization and across borders. Next, we deal with the capstone topic of developing leaders and choosing successors for executives.

## SUMMARY

The modern leader must be multicultural because corporate success, profit, and growth depend increasingly on the management of a diverse work force. The ethical and social responsibility goals of leaders and their organizations include providing adequately for the members of the diverse work force.

Managing for diversity brings a competitive advantage to the firm in several ways. Turnover and absenteeism costs may be lower because minorities are more satisfied. Marketing can be improved because a representational work force facilitates selling products and services, and a good reputation for diversity management may attract customers. Companies with a favorable record in managing diversity are at an advantage in recruiting and retaining talented minority-group members. Managing diversity also helps unlock the potential for excellence among employees who might otherwise be overlooked. A heterogeneous work force may also offer an advantage in creativity and problem solving.

To influence, motivate, and inspire culturally diverse people, the leader must be aware of overt and subtle cultural differences. Differences in cultural values help explain differences among people. Ten of these values are as follows: performance orientation; assertiveness; future orientation; time orientation; humane orientation; in-group collectivism; gender egalitarianism; power distance (acceptance of formal authority); uncertainty avoidance; and work orientation.

Cultural values influence leadership style as well as the behavior of other workers. For example, French managers believe in a class system. Another way to understand how culture influences leadership is to compare leadership styles across cultural groups. For Malaysian managers, the preferred organizational leadership style is to show compassion while at the same time being more autocratic than participative. Cultural differences in leadership style within the same country exist also, such as the stereotype of U.S. Southern managers being more interested in building relationships than their Northern counterparts.

Cultural sensitivity is essential for inspiring people from different cultures. Part of this sensitivity is the leader's willingness to acquire knowledge about local customs and to learn to speak the native language. A person with cultural sensitivity will recognize certain nuances in customs that help him or her build better relationships with people from different cultures. Cultural misunderstandings tend to cluster in five key areas: language differences, religious differences, work habits, women's roles, and personal appearance and behavior. Choosing appropriate attire for conducting business in another culture requires careful observation. Generational differences are another manifestation of cultural differences.

Cultural intelligence helps an outsider interpret someone's unfamiliar and ambiguous gestures the way that person's compatriots would. Such intelligence has three facets: cognitive (head), physical (body), and emotional/motivational (heart).

Global leadership skills help improve a company's reputation and contribute to a sustainable competitive advantage. One model of such skills contends that behavioral complexity helps a leader attain high organizational performance. To tap into universal needs, global leaders should satisfy three metavalues: community, pleasure, and meaning. Among the success factors for international management positions are cultural sensitivity; cultural adventurousness (or being a global explorer); being a contextual chameleon (adaptation to the unfamiliar); emotional intelligence; and tolerance for ambiguity. Having a command of a second language is helpful for influencing a person from another culture.

Top management commitment to valuing diversity is clearest when valuing diversity is embedded in organizational strategy. Specific leadership initiatives for valuing diversity can be divided into seven categories: (1) hold managers accountable for diversity; (2) establish minority recruitment, retention, and mentoring programs; (3) conduct diversity training; (4) conduct cross-cultural training, (5) encourage the development of employee networks; (6) avoid group characteristics when hiring for person–organization fit, and (7) attain diversity among organizational leaders.

## KEY TERMS

| | | |
|---|---|---|
| Multicultural leader | Humane orientation | Work orientation |
| Performance orientation | In-group collectivism | Cultural sensitivity |
| Assertiveness | Gender egalitarianism | Multicultural worker |
| Future orientation | Power distance | Cultural intelligence (CQ) |
| Time orientation | Uncertainty avoidance | Global leadership skills |

**Diversity training**
**Cross-cultural training**

**Employee network (or affinity)**
  **groups**

**Leadership diversity**

 ## GUIDELINES FOR ACTION AND SKILL DEVELOPMENT

A major problem to manage in developing a diverse work force is for company leadership to reduce turnover among the employees they have worked so hard to recruit. A report that surveyed 490 minority professionals in finance suggests that companies that work so hard to get diverse employees in the building don't try nearly hard enough to keep them from leaving. Among the suggestions made in the report were to include communicating a clear path for employee advancement and providing suggestions for development as part of performance evaluation. The report also stated that "Professionals of color are, or perceive themselves to be, outside of the informal mechanisms of information sharing and social networks, including lunch or coffee with peers, being invited to drinks, and socializing with managers."[55]

A caution in implementing diversity management is for managers and other interviewers not to go overboard in trying to make a minority-group member feel comfortable. "When interviewers try too hard to be black, Latin, or Asian," says Martin de Campo, managing consultant with an executive search firm, "they come across as hokey." John Fujii, the president of a diversity recruiting firm, says, "The best way to make minority candidates feel comfortable is to make them feel that they have an equal opportunity to compete for a position. That's all they want."[56]

### Discussion Questions and Activities

1. Given that the U.S. work force is becoming increasingly Hispanic (or Latino), should managers all be required to speak and read Spanish?
2. How does the concept of diversity in organizations relate to *political correctness?*

3. If a business leader is regarded as charismatic by many people in one culture, to what extent do you think the leader would be perceived as charismatic in many other cultures?
4. What actions might a leader take to demonstrate that his or her interest in diversity goes beyond rhetoric?
5. Assume that a manager becomes the leader of a division in which the vast majority of the workers are under 25, such as a restaurant chain. Would you recommend that the leader get some body piercing to help establish rapport with the division work force? Explain your reasoning.
6. Imagine that your company is going to establish a major facility in the Democratic Republic of the Congo, Africa. Explain whether or not you should give preference to hiring a Republic of the Congo citizen to lead that operation.
7. Assume that an outstanding sales representative works for a company that considers it unethical to bribe officials to make a sale. The sales representative is about to close a major deal in a country where bribing is standard practice. Her commission will be $60,000 for a signed contract. What should the representative do if an official demands a $4,000 *gift* before closing the deal?
8. With so much business being conducted over the Internet, including email, why is it important to understand cross-cultural differences in values?
9. Suppose you are a team leader and one of your team members has a strong work ethic, based on his or her cultural values. Is it fair to assign this member much more work just because he or she is willing to work longer and harder than the other team members?
10. What can you do this week to help prepare yourself to become a multicultural leader?

## Leadership Case Problem A

### Can Howard Stringer Fix Sony?

Howard Stringer is annoyed. Since becoming Sony Corp.'s first foreign executive in 2005, he has been slammed by Japanese financial analysts and Sony employees for being disconnected from the company's daily operations, especially during two big crises. Investors in the United States, meanwhile, have put him under constant pressure to fix Sony's problems more quickly. And he was hearing conflicting advice from both sides.

"Look, in America, I was told to cut costs," Stringer says. "In Japan I was told not to cut costs. Two different worlds. In this country you can't lay people off very easily. In America, you can." Stringer says he balanced those competing demands to recently squeeze 4 percent growth out of Sony's electronics business and beat earnings estimates for four consecutive quarters. He bristles at criticism, mostly from Japanese, that he lives in a hotel when in Tokyo and spends much too much time in New York and London to run the company effectively. Says Stringer, sitting in a conference room in Sony's Tokyo headquarters: "If I'm not running the company, who the _____ is?"

Fixing this iconic Japanese company is considered to be one of the biggest challenges in business. Stringer's dilemma is that he is caught between two different management styles and cultures. He says he recognizes the risk of falling behind amid breakneck changes in electronics. But he says there's an equal risk in moving too aggressively.

"I don't want to change Sony's culture to the point where it's unrecognizable from the founder's vision," Stringer says. "That's the balancing act I'm doing."

Critics believe that whether he can pull it off is still an open question. For the Welsh-born executive, the task is complicated by having to navigate a sea of obstacles, from uncommunicative top executives—one surprised Stringer with bad news at a board meeting—to poor public relations advice. The critics say that the risk to Sony from his management-through-persuasion is that the company could fall further behind nimbler and more aggressive rivals. Stringer has already shifted

gears once, adopting a more assertive stance after his softly-softly approach faltered.

When he became CEO, Stringer started cautiously. He knew that despite its global brand name, Sony remained a traditional Japanese company, full of employees with lifetime tenure who were suspicious of change. Japan had opened up to the idea of having foreign managers run Japanese companies, notably Carlos Ghosn at Nissan Motor Co., but it hadn't necessarily embraced the Western style of management.

Stringer, 65 years old, stuck with the executive team he inherited. He tried gently persuading managers to cooperate with one another and urged them to think about developing products in a new way. The dangers of that approach quickly became clear. Two big missteps—a delayed launch of the PlayStation 3 video-game console and an embarrassing battery recall—tarnished Stringer's first five years in charge. In both cases, managers tried handling problems in the traditional Sony way: quietly and without informing top executives. After a shuffling of executives, Stringer now receives every report about manufacturing problems—"more emails that I care to read," he says.

Stringer has counseled patience to his critics, noting that his turnaround of Sony's U.S. operations took five years to complete. "You can't go through a Japanese company with a sledgehammer," he said. In a later interview, Stringer said, "I'm going to do what I want to do now. I'm not going to be following everybody's suggestions. I've got to be true to myself in some ways."

Stringer says nothing has changed in his management style. The perception of him as a hands-off manager was ruled by his decision to live in a Tokyo hotel. The CEO says he now regrets the decision, but also rejects as "insane" the notion that he wasn't firmly in control. He says his response to the crises wasn't a change of heart but a quickening of his long-term plans. He adds that his record has been obscured by the battery crisis, "which took too long for bizarre reasons that I don't want to spend the rest of my life discussing."

After being appointed CEO, one of Stringer's goals was to encourage Sony's hardware engineers to treat software seriously when developing products. But Sony's culture celebrates proud innovators who do what they want. Many still quote an admonition by one Sony veteran: If you have the misfortune to be under a clueless boss, don't tell him about new ideas—just execute them.

In the old Sony way of doing business, executives ran independent fiefs. "We learned from the lesson that we are not developing software that way any-more," Stringer says.

Stringer bristles at the idea that he isn't committed to Tokyo. "I have a home in England and I have a home in New York—I'm already bloody cross-cultural—and I just didn't want to be in a lonely apartment somewhere in Tokyo even for symbolic reasons."

The two crises were a wake-up call. In video games, Stringer says he persuaded Ken Kutargi to give up day-to-day control of the division. He remains chair-man and chief executive, focused on next-generation games. Stringer replaced him with the U.S. head of the video-game unit, a longtime ally. In electronics, Stringer moved Nakagawa, the executive who ques-tioned the role of software, to a unit overseeing batter-ies, chips, and other components. Stringer and Ryoji Chubachi receive daily emails alerting them about manufacturing problems companywide via a product-safety officer.

One of the new developments at Sony stemming from shuffling managers is a module for TVs that allows users to watch video from the Internet using a remote control. It uses some of the same software as the PlayStation 3 console.

Stringer said the rough experiences gave him an opening to speed up his plans. "All crises create opportunities," he says. "While we were being beaten up on the one hand, it was an opportunity to acceler-ate the transformation."

Stringer's overall plan to improve Sony includes the slogan "Sony United" to encourage employees to work more closely together. He has also trimmed down the company by closing factories, eliminating jobs, and getting rid of unprofitable businesses. At the same time, Stringer has encouraged innovation and speed to help Sony regain its leadership position in the elec-tronics industry. At a management conference in 2008, he told the audience, "I'm asking you to get mad." He also asked the managers to be more energetic, bold, and imaginative in running their businesses.

### Questions

1. What leadership style should Stringer use for best effectiveness at Sony?
2. What major cross-cultural issues is Stringer facing?
3. Based on your familiarity with Sony products, what business strategy do you recommend that Stringer employ to help Sony accelerate its busi-ness progress?
4. How much sense does it make for an Ameri-canized Welshman to run an iconic Japanese company?

*Source*: Excerpted from Yukari Iwatani Kane and Phred Dvorak, "Howard Stringer, Japanese CEO: Caught Between Two Worlds, the Sony Chief Tightens His Management Grip. Will It Work?" *Wall Street Journal (Central Edition)*, March 3–4, 2007, pp. A1, A6. Copyright 2007 by Dow Jones & Company, Inc. Reproduced with permission of Dow Jones & Company, Inc. in the format Textbook via Copyright Clear-ance Center. Yukari Iwatani Kane, "Sony CEO Urges Manag-ers 'to Get Mad,'" *Wall Street Journal*, May 23, 2008, p. B8.

## Leadership Case Problem B

### Curses, Foiled Again in France

An American manufacturer of kiosk photo printers with an affiliate in Dijon, France, decided to create the position of "international liaison." This person would spend about five days per month in Dijon in the role of home-office representative. The liaison would offer some advice to European operations and function as the intermediary between the home office and Dijon.

Erin Barker, a product development manager, was a logical choice for the new position. In addition to being technically competent, Barker had good interpersonal skills and spoke French. She had studied French in high school and college and had spent one semester in France as part of her college program. In recent years, she had taken two vacations in France.

Erin still retained her position as product development manager. She planned to work at her new position about half time. Some of her responsibilities as product development manager were delegated to two specialists in the product development department. Erin was somewhat skeptical about occupying a liaison position, because it was by nature nebulous. The Dijon group would have to respect her authority because she represented company headquarters. However, the Dijon group really reported to the company CEO, not to her.

Erin prepared herself mentally for her first trip to Dijon. She gathered relevant facts and figures about the company's European business headquartered in Dijon, and listened to French language-learning CDs for two weeks. With a dry throat, and determination in her heart, Erin walked into the Dijon conference room one Monday morning for her first meeting with the French group.

Barker greeted the management team at the plant in French: "Bonjour. Je suis enchanté de faire votre connaissance. Mon séjour sera pour plusieurs jours. Je voudrais apprendre votre opération. Aussi, je voudrais expliquer les opérations du siège, et répondre à vos questions." [Hello. It's a pleasure to meet you. My stay will be several days. I would like to learn about your operation. Also, I would like to explain the operations of headquarters and answer your questions.]

"Oh, how nice, you speak a little French," said plant manager Gilles Naulleau, in English. Erin was taken aback that Naulleau and the other French managers seemed intent on speaking English. She interpreted it as a sign of their not taking her interest in them seriously. Erin also thought that her first few days in Dijon were strictly ceremonial. She felt more like a visitor on a plant tour than an executive conducting business. When Erin touched on business topics such as sales and production forecasts, the Dijon representative would typically shrug and change the subject.

The following month, Erin revisited Dijon and again met with Naulleau and Pierre Chevalier, the sales manager for France. She opened the meeting with these words: "Ma dernière visite chez vous était très agréable. J'ai apprécié l'opportunité à connaître les cadres de Dijon. Maintenant je voudrais discuter les projets liés au succès de notre entreprise." [My last visit here was very pleasant. I appreciated the opportunity to get to know the Dijon managers. Now, I would like to discuss projects linked to the success of our business.] Again, Naulleau talked mostly about superficial topics, but he did respond in a few words of French. The other managers spoke among themselves in French in her presence but held back on talking about serious business issues.

Back at headquarters, Erin met with the CEO. She discussed her seemingly slow progress in getting down to serious business with the Dijon managers. The CEO then asked whether she would like the company to assign somebody else to the job. Erin responded, "I'm not willing to say goodbye to Dijon quite yet. Give me more time to prove myself."

## Questions

1. How should Erin conduct herself in her future visits to the Dijon operation in order to get down to business?

2. Should the company replace Erin with another person for the position of international liaison? Explain your answer.

3. What message or messages about global business relationships do you extract from this case history?

## ◎ Leadership Skill-Building Exercise 14-3

### My Leadership Portfolio

To be an effective cross-cultural leader, you need to work effectively with people from demographic and cultural groups different from your own. Describe what experiences you have had lately in working with and/or relating effectively to a person quite different from you. If you have not had such an experience, take the initiative during the next week to relate meaningfully to a person quite different from you in terms of culture or demographic group membership. Finance major Stephanie had this to say:

> Claire, a special ed teacher, lives on my block. Claire goes to work every school day in spite of being legally blind. She can read with visual assists, including reading what is on her computer screen. Yet paper forms are difficult for Claire to navigate. I telephoned Claire one night and asked her if she could use my assistance in preparing her income tax this year. Claire agreed, and it worked out well. I now feel more comfortable working side by side with a visually handicapped person. Also, I picked up some practical experience in preparing a complicated tax form.

## Internet Skill-Building Exercise

### Test Yourself for Hidden Bias

To be an effective multicultural leader and to promote diversity, it is helpful to be aware of your own biases. Visit www.tolerance.org/hidden_bias, a web project of the Southern Poverty Law Center. Go to Test Yourself for Hidden Biases. Created by psychologists at Yale University and the University of Washington, this collection of Implicit Association Tests claims to measure unconscious bias in the following eleven areas: Native Americans; sexual orientation; six types of racial bias (Arab Muslims, weapons, black/white children, black/white adults, skin tone, Asian Americans); age bias; gender bias; and body image bias. After reflecting on the results of these tests, what ideas did you gather that might help you be less biased in your dealings with other people in the workplace?

**Apply the chapter concepts! Visit the Web and complete this Internet skill-building exercise to learn more about current leadership topics and trends.**

## CHAPTER 15

# Leadership Development and Succession

## LEARNING OBJECTIVES

After studying this chapter and doing the exercises, you should be able to

- Explain how leaders develop through self-awareness and self-discipline.
- Explain how leaders develop through education, experience, and mentoring.
- Summarize the nature of leadership development programs.
- Describe the nature of leadership succession.

Rich Milgram finds the psychological aspect of business *really* fascinating—the idea of examining the company as an organism, affected by its patterns and personalities. Luckily for Milgram, he owns his own business, and so, as a person with a mathematical mind and a head full of psychology, he can run Beyond.com and experiment on the human race at the same time. And he's the biggest guinea pig in the lab. (Beyond.com operates online job search systems and creates its own specialty sites.)

At one time Milgram, 39, turned a video camera on his employees during a team-building game at the company's King of Prussia, Pennsylvania, offices. When he watched the recording alone later, he noticed something: "Someone was getting frustrated too easily in the game," he said. "It related to how he interacts at work. He gets too frustrated at work, too. So now I can guide him differently, giving him smaller wins along the way."

Milgram teaches the employees; they teach him. "Learning from other people to understand myself and how to better understand my company, learning from them how to make myself a better leader—it's a constant process," he said. One time, for example, he asked his employees to describe his personality. His aggressive sales manager said Milgram was detail oriented. No way, disagreed his manager of data services. Milgram's a big-picture thinker. Perfect, Milgram thought.

Milgram knew that the sales manager loved to start new projects but needed Milgram to ground him on details. Of necessity, the data manager often became mired in detail. She needed Milgram's view of a wider horizon.[1]

The leader just described uses feedback from employees to hone his leadership approach, illustrating the importance that managers place on developing their leadership ability. The previous chapters in this book have included information and activities designed to develop leaders and enhance their effectiveness. This chapter describes how self-development can enhance leadership effectiveness, as well as the processes organizations use to develop current and future leaders. Such activities and processes are typically referred to as leadership development, or management development. One reason that leadership development is important is because unless top-level management assigns high priority to leadership development and succession planning, the company will experience a steady attrition in talent. As a result, it will be difficult for the company to cope with an upheaval such as acquiring a company with a different operating style and organizational culture.[2]

Having a separate chapter about leadership development is based on the belief expressed in Chapter 1 that leaders are both born and made. Leadership talent can therefore be developed. As Sharon Daloz Parks observes, leadership is not exclusively about having the right traits, but also involves behaviors. And these behaviors can be taught because they can be translated into doable tasks, such as learning to coach.[3] We add that traits can also be developed to some degree, as described in this chapter.

In addition to describing various approaches to leadership development, this chapter also describes leadership succession. Leadership succession is included here because an important part of leadership development is being groomed for promotion. The text concludes with a glimpse of the challenges newly appointed leaders face.

# DEVELOPMENT THROUGH SELF-AWARENESS AND SELF-DISCIPLINE

Leadership development is often perceived in terms of education and training, job experience, and coaching. Nevertheless, self-help also contributes heavily to developing leadership capabilities. Self-help takes many forms, including working on one's own to improve communication skills, to develop charisma, and to model the behavior of effective leaders. Two major components of leadership self-development are self-awareness and self-discipline.

## Leadership Development Through Self-Awareness

An important mechanism underlying self-development is **self-awareness**, insightfully processing feedback about oneself to improve one's effectiveness. Business ethicist Joseph L. Badaracco Jr. points out that leaders should learn more about themselves if they want to succeed. An example is that if you want to lead other people, you first need to reflect on how well you can manage yourself.[4]

According to two specialists in leadership assessment, many big mistakes in careers and organizations result from gaps in self-awareness.[5] For example, a managerial leader might observe that three key group members left her group over a six-month time span. The leader might defensively dismiss this fact with an analysis such as, "I guess we just don't pay well enough to keep good people." Her first analysis might be correct. With a self-awareness orientation, however, the leader would dig deeper for the reasons behind the turnover. She might ask herself, "Is there something in my leadership approach that creates turnover problems?" She might ask for exit-interview data to sharpen her perceptions about her leadership approach.

Chris Argyris has coined the terms *single-loop learning* and *double-loop learning* to differentiate between levels of self-awareness.[6] **Single-loop learning** occurs when learners seek minimum feedback that might substantially confront their basic ideas or actions. As in the example of the high-turnover leader, single-loop learners engage in defensive thinking and tend not to act on the clues they receive. Argyris offers the example of a thermostat that automatically turns on the heat whenever the room temperature drops below 68 degrees Fahrenheit (20 degrees Celsius).

**Double-loop learning** is an in-depth type of learning that occurs when people use feedback to confront the validity of the goal or the values implicit in the situation. The leader mentioned earlier was engaged in double-loop learning when she

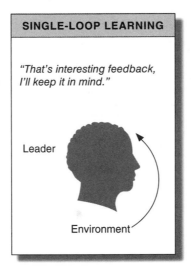
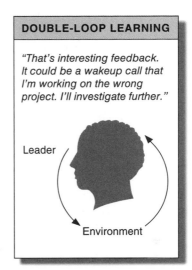

**FIGURE 15-1** Single-Loop Learning Versus Double-Loop Learning.

questioned the efficacy of her leadership approach. To achieve double-loop learning, one must minimize defensive thinking. Many people are blind to their incompetencies and do not know their vision is blocked. Argyris explains that a double-loop learning thermostat would ask, "Why am I set at 68 degrees?" The thermostat would then ask whether another temperature might more economically achieve the goal of heating the room. Figure 15-1 illustrates the difference between single-loop and double-loop learning.

An important contribution of double-loop learning is that it enables the leader to learn and profit from setbacks. Interpreting the reason that a setback occurred may help the leader to do better the next time. Faced with a group in crisis, a leader might establish a vision of better days ahead for group members. The leader observes that the vision leads to no observable changes in performance and behavior. Perhaps the group was not ready for a vision. In a comparable situation in the future, the leader might hold back on formulating a vision until the group is headed out of the crisis.

A promising new area of self-awareness is for leaders to recognize their standing on two key dimensions of leadership: forceful versus enabling leadership, and strategy versus operational. Bob Kaplan explains that the leader should not go overboard on each dimension, such as being too forceful or too enabling (empowering). A leader should also not spend so much time strategizing that operations become neglected, or so much time focusing on operations that strategy is neglected. The process of self-awareness on these two dimensions is much like volume control—raise or lower the volume to get the best result. Figure 15-2 outlines this area of self-awareness in terms of the extremes, or being lopsided. Leaders can take the Leadership Versatility Index®, which enables them to find their standing on the

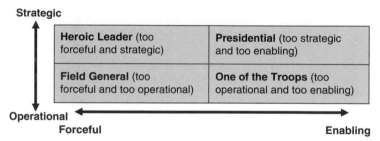

**FIGURE 15-2** Four Kinds of Lopsided Leaders.

*Source:* Based on concepts from Bob Kaplan with Rob Kaiser, *The Versatile Leader: Make the Most of Your Strengths—Without Overdoing It* (San Francisco: Pfeiffer, 2006).

two dimensions of leadership. The ideal point is to be "just right" in forcefulness versus enabling, and strategic versus operational. Feedback from others helps a leader become self-aware of his or her standing on these two dimensions.[7]

## Leadership Development Through Self-Discipline

As with other types of personal development, leadership development requires considerable self-discipline. In the present context, **self-discipline** is mobilizing one's effort and energy to stay focused on attaining an important goal. Self-discipline is required for most forms of leadership development. Assume, for example, that a leader is convinced that active listening is an important leadership behavior. The leader reads about active listening and also attends a workshop on the subject. After the reading and workshop are completed, the leader will need to concentrate diligently in order to remember to listen actively. Self-discipline is particularly necessary because the pressures of everyday activities often divert a person's attention from personal development.

Self-discipline plays an important role in the continuous monitoring of one's behavior to ensure that needed self-development occurs. After one identifies a developmental need, it is necessary to periodically review whether one is making the necessary improvements. Assume that a person recognizes the developmental need to become a more colorful communicator as a way of enhancing charisma. The person would need self-discipline to make the conscious effort to communicate more colorfully when placed in an appropriate situation. Leadership Self-Assessment Quiz 15-1 contains an interpersonal skills checklist that will help you identify your own developmental needs related to interpersonal relationships.

A key part of making self-awareness and self-discipline vehicles for personal development is to have a healthy belief in personal growth. According to psychology professor Carol Dweck, some people have a healthy belief in growth, whereby they assume that they will develop their talents during their personal and work lives. In contrast, others possess a fixed mindset, whereby they believe that talents are innate and will carry them to the top without the need for modification.[8]

## Leadership Self-Assessment Quiz 15-1

### The Interpersonal Skills Checklist

**Instructions:** Following are a number of specific aspects of behavior that suggest that a person needs to improve his or her interpersonal skills related to leadership and influence. Check each statement that is generally true for you. You can add to the reliability of this exercise by asking one or two other people who know you well to rate you. Then compare your self-analysis with their analysis of you.

#### Developmental Needs and Areas for Improvement

1. I am too shy and reserved. ☐
2. I bully and intimidate others frequently. ☐
3. I tell others what they want to hear rather than emphasizing the truth. ☐
4. I have trouble expressing my feelings. ☐
5. I make negative comments about group members too readily. ☐
6. Very few people pay attention to the ideas I contribute during a meeting. ☐
7. My personality is not colorful enough. ☐
8. People find me boring. ☐
9. I pay too little attention to the meaning behind what team members and coworkers are saying. ☐
10. It is very difficult for me to criticize others. ☐
11. I am too serious most of the time. ☐
12. I avoid controversy in dealing with others. ☐
13. I do not get my point across well. ☐
14. It is difficult for me to make small talk with others. ☐
15. I boast too much about my accomplishments. ☐
16. I strive too much for individual recognition instead of looking to credit the team. ☐
17. Self-confidence is my weak point. ☐
18. My spoken messages are too bland. ☐
19. My written messages are too bland. ☐
20. I relate poorly to people from cultures different from my own. ☐
21. I read people poorly. ☐
22. I display a lot of nervous mannerisms when I am working in a group. ☐
23. I do a poor job of making a presentation in front of others. ☐
24. _____ ☐

(Fill in your own statement.)

## Quiz 15-1 (continued)

Now that you (and perhaps one or two others) have identified specific behaviors that may require change, draw up an action plan. Describe briefly a plan of attack for bringing about the change you hope to achieve for each statement that is checked. Ideas might come from personal development books or from leadership development and human relations workshops. After formulating an action plan, you will need self-discipline for its successful implementation. For example, if you checked, "People find me boring," you might want to expand your fund of knowledge by extensive reading and by talking to dynamic people. You will then need the self-discipline to continue your quest for ideas and to incorporate some of these ideas into your conversation.

Another approach to this exercise is for each student to choose one developmental need, combined with an action plan, that he or she is willing to share with others. Next, students present their developmental need and action plan to the rest of the class. After all students have presented, a class discussion is held about whatever observations and generalizations students have reached.

# DEVELOPMENT THROUGH EDUCATION, EXPERIENCE, AND MENTORING

Much of leadership development takes place through means other than self-awareness and self-discipline or leadership development programs. Leadership is such a comprehensive process that almost any life activity can help people prepare for a leadership role. Three important life and work experiences that contribute to leadership development are education, experience as a leader, and mentoring. In the next several pages, we look at the link between each of these three factors and leadership.

### Education

Education generally refers to acquiring knowledge without concern about its immediate application. If a potential leader studies mathematics, the logical reasoning acquired might someday help him or her solve a complex problem facing the organization. As a result, the leader's stature is enhanced. Reading biographies and autobiographies about successful people is a good source of ideas about leadership. Formal education is positively correlated with achieving managerial and leadership positions. Furthermore, there is a positive relationship between the amount of formal education and the level of leadership position attained.

The correlation between education and leadership status, however, may not reflect causation. Many people get the opportunity to hold a business leadership position *only if* they have achieved a specified level of education. A more important issue than the statistical association between leadership and formal education is *how* education contributes to leadership effectiveness.

Most high-level leaders are intelligent, well-informed people who gather knowledge throughout their career. The knowledge that accrues from formal education and self-study provides them with information for innovative problem solving. Being intellectually alert also helps them exert influence through logical persuasion.

## Experience

On-the-job experience is an obvious contributor to leadership effectiveness. Without experience, knowledge cannot readily be converted into skills. For example, you will need experience to put into practice the appropriate influence tactics you studied in Chapter 8. Leadership experience also helps build skills and insights that a person may not have formally studied. Many company leadership development programs focus on giving participants varied experiences, such as Yum Brands requiring that executive leaders obtain experience managing a store.

***Challenging Experiences*** Based on the research of Morgan W. McCall, the best experiences for leadership development are those that realistically challenge the manager. Creating an environment for development requires that an organization first rid itself of the belief in survival of the fittest. The goal of leadership development is to provide meaningful development opportunities, not to push managers to the point where they are most likely to fail.[9] An example of a stretch experience for many managers would be to be placed in charge of an organizational unit with low productivity and morale. The manager would need to apply many leadership skills to improve the situation.

Failure is a special type of challenging experience that contributes enormously to reaching one's leadership potential. One reason is that people who have never failed have avoided taking big risks. Richard Branson, the flamboyant chairman of Virgin Atlantic Airways Limited, claims that "the best developer of a leader is failure." An effective way of capitalizing on failure is to reflect on what you might do differently in the future. Ask yourself questions such as "What would have to change inside me to enable me to do things differently?"[10] For example, perhaps the project failed because you did not provide enough guidance to the group and did not communicate a sense of urgency. In the future, you might lead with more control and assertion. Table 15-1 lists a number of powerful learning experiences for developing leadership and managerial skills.

An important part of capitalizing on challenging experiences is for the leader or manager to be given leeway in choosing how to resolve the problem. A team leader, for example, might be told, "Increase productivity by 10 percent and, at the same time, decrease costs by 10 percent." The team leader would have the developmental opportunity of finding a solution to this challenge.

***Sources of Experience*** The two major developmental factors in any work situation are work associates and the task itself.[11] Work associates can help a person develop in myriad ways. An immediate superior can be a positive or negative model of effective leadership. You might observe how your boss skillfully confronts a cost

**TABLE 15-1** Powerful Learning Experiences for Developing Leadership Skills

Research with managers has revealed fifteen types of powerful learning experiences that contribute to one's development as a leader and manager.

1. *Unfamiliar responsibilities.* Responsibilities are new, quite different, or much broader than previous ones. As a result the situation requires skills and abilities beyond a person's current competencies.

2. *Proving yourself.* There is pressure to show others that one can get the job done.

3. *Developing new directions.* The leader is responsible for starting something new, implementing a reorganization, or responding to rapid changes in the business environment.

4. *Inherited problems.* The manager must fix problems created by a former manager or is handed the responsibility for problem employees.

5. *Downsizing decisions.* The manager must make decisions about shutting down operations or reducing staff.

6. *Dealing with problem employees.* The group members lack adequate experience, are incompetent, or are resistant.

7. *Facing high stakes.* The manager is faced with tight deadlines, pressure from senior management, high visibility, and responsibility for success and failure.

8. *Managing business complexity.* The job is large in scope, and the manager is responsible for multiple functions, groups, products, customers, or markets.

9. *Role overload.* The size of the job requires a large investment of time and energy. An example is that suddenly you deal with a customer request way beyond the capacity of the company to handle.

10. *Handling external pressure.* The manager is forced to deal with external factors that affect the business, such as negotiating with unions or government agencies or coping with serious community problems.

11. *Having to exert influence without authority.* To accomplish the job, it is necessary to influence peers, higher management, external parties, or other key people over whom one has no formal control.

12. *Adverse business conditions.* The business unit faces a drop in revenues or a drastic budget cut. For example, it becomes necessary to raise funds from investors and you have to be humble and almost beg for money.

13. *Lack of top management support.* Senior management is reluctant to provide direction, support, or resources for the manager's major work activities or for a new project.

14. *Lack of personal support.* The manager is excluded from key networks and receives little encouragement from others about the work activities.

15. *Difficult boss.* A personality clash with the boss is evident, or he or she is incompetent.

*Source*: Adapted from C. McCauley, M. Ruderman, P. Ohlott, and J. Morrow, "Assessing the Developmental Components of Managerial Jobs," *Journal of Applied Psychology* 79, 4 (1994), 544–560. Copyright © 1994 by the American Psychological Association. Adapted with permission. Point 1 is also derived from Gretchen M. Spreitzer, "Leadership Development Lessons from Positive Organizational Studies," *Organizational Dynamics*, Issue No. 4, 2006, p. 307. Points 7 and 12 are also derived from "Moments of Truth: Global Executives Talk About the Challenges That Shaped Them as Leaders," *Harvard Business Review*, January 2007, pp. 16, 17.

overrun problem during a staff meeting. You observe carefully and plan to use a similar technique when it becomes necessary for you to confront a problem with a group. In contrast, assume that your boss's confrontational approach backfires and the group becomes defensive and recalcitrant. You have learned how *not* to confront. Members of upper management, peers, and reporting staff can also help a worker profit from experience. For example, by trial and error the worker might learn which type of praise is best for influencing others.

Work-related tasks can also contribute to leadership development because part of a leader's role is to be an effective and innovative problem solver. The tasks that do most to foster development are those that are more complex and ambiguous than a person has faced previously. Starting a new activity for a firm, such as establishing a dealer network, exemplifies a developmental experience.

An extreme approach to developing leadership skills is to be assigned responsibility for an area in which you lack the appropriate skills or knowledge of the business. An example would be appointing an operations manager as the director of marketing. According to Matt Paese of Development Dimensions International, leadership ability is the most effective way of succeeding in areas where you lack technical expertise. Among the specific leadership skills would be consulting with people who have the necessary expertise and exuding self-confidence, yet not being arrogant.[12]

*Broad Experience*   Many aspects of leadership are situational. A sound approach to improving leadership effectiveness is therefore to gain managerial experience in different settings. An aspirant to executive leadership is well advised to gain management experience in at least two different organizational functions, such as marketing and operations. **Multifunctional managerial development** is an organization's intentional efforts to enhance the effectiveness of managers by giving them experience in multiple functions within the organization.[13]

As shown in Figure 15-3, the most modest level of commitment to multifunctional management development would be for managers merely to study other functions. Studying other functions, however, is quite useful because it provides a person with the necessary background to profit from experience. Participation in multifunctional task forces indicates more commitment to the acquisition of breadth.

**High commitment**

- Complete mobility across functions, i.e., "career maze"

- Temporary (six-month to two-year) assignments outside the person's "home function"

- Brief, orientational rotation through functions

- Exposure to other functions on task forces' project teams

- Classroom education about other functions

**Low commitment**

**FIGURE 15-3** Continuum of Practical Options for Multifunctional Managerial Development.

*Source:* "Continuum of Practical Options for Multifunctional Managerial Development." Reprinted from *Organizational Dynamics*, Autumn 1992, Copyright © *1992*, with permission from Elsevier Science.

The highest level of commitment is complete mobility across functions. For example, an employee may begin in product design and then move on to assignments in marketing, manufacturing, customer service, purchasing, human resources, and so forth. Employees judged to have leadership potential are the most likely to be offered complete mobility.

A widespread practice is to assign managers to cross-functional teams to give them experience in working with other disciplines. The more urgent the purpose of the team, the more likely meaningful leadership development will take place. A case in point is the business incubator project at Schneider Electric SA, a company of 15,000 employees. The project selects about fifty high-potential employees to join "SWAT teams" that have the authority and capability to move quickly within the organization to find new opportunities and solve problems. The team leader works full-time at the project, whereas group members devote only a quarter of their time to the project. The company believes that the incubator project will become its primary sales-growth engine while giving high-potential employees experience that helps them to develop into future leaders.[14]

Achieving broad experience fits well with the current emphasis on growth through learning new skills rather than a preoccupation with vertical mobility. For example, more professionals today than in the past are willing to take a lateral move instead of a promotion if there is an opportunity to acquire new skills. For example, the manager of market research might be content to become a sales manager (a position at about the same level) in order to enhance his or her skill portfolio.

The leadership portfolio that you have been maintaining will help you capitalize on experience as a source of leadership development.

## Mentoring

Another experience-based way to develop leadership capability is to be coached by an experienced, knowledgeable leader. Quite often this person is a **mentor**, a more experienced person who develops a protégé's abilities through tutoring, coaching, guidance, and emotional support. Mentoring others is an important leadership responsibility. In some companies, such as Safeway, every manager from the CEO on down is supposed to be an active mentor.[15] The mentor, a trusted counselor and guide, is typically a person's manager. However, a mentor can also be a staff professional or coworker. An emotional tie exists between the person mentored and the mentor. To personalize the subject of mentoring, test your attitudes toward the process by taking Leadership Self-Assessment Quiz 15-2.

*Informal Versus Formal Mentoring*   Mentoring is traditionally thought of as an informal relationship based on compatibility or spark between two personalities. In reality it is a widespread practice for employers to formally assign a mentor to a new employee to help him or her adjust well to the organization and to succeed. Belle Rose Ragins and John L. Cotton conducted a study comparing the effectiveness of informal versus formal mentoring programs for men and women.[16] Three occupations were studied: engineering (male dominated); social work (female dominated); and journalism (gender integrated). Formal mentoring programs were used in all three of these occupations.

Leadership Self-Assessment Quiz 15-2

## My Attitudes Toward Mentoring

*Instructions:* Answer "Generally Agree" or "Generally Disagree" to the following ten statements.

|  | Generally Agree | Generally Disagree |
|---|---|---|
| 1. Many times in life I have taught useful skills to younger family members or friends. | ☐ | ☐ |
| 2. Few people would be successful if somebody else had not given them a helping hand. | ☐ | ☐ |
| 3. I would enjoy (or have enjoyed) being a Big Brother or Big Sister. | ☐ | ☐ |
| 4. Experienced workers should be willing to show the ropes to less experienced workers. | ☐ | ☐ |
| 5. I would like to be considered a good role model for others in my field. | ☐ | ☐ |
| 6. I have very little concern that if I shared my knowledge with a less experienced person, he or she would replace me. | ☐ | ☐ |
| 7. At least one of my teachers has been an inspirational force in my life. | ☐ | ☐ |
| 8. I am willing to drop what I am doing to help somebody else with a work or study problem. | ☐ | ☐ |
| 9. I am willing to share my ideas with others, even if I do not receive any credit. | ☐ | ☐ |
| 10. Helping others contributes toward becoming immortal. | ☐ | ☐ |

*Scoring and Interpretation:* This quiz does not have a precise scoring key. However the more of the statements that you agree with, the more likely you have the proper mental set to be a mentor.

*Source:* Andrew J. DuBrin, Coaching and Mentoring Skills, First Edition, © 2005, p. 161. Adapted with permission of Pearson Education, Inc., Upper Saddle River, N.J.

Protégés with informal mentors received greater benefits than protégés with formal mentors. Informal mentors were also perceived as more effective. The protégés with informal mentors reported that their mentors provided more career development and psychological and social support than protégés with formal mentors. Protégés with informal mentors also reported higher incomes. A possible explanation for these findings is that people who are able to attract their own mentor are more career-driven and have the type of interpersonal skills that help one earn a higher income.

Three key human resource elements are associated with a successful mentoring program. First, the human resource department in conjunction with senior management needs to set the goals of the program and base its design on those goals. Second, the program administrators must carefully pair the mentors and protégés, set realistic expectations for both parties, and follow up with the pairs to ensure that the arrangement is satisfactory. Third, top management must be committed to the program.[17] An example of a realistic goal for a given protégé might be to develop better interpersonal and strategic leadership skills.

Another approach to mentoring is **shadowing**, or directly observing the work activities of the mentor by following the person around for a stated period of time, such as one day per month. The protégé might be invited to strategy meetings, visits with key customers, discussions with union leaders, and the like. The protégé makes observations about how the mentor handles situations, and a debriefing session might be held to discuss how and why certain tactics were used.

Online, or virtual, mentoring is popular because sending email messages helps overcome barriers created by geography, limited time, and voice mail. The protégé might pose a career or work question to the mentor and receive a helpful reply that day. A major advantage of online mentoring is that it offers a wide pool of possible mentors and better matches between the mentor and the person mentored. Going online, you might be working in Chicago, yet have a good fit with a manager in San Francisco or London.

One innovation in online mentoring are web sites that link mentors and mentored employees via profiling software, modeled after dating web sites. Another innovation is virtual mentoring that makes face-to-face contact rare. With one system, an employee searching for a mentor logs onto an intranet and enters up to three career interests or skills he or she wants to develop. "Literally, in a matter of seconds you get a list of possible mentors throughout the company all over the world," says Kevin D. Gazzara, program manager of "Leading Through People" at Intel.[18]

Despite the efficiency advantage of online mentoring, some face-to-face contact with a mentor is recommended to help keep the relationship vibrant. Can you imagine somebody recommending you for promotion after having communicated with you exclusively by email and a web site?

*Impact on Leadership* Mentors enhance the career of protégés in many ways, such as by recommending them for promotion and helping them establish valuable contacts. A survey of large companies found that 96 percent of executives credited mentoring as an important developmental method, and 75 percent said mentoring played a key role in their career success.[19] High-level leaders sometimes use mentors as a way of obtaining useful feedback. For example, Melissa Dyrdhal, an Adobe systems executive, says she uses mentors because "they provide a mirror for me to reflect back on, presenting perspectives that I am unable or unwilling to see."[20] The roles of a coach and mentor can blur.

A high level of mentor involvement is to coach the apprentice on how he or she handles certain leadership assignments. The mentor is usually not physically present when the protégé is practicing leadership. A substitute is for the protégé to recap a leadership situation and ask for a critique. Wendy Lopez, the operations manager for a payroll services firm, recounts a mentoring session with her boss about a leadership incident:

> I explained to Max [her mentor and the vice president of administration] that I had some trouble motivating my supervisors to pitch in with weekend work. We had received a surge of new clients because many firms had decided to downsize their own payroll departments. Our group was having trouble adjusting to the new workload. Instead of operations running smoothly, things were a little spastic. Although I tried to explain the importance of getting out the work, the supervisors were still dragging their heels a little.
>
> Max reviewed the incident with me. He told me that I might have helped the supervisors take a broader view of what this new business meant to the firm. Max felt I did not communicate clearly enough how the future of our firm was at stake. He also suggested that I should have been more specific about how pitching in during an emergency would benefit the supervisors financially.
>
> With Max's coaching behind me, I did a much better job of enlisting cooperation the next time an emergency surfaced.

Another way in which a mentor helps a person develop as a leader is to help him or her understand the political aspects of the organization. Many career professionals search for ways to navigate the tough and competitive terrain of the world of business, and such navigation is difficult without being mentored.[21]

A challenge in having a strong mentor is to at some point no longer be regarded as his or her protégé. The mentor may have given you credibility and connections for a long time, but at some point you have to get away from the mentor's shadow in order to be perceived as a leader with your own strengths. Detaching yourself from a strong mentor is often facilitated by a few accomplishments of your own, outside the jurisdiction of the mentor.[22]

The accompanying Leader in Action profile will give you additional insight into how mentoring assists in a manager's development as a leader.

## LEADERSHIP DEVELOPMENT PROGRAMS

A time-honored strategy for developing prospective, new, and practicing leaders is to enroll them in leadership development programs. These programs typically focus on such topics as personal growth, strategy formulation, influence, motivation, persuasive communication, and diversity management. Offsite training, as described in Chapter 9, is one important type of leadership training. Many management development programs are also aimed at leadership development. The difference, however, is that management development programs offer courses that cover hundreds of topics within the functions of planning, organizing, controlling, and leading. Table 15-2 lists a sample of leadership development programs.

Leadership development has become a heavy priority for many major business and government organizations. An analysis conducted by *Fortune* concluded that no matter what business a company is in, the real business is building leaders. Without a cadre of effective current and future leaders, a company would lose

**Leader in Action**

## Compensation Consultant Kathy Van Neck Benefits from Formal Mentoring

The first time Kathy Van Neck participated in a formal mentoring program, the pairing was a flop. Van Neck, a compensation consultant, met her assigned mentor over lunch one day about six years ago. The conversation was perfectly pleasant. But neither person knew what to do or say. They never met again.

She got another shot at an arranged mentoring relationship—and that time it worked. For one year she participated in a program that paired her with Keith Hauschildt, an executive at an insurance company. In their first meeting, they talked about logistics, agreeing to meeting one Friday a month for lunch. A few days later Van Neck emailed Hauschildt a year-long schedule of proposed dates. It helped them stay on track; they rarely rescheduled their lunch dates. Setting dates far in advance is "critical to that commitment," Hauschildt says.

In their first meeting, they also discussed personal backgrounds and work styles. They talked about where they grew up, their families, and their career paths. They learned they both have nonconfrontational work styles, and that they both tend to trust people until the other breaks that trust. The conversation made Van Neck feel comfortable opening up to her mentor. "We could move as quickly as we wanted to into the heart of the matter. We didn't have to continually get to know each other," she says. The groundwork at their first meeting helped to set the foundation.

That proved invaluable when Van Neck talked with Hauschildt about the prospect of becoming a principal at her firm. She had two young children and was worried about balancing work and family. "He finally looked at me and said, 'Kathy, do you want this or not?'" Van Neck says. "I said, 'I think so,' and he said, 'You need want this more than just think so.'"

He pointed out that her bosses would sense any hesitation on her part, and probably wouldn't select her for the role. He knew she has a tendency to evaluate all sides and perspectives of an issue, which sometimes makes her seem as though she isn't being assertive or self-confident enough. "You have to understand the person's personality in order to make suggestions," Hauschildt says.

Van Neck reassessed the image she was projecting. She decided she did want to be a principal, and got it. "I made a conscious effort to become more confident in the way I was coming across," she says.

She felt comfortable asking Hauschildt for advice on more nitty-gritty matters as well. She wanted her firm to host a networking conference for participants and alumni of the mentoring program. She needed senior managers to approve the event and a modest amount of funding. She typed up a proposal and sent it to Hauschildt. He suggested she spell out the benefits for her firm more directly. She did, in five straightforward points.

"What we had set forth early on helped us naturally and quickly get into other issues we needed to deal with," Van Neck says.

### Questions

1. In what way might the advice Van Neck received about evaluating all sides and perspectives on issues help her as a leader?
2. What did Hauschildt do that made him a valuable mentor?
3. What did Van Neck do that made her enjoyable to mentor?

*Source:* Excerpted from Erin White, "Making Mentorships Work," *Wall Street Journal (Central Edition),* October 23, 2007, p. B11. Copyright 2007 by Dow Jones & Company, Inc. Reproduced with permission of Dow Jones & Company, Inc. In the format Textbook via Copyright Clearance Center.

**TABLE 15-2** A Sampling of Leadership Development Programs Offered by Universities and Training and Development Firms

The Executive Program (four-week program for senior executives involved in the strategic management of their firms)

Leadership: The New Challenges

Strategic Business Leadership: Creating and Delivering Value

Business Ethics for the Professional Manager

The Disney Approach to Leadership Excellence

Leading Change and Innovation

Leadership for an Uncertain Time

Building Better Work Relationships

Implementing Successful Organizational Change

Managing People for Maximum Performance

Portfolio Management

Developing Exemplary Leaders: Key Practices for Achieving Results

The Voice of Leadership: How Leaders Inspire, Influence, and Achieve Results

Outdoor Training

*Note:* Organizations offering such seminars and courses are the Wharton School of the University of Pennsylvania, the University of Michigan Business School, the University of Chicago Graduate School of Business, the Cornell University School of Industrial and Labor Relations, the Center for Creative Leadership, the Center for Management Research, the American Management Association, Dale Carnegie Training, the World Business Forum, the Cape Cod Institute, and the Disney Institute.

**KB Knowledge Bank**
Presents a description of key things that a leadership development program should do.
**www.cengage.com/management/dubrin**

its competitive edge. Part of the reason is that leaders are either responsible for providing innovative ideas or for creating the conditions that foster innovation (refer back to Chapter 11). One of the forces compelling companies to develop leaders is the world economy's shift from dependency on financial capital toward human capital. Hewitt global practices leader Robert Gandossy says, "Organizations need talented people a lot more than talented people need organizations." The general picture of developing leaders is to make such development part of the culture, including mentoring and offering constructive feedback on performance.[23] The more specific picture of leadership development is presented next.

Developing and training leaders is far more complex than merely sending aspiring leaders to a one-week seminar. The leadership development program has to be appropriately sponsored, carefully designed, and professionally executed.

## Types of Leadership Development Programs

In practice, the various programs for developing leaders often overlap. For ease of comprehension, we divide these programs into seven categories: feedback-intensive programs, and those based on skills, conceptual knowledge and awareness, personal growth, socialization, action learning, and coaching and psychotherapy.

***Feedback-Intensive Programs***   As implied at many places in this text, an important vehicle for developing as a leader is to obtain feedback on various aspects of your behavior. A **feedback-intensive development program** helps leaders develop by seeing more clearly their patterns of behaviors, the reasons for such behaviors, and the impact of these behaviors and attitudes on their effectiveness. Such a program also helps leaders or potential leaders find more constructive ways of achieving their goals.

The Hasbro Global Leadership Development Program includes intensive feedback. (Hasbro's successes include Mr. Potato Head, G.I. Joe, Monopoly, and Scrabble.) Each participant receives a sealed envelope containing his or her individual 360-degree assessment report. No one but the participant sees the report. Each participant chooses at least one behavior he or she would like to change. The general manager of international brands at Hasbro, for example, found out that her blind spot was listening. She was a multitasker who is always doing three things at once, and therefore was perceived as not listening. She said, "I learned that I need to stop what I am doing, look a person in the eye and focus on [him or her] when we talk to counteract that perception."[24]

An instructive point about feedback-intensive programs, as well as practically all forms of leadership development, is that the person being developed needs to follow up. If you learn that you tend to shut people off with an angry smirk on your face, unless you practice removing that smirk you have not gained much from the feedback. In the words of leadership coach Marshall Goldsmith, "If you go to a class and don't do any follow-up, it's a complete waste of time."[25]

***Skill-Based Programs***    Skill training in leadership development involves acquiring abilities and techniques that can be converted into action. Acquiring knowledge precedes acquiring skills, but in skill-based training the emphasis is on learning how to apply knowledge. A typical example would be for a manager to develop coaching skills so he or she can be a more effective face-to-face leader. Skills training, in short, involves a considerable element of "how to."

Five different methods are often used in skill-based leadership training: lecture, case study, role play, behavioral role modeling, and simulations. Since the first three methods are quite familiar, only the last two are described here. *Behavioral role modeling* is an extension of role playing and is based on social learning theory. You first observe a model of appropriate behavior, and then you role-play the behavior and gather feedback. A person might observe a video of a trainer giving positive reinforcement, then role-play giving positive reinforcement. Finally, the classroom trainer and the other participants would offer feedback on performance.

*Simulations* give participants the opportunity to work on a problem that simulates a real organization. In a typical simulation participants receive a hard copy or computerized packet of information about a fictitious company. The participants are given details such as the organization chart, the company's financial status, descriptions of the various departments, and key problems facing the organization and/or organizational units. Participants then play the roles of company leaders and devise solutions to the problems. During the debriefing, participants receive feedback on the content of their solutions to problems and the methods they used. The group might be told, for example, "Your decision to form a strategic alliance was pretty good, but I would have liked to have seen more group decision making."

A pioneering approach to simulations for leadership development is the use of multiple online role-playing fantasy games such as *Star Wars Galaxies*. One component of *Galaxies* is to make useful products and then market the products on game planets. Players advance by keeping the supply chain filled and satisfying customer demands. The players who lead teams in these online fantasies hone their business leadership skills. According to the developers of this type of simulation, the computer game helps develop the leadership skills of speed, risk taking, and the acceptance of leadership roles as being temporary.[26] Participants who have previously acquired gaming skills are fascinated by this approach to leadership development.

***Conceptual Knowledge and Awareness Programs*** A standard university approach to leadership development is to equip people with a conceptual understanding of leadership. The concepts are typically supplemented by experiential activities such as role playing and cases. Non-university learning firms such as the American Management Association and the Brookings Institution also offer conceptually based leadership development programs. Conceptual knowledge is very important because it alerts the leader to information that will make a difference in leadership. For example, if a person studies how a leader brings about transformations, he or she can put these ideas into practice. The World Business Forum is a leadership development program for well-established managers that offers considerable conceptual knowledge. The presenters are well-known executives, business professors, and authors. For example, Jack Welch, the former chairman and CEO of General Electric, makes a presentation called "Leading Successful Organizations." Table 15-2 presents examples of the types of conceptual knowledge contained in leadership development programs.

***Personal Growth Programs*** Leadership development programs that focus on personal growth assume that leaders are deeply in touch with their personal dreams and talents and that they will act to fulfill them. Therefore, if people can get in touch with their inner desires and fulfill them, they will become leaders. A tacit assumption in personal-growth training programs is that leadership is almost a calling. The executive leadership development program at PepsiCo, Inc., focuses on personal growth and business topics such as corporate strategy, ethics, and bringing about change and innovation. Jim Loehr, the psychologist heading the program, challenges the participants to reflect about their lives and identify something they want to change that will give them more energy and improved motivational skills.[27]

***Socialization Programs*** From the company standpoint, an essential type of leadership development program emphasizes becoming socialized—becoming acclimated to the company and accepting its vision and values. Senior executives make presentations in these programs because they serve as role models who thoroughly understand the vision and values participants are expected to perpetuate.[28] Many of the other types of programs presented so far also include a segment on socialization, particularly in the kickoff session. Quite frequently the chief executive makes a presentation of the company's vision and values.

***Action Learning Programs***    A directly practical approach to leadership development is for leaders and potential leaders to work together in groups to solve organizational problems outside their usual sphere of influence. You will recall that action learning is part of the learning organization, as described in Chapter 13. Much of the development relates to problem solving and creativity, yet collaborating with a new set of people from your firm can also enhance interpersonal skills.

Action learning is also referred to as experiential learning, and a key player proponent is IBM. Several years ago, the company commissioned three different teams of about thirty people to investigate three practical problems facing the company. One of these problems was "how do we add client value?" Team members sometimes do not have subject matter expertise, so they are forced to acquire new knowledge rapidly. At the same time, team members have ample opportunity to develop team leadership skill.[29]

A variation on action learning for leadership development is to send leaders abroad to work on volunteer projects. The projects are long and complex enough to develop a wide range of leadership and management skills. An example is Project Ulysses, a global leadership development program sponsored by Pricewaterhouse-Coopers. In one assignment, a partner named Tahir Ayub spent two-and-one-half months in Namibia, working with two other PwC partners helping local villages draft funding proposals for AIDS/HIV. As a consequence of this program, the participants develop global leadership skills and PwC engages in social responsibility.[30]

***Coaching and Psychotherapy***    Executive coaching as described in Chapter 10 is clearly a form of leadership development because the managers coached receive advice and encouragement in relation to their leadership skills. A coach, for example, might advise a leader that giving more recognition for good performance would make him a more dynamic leader.

Another highly personal way of enhancing leadership effectiveness is to undergo treatment for emotional problems that could be blocking leadership effectiveness. For example, a leader who has difficulty giving recognition might not improve in response to coaching. The person might have underlying problems of being so hostile toward people that he or she really does not want to boost their morale. Psychotherapy might help, but positive changes are not always forthcoming. Psychiatrist Kerry Sulkowicz notes that change does not always take place quickly. However, executives are accustomed to getting quick results, which can make them highly motivated patients.[31] In general, leaders who score low on the personality dimension of emotional stability might become more effective in their interpersonal relationships with the benefit of psychotherapy. Some of the bizarre behavior exhibited by executives, such as swearing at and belittling subordinates and arbitrarily firing workers, are symptoms of psychological problems.

Leadership development is a process that continues to evolve. The content of these programs varies to fit new opinion and research as to what is most relevant for leaders to know. For example, if the dollar is declining, seminars about dealing with the impact of this decline might be popular, as well as seminars on making the most of intuition in decision making. Although online learning supplements leadership development, face-to-face interaction with other leaders and course presenters will most likely remain popular. Leadership development programs for C-level executives are unlikely to be conducted online because executives believe that face-to-face contact with professors and other executives is an important part of the learning process.

Many companies evaluate their leadership development programs to see if they are cost effective. In a large company, for example, a comparison would be made of the ratings from superiors and subordinates for those leaders who participated in the program versus those who did not. Another method of evaluating the outcome of a leadership development program would be to compare the financial results of participants versus nonparticipants. The Knowledge Bank presents more details about program evaluation.

**KB Knowledge Bank**
Presents a description of the evaluation of leadership development efforts.

**www.cengage.com/ management/dubrin**

# LEADERSHIP SUCCESSION

In a well-managed organization, replacements for executives who quit, retire, or are dismissed are chosen through **leadership succession**, an orderly process of identifying and grooming people to replace managers. Succession planning is linked to leadership development in two important ways. First, being groomed as a successor is part of leadership development. Second, the process of choosing and fostering a successor is part of a manager's own development.

Succession planning is vital to the long-term health of an organization, and therefore an important responsibility of senior leadership. Consultant Chris Pierce-Cooke observes that companies lacking succession plans are fragile enterprises. They lose the intellectual capital that goes with the people who have left. They also lose traction, momentum, productivity, morale, and customer service. In addition, when a capable leader departs and no well-regarded replacement is named, the stock price might plunge as much as 10 percent.[32] Despite the importance of succession planning, a survey indicates only about half of public and private corporations have CEO-succession plans in place. Furthermore, most companies have not been grooming and training enough employees for promotions, and now lack the right talent for managerial positions.[33]

A concern about succession planning is that it is often done poorly, which results in leaders who are a poor fit for their responsibilities. Ram Charan reports that two out of five CEOs fail in their first eighteen months. The failure results from a variety of factors, such as making poor decisions about new products, demoralizing the organization, or engaging in highly unethical practices. One of the most important approaches to successful succession planning is to develop enough strong leaders within the company.[34] Our approach to understanding the leadership aspects of succession focuses on five topics: (1) how the board chooses a new chief officer; (2) succession planning at GE; (3) the emotional aspects of leadership succession; (4) developing a pool of successors; and (5) growing inside-out leaders. Understanding these factors should lead to more success in new appointments to leadership positions.

## How the Board Chooses a Successor

A major responsibility of the board of directors is to select a successor to the chief executive, typically a CEO. The general approach is to follow standard principles of human resource selection, such as thoroughly screening candidates, including speaking to several people who have worked with the individual. Conducting a background investigation to uncover any possible scandalous or illegal behavior is also important. When the successor is an outsider, boards consistently use executive search firms (also known as *headhunters*) to locate one or several candidates. Even when the board has an outside candidate in mind, a search firm might be hired to act as an intermediary.

George D. Kennedy, a person with experience on many boards, provides a few specifics of a representative approach to selecting an internal candidate for the top executive position. First, the information from a development program for successors must be carefully reviewed, including documentation of performance. Second, the board should have direct and regular contact with all of the promising candidates. Some of the contact should be formal; for example, the candidate should make regular presentations at board meetings. Informal connections are also important. Board members should invest the time to develop a feel for the personal chemistry of the candidates through such means as casual conversations over dinner and lunch.[35] (Because some of the decision making about succession is based on subjective judgments, it is imperative for CEO candidates to be skilled at organizational politics and influence tactics.)

## Succession Planning at General Electric

General Electric is often noted for its progressive and thorough management techniques. Its system for identifying and developing talent is considered exemplary. Leadership development is so important to the company that CEO Jeffrey Immelt reportedly invests 30 percent of his time to the process. GE-trained executives are in high demand at other business firms.

Much of this activity is linked closely to succession planning. Board members are closely involved in an ongoing evaluation of the company's 130 highest-ranking managers. Twice a year, directors scrutinize about 15 of these people. The information they use comes from lengthy interviews with the managers, their managers, former associates, and group members. Directors investigate the managers' strengths and weaknesses, make suggestions for leadership development, and discuss future assignments. Should the day arrive when a manager must be chosen to replace a higher-level manager, the board will be prepared to make an independent decision rather than have to give automatic approval to an insider's recommendations.[36]

Key advantages of the GE system for identifying successors are that it is based on multiple opinions and that it tracks longitudinal performance. Yet the system may still be replete with political biases. The board members, for example, are not exempt from giving high ratings to the people they like the best or to people who have personal characteristics similar to theirs.

## The Emotional Aspects of Leadership Succession

Leadership succession should not be regarded as a detached, objective management process. Even financially independent executives are likely to experience an emotional loss when they are replaced; they might yearn for the power and position they once possessed. Leadership succession in family-owned firms is a highly emotional process for many reasons. Family members may fight over who is best qualified to take the helm, or the owner and founder may not feel that any family member is qualified. An intensely emotional situation exists when the owner would like a family member to succeed him or her, yet no family member is willing. The business may therefore have to be sold or simply abandoned; in any case, its identity will be lost.

The emotional aspects of leadership succession are also evident when a business founder is replaced by another leader, whether or not the enterprise is a family business. After the sale of his or her company, the business founder often stays on in some capacity, perhaps as a consultant or chairperson. Watching the new owner manage the business can be uncomfortable for the founder. The issue transcends concerns about delegation. The entrepreneurial leader is typically emotionally involved in the firm he or she has founded and finds it difficult to look on while somebody else operates the firm.

Emotional reactions to leadership succession also take place at the work group level, as described in a theory recently developed by Gary A. Ballinger and F. David Schoorman. A good example is that when a departing leader is well liked by the group or team, it will be more difficult for the new leader to exert his or her authority or to be accepted. Another problem is that when the previous leader was well liked, turnover in the group will be higher, and productivity might be lower. Yet, on the positive side if the previous leader was disliked, turnover might be lower, and productivity might be higher.[37]

## Developing a Pool of Successors

Developing a pool of successors goes beyond succession planning, which usually involves identifying one or two candidates for a specific job. The steps involved in developing a pool of successors (or succession management) are as follows:[38]

- Evaluate the extent of an organization's pending leadership shortage.
- Identify needed executive competencies based on the firm's future business needs, values, and strategies.
- Identify high-potential individuals for possible inclusion in the pool, and assess these individuals to identify strengths and developmental needs to determine who will stay in the high-potential pool.
- Establish an individually tailored developmental program for each high-potential candidate that includes leadership development programs, job rotation, special assignments, and mentoring. Rising stars should be given the opportunity to change responsibilities every three to five years.
- Select and place people into senior jobs based on their performance, experience, and potential. While in these positions, the leaders should have access to board members including making presentations. The managers develop a sense of what matters to directors, and directors get to see firsthand the talent in the pipeline.
- Continuously monitor the program and give it top management support.

Developing a pool of candidates, therefore, combines evaluating potential with giving high-potential individuals the right type of developmental experiences. To the extent that these procedures are implemented, a leadership shortage in a given firm is less likely to take place.

One analysis suggests that large, family-owned businesses often have an edge in leadership succession. The reason is that potential leaders have the benefit of years of experience under the watchful eyes of their elders. Successors are identified early and provided with all of the choice assignments and mentoring they need. An example of a large family business that emphasizes succession planning is Cintas, a business uniform powerhouse that began as a rag reclamation company.[39]

A concern expressed about most methods of succession planning is that minority group members are often overlooked. People whose personality type differs from those in power might also be overlooked. The problem often arises because people nominated for key leadership positions are often those who have performed well in the best opportunities and assignments. It is often likely that these high-power experiences came about because of the candidates' resemblance to those they hope to replace. According to the Mini-Me syndrome, executives feel more comfortable when critical organizational roles are given to people similar to the incumbent.[40] When top management is sensitive to the need for more diversity in choosing successors, the problem is on the way toward resolution.

### Growing Inside-Outside Leaders

A continuing debate related to succession planning is whether a company should promote an insider or an outsider, to a top position. Recent research and analysis suggest that promoting insiders with an outside perspective may be the best solution. Joseph Bower found in his analysis of 1,800 successions that companies performed substantially better when they appointed insiders to CEO. Other researchers have reached similar conclusions. Promotion from within also offers the advantage of more hope to insiders because they believe they have more opportunity for advancement within their own company.

Company insiders promoted to a top position know the company, its culture, and its people but often do not see clearly the need for radical change. Also, their many political ties may inhibit them from making some necessary personnel shifts. Outsiders may recognize the need for a new approach but may be limited because they do not understand the company culture or the industry. Bower recommends that companies nurture *insider-outsiders*—internal candidates who have developed an outside perspective.

Insider-outsiders are frequently those who have considerable experience away from the company mainstream (and away from headquarters), and experience in taking on challenging opportunities. Before being selected as CEO of Procter & Gamble, A. G. Lafley, for instance, worked for years building the Chinese cosmetics division of the company rather than P&G's core business.[41]

## CHALLENGES OF BEING A NEW LEADER

People participate in leadership development programs for two broad purposes: (1) preparing to become a leader for the first time, or (2) enhancing their leadership skills for a current position or advancement into more leadership responsibility.

All that has been written in this book and discussed in its related course fits these two broad purposes. Another way of preparing for becoming a leader for the first time is to think through some of the inevitable challenges in the role. The information presented about the rewards and frustrations of occupying a leadership role presented in Chapter 1 points to the challenges of occupying a formal leadership position for the first time. In addition, consider these five additional challenges for the first time leader:

**1. *Uncertainty about how much time to spend leading versus doing individual tasks.*** From the first-level supervisor of entry-level workers to the chairperson of the board, leaders spend some time as individual contributors, including preparing budgets, thinking of ideas for new products, and making financial deals. As a new leader you have to work with your manager and perhaps your direct reports to find the right balance between doing and leading.

**2. *Overcoming the resentment of the people in the group who wanted your leadership position.*** If you are selected from among the group to be the new leader, you will have to deal with the resentment and envy of several direct reports who wanted your position. It can be helpful to deal openly with the issue with such statements as, "I know that other people would be equally qualified to be the leader of the group. Yet management has chosen me for this position, at least for now. I respect your expertise and I need your contribution. I also want your respect for me in my job as the chosen leader."

**3. *Building relationships and fostering teamwork quickly enough.*** As a new leader, a high priority is to build constructive relationships with subordinates as quickly as possible, using many of the techniques described in Chapter 9. Several direct reports who were your former coworkers may attempt to manipulate you and take advantage of prior friendships to receive special treatment. It is essential to build a professional, merit-based team climate as soon as possible. In the words of career coach Aya Fubara Eneli: "Friendships work best between equals. If you were already friends with some of the staff, expect those relationships to change. It's difficult to be a friend while giving orders and judging performance."[42]

**4. *Having realistic expectations about how much you can accomplish right away.*** The role of a leader/manager is not like that of a house painter—you typically do not see sparkling results right away. Patience is necessary. Many organizational leaders as well as elected officials proclaim, "Everything will be different from day one." Leadership involves building relationships, so the process will take time.

**5. *Overcoming the need to be liked by everybody.*** The most admired leaders at every level are rarely liked by everybody. By the nature of their roles, leaders make decisions that not everybody agrees with. The changes you bring about may hurt the feelings of some people and jeopardize their positions. Your role is to establish and implement goals that will result in the greatest good.

Leadership Skill-Building Exercise 15-1 may give you a few good insights into the type of leader you are becoming and how well you fit the role of a new or experienced leader.

## ◎ Leadership Skill-Building Exercise 15-1

### Building for the Future

Our final skill-building exercise, the use of a feedback circle, encompasses many aspects of leadership covered in this and the previous fourteen chapters. Ten members of the class arrange their chairs in a circle. One person is selected as the feedback "target," and the other nine people take turns giving him or her supportive feedback. Assume it is "Linda's" turn. Each person in the circle gives Linda two pieces of feedback: (a) her best leadership attribute, and (b) how she needs to develop for the future. The feedback should take about thirty seconds per feedback giver. After receiving input from all of the circle members, Linda is free to comment. It is then the next person's turn to be the feedback target.

Class members who are not in the circle observe the dynamics of what is happening and report their observations after the circle finishes. With diligence, the whole process will take about ninety minutes. If time permits, a new feedback circle can form. Alternatively, the class can break into several circles that operate simultaneously, or run just one circle with ten volunteers.

## SUMMARY

Leadership and management development are widely practiced in a variety of organizations and take many forms, including self-development. Self-awareness involves the insightful processing of feedback about oneself to improve personal effectiveness. Single-loop learning occurs when learners seek minimum feedback that may substantially confront their basic ideas or actions. Double-loop learning occurs when people use feedback to confront the validity of the goal or values implicit in the situation; it enables the leader to learn and profit from failure. A promising new area of self-awareness is for leaders to recognize their standing on two key dimensions of leadership: forceful versus enabling, and strategy versus operational.

Leadership development requires considerable self-discipline. For example, self-discipline is needed to monitor one's behavior to ensure that the necessary self-development takes place.

Education, leadership experience, and mentoring are all major contributors to leadership development.

Most high-level leaders are intelligent, well-informed people who gather knowledge throughout their career. The best experiences for leadership development are those that realistically challenge the manager. An important part of capitalizing on challenging experiences is for the leader/manager to be given leeway in how to resolve the problem. Two important aspects of leadership experience are work associates and the task itself (such as a complex and ambiguous assignment). An extreme approach to developing leadership skills is to be assigned responsibility for an area in which you lack the appropriate skills or knowledge of the business.

Broad experience is important for leadership development, as suggested by multifunctional managerial development and membership on a cross-functional team. Broad experience is also effective for career development through skill acquisition.

Another experience-based way to develop leadership capability is to receive mentoring. Although usually an informal relationship, mentoring can also be assigned. A study showed that informal mentors typically were more helpful to a person's career than formal mentors, and informal mentoring is also associated with higher income. The human resource department often coordinates a formal mentoring program. Shadowing is a form of mentoring. Mentors enhance the career of protégés in many ways, such as by recommending them for promotion and helping them establish valuable contacts. Also, the mentor can serve as a model for effective (or ineffective) leadership.

Feedback-intensive development programs help leaders develop by seeing more clearly their patterns of behavior, the reasons for such behaviors, and the impact of these behaviors and attitudes on their effectiveness. Skill training in leadership development involves acquiring abilities and techniques that can be converted into action. Such training involves a considerable element of "how to." Five methods of skill-based training are lecture, case study, role play, behavior role modeling, and simulations. During simulations, participants play the role of company leaders and devise solutions to problems. Feedback on performance is provided.

A standard university approach to leadership development is to equip people with a conceptual understanding of leadership. The concepts can be applied to leadership situations. Personal growth experiences for leadership development assume that leaders are deeply in touch with their personal dreams and talents and will act to fulfill them. Another emphasis in these programs is learning who you need to be. From the company standpoint, an essential type of leadership development is becoming socialized in the company vision and values. Action learning is a directly practical approach to leadership development and may be directed at areas outside the participant's expertise. Coaching and psychotherapy are two highly personal ways of developing as a leader. Psychotherapy is called for when the leader has emotional problems that lower his or her effectiveness.

Leadership succession is linked to leadership development because being groomed as a successor is part of a leader's development. Boards of directors use standard selection methods in choosing a CEO. In addition, they look for both formal and informal contact with insiders. When recruiting an outsider, organizations often employ executive search firms. General Electric is an example of a company that uses rigorous succession planning. Leadership succession is highly emotional for the leader who is being replaced, especially when a founder sells a business. The succession problem in a family business often leads to conflict among family members. Large family-run businesses are more likely to identify leadership successors. One way to cope with potential shortages of leaders is to identify a pool of high-potential individuals and provide them with developmental experiences. Recent research and analysis suggest that promoting company insiders with an outside perspective may be the best solution to succession through an internal versus an external candidate.

One way of preparing for becoming a first-time leader is to think through some of the inevitable challenges in the role, including the following: uncertainty about how much time for leading versus doing individual tasks; overcoming resentment of people who wanted your job; quickly building relationships and fostering teamwork; having realistic expectations about quick accomplishments; and overcoming the need to be liked by everybody.

## KEY TERMS

Self-awareness
Single-loop learning
Double-loop learning
Self-discipline

Multifunctional managerial
    development
Mentor
Shadowing

Feedback-intensive development program
Leadership succession

## ✔ GUIDELINES FOR ACTION AND SKILL DEVELOPMENT

An important method for enhancing both the acceptance and the effectiveness of leadership development is **needs analysis**, the diagnosis of the needs for development. A needs analysis is based on the idea that there are individual differences among leaders and future leaders. For example, Jennifer might have excellent conceptual knowledge about leadership but limited team experience. She might be a good candidate for outdoor training. Jack might be an excellent team leader with limited conceptual knowledge. He might be a good candidate for a leadership development program concentrating on formal knowledge about leadership. Sources of data for assessing leadership developmental needs include the following:

1. Self-perceptions of developmental needs, including the results of many of the diagnostic instruments presented in this text
2. Perceptions by superiors, subordinates, and peers of the person's developmental needs, including 360-degree survey results
3. Psychological evaluation of developmental needs
4. A statement of organizational needs for development, such as the importance of leaders who can deal effectively with diversity (within the company, with customers, and globally)

Multiple sources of data are useful because of possible errors in perception, biases, and favoritism.

### Discussion Questions and Activities

1. A reviewer commented that the information in this chapter is useful mostly for people in HR (human resources). How do you think the information in this chapter would be useful to leaders and potential leaders not working in HR?
2. Many business executives believe that playing team sports helps a person develop as a leader. Based on your knowledge of leadership development, where do you stand on this issue?
3. Where can a person get some honest feedback about his or her leadership ability?
4. Give an example from your own life in which you engaged in double-loop learning, or in which you *should* have engaged in such learning.
5. Suppose you aspired to become a senior manager in a large company. How would working as an office supervisor, production supervisor, or manager in a fast-food restaurant help you achieve your goal?
6. Why is being a member of a cross-functional team considered to be helpful experience for a future leader?
7. What are the advantages and disadvantages of having an outsider succeed the top executive in an organization?
8. What can you as a parent, future parent, or close relative do to help a child under 10 years old become a leader later in life?
9. Ask an experienced leader what he or she thinks is the most effective method of developing leadership skills. Bring your findings back to class.
10. Now that you have completed a course in leadership, what do you think of this ancient adage: "Leadership shouldn't be a popularity contest."

## Leadership Case Problem A

### The Leadership Inventory Chart at Pine Grove

Pine Grove HealthCare is a multiservice health care company providing such services as administration of company health care plans, health maintenance organizations (HMOs), employee assistance programs, and assisted living retirement communities. Last year CEO Mandy Ming recognized that Pine

Grove had grown so much that the firm needed a systematic method of identifying candidates to occupy future leadership positions in the company. To assist in this process, Ming hired human resources consultant Perry Watson.

After meeting with Ming and her staff for several hours, Watson recommended that Pine Grove implement a system of Leadership Inventory Charts. These charts, which are developed by the consultant working with top management, take an inventory of current and future leadership capability. The charts are based on performance information the company already has on hand as well as on the formulation of new judgments.

Ratings are made of both current performance and judgments about a candidate's potential for new responsibility. "Leadership potential" is a summary judgment based on such factors as current performance, charisma, conceptual thinking, and interpersonal skills. The Leadership Inventory Chart is supplemented with narrative descriptions backing up the ratings. A portion of the Leadership Inventory Chart for Pine Grove HealthCare is shown in Exhibit A.

**Exhibit A**  Pine Grove HealthCare Management Inventory Chart (Top Secret)

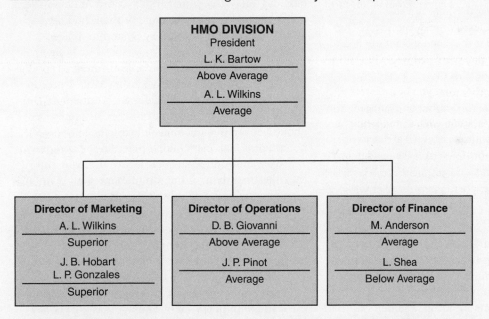

Code for ratings and names with boxes:
Rating at top of the box refers to job performance. Rating at bottom refers to potential for additional responsibility and a higher-level leadership position. Names within lower part the boxes refer to individuals considered promotable (or not promotable) to the position in question.

## Description of Performance Ratings

| | |
|---|---|
| *Superior:* | The unique, exceptional top performer. |
| *Above Average:* | Standards are usually exceeded. Carries out almost all responsibilities well. |
| *Average* | Performs most responsibilities in a satisfactory manner. Results are acceptable. |
| *Below Average* | Carries out several responsibilities unsatisfactorily. Achieves poor results. Job tenure is doubtful. |

*Continued*

**Exhibit A (*continued*)**

**Description of Potential Ratings**

*Superior:*          Person of general management potential. Exceptional leadership qualities.
*Above Average:*     Promotable person. Should be able to advance one or two levels.
*Average:*           With average growth and development is promotable to at least one higher level.
*Below Average:*     Has achieved a plateau. Considered to be nonpromotable.

Watson repeated several times to Ming and her team that the Leadership Inventory Chart should be highly confidential, that it was a succession-planning document that was not part of a person's personnel record.

I caution you not to send this information to each other by email, or to keep several copies of the Inventory Chart at several different places in company hard-copy files. Classify the document as "Top Secret." If word gets out that such a planning document exists, all of the managers involved will want to see how they rate on the chart.

I am not recommending that you be a secretive top management team. You should be discussing your evaluation of key staffers with them during performance evaluation and more informal discussions. Yet, you can create a hornet's nest if the Leadership Inventory Chart gets out.

Within one month, Ming and her staff, assisted by Watson, had prepared the Leadership Inventory Chart. Ming advised her staff, "Note that we have attached a date to this chart. The chart will be updated every quarter to reflect performance changes and perhaps any updated opinion we have about the leadership potential of our managers."

A few days before Watson, Ming, and her staff had completed the Leadership Inventory Chart, Michael Anderson, the director of finance at the HMO division, passed Perry Watson in the parking lot. After a little recollecting, he recalled that Watson was a human resources consultant specializing in leadership succession issues. Watson had consulted with Anderson's previous firm.

That night Anderson searched the Internet to find out whether Watson was still consulting in the area of management succession and preparing Leadership Inventory Charts. His findings were affirmative. Later that night, Anderson sent email messages to several other managers at HealthCare, asking them if they had heard about a Leadership Inventory System being implemented at the company. By 10:00 A.M. the next day, all of the managers to whom Anderson sent messages had replied. Not one of them had heard about a Leadership Inventory System in place.

Within fifteen minutes, Anderson sent Ming an email message requesting an appointment as soon as possible to discuss a sensitive issue. Ming freed up time at 4:45 P.M. to meet briefly with Anderson. During the meeting, Anderson explained his concerns about a covert system of evaluating the succession potential of managers taking place in the company.

"My well-founded suspicions are that you and the other members of the top management team are making judgments about the promotion potential of key members of your staff. I understand that it is part of your job to plan for the future of Pine Grove, but I think each manager should receive honest feedback about your conclusions. I, for one, want to know if I have much of a future here."

"I am not denying that making judgments about the leadership potential of managers is part of my job," replied Ming. "Yet, I am not yet ready to discuss the specifics of our system."

Ming reflected quickly that because Anderson was thought to have below-average potential, it would be awkward to discuss the Leadership Inventory with him. At the same time, Anderson was a major contributor in his present role. After these few moments of reflection, Ming said to Anderson, "Let me get back to you in a few days about this topic."

## Questions

1. What should Ming tell Anderson at their next meeting?
2. What do you see as the advantages and disadvantages of the Leadership Inventory Chart? Comment also about the confidentiality issue.
3. What should L. Shea do from a career management standpoint if he finds out that he is considered to have below-average leadership potential at Pine Grove?

## Leadership Case Problem B

### No-Holds-Barred Feedback in Aspen

Ten managers representing ten different organizations gathered at a resort in Aspen, Colorado, during late summer. The purpose was a three-day leadership development seminar, with Virginia Abrazzo as the seminar leader. For two-and-one-half days, the group engaged in a variety of activities, including lectures about strategic leadership, problem-solving groups, and scavenger hunting. The group also dined together and went on nature hikes in the mountains.

As the group gathered for its final leadership-development session, Abrazzo instructed the group, "Here we are for the grand finale. All of you have been working together, and most likely observing each other, since you arrived here two-and-one-half days ago. You are now going to experience something that could change your life, as well as make you a better leader.

"Every manager in this room is going to receive candid feedback from the nine other managers who have worked with you at our leadership development seminar. We begin by placing one of you in the center of a circle, or the hot seat. Each of the other nine participants, one by one, will look you in the eye and give you feedback about you, as a person and as a leader. After you have received your feedback from the nine other participants, you will be given a few minutes to respond."

Loads of nervous laughter arose from the group. One of the participants, Gary, said, "What's going on here? How is this ridiculous exercise going to help me get a better return on investment for our stockholders?"

Virginia replied, "Gary, you are being too defensive. Let's give this a try. You'll see the value later."

Next, Virginia smiled and said, "Who would like to go first?" Stan, an operations head from an office-building construction company, said, "I feel suicidal today, so I'll go first." Stan's feedback proceeded as follows:

*Marilyn:*  Stan, I think you are a nice guy. I would like to have a beer with you. But I think you try too hard to be liked. Ease up a bit on your likeableness.

*Bud:*  Stan, I don't think you are as nice as you appear on the surface. It's a little bit of a façade. When you get serious, you are a determined tiger. I think the combo makes you a really effective leader.

*Derek:*  Hey Stan, I noticed that you look a little nervous when you are under pressure. Like right now. If you could control your nervous tics, you would be a better leader. Look, you are scratching your face right now.

*Sara:*  Stan, I think you really have it as a leader. I notice that you can talk financials with the best of us. Yet at the same time you are likeable and approachable. I'm going to give you a gold star and a hug.

*Gerry:*  You didn't make much of an impression on me, either good or bad, Stan. And that could be a problem. A leader should stand out. You need to have a stronger presence.

*Bill:*  Stan, I notice that you are hesitant to criticize, even when you know the other person is wrong.

Remember the other day when Marilyn had the wackiest idea about downsizing I ever heard? I could tell from your face that you disagreed with her strongly, yet you just smiled.

*Lori:* Don't let all this negativity get you down, Stan. You are a straight shooter with lots of potential. I think you just need to tweak your being firm with people a little. You could be just a little more assertive.

*Hugh:* You look pretty good to me as a leader. But can't you change your hairdo? The way you set your hair makes you look like Donald Trump. Are you imitating "The Donald," because you are in the building development business? [Burst of laughter from the group.]

*Nancy:* I find it interesting that another man would be so concerned about your hairdo, Stan. I think you have loads of leadership qualities. Yet, I think you need to improve a little on how comfortably you feel working with woman as equals. I noticed a little sexist behavior, like pulling out the chair for me when I entered the conference room.

*Stan:* Thanks for all the feedback. Maybe I felt suicidal for a good reason. But seriously, I have learned a lot that will help me. I recognize that I also have a lot to work on to develop further as a leader.

Stan left the hot seat with a smile. Attention then shifted to giving feedback to the other nine participants.

## Questions

1. What value, if any, do you see in this type of feedback for purposes of leadership development?
2. What specific suggestions for development do you think Stan should take away from this feedback session?
3. If you were Virginia, the seminar leader, would you have reacted to Hugh's feedback about Stan's hairdo? Why or why not?

---

 Leadership Skill-Building Exercise 15-2

### My Leadership Portfolio

The final entry for your leadership portfolio deals more with the future than the present. As you build your leadership career in either a formal or informal leadership position, update your journal from time to time, perhaps once a quarter. Review what experiences you have had that contribute to your development as a leader. Entries might take forms such as the following:

■ In January, my company sent me to a seminar about dealing with difficult people. I came away with a few good insights about helping to turn around a difficult person, such as explaining how his or her behavior was hurting productivity and morale. I also learned that many difficult people are crying out for attention, so I will try to pay more attention to a difficult person should I encounter one.

■ We had a major flood in the area last week, and our office became inundated. We had to do something quick before we were damaged so badly that we could not serve our customers. Our supervisor was out of town. I called her on her cell phone and asked for her authorization to be in charge of organizing our salvage operation. I spearheaded an effort that helped salvage a lot of equipment and computer records. I think I really polished my crisis management skills.

## Internet Skill-Building Exercise

### A Scientific Approach to Succession Planning

Visit www.successionwizard.com, a human resources consultancy located in the United Kingdom. Go to "animated tutorials" to see a demonstration of how the Succession Wizard works. You will have a choice of six different tutorials to view. Begin with "1. Introduction," which gives a quick demonstration of the key program features. The tutorial will take you through an elaborate series of charts and dialogue boxes that help executives and human resource specialists engage in succession planning. Imagine that you are a senior executive of a company that wants to engage in serious succession planning.

1. What do you think of the potential value of the Succession Wizard?
2. Do you think it will be possible for your firm to do succession planning with such precision?
3. Why would any medium-size or large firm *not* use such a system?

**Apply the chapter concepts! Visit the Web, and complete this Internet skill-building exercise to learn more about current leadership topics and trends.**

# End Notes

## Chapter 1

1. Vanessa Fuhrmans, "The 50 Women to Watch— 1: Angela Braly, *President and Chief Executive*, WellPoint," *The Wall Street Journal*, November 19, 2007, p. R3.
2. W. Kan Kim and René A. Maubourgne, "Parables of Leadership," *Harvard Business Review*, July–August 1992, p. 123.
3. Derived from a literature review in Bernard Bass, *Bass & Stogdill's Handbook of Leadership: Theory, Research, and Managerial Applications* (New York: The Free Press, 1990), pp. 11–18.
4. Jeffrey Zaslow, "Joe Montana: Leadership, Says the Legendary Quarterback of Four Super Bowls, Means 'Being Willing to Take the Blame,'" *USA Weekend*, January 30–February 1, 1998, p. 15.
5. Brian M. Carney, "Of Tax Cuts and Terror," *The Wall Street Journal*, June 30–July 1, 2007, p. A7.
6. James Kelly and Scott Nadler, "Leading from Below," *The Wall Street Journal*, March 3–4, 2007, p. R4.
7. Keith M. Hammonds, "Leaders for the Long Haul," *Fast Company*, July 2001, p. 56; www.hoovers.com, December 6, 2007.
8. Peter Block, *Stewardship: Choosing Service over Self-Interest* (San Francisco: Berrett-Koehler Publishers, 1993), pp. 27–32.
9. Ibid., pp. 29–31.
10. Quoted on page 2 of the February 2006 issue of *Black Enterprise*.
11. James M. Kouzes and Barry Z. Posner, *The Leadership Challenge*, 3rd ed. (San Francisco: Jossey-Bass, 2002), p. 20.
12. John P. Kotter, *A Force for Change: How Leadership Differs from Management* (New York: The Free Press, 1990); "Managing + Leading = True Leadership," *Executive Leadership*, September 2004, p. 8; Edwin A. Locke and Associates, *The Essence of Leadership: The Four Keys to Leading Successfully* (New York: Lexington/Macmillan, 1991), p. 4.
13. David A. Waldman, Gabriel G. Ramirez, Robert J. House, and Phanish Puranam, "Does Leadership Matter? CEO Leadership Attributes and Profitability Under Conditions of Perceived Environmental Uncertainty," *Academy of Management Journal*, February 2001, pp. 134–143.
14. Nitin Nohria, William Joyce, and Bruce Roberson, "What Really Works," *Harvard Business Review*, July 2003, p. 51.
15. Ellen Shubart, "Success Hinges on Vital Skills Like the Human Factor," *The Wall Street Journal* (Special Advertising Section), March 29, 2007, p. D6.
16. Robert B. Kaiser, Robert Hogan, and S. Bartholomew Craig, "Leadership and the Fate of Organizations," *American Psychologist*, February–March 2008, p. 103.
17. Gary A. Yukl, *Leadership in Organizations*, 3rd ed. (Upper Saddle River, N.J.: Prentice Hall, 1994), pp. 384–387.
18. Jon P. Howell, David E. Bowen, Peter W. Dorfman, Steven Kerr, and Philip Podaskoff, "Substitutes for Leadership: Effective Alternatives to Ineffective Leadership," *Organizational Dynamics*, Summer 1990, p. 23.
19. Bass, *Bass & Stogdill's Handbook*, p. 686.

20. Shelly D. Dionne, Francis J. Yammarino, Leanne E. Atwater, and Lawrence R. James, "Neutralizing Substitutes for Leadership Theory: Leadership Effects and Common-Source Bias," *Journal of Applied Psychology,* June 2002, pp. 454–464.

21. Jeffrey Pfeffer, "The Ambiguity of Leadership," *Academy of Management Review,* April 1977, pp. 104–112.

22. Cited in Jerry Useem, "Conquering Vertical Limits," *Fortune,* February 19, 2001, p. 94.

23. Jeffrey S. Nielsen, *The Myth of Leadership: Creating Leaderless Organizations* (Palo Alto, Calif.: Davies-Black Publishing, 2004).

24. Thomas H. Hout, "Are Managers Obsolete?" *Harvard Business Review,* March–April 1999, pp. 161–162. (Books in Review)

25. J. Richard Hackman and Ruth Wageman, "Asking the Right Questions About Leadership," *American Psychologist,* January 2007, p. 43.

26. Updated and expanded from Henry Mintzberg, *The Nature of Managerial Work* (New York: Harper & Row, 1973); Kenneth Graham Jr. and William M. Mihal, *The CMD Managerial Job Analysis Inventory* (Rochester, N.Y.: Rochester Institute of Technology, Center for Management Development, 1987), pp. 132–133; Mary Jo Hatch, Monika Kostera, and Andrzej K. Koźmiński, "The Three Faces of Leadership: Manager, Artist, Priest," *Organizational Dynamics,* vol. 35, no. 1, 2006, pp. 49–68.

27. Christopher A. Bartlett and Sumantra Ghosal, "Changing the Role of Top Management Beyond Systems to People," *Harvard Business Review,* June 2002, pp. 132–133.

28. Joel Russell, "A Day in the Life of the Woman of the Year," *Hispanic Business,* April 2006, p. 30.

29. Emily Thornton, "Perform or Perish," *Business-Week,* November 5, 2007, p. 040.

30. Ronald A. Heifetz and Mary Linsky, "A Survival Guide for Leaders," *Harvard Business Review,* June 2002, pp. 65–74.

31. Thomas A. Stewart, "The Nine Dilemmas Leaders Face," *Fortune,* March 18, 1996, pp. 112–113.

32. Three examples are Martin M. Chemers, *An Integrative Theory of Leadership* (Mahwah, N. J.: Lawrence Erlbaum Associates, 1997), pp. 151–173; Francis Yammarino, Fred Dansereau, and Christina J. Kennedy, "A Multiple-Level Multidimensional Approach to Leadership: Viewing Leadership Through an Elephant's Eye,"

*Organizational Dynamics,* Winter 2001, pp. 149–162; Bruce J. Avolio, "Promoting More Integrative Strategies for Leadership Theory-Building," *American Psychologist,* January 2007, pp. 25–33.

33. Avolio, "Promoting More Integrative Strategies," pp. 25, 31.

34. Cited in "Firms Cite People Skills as Essential for Leaders," *Human Resource Management,* July 2002, p. 11.

35. Hackman and Wageman, "Asking the Right Questions," p. 45.

36. Barbara Kellerman, "What Every Leader Needs to Know About Followers," *Harvard Business Review,* December 2007, pp. 84–91.

37. Robert E. Kelley, "In Praise of Followers," *Harvard Business Review,* November–December 1988, pp. 142–148.

38. Warren Bennis, "The End of Leadership: Exemplary Leadership Is Impossible Without Full Inclusion, Initiatives, and Cooperation of Followers," *Organizational Dynamics,* Summer 1999, pp. 76–78.

### Chapter 2

1. Excerpted from Alan Huges, "Bringing the Sizzle Back to McDonald's," *Black Enterprise,* September 2007, pp. 100–106.

2. Stephen J. Zaccaro, "Trait Based Perspectives of Leadership," *American Psychologist,* January 2007, p. 6.

3. Shelley A. Kirkpatrick and Edwin A. Locke, "Leadership: Do Traits Matter?" *Academy of Management Executive,* May 1991, pp. 48–60; Zaccaro, "Trait Based Perspectives," p. 11.

4. George P. Hollenbeck and Douglas T. Hall, "Self-Confidence and Leader Performance," *Organizational Dynamics,* no. 3, 2004, p. 254.

5. Ibid., pp. 254–269; Rosabeth Moss Kanter, *Confidence* (New York: Crown Business, 2004).

6. Stephen G. Harrison, "Leadership and Hope Go Hand in Hand," *Executive Leadership,* June 2002, p. 8.

7. Jim Collins, "Level 5 Leadership: The Triumph of Humility and Fierce Resolve," *Harvard Business Review,* January 2001, p. 70.

8. Gareth R. Jones and Jennifer M. George, "The Experience and Evolution of Trust: Implications for Cooperation and Teamwork," *Academy of Management Review,* July 1998, pp. 531–546;

Jenny C. McCune, "That Elusive Thing Called Trust," *Management Review*, August 1998, pp. 10–16.

9. Roy J. Lewicki, Daniel McAllister, and Robert J. Bies, "Trust and Distrust: New Relationships and Realities," *Academy of Management Review*, July 1998, p. 439.

10. Survey reported in Eric Krell, "Do They Trust You?" *HR Magazine*, June 2006, p. 60.

11. Robert Glaser, "Paving the Road to Trust," *HRfocus*, January 1997, p. 5; Thomas A. Stewart, "Whom Can You Trust? It's Not So Easy to Tell," *Fortune*, June 12, 2000, p. 334; "4 Keys to Building Trust Quickly," *Manager's Edge*, March 2005, p. 4.

12. Kurt T. Kirks and Donald L. Ferrin, "Trust in Leadership: Meta-Analytic Findings and Implications for Research and Practice," *Journal of Applied Psychology*, August 2002, pp. 611–628.

13. Linda Tischler, "IBM's Management Makeover," *Fast Company*, November 2004, pp. 112–113.

14. Bill George, Peter Sims, Andrew N. McClean, and Diana Mayer, "Discovering Your Authentic Leadership," *Harvard Business Review*, February 2007, p. 130.

15. Ibid., pp. 129–138.

16. Timothy A. Judge, Joyce E. Bono, Remus Ilies, and Megan W. Gerhardt, "Personality and Leadership: A Qualitative and Quantitative Review," *Journal of Applied Psychology*, August 2002, pp. 765–780.

17. "The Hot Seat: Leadership in the 90s Is a Different Ball Game," *Executive Strategies*, September 1992, p. 1.

18. Jared Sandberg, "The Office Pessimists May Not be Lovable, But Are Often Right," *The Wall Street Journal*, November 27, 2007, p. B1.

19. Quoted in "Leadership Concepts," *Executive Strategies*, July 9, 1991, p. 1.

20. Eric J. Romeo and Kevin W. Cruthirds, "The Use of Humor in the Workplace," *Academy of Management Perspectives*, May 2006, pp. 60, 63–64.

21. "Randy Komisar: Virtual CEO," *Success*, December–January 2001, p. 29.

22. "Starbucks: More Than a Caffeine High," *Executive Leadership*, August 2006, p. 4.

23. Daniel Goleman, "What Makes a Leader?" *Harvard Business Review*, November–December 1998, p. 94. For more research supporting the same conclusion, see Jennifer Laabs, "Emotional Intelligence at Work," *Workforce*, July 1999, pp. 68–71.

24. Daniel Goleman, Richard Boyatzis, and Annie McKee, "Primal Leadership: The Hidden Driver of Great Performance," *Harvard Business Review*, December 2001, pp. 42–51.

25. "How Coke Bottled Up Heyer's Flair," *Executive Leadership*, August 2004, p. 4.

26. Marcus Baram, "Misconduct in the Corner Office," abcnews.go.com, April 11, 2007.

27. Lynette M. Loomis, "Use Emotions to Guide Thinking, Enhance Results," Rochester, New York, *Democrat and Chronicle*, October 21, 2007, p. 2E.

28. Goleman, Boyatzis, and McKee, "Primal Leadership," pp. 42–51.

29. Kathleen K. Reardon, "Courage as a Skill," *Harvard Business Review*, January 2007, p. 63.

30. David C. McClelland and Richard Boyatzis, "Leadership Motive Pattern and Long-Term Success in Management," *Journal of Applied Psychology*, December 1982, p. 727.

31. Locke and Associates, *The Essence of Leadership: The Four Keys to Leading Successfully* (New York: Lexington/Macmillan, 1992), p. 22.

32. Quoted in Jeffrey Pfeffer, "The Courage to Rise Above," *Business 2.0*, May 2006, p. 86.

33. Locke and Associates, *The Essence of Leadership*, p. 22.

34. John B. Miner, Normal R. Smith, and Jeffrey S. Bracker, "Role of Entrepreneurial Task Motivation in the Growth of Technologically Innovative Firms," *Journal of Applied Psychology*, August 1989, p. 554.

35. Matthew Rand, "Medicine Man," *Forbes*, November 27, 2006, p. 152.

36. Cited in Julie Cohen Mason, "Leading the Way to the 21st Century," *Management Review*, October 1992, p. 19.

37. Timothy A. Judge, Amy E. Colbert, and Remus Ilies, "Intelligence and Leadership: A Quantitative Review and Test of Theoretical Propositions," *Journal of Applied Psychology*, June 2004, pp. 542–552.

38. Pete Engardio, "The Last Rajah," *BusinessWeek*, August 13, 2007, p. 049.

39. Alex Taylor III, "Toyota's Secret Weapon," *Fortune*, August 23, 2004, pp. 60, 62; "Chrysler Executive Seeks Vehicle Tuneup," detnews.com, October 2, 2007.

40. Quoted in Carol Hymowitz, "Leaders Must Produce Bold New Blueprints in Era of Architect CEO," *The Wall Street Journal*, April 17, 2006, p. B1.

41. Robert D. Hof, "Back to the Future at Yahoo!" *BusinessWeek*, July 2, 2007, p. 035.

42. From Jeffrey E. Garten, *The Mind of the C.E.O.* (Cambridge, Mass.: Perseus Publishing, 2001), as quoted in "Random Wisdom," *Executive Leadership*, April 4, 2002, p. 1.

43. Justin Menkes, *Executive Intelligence: What All Great Leaders Have* (New York: Collins, 2006); Dean Foust, "How to Pick a Business Brain," *BusinessWeek*, February 20, 2006, p. 104.

44. Robert J. Sternberg, "A Systems Model of Leadership: WICS," *American Psychologist*, January 2007, pp. 34–42; "The WICS Approach to Leadership: Stories of Leadership and the Structures and Processes that Support Them," *The Leadership Quarterly*, June 2008, pp. 360–371.

45. "How Stanford Is Grooming Next Business Leaders," *The Wall Street Journal*, May 29, 2007, p. B6.

46. Goleman, "What Makes a Leader?" p. 97.

47. Quoted in "Practice Makes Perfect for Leaders, Too," *HR Magazine*, December 2005, p. 14.

48. Kirkpatrick and Locke, "Leadership: Do Traits Matter?" p. 59.

49. Cited in Frances Hesselbein, Marshall Goldsmith, and Richard Beckhard, eds., *The Leader of the Future* (San Francisco: Jossey-Bass, 1996).

50. Zacarro, "Trait-Based Perspectives," p. 14.

### Chapter 3

1. Geoff Colvin, "Xerox's Inventor-in-Chief," *Fortune*, July 9, 2007, pp. 69, 70.

2. Jack and Suzy Welch, "It's Not About Empty Suits," *BusinessWeek*, October 16, 2006, p. 032.

3. Jay A. Conger and Rabindra N. Kanungo, *Charismatic Leadership in Organizations* (Thousand Oaks, Calif.: Sage Publications, 1998).

4. Comment by Hugh Hefner, founder and editor-in-chief of Playboy Enterprises, included in advertisement in *The Wall Street Journal*, December 13, 2007, p. C8.

5. Daniel Lyons, "Digital Tools: Big Brother," *Forbes*, October 1, 2007, p. 51.

6. Juan-Carlos Pastor, James R. Meindl, and Margarit C. Mayo, "A Network Effects Model of Charisma Attributions," *Academy of Management Journal*, April 2002, pp. 410–420.

7. Cited in Jay A. Conger, *The Charismatic Leader: Beyond the Mystique of Exceptional Leadership* (San Francisco: Jossey-Bass, 1989).

8. William L. Gardner and Bruce J. Avolio, "The Charismatic Relationship: A Dramaturgical Perspective," *Academy of Management Review*, January 1998, pp. 32–58.

9. Angelo Fanelli and Vilmos F. Misangyi, "Bringing Out Charisma: CEO Charisma and External Stakeholders," *Academy of Management Review*, October 2006, p. 1053.

10. Eugene Schmuckler, book review in *Personnel Psychology*, Winter 1989, p. 881.

11. Jane A. Halpert, "The Dimensionality of Charisma," *Journal of Business Psychology*, Summer 1990, p. 401.

12. Jeffrey D. Kudisch et al., "Expert Power, Referent Power, and Charisma: Toward the Resolution of a Theoretical Debate," *Journal of Business and Psychology*, Winter 1995, pp. 177–195.

13. Randall Smith and Ann Davis, "In Bloodletting on Street, Cruz Is Latest Casualty," *The Wall Street Journal*, November 30, 2007, p. C1.

14. Conger, Kanungo, and Associates, *Charismatic Leadership*; Bernard M. Bass, *Bass & Stogdill's Handbook of Leadership: Theory, Research, & Managerial Applications*, 3rd ed. (New York: The Free Press, 1990), pp. 185–186.

15. Michael E. Brown and Linda K. Treviño, "Socialized Charismatic Leadership, Values Congruence, and Deviance in Work Groups," *Journal of Applied Psychology*, July 2006, pp. 954–962.

16. Jane M. Howell and Boas Shamir, "The Role of Followers in the Charismatic Leadership Process: Relationships and Their Consequences," *Academy of Management Review*, January 2005, p. 100.

17. Ibid.

18. Mark Greer, "The Science of Savoir Faire," *Monitor on Psychology*, January 2005, pp. 28–39; Jane M. Howell and Bruce Avolio, "The Ethics of Charismatic Leadership: Submission or Liberation?" *The Academy of Management Executive*, May 1992, pp. 43–52.

19. Research reported in "This Is Your Brain on the Job," *The Wall Street Journal*, September 20, 2007, pp. B1, B6.

20. Cited in "Vision and Mission: Know the Difference," *Executive Leadership*, February 2006, p. 1.

21. Jim Collins, "Aligning Action and Values," Leader to Leader Institute, http://leadertoleader.org, as reported in "Actions: Louder Than Vision Statements," *Executive Leadership*, May 2004, p. 8.

22. A couple of the ideas in the list are from "Nailing Down Your Vision: 8 Steps," *Executive Leadership*, September 2007, p. 2.

23. Howell and Avolio, "The Ethics of Charismatic Leadership," p. 46.

24. Noel Tichy and Christopher DeRose, "Roger Enrico's Master Class," *Fortune*, November 27, 1995, p. 406.

25. Jay A. Conger, "Inspiring Others: The Language of Leadership," *The Academy of Management Executive*, February 1991, p. 39.

26. Ibid.

27. Peter Guber, "The Four Truths of the Storyteller," *Harvard Business Review*, December 2007, p. 56.

28. Mark Lasswell, "Fabulists at the Firm," *The Wall Street Journal*, January 9, 2004, p. W11; Stephen Denning, *The Secret Language of Leadership: How Leaders Inspire Action Through Narrative* (New York: Wiley, 2007).

29. Dennis A. Romig, *Side by Side Leadership: Achieving Outstanding Results Together* (Marietta, Ga.: Bard Press, 2001), p. 157.

30. Research cited in Greer, "The Science of Savoir Faire," p. 30.

31. Jeninne Lee-St. John, "It's a Brand-You World," *Time*, November 6, 2006, pp. 60–61, 78.

32. Karl Taro Greenfield, "Ralph's Rough Ride," *Time*, March 15, 1999, p. 50.

33. Kris Maher, "The Jungle: Focus on Recruitment, Pay and Getting Ahead," *The Wall Street Journal*, July 13, 2004, p. B6; Suzanne Hoppough, "Image Doctor," *Forbes*, February 26, 2007, p. 60.

34. Marshall Sashkin and Molly G. Sashkin, *Leadership That Matters: The Critical Factors for Making a Difference in People's Lives and Organizations' Success* (San Francisco: Berrett-Koehler, 2003).

35. Bernard M. Bass, "Does the Transactional-Transformational Leadership Paradigm Transcend National Boundaries?" *American Psychologist*, February 1997, p. 130.

36. "Greg Brenneman Named Quiznos President and CEO," www.qsrmagazine.com, January 9, 2007.

37. Joann S. Lublin and Steven Gray, "Burger King Set to Put Brenneman in CEO's Office," *The Wall Street Journal*, July 13, 2004, pp. A3, A6; Brian Grow, "Fat's in the Fire for This Burger King," *BusinessWeek*, November 8, 2004, pp. 069–070.

38. John J. Hater and Bernard M. Bass, "Superiors' Evaluations and Subordinates' Perceptions of Transformational and Transactional Leadership," *Journal of Applied Psychology*, November 1988, p. 65; Noel M. Tichy and Mary Anne Devanna, *The Transformational Leader* (New York: Wiley, 1990).

39. Peter Koestenbaum, *Leadership: The Inner Side of Greatness* (San Francisco: Jossey-Bass, 1991).

40. Alan J. Dubinsky, Francis J. Yammarino, and Marvin A. Jolson, "An Examination of Linkages Between Personal Characteristics and Dimensions of Transformational Leadership," *Journal of Business and Psychology*, Spring 1995, p. 316.

41. Carlos Ghosn, "First Person: Saving the Business Without Losing the Company," *Harvard Business Review*, January 2002, p. 40.

42. W. Chan Kim and Renée Mauborgne, "Tipping Point Leadership," *Harvard Business Review*, April 2003, pp. 65–66.

43. Literature reviewed in Sally A. Carless, Alexander J. Wearing, and Leon Mann, "A Short Measure of Transformational Leadership," *Journal of Business and Psychology*, Spring 2000, pp. 389–405; Joyce E. Bono and Timothy A. Judge, "Personality and Transformational and Transactional Leadership: A Meta-Analysis," *Journal of Applied Psychology*, October 2004, pp. 901–910; Taly Dvir, Dov Eden, Burce J. Avolio, and Boas Shamir, "Impact of Transformational Leadership on Follower Development and Performance: A Field Experiment," *Academy of Management Journal*, August 2002, pp. 735–744.

44. Timothy A. Judge and Joyce E. Bono, "Five-Factor Model of Personality and Transformational Leadership," *Journal of Applied Psychology*, October 2000, pp. 751–765; Bono and Judge, "Personality and Transformational and Transactional Leadership," pp. 901–910.

45. Barbara Mandell and Shilpa Pherwani, "Relationship Between Emotional Intelligence and Transformational Leadership Style: A Gender Comparison," *Journal of Business and Psychology*, Spring 2003, pp. 387–404; Robert S. Rubin, David C. Munz, and William H. Bommer, "Leading from Within: The Effects of Emotional Recognition and Personality on Transformational Leadership Behavior," *Academy of Management Journal*, October 2005, pp. 845–856.

46. Nick Turner et al., "Transformational Leadership and Moral Reasoning," *Journal of Applied Psychology*, April 2002, pp. 304–311.

47. Ronald F. Piccolo and Jason A. Colquitt, "Transformational Leadership and Job Behaviors: The Mediating Role of Core Job Characteristics," *Academy of Management Journal*, April 2006, p. 327.

48. Joyce E. Bono, Hannah Jackson Foldes, Gregory Vinson, and John P. Muros, "Workplace Emotions: The Role of Supervision and Leadership," *Journal of Applied Psychology*, September 2007, pp. 1357–1367.

49. Timothy A. Judge and Ronald F. Piccolo, "Transformational and Transactional Leadership: A Meta-Analytic Test of Their Relative Validity," *Journal of Applied Psychology*, October 2004, pp. 755–768.

50. Jane M. Howell and Bruce J. Avolio, "Transformational Leadership, Transactional Leadership, Locus of Control, and Support for Innovation: Key Predictors of Consolidated-Business-Unit Performance," *Academy of Management Journal*, August 1998, pp. 387–409.

51. John Schaubroeck, Simon S. K. Lam, and Sandra E. Cha, "Embracing Transformational Leadership: Team Values and the Impact of Leader Behavior on Team Performance," *Journal of Applied Psychology*, July 2007, pp. 1020–1030.

52. Warren G. Bennis and Burt Nanus, *Leaders: Strategies for Taking Charge* (New York: Harper & Row, 1985), p. 223.

53. Bradley R. Agle, Nandu J. Nagarajan, Jeffrey A. Sonnefeld, and Dhinu Srinivasan, "Does CEO Charisma Matter? An Empirical Analysis of the Relationships Among Organizational Performance, Environmental Uncertainty, and Top Management Team Perceptions of CEO Charisma," *Academy of Management Journal*, February 2006, pp. 161–174.

54. Robert C. Tucker, "The Theory of Charismatic Leadership," *Daedalus*, Summer 1968, pp. 731–756.

55. Quoted in Greer, "The Science of Savoir Faire," p. 30.

56. The first six items on the list are from Roger Dawson, *Secrets of Power Persuasion: Everything You'll Need to Get Anything You'll Ever Want* (Upper Saddle River, N.J.: Prentice Hall, 1992), pp. 179–194; the last item is from James M. Kouzes and Barry Z. Posner, *The Leadership Challenge*, 3rd ed. (San Francisco: Jossey-Bass, 2002), p. 158.

## Chapter 4

1. Excerpted from Carol Hymowitz, "Two Football Coaches Have a Lot to Teach Screaming Managers," *The Wall Street Journal (Central Edition)*, January 29, 2007, p. B1. Copyright 2007 by Dow Jones & Company, Inc. Reproduced with permission of Dow Jones & Company, Inc. In the format Textbook via Copyright Clearance Center.

2. Ralph M. Stogdill and Alvin E. Coons, eds., *Leader Behavior: Its Description and Measurement* (Columbus, O.: The Ohio State University Bureau of Business Research, 1957); Carroll L. Shartle, *Executive Performance and Leadership* (Upper Saddle River, N.J.: Prentice Hall, 1956).

3. Margaret Littman, "Best Bosses Tell All," *Working Woman*, October 2000, p. 50; *Chain Leader* (www.chainleader.com), November 1, 2007, p. 1.

4. Terry Leap, "Keys to Spotting a Flawed CEO—Before It's Too Late," *The Wall Street Journal*, December 1–2, 2007, p. R3.

5. Stanley Holmes, "Boeing's Favorite Supergeek," *BusinessWeek*, September 6, 2004, p. 101; www.boeing.com, October 2007.

6. Timothy A. Judge, Ronald F. Piccolo, and Remus Ilies, "The Forgotten Ones? The Validity of Consideration and Initiating Structure in Leadership Research," *Journal of Applied Psychology*, February 2004, pp. 36–51.

7. Larry Bossidy, "What Your Leader Expects of You, and What You Should Expect in Return," *Harvard Business Review*, April 2007, p. 64.

8. Geoffrey Colvin, "What Makes GE Great?" *Fortune*, March 6, 2006, p. 96.

9. Marcus Buckingham, "What Great Managers Do," *Harvard Business Review*, March 2005, pp. 70–79.

10. Desa Philadelphia, "Q&A: Larry Bossidy on Execution." *Time Global Business*, July 2002, p. B5. See also Larry Bossidy and Ram Charan, *Execution: The Discipline of Getting Things Done* (New York: Crown Business, 2002).

11. Cited in Jacinthe Tremblay, <<Les Ravages de la Macro Gestion,>> *Lapressaffaires.cyberpresse*, le 10 juin, 2007, p. 1. ["The Ravages of Macromanagement," June 10, 2007.]

12. Joann S. Lublin, "Top Brass Try Life in the Trenches," *The Wall Street Journal*, June 25, 2007, p. B1.

13. Quoted in David Kiley, "The New Heat on Ford," *BusinessWeek*, June 4, 2007, p. 035.

14. "A CEO on the Go: Randy Komisar on the Art of Snap Leadership," *Executive Strategies*, July 2000, p. 3.

15. John P. Kotter, "What Leaders Really Do," *Harvard Business Review*, May–June 1990, pp. 105–106.

16. Tom Lowry, "The NFL Machine," *BusinessWeek*, January 27, 2003, p. 088.

17. James R. Detert and Ethan R. Burris, "Leadership Behavior and Employee Voice: Is the Door Really Open?" *Academy of Management Journal*, August 2007, p. 871.

18. David Kirkpatrick, "Inside Sam's $100 Billion Growth Machine," *Fortune*, June 14, 2004, p. 88.

19. Geoffrey Colvin, "How One CEO Learned to Fly," *Fortune*, October 30, 2006, p. 98.

20. Jerry Newman, *My Secret Life on the McJob* (New York: McGraw-Hill, 2007).

21. "Carrot & Stick Failing? Try Encouragement," *Executive Leadership*, July 2007, p. 4.

22. "Covey Proposes Principle-Based Leadership," *Management Review*, September 1995, p. 21.

23. Bill George, *Authentic Leadership* (San Francisco: Jossey-Bass, 2003).

24. George, *True North* (New York: Wiley, 2007); Erin White, "'Authentic' Ways of Leading," *The Wall Street Journal*, December 3, 2007, p. B3.

25. Robert K. Greenleaf, *The Power of Servant Leadership* (San Francisco: Berrett-Koehler Publishers, 1998).

26. Based on Robert K. Greenleaf, *Servant Leadership: A Journey into the Nature of Legitimate Power and Greatness* (Mahwah, N.J.: Paulist Press, 1997); Michael Useem, "The Leadership Lessons of Mt. Everest," *Harvard Business* (Paulist Press, 1997); Robert C. Liden, Sandy J. Wayne, Hao Zhao, and David Henderson, "Servant Leadership: Development of a Multidimensional Measure and Multi-Level Assessment," *The Leadership Quarterly*, April 2008, pp. 161–177.

27. "Be a Leader, Not a Pal," *Manager's Edge*, March 2007, p. 3.

28. "The Essence of Servant Leadership," *Manager's Edge*, January 2004, p. 3.

29. Liden et al., "Servant Leadership: Development of a Multidimensional Measure," p. 172.

30. Ginka Toegel and Jay A. Conger, "360-Degree Assessment: Time for Reinvention," *Academy of Management Learning and Education*, September 2003, pp. 297–311.

31. Bruce Pfau and Ira Kay, "Does 360-Degree Feedback Negatively Affect Company Performance?" *HR Magazine*, June 2002, pp. 58–59.

32. The research of Michael Useem reported in Bill Breen, "Trickle-Up Leadership," *Fast Company*, November 2001, p. 70.

33. Craig L. Pearse, "The Future of Leadership: Combining Vertical and Shared Leadership to Transform Knowledge Work," *Academy of Management Executive*, February 2004, pp. 47–57.

34. "Ricardo Semler's Huge Leap of Faith," *Executive Leadership*, April 2006, p. 6.

35. Anders Skogstad et al., "The Destructiveness of Laissez-faire Leadership Behavior," *Journal of Occupational Health Psychology*, no. 1, 2007, pp. 80–92.

36. Hector Ruiz, "Chipping Away at Intel," *Fortune*, November 1, 2004, p. 112.

37. Gina Chon and Joann S. Lublin, "Chrysler's New Era Begins Under Nardelli," *The Wall Street Journal*, August 7, 2007, p. A7; David Welch and David Kiley, "'Fresh Eyes'—and a Sharp Ax," *BusinessWeek*, August 20 and 27, 2007, p. 035.

38. Brian Grow, "Out at Home Depot," *BusinessWeek*, January 15, 2007, p. 060.

39. Robert R. Blake and Anne Adams McCanse, *Leadership Dilemmas—Grid Solutions* (Houston: Gulf Publishing, 1991); http://www.gridinternational .com/gridtheory.html, 2007.

40. J. Robert Baum and Edwin A. Locke, "The Relationship of Entrepreneurial Traits, Skill, and Motivation to Subsequent Venture Growth," *Journal of Applied Psychology*, August 2004, pp. 587–598; Gayle Sato Stodder, "Goodbye Mom & Pop: The Neighborhood's Not Big Enough for Today's Entrepreneur. Only the World Will Do," *Entrepreneur*, May 1999, pp. 145–151.

41. Pui-Wing Tam, "The Other Tech CEOs Find It's Not Easy to Keep the Faith," *The Wall Street Journal*, December 12, 2007, p. B1.

42. Judy Rosener, "Ways Women Lead," *Harvard Business Review*, November–December 1990, pp. 119–125.

43. Debra Phillips, "The Gender Gap," *Entrepreneur*, May 1995, pp. 110, 111.

44. Robert J. Kabacoff, "Gender Differences in Organizational Leadership," Management Research

Group, Portland, Me., as reported in "Do Men and Women Lead Differently?" *Leadership Strategies,* Premier Issue, copyright 2001, Briefings Publishing Group.

45. Research reported in Michael Schrage, "Why Can't a Woman Be More Like a Man?" *Fortune,* August 16, 1999, p. 184.

46. Much of the research on this topic is summarized in Mary Crawford, *Talking Difference: On Gender and Language* (London: Sage Publications, 1995).

47. Jan Grant, "Women Managers: What Can They Offer Organizations?" *Organizational Dynamics,* Winter 1988, pp. 56–63.

48. Carol Hymowitz, "Women Swell Ranks as Middle Managers, But Are Scarce at the Top," *The Wall Street Journal*, July 24, 2006, p. B1.

49. Alice H. Eagly and Linda L. Carli, "Women and the Labyrinth of Leadership," *Harvard Business Review*, September 2007, p. 66.

50. Daniel Goleman, "Leadership That Gets Results," *Harvard Business Review,* March–April 2000, pp. 78–90.

51. Felix Brodbeck, Michael Frese, and Mansour Havidan, "Leadership Made in Germany: Low on Compassion, High on Performance," *Academy of Management Executive*, February 2002, pp. 16–30.

52. Ralph M. Stogdill, "Historical Trends in Leadership Theory and Research," *Journal of Contemporary Business*, Autumn 1974, p. 7.

53. "Directive Management or Not?" *Working SMART*, December 1992, p. 3.

### Chapter 5

1. "The 101 Dumbest Moments in Business: They Had Such High Hopes," *Fortune*, December 24, 2007, p. 152.

2. "Surprising and Effective Cure for Today's Biggest Workplace Crisis," *Executive Focus*, September 2004, p. 21.

3. Victor H. Vroom and Arthur G. Jago, "The Role of the Situation in Leadership," *American Psychologist*, January 2007, pp. 6–16.

4. For a synthesis of contingency theory by one of its key researchers, see Martin M. Chemers, *An Integrative Theory of Leadership* (Mahwah, N.J.: Erlbaum, 1997), pp. 28–38. See also Fred E. Fiedler, Martin M. Chemers, and Linda Mahar, *Improving Leadership Effectiveness*: *The*

*Leader-Match Concept*, 2nd ed. (New York: Wiley, 1994).

5. Vroom and Jago, "The Role of the Situation," p. 20.

6. Robert J. House, "A Path-Goal Theory of Leader Effectiveness," *Administrative Science Quarterly,* September 1971, pp. 321–328; Robert T. Keller, "A Test of the Path-Goal Theory with Need for Clarity as a Moderator in Research and Development Organizations," *Journal of Applied Psychology*, April 1989, pp. 208–212; Robert J. House and Terence R. Mitchell, "Path-Goal Theory of Leadership," *Journal of Contemporary Business,* Autumn 1974, pp. 81–97.

7. Vroom and Jago, "The Role of the Situation," p. 20.

8. Robert House, "Path-Goal Theory of Leadership: Lessons, Legacy, and a Reformulated Theory," *Leadership Quarterly,* no. 3, 1996, p. 348.

9. House and Mitchell, "Path-Goal Theory," p. 84; Bernard M. Bass, *Bass & Stogdill's Handbook of Leadership: Theory, Research, and Managerial Applications,* 3rd ed. (New York: The Free Press, 1990), p. 633.

10. Chemers, *An Integrative Theory of Leadership*, p. 48.

11. Kenneth H. Blanchard, David Zigarmi, and Robert Nelson, "Situational Leadership After 25 Years: A Retrospective," *Journal of Leadership Studies,* vol. 1, 1993, pp. 22–26; Kenneth Blanchard and Robert Nelson, "Recognition and Reward," *Executive Excellence*, no. 4, 1997, p. 15; "Building Materials Leader Builds Better Leaders," kenblanchard.com/casestudies/certainteed.pdf, accessed November 26, 2004.

12. Victor H. Vroom, "Leadership and the Decision-Making Process," *Organizational Dynamics,* Spring 2000, pp. 82–93; Vroom, "Educating Managers in Decision Making and Leadership," *Management Decision*, vol. 10, 2003, pp. 968–978.

13. Richard H. G. Field and Robert J. House, "A Test of the Vroom–Yetton Model Using Manager and Subordinate Reports," *Journal of Applied Psychology,* June 1990, pp. 362–366.

14. Fred F. Fiedler and Joseph E. Garcia, *New Approaches to Effective Leadership: Cognitive Resources and Organizational Performance* (New York: Wiley, 1987); Robert P. Vecchio, "Theoretical and Empirical Examination of Cognitive Resource Theory," *Journal of Applied Psychology,* April 1990, p. 141; Chemers, *An Integrative Theory of Leadership*, pp. 38–40.

15. Vecchio, "Theoretical and Empirical Examination of Cognitive Resource Theory," pp. 141–147.

16. Robert Vecchio, "Cognitive Resource Theory: Issues for Specifying a Test of the Theory," *Journal of Applied Psychology,* June 1992, p. 66.

17. Charles M. Farkas and Suzy Wetlaufer, "The Ways Chief Executive Officers Lead," *Harvard Business Review,* May–June 1996, pp. 110–122; Charles M. Farkas and Philippe DeBacker, *Maximum Leadership: The World's Leading CEOs Share Their Five Strategies for Success* (New York: Holt, 1996).

18. Farkas and Wetlaufer, "The Ways Chief Executive Officers Lead," p. 116.

19. Anthony J. Mayo and Nitin Nohria, "Zeitgeist Leadership," *Harvard Business Review*, October 2005, p. 55.

20. Research cited in Gary Yukl, *Leadership in Organizations*, 5th ed. (Upper Saddle River, N.J.: Prentice Hall, 2002), p. 344.

21. Kate Kelly, "Bear CEO's Handling of Crisis Raises Issues," *The Wall Street Journal,* November 1, 2007, p. A1.

22. James E. Dutton et al., "Leading in Times of Trauma," *Harvard Business Review,* January 2002, p. 56.

23. Suzanne Koudsi, "How to Cope with Tragedy," *Fortune,* October 1, 2001, p. 34.

24. Chester Dawson, "What Japan's CEOs Can Learn from Bridgestone," *BusinessWeek,* January 29, 2001, p. 050.

25. Barbara Baker Clark, "Leadership During a Crisis," *Executive Leadership*, December 2001, p. 8.

26. Joyce M. Rosenberg, "Business Must Be Ready for Disasters," Associated Press, April 19, 2004; "Have Disaster Plan Ready to Go," Associated Press, May 98, 2005.

27. Michael M. Grynbaum, "Citi Names Executive to Repair Mortgage Problems," nytimes.com, November 6, 2007, p. 1.

28. Jia Lynn Yang, "A Recipe for Consistency," *Fortune*, October 29, 2007, p. 58.

29. Erika Hayes James and Lynn Perry Wooten, "How to Display Competence in Times of Crisis," *Organizational Dynamics*, vol. 34, no. 2, 2005, p. 146.

30. Denis M. Rousseau, "Presidential Address: Is There Such a Thing as 'Evidence-Based Management'?" *The Academy of Management Review,* April 2006, pp. 256–269; Wayne F. Cascio, "Evidence-Based Management and the Marketplace for Ideas," *Academy of Management Journal,* October 2007, pp. 1009–1012.

31. Alan Murray, "Executive's Fatal Flaw: Failing to Understand New Demands on CEOs," *The Wall Street Journal*, January 4, 2007, p. A1.

Suggested path for Leadership Skill-Building Exercise 5-2: Applying the Time-Driven Model: H H H L H H L CONSULT GROUP.

## Chapter 6

1. Tyler Hamilton, "Branson's $3B Pledge," *Toronto Star* (www.thestar.com), September 22, 2006, pp. 1–2.

2. James G. Clawson, *Level Three Leadership: Getting Below the Surface*, 2nd ed. (Upper Saddle River, N.J.: Prentice Hall, 2002), p. 54.

3. Cited in Joanne B. Ciulla, ed., *Ethics: The Heart of Leadership*, 2nd ed. (Westport, Conn.: Praeger, 2004), p. 119.

4. "New Report Details Findings of LRN Ethics Study," www.lrn.com, accessed August 14, 2006.

5. "Workers Lack Trust in Bosses and Colleagues," Associated Press, September 6, 2004.

6. Chris Prystay, "Most Workers in Asia Distrust Bosses," *The Wall Street Journal*, November 24, 2004, p. B8.

7. Thomas E. Becker, "Integrity in Organizations: Beyond Honesty and Conscientiousness," *Academy of Management Review,* January 1998, pp. 154–161.

8. Robert Simons, Henry Mintzberg, and Kunal Basu, "Memo to CEOs Re Five Half-Truths of Business," *Fast Company,* June 2002, p. 118.

9. Tricia Bisoux, "Corporate Counter Culture," *BizEd*, November/December 2004, p. 18.

10. Douglas R. May, Adrian Y. L. Chan, Timothy D. Hodges, and Bruce J. Avolio, "Developing the Moral Component of Authentic Leadership," *Organizational Dynamics*, no. 3, 2003, p. 248.

11. Peter G. Northouse, *Leadership: Theory and Practice,* 2nd ed. (Thousand Oaks, Calif.: Sage Publications, 2001), p. 263.

12. Pete Engardio, "Global Compact, Little Impact," *BusinessWeek*, July 12, 2004, p. 086; "Global Compact Strengthens Efforts to Promote Human Rights in Business," www.unglobalcompact.org, December 10, 2007.

13. Clawson, *Level Three Leadership*, p. 57.

14. Joseph L. Badaracco Jr., "We Don't Need Another Hero," *Harvard Business Review,* September 2001, pp. 120–126.

15. "Fed Chief Points to Cautious Recovery," Gannett News Service, July 17, 2002.

16. "KPMG's Timothy Flynn: Restoring Credibility and Not Looking Back," *Knowledge @ Wharton*, December 12, 2007, p.1.

17. Research synthesized in Richard L. Daft, *Leadership: Theory and Practice* (Fort Worth, Tex.: The Dryden Press, 1999), pp. 369–370.

18. Susan Chandler, "Why Do Rich CEOs Steal? Entitlement," Knight Ridder News Service, September 19, 2004; "2006 Trends in CEO Pay," www.aflcio.org/corporatewatch, 2007.

19. Aaron Lucchetti and Monica Langley, "Perform-or-Die Culture Leaves Thin Talent Pool for Top Wall Street Jobs," *The Wall Street Journal*, November 5, 2007, p. A1.

20. "The Ethical Mind: A Conversation with Psychologist Howard Gardner," *Harvard Business Review*, March 2007, pp. 51–56.

21. Timberly Ross, "Buffet Warns Execs to Avoid Temptation," The Associated Press, October 10, 2006.

22. James L. Bowditch and Anthony F. Buono, *A Primer on Organizational Behavior*, 5th ed. (New York: Wiley, 2001), p. 4.

23. Kate Kelly, "How Goldman Won Big on Mortgage Meltdown," *The Wall Street Journal*, December 14, 2007, pp. A1, A18.

24. Kris Maher, "Wanted: Ethical Employer," *The Wall Street Journal*, July 9, 2002, p. B1.

25. Kunal Basu and Guido Palazzo, "Corporate Responsibility: A Process Model of Sensemaking," *Academy of Management Review*, January 2008, p. 124.

26. R. Edward Freeman, "From the Boardroom to the Classroom: An Ethics Revolution," *The Wall Street Journal*, December 10, 2007, p. A15.

27. Richard L. Schmalensee, "The 'Thou Shalt' School of Business," *The Wall Street Journal*, December 30, 2003, p. B4.

28. Terry Thomas, John R. Schermerhorn Jr., and John W. Dienhart, "Strategic Leadership of Ethical Behavior in Business," *Academy of Management Executive*, May 2004, pp. 56–66.

29. Linda Klebe Treviño and Michael E. Brown, "Managing to Be Ethical: Debunking Five Business Ethics Myths," *Academy of Management Executive*, May 2004, p. 79.

30. Robert Levering and Milton Moskowitz, "The 2008 List," *Fortune*, February 4, 2008, p. 75; Levering and Moskowitz, "The 100 Best Companies to Work For," *Fortune*, January 24, 2005, pp. 72–78.

31. Stephen Power, "Green Push Hits Tire Makers," *The Wall Street Journal*, December 11, 2007, p. A18.

32. "Women in Charge: Bold Moves," *Entrepreneur*, January 2008, pp. 33–34.

33. Marc Gunther, "The Green Machine," *Fortune*, August 7, 2006, p. 44; Pallavi Gogoi and Moira Herbst, "Wal-Mart's Bold Environmental Move—Maybe," *MSNBC.com*, September 26, 2007, p. 1.

34. Erika Brown, "Rehab, Reuse, Recycle," *Forbes*, April 21, 2008, pp. 70, 72.

35. For details see www.gatesfoundation.org; Robert A. Guth, "Bill Gates Issues Call for Kinder Capitalism," *The Wall Street Journal*, January 24, 2008, p. A1.

36. Sarah E. Needleman, "Firm Decisions," *The Wall Street Journal*, December 10, 2007, p. R8.

37. Robert J. Bies, Jean M. Bartunek, Timothy L. Fort, and Mayer N. Zald, "Corporations as Social Change Agents: Individual, Interpersonal, Institutional, and Environmental Dynamics," *Academy of Management Review*, July 2007, pp. 788–793.

38. Amy Merrick, "Gap Offers Unusual Look at Factory Conditions," *The Wall Street Journal*, May 12, 2004, pp. A1, A12.

39. Quoted in Joanne Lozar Glenn, "Making Sense of Ethics," *Business Education Forum*, October 2004, p. 10.

40. Mike Esterlk, "Siemens Polishes Image," *The Wall Street Journal*, November 29, 2007, p. B5.

41. Jonathan Karp, "At the Pentagon, An 'Encyclopedia of Ethical Failure,'" *The Wall Street Journal*, May 14, 2007, p. A15.

42. Lara Lakes Jordan, "Whistle-Blowers Identified $1.3 in Fraud over Year," The Associated Press, November 22, 2006.

43. "A Tip for Whistleblowers: Don't," *Mother Jones*, June 2007, reprinted in *The Wall Street Journal*, May 31, 2007, p. B6.

44. Jean Thilmany, "Supporting Ethical Employees," *HR Magazine*, September 2007, p. 108.

45. Jonathan M. Tisch, "From 'Me' Leadership to 'We' Leadership," *The Wall Street Journal*, October 26, 2004, p. B2.

46. Alison Mackey, Tyson B. Mackey, and Jay B. Barney, "Corporate Social Responsibility and Firm Performance: Investor Preferences and Corporate Strategies," *Academy of Management Review*, July 2007, p. 833.

47. Sandra A. Waddock and Samuel B. Graves, "The Corporate Social Performance–Financial Performance Link," *Strategic Management Journal*, Spring 1997, pp. 303–319.

48. Peter A. Heslin and Jenna D. Ocha, "Understanding and Developing Strategic Corporate Social Responsibility," *Organizational Dynamics*, April–June 2008, p. 141.

49. Anne Field, "Mission Possible," *BusinessWeek SmallBiz*, December 2007–January 2008, pp. 41–42.

50. Daniel J. Brass, Kenneth D. Butterfield, and Bruce C. Skaggs, "Relationships and Unethical Behavior: A Social Network Perspective," *Academy of Management Review*, January 1998, pp. 14–31.


*Chapter 7*

1. Excerpted from Roy S. Johnson, "Build 'Em, Cowboy," *Fortune*, February 5, 2007, pp. 25–27.

2. John R. French and Bertram Raven, "The Basis of Social Power," in Dorwin Cartwright, ed., *Studies in Social Power* (Ann Arbor, Mich.: Institute for Social Research, 1969); Timothy R. Hinkin and Chester A. Schriescheim, "Power and Influence: The View from Below," *Personnel*, May 1988, pp. 47–50.

3. Mark Jewell, "Fidelity Investments' Leadership, Structure, Questioned," www.miamihearald.com, January 3, 2008, p. 1.

4. Ann Davis and Randall Smith, "Merrill Switch: Popular Veteran Is In, Not Out," *The Wall Street Journal*, August 13, 2003, p. C1; Landon Thomas Jr., "Dismantling a Wall Street Club," www.nytimes.com, November 2, 2003; George Anders, "Is There a Second Act for O'Neal After Merrill?" *The Wall Street Journal*, October 31, 2007, p. A2.

5. Frank Gibney Jr., "Vroooom at the Top," *Time*, January 14, 2002, p. 42; Katie Merx, "Vice Chairman Bob Lutz Declares: 'A New Era' Nears for GM," *Detroit Free Press* (www.freep.com), October 31, 2007, pp. 1–3.

6. Sydney Finkelstein, "Power in Top Management Teams: Dimensions, Measurement, and Validation," *Academy of Management Journal*, August 1992, p. 510.

7. Finkelstein, "Power in Top Management Teams," p. 510.

8. Richard M. Emerson, "Power-Dependence Relations," *American Sociological Review*, vol. 27, 1962, p. 32.

9. Quoted in Jeremy Smerd, "Wal-Mart Betting on Tech Clinics," *Workforce Management*, May 7, 2007, p. 3.

10. Jeffrey Pfeffer, *Managing with Power: Power and Influence in Organizations* (Boston: Harvard Business School Press, 1992), pp. 100–101.

11. Diane Brady, "It's All Donald, All the Time," *BusinessWeek*, January 22, 2007, p. 051; "The Forbes 400 Landlords," *Forbes*, October 9, 2006, p. 110.

12. C. R. Hinings, D. J. Hickson, C. A. Lee, R. E. Schenck, and J. W. Pennings, "Strategic Contingencies Theory of Intraorganizational Power," *Administrative Science Quarterly*, 1971, pp. 216–229.

13. "Lessons in Power: Lyndon Johnson Revealed: A Conversation with Historian Robert A. Caro," *Harvard Business Review*, April 2006, pp. 47–52.

14. Gregory G. Dess and Joseph Picken, "Changing Roles: Leadership in the 21st Century," *Organizational Dynamics*, Winter 2000, p. 22.

15. "The Secrets of His Success," *Fortune*, November 29, 2004, p. 158.

16. George Anders, "Overseeing More Employees—With Fewer Managers," *The Wall Street Journal*, March 24, 2008, p. B6.

17. Gretchen M. Spreitzer, "Psychological Empowerment in the Workplace: Dimensions, Measurement, and Validation," *Academy of Management Journal*, October 1995, pp. 1442–1465.

18. Scott E. Seibert, Seth R. Silver, and W. Alan Randolph, "Taking Empowerment to the Next Level: A Multiple-Level Model of Empowerment, Performance, and Satisfaction," *Academy of Management Journal*, June 2004, pp. 332–349.

19. Jay A. Conger, "Leadership: The Art of Empowering Others," *Academy of Management Executive*, August 1995, pp. 21–31.

20. Barbara Ettorre, "The Empowerment Gap: Hype vs. Reality," *HRfocus*, July 1997, p. 5.

21. Quoted in Phillip M. Perry, "Seven Errors to Avoid When Empowering Your Staff," *Success Workshop* (a supplement to *Manager's Edge*), March 1999, p. 3.

22. Craig L. Pearce and Charles C. Manz, "The New Silver Bullets of Leadership: The Importance of Self- and Shared-Leadership in Knowledge Work," *Organizational Dynamics*, no. 2, 2005, pp. 130–140.

23. Kyle Dover, "Avoiding Empowerment Traps," *Management Review*, January 1999, p. 52.

24. Dimitry Elias Léger, "Tell Me Your Problem, and I'll Tell You Mine," *Fortune*, October 6, 2000, p. 408.

25. Christopher Robert et al., "Empowerment and Continuous Improvement in the United States, Mexico, Poland, and India: Predicting Fit on the Basis of the Dimensions of Power Distance and Individualism," *Journal of Applied Psychology*, October 2000, pp. 751–765.

26. Abhishek Srivastava, Kathryn M. Bartol, and Edwin A. Locke, "Empowering Leadership in Management Teams: Effects on Knowledge Sharing, Efficacy, and Performance," *Academy of Management Journal*, December 2006, pp. 1239–1251.

27. Jay B. Carson, Paul E. Telsuk, and Jennifer A. Marrone, "Shared Leadership in Teams: An Investigation of Antecedent Conditions and Performance," *Academy of Management Journal*, October 2007, pp. 1217–1234.

28. Stanley Holmes, "Inside the Coup at Nike," *BusinessWeek*, February 6, 2006, pp. 034–037.

29. Gerald R. Ferris et al., "Political Skill at Work," *Organizational Dynamics*, Spring 2000, p. 25.

30. Gerald Biberman, "Personality Characteristics and Work Attitudes of Persons with High, Moderate, and Low Political Tendencies," *Psychological Reports*, vol. 57, 1985, p. 1309.

31. Marshall Goldsmith, "All of Us Are Stuck on Suck-Ups," *Fast Company*, December 2003, p. 117.

32. Pamela L. Perrewé et al., "Political Skill: An Antidote for Workplace Stressors," *Academy of Management Executive*, August 2000, p. 115.

33. Tom Peters, "Power," *Success*, November 1994, p. 34.

34. Stanley Holmes, "EADS' Unlikely American Ascent," *BusinessWeek*, April 9, 2007, p. 068.

35. Nanette Byrnes and David Kiley, "Hello, You Must Be Going," *BusinessWeek*, February 12, 2007, p. 030.

36. Michael Warshaw, "The Good Guy's (and Gal's) Guide to Office Politics," *Fast Company*, April 1998, p. 160.

37. Robin J. Ely, Debra Meyerson, and Martin N. Davidson, "Rethinking Political Correctness," *Harvard Business Review*, September 2006, p. 80.

38. Joann S. Lublin, "To Win Advancement, You Need to Clean Up Any Bad Speech Habits," *The Wall Street Journal*, October 3, 2004, p. B1.

39. An example of such research is Zoe I. Barsness, Kristina A. Diekmann, and Marc-David L. Seidel, "Motivation and Opportunity: The Role of Remote Work, Demographic Dissimilarity, and Social Network Centrality in Impression Management," *Academy of Management Journal*, June 2005, pp. 401–419.

40. James D. Westphal and Ithai Stern, "Flattery Will Get You Everywhere (Especially If You Are a Male Caucasian): How Ingratiation, Board-room Behavior, and Demographic Minority Status Affect Additional Board Appointments at U. S. Companies," *Academy of Management Journal*, April 2007, pp. 267–288.

41. Quoted in Joann S. Lublin, "Did I Just Say That?! How You Can Recover from Foot-in-Mouth," *The Wall Street Journal*, June 18, 2002, p. B1.

42. Tracy Minor, "Office Politics: Master the Game by Making Connections," *Monster: Diversity & Inclusion*, October 30, 2002 (monster.com).

43. Devin Leonard, "How Wal-Mart Got the Love E-Mail," *Fortune*, April 30, 2007, p. 52.

44. Annette Simmons, *Territorial Games: Understanding & Ending Turf Wars at Work* (New York: AMACOM, 1998); Robert J. Herbold, *The Fiefdom Syndrome* (New York: Currency Doubleday, 2004).

45. Graham Brown, Thomas B. Lawrence, and Sandra L. Robinson, "Territoriality in Organizations," *Academy of Management Review*, July 2005, pp. 577–594.

46. Jared Sandberg, "Office Superheroes: Saving the Rest of Us from Unseen Dangers," *The Wall Street Journal*, December 10, 2003, p. B1.

47. John M. Maslyn and Donald B. Fedor, "Perceptions of Politics: Does Measuring Foci Matter?" *Journal of Applied Psychology*, August 1998, pp. 666–674.

48. L. A. Witt, "Enhancing Organizational Goal Congruence: A Solution to Organizational Politics," *Journal of Applied Psychology*, August 1998, pp. 666–674.

49. Robert P. Vecchio, *Organizational Behavior*, 4th ed. (Fort Worth, Tex.: The Dryden Press, 2000), p. 136.

50. "Throw Politics Out of Your Office," *Manager's Edge*, July 2001, p. 8.

51. Adapted from Sarah Myers McGinty, *Power Talk: Using Language to Build Authority* (New York: Warner Books, 2001), as cited in "6 Ways to Judge Internal Dynamics," *Executive Leadership*, August 2001, p. 7.

## Chapter 8

1. Excerpted and adapted from Jia Lynn Yang, *Fortune*, November 26, 2007, p. 42.
2. Allan R. Cohen, Stephen L. Fink, Herman Gadon, and Robin D. Willits, *Effective Behavior in Organizations: Cases, Concepts, and Student Experiences*, 5th ed. (Homewood, Ill.: Irwin, 1992), p. 139.
3. Linda Tischler, "IBM's Management Makeover," *Fast Company*, November 2004, pp. 112–113.
4. Cited in Adam Lashinsky, "Where Does Google Go Next?" *Fortune*, May 26, 2008, p. 108.
5. Geoff Colvin, "Power: A Cooling Trend," *Fortune*, December 10, 2007, p. 114.
6. Gary Yukl, *Leadership in Organizations*, 5th ed. (Upper Saddle River, N.J.: Prentice Hall, 2002), p. 143.
7. "Steven Cohen: Speaking Softly but Carrying a Big Hedge Fund," *Time*, May 14, 2007, p. 165.
8. Gary Yukl and J. Bruce Tracey, "Consequences of Influence Tactics Used with Subordinates, Peers, and the Boss," *Journal of Applied Psychology*, August 1992, p. 526.
9. Mitchell S. Nesler, Herman Aguinis, Brian M. Quigley, and James T. Tedeschi, "The Effect of Credibility on Perceived Power," *Journal of Applied Social Psychology*, 1993, vol. 23, no. 17, pp. 1407–1425.
10. "Steve Jobs: The Information-Age Iconoclast Who Became an Icon," *Time*, May 14, 2007, p. 160.
11. "You Scratch My Back . . . Tips on Winning Your Colleague's Cooperation," *Working Smart*, October 1999, p. 1.
12. Gary Yukl, *Skills for Managers and Leaders: Texts, Cases, and Exercises* (Upper Saddle River, N.J.: Prentice Hall, 1990), pp. 58–62.
13. Jeffrey Pfeffer, *Managing with Power: Power and Influence in Organizations* (Boston: Harvard Business School Press, 1992), p. 224.
14. Nelson D. Schwartz, "Wall Street's Man of the Moment," *Fortune*, March 5, 2007, p. 76.
15. Cited in "Choose Words that Inspire," *Executive Leadership*, March 2001, p. 2.
16. Yukl, *Skills for Managers*, p. 65.
17. George Anders, "Tough CEOs Often Most Successful, a Study Finds," *The Wall Street Journal*, November 19, 2007, p. B3.
18. David Welch, "Renault-Nissan: Say Hello to Bo," *BusinessWeek*, July 31, 2006, p. 056.
19. Bernhard M. Bass, *Bass & Stogdill's Handbook of Leadership: Theory, Research, & Managerial Applications*, 3rd ed. (New York: The Free Press, 1990), p. 134.
20. "Create an Arsenal of Influence Strategies," *Manager's Edge*, March 2003, p. 1.
21. David M. Buss, Mary Gomes, Dolly S. Higgins, and Karen Lauterbach, "Tactics of Manipulation," *Journal of Personality and Social Psychology*, December 1987, p. 1222.
22. Anthony Bianco and Tom Lowry, "Can Dick Parsons Rescue AOL Time Warner?" *BusinessWeek*, May 19, 2003, p. 089.
23. Buss et al., "Tactics of Manipulation," p. 1222.
24. Linda Himelstein, "Frank's Life in the Rough," *BusinessWeek*, March 31, 2003, pp. 088–089; "After Four Years, Last Charges Dropped in Quattrone Case," *Bloomberg News*, August 30, 2007.
25. David Kipnis and Stuart Schmidt, "Intraorganizational Influence Tactics: Explorations in Getting One's Way," *Journal of Applied Psychology*, August 1980, p. 445.
26. Amy Cortese, "I'm Humble, I'm Respectful," *BusinessWeek*, February 9, 1998, p. 040.
27. Gary Yukl and Cecilia M. Falbe, "Influence Tactics and Objectives in Upward, Downward, and Lateral Influence Attempts," *Journal of Applied Psychology*, April 1990, p. 133.
28. Comment contributed anonymously to author by a professor of organizational behavior.
29. Mara Der Hovanesian, Roben Farzad, and Aaron Pressman, "He Fixed the NYSE, Can He Fix Merrill?" *BusinessWeek*, November 26, 2007, p. 029.
30. Mimi Bacilek, "To Change Organization, the Leaders Can't Let Up," Rochester, New York, *Democrat and Chronicle*, December 23, 2007.
31. Diane Brady, "The Immelt Revolution: He's Turning GE's Culture Upside Down, Demanding Far More Risk and Innovation," *BusinessWeek*, March 28, 2005, pp. 064–066, 071–073.
32. Stanley Holmes, "Cleaning Up Boeing," *BusinessWeek*, March 13, 2006, p. 064.
33. Michael Barbaro, "Sears Chairman Works to Emphasize Selling," *The New York Times* (www.nytimes.com), April 13, 2006.
34. Yukl and Tracey, "Consequences of Influence Tactics," pp. 525–535.
35. Martin M. Chemers, *An Integrative Theory of Leadership* (Mahwah, N.J.: Lawrence Erlbaum Associates, 1997), p. 76.

36. Carole V. Wells and David Kipnis, "Trust, Dependency, and Control in the Contemporary Organization," *Journal of Business and Psychology,* Summer 2001, pp. 593–603.

37. Raymond T. Sparrowe, Budi W. Soetjipto, and Maria L. Kraimer, "Do Leaders' Influence Tactics Relate to Members' Helping Behavior? It Depends on the Quality of the Relationship," *Academy of Management Journal*, December 2006, pp. 1194–1208.

38. Olga Epitropaki and Robin Martin, "Implicit Leadership Theories in Applied Settings: Factor Structure, Generalizability, and Stability over Time," *Journal of Applied Psychology*, April 2004, pp. 297–299.

39. Epitropaki and Martin, "From Real to Ideal: A Longitudinal Study of Implicit Leadership Theories in Leader–Member Exchanges and Employee Outcomes," *Journal of Applied Psychology,* July 2005, pp. 659–676.

40. Study described in Chester A. Schriesheim and Linda L. Neider, eds., *Power and Influence in Organizations: New Empirical and Theoretical Perspectives* (Greenwich, Conn.: IAP, 2006), Chapter 1.

### Chapter 9

1. Excerpted from Phred Dvorak, "How Teams Can Work Well Together from Far Apart," *The Wall Street Journal*, September 17, 2007, p. B4.

2. Edwin A. Locke and Associates, *The Essence of Leadership: The Four Keys to Leading Successfully* (New York: Lexington/Macmillan, 1991), p. 94.

3. W. Dyer, *Team Building: Issues and Alternatives* (Reading, Mass.: Addison-Wesley, 1977), as cited in Lynn R. Offerman and Rebecca K. Spiros, "The Science and Practice of Team Development: Improving the Link," *Academy of Management Journal,* April 2001, p. 380.

4. Jon R. Katzenbach and Douglas K. Smith, "The Discipline of Teams," *Harvard Business Review,* March–April 1993, p. 112.

5. Shari Caudron, "Teamwork Takes Work," *Personnel Journal*, February 1994, p. 45; Andrew J. DuBrin, *The Reengineering Survival Guide: Managing and Succeeding in the Changing Workplace* (Mason, OH.: Thomson Executive Press, 1996), pp. 129–144.

6. Frederick P. Morgeson, "The External Leadership of Self-Managing Teams: Intervening in the Context of Novel and Disruptive Events," *Journal of Applied Psychology,* May 2005, pp. 497–508.

7. David De Cremer and Daan van Knippenberg, "How Do Leaders Promote Cooperation? The Effects of Charisma and Procedural Fairness," *Journal of Applied Psychology*, October 2002, pp. 858–866.

8. "Clarify Team Roles to Ensure Success," *Manager's Edge*, August 2005, p. 6.

9. James M. Kouzes and Barry Z. Posner, *The Leadership Challenge*, 3rd ed. (San Francisco: Jossey-Bass, 2002), p. 244.

10. Stephen Baker, "Nokia: Can CEO Ollila Keep the Cellular Superstar Flying High?" *BusinessWeek,* August 10, 1998, p. 056.

11. Dean Tjosvold and Mary M. Tjosvold, *The Emerging Leader: Ways to a Stronger Team* (New York: Lexington Books, 1993); "Improve Teamwork with a 'Code of Conduct,'" *Manager's Edge*, February 2005, p. 1.

12. Vanessa Urch Druskat and Steven B. Wolff, "Building the Emotional Intelligence of Groups," *Harvard Business Review,* March 2001, pp. 80–90.

13. William A. Cohen, *The Art of the Leader* (Upper Saddle River, N.J.: Prentice Hall, 1990).

14. Paul S. George, "Teamwork Without Tears," *Personnel Journal,* November 1987, p. 129.

15. Clive Goodworth, "Some Thoughts on Creating a Team," in Michel Syrett and Clare Hogg, eds., *Frontiers of Leadership* (Oxford, England: Blackwell Publishers, 1992), p. 472.

16. "How Jon Gruden Pounds the Rock," *Executive Leadership*, November 2004, p. 4, as adapted from Jon Gruden with Vic Carducci, *Do You Love Football?* (New York: HarperCollins, 2004).

17. Quoted in Nancy Hatch Woodward, "The Coming of the X Managers," *HR Magazine*, March 1999, pp. 75, 76.

18. Susan Sonnesyn Brooks, "Managing a Horizontal Revolution," *HR Magazine,* June 1995, p. 56.

19. Katzenbach and Smith, "The Discipline of Teams," pp. 118–119.

20. Lee G. Bolman and Terrence E. Deal, "What Makes a Team Work?" *Organizational Dynamics,* Autumn 1992, p. 6.

21. Reported in Jared Sandberg, "Bosses Who Fiddle with Employees' Work Risk Ire, Low Morale," *The Wall Street Journal*, April 25, 2006, p. B1.

22. Anne Fisher, "In Praise of Micromanaging," *Fortune*, August 23, 2004, p. 40.

23. Bruce J. Avolio and Surinder S. Kahai, "Adding 'E' to E-Leadership: How It May Impact Your Leadership," *Organizational Dynamics*, vol. 31, no. 4, 2003, p. 325.

24. Arvind Malhotra, Ann Majchzak, and Benson Rosen, "Leading Virtual Teams," *Academy of Management Perspectives*, February 2007, pp. 60–70; study reported in Lynda Gratton, "Working Together . . . When Apart," *The Wall Street Journal*, June 16–17, 2007, p. R4.

25. "Build Team Bonds with 'No E-Mail Fridays,'" *Manager's Edge*, February 2007, p. 1.

26. Bolman and Deal, "What Makes a Team Work?" pp. 41–42.

27. Thomas J. McCoy, *Creating an "Open Book" Organization . . . Where Employees Think & Act Like Business Partners* (New York: AMACOM, 1999); John Case, "HR Learns How to Open the Books," *HR Magazine,* May 1998, pp. 71–76.

28. Study cited in "Poll Says Sports Helps Women's Career Paths," Rochester, New York, *Democrat and Chronicle,* March 3, 2002, p. 1E.

29. Faith Keenan and Spencer E. Ante, "The New Teamwork," *BusinessWeek e.biz*, February 18, 2002, pp. EB12–EB16.

30. Joyce Gannon, "Horses Help People Learn to Work Better with Others," *Pittsburgh Post-Gazette*, June 4, 2004.

31. Jeffrey M. O'Brien, "Team Building in Paradise," *Fortune*, May 26, 2008, pp. 112–116.

32. Jared Sandberg, "Can Spending a Day Stuck to a Velcro Wall Help Build a Team?" *The Wall Street Journal*, December 26, 2006, p. B1.

33. Jay A. Conger, *Learning to Lead: The Art of Transforming Managers into Leaders* (San Francisco: Jossey-Bass, 1992), p. 159.

34. Cited in Michael P. Regan, "Radical Steps to Help Build Teamwork," Associated Press, February 20, 2004.

35. Quoted in Nancy Hatch Woodward, "Make the Most of Team Building," *HR Magazine*, September 2006, p. 76.

36. George Graen and J. E. Cashman, "A Role-Making Model of Leadership in Formal Organizations: A Developmental Approach," in J. G. Hunt and L. L. Larson, eds., *Leadership Frontiers* (Kent, O.: Kent State University Press, 1975), pp. 143–165;

Robert P. Vecchio, "Leader–Member Exchange, Objective Performance, Employment Duration, and Supervisor Ratings: Testing for Moderation and Mediation," *Journal of Business and Psychology,* Spring 1998, p. 328.

37. Elaine M. Engle and Robert G. Lord, "Implicit Theories, Self-Schemas, and Leader–Member Exchange," *Academy of Management Journal,* August 1997, pp. 988–1010.

38. Robert P. Vecchio, "Are You IN or OUT with Your Boss?" *Business Horizons,* 1987, pp. 76–78. See also, Charlotte R. Gerstner and David W. Day, "Meta-Analytic Review of Leader–Member Exchange Theory: Correlates and Construct Issues," *Journal of Applied Psychology,* December 1997, pp. 827–844.

39. Howard J. Klein and Jay S. Kim, "A Field Study of the Influences of Situational Constraints, Leader–Member Exchange, and Goal Commitment on Performance," *Academy of Management Journal,* February 1998, pp. 88–95.

40. Randall P. Settoon, Nathan Bennett, and Robert C. Liden, "Social Exchange in Organizations: Perceived Organizational Support, Leader–Member Exchange, and Employee Reciprocity," *Journal of Applied Psychology,* June 1995, pp. 219–227.

41. Pamela Tierney and Talya N. Bauer, "A Longitudinal Assessment of LMX on Extra-Role Behavior," *Academy of Management Best Papers Proceedings,* 1996, pp. 298–302.

42. David A. Hofman and Frederick P. Morgeson, "Safety-Related Behavior as a Social Exchange: The Role of Perceived Organizational Support and Leader–Member Exchange," *Journal of Applied Psychology,* April 1999, pp. 286–296.

43. Ronald F. Piccolo and Jason A. Colquitt, "Transformational Leadership and Job Behaviors: The Mediating Role of Core Job Characteristics," *Academy of Management Journal*, April 2006, pp. 327–340.

44. Robert C. Liden, Sandy J. Wayne, and Deal Stilwell, "A Longitudinal Study on the Early Development of Leader–Member Exchanges," *Journal of Applied Psychology,* August 1993, pp. 662–674.

45. "Promote Teamwork by Rearranging the Office," *people@work*, sample issue, 1999, published by Texas Professional Training Associates, Inc.; Diana Louise Carter, "Global Crossing Fuses Staff," Rochester, New York, *Democrat and Chronicle*, January 18, 2008, pp. 6D, 5D.

*Chapter 10*

1. Excerpted from Dorothy Bourdet, "Domino Effect: David Brandon Has Pizza Chain Shaking and Baking," *The Detroit News* (detnews.com), December 9, 2006.

2. Thad Green, *Motivation Management: Fueling Performance by Discovering What People Believe About Themselves and Their Organizations* (Palo Alto, Calif.: Davies-Black Publishing, 2000). An original version of expectancy theory applied to work motivation is Victor H. Vroom, *Work and Motivation* (New York: Wiley, 1964).

3. Jack and Suzy Welch, "Battle Stations in a Dead Calm," *BusinessWeek*, August 7, 2006, p. 100.

4. Wendelien Van Eerde and Hank Thierry, "Vroom's Expectancy Models and Work-Related Criteria: A Meta-Analysis," *Journal of Applied Psychology*, October 1996, pp. 548–556.

5. David A. Nadler and Edward E. Lawler III, "Motivation: A Diagnostic Approach," in Richard Hackman, Edward E. Lawler III, and Lyman W. Porter, eds., *Perspectives on Behavior in Organizations,* 2nd ed. (New York: McGraw-Hill, 1983), pp. 67–78; James A. F. Stoner and R. Edward Freeman, *Management,* 4th ed. (Upper Saddle River, N.J.: Prentice Hall, 1989), p. 448.

6. Amir Erez and Alice M. Isen, "The Influence of Positive Affect on the Components of Expectancy Motivation," *Journal of Applied Psychology*, December 2002, pp. 1055–1067.

7. "The Secret to Meeting Your Goals," *Manager's Edge*, Special Issue, 2008, p. 3.

8. Literature reviewed in Gerard H. Seitjts, Gary P. Latham, Kevin Tasa, and Bradon W. Latham, "Goal Setting and Goal Orientation: An Integration of 'Two Different Yet Related Literatures,'" *Academy of Management Journal*, April 2004, pp. 227–228.

9. Edwin A. Locke and Gary P. Latham, *A Theory of Goal Setting and Task Performance* (Upper Saddle River, N.J.: Prentice Hall, 1990); Latham, *Work Motivation: History, Theory, Research, and Practice* (Thousand Oaks, Calif.: Sage Publications, 2007).

10. "Motivate Staff with Noble Cause," *Manager's Edge*, June 2005, p. 1.

11. Cited in "Set Outrageous Goals," *Executive Leadership*, June 2001, p. 7.

12. John J. Donavan and David J. Radosevich, "The Moderating Role of Goal Commitment on the Goal Difficulty–Performance Relationship: A Meta-Analytic Review and Critical Reanalysis," *Journal of Applied Psychology*, April 1998, pp. 308–315.

13. Don VandeWalle, Steven P. Brown, William L. Cron, and John W. Slocum Jr., "The Influence of Goal Orientation and Self-Regulation Tactics on Sales Performance: A Longitudinal Field Test," *Journal of Applied Psychology*, April 1999, pp. 249–259.

14. P. Christopher Earley and Terri Lituchy, "Delineating Goal and Efficacy Effects: A Test of Three Models," *Journal of Applied Psychology*, February 1991, p. 83.

15. Maurcie E. Schweitzer, Lisa Ordoñez, and Bambi Douma, "Goal Setting as a Moderator of Unethical Behavior," *The Academy of Management Journal*, June 2004, p. 430.

16. Study cited in Adrian Gostick and Chester Elton, *The Carrot Principle: How the Best Managers Use Recognition to Engage Their People, Retain Talent, and Accelerate Performance* (New York: The Free Press, 2007).

17. Jennifer Laabs, "Satisfy Them with More Than Money," *Workforce*, November 1998, p. 43.

18. "Motivate Staffers with a Twist," *Manager's Edge*, April 2003, p. 2.

19. Leslie Gross Klaff, "Getting Happy with the Rewards King," *Workforce*, April 2003, p. 47.

20. Andrew J. DuBrin, "Self-Perceived Technical Orientation and Attitudes Toward Being Flattered," *Psychological Reports*, 96, 2005, pp. 852–854.

21. Gostick and Elton, *The Carrot Principle.*

22. Adapted from Marshall Goldsmith with Mark Reiter, *What Got You Here Won't Get You There* (New York: Hyperion, 2007).

23. Cited in John A. Byrne, "How to Lead Now," *Fast Company*, August 2003, p. 66.

24. J. Stacy Adams, "Toward an Understanding of Inequality," *Journal of Abnormal and Social Psychology* 67, 1963, pp. 422–436; M. R. Carrell and J. E. Dettrick, "Equity Theory: The Recent Literature, Methodological Considerations, and New Directions," *Academy of Management Review*, April 1978, pp. 202–210.

25. David Novak with John Boswell, *The Education of an Accidental CEO* (New York: Crown Business, 2007).

26. Bruce Tulgan, "The Under-Management Epidemic," *HR Magazine*, October 2004, p. 119.

27. Cited in Carol Hymowitz, "Managers Lose Talent When They Neglect to Coach Their Staffs," *The Wall Street Journal*, March 19, 2007, p. B1.

28. James M. Hunt and Joseph R. Weintraub, *The Coaching Manager: Developing Top Talent in Business* (Thousand Oaks, Calif.: Sage Publications, 2002).

29. "The Best Approach to Coaching," *Manager's Edge*, September 2006, p. 3; Douglas Riddle, "Prepping Tomorrow's Leaders Today," *Leading Effectively*, www.ccl.org, September 2006.

30. Robert D. Evered and James E. Selman, "Coaching and the Art of Management," *Organizational Dynamics*, Autumn 1989, p. 15.

31. Ian Cunningham and Linda Honold, "Everyone Can Be a Coach," *HR Magazine*, June 1998, pp. 63–66.

32. "Coaching—One Solution to a Tight Training Budget," *HRfocus*, August 2002, p. 7.

33. "Request Permission to Coach," *Manager's Edge*, June 2003, p. 5.

34. Richard J. Walsh, "Ten Basic Counseling Skills," *Supervisory Management*, November 1990, p. 6.

35. "Fast Tips for Savvy Managers," *Executive Strategies*, April 1998, p. 1.

36. Anna Marie Valerio and Robert J. Lee, *Executive Coaching: A Guide for the HR Professional* (San Francisco: Pfeiffer, 2005).

37. Douglas P. Shuit, "Huddling with the Coach," *Workforce Management*, February 2005, pp. 53–57.

38. This last item is from Joann S. Lublin, "Now, Add One More to the Hiring Process: The Boss's Coach," *The Wall Street Journal*, April 3, 2007, p. B1.

39. Amy Joyce, "Career Coaches Nurture Executives," *Washington Post* syndicated story, August 16, 2004.

40. Interview by Bob Rosner, "'Team Players' Expect Real Choices," *Workforce*, May 2001, p. 63.

41. Annie Fisher, "Readers Weigh In on Coaches, Crazy Colleagues," *Fortune*, July 23, 2001, p. 272.

42. Stratford Sherman and Alyssa Freas, "The Wild West of Executive Coaching," *Harvard Business Review*, November 2004, pp. 86–88.

43. Jared Sandberg, "Some Office Coaches Whitewash Miseries with Sunny Platitudes," *The Wall Street Journal*, September 27, 2005, p. B1.

44. Steve Berglas, "The Very Real Dangers of Executive Coaching," *Harvard Business Review*, June 2002, pp. 86–92.

### Chapter 11

1. Julie Bennett, "Finding Success with Franchisee-Centered Survival Strategies," *The Wall Street Journal*, April 7, 2003, p. A25.

2. Jena McGregor, "The World's Most Innovative Companies," *BusinessWeek*, April 24, 2006, p. 064.

3. Warren Bennis, "The Challenges of Leadership in the Modern World," *American Psychologist*, January 2007, p. 2.

4. Susan Meisinger, "Creativity and Innovation: Key Drivers for Success," *HR Magazine*, May 2007, p. 10.

5. G. Wallas, *The Art of Thought* (New York: Harcourt Brace, 1926).

6. Anna Esaki-Smith and Michael Warshaw, "Renegades 1993: Creating the Future," *Success*, January/February 1993, p. 36.

7. Janet Rae-Dupree, "Eureka! It Really Takes Years of Hard Work," newyorktimes.com, February 2, 2003, p. 1.

8. John A. Gover, Royce Ronning, and Cecil R. Reynolds, eds., *Handbook of Creativity* (New York: Plenum Press, 1989); Teresa M. Amabile, "How to Kill Creativity," *Harvard Business Review*, September–October 1998, pp. 78–79.

9. Michael Gibbert and David Mazursky, "A Recipe for Creating New Products," *The Wall Street Journal*, October 27–28, 2007, p. R4.

10. "The Talent Hunt: Desperate to Innovate, Companies Are Turning to Design Schools for Nimble, Creative Thinkers," *BusinessWeek*, October 9, 2006, p. 072.

11. Cited in Anita Bruzzi, "Seek Out Creative Free Spirit," Gannett News Service, October 31, 2000. See also, William C. Taylor and Polly LaBarre, *Mavericks at Work: Why the Most Original Minds in Business Win* (New York: William Morrow, 2006).

12. Amabile, "How to Kill Creativity," p. 79.

13. Mihaly Csikszentmihalyi, "If We Are So Rich, Why Aren't We Happy?" *American Psychologist*, October 1999, p. 824.

14. Cited in Bill Breen, "The Six Myths of Creativity," *Fast Company*, December 2004, pp. 77–78.

15. Amabile, "How to Kill Creativity," pp. 78–79.

16. "Putting Creativity into Action," *Success Workshop*, supplement to *The Pryor Report*, April 1996, p. 1.

17. Cynthia D. McCauley, Russ S. Moxley, and Ellen Van Velsor, *The Center for Creative Leadership Handbook of Leadership Development* (San Francisco: Jossey-Bass, 1998) p. 111.

18. Quoted in Duane D. Stanford, "Coke's Chief Innovator Brings Together Consumer Need and Business Fit," *The Atlanta Journal-Constitution* (ajc.com), November 11, 2007.

19. Fara Warner, "How Google Searches Itself," *Fast Company*, July 2002, pp. 50, 52; Carl Hymowitz, "Google Founders Face Wealth, Resentment and a Changed Culture," *The Wall Street Journal*, May 18, 2004, p. B1.

20. "Special: CEOs on Innovation: A. G. Lafley, Procter & Gamble," *Fortune*, March 8, 2004.

21. Michael Orey, "Inside Nathan Myhrvold's Mysterious New Idea Machine," *BusinessWeek*, July 3, 2006, pp. 054, 057.

22. Robert C. Litchfield, "Brainstorming Reconsidered: A Goal-Based View," *Academy of Management Review*, July 2008, pp. 649–668.

23. "Brainstorm Better Ideas with the 6-3-5 Method," *Manager's Intelligence Report*, undated sample distributed in September 1996.

24. "Hold a Creativity Session," *Manager's Edge*, May 2006, p. 6.

25. Michael Schrage, "Playing Around with Brainstorming," *Harvard Business Review*, March 2001, pp. 149–154. Review of Tom Kelley with Jonathan Littman (New York: Doubleday/Currency, 2001).

26. Anne Sagen, "Creativity Tools: Versatile Problem Solvers That Can Double as Fun and Games," *Supervisory Management*, October 1991, pp. 1–2.

27. Cited in Robert McGarvey, "Turn It On: Creativity Is Crucial to Your Business' Success," *Entrepreneur*, 1996, p. 156.

28. Juanita Weaver, "The Mental Picture: Bringing Your Definition of Creativity into Focus," *Entrepreneur*, February 2003, p. 69.

29. Scott S. Smith, "Grounds for Success," *Entrepreneur*, May 1998, p. 120.

30. Alex F. Osburn, quoted in "Breakthrough Ideas," *Success*, October 1990, p. 38.

31. Breen, "The Six Myths of Creativity," p. 78.

32. Chuck Frey, "Ten Power Tools for Recording Your Best Ideas," *Innovation Tools* (www.innovationtools.com), December 10, 2003.

33. "Be a Creative Problem Solver," *Executive Strategies*, June 6, 1989, pp. 1–2.

34. Richard A. Lovett, "Jog Your Brain: Looking for a Creative Spark? Hop to the Gym," *Psychology Today*, May/June 2006, p. 55.

35. Amabile, "How to Kill Creativity," pp. 80–81; Teresa M. Amabile, Constance N. Hadley, and Steven J. Kramer, "Creativity Under the Gun," *Harvard Business Review*, August 2002, pp. 52–61; G. Pascal Zachary, "Mighty Is the Mongrel," *Fast Company*, July 2000, pp. 270–274; Breen, "The Six Myths of Creativity," pp. 77–80.

36. "Creative People Are Found, Not Made," *Executive Leadership*, March 2006, p. 1.

37. Quoted in Jena McGregor, "25 Most Innovative Companies," *BusinessWeek*, May 14, 2007, p. 052.

38. Pamela Tierney, Steven M. Farmer, and George B. Graen, "An Examination of Leadership and Employee Creativity: The Relevance of Traits and Relationships," *Personnel Psychology*, Autumn 1999, pp. 591–620.

39. Shari Caudron, "Strategies for Managing Creative Workers," *Personnel Journal*, December 1994, pp. 104–113; Chris Pentila, "An Art in Itself," *Entrepreneur*, December 2003, pp. 96–97.

40. Marissa Ann Mayer, "Creativity Loves Constraints," *BusinessWeek*, February 13, 2006, p. 102.

41. Keith H. Hammonds, "No Risk, No Reward," *Fast Company*, April 2002, pp. 81–93.

42. Rob Cross, Andrew Hargadon, Salvatore Parise, and Robert J. Thomas, "Together We Innovate," *The Wall Street Journal*, September 15–16, 2007, p. R6.

43. Ben Elgin, "A Do-It-Yourself Plan at Cisco," *BusinessWeek*, September 10, 2001, p. 052.

44. Survey cited in Richard Evans, "A Cost–Benefit View of Innovation," *Los Angeles Times* (www.latimes.com), March 4, 2007.

45. George Anders, "How Innovation Can Be Too Much of a Good Thing," *The Wall Street Journal*, June 11, 2007, p. B3.

46. Robert McGarvey, "Idea Inc.," *Entrepreneur*, March 1998, pp. 127, 129.

47. Sebastian Moffett, "Separation Anxiety," *The Wall Street Journal*, September 27, 2004, p. R11.

48. Jena McGregor, "How Failure Breeds Success," *BusinessWeek*, July 10, 2006, pp. 042–045.

49. Matthew Karnitschnig, "Mr. MTV Moves Up," *The Wall Street Journal*, January 9, 2006, B1.

**Solutions to Leadership Skill-Building Exercise 11-3, Word Hints to Creativity**

| 1. party | 5. club | 9. high | 13. make |
| 2. ball | 6. dog | 10. sugar | 14. bean |
| 3. cheese | 7. paper | 11. floor | 15. light |
| 4. cat | 8. finger | 12. green | |

## Chapter 12

1. Quoted in Carol Hymowitz, "Sometimes, Moving Up Makes It Harder to See What Goes on Below," *The Wall Street Journal*, October 15, 2007, p. B1.
2. Peter de la Billiere, "Leadership," in *Business: The Ultimate Resource* (Cambridge, Mass.: Perseus Publishing, 2002), p. 226.
3. John Hamm, "The Five Messages Leaders Must Manage," *Harvard Business Review*, p. 116.
4. Stephen P. Robbins and Phillip L. Hunsaker, *Training in Interpersonal Skills: Tips for Managing People at Work* (Upper Saddle River, N.J.: Prentice Hall, 1996), p. 115.
5. Mark Hendricks, "Wag Your Tale," *Entrepreneur*, February 2001, pp. 78–81.
6. Several of these examples are from "Avoid These Top Ten Language Errors," *Working Smart*, October 1991, p. 8; Joann S. Lublin, "Readers Agree Speech Needs Cleaning Up, and They Provide Tips," *The Wall Street Journal*, October 19, 2004, p. B1.
7. William Strunk Jr., E. B. White, and Maira Kalman, *The Elements of Style*, 6th ed. (Boston: Allyn and Bacon, 2007).
8. Christopher Rhoads, "Business Types Get a New Kick out of the 'Bucket,'" *The Wall Street Journal*, March 27, 2007, p. A1.
9. Sherry Sweetham, "How to Organize Your Thoughts for Better Communication," *Personnel*, March 1986, p. 39.
10. Deborah Tannen, "The Power of Talk: Who Gets Heard and Why?" *Harvard Business Review*, September–October 1995, pp. 138–148.
11. Tannen, "The Power of Talk," pp. 138–148; "How You Speak Shows Where You Rank," *Fortune*, February 2, 1998, p. 156; "Speak Like You Mean Business," *Working Smart* (www.nibm.net), March 2004; "Weed Out Wimpy Words: Speak Up Without Backpedaling, Qualifying," *Working SMART*, March 2000, p. 2.
12. Erin White, "Art of Persuasion Becomes Key," *The Wall Street Journal*, May 19, 2008, p. B5.
13. Robert B. Cialdini, "Harnessing the Science of Persuasion," *Harvard Business Review*, October 2001, pp. 72–79.
14. Ibid., p. 79.
15. Several of the suggestions here are from *Body Language for Business Success* (New York: National Institute for Business Management,

1989), pp. 2–29; "Attention All Monotonous Speakers," *Working SMART*, March 1998, p. 1.
16. Cited in Joann S. Lublin, "Some Dos and Don'ts to Help You Hone Videoconference Skills," *The Wall Street Journal*, February 7, 2006, p. B1.
17. Ibid.
18. Richard M. Harris, *The Listening Leader: Powerful New Strategies for Becoming an Influential Communicator* (Westport, Conn.: Praeger, 2006).
19. Erika H. James, "Selective Hearing Can Lead to a Blind Eye," *The Darden Perspective in First Person*, published in *The Wall Street Journal*, December 4, 2007, p. A16.
20. Linda Dulye, "Get Out of Your Office," *HR Magazine*, July 2006, pp. 99–100; "'Making Rounds' Like a Physician," *Manager's Edge*, February 2006, p. 8.
21. Trudy Milburn, "Bridging Cultural Gaps," *Management Review*, January 1997, pp. 26–29.
22. Gunnar Beeth, "Multicultural Managers Wanted," *Management Review*, May 1997, p. 17.
23. "When English Is Not Their Native Tongue," *Manager's Edge*, April 2003, p. 5.
24. Kathryn Kranhold, "Lost in Translation," *The Wall Street Journal*, May 18, 2004, p. B1.
25. "Cross-Cultural Communication: An Essential Dimension of Effective Education," *Northwest Regional Educational Library: CNORSE* (www.nwrel.org/cnorse).
26. Siri Carpenter, "Why Do 'They All Look Alike'?" *Monitor on Psychology*, December 2000, p. 44.
27. Howard M. Guttman, "Conflict at the Top," *Management Review*, November 1999, p. 50.
28. Chris Penttila, "Turf Wars," *Entrepreneur*, March 2007, p. 90.
29. Jeff Weiss and Jonathan Hughes, "Want Collaboration? Accept—and Actively Manage—Conflict," *Harvard Business Review*, March 2005, pp. 92–101.
30. Kenneth Thomas, "Conflict and Conflict Management," in Marvin D. Dunnette, ed., *Handbook of Industrial and Organizational Psychology* (Chicago: Rand McNally, 1976), pp. 900–922.
31. "Replace Criticism with Agreement," *Manager's Edge*, May 1999, p. 50
32. Barbara Kellerman, "When Should a Leader Apologize and When Not?" *Harvard Business Review*, April 2006, pp. 72–81.
33. Elizabeth A. Mannix, Leigh L. Thompson, and Max H. Bazerman, "Negotiation in Small

Groups," *Journal of Applied Psychology,* June 1989, pp. 508–517.

34. Patrick S. Nugent, "Managing Conflict: Third-Party Interventions for Managers," *Academy of Management Executive*, February 2002, p. 152.

35. "Questions for Michael Watkins," *Workforce,* December 11, 2006, p. 11.

36. Brenda Goodman, "The Art of Negotiation," *Psychology Today*, January/February 2007, p. 65.

37. Deepak Malhotra and Max H. Bazerman, "Investigative Negotiation," *Harvard Business Review*, September 2007, pp. 72–78.

38. John Heister, "Collaborate to Solve Societal Ills," Rochester, New York, *Democrat and Chronicle*, May 14, 2004, p. 18A.

39. James K. Sebenius, "Six Habits of Merely Effective Negotiators," *Harvard Business Review,* April 2001, pp. 91–92.

40. Frank Acuff, *The World-Class Negotiator: An Indispensable Guide for Anyone Doing Business with Those from a Foreign Culture* (New York: AMACOM, 1992).

41. Wendi L. Adair, Tetsushi Okumura, and Jeanne M. Brett, "Negotiation Behavior When Cultures Collide: The United States and Japan," *Journal of Applied Psychology*, June 2001, pp. 371–385.

42. "Roger Fisher: Master Negotiator and Best-Selling Author," *In Their Own Words,* National Institute of Business Management Special Report 250, 1997, p. 7.

43. "Avoid Language That Shuts People Up," *Executive Leadership*, January 2008, p. 8.

### Chapter 13

1. Janet Adamy, "How Jim Skinner Flipped McDonald's: Big Chain's CEO Focused on Getting Better, Not Bigger; 'We Have to Provide Choices,'" *The Wall Street Journal*, January 5, 2007, p. B1.

2. Donald C. Hambrick and James W. Fredrickson, "Are You Sure You Have a Strategy?" *Academy of Management Executive,* November 2001, p. 48.

3. Richard L. Hughes and Katherine C. Beatty, *Becoming a Strategic Leader: Your Role in Your Organization's Enduring Success* (San Francisco: Jossey-Bass, 2005).

4. Robert A. Guth, "Behind Microsoft's Bid to Gain Cutting Edge," *The Wall Street Journal*, July 30, 2007, p. A1.

5. Cynthia Montgomery, "Putting Leadership Back in Strategy," *Harvard Business Review*, January 2008, pp. 54–80.

6. Bruce J. Avolio and David A. Waldman, "An Examination of Age and Cognitive Test Performance Across Job Complexity and Occupational Types," *Journal of Applied Psychology*, February 1990, pp. 43–50.

7. Matthew Boyle, "The Man Who Fixed Kellogg," *Fortune*, September 6, 2004, p. 220.

8. Quoted in John A. Byrne, "Three of the Busiest New Strategists," *BusinessWeek*, August 26, 2002, p. 050.

9. Julia Kirby and Thomas A. Stewart, interview with Jeff Bezos, "The Institutional Yes," *Harvard Business Review*, October 2007, p. 76.

10. Samuel Greengard, "Leveraging a Low-Wage Workforce," *Workforce Online,* February, 2004.

11. Pierre Briacon and Anthony Currie, "Are Alcatel's Cuts Enough? CEO Russo Needs to Tackle Market, Product Problems, Not Just Hope for the Best," *The Wall Street Journal*, November 1, 2007, p. C14.

12. Strategy Session with C. K. Prahalad, *Management Review*, April 1995, pp. 50–51.

13. Gary Hamel, "Revolution vs. Evolution: You Need Both," *Harvard Business Review*, May 2001, p. 150.

14. Geoffrey Colvin, "Managing on the Edge," *Fortune*, October 2, 2006, p. 78.

15. Keith H. Hammonds, "Michael Porter's Big Ideas," *Fast Company*, March 2001, p. 153.

16. Dennis Kneale, "Whitacre's Way," *Forbes*, January 8, 2007, pp. 84–85.

17. Susanna Hamner and Tom McNichol, "Ripping Up the Rules of Management," *Business 2.0*, May 2007, p. 63.

18. James R. Lucas, "Anatomy of a Vision Statement," *Management Review*, February 1998, p. 26.

19. Carmine Gallo, "Be a Visionary Leader," *The Ladders.com Executive Coach* (TheLadders.com), January 23, 2008.

20. Sarah Fister Gale, "Share the Vision: Strategic Thinking Can't Just Be the Province of the Executive Suite," *PM Network*, December 2007, pp. 33–35.

21. Several ideas for this version of SWOT are from "SWOT Analysis," *Business Owner's Tool Kit,* November 8, 1999 (www.toolkit.cch.com/text/p02_4341.asp); "Performing a SWOT Analysis," in *Business: The Ultimate Resources* (Cambridge, Mass.: Perseus Publishing, 2002), pp. 226–227.

22. Christopher Lawton, "How H-P Reclaimed Its PC Lead over Dell: Shifting Battlefield to Stores

Was Key; Help from Vera Wang," *The Wall Street Journal*, June 4, 2007.

23. A representative example of a complex strategic planning scheme is Joseph C. Picken and Gregory G. Dess, "Right Strategy—Wrong Problem," *Organizational Dynamics*, Summer 1998, pp. 35–49.

24. Michael Porter, *Competitive Strategy* (New York: The Free Press, 1980), pp. 36–46.

25. Nick Wingfield, "Taking on eBay," *The Wall Street Journal*, September 15, 2004, p. R10.

26. Joe Sharkey, "Gun or Bug Spray Not Needed, but You Do Make Your Own Bed," *The New York Times* (nytimes.com), September 26, 2006.

27. Based on information in advertisement appearing in *The Wall Street Journal*, November 8, 2006, p. A19.

28. Melanie Haiken, "Innovative Partnering: Papa John's and Six Flags," *Time* (*Business 2.0* insert), December 11, 2006, p. 2.

29. A. Gary Schilling, "First-Mover Disadvantage," *Forbes*, June 18, 2007, p. 15.

30. Rob Cox, John Cristy, and Aliza Rosenbaum, "Coke's New Fizz," *The Wall Street Journal*, December 10, 2007, p. C10.

31. Bobby White, "No Longer Just 'Plumbers': Aiming to Rival Sony, Apple, John Chambers Takes Cisco Beyond Routers and Switches," *The Wall Street Journal*, August 7, 2007, p. B1.

32. Matthew Karnitschnig, "Montblanc, Famed for Pens, Targets Wrists," *The Wall Street Journal*, December 23, 2004, p. B1.

33. George Anders, "Homespun Strategist," *The Wall Street Journal*, January 6, 2004, p. B1.

34. Robert Guy Matthews, "Why Firms Are Returning to Their Roots," *The Wall Street Journal*, October 22, 2007, p. A2.

35. "The 100 Top Brands," *BusinessWeek*, August 6, 2007, p. 059.

36. Alison Overholt, "Smart Strategies: Putting Ideas to Work" *Fast Company*, April 2004, p. 63.

37. Michael Beer and Russell A. Eisenstat, "How to Have an Honest Conversation About Your Business Strategy," *Harvard Business Review*, February 2004, pp. 82–89.

38. Thomas H. Davenport, Laurence Prusak, and Bruce Strong, "Putting Ideas to Work: Knowledge Management Can Make a Difference, but It Needs to Be More Pragmatic," *The Wall Street Journal*, March 10, 2008, p. R11.

39. David A. Garvin, "Building a Learning Organization," *Harvard Business Review*, July–August 1993, p. 80.

40. Davenport, Prusak, and Strong, "Putting Ideas to Work," p. R11.

41. Pamela Babcock, "Shedding Light on Knowledge Management," *HR Magazine*, May 2004, p. 7.

42. Bill Breen, "Hidden Asset," *Fast Company*, March 2004, p. 95.

43. Thomas H. Davenport and John Glaser, "Just-in-Time Delivery Comes to Knowledge Management," *Harvard Business Review*, July 2002, pp. 107–111.

44. Morten T. Hansen, Marie Louise Mors, and Bjorn Lovas, "Knowledge Sharing in Organizations: Multiple Networks, Multiple Phases," *Academy of Management Journal*, October 2005, p. 790.

45. David W. De Long and Liam Fahey, "Diagnosing Cultural Barriers to Knowledge Management," *Academy of Management Executive*, November 2000, pp. 115–117.

46. Megan Santosus, "Information Micromanagement," *CIO Enterprise Magazine*, April 15, 1998 (www.cio.com/archive/enterprise/041598_reality.html).

47. Alton Y. K. Chua, "The Curse of Success: Knowledge Management Projects Often Look Good in the Beginning, but Then Problems Arise," *The Wall Street Journal*, April 28–29, 2007, pp. R8, R9.

48. Robert M. Fulmer and J. Bernard Keys, "A Conversation with Peter Senge: New Developments in Organizational Learning," *Organizational Dynamics*, Autumn 1998, p. 35.

49. Lester Thurow, "Help Wanted: A Chief Knowledge Officer," *Fast Company*, January 2004, p. 91.

50. Dusya Vera and Mary Crossan, "Strategic Leadership and Organizational Learning," *Academy of Management Review*, April 2004, p. 235.

51. Robert M. Fulmer and Philip Gibbs, "The Second Generation Learning Organizations: New Tools for Sustainable Competitive Advantage," *Organizational Dynamics*, Autumn 1998, pp. 7–20; Peter M. Senge, *The Fifth Discipline* (New York: Doubleday, 1990); Thomas P. Lawrence, Michael M. Mauws, Bruno Dyck, and Robert F. Kleysen, "The Politics of Organizational Learning: Integrating Power into the 4I Framework," *Academy of Management Review*, January 2005, pp. 180–191; Constance James, "Designing Learning Organizations," *Organizational Dynamics*, vol. 32, no. 1, 2003, pp. 46–61; Joe Raelin, "Does Action Learning Promote Collaborative Leadership?" *Academy of*

*Management Learning & Education*, June 2006, pp. 152–168.

52. Neil Gross, "Mining a Company's Mother Lode of Talent," *BusinessWeek*, August 28, 2000, p. 137.

53. "Making Vision Statements 'Visionary,'" *Manager's Edge*, December 1998, p. 1.

### Chapter 14

1. Adapted and excerpted from "The Borderless Leader: Cross-Cultural Skills Are Needed Just to Survive in Today's Global Economy," *2008 Leadership in Project Management* (Project Management Institute), pp. 12–13.

2. Jennifer Schramm, "Acting Affirmatively," *HR Magazine*, September 2003, p. 192.

3. Erin White, "Executives with Global Experience Are Among the Most In-Demand," *The Wall Street Journal*, January 25, 2005, p. B6.

4. Patti Bond and Leon Stafford, "Kent to Succeed Isdell as Coke's Chief Executive," *The Atlanta Journal-Constitution* (ajc.com), December 6, 2007.

5. Fay Hansen, "Diversity's Business Case Doesn't Add Up," *Workforce*, April 2003, pp. 28–32.

6. Susan Meisinger, "Diversity: More Than Just Representation," *HR Magazine*, January 2008, p. 8.

7. Irwin Speizer, "Diversity on the Menu," *Workforce Management*, November 2004, pp. 41–45; Louisa Wah, "Diversity at Allstate: A Competitive Weapon," *Management Review*, July–August 1999, p. 24.

8. Jim Kirk, "PepsiCo Wants Hispanics to Feel at Home," *Chicago Tribune* online edition, June 20, 2004, p. 1.

9. Leanndra Martinez, "Banking on Diversity: HSBC Attributes Its Success to Its Multicultural Workforce," *Hispanic Business*, November 2006, p. 74.

10. Nicole Ibarra, "Some Companies Turn to Their Diverse Workforce to Help with the Bottom Line," *Hispanic Business*, December 2007, p. 56.

11. Scott E. Page, "Making the Difference: Applying a Logic of Diversity," *Academy of Management Perspective*, November 2007, p. 9.

12. Anthony Limon, "Back to the Future," *Hispanic Business*, November 2004, p. 66.

13. Frances J. Milliken and Luis L. Martins, "Searching for Common Threads: Understanding the Multiple Effects of Diversity in Organizational Groups," *Academy of Management Review*, April 1996, p. 403. See also, Daan van Knippenberg, Carsten K. W. De Dreu, and Astrid C. Homan, "Work Group Diversity and Group Performance: An Integrative Model and Research Agenda," *Journal of Applied Psychology*, December 2004, pp. 1008–1022.

14. Katherine J. Klein and David A. Harrison, "On the Diversity of Diversity: Tidy Logic, Messier Realities," *Academy of Management Perspectives*, November 2007, p. 31.

15. Mansour Javidan, Peter W. Dorfman, May Sully de Luque, and Robert J. House, "In the Eye of the Beholder: Cross Cultural Lessons in Leadership from Project GLOBE," *Academy of Management Perspectives*, February 2006, pp. 69–70. Similar dimensions were described in Geert Hofstede, *Culture's Consequences: International Differences in Work Related Values* (Beverly Hills, Calif.: Sage Publications, 1980); updated and expanded in "A Conversation with Geert Hofstede," *Organizational Dynamics*, Spring 1993, pp. 53–61. Dimension 10 is not included in the above research.

16. Study reported in Bradley S. Klapper, "Report: U.S. Workers Are the Most Productive," Associated Press, September 2, 2007.

17. Geert Hofstede, "The Universal and the Specific in 21st-Century Global Management," *Organizational Dynamics*, Summer 1999, pp. 35–37.

18. The observation about bureaucracy is from Javidan, Dorfman, de Luque, and House, "In the Eye of the Beholder," p. 79.

19. Felix C. Brodbeck, Michael Frese, and Mansour Javidan, "Leadership Made in Germany: Low on Compassion, High on Performance," *Academy of Management Executive*, February 2002, pp. 16–30.

20. Jeffrey C. Kennedy, "Leadership in Malaysia: Traditional Values, International Outlook," *Academy of Management Executive*, August 2002, pp. 15–26.

21. Del Jones, "North vs. South: Leaders from Both Sides of the Mason-Dixon Line Have Strong Opinions About the Styles of Their Regionally Different Peers," *USA Today*, July 9, 2004, p. 5B.

22. Ibid.

23. Robert J. House, Paul J. Hanges, Mansour Javidan, Peter W. Dorfman, and Vipin Gupta, eds., *Culture, Leadership, and Organizations: The GLOBE Study of 62 Societies* (Thousand Oaks, Calif.: Sage Publications, 2004), p. 7.

24. Gunnar Beeth, "Multicultural Managers Wanted," *Management Review*, May 1997, p. 17.

25. Carla Johnson, "Cultural Sensitivity Adds Up to Good Business Sense," *HR Magazine*, November 1995, pp. 83–85.

26. Christina Binkley, "Where Yellow's a Faux Pas and White Is Death," *The Wall Street Journal*, December 6, 2007, p. D8.

27. "Managing Diversity: When Cultures Collide," *Managing People at Work*, sample issue, 2008, p. 7.

28. P. Christopher Earley and Elaine Mosakowski, "Cultural Intelligence," *Harvard Business Review*, October 2004, pp. 139–146.

29. Javidan, Dorfman, de Luque, and House, "In the Eye of the Beholder," p. 85.

30. Joseph A. Petrick, Robert E. Scherer, James D. Bodzinski, John F. Quinn, and M. Fall Ainina, "Global Leadership Skills and Reputational Capital: Intangible Resources for Sustainable Competitive Advantage," *The Academy of Management Executive*, February 1999, pp. 58–69.

31. Manfred F. R. Kets De Vries, and Elizabeth Florent-Treacy, "Global Leadership from A to Z: Creating High Commitment Organizations," *Organizational Dynamics*, Spring 2002, pp. 295–309.

32. Gretchen M. Spreitzer, Morgan W. McCall Jr., and Joan D. Mahoney, "Early Identification of International Executive Potential," *Journal of Applied Psychology*, February 1997, pp. 6–29.

33. David Tessmann-Keys and Richard S. Wellins, *The CEO's Guide to Preparing Future Global Leaders* (Pittsburgh, Penn.: DDI, 2008), pp. 18–19.

34. Research cited in Douglas T. Hall, Guorong Zhu, and Amin Yan, "Developing Global Leaders: To Hold On to Them, Let Them Go," *Advances in Global Leadership*, vol. 2, 2001, p. 331.

35. Javidan, Dorfman, de Luque, and House, "In the Eye of the Beholder," p. 85.

36. Jeanne Brett, Kristin Behfar, and Mary C. Kern, "Managing Multicultural Teams," *Harvard Business Review*, November 2006, p. 87.

37. Daren Fonda, "Selling in Tongues," *Time*, November 26, 2001, pp. B12–B15.

38. Simon Kent, "Go Team, Go!" *PM Network*, November 2007, p. 41.

39. Paul Ingrassia and John Stoll, "Hottest Car Guy on Earth," *The Wall Street Journal*, January 14–15, p. A8; Alex Taylor III, "The World According to Ghosn," *Fortune*, December 11, 2006, p. 116.

40. Todd Campbell, "Diversity in Depth," *HR Magazine*, March 2003, p. 152.

41. Ann Zimmerman, "Defending Wal-Mart," *The Wall Street Journal*, October 6, 2004, p. B1.

42. Louisa Wah, "Diversity at Allstate," *Management Review*, July–August 1999, p. 28; "Allstate Insurance Company," *Vault/INROADS Guide to Diversity Internship, Co-op and Entry-Level Programs, 2007 Edition*, pp. 65–66.

43. Cora Daniels, "50 Best Companies for Minorities," *Fortune*, June 28, 2004, p. 138.

44. Marc Adams, "Building a Rainbow One Stripe at a Time," *HR Magazine*, August 1998, pp. 73–74.

45. Sarah E. Needleman, "More Programs Move to Halt Bias Against Gays," *The Wall Street Journal*, November 26, 2007, p. B3.

46. Phred Dvorak, "Firms Push New Methods to Promote Diversity," *The Wall Street Journal*, December 18, 2006, p. B3.

47. Research reported in Shankar Vedantam, "Most Diversity Training Ineffective, Study Finds," *Washington Post* (washingtonpost.com), January 22, 2008.

48. Deborah Steinborn, "Cross-Cultural Training Gains," *The Wall Street Journal*, April 4, 2007, p. B5D.

49. Christina Binkley, "Americans Learn the Global Art of the Cheek Kiss," *The Wall Street Journal*, March 27, 2008, p. D1.

50. P. Christopher Earley and Randall S. Peterson, "The Elusive Cultural Chameleon: Cultural Intelligence as a New Approach to Intercultural Training for the Global Manager," *Academy of Management Learning and Education*, March 2004, p. 105.

51. Ibarra, "Some Companies Turn to Their Diverse Workforce," p. 56.

52. Robert Rodriguez, "Diversity Finds Its Place," *HR Magazine*, August 2006, pp. 56, 58.

53. Lin Grensing-Pophal, "Hiring to Fit Your Corporate Culture," *HR Magazine*, August 1999, p. 52.

54. Derek T. Dingle, "Parson's Time," *Black Enterprise*, February 2008, p. 122.

55. Michael Todd, "Report: Companies Should Help Workers Get Comfortable, Stay Awhile," *Hispanic Business*, March 2007, p. 44.

56. Julie Bennett, "'Corporate Angst' Can Generate Gaffes That Turn Off Coveted Candidates," *The Wall Street Journal*, October 21, 2003, p. D9.

### Chapter 15

1. Excerpted from "Experiments in Managing," *Philadelphia Inquirer* (www.philly.com), November 23, 2007.

2. Jeffrey M. Cohn, Rakesh Khurana, and Laura Reeves, "Growing Talent as If Your Business

Depended on It," *Harvard Business Review*, October 2005, p. 64.

3. Sharon Daloz Parks, *Leadership Can Be Taught: A Bold Approach for a Complex World* (Boston: Harvard Business School Press, 2005).

4. "Leadership in Literature: A Conversation with Business Ethicist Joseph L. Badaracco, Jr.," *Harvard Business Review*, March 2006, p. 55.

5. Robert Hogan and Rodney Warrenfeltz, "Educating the Modern Manager," *Academy of Management Learning and Education*, March 2003, p. 74.

6. Chris Argyris, "Teaching Smart People How to Learn," *Harvard Business Review*, May–June 1991, pp. 99–109; Argyris, "Double-Loop Learning, Teaching, and Research," *Academy of Management Learning and Education*, December 2002, p. 206.

7. Bob Kaplan with Rob Kaiser, *The Versatile Leader: Make the Most of Your Strengths—Without Overdoing It* (San Francisco: Pfeiffer, 2006).

8. Cited in Jared Sandberg, "Cubicle Culture: Why Learn and Grow on the Job? It's Easier to Feign Infallibility," *The Wall Street Journal*, January 22, 2008, p. B1.

9. Cynthia D. McCauley, Russ S. Moxley, and Ellen Van Velsor, *Handbook of Leadership Development* (San Francisco: Jossey-Bass, 1998), pp. 132–133. The same theme is found in Morgan W. McCall, "Leadership Development Through Experience," *Academy of Management Executive*, August 2004, pp. 127–130.

10. "How Great Leaders Benefit from Failure," *Manager's Edge*, November 2004, p. 3.

11. Richard L. Hughes, Robert C. Ginnett, and Gordon J. Curphy, *Leadership: Enhancing the Lessons of Experience* (New York: McGraw-Hill/Irwin, 2006) pp. 58–61.

12. Joann S. Lublin, "Leadership Skills Ease Stressful Promotion to Uncharted Area," *The Wall Street Journal*, July 3, 2007, p. A7.

13. Daphna F. Raskas and Donald C. Hambrick, "Multifunctional Managerial Development: A Framework for Evaluating the Options," *Organizational Dynamics*, Autumn 1992, p. 5.

14. Joe Mullich, "Warming Up for Leadership," *Workforce Management*, November 2004, p. 64.

15. Ann Pomeroy, "Cultivating Female Leaders," *HR Magazine*, February 2007, p. 48.

16. Belle Rose Ragins and John L. Cotton, "Mentor Functions and Outcomes: A Comparison of Men and Women in Formal and Informal Mentoring Relationships," *Journal of Applied Psychology*, August 1999, pp. 529–550. Similar observations are reported by Kathy Kram in Jared Sandberg, "With Bad Mentors, It's Better to Break Up Than to Make Up," *The Wall Street Journal*, March 18, 2008, p. B1.

17. Andrea C. Poe, "Establish Positive Mentoring Relationships," *HR Magazine*, February 2002, p. 65.

18. Donna M. Owens, "Virtual Mentoring," *HR Magazine*, March 2006, p. 106.

19. Shimon-Craig Van Collie, "Moving Up Through Mentoring," *Workforce*, March 1998, p. 36.

20. Joann S. Lublin, "Even Top Executives Could Use Mentors to Benefit Their Careers," *The Wall Street Journal*, July 1, 2003, p. B1.

21. Wendy Harris, "Making the Connection: Mentors, Sponsors, and a Network You Can Count On," *Black Enterprise*, February 2007, p. 114.

22. Lublin, "Protégé Finds Mentor Gave Her a Big Boost, but Shadow Lingers," *The Wall Street Journal*, September 7, 2004, p. B1.

23. Geoff Colvin, "Leader Machines," *Fortune*, October 1, 2007, pp. 98, 101–102.

24. Ann Pomeroy, "Head of the Class," *HR Magazine*, January 2005, p. 57.

25. Jared Sandberg, "The Sensitive Me," *The Wall Street Journal*, April 11, 2006, p. B1.

26. Byron Reeves, Thomas W. Malone, and Tony O'Driscoll, "Leadership Online Labs," *Harvard Business Review*, May 2008, pp. 58–66.

27. Carol Hymowitz, "PepsiCo Chief Executive Asks Future Leaders to Train Like Athletes," *The Wall Street Journal*, September 9, 2003, p. B1.

28. Jay A. Conger and Beth Benjamin, *Building Leaders: How Successful Companies Develop the Next Generation* (San Francisco: Jossey-Bass, 1999), p. 79; Conger, "Can We Really Train Leadership, www.strategy+leadership.com, 2006.

29. Ed Frauenheim, "Upgrading IBM," *Workforce Management*, May 21, 2007, p. 22.

30. Jessica Marquez, "Companies Send Employees on Volunteer Projects Abroad to Cultivate Leadership Skills," *Workforce Management*, November 21, 2005, pp. 50–51.

31. Cited in Carol Hymowitz, "More CEOs Seek Psychotherapy," *The Wall Street Journal*, June 22, 2004, pp. B1, B3.

32. Shelia Anne Feeney, "Irreplaceable You," *Workforce Management*, August 2003, p. 38.

33. Carol Hymowitz, "Too Many Companies Lack Succession Plans, Wasting Time, Talent," *The Wall Street Journal*, November 26, 2007, p. B1; Hymowitz, "They Ponder Layoffs, but Executives Still Face Gaps in Talent," *The Wall Street Journal*, January 28, 2008, p. B1.

34. Ram Charan, "Ending the Succession Crisis," *Harvard Business Review*, February 2005, pp. 72–81; Charan, *Leaders at All Levels* (San Francisco: Jossey-Bass, 2008).

35. Jay W. Lorsch and Rakesh Khurana, "Changing Leaders: The Board's Role in CEO Succession," *Harvard Business Review,* May–June 1999, p. 100.

36. Linda Grant, "GE: The Envelope, Please," *Fortune,* June 26, 1995, pp. 89–90; George Anders, "When Filling Top Jobs Inside Makes Sense—And When It Doesn't," *The Wall Street* Journal, January 16, 2006, p. B1; Fay Hansen, "Training the Top at GE," *Workforce Management*, June 9, 2008, p. 26.

37. Gary A. Ballinger and F. David Schoorman, "Individual Reactions to Leadership Succession in Workgroups," *Academy of Management Review*, January 2007, pp. 118–136.

38. William C. Byham, "Grooming Next-Millennium Leaders," *HR Magazine,* February 1999, pp. 46–50; Joseph Weber, "The Accidental CEO," *Business-Week*, April 23, 2007, p. 068.

39. Joseph Weber, "Family, Inc." *BusinessWeek,* November 10, 2003, p. 108.

40. Martha Frase-Blunt, "Moving Past 'Mini-Me,'" *HR Magazine*, November 2003, pp. 95–98.

41. Joseph L. Bower, "Solve the Succession Problem by Growing Inside-Outside Leaders," *Harvard Business Review*, November 2007, pp. 90–96.

42. Quoted in Sonja D. Brown, "Congratulations, You're a Manager, Now What?" *Black Enterprise,* April 2006, p. 104.

# Glossary

*NOTE:* The number in brackets following each term refers to the chapter in which the term first appears.

**Achievement motivation** Finding joy in accomplishment for its own sake. [2]

**Assertiveness** Forthrightness in expressing demands, opinions, feelings, and attitudes. [2] As a cultural value, the degree to which individuals are (and should be) assertive, confrontational, and aggressive in their relationships with one another. [14]

**Attribution theory** The theory of how we explain the causes of events. [1]

**Authenticity** Being genuine and honest about your personality, values, and beliefs, as well as having integrity. [2]

**Autocratic leader** A person in charge who retains most of the authority for himself or herself. [4]

**Bandwagon technique** A manipulative approach in which one does something simply because others are doing likewise. [8]

**Centrality** The extent to which a unit's activities are linked into the system of organized activities. [7]

**Charisma** A special quality of leaders whose purposes, powers, and extraordinary determination differentiate them from others. [3]

**Coalition** A specific arrangement of parties working together to combine their power. [8]

**Coercive power** The power to punish for noncompliance; power based on fear. [7]

**Cognitive factors** Problem-solving and intellectual skills. [2]

**Cognitive resource theory** An explanation of leadership emphasizing that stress plays a key role in determining how a leader's intelligence is related to group performance. [5]

**Commitment** The most successful outcome of a leader's influence tactic: The person makes a full effort. [8]

**Compliance** Partial success of an influence attempt by a leader: The person makes a modest effort. [8]

**Consensus leader** The person in charge who encourages group discussion about an issue and then makes a decision that reflects general agreement and that group members will support. [4]

**Consideration** The degree to which the leader creates an environment of emotional support, warmth, friendliness, and trust. [4]

**Consultative leader** A person in charge who confers with group members before making a decision. [4]

**Contingency approach to leadership** The contention that leaders are most effective when they make their behavior contingent upon situational forces, including group member characteristics. [5]

**Cooperation theory** A belief in cooperation and collaboration rather than competitiveness as a strategy for building teamwork. [9]

**Corporate social responsibility** The idea that organizations have an obligation to groups in society other than owners or stockholders and beyond that prescribed by law or union contract. [6]

**Creativity** The production of novel and useful ideas. [11]

**Crisis leadership** The process of leading group members through a sudden and largely unanticipated, intensely negative, and emotionally draining circumstance. [5]

**Cross-cultural training** A set of learning experiences designed to help employees understand the customs, traditions, and beliefs of another culture. [14]

**Cultural intelligence (CQ)** An outsider's ability to interpret someone's unfamiliar and ambiguous gestures the way that person's compatriots would. [14]

**Cultural sensitivity** An awareness of and a willingness to investigate the reasons why people of another culture act as they do. [14]

**Debasement** The act of demeaning or insulting oneself to control the behavior of another person. [8]

**Delegation** The assignment of formal authority and responsibility for accomplishing a specific task to another person. [7]

**Democratic leader** A person in charge who confers final authority on the group. [4]

**Dependence perspective** The point of view that a person accrues power by others being dependent on him or her for things they value. [7]

**Diversity training** A learning experience designed to bring about workplace harmony by teaching people how to get along better with diverse work associates. [14]

**Double-loop learning** An in-depth style of learning that occurs when people use feedback to confront the validity of the goal or the values implicit in the situation. [15]

**Drive** A propensity to put forth high energy into achieving goals and persistence in applying that energy. [2]

**Effective leader** One who helps group members attain productivity, including good quality and satisfaction. [4]

**E-leadership** A form of leadership practiced in a context where work is mediated by information technology. [9]

**Emotional intelligence** The ability to do such things as understand one's feelings, have empathy for others, and regulate one's emotions to enhance one's quality of life. [2]

**Employee network (or affinity) group** A group of employees throughout the company who affiliate on the basis of a group characteristic such as race, ethnicity, sex, sexual orientation, or physical ability status. [14]

**Empowerment** Passing decision-making authority and responsibility from managers to group members. [7]

**Entitlement** In relation to unethical behavior by executives, the idea that some CEOs lose their sense of reality and feel entitled to whatever they can get away with or steal. [6]

**Equity theory** An explanation of motivation contending that employee satisfaction and motivation depend on how fairly the employees believe they are being treated in comparison to peers. [10]

**Ethical mind** A point of view that helps the individual aspire to good work that matters to his or her colleagues, companies, and society in general. [6]

**Ethics** The study of moral obligations, or separating right from wrong. [6]

**Evidence-based leadership or management** The approach whereby managers translate principles based on best evidence into organizational practices. [5]

**Executive coaching** A one-on-one development process formally contracted between a coach and a management-level client to help achieve goals related to professional development and/or business performance. [10]

**Executive intelligence** Superior reasoning and problem-solving skills that enable the executive to cut through conflicting data to create a solution that uniquely fits the situation at hand. [2]

**Expectancy** An individual's assessment of the probability that effort will lead to correct performance of the task. [10]

**Expectancy theory** A theory of motivation based on the premise that the amount of effort people expend depends on how much reward they can expect in return. [10]

**Experience of flow** An experience so engrossing and enjoyable that the task becomes worth doing for its own sake regardless of the external consequences. [11]

**Expert power** The ability to influence others because of one's specialized knowledge, skills, or abilities. [3]

**Farsightedness** The ability to understand the long-range implications of actions and policies. [2]

**Feedback-intensive development program** A learning experience that helps leaders develop by seeing more clearly their patterns of behaviors, the reasons for such behaviors, and the impact of these behaviors and attitudes on their effectiveness. [15]

**Flexibility** The ability to adjust to different situations. [2]

**Future orientation** As a cultural value, the extent to which individuals engage (and should engage) in future-oriented behaviors such as delaying gratification, planning, and making investments for the future. [14]

**Gender egalitarianism** As a cultural value, the degree to which a culture minimizes, and should minimize, gender inequality. [14]

**Global leadership skills** The ability to exercise effective leadership in a variety of countries. [14]

**Goal** What a person is trying to accomplish. [10]

**Hands-on leader** A leader who gets directly involved in the details and process of operations. [8]

**Humane orientation** As a cultural value, the degree to which a society encourages and rewards, and should encourage and reward, individuals for being fair, altruistic, and caring toward others. [14]

**Implicit leadership theories** Personal assumptions about the traits and abilities that characterize an ideal organizational leader. [8]

**Influence** The ability to affect the behavior of others in a particular direction. [8]

**Information power** Power stemming from formal control over the information people need to do their work. [7]

**In-group collectivism** As a cultural value, the degree to which individuals express, and should express, pride, loyalty, and cohesiveness in their organizations and families. [14]

**Initiating structure** Organizing and defining relationships in the group by activities such as assigning specific tasks, specifying procedures to be followed, scheduling work, and clarifying expectations of team members. [4]

**Innovation** The process of creating new ideas and their implementation. [11]

**Insight** A depth of understanding that requires considerable intuition and common sense. [2]

**Instrumentality** An individual's assessment of the probability that performance will lead to certain outcomes. [10]

**Integrity** Loyalty to rational principles, thereby practicing what one preaches, regardless of emotional or social pressure. [6]

**Internal locus of control** The belief that one is the primary cause of events happening to oneself. [2]

**Job involvement** The experience of being excited about work. [3]

**Kitchen for the mind** A space designed to nurture creativity. [11]

**Knowledge management (KM)** The systematic sharing of information to achieve goals such as innovation, nonduplication of effort, and competitive advantage. [13]

**Leader–member exchange model (LMX)** An explanation of leadership proposing that leaders develop unique working relationships with group members. [9]

**Leadership** The ability to inspire confidence and support among the people who are needed to achieve organizational goals. [1]

**Leadership diversity** The presence of a culturally heterogeneous cadre of leaders. [14]

**Leadership effectiveness** Attaining desirable outcomes such as productivity, quality, and satisfaction in a given situation. [1]

**Leadership Grid™** A framework for specifying the extent of a leader's concern for production and people. [4]

**Leadership polarity** The disparity in views of leaders: They are revered or vastly unpopular, but people rarely feel neutral about them. [3]

**Leadership style** The relatively consistent pattern of behavior that characterizes a leader. [4]

**Leadership succession** An orderly process of identifying and grooming people to replace executives. [15]

**Leading by example** Influencing others by acting as a positive role model. [8]

**Learning organization** An organization that is skilled at creating, acquiring, and transferring knowledge and at modifying behavior to reflect new knowledge and insights. [13]

**Legitimate power** The lawful right to make a decision and expect compliance. [7]

**Linguistic style** A person's characteristic speaking pattern. [12]

**Machiavellians** People in the workplace who ruthlessly manipulate others. [8]

**Management openness** A set of leadership behaviors particularly relevant to subordinates' motivation to voice their opinion. [4]

**Management by storytelling** The technique of inspiring and instructing group members by telling fascinating stories. [3]

**Making the rounds** The leader casually dropping by constituents to listen to their accomplishments, concerns, and problems and to share information. [12]

**Mentor** A more experienced person who develops a protégé's abilities through tutoring, coaching, guidance, and emotional support. [15]

**Micromanagement** The close monitoring of most aspects of group member activities by the manager or leader. [9]

**Morals** An individual's determination of what is right or wrong influenced by his or her values. [6]

**Multicultural leader** A leader with the skills and attitudes to relate effectively to and motivate people across race, gender, age, social attitudes, and lifestyles. [14]

**Multicultural worker** A worker who is convinced that all cultures are equally good and enjoys learning about other cultures. [14]

**Multifunctional managerial development** An organization's intentional efforts to enhance the effectiveness of managers by giving them experience in multiple functions within the organization. [15]

**Normative decision model** A view of leadership as a decision-making process in which the leader examines certain factors within the situation to determine which decision-making style will be the most effective. [5]

**Open-book management** An approach to management in which every employee is trained, empowered, and motivated to understand and pursue the company's business goals. [9]

**Organizational politics** Informal approaches to gaining power through means other than merit or luck. [7]

**Outcome** Anything that might stem from performance, such as a reward. [10]

**Participative leader** A person in charge who shares decision making with group members. [4]

**Partnership** A relationship between leaders and group members in which power is approximately balanced. [1]

**Path-goal theory** An explanation of leadership effectiveness that specifies what the leader must do to achieve high productivity and morale in a given situation. [5]

**Performance orientation** As a cultural value, the degree to which a society encourages (or should encourage) and rewards group members for performance improvement and excellence. [14]

**Personal brand** Also the *brand called you*, or your basket of strengths that make you unique. [3]

**Personal magnetism** A captivating, inspiring personality with charm and charismatic-like qualities. [8]

**Personal power** Power derived from the person rather than from the organization. [7]

**Personalized charismatic** A charismatic leader who exercises few restraints on the use of power in order to best serve his or her own interests. [3]

**Pet-peeve technique** A method of brainstorming in which a group identifies all the possible complaints others might have about the group's organizational unit. [11]

**Power** The potential or ability to influence decisions and control resources. [7]

**Power distance** As a cultural value, the degree to which members of a society expect, and should expect, power to be distributed unequally. [14]

**Prestige power** The power stemming from one's status and reputation. [7]

**Pygmalion effect** The situation that occurs when a managerial leader believes that a group member will succeed, and communicates this belief without realizing it. [4]

**Referent power** The leader's ability to influence others through his or her desirable traits and characteristics. [3]

**Resistance** The state that occurs when an influence attempt by a leader is unsuccessful: The target is opposed to carrying out the request and finds ways to either not comply or do a poor job. [8]

**Resource dependence perspective** The view that an organization requires a continuing flow of human resources, money, customers and clients, technological inputs, and materials to continue to function. [7]

**Reward power** The authority to give employees rewards for compliance. [7]

**Self-awareness** Insightfully processing feedback about oneself to improve personal effectiveness. [15]

**Self-discipline** The ability to mobilize one's efforts to stay focused on attaining an important goal. [15]

**Self-efficacy** The confidence in one's ability to carry out a specific task. [10]

**Self-leadership** The idea that all organizational members are capable of leading themselves at least to some extent. [7]

**Servant leader** One who serves constituents by working on their behalf to help them achieve their goals, not the leader's own goals. [4]

**Shadowing** An approach to mentoring in which the trainee follows the mentor around for a stated period of time. [15]

**Single-loop learning** A situation in which learners seek minimum feedback that might substantially confront their basic ideas or actions. [15]

**Situational Leadership II (SLII)** A model of leadership that explains how to match the leadership style to capabilities of group members on a given task. [5]

**Socialized charismatic** A charismatic leader who restrains the use of power in order to benefit others. [3]

**Strategic contingency theory** An explanation of sources of power suggesting that units best able to cope with the firm's critical problems and uncertainties acquire relatively large amounts of power. [7]

**Strategic leadership** The process of creating or sustaining an organization by providing the right direction and inspiration. [13]

**Strategic planning** Those activities that lead to the statement of goals and objectives and the choice of strategy. [13]

**Strategy** An integrated, overall concept of how the firm will achieve its objectives. [13]

**Substitutes for leadership** Factors in the work environment that provide guidance and incentives to perform, making the leader's role almost superfluous. [1]

**SWOT analysis** A method of considering internal strengths and weaknesses, and external opportunities and threats in a given situation. [13]

**Team** A work group that must rely on collaboration if each member is to experience the optimum success and achievement. [9]

**Teamwork** Work done with an understanding and commitment to group goals on the part of all team members. [9]

**Territorial games** Also referred to as turf wars, political tactics that involve protecting and hoarding resources that give one power, such as information, relationships, and decision-making authority. [7]

**360-degree feedback** A formal evaluation of superiors based on input from people who work for and with them, sometimes including customers and suppliers. [4]

**Time orientation** As a cultural value, the importance nations and individuals attach to time. [14]

**Tough question** One that makes a person or group stop and think about why they are doing or not doing something. [4]

**Transformational leader** A leader who brings about positive, major changes in an organization. [3]

**Uncertainty avoidance** As a cultural value, the extent to which members of a society rely (and should rely) on social norms, rules, and procedures to lessen the unpredictability of future events. [14]

**Upward appeal** A means of influence in which the leader enlists a person with more formal authority to do the influencing. [8]

**Valence** The worth or attractiveness of an outcome. [10]

**Virtuous circle** The idea that corporate social performance and corporate financial performance feed and reinforce each other. [6]

**Vision** The ability to imagine different and better conditions and ways to achieve them. [3]

**Whistleblower** An employee who discloses organizational wrongdoing to parties who can take action. [6]

**WICS** A systems model of leadership that provides an understanding of leadership as a set of decision processes that embodies wisdom, intelligence, and creativity as well as other cognitive processes. [2]

**Win–win approach to conflict resolution** The belief that after conflict has been resolved, both sides should gain something of value. [12]

**Work orientation** As a cultural value, the number of hours per week and weeks per year people expect to invest in work versus leisure, or other nonwork activities. [14]

# Name Index

# Organization Index

# Subject Index